DAVID ROHL is the author of three best-selling books: *A Test of Time: The Bible – From Myth to History* (also published in the USA as *Pharaohs and Kings*); *Legend: The Genesis of Civilisation*; and *The Lost Testament: From Eden to Exile – A 5,000-year History of the People of the Bible.* These volumes have been published in nine different languages. David also presented the internationally acclaimed three-part television series 'Pharaohs and Kings' and the one-hour documentary 'In Search of Eden'. He is currently completing another archaeological series entitled 'The Egyptian Genesis' dealing with the origins of Egyptian civilisation.

David is Director of the Eastern Desert Survey, which is responsible for recording the rock-art of Egypt's desert mountains between the Nile Valley and Red Sea. He is the organiser of 'Legend Conferences' in the UK and Egypt, as well as giving lectures himself all around the world.

Paperbacks also by David Rohl:

A Test of Time: The Bible – From Myth to History

Legend: The Genesis of Civilisation

From Eden to Exile: A 5,000-year History of the People of the Bible

The
Lords of Avaris

Uncovering the Legendary
Origins of Western Civilisation

David M. Rohl

arrow books

Published in the United Kingdom by Arrow Books in 2008

1 3 5 7 9 10 8 6 4 2

Copyright © David Rohl 2007

First published in the United Kingdom in 2007 by Century
First published in paperback in 2008 by Arrow Books

Arrow Books
The Random House Group Limited
20 Vauxhall Bridge Road, London SW1V 2SA

Addresses for companies within The Random House Group Limited
can be found at: www.randomhouse.co.uk/offices.htm

Random House Group Limited Reg. No. 954009

www.rbooks.co.uk

A CIP catalogue record for this book
is available from the British Library

ISBN 9780099177623

The Random House Group Limited makes every effort to ensure that
the papers used in its books are made from trees that have been legally
sourced from well-managed and credibly certified forests. Our paper
procument policy can be found at: www.randomhouse.co.uk/paper.htm

Printed and bound in Great Britain by
CPI Cox & Wyman, Reading, RG1 8EX

Typeset by
Ditas Rohl

To the future:

Mohan
Iain
Vanessa
Rebecca
Robert
Maya

Contents

Part One
The Lords of Chaos

Part Two
Divine Pelasgians

PREFACE

The morning of 27 April 1991 began with a typical grey sky hanging over central London as I headed through the streets of Bloomsbury towards the equally grey Ionic splendour which is the British Museum. I was already late for the ISIS 1991 Fellowship Lecture as I headed up the steps of the portico and through the doors into the atrium of that august institution. A sharp left turn quickly took me to the Egyptian sculpture gallery and another left turn by the Rosetta Stone led to the corridors of ORTHOSTATS from the palace of King ASHURBANIPAL of Assyria, decorated with masterful reliefs of his famous lion hunt (above). At the end of the exhibit from the state apartments of Nineveh you come to the rear ends of a pair of giant cherubim – winged bulls with human heads – guarding the Assyrian collection of the museum. At this point to the right is the Egyptian Sculpture Gallery and, through a door on the left, a large room containing the façade of the elegant Classical temple-tomb (built between 390 and 380 BC) known as the 'Nereid Monument', discovered by Charles FELLOWS in the 1840s whilst exploring the ruined city of Xanthus in Lycia (south-west Anatolia). Beyond here you will find the notorious Elgin Marbles, removed from the Parthenon in Athens by Lord Elgin between 1801 and 1806.

But I was not 'going Greek' today. My destination was down an unobtrusive stairway, beneath the stern gaze of the cherubim, which led to the basement lecture theatre of the British Museum. I could hear the muffled buzz of excitement beyond the closed double doors as I approached.

Things were just about to get under way as I slipped apologetically into my seat with just enough time to acknowledge the nods and waves of my teachers and academic colleagues. You see, I was a postgraduate student at University College London at the time and fortunate enough to have been under the tutelage of some of the greatest ancient world scholars of the late twentieth century. I sat next to Peter Parr, the excavator of KADESH-ON-THE-ORONTES. Peter had taught me Levantine archaeology at the Institute of Archaeology, London, and had the good grace to invite me to participate in his excavations in Syria. Next to him was Professor Nicholas Coldstream, the leading authority on GEOMETRIC GREECE.[1] This exceptional and ebullient scholar had introduced me to the splendours of Bronze Age Crete and Greece through his famous archaeology courses and Mycenaean seminars at UCL. One row back and to my right sat Vronwy Hankey and Professor Peter Warren, co-authors of the standard research volume on the pottery chronology of the Aegean world.[2] The row in front was crammed with my tutors and honorary research fellows from the Department of Ancient History; next to them my Egyptology professors – the much-loved Harry Smith and Geoffrey Martin. This galaxy of stars from the academic world was here for one reason: to hear the lecture of a remarkable man – a scholar whom I had recourse to introduce, at some length, in *A Test of Time*, Volume One, when writing about the archaeological evidence for the Israelites in Egypt.

The Man from Avaris

Professor Manfred Bietak, the Director of the Institute for Egyptology in Vienna and Field Director of the Austrian mission to TELL ED-DABA in Egypt, is a hero to many an aspiring young Egyptologist and archaeologist – including myself. He has excavated in Egypt, year in year out, for the best part of half a century, steadily (and sometimes sensationally) revealing Egypt's greatest discovery since the days of Howard Carter and the tomb of Tutankhamun. With the help of his international team of experts (including archaeologists, surveyors, anthropologists, architects and restorers) Bietak has brought one of Egyptian civilisation's darkest and most mysterious eras into the bright daylight of modern scientific endeavour. Thanks to Professor Bietak, the Second Intermediate Period – encompassing the 13th Dynasty and the Hyksos Age – is now a hot topic of debate within academia and has become a fascinating aspect of Egyptian history for study amongst both students and amateur Egyptologists alike.

As Director of ISIS (the Institute for the Study of Interdisciplinary Sciences), I had invited Professor Bietak to give the 1991 ISIS Fellowship Lecture at the British Museum so that a British scholarly audience could hear about the latest discoveries at Tell ed-Daba – a little village which marks the location of ancient Avaris, capital of the Hyksos empire. Manfred Bietak had not spoken in the UK since his British Academy lecture way back in 1969 and so this was a bit of a coup on my part. He had, in fact, flown directly from the Austrian Institute headquarters in Cairo – having departed from the site of Avaris the day before, where he had left his team of site supervisors hard at work at a new excavation site just a kilometre to the west of the main ruin-mound at Tell ed-Daba. Now he was standing before a large expectant crowd in the basement lecture theatre of the BM and nobody in the audience had any inkling of what he was about to reveal.

The lights were dimmed as the first of a hundred slides cast their magic onto the big screen before us. Initially the material was familiar to those who had studied the Austrian excavations and read the regular site reports. The people in the audience who were not so familiar with the Second Intermediate Period were introduced to the houses and graves of a population of Western Asiatic (that is, Semitic-speaking) folk who had migrated across Sinai into Egypt at the end of the 12th Dynasty and settled in the eastern delta. There they had gradually become Egyptianised – but, interestingly, these pastoralists had retained their burial customs, placing Middle Bronze IIA pottery in simple mudbrick graves along with bronze daggers of exceptional quality to protect the deceased, bodies lying on their sides in semi-foetal position. These were the folk of the Tell ed-Daba Middle Bronze IIA Strata H and G.

Then in the next (higher) stratum came a break in the stratigraphic sequence. The last phase of G had come to a sudden and dramatic end. A catastrophe had struck Avaris – readily apparent from the scores of shallow burial pits found all over the site. Bodies had been thrown into hastily dug graves, face down and on top of each other. There were no burial goods to accompany the deceased; no pottery for the afterlife; and no bronzes to protect the dead in the other world. Bietak surmised that a devastating plague had struck the town, causing hundreds of deaths and an emergency interment of the victims. This might also explain why the main part of the settlement, where the Asiatics were concentrated, was equally suddenly abandoned and left deserted for a period of time.

The next stratum (F) marked the reoccupation of Avaris by a new wave of Asiatics from the north – people very different from those who had departed from the site at the end of Stratum G. Their pottery represents the approximate beginning of a new archaeological sub-phase known as Middle Bronze IIB (or MB IIB for short) – a development from, but just about recognisably different to, the previous MB IIA ceramic culture. These were warriors – men who went into the netherworld accompanied by slave-girls buried alongside them. The newcomers soon set about demolishing the mudbrick houses of the old town in order to make space for a cemetery, replete with small funerary chapel (Stratum E/3).

The next three strata (E/2, E/1 and D/3) saw the new Asiatics growing in power and the settlement expanding. The community built a larger Egyptian-style mortuary chapel in the cemetery and a huge ritual compound with, at its centre (begun in Stratum E/3), 'one of the largest sanctuaries known from the Middle Bronze Age world'.[3] Bietak believes that this temple was dedicated to Baal/Hadda, the storm-god of the north, assimilated with the Egyptian god of chaos – 'Seth, Lord of Avaris'.

The so-called 'Greater Hyksos' royal line – identified with Manetho's 15th Dynasty – are, according to Bietak, represented in the last Middle Bronze Age strata at Avaris (E/1, D/3 & D/2) before the fall of the fortified city to Pharaoh AHMOSE 'the liberator' and founder of the 18th Dynasty. With the expulsion of the Hyksos from Egypt, Avaris (Stratum D/2) was abandoned for a second time (or so it was thought in 1991) as the New Kingdom pharaohs rebuilt their royal capitals at Memphis and Thebes. All this was known and pretty much accepted amongst Bietak's scholarly audience.

Now came the surprise which Professor Bietak was holding back to the end of his presentation. This season he had 'rented' what appeared to be an ordinary field adjacent to the houses of the small hamlet known as Ezbet Helmi. He had two months to excavate the site before handing the field back to the farmer for cultivation. Helmi village is located just off the main road to Tanis which, in this area near Tell ed-Daba, follows the left bank of the Didamun canal. A dirt track runs west from the asphalt road, across a shallow ditch in which Bietak and his surveyor, Josef Dorner, had spotted well-cut limestone blocks from some lost pharaonic building. This was one of the indications that something important lay nearby.

The mudbrick houses of Ezbet Helmi had themselves been built around three massive blocks of pink Aswan granite which represented the collapsed remnants of a great doorway. On the blocks were inscribed the cartouches of two 12th Dynasty pharaohs – AMENEMHAT I (founder of the dynasty) and SENUSERET III who, in the inscription carved in the granite, claimed to have restored an ancient ceremonial hall of the former king, known as the 'Djadja of Amenemhat'. Surely this building must have been located around here.

These were the clues which led Bietak to chance his luck and rent the field for a quick investigative excavation. As I said in *A Test of Time*, Manfred Bietak seems to have a sixth sense when it comes to archaeology – either a built-in ground radar which comes from years of experience or a magic trowel straight out of a Harry Potter novel. Wherever he and his team dig they seem to turn up amazing new discoveries which invariably change our understanding of the ancient past. And, on this occasion too, the Bietak trowel – passed into the capable hands of Site Director Peter Jánosi – had worked its magic.

Just before their leader's departure for the UK the Austrian mission had uncovered an eight-metre-thick fortress wall extending off east under the houses of the village. Within the wall they found a garden with tree-pits and post-holes, perhaps belonging to a vineyard. The great wall appeared to bound the east bank of the Pelusiac branch of the Nile which, having silted up in the late New Kingdom, had been buried under the fields for millennia. Archaeological surveyor, Josef Dorner, had located this long-lost delta river by drilling over six hundred cores into the ground around Tell ed-Daba (Avaris) and Kantir (the site of Pi-Ramesse, further to the north). He had thus been able to profile the ancient topography, lying buried under thousands of years of Nile flood silt deposits, revealing the landscape of the area as it must have appeared in the times of Ramesses II of the 19th Dynasty, Ahmose, founder of the 18th Dynasty, and the 12th Dynasty pharaohs Amenemhat I and Senuseret III.

In the following season Bietak's team would come upon massive mudbrick foundations, next to the garden, laid out in a complex pattern of sealed compartments (known as casemates in archaeology). This turned out to be a giant platform which once supported a palace. One set of walls appeared to form the sub-structure of a ramp leading down to the fortress wall. The granite blocks of the Middle Kingdom doorway lay very close to the end of the ramp and adjacent to the fortress wall foundations. Bietak would later come to the logical conclusion that these imposing blocks had been reused here to make a new river-gate leading from the inside of the great wall out to the east bank of the Pelusiac branch of the River Nile which once flowed past the fortress wall on its northern side. But all this was still buried and unknown in April 1991 as Bietak announced the discovery of the fortified enclosure wall and garden/vineyard at Ezbet Helmi.

Listening to Bietak describing these fascinating discoveries of the fortress wall and the long-lost river, I could not help but recall the famous stela inscription of King KAMOSE, last ruler of the 17th Dynasty. He was the paternal uncle of Ahmose and the first of the native pharaohs to assault Avaris in a prolonged and vicious struggle to liberate Egypt from the despised Aamu ('Asiatics'). Standing on the deck of his warship before the high mudbrick wall surrounding the stronghold of Avaris, the Egyptian pharaoh observed the frightened women-folk of the Hyksos king APOPHIS, comparing them to lizards poking their heads out of their holes in the banks of the River Nile.

> I caught eight of his women on the top of his palace looking out of their embrasures towards the riverbank (their bodies not stirring when they saw me) as they peeped out between the crenulations on their (fortress) walls like young of lizards from within their holes.

Had Bietak found the great fortress wall of Hyksos Avaris? By now the audience was on the edge of its collective seat. For a bunch of dusty academics this was heart-fluttering

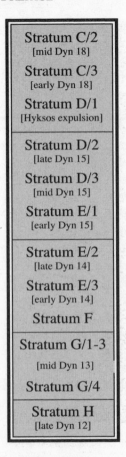

| Stratum C/2 [mid Dyn 18] |
| Stratum C/3 [early Dyn 18] |
| Stratum D/1 [Hyksos expulsion] |
| Stratum D/2 [late Dyn 15] |
| Stratum D/3 [mid Dyn 15] |
| Stratum E/1 [early Dyn 15] |
| Stratum E/2 [late Dyn 14] |
| Stratum E/3 [early Dyn 14] |
| Stratum F |
| Stratum G/1-3 [mid Dyn 13] |
| Stratum G/4 |
| Stratum H [late Dyn 12] |

Chart showing a simplified scheme of the Tell ed-Daba and Ezbet Helmi stratigraphy.

1. The Second Kamose Stela, found at Karnak in 1954. Originally one of a pair set up to record the king's victories over the Hyksos Apophis of Avaris and the Kushite ruler of Kerma (Luxor Museum).

stuff. Here was legend and archaeology coming together in tantalising detail. But Bietak wasn't finished yet. Up came the final slide to an audible gasp from the row of dignitaries in front of me. On the screen was the giant image of a piece of painted plaster. Crystal clear, for all to see, we were confronted by the profile of a man's face with red coloured skin and jet-black hair, slightly curled up

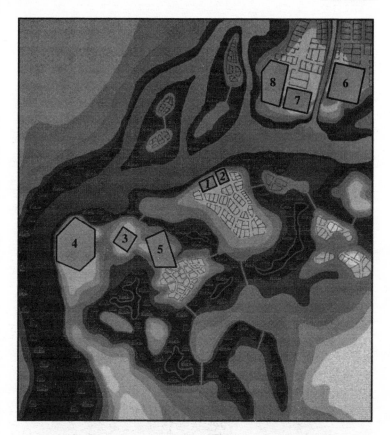

2. A simplified map of Avaris (and the later Pi-Ramesse) based on the drill-cores recorded by Josef Dorner.

1 & 2: The sacred and royal precincts of the Middle Kingdom located at the modern village of Ezbet Rushdi.

3: Area F where the palace and tomb of an Asiatic official of the late 12th Dynasty was found. The colossal seated funerary statue was decorated with a multi-coloured coat.

4: The huge military compound of Hyksos Avaris which was subsequently transformed into a palace district for the 18th Dynasty riverine trading port of Perunefer.

5: The sacred enclosure of the New Kingdom temple of Seth.

6: Chariot stables for the army of Seth based at Pi-Ramesse.

7 & 8: The royal palace and workshops of the 19th Dynasty Pi-Ramesse.

at the fringe. We could even see the strokes of the artist's brush which had given our ancient subject a beard. This was a remarkable piece of art – a fresco almost as fresh as the day it was painted – which Bietak now explained had just been dug up from the garden area inside the Hyksos wall of Avaris. In addition, a telegram he had received the previous evening from his colleagues in Egypt simply read 'Amazing discovery … contact the Cairo office a.s.a.p.'. Clearly something big was happening at the very instant that Bietak was giving his presentation to ISIS – of which the fresco of the man's head was just the first discovery.

I turned around to catch the eye of Professor Warren and mouthed the single word – 'Minoan?'. The professor

3. Plaster fragment of the Minoan face found at Ezbet Helmi in 1991.

from Bristol University shrugged his shoulders and smiled in a puzzled sort of way. UCL Honorary Research Fellow, Vronwy Hankey, whom I had known for many years, winked and gave a subtle nod of approval. Right on cue, Bietak confirmed that we were looking at a piece of Minoan fresco. The theatre suddenly erupted with excited chatter. The normally reserved academics simply could not help themselves. The implications of full-blown Cretan art discovered in Egypt were huge for Egyptology and Ancient World studies across the eastern Mediterranean. This certainly had not been anticipated. Nothing of its kind had ever turned up in the Nile valley or delta before in two centuries of excavation. I cannot overstress the significance of this. To turn the coin over, just imagine the sort of impact that the discovery of an Egyptian royal tomb would have if it turned up within the walls of the labyrinthine palace of Knossos on Crete. This may give you a sense of the excitement this Tell ed-Daba discovery generated amongst ancient historians gathered in the British Museum that wet spring day in 1991.

If the bearded face of the man in the slide before us really was an example of Minoan fresco-art, painted by artists from the Aegean, what on Earth were these exotic and mysterious people doing in Hyksos Avaris during the Egyptian Second Intermediate Period? I don't think anyone quite knew what to do with this remarkable piece of news. But I was in the fortunate position of being able to grasp the bull by the horns (so to speak – see later). The very next day I was flying out to Egypt for an exploration of the eastern delta and so would get to Avaris even before Professor Bietak could return to the dig. He was heading back to Vienna for meetings before returning to Cairo and had given me his blessing to visit the site to see the ongoing work at first hand. What a chance this was for a student of Egyptology – to be an eyewitness at one of the greatest archaeological discoveries made within my own lifetime. I could not wait to be on the plane heading for the Land of the Pharaohs.

The drive out to the eastern delta from Cairo was hot and dusty. I was travelling with Roy SPENCE – an experienced Egyptophile and, though getting on in years, an avid explorer of untrodden paths in the Black and Red Lands. By the time we reached Fakus, regional capital of Sharkiya province, it was getting on for 10 am. The large modern town of Fakus is named after the ancient Egyptian city of Pa-Kusa (Classical period Phacusa), known in the book of Genesis as 'The Goshen' (Kessan of the SEPTUAGINT). As we turned left onto the Tanis road beside the Didamun canal, I reminded Roy that we were in the land of the Israelite sojourn in Egypt – the area where Joseph had settled his father Jacob and the place of the terrible plagues of Exodus.

Those momentous days seemed far away as we sped along the asphalt track lined with Gazwarina trees, their trunks whitewashed by the modern Egyptians to mark out the road as an aid to night travelling. In between the trees, flashing by, I could see the canal on my right and, beyond, the lush fields of wheat swaying in the spring breeze. In a clearing I even caught a brief glimpse of a magnificent Egyptian falcon swooping down to pounce on some poor unsuspecting field mouse. In all my years of travelling in Egypt, I had never seen a bird of prey so large and colourful – exactly like the paintings of the Horus falcon adorning the royal tombs in the Valley of the Kings.

Ten minutes on and I could just make out the whitewashed walls of the Austrian dig house a few hundred yards across the fields off to our right. We soon reached the narrow dirt track on the left side of the road and turned to cross the little bridge over the ditch containing the limestone blocks observed by Bietak and Dorner. Two hundred metres further down the lane we came to the first house of around twenty which make up the village of Ezbet Helmi. The taxi driver found a spot to pull his Peugeot off the track and we clambered out, bedecked in cameras, gingerly negotiating our way through the placid village dogs and ferocious, man-eating chickens.

The excavation site was close by, set against the backdrop of a large mound of earth – the excavation dump of waste material removed from the field to reach the Hyksos levels of ancient Avaris. A procession of village girls, clad in their brightly coloured GALABEYAS, was snaking up the hill, each carrying her ZAMBEEL full of dirt. As the girls reached the summit they would pour out the contents in a cloud of dust before scampering down the slope for another load. I could just make out the heads of the excavators popping up above the ground as they moved about in the one-metre-deep excavation trenches.

Roy and I set out across the field, leaping across a shallow water channel of the basin irrigation system used in both modern and ancient Egypt. Halfway to our destination we were spotted by Site Director, Peter Jánosi, who climbed out of his hole in the ground and came to greet us with a friendly smile.

I had first met Peter in Vienna a couple of years earlier when Professor Bietak invited me to give two lectures on the New Chronology to the University of Vienna and the Austrian Institute for Egyptology. Needless to say, it was not the normal state of affairs for undergraduate students to present their work to such distinguished bodies, but I was rapidly getting myself a 'reputation' within Egyptological circles because of my somewhat unorthodox thinking on ancient chronology. In the previous year I had addressed the Egypt Exploration Society in London and had also given papers in the University College London Egyptology postgraduate seminars, as well as in Professor Coldstream's Mycenaean seminar series. The New Chronology had not reached the ears of the general public yet – but it was being discussed and debated in the academic forum.

In Vienna, Dr (now Professor) Peter Jánosi had been assigned to look after me during my three-day stay. We spent long hours over dinners in elegant Viennese restaurants, in the company of Dr Zbigniew Szafranski of Warsaw University (currently Director of the Polish mission reconstructing the temples of Deir el-Bahri). The conversation ranged over the New Chronology thesis and its implications for ancient world studies. Peter and Zbigniew are both open-minded scholars, so they found the issues both interesting and challenging. But, at that time, none of us knew what chronological time bomb awaited us all, buried in the earth of Ezbet Helmi – a time bomb which would set archaeologist against scientist and Egyptologist against Aegean historian. That is for later. ... Back to Egypt and our visit to the Austrian excavations.

Peter was delighted that we had come to see the Ezbet Helmi site and generously offered to give us a guided tour of the excavations. As we took the final few strides towards the edge of the first ten-metre test square, Peter announced that he had a big surprise in store for us. I replied 'Yes, I know, Minoan frescoes!' The Austrian archaeologist was taken aback. 'How did you know that?' he asked. I then explained that I had seen the slide in Bietak's lecture of the painted plaster fragment depicting the man with red skin, beard and black hair. I explained that I had instantly recognised the style as Aegean in origin and that Bietak himself had confirmed the discovery to an astonished academic world back in London a little over twenty-four hours earlier.

By now we had reached the trench and, looking down, the most amazing sight greeted us. There, a metre below the surface of the field, was a swathe of plaster fragments, glinting with vivid colours. An Egyptian worker in sky-blue galabeya was carefully extricating a large fragment from its earthly prison after more than three thousand years of captivity. I could see brilliant blue leaves painted on an ochre background. Behind the man was another substantial fragment of what appeared to be a large eye with eyebrow and red hair or colouring above it. It looked to me like part of the face of a bull ... but I could not be sure. What was obvious was that there were thousands of plaster fragments lying here, some face up, some face down, close to the great mudbrick fortress wall from the Hyksos period.

The whole world would soon come to hear of the

wonderful 'Minoan' frescoes found in the Egyptian delta by the Austrians. Their discovery has not only caused a sensation in the press but has really set the cat amongst the pigeons within scholarly circles because of the dramatic implications an associated find is having on the debate over the dating of the eruption of Thera (see *Chapter Eight*). It also radically alters our understanding of the influence of Minoan/Aegean culture on the rest of the ancient world at the beginning of the Late Bronze Age – the time when Egypt was casting off the shackles of Hyksos domination and when Agamemnon's ancestors were arriving in the Argolid to found Golden Mycenae – the event which marks the birth of the Heroic Age of Bronze Age Greece.

A single author cannot speak with the high authority of a panel of experts, but he may succeed in giving to his work an integrated and even an epical quality that no composite volume can achieve. Homer as well as Herodotus was a Father of History – as Gibbon, the greatest of our historians, was aware – and it is difficult, in spite of certain critics, to believe that Homer was a panel. History writing today has passed into an Alexandrian age, where criticism has overpowered creation. Faced by the mountainous heap of the minutiae of knowledge and awed by the watchful severity of his colleagues, the modern historian too often takes refuge in learned articles or narrowly specialised dissertations – small fortresses that are easy to defend from attack. His work can be of the highest value; but it is not an end in itself. I believe that the supreme duty of the historian is to write history, that is to say, to attempt to record in one sweeping sequence the greater events and movements that have swayed the destinies of Man.

[Steven Runciman: *The First Crusade* (London, 1951)]

INTRODUCTION

For more than two thousand years Europe and its offspring (collectively labelled the 'Western World') have played a significant role in the history and cultural development of our planet. From Classical Greece to Rome and on into Renaissance Europe – which saw a revival in the arts of those two remarkable civilisations – the people of the West have steadily come to dominate humankind (for good or ill). Western Civilisation has created its own particular character and perspectives – admittedly influenced over the centuries by its many cultural strands but, even so, retaining an over-arching culture which makes 'Westerners' quite distinct from their eastern neighbours whose traditions grew out of the civilisations of ancient Mesopotamia, pharaonic Egypt and Arabian Islam. Towards the Far East, oriental culture developed independently of Old World Mediterranean and Levantine influences and does not play a part in our story. So, when I mention Easterners in the context of *The Lords of Avaris* I am referring to the peoples of what has become known as the Middle East – in other words the Semitic- and Hamito-Semitic-speaking civilisations of the ancient world.

Archaeology and history inform us that we all origi-nated from the same Bronze Age milieu of the eastern

Mediterranean in the third and second millennia before the birth of Christ, yet the peoples of 'East' and 'West' have always been undeniably separate in respect of their languages, cultural backgrounds and heritage. Why? What made our Indo-European-speaking ancestors – the Anatolians, Greeks and Romans – so different from the Semitic-speaking Assyrians, Babylonians and Canaanites, and the Hamito-Semitic Egyptians?

The traditions which our ancestors have passed down to us overflow with stories of legendary heroes and their mighty deeds. What child of the West has not heard of King Minos and his mysterious Labyrinth, or Hercules – the world's strongest man? What young imagination remains unmoved by the Homeric tales of Agamemnon, king of Golden Mycenae, ferocious Achilles, honourable Hector and the bloody Trojan War? And we must not forget wily Odysseus and his ten-year wanderings across the Mediterranean, or, last but not least, the Trojan refugee Aeneas – legendary founder of Roman civilisation. These mighty heroes and events were all part of the 'Heroic Age' of Man (as Hesiod put it) which the citizens of Athens and Rome held to be their historical heritage – and, yes, they really did believe it. Yet, for the past two hundred years, scholars have labelled these traditions as 'mythological' and generally disassociated them from 'real history', preferring to draw only upon the 'facts' of archaeology. You may have always believed that the Trojan War was an historical reality but you will rarely find a scholarly work written in our scientific age prepared to give historical credence to any of these marvellous tales. They are merely legends – and legends cannot be the stuff of history. Yet these stories are undeniably the foundation of our cultural origins. So are we merely the offspring of myth?

The origins of Western Civilisation are traditionally founded in the Classical Greek and Roman worlds which themselves trace their history back to the Heroic Age of Minoan Crete, Mycenaean Greece and Trojan Anatolia (modern Turkey). The rich and, it has to be said, complex legendary history of southern European civilisation, bordering the north Mediterranean coast, is laced throughout with strands of what the Greeks called *muthos*, inevitably involving the difficult relationship between Man and gods. And for centuries these 'myths' were regarded as nothing more than that. No real history was credited to the ancient poets and orators such as Homer and Hesiod. Little more respect was given to Roman poets such as Virgil who dramatised the adventures of the Trojan hero Aeneas. To Victorian scholars of Classical History all this was patent myth reflecting the constant struggle between early human activity and uncompromising nature. Then along came Heinrich SCHLIEMANN who, almost single-handedly, began to transform legend into history.

In 1870 he commenced his excavations at the little mound of Hissarlik, beside the Hellespont in north-west Turkey. Within decades the extraordinary ancient world of Mycenaean Bronze Age Greece had been revealed to the modern world: a high-bastioned city of Troy to substantiate Homer's epic saga of the Trojan War; and a brooding, Cyclopean citadel at Mycenae, replete with royal burials, to put historical flesh on the Heroic Age of Achaean Greece.

Soon after, at the turn of the twentieth century, Arthur EVANS was exhilarating the Edwardian public with his amazing discoveries at Knossos, labyrinthine home of King Minos and the terrible Minotaur – supposedly a place which also existed only in the dream-like world of mythology. Then, in 1906, came the unearthing of the mighty city of Hattusha at Boghazköy in central Anatolia by the German archaeologist Hugo WINCKLER which, for the first time, produced tangible archaeological evidence (including a huge archive of cuneiform tablets) to confirm the existence of the mysterious Hittites of the Bible. Indo-European archaeology, from the Anatolian highlands, across the Aegean to the

Greek mainland, was rising, phoenix-like, from the ashes of the past. By the middle of the twentieth century, this new and vigorous avenue of scholarly research had transformed our understanding of the origins of Western Civilisation and was destined to rival the already well-established Near Eastern disciplines centred on Egypt, the Levant and Mesopotamia.

But there was a problem. This early western world had no timeline. The Indo-European civilisations of Greece, Crete, Hatti (the Hittites) and Troy were all dependent on Egypt and Mesopotamia for their dating. This was simply because these two older cultures already possessed a well-established chronology (from here on referred to as the Orthodox Chronology or OC) based on nearly a century of scholarly endeavour. The Egyptian timeline, especially, was 'fixed to within a decade or so' according to conventional Egyptological wisdom. It is important to understand that, as Professors Anthony Harding and John Tait put it in 1989, chronology 'is the lynch-pin on which our interpretations of the past depend'.[1] So, constructing the right timeline is crucial to achieving a proper understanding of events and personalities in the distant past and their historical relationship to each other.

In the first book of this series, *A Test of Time: The Bible – From Myth to History* (1995), I proposed a radical down-dating of Egyptian history (known as the New Chronology or NC), removing some three centuries of 'artificial' time from the era of the NEW KINGDOM and THIRD INTERMEDIATE PERIOD. This produced a remarkable re-alignment with events and personalities described in the biblical narratives and, for the first time, gave these Old Testament stories a genuine archaeological background – something which the Orthodox Chronology had plainly failed to achieve over the previous century.

Since *A Test of Time* appeared, a whole raft of scholarly books has been published which question the historicity of the Bible – sadly based on the old chronological scheme which offers virtually no archaeological evidence in support of biblical history. The New Chronology has been ignored by these writers despite the clear advantages it offers for an historical interpretation of the Old Testament narratives. The principal reason given for this rejection is that the NC is simply too radical – the currently accepted chronology cannot be *that* wrong surely? Instead scholars prefer to adopt what many would regard as an even more radical stance – that the Bible is all wrong. The Israelite Sojourn in Egypt has been questioned; the Conquest of the Promised Land denied; the empire of David and Solomon reduced to a tiny rustic chiefdom. Thus the Old Testament has been cast into the murky depths of mythology and fable – ironically enough, just as the legendary past of the Indo-European world is beginning to surface into the light of real history.

But the New Chronology is not just about Egypt and the Bible. It holds dramatic consequences for the subject of this book – the origins and history of our Indo-European forebears. Applying the New Chronology to Anatolia, Greece and Rome produces astonishing results which give real credence to the Classical legends and remove in a single brush-stroke the many imperfections in the archaeological picture of our ancestral past.

Flinders Petrie and the Dark Age of Greece

Sir William Matthew Flinders PETRIE is regarded as the 'Father of Egyptian Archaeology' because he was the first Egyptologist to treat *everything* he excavated as relevant for the better understanding of Egyptian civilisation. Above all, he recognised the importance of pottery – broken or intact – for establishing a relative chronology in different parts of Egypt and the rest of the ancient world. Prior to Petrie's first visit to Egypt in 1880 (and it has to be said for some time after) other excavators were only interested in trophies for their financial sponsors and museums. What they were after was fine statuary and reliefs – anything monumental. They were simply unimpressed by the huge quantities of broken pot-sherds scattered over the sites which they were digging. Petrie, on the other hand, realised that this pottery held the key to dating the strata or occupation levels of the sites by means of a fairly straightforward and understandable logic.

(1) Pots are made of different fabrics (clays) and are decorated in many different ways/styles (colours, glazes, designs). They can be hand-made or wheel-made. Firing techniques vary. And, obviously, ceramic vessels can be formed into a large variety of different shapes and sizes (depending on their function). These attributes were dictated by the then-current technology and fashion and were therefore symptomatic of different eras (some lasting only a short time and others for centuries). In principle, therefore, a study of all these characteristics allows a pottery specialist to determine contemporary levels at different sites throughout Egypt and even neighbouring countries where a set of characteristics corresponds. Even broken fragments (sherds) can be dated – if they are from key parts of the pot (such as rim, base, handle or shoulder). These elements characterise what we call the 'diagnostics' of the pottery.

(2) In Egypt strata can often be dated by the recovery of inscribed material bearing the names of pharaohs or well-known members of the royal family and government. If you find a pot of a certain style, archaeologically associated with an inscription naming a king, then this type of ceramic must have been manufactured when that king was on the throne (or thereabouts). Find an identical pot in a stratum of a Canaanite/Israelite city such as Megiddo, for example, and you might be justified in assuming that this city level was also contemporary with that Egyptian monarch (depending on how long the pottery style lasted).

(3) Absolute dates for the Egyptian kings were the first dates to be determined by scholars specialising in the pre-Graeco-Roman world. Egyptologists are thus the *de facto* high priests of chronology and bequeath their Egyptian dates to the pottery styles of the ancient world and, therefore, to many of its civilisations – especially those which are not so rich in inscribed monuments compared to Egypt.

The classic example of this dating technique was initiated by Petrie himself when he almost single-handedly established the dates for the Mycenaean Late Bronze Age which, at the same time, led to the 'discovery' of the Greek Dark Age. Quite an achievement. He is therefore not only rightly regarded as the father of Egyptian archaeology but also the father of all the chronological conundrums of the Indo-European world with which *The Lords of Avaris* is concerned.

I hasten to say that this is not entirely Petrie's fault. He was not solely responsible for the high Egyptian dates of the Orthodox Chronology which I exposed in *A Test of Time*. These were already pretty much in use by Petrie's day. What he did was to find Greek Bronze Age pottery – identical to that found by Heinrich Schliemann at Mycenae – in datable Egyptian contexts. He then, quite correctly, proposed that Golden Mycenae could be dated by the Egyptian evidence.

Petrie first arrived in Egypt in 1880, commissioned with the task of measuring the Great Pyramid in order to test out the theories of his sponsor, Piazzi Smyth – the somewhat eccentric Astronomer Royal of Scotland. He was back in Egypt two years later in the company of Archibald Sayce, Professor of Assyriology at Oxford University. The two men sailed up the Nile in a DAHABIYA, exploring the sites and collecting samples of pottery for study as they went. At Tell el-Amarna Petrie picked up large quantities of vivid blue painted pottery typical of the late 18th Dynasty and he determined to return to excavate at the site of Akhenaten's royal city at some time in the future.

Between 1882 and 1890 the young English Egyptologist obtained concessions to dig at various sites. In 1885 he was excavating at Naucratis – the first known Aegean trading colony in Egypt's western delta, founded by Greek merchants during the reign of Pharaoh PSAMTEK I according to Herodotus.[2] The Greek pottery unearthed there was subsequently used to date many of the Greek colony sites around the Mediterranean (where similar ceramics were found) to the last decades of the 26th Dynasty (just prior to the Persian invasion of Egypt in 525 BC).

Then, in the winter season of 1889-90, Petrie found himself working at Kahun in the Faiyum, close to the waterway known as the Bahr Yussef which, in *A Test of Time*, I identified as the work of the Israelite patriarch Joseph when he was vizier for King Amenemhat III of the late 12th Dynasty. Here Petrie excavated a shaft tomb from the New Kingdom which contained ten coffins and around forty burials. The principal named individual in the central burial chamber was 'the lady of the house, Maket' and so the tomb has gone down in the literature as the 'Tomb of Maket'.

Amongst the ceramic repertoire in the tomb were a number of vessels which Petrie recognised as 'Aegean' in origin (twelve of which were of a class we now call Late Cypriot ware). The most significant vessel came from coffin number nine. This was a Mycenaean squat jar with single handle, decorated in an ivy-leaf design (a rare type now classified within Late Helladic or Mycenaean IIB). Also associated with the burials were scarabs bearing the cartouches of Thutmose I, Thutmose II and Thutmose III (conventionally dated from 1493 to 1425 BC). In the same season, Petrie excavated at nearby Gurob and found more of this 'Aegean' pottery.

Moving on to Tell el-Hesi in southern Palestine, Petrie worked through the summer of 1890, finding Bronze Age Aegean pottery in the deeper levels and Iron Age Greek pottery, identical to that at Naucratis, in the upper levels of the mound. A chronology for Greek pottery, and therefore Greek civilisation, was beginning to emerge.

In April 1891 Petrie felt that it was crucial to make a special trip to Greece in order to study the pottery found by Schliemann at Mycenae before confidently declaring to the world that the matter of Greek chronology had been resolved.

> ... hundreds of pieces of pottery, purely Mycenaean in style, have been found in various dateable discoveries in Egypt, and without exception every datum for such lies between 1500 and 1100 BC, and earlier rather than later in that range. So far I have not heard of a single fragment of dated evidence to set against these facts.[3]

The Heroic Age of Agamemnon and his capital, Mycenae, had to be dated to the Egyptian New Kingdom – in other words from the fifteenth to twelfth centuries BC – whilst the Iron Age pottery of the Greek colonies (typified by the material from Naucratis) was securely anchored to the Egyptian 26th Dynasty (from 664 BC onwards). Earlier Iron Age pottery would later be identified which took the date for the beginning of Archaic Greece back to around 800 BC. But this still appeared to leave a gap of several centuries between the Bronze Age Greeks (with their Mycenaean pottery) and the later Iron Age Greeks of the 'historical' era. There was only one way to reconcile Petrie's dating, based on the archaeological evidence and the written sources from the Graeco-Roman world. There had to have been an extended collapse in Greek culture to explain the archaeological gap – a long period of darkness which seemed to have been forgotten by the Greeks themselves. Thus the Greek Dark Age was born – with all its controversial historical consequences.

That controversy began almost immediately when antiquarian scholar Cecil Torr launched into a ferocious attack upon Petrie and his new chronology for the Greek world. It has to be remembered that before Petrie's announcement it was generally thought that the Heroic Age of Homer's Greece, unearthed by Schliemann, had been followed immediately by the 'historical age' (consisting of the Archaic and Classical periods) – without a gap. In a series of letters published in the *Classical Review*[4] and *The Academy*[5] the two combatants slugged it out with little give or take. Torr eventually became the 'last man standing', not because he had won the argument but simply because he had ground Petrie into submission with his constant barrage of letters. The Egyptologist had made his case for a new Aegean chronology to his own satisfaction and retired from the ring, leaving the antiquarian to shadow-box amongst the ghosts of the old Classical chronology.

> A repetition of attacks already answered naturally leads to a repetition of answers. But as I have now fully noticed every fact alleged against my views on the Aegean pottery, I fail to see that I am called on to take further notice of the subject at present.[6]

Petrie simply gave up the contest, through frustration and boredom with the never-ending debate. He had better things to do with his time. Torr briefly relished his moment.

> Mr Petrie's collapse seems to be tolerably complete.[7]

However, the Egyptologist soon had the last word when he finally settled the argument to most scholars' satisfaction, having secured his long-sought concession to dig at Amarna for the winter season of 1891-92. There, in the central city, he collected a grand total of 1,329 Mycenaean sherds, proving unequivocally that this Bronze Age pottery had to be dated to the time of Akhenaten (OC – *c*. 1350 BC) and for a period either side of his reign. The particular type of Mycenaean pottery found at Amarna by Petrie has now been more narrowly classified as LH IIIA:2 (i.e. Late Helladic period III, phase A, sub-phase 2). By 1894 Petrie was able to proclaim his Greek Bronze Age dating with complete assuredness.

> There are few facts in all archaeology determined
> with a more overwhelming amount of evidence
> than the dating of this earlier stage of Aegean
> pottery.[8]

The debate was over. There was now no doubt that the Heroic/Mycenaean Age of Greece had come to an end long before the rise of Archaic Greece. The Dark Age was a fact. A chronological scheme was soon devised which determined that Bronze Age Mycenaean pottery was manufactured between *circa* 1500 BC and *circa* 1100 BC; the Dark Age followed, lasting for about three centuries; then the Iron Age Archaic period had its beginnings in around 800 BC.

Before we begin to unpick and unravel this now conventional dating scheme, I think it might be useful to provide a general history of the period under discussion. Here I will be telling the story from within the *A Test of Time* model (that is, using the New Chronology or NC framework) so that you can get to grips with the scheme and, thus armed, cope admirably with this marvellous historical era in which you are about to be immersed. By adopting an identical NC approach to the question of the Indo-European-speaking civilisations as I did for the Egyptian dynasties, I will be revealing a very different historical picture, much closer to that envisaged by the historians of Classical Greece and Rome themselves – a history, moreover, which does not require a long Greek Dark Age.

A Brief History

Our story begins in the opening years of the second millennium BC. Many of the rich Middle Eastern cities of the Early Bronze Age have already been destroyed and abandoned as a result of some great but, as yet, unidentified cataclysm involving earthquakes and fire. A series of severe famines had reduced the population of the ancient world to a tiny percentage of what it had been in the prosperous days of the Early Bronze II era. People were on the move, searching for new homelands where conditions afforded them a better chance of survival. These were truly difficult times.

In Egypt, a tomb inscription of a local governor from this period (7th to 11th Dynasties) chillingly recalls the days when parents ate their own children to keep themselves alive.

> It was the beginning and end of Mankind … the sky was clouded and the Earth […] of hunger on this sandbank of Apophis. … All of Upper Egypt was dying of starvation and people were eating their children, but I did not allow anyone to die of hunger in this district. [Inscription of Ankhtify from Moalla]

The wealthy bureaucratic civilisation of Ur III in central and southern Mesopotamia was under constant attack and being seriously undermined by Amorite raiders from the northwest. In the historical scenario I have been developing over the last twenty years or so, we find Abraham and his clan forming part of that Amorite diaspora, moving south from the region of Harran to the relative safe haven of Canaan and, in Abraham's case, the Nile delta where food was more abundant in the years following the Egyptian famine recorded in the FIRST INTERMEDIATE PERIOD inscriptions. At the same instant, Indo-European-speaking tribes were appearing on the historical stage for the first time in eastern Anatolia.

The Arrival of the Indo-Europeans

Within a couple of centuries the political picture in the ancient world had changed utterly. The gradual surfacing of the ancestors of Western Civilisation – the Hittites, Mitannians, Minoans and Greeks – had produced a new mix of linguistic and ethnic groups. The old two-power axis of Egypt and Mesopotamia was replaced by a three-way struggle with the arrival of the Indo-European elites.

The Bible refers to these exotic peoples by various names – the Anakim, the Rephaim, the Kretim (Cretans), the Kaptorim (later known as the Philistines), the Hittim (Hittites), and the Yawanim (Greeks). In addition we hear of their allies from the northern mountains of the Middle East – people such as the Horim (Horites = Hurrians). The 'aliens' had taken control of the Middle Bronze Age Levantine towns, slowly establishing themselves over the ruins of the Early Bronze Age cities. With the arrival of these Indo-European ruling elites came the introduction of a new kind of settlement in Canaan – the heavily fortified city with massive rampart defences (the latter sometimes coated in gleaming white lime plaster) known as the sloping glacis.

The Israelites in Egypt

In Egypt the Theban rulers of the 12TH DYNASTY had re-established pharaonic rule over the whole country once more, following the post-Old Kingdom collapse which scholars refer to as the First Intermediate Period. The MIDDLE KINGDOM, which began with the reunification of Egypt under MONTUHOTEP II of the 11th Dynasty, was markedly different to the 'Pyramid Age' of the Old Kingdom. The pharaohs still built pyramids for themselves, but these were more practical affairs – smaller in size and less demanding in construction. Monumental architecture was now less monumental. Literature and exquisite life-size sculpture were the order of the day. The brutal grandeur and economic folly of KHUFU and KHAFRE were replaced by the human face of kingship, as expressed in the painfully honest statuary of Senuseret III and his son Amenemhat III – perhaps the greatest kings of the 12th Dynasty.

This was a key time in biblical history, for it was during the co-regency period of these two pharaohs (between 1678 and 1658 BC) that Jacob and Joseph settled their small clan in the eastern delta region of 'the Goshen' at a place called ROWATY. Gradually, over the next half-century, their small settlement grew into a large town, made up almost entirely of Semitic-speaking people of Western-Asiatic origin (that is to say, from Canaan and Syria). When Joseph became Egypt's vizier in Year 13 of Amenemhat III (1666 BC), the name of the place was changed to HA(T)WARE(T), which meant the 'House (i.e. Office) of the Department (of the North)' because it had become not only the family home of the vizier but also the centre of government for the entire delta. The later Greek writers knew the city as Auaris and our modern Egyptological literature refers to it as Avaris.

The Israelite Sojourn in Egypt began with the arrival of Jacob in Goshen during the second year of the great famine (c. 1658 BC) and ended with Moses leading his people out of enslavement and into the Sinai wilderness in the days of Exodus (c. 1447 BC). During this roughly 215-year period the 12th Dynasty came to an end and was replaced by the 13th Dynasty – an era of short-reigned kings (many of Asiatic origin or descent) and politically unstable government. Egyptologists refer to this dark era as the SECOND INTERMEDIATE PERIOD or SIP.

In the New Chronology, the SIP itself is divided up into two phases. The first part, lasting nearly two centuries, encompasses the whole of the 13th Dynasty with its population of Asiatic immigrants who eventually became slaves under the native Egyptian pharaohs from Sobekhotep III onwards (*c.* 1545 BC). The second part of this little-understood period in pharaonic history was marked by the arrival of foreign kings from the north who, having overthrown the last kings of the 13th Dynasty, took over all of LOWER EGYPT and the Nile valley as far as Cusae (south of Tell el-Amarna and Hermopolis), leaving the native Egyptian pharaohs confined to UPPER EGYPT trapped between 'a Kushite' in the south and 'an Asiatic' in the north.[9]

The northern Asiatic pharaohs were later called 'Hyksos' by the third-century BC priest-historian, Manetho, and that name has become common currency in Egyptology, with the second part of the SIP being referred to simply as the 'Hyksos Age'. It is this Second Intermediate Period (13th to 17th Dynasties) upon which we are going to concentrate in the first part of *The Lords of Avaris* as we go in search of the origins of these Hyksos kings.

Legends and Traditions

> There are two things to avoid in dealing with a legend. One is to make too much of it, the other is to disbelieve it entirely.[10]

With the appearance of 'Greeks' in the eastern Mediterranean we find ourselves confronted by a wealth of puzzling and apparently 'unhistorical' legends. The majority of scholars would strongly resist using such traditions as a tool for historical reconstruction. However, I would concur with the quote from Harold Mellersh above, commenting on the legends of Minoan Crete, and argue that we should perhaps take a less negative view of such material. Time and again legendary tales have been dismissed as fiction – only, subsequently, to be demonstrated by archaeological discovery to have a basis in truth. The least one could say is

4. Heinrich Schliemann presenting his discoveries at Hissarlik to the Society of Antiquavies, London, on 31 March 1877.

that archaeology often provides plausible historical settings for the legends of our ancestral past.

The most famous example of such an about-turn is that of the Greek ten-year war against Troy, as epitomised in Homer's magnificent poem the *Iliad*. As I have already mentioned, this celebrated piece of Western literature was regarded by nineteenth-century scholars as nothing more than a fantastical myth without historical foundation – that is, until Heinrich Schliemann, with dogged determination, resurrected the real city of Troy from the earth of north-west

Anatolia between 1870 and 1890. This 'amateur' German archaeologist, with an all-consuming passion for Homerica (and a bank balance to pursue his dream), did not, in the end, *prove* that the Trojan War was an actual historical event (that is still a matter of scholarly debate) – but he *did* dramatically reveal a Bronze Age Greek world broadly consistent with the heroic epics. Follow-up excavations and research (especially over the last decade) have confirmed, to the complete satisfaction of academia, that Schliemann is to be credited with the discovery of the city of Troy at the ruin-mound of Hissarlik, and that this location was the focus of the Homeric tradition. Indeed, tantalising evidence of the sacking of the Late Bronze Age city has been revealed. Legend has thus been given an entirely credible historical setting through archaeology. Moreover, the ancient name of that city has at last been determined by a detailed analysis of the geography of western Anatolia as given in Hittite state documents. The kingdom of Troy was known as 'Wilusa' – the Anatolian version of Homer's (W)Ilios from which the title *Iliad* derives.

> Since 1996 not only research on Troy but research on Homer too – in so far as these deal with the material base of the *Iliad* – have faced a new situation: before 1996 it was not established beyond doubt that Troy/Ilios, the setting for Homer's epic, could be equated with the ruins on the hill above the Dardanelles known as Hissarlik. ... Since 1996, however, there has been no doubt that the setting for the *Iliad* and the excavated ruins at Hissarlik must be equated: Homer's (W)Ilios is Wilusa, the city associated with the empire of the Hittites.[11]

So, if Ilios/Troy has a basis in history, what about the other Greek legends, many of which are connected to the events leading up to and following on from the *Iliad*? Could there be further material here to enlighten us about the origins of Western Civilisation?

The collection of myths and legends from ancient Greece includes a number of epics which deal with the rise and fall of the Late Bronze Age Achaeans (Mycenaeans) – the deeds of Heracles (Roman Hercules) and the adventures of Odysseus, for example – whilst others relate to the arrival of the Dorians – an event which, according to the Greeks themselves, marked the end of the Heroic Age.

However, there are also more ancient sagas, shrouded in mythological language and metaphor, which deal with the birth of Bronze Age Greek civilisation. These texts hint at distant events – memories of a sea journey and political intermarriage between an Indo-European princess and an Egyptian pharaoh, and of the settlement of Indo-European speakers along the Levantine coast. We also have the legend of Danaos in which the foundation of Mycenaean Greece is attributed to an eponymous ancestor of Homer's Danaoi who arrived in the Peloponnese from Egypt many generations earlier. What is perhaps the oldest narrative painting in the world – the West House miniature fresco at Akrotiri on the island of Santorini – may also hold the key to a long-lost epic of Homeric dimensions, concerning the migration to, and domination of, Egypt in the latter part of the Middle Bronze Age by the forebears of Agamemnon's Mycenaean Greeks.

In this book I will attempt to put these stories into an historical context which both explains them and, at the same time, casts new light on the 'shadowy period' of Hyksos rule which falls between the Middle and New Kingdoms of Egyptian dynastic history. The identity of the Hyksos kings themselves will be unearthed – and you may be surprised how their history is so colourfully woven into our legendary past. Hyksos rule in Egypt is not just a matter for Egyptologists but reaches deep down to the very roots of Western Civilisation. We will expose those hidden roots through recent archaeological discovery and an in-depth study of Bronze Age art-history. The Hyksos era will be shown to be the historical foundation underlying the Greek and Roman legends. I shall also attempt to date these events by using the New Chronology timeline and by employing the 'imaginative' way of thinking common to the growing body of NC researchers. Yes, ancient history can be fun and exciting!

The Late Bronze Age in Egypt

The Greater Hyksos dynasty (conventionally referred to as the 15th Dynasty) was eventually expelled from Egypt by Pharaoh Ahmose, the founder of the 18th Dynasty, in the early years of his second decade as ruler of Upper Egypt. This event (NC – *c*. 1181 BC[12]) marks the end of the Second Intermediate Period and the beginning of the New Kingdom.

The next four centuries saw Egypt at its zenith of power and influence. This was the age of warrior pharaohs (Ahmose I 'the Liberator'; Thutmose III 'the Napoleon of ancient Egypt', Ramesses II 'the Great') and of wealth beyond indulgence (Amenhotep III, Akhenaten and Tutankhamun). It was a time when the Land of the Pharaohs extended its political boundaries to their historical limits – as far as the Fourth Cataract of the Nile in the south and to Kadesh-on-the-Orontes on the Syrian plain in the north. Wars were fought with their new Indo-European enemies – first (during the 18th Dynasty) against the 'Indo-Aryan' kings of Mitanni in the region of the Upper Euphrates, then (during the 19th Dynasty) against the Indo-European Hittite emperors of central Anatolia. These wars were often followed by peace treaties and diplomatic marriages of foreign princesses to pharaohs (Thutmose IV, Amen-hotep III, Akhenaten, Ramesses II). Archaeology has also revealed that gift-exchange was taking place between Egypt and the Mycenaean world of mainland Greece. In addition, there is tantalising evidence that Mycenaean and Shardana mercenary troops (the latter from western Anatolia) were being hired by Pharaoh to police the New Kingdom empire.

The Close of the Bronze Age

All this came to an abrupt and calamitous end with the collapse of the Late Bronze Age kingdoms of the Near East. The Hittites of Anatolia were overthrown in an instant by anonymous marauders from the north; the wealthy Levantine city-states were burnt and destroyed by the Sea Peoples and other rogue elements (Tyre, Hamath, Hazor, Tell Abu Hawam), some never to be reoccupied (Ugarit). Famine was rife once more – even in the Nile valley where the last vestiges of New Kingdom power and authority dwindled away throughout the 20th Dynasty and completely collapsed into anarchy and civil war towards its end (following the assassination of Ramesses III in the NC model *c.* 832 BC).

What followed in Egypt was an era of division and political instability known as the Third Intermediate Period, ruled over by ineffectual pharaohs of Libyan and KUSHITE descent whose reigns constituted the 21st to 25th Dynasties. Throughout this period and beyond, Egypt rarely looked outside its own desert borders. The pharaonic empire was gone for ever, along with the other Late Bronze Age super-powers of Hatti, Crete and Mycenaean Greece. The new masters of the ancient world would come from the north – Dorian Greeks and Phrygians; and the east – Neo-Assyrians, Neo-Babylonians and Persians.

The destructions of the Late Bronze Age once more mark a major archaeological transition as we enter a new era which archaeologists have dubbed the 'Iron Age'. This began in poverty with a marked decline in the quality of archaeological remains. In the NC this is the post-Solomonic era of the Divided Monarchy when kings such as Omri, Ahab and Jeroboam II ruled over the Northern Kingdom of Israel, often at war with their neighbour, the Southern Kingdom of Judah and its kings – principally Asa, Joash and Uzziah.

It is also the period of the Greek Dark Age and its Anatolian counterpart – the time of the Mycenaean collapse, Ionian migrations and the Neo-Hittite city-states; the era when Greeks, Anatolians and Phoenicians departed by sea to the west to found colonies along the coast of North Africa, the islands of Sicily and Sardinia, and the coastal lowlands of Italy and Spain. In the Orthodox Chronology the events I have just described are stretched out over centuries but in the NC all this is compressed into a shorter and much more dynamic epoch with the migrations away from the old eastern world appearing far closer, in historical terms, to the seafaring adventures of Classical legend. You will see that the Trojan War was not just an over-exaggerated quarrel between Mycenaean Greeks and a city in northern Anatolia but an event of dramatic proportions, the consequences of which were to change the ancient world utterly. The disturbances which followed led to major movements of peoples and the collapse of long-lived and powerful civilisations – the Hittites and Egyptians amongst them. The future lay in the Aegean and western Mediterranean in the wake of Odysseus' black ship – a future for Greeks and Trojans alike on the plains of Hesperia and seven unprepossessing hills beside the River Tiber.

As the nineteenth-century German philosopher, Arthur SCHOPENHAUER, wryly commented:

> All truth passes through three stages: first, it is ridiculed; second, it is violently opposed; and third, it is accepted as self-evident.

Interestingly enough, as I write this *Introduction* in the late summer of 2004, the New Chronology theory appears to be moving gradually into phase three of Schopen-hauer's incisive observation. Some stubborn and usually conservative scholars remain in the ridicule mode, others try desperately to ignore such controversies which threaten to disturb their comfortable existence, but a few are now beginning to see the possibilities of resetting the biblical narratives in an earlier archaeological and historical period. Many of this last group of more liberally minded academics cannot, as yet, find it in themselves to accept the revised chronology without justifiable concerns – but they are now beginning to acknowledge the similarities between the Sojourn, Exodus and Conquest stories, as presented in the Bible, and the archaeology of the Middle Bronze Age.

In July 2004 I attended a British Museum colloquium on 'The Second Intermediate Period in Egypt' and had an opportunity to discuss one particular aspect of the *A Test of Time* historical model with one of the UK's most eminent and influential Egyptologists – Professor Alan Lloyd of Swansea University, who also happens to be Chairman of the Academic Committee of the Egypt Exploration Society, and a Fellow of the Society of Antiquaries of London.

In the afternoon lecture session, art historian and archaeologist Dorothea Arnold of the Metropolitan Museum in New York had focused much of her talk on the severely mutilated head and shoulders from a colossal statue of an Asiatic official of the 12th Dynasty (contemporary with the reign of Amenemhat III and his successors). She pointed out the significance of this remarkable image, found by Manfred Bietak in a tomb located behind a palace belonging to the earliest settlement at Avaris. According to Arnold, this was one of the most important discoveries of the last quarter of a century in Egypt. The high official of state was no ordinary person with his flame-red hair, pale yellow skin, and multi-coloured coat. She drew parallels, in terms of the artistic quality of the statue, to royal sculptures of Amenemhat III, announcing that she believed the Avaris statue had come from the same sculpture workshop as the royal statues of

Hawara (the pyramid site of Amenemhat). Then Arnold surprised us all by proclaiming, 'Some have identified this statue as Joseph, the Israelite vizier of Pharaoh in the book of Genesis.' This was quite an amazing thing to hear, coming out of the mouth of such an eminent scholar – and in such a distinguished gathering of international Egyptologists. Was this some sort of tacit acceptance that I may be on the right track? After all, this is precisely what I had proposed in 1995. The heresy of *A Test of Time* was normally a taboo subject in academic circles – but here was one of the great figures of Egyptology daring to remind her colleagues that this might not be such an outlandish idea.

During the post-conference reception in the Egyptian sculpture gallery, Professor Lloyd sidled up to me and we chatted about the day's lectures. I thought to myself, here's my opportunity to broach the subject of the 'Joseph statue' and get the professor's valued opinion. So I tentatively asked what he thought of Dorothea Arnold's comment. To my surprise Alan Lloyd was quite positive about the whole thing. There was no problem, in his view, with the idea of labelling this statue of a Middle Kingdom Asiatic official as 'Proto-Joseph'. In other words (and I asked him to clarify what he meant), the biblical story of Joseph in Egypt may well have derived from a real (i.e. historical) Asiatic official working for Pharaoh Amenemhat at the end of the 12th Dynasty. And this impressive statue, with its coat of many colours, could indeed be an image of that man. So, as long as we insert the word 'Proto' in front of the name Joseph, the proposition was quite acceptable.

'Well', I replied, 'taking this way of looking at things a step further, does this mean that the Asiatic population living at Avaris in the late-12th and 13th Dynasties could just as easily be labelled "Proto-Israelite"?'

The answer was, 'Yes, I don't see why not.'

'And so could there have been a "Proto-Exodus" of these Asiatic "Proto-Israelites" during the Second Intermediate Period?'

Again 'Yes.'

I could see Professor Lloyd turning this over in his mind and I chanced my arm one more time.

'So, I assume it is therefore acceptable to identify the destructions of the Middle Bronze Age cities of Canaan with a "Proto-Conquest" and to have a "Proto-Joshua" as the leader of the invaders?'

'Hmm.'

The professor pondered over the implications of the point I was making. If all these events had actually happened and then, some time later, had been collated together to form the basis of the story of Israelite origins in Egypt and Canaan, then why don't we do away with all the 'Protos' and simply accept that the events described in the biblical narratives were based on real history?

The answer is actually quite straightforward. In order to have a genuine history of the Sojourn, Exodus and Conquest – not simply a memory – it is necessary to realign ancient Near Eastern archaeology with the Old Testament timeline, and this means removing several centuries from Egyptian chronology which forms the backbone of that archaeological framework. After all, a history must be founded on clear dates and a reasonably precise chronological structure. A 'cultural memory' can remain safely nebulous in terms of its historical origins whereas a history is fixed to a secure dating framework. And that is where the problem lies. In accepting an historical Sojourn, Exodus and Conquest during the Middle Bronze Age, scholars are required to take on board a three-century downward adjustment to Egyptian chronology – a concept that is simply not acceptable as things currently stand.

The best we can expect at the moment is the sort of positive approach on offer from scholars such as Dorothea Arnold and Alan Lloyd: an acknowledgement that a series of historical personalities and events from the Middle Bronze Age era may have formed the basis or core foundation of the biblical stories.

Introduction

tion. So, I think we can say that the battle to convince people of the merits of this reworking of biblical history is a little closer to being half won. Now it is time to concentrate on winning the chronological argument and complete a Pyrrhic victory for common sense and reasoned argument. After all:

> Research is to see what everybody else has seen,
> and to think what nobody else has thought.[13]

The New Chronology revision of the ancient world is not just an issue which concerns the Egyptological fraternity (perhaps a bad choice of word). As we have seen, it matters a great deal to other disciplines such as Old Testament studies, Bronze Age Greek and Minoan archaeology, and the Classical disciplines of Homeric studies and the origins of Roman civilisation.

Time then to begin a new adventure – an odyssey of our own to rival that of Odysseus – as we go in search of a new foundation story for the Western World. Our voyage will be full of twists and turns, and, no doubt, puzzlement over strange names and places. But no adventure is worth the effort without its own set of challenges. I hope you enjoy the journey.

Part One

The Lords of Chaos

Chapter One

THE WALLS CAME TUMBLING DOWN

Discovering Jericho Tomb H13 -- The H13 Sheshi Scarab
-- The Conventional Dating of Exodus and Conquest
-- Pithom and Raamses -- The Israelite Sojourn
-- Papyrus Ipuwer -- The Fall of the 13th Dynasty

t is a clear spring morning in 1954. By 8 am the sun
has already risen high above the steep escarpment
of the Transjordanian plateau and is bathing the
Jordan valley in its warm light. Kathleen KENYON, with her
team of archaeologists and Palestinian helpers, has already
been hard at work for an hour. The archaeologists have
located a large shaft in the northern cemetery at Jericho in
what Kenyon has designated 'Area H'. This is the thirteenth
tomb to have been unearthed in that part of the site and is
thus labelled 'H13'.

The routine for clearing this type of rock-cut tomb has
already been well established. The roughly circular shaft,
cut into the flat ground north of the great mound of Middle
Bronze Age Jericho, is soon cleared of its fill of powdery earth
and rubble. In ancient times the shaft had been emptied and
refilled on several occasions as new burials were placed in

this family sepulchre. With the very last interment, a large storage jar with pointed base, two handles on the shoulder and high neck with flared rim, had been placed at the bottom of the shaft in front of the boulder which blocked the tomb entrance. The large jar is intact and even displays a skin of residue from the original evaporated contents of the vessel. Kenyon concludes that this must have formed a part of the final burial offerings which had been placed in the shaft simply because there was no room left in the chamber itself.[1]

The boulder blocking the narrow tomb entrance is pushed to one side and the stagnant air, last breathed nearly three and a half millennia ago, is allowed to escape skyward. Kenyon and her team cast their eyes across the chaotic scene which awaits them inside the burial chamber. The first thing they note is that the roof of the cave has collapsed, obliterating anything which had lain at the centre of the floor. But around the periphery of the fallen rock are numerous skeletons. Kenyon quickly realises that this is another example of something she has already found in half a dozen other tombs belonging to the Middle Bronze Age cemetery – a simultaneous burial of several bodies in a single act of interment.[2]

Four bodies lie on the right side of the chamber, their legs extended towards the centre; against the back wall the remains of another three bodies; and to the left two more. A further twenty-nine skulls are later identified in the mêlée of bones which had been brushed to one side in order to accommodate the multiple burials at the final sealing of the tomb. These are the skulls of earlier burials in H13 – but all from the last decades of Middle Bronze Age Jericho (what Kenyon calls tomb Group V). They had not been buried simultaneously like the final nine occupants.

Why were so many bodies in H13 and other tombs (such as H18, H22, G1 and J7) all buried at the same time and, clearly, at the very end of Jericho's existence as a major Middle Bronze Age city? What sort of disaster had befallen the citizens of Jericho at this time? Kenyon, in the official publication of the excavations, suggested that a disease or plague had caused the multiple deaths in the last days of the settlement, just prior to its destruction by earthquake and fire.

> It is therefore probable that disease of some sort was responsible for the simultaneous death of entire families. This may have taken place very shortly before the final destruction of the town. On this evidence from the tell (city mound), the site was then completely abandoned for a considerable period, and therefore no subsequent burials were made in these tombs.[3]

This view is now generally accepted and adds an interesting detail to the story of Jericho's destruction some time before the advent of what archaeologists call the Late Bronze Age (conventionally dated to *c.* 1550 BC). The question is *precisely* when, in the latter part of the Middle Bronze Age, this famous biblical city met its end.

The Sheshi Scarab

After several hours of work in the claustrophobic conditions of H13, Kenyon's team discovers a tiny artefact, lying on the floor between two of the last bodies to be interred in the tomb.[4] It is a scarab seal, later catalogued as 3281.

Scarabs were generally used in the ancient world to impress designs or hieroglyphs or royal cartouches into soft clay seals (*bullae*) as a means of identifying the owners of sealed jars and documents. Others – predominantly the ones bearing royal names – were perhaps status symbols or simply decorative ornaments in jewellery and clothing. This particular scarab had almost certainly fallen from the adjacent body, having been originally attached to a TOGGLE-PIN or leather necklace which had subsequently perished.[5]

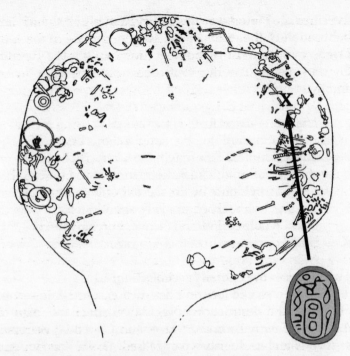

5. *Plan of Tomb H13 with the approximate position of the scarab marked by the X. The drawing of the H13 Sheshi scarab is taken from the Jericho Volume II publication and is the best version of it I could find [after Kenyon].*

6. *A typical Sheshi scarab similar to the one found in tomb H13 [photo Richard Wiskin].*

Scarab 3281 was thus a possession of one of the last inhabitants of Jericho before the Middle Bronze Age city had been destroyed and abandoned.

The underside of the tiny scarab seal (now in the Australian Institute of Archaeology collection in Melbourne) is carved with a king's name, spelt with three Egyptian hieroglyphic symbols – *sh-sh-i.* This name is well known to Egyptologists.

Pharaoh Maibre Sheshi was one of the Hyksos kings of the Second

Intermediate Period – an era of Egyptian history which lies between the fall of the Middle Kingdom (close of the 12th Dynasty) and the rise of the New Kingdom (start of the 18th Dynasty). More specifically, Sheshi was an 'Asiatic' ruler who is thought to have reigned following the collapse of the 13th Dynasty in what Egyptologists call the 'Hyksos period' (conventionally dated from c. 1640 to 1530 BC). Of course, in the New Chronology the dates for the entire Hyksos period are somewhat different (c. 1445-1181 BC) – but more on that later. For now, all you need to take on board is that Sheshi ruled some time before the expulsion of the foreign Hyksos kings by the Theban pharaohs of the late 17th and early 18th Dynasties. Precisely when, in relative terms, this King Sheshi controlled northern Egypt and southern Canaan is of paramount importance because it is the strongest clue we have as to the date of Jericho's demise.

The tiny scarab bearing Sheshi's cartouche found in H13 dates the destruction of Jericho to either the reign of this king or fairly soon after. How can I say this? Because, as several archaeologists have realised, Sheshi was not one of the renowned pharaohs of the great kingdom periods in Egyptian history and his scarabs would hardly have been regarded as 'heirlooms' to be kept and worn for centuries after his reign. That was what happened with the scarabs of great warrior kings such as Thutmose III and Ramesses II – but it is surely unreasonable to claim any prestige value for artefacts belonging to the time of the Asiatic ruler Maibre Sheshi. So, we may conclude (as did the excavators of Jericho[6]) that the finding of Sheshi's scarab in an archaeological context dates that context to this king's time or shortly after. Piotr Bienkowski, a recognised specialist in the archaeology of Jericho, makes the point.

> Scarabs of obscure Hyksos kings are not known to have been kept as heirlooms or manufactured later, and thus are a better guide to the absolute date of burial.[7]

Thus the closing of H13 and subsequent destruction of Jericho can be dated, with reasonable confidence, to the time of Sheshi or his immediate successors.

The Destruction of Joshua's Jericho

Why does it actually matter when Middle Bronze Age Jericho came to an end? Well, because this is the Jericho which was destroyed by Joshua and the Israelites – according to the New Chronology – and, as a result, the date of its destruction places not only the Conquest of the Promised Land but also the Israelite Exodus from Egypt and Moses himself in their proper historical and archaeological context.

Of course, virtually every book you will read on the subject (and the Hollywood movies) claims that Ramesses II was Pharaoh of the Exodus – the stubborn opponent of Moses. And, given that Ramesses is a Late Bronze Age king belonging to Egypt's New Kingdom, Jericho must have been destroyed by Joshua at the end of the Late Bronze Age (towards the end of the 19th Dynasty in Egyptian terms, conventionally dated to c. 1200 BC). This is obviously very different to what I am proposing with Joshua's destruction of Jericho during the Middle Bronze IIB (MB IIB) era.

So let us take a look at how historical dates have been assigned to the biblical stories – specifically how Ramesses came to be identified as the Pharaoh of the Exodus and Joshua's Jericho ended up being placed by scholars at the transition from Late Bronze IIB (LB IIB) to Iron Age IA (IA IA).

Dating Biblical Events

It all began in the nineteenth century with the initial establishment of the historical dates for the Egyptian kings, following the decipherment of hieroglyphics by Thomas YOUNG and Jean François CHAMPOLLION in the early 1820s.

Archaeology	Egypt	OC	NC
IA IIA	22nd Dynasty	**Monarchy Period**	Jeroboam II
IA IB	21st Dynasty	Solomon David Saul	
IA IA	20th Dynasty	**Judges Period** Joshua	Omri Ahab
LB IIB	19th Dynasty Ramesses II	**Exodus** Moses	**Monarchy Period** Solomon David Saul
LB IIA	Amarna Period	**Sojourn Period**	
LB I	18th Dynasty Ahmose		**Judges Period**
	15th Dynasty	Joseph	
MB IIB	14th Dynasty		Joshua
	Dudimose		**Exodus** Moses
MB IIA	13th Dynasty Amenemhat III 12th Dynasty		**Sojourn Period** Joseph

Comparison between the Orthodox Chronology (OC) and the New Chronology (NC), set against the major archaeological periods and Egyptian dynastic history. The principal differences are: (a) that in the NC the Israelite Sojourn occurs during the Middle Bronze Age (Egyptian Second Intermediate Period) rather than the Late Bronze Age (Egyptian 18th & 19th Dynasties) as in the OC; and (b) the Israelite United Monarchy period falls during the Amarna period and early 19th Dynasty in the NC whilst in the OC it occurs during the 21st Dynasty.

It was quickly determined that Ramesses II reigned in the thirteenth century BC by adding up the kings' reigns, working backwards from Shoshenk I of the 22nd Dynasty.

This Libyan pharaoh had been identified by Champollion as the biblical Shishak – the plunderer of the Temple of Solomon in 926 BC [2 Chronicles 12:1-9] according to the Bible's own internal chronology.

Ramesses II's recently refined dates of 1279-1213 BC, as proposed by Professor Kenneth Kitchen, continue to entrench this view. But it is important to understand the methodology which lies behind these apparently secure and immovable dates for Ramesses the Great.

(1) Shoshenk I's own dates (OC – 945-925 BC) are almost entirely derived from biblical chronology – not from the internal and independent Egyptian archaeological and textual evidence which rather suggests that Shoshenk should be placed in the last quarter of the ninth century BC (NC – *c.* 822-802 BC).[8]

(2) The starting point for dating the Exodus, according to the Orthodox Chronology, is therefore the *biblical date* for Shishak, who is identified with Shoshenk (based on the similarity of names). This is, in itself, an assumption without confirmatory historical evidence. Indeed, what evidence there is contradicts this crucial starting point.[9]

(3) The biblical date for Shoshenk I, founder of the 22nd Dynasty, then provides the date for Ramesses II of the 19th Dynasty, by counting backwards through the regnal years of the intervening kings belonging to 21st, 20th and late 19th Dynasties – all of which are assumed to have ruled in a single sequential line.

(4) Thus we arrive at a date for Exodus of *circa* 1260 BC in the mid-reign of Ramesses II – a date completely inconsistent with *biblical* chronology which places Exodus in *circa* 1447 BC.

Talk about two ends of a circle failing to meet! If you are going to employ a circular argument, you should at least end up completing the circle. It is important to stress how embarrassing this is. Scholars take a biblical date as their starting point, make a number of unsupported assumptions, and end up rejecting another biblical date (as well as a whole section of the Bible) because of where those assumptions have led them. This is not a convincing methodology. The proper historical approach is surely to arrive at dates for both Shoshenk I and Ramesses II based on the internal Egyptian evidence (in conjunction, of course, with known and verifiable synchronisms with other civilisations), then – and only then – having established an Egyptian chronology quite independent of the Bible, should one search for links with the Old Testament narratives to see if the stories contained in that work are verifiable through the Egyptian historical records. If the Bible has any history in it, then this will be revealed only by means of a methodological approach which does not rely on the Bible itself as a starting point.

Raamses

As a witness to how tenuous the whole process of dating the biblical stories historically has been, I shall now explain why Ramesses the Great ended up being cast in the role of the Pharaoh of the Exodus in the first place.

> Then a new king, who did not know Joseph, came to power in Egypt. 'Look', he said to his people, 'the Israelites have become much too numerous for us. Come, we must deal shrewdly with them or they will grow even more numerous and, if war breaks out, will join our enemies, fight against us and leave the country.' So they put slave masters over them to oppress them with forced labour, and they (the Israelite slaves) built Pithom and Raamses as store-cities for Pharaoh. [Exodus 1:8-11]

CHAPTER ONE

Here, in the first chapter of the book of Exodus, we read that Israelite slaves built store-cities for Pharaoh before they were able to cast off their bondage in Egypt following the Ten Plagues. The two Egyptian cities built by these Asiatic slaves are specifically named as 'Pithom and Raamses'. The first biblical name appears to represent an Egyptian foundation known as Pi-Atum (the 'Estate of Atum') and is usually identified these days with Tell er-Retaba in the Wadi Tumilat. Raamses, on the other hand, seems to be the biblical version of Pi-Ramesse – the 'Estate of Ramesses' located in the eastern delta and centred on the modern village of Kantir.

This Pi-Ramesse was the family seat and royal capital of Ramesses II. So the mention of it in Exodus 1:11 logically dates the Israelite bondage period to the time of Ramesses the Great. This has certainly been the assumption from the early days of Egyptology. But is it right?

The first reason to doubt this synchronism between Egyptian history and the Bible is the dating mismatch. As we have seen, Ramesses II is dated to the mid-thirteenth century by Egyptologists and thus the Exodus is conventionally placed in *circa* 1260 BC. However, the series of dates for the kings of Israel, provided in the Old Testament narratives, places Solomon's first year in *circa* 971 BC and the foundation of the Solomonic temple (in this king's fourth year) in 968 BC. Then, 1 Kings 6:1 states that the Exodus from Egypt took place some 480 years before the temple of Yahweh was founded in Jerusalem – which thus gives us a biblical date for the Exodus of 1447 BC (or thereabouts). Clearly 1447 BC (the Bible's date for the end of the Israelite bondage) is two hundred years *too early* for the Egyptologist's date for an Exodus in the time of Ramesses II.

Second, there is every reason to believe that the mention of the building of Pithom and Raamses in Exodus 1:11 is anachronistic – a later addition to the biblical text by a redactor or editor (possibly of the seventh century BC, during the reign of King Josiah of Judah). The reason why I think this is the case is that we have just such an example of an editorial anachronism in the book of Genesis which mentions the 'region of Ramesses' centuries before any pharaohs of that name. This is true for *any* chronology – including the conventional scheme which (according to Kitchen) places Ramesses II in 1279-1213 BC and therefore Ramesses I (founder of the 19th Dynasty) in 1295-1294 BC.

Combining two related passages in Genesis, we learn that, in the time of Pharaoh's vizier Joseph (who lived more than two centuries before Moses), the extended family of his father, Jacob, was settled in a place called Goshen – a region of the eastern delta which was also known as Ramesses.

> Your son Joseph says this: 'God has made me lord of all Egypt. Come down to me without delay. You will live in the region of Goshen where you will be near me, you, your children and your grandchildren, your flocks, your cattle and all your possessions.' [Genesis 45:9-10]

> Joseph then settled his father and brothers, giving them land holdings in Egypt, in the best part of the country, the region of Ramesses, as Pharaoh had ordered. [Genesis 47:11]

So Goshen and Ramesses are one and the same location. But why *two* names for the place where the Israelites settled? Clearly pharaohs named Ramesses did not reign until long after the settlement of the Israelites in Goshen at the time of Joseph and Jacob. Most scholars therefore accept that the mention of the 'region of Ramesses' in this passage is a later amendment or addition to the original text, made by a biblical editor in order to indicate to his readership precisely where Goshen was located in the editor's own time – that is, in the region of Egypt known as Ramesses. It is clear that the area around Kantir (anciently known as Goshen) was known as Pi-Ramesse (or simply

Ramesses) from the reign of Ramesses II right down into the early centuries AD.

Retaining a Late Bronze Age Israelite Bondage and Exodus in the time of Ramesses II begs a number of questions.

(1) If the 'region of Ramesses' in Genesis 47:11 is an anachronism, why then is the 'city of Raamses' of Exodus 1:11 regarded as historically accurate and not also anachronistic?

(2) Why do scholars hang the chronology of Sojourn, Exodus and Conquest entirely on this single passage when the Old Testament text clearly states that the Exodus took place in *circa* 1447 BC (480 years before Solomon) rather than *circa* 1260 BC (the reign of Ramesses II)?

(3) What other evidence is there that Ramesses II ruled over a large Asiatic population of slaves? Where are their houses and graves in the city of Pi-Ramesse (currently being excavated by Edgar Pusch's German archaeological mission at Kantir)? Where are the Ramesside slave lists of the 19th Dynasty? Has all this simply disappeared along with the Israelites who wandered off into oblivion across the Sinai wilderness?

(4) Apparently, according to archaeologists working in Israel, these refugees from Egyptian slavery did not turn up there. Professor Israel Finkelstein of Tel Aviv University – the doyen of Israeli archaeology – having (along with his colleagues) undertaken a detailed survey of the hill country of the Holy Land, continues to make it quite clear that no newcomers from Egypt arrived at the end of the Late Bronze Age to usurp the indigenous population of Canaanites. The people who settled in the hills of Ephraim during the Early Iron Age were

culturally identical to the Late Bronze Age 'Canaanites' who lived there before them.

> The process ... is, in fact, the opposite of what we have in the Bible: the emergence of early Israel was an outcome of the collapse of the Canaanite culture, not its cause. And most of the Israelites did not come from outside Canaan – they emerged from within it. There was no mass Exodus from Egypt. There was no violent conquest of Canaan. Most of the people who formed early Israel were local people – the same people whom we see in the highlands throughout the Bronze and Iron Ages. The early Israelites were – irony of ironies – themselves originally Canaanites![10]

(5) Finkelstein also points out another obvious problem with the theory of a Late Bronze Age Conquest by the Israelites. Why does this major disturbance (with numerous Canaanite cities being attacked and destroyed according to the book of Joshua) not reveal itself in the administrative records of the 19th Dynasty – a group of kings that exercised widespread military control over its northern province?

> It is highly unlikely that the (19th Dynasty) Egyptian garrisons throughout the country would have remained on the sidelines as a group of refugees (from Egypt) wreaked havoc throughout the province of Canaan. And it is inconceivable that the destruction of so many loyal vassal cities (of Egypt) by the (Israelite) invaders would have left absolutely no trace in the extensive records of the Egyptian empire. ... Something clearly doesn't add up when the biblical account, the archaeological evidence, and the Egyptian records are placed side by side.[11]

(6) And, most tellingly, where is the Late Bronze Age Jericho destroyed by Joshua according to the Bible? It certainly does not exist at Tell es-Sultan where the archaeologists were unable to identify the remains of any walled city between the destruction of the mighty Middle Bronze Age stronghold and the modest town of the Iron Age.[12]

(7) What happened to all the cities supposedly destroyed by the Israelite tribes during the Conquest of the Promised Land? John Bimson and, subsequently, a number of authorities have demonstrated that few, if any, of the towns claimed as destroyed by Joshua were in fact destroyed at this time, or even existed at the end of the Late Bronze Age.

(8) Moreover, what cities did exist in this era were not even walled (as described in the Joshua narrative). Why? Because the local rulers enjoyed the protection of the Egyptian 19th Dynasty military network. This is the antithesis of the picture presented in the Conquest story.

> In the Bible, no Egyptians are reported outside the borders of Egypt and none are mentioned in any of the battles within Canaan. Yet contemporary texts and archaeological finds indicate that they managed and carefully watched over the affairs of the country. ... there were no city walls. The formidable Canaanite cities described in the conquest narrative were not protected by fortifications! The reason apparently was that, with Egypt firmly in charge of security for the entire province, there was no need of massive defensive walls.[13]

It seems to me and many observers that, by uncritically adopting Exodus 1:11 as the single dating criteria for the

EARLY IRON AGE TOWN
NC – *c.* 860 BC
OC – *c.* 1100 BC
LATE BRONZE AGE
No Fortified Settlement
MB IIB (late)
NC – *c.* 1407 BC – destroyed
OC – *c.* 1550 BC
MB IIB (early) CITY
MB IIA CITY
NC – *c.* 1750 BC
OC – *c.* 2000 BC
EARLY BRONZE AGE CITY

A simplified chronological chart showing the successive settlements on the mound of Jericho with the period of abandonment, during the last part of the Middle Bronze IIB and Late Bronze Age, indicated by the darker shading.

Exodus, scholars have created for themselves a bed of nails that is not only hurting their own credibility but also doing untold damage to the authority of the Old Testament as an historical document worthy of further study and research. Such doubts about the accuracy of the Exodus and Conquest narratives lead Finkelstein legitimately to question the historical value of the entire early Old Testament epic.

> Did the Conquest of Canaan really happen? Is this
> central saga of the Bible – and of the subsequent
> history of Israel – history or myth?[14]

Conservative scholars have a lot to answer for if they continue stubbornly to hold on to the idea that the Israelites built the city of Pi-Ramesse of the 19th Dynasty – a statement which is almost certainly anachronistic. Following the pattern of Genesis 47:11, the Israelites may well have built a city at or near the place where the later royal estate of Ramesses II was constructed – but they did not build *that* city.

It just so happens that there is another city located in the immediate vicinity of Kantir – a much older settlement known as Avaris. This huge Middle Bronze Age population centre consisted principally of Asiatic people originating from Syria and Canaan. They lived in mudbrick houses within farming compounds where they kept their animals, baked bread and buried their dead. The vast majority of these Asiatics then abandoned Avaris towards the end of the MB IIA archaeological period after a plague. According to the scarab evidence and archaeological finds at Tell ed-Daba (the site of the main tell of Avaris), this abandonment appears to have taken place just prior to the reigns of pharaohs Sheshi and Nehesi (with whom we shall be dealing in some detail in the next chapter). Within a couple of generations we also see the destruction of MB IIB Jericho with its Tomb H13 Sheshi scarab.

All this seems to fit the stories of Exodus and Conquest remarkably well – especially when we examine the nature of the MB IIA settlement at Tell ed-Daba (Avaris) and the MB IIB Jericho destruction.

Remarkable Parallels

It is interesting to compare what the Bible has to say about the Sojourn and Exodus with the comments of the Field Director in respect of Strata H and G at Avaris.

The Israelite settlement and subsequent departure from Egypt as described in the book of Exodus:

> Then Joseph died, and his brothers, and all that generation. But the Israelites were fruitful and prolific; they became so numerous and powerful that eventually the whole land was full of them. [Exodus 1:6-7]

> And at midnight Yahweh struck down all the first-born in Egypt from the first-born of Pharaoh, heir to the throne, to the first-born of the prisoner in the dungeon ... and there was great wailing in Egypt, for there was not a house without its dead. It was still dark when Pharaoh summoned Moses and Aaron and said, 'Up, leave my subjects, you and the Israelites! Go and worship Yahweh as you have asked! And take your flocks and herds as you have asked, and go! And bless me too!' The Egyptians urged the people on and hurried them out of the country ... [Exodus 12:29-33]

Professor Manfred Bietak on the Asiatic settlement of Stratum H and Stratum G at Tell ed-Daba:

> Over the course of this period, the (Asiatic) settlement expanded considerably but suffered a crisis near its end. Tombs found in excavation

> areas F/1 and A/II, areas which are more than
> five hundred metres apart from each other, were
> obviously emergency graves. Some of them are
> merely pits into which bodies were thrown. Most
> were without offerings. We think the evidence
> suggests that an epidemic swept through the
> town.[15]

> On Tell A ... a drastic reduction of the settlement
> activity can be found immediately afterwards.[16]

Here then we see clear parallels between the Old Testament
narrative and the modern archaeologists' findings: the
initial settlement of Asiatics – that is, Semitic-speaking
peoples – beginning in the late 12th Dynasty at the site of
Avaris in Goshen (= the arrival of the Israelites under the
patriarchs Joseph and Jacob); the rapid expansion of that
Asiatic population during the 13th Dynasty (= the prolific
increase in Israelite numbers following Joseph's death);
and, finally, a terrible epidemic with numerous death-pits,
followed immediately by the abandonment of the main
(eastern) suburb of the town by the foreigners (= the Tenth
Plague and Exodus).

A similar comparison can be made at Jericho perhaps
no more than a couple of generations later.

The Israelite tribes destroy Jericho in the book of Joshua:

> At once the people stormed the city, each man
> going straight forward, and they captured the
> city. They enforced the curse of destruction on
> everyone in the city: men and women, young
> and old, including the oxen, the sheep and the
> donkeys, slaughtering them all. ... They burned
> the city and everything inside it ... 'Accursed
> before Yahweh be the man who rises up and
> rebuilds this city!' [Joshua 6:20-26]

Piotr Bienkowski on the end of MB IIB Jericho:

> The final MB II buildings at Jericho were destroyed violently by fire. The walls were covered by a thick layer of burnt debris washed down from higher up the slope during the subsequent period of abandonment and erosion. ... There is no material on the tell or in the tombs which can be dated between the early sixteenth and the late fifteenth centuries BC (in the OC).[17]

Here Kenyon even found that the mighty Middle Bronze Age mudbrick wall which surmounted the city mound, ringing the settlement, had collapsed and literally tumbled down the slope to the base of the mound where it effectively acted as a ramp leading 'up into the city' [Joshua 6:20]. And so, in dramatic parallel to our understanding of Jericho's fall, 'the walls came a-tumblin' down' – just as in the old spiritual bemoaning the bondage of the American cotton slaves.

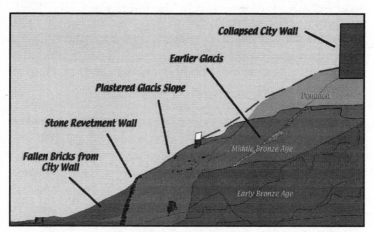

7. Cross-section of the sloping glacis defences of MB Jericho showing the remains of the mudbrick defensive wall which collapsed and rolled down the slope ending up below the lower revetment wall of the glacis [after Kenyon].

The Israelites in Egypt

Allow me to briefly tell (because split infinitives are now permitted) the story of the Israelite sojourn in the New Chronology archaeological and historical context. We are now in the Middle Bronze II period (archaeologically) and coming towards the end of the Middle Kingdom (historically).

(1) In the reign of Senuseret II (NC – *c.* 1716-1698 BC) Asiatic traders are entering Egypt, their donkey caravans crossing Sinai loaded with Canaanite goods to barter in the Nile valley. The scene of Abishai and his thirty-seven-strong caravan bringing eye make-up, depicted in the tomb of Khnumhotep at Beni Hassan, reflects this contact between Canaan and Egypt. Shortly after (in the reigns of the co-regents Senuseret III and Amenemhat III) the boy Joseph is brought into Egypt by just such 'Midianite' caravaneers to be sold into domestic servitude.

(2) After a series of trials and adventures the young Israelite rises to the exalted position of vizier and right-hand man to Pharaoh (identified in the NC as Amenemhat III). Towards the end of the 12th Dynasty (and subsequently) the historical records begin to reveal high officials of state with Semitic names.

(3) Joseph settles his family (the tribe of Jacob) in the land of Goshen in the eastern delta. Archaeological excavations in the eastern delta have produced clear evidence of an influx and settlement of Asiatics in the region around Tell ed-Daba/Kantir at this time (late 12th Dynasty).

(4) Jacob's sons bring their flocks with them. The burials of the Asiatic chieftains at Avaris are accompanied by donkey and sheep sacrifice. The sheep are of the long-haired Levantine variety.

8. Colourfully clad caravaneers entering Egypt during the reign of Senuseret II [tomb of Khnumhotep, Beni Hassan].

(5) Joseph dies in old age but his people continue to prosper and multiply. During the 13th Dynasty, the site of Avaris/Tell ed-Daba expands dramatically as the Asiatic/Semitic population increases.

(6) The Israelites are enslaved by a pharaoh who 'did not know Joseph'. In the reign of Sobekhotep III (twentieth ruler of the 13th Dynasty) documents record lists of Asiatic domestic slaves bearing Semitic names, several of which are attested in biblical Hebrew.

(7) The Israelite slaves are forced into hard labour, overseen by Egyptian taskmasters. Anthropological examination of the skeletal remains of the Asiatics buried at Avaris reveal signs of ill-health and malnourishment. Life expectancy amongst these people is as low as thirty-four years.

(8) According to Artapanus, Moses is born in the reign of Khenophres (identified in the NC with Khaneferre Sobekhotep IV, twenty-third ruler of the 13th Dynasty) and eventually leads his people out of Egypt following

a series of devastating plagues. At the end of Stratum G at Tell ed-Daba the archaeologists have discovered mass burials in shallow pits. They believe that these emergency burials are the result of plague. The Asiatic settlement is then abandoned, leaving only Egyptian houses still occupied.

(9) The Israelites cross Sinai and head for the Promised Land, meeting Amalekites from the north on their way. Avaris (Stratum F) sees the arrival of Asiatic warriors who settle in the ruins of the abandoned Stratum G settlement. They build a temple to Baal/Seth.

The parallels I have drawn here between the biblical narrative and the archaeological record are, I think, you will agree, remarkable. The question is, are they merely coincidence?

The Ipuwer Papyrus

'The Admonitions of an Egyptian Sage', as Sir Alan GARDINER has called the text of Papyrus Leiden 344 (recto), is a plea to an unnamed king of Egypt by a sage named Ipuwer, who relates to his lord how the land of Egypt has degenerated into chaos. The papyrus itself was found at Memphis and, according to Gardiner, is to be dated to the 19th Dynasty at the earliest. However, the PALAEOGRAPHY and ORTHOGRAPHY suggest that this 19th Dynasty version was a copy of an earlier 18th Dynasty text, whereas the language is typical of the Middle Kingdom. Gardiner, on somewhat tenuous grounds, proposed a date at the beginning of the First Intermediate Period for the original story. Because of his authority in the discipline of ancient Egyptian linguistics, Gardiner's view held sway for many years. On the other hand, he himself conceded that a date as late as the early 18th Dynasty could not be excluded[18] and, more recently, a number of respected scholars have come to the conclusion that Gardiner's First-Intermediate-Period date for the Ipuwer story appears 'contradictory and untenable'.[19]

In 1966 John van Seters convincingly argued that the original Ipuwer text belonged securely in the late Middle Kingdom or Second Intermediate Period.[20] He has shown that the orthography and language are, in fact, not typical of Old Kingdom texts and that, if Gardiner's view holds, then 'the many intimate connections with the Middle Kingdom' would have to be 'considered merely as anticipations'. There are so many points of language, social structure and ethnic terminology which favour the later period that our current view of Egyptian cultural and social history would have to be turned on its head if a First-Intermediate-Period date is to be retained.

I shall briefly summarise van Seters' arguments concerning the Admonitions of Ipuwer here and rely on the reader to pursue the points in more detail in the original work. His telling observations include the following.

(1) The *Medjai* (Nubian mercenaries) are not attested as a pro-Egyptian military force until the Middle Kingdom, yet they appear in the Ipuwer text as friendly to the Egyptian authorities and to be relied upon during troubled times (unlike other neighbouring peoples).[21]

> Every man fights for his sisters and protects himself. Is it Kushites? Then we will protect ourselves! There are plenty of fighters to repel the *Setetyu* (Bowmen). Is it Libyans? Then we will turn them back! However, the Medjai are content with Egypt. [Admonitions 14:10[22]]

(2) The term *Setetyu,* used to designate Asiatics who carry the bow, is common during the Middle Kingdom but does not occur in this form during the Old Kingdom and rarely in the New Kingdom.[23]

There are plenty of fighters to repel the *Setetyu*.
[Admonitions 14:11]

The troops we raised for ourselves have become
Setetyu bent on destroying! What has come of it
is to let the Asiatics know the state of the land.
[Admonitions 15:1]

(3) Winlock[24] noted that there was a shortage of coffin wood
from Syria and Lebanon (specifically the port of Byblos)
near the beginning of the Second Intermediate Period
– a situation which is reflected in the Admonitions.

   None indeed sail north to Byblos today. What
   shall we do for the cedar wood for the making
   of coffins? [Admonitions 3:6]

(4) The term *Keftiu*, used to describe a people of the eastern
Mediterranean, does not occur in the Old Kingdom
and is even quite rare in the 12th Dynasty.[25] To my
knowledge, Minoan Kamares ware does not appear in
Egypt before the late 12th Dynasty.

   Free men are buried with their produce, nobles
   are embalmed with their oil. As for the Keftiu,
   they come no more. [Admonitions 3:9]

(5) 'The institution of slavery, apart from a type of serfdom
associated primarily with royal land estates, is not
attested for the Old Kingdom. Slavery is, at the earliest,
a product of the Middle Kingdom; in this period there
is clear evidence for privately owned household slaves,
male and female, who were considered as transferable,
moveable property.' The term *hem/hemet* (male/female
servant) is used seven times in the Admonitions in the
context of household slaves, exactly as it is used in the
slave-list of the Brooklyn Papyrus which is dated to the
13th Dynasty (during the reign of Sobekhotep III).

In summation of his findings van Seters makes the following statement:

> One date seems to fit all the requirements: late 13th Dynasty. The orthography and the linguistic evidence have always pointed toward this later date, and our present knowledge of the social and political history of this period confirms this opinion.[26]

Thus the Admonitions of Ipuwer should more justifiably be utilised in the elaboration of Second-Intermediate-Period history than the First Intermediate Period. Even if one were to argue that this class of literature is of the 'pessimistic' variety, there is no reason why it should not reflect, to some degree, the conditions in which Egypt found itself at the time of the writing of the original text. Sir Alan Gardiner himself argued that 'the pessimism of Ipuwer was intended to be understood as the direct and natural response to a real national calamity'. Unfortunately we now know that he attributed it to the wrong era. Thanks to the work of John van Seters and others, we can say with reasonable confidence that Ipuwer was describing the suffering of the Egyptians some time during the mid- to late-13th Dynasty – at least partly due to the machinations of the large Asiatic population resident in the delta which looms large in the Admonitions text.

It is, therefore, also my own view that Gardiner was wrong in his dating of this important text, and to continue to regard Ipuwer as reflecting the troubles at the end of the Old Kingdom, as most reference works still do, is to perpetuate a serious misconception concerning the nature of the era known as the First Intermediate Period and deprive the 13th Dynasty of an important document relating to the troubled conditions that pertained at that time. One may legitimately argue that the Admonitions has no real historical value (as some have done), but this would be to ignore the obvious point that pessimistic writings tend to be born out of periods of political instability and can justifiably be used, to some degree, to create a picture of the era which spawned them. In the case of Ipuwer it is the continuous references to Aamu ('Asiatics'), who seem to be at the focus of the troubles, which can add colour and drama to the more 'historical' information from other sources pointing to a general decline during the second half of the 13th Dynasty.

It has been suggested that one major element in this scenario of decline was Asiatic expansion in the delta and this appears to be precisely the sort of political picture described in the Ipuwer papyrus – and the biblical passage describing the era following Joseph's death.

> Then Joseph died, and his brothers, and all that generation. But the Israelites were fruitful and prolific; they became so numerous and powerful that eventually the whole land was full of them. [Exodus 1:6-7]

With the book of Exodus in mind, we can see how similar the Ipuwer laments are to either the time of the Israelite rise in population and resultant increase in power after Joseph's death, or the desperate state of Egypt immediately following the Ten Plagues.

> Foreigners have become Egyptian citizens (literally 'people') everywhere. ... The servant takes what he finds. ... Lo, poor men have become men of wealth; he who could not afford sandals owns riches. Lo, men's slaves – their hearts are greedy ...

> Lo, hearts are violent, storm sweeps the land, there is blood everywhere – no shortage of dead. The shroud calls out before one comes near it. Lo, many dead are buried in the river ... Lo, nobles lament whilst the poor rejoice ...

Lo, the river is (turned to) blood. As one drinks of it, one shrinks from people and thirsts for water. ...

Foreign bowmen have come into Egypt. ... Lo, gold, lapis-lazuli, silver, and turquoise, carnelian, amethyst, *ibht*-stone and [...] are strung on the necks of female slaves. ... What belongs to the palace has been stripped. ...

Lo, merriment has ceased – is made no more. Groaning is throughout the land, mingled with laments. Lo, every have-not is one who has ... Lo, children of nobles are dashed against the walls ... Lo, the whole delta cannot be seen (i.e. is in darkness); Lower Egypt puts trust in trodden roads. What can one do? ...

Foreigners are skilled in the works of the delta. ... See now, the land is deprived of kingship by a few people who ignore custom. See now, men rebel against the Uraeus Serpent; [stolen] is the crown of Re, who pacifies the Two Lands ... If the royal palace is stripped, it will collapse in a moment. ...

Those who had shelter are in the dark of the storm. ... See, the poor of the land have become rich; the man of property is a pauper. ... There is fire in their hearts! If only he (an earlier Pharaoh?) had perceived their nature in the first generation! Then he would have smitten the evil, stretched out his arm against it, and would have destroyed their seed and heirs! But since giving birth is desired, grief has come and misery is all around. ... It means reducing their numbers everywhere.

This last section (and some of the earlier descriptions) seems to place us in the time when Pharaoh took the advice of his counsellors (perhaps Ipuwer amongst them) to cull the male Israelite children and enslave the population far beyond the servitude of the previous generation which had retained certain freedoms under the earlier rulers of the 13th Dynasty. It is therefore tempting to place Ipuwer in the time of Sobekhotep III and the rise of the powerful native sub-dynasty of Sobekhotep III, Neferhotep, and Sobekhotep IV. In the New Chronology it is Khaneferre Sobekhotep IV who raises Moses as a prince of Egypt. On the other hand, one is also immediately struck by the parallels to certain of the Exodus plagues – the river turning blood-red, darkness over the delta, the slaves who have become rich and adorn themselves in Egyptian gold – all this seemed remarkable confirmation of the events of Exodus in the mind of Immanuel Velikovsky in the 1950s[27] and still holds true today.

So the papyrus known as the 'Admonitions of an Egyptian Sage' appears to provide further Egyptian parallels to the Sojourn and Exodus stories found in the Old Testament – but, once again, placed much earlier than required by the Orthodox Chronology (with an Exodus date set during the Ramesside era) and precisely during the time of the Second Intermediate Period (the Exodus date proposed in the New Chronology).

The walls of the Ramesside Exodus date have just about crumbled into dust, following the onslaught of the Levantine and Egyptian archaeologists over the last decade, and a new, much stronger, alternative is rising out of the ashes of Middle Bronze Age Jericho. The most convincing archaeological and historical period for the Israelite Sojourn and Exodus is the Second Intermediate Period, beginning in the late 12th Dynasty and ending some time towards the end of the 13th Dynasty.

Kenyon's Dating for the Fall of Jericho

We started this chapter in the Middle Bronze Age cemetery of Jericho amongst the final tombs of City IV where Kenyon discovered a whole series of multiple, simultaneous burials. These marked the end of the city which had been overthrown by earthquake and burnt to the ground. The collapsed and charred walls had been left to crumble into ruin for centuries, before a new Iron Age town was rebuilt on the old Middle Bronze Age mound.

In Kenyon's day it was believed that the city destructions which brought Middle Bronze Age Canaan to an end and which gave birth to the Late Bronze Age were the work of Egyptian armies bent on retribution for years of oppression by the Asiatic Hyksos kings of that region. Scholars thought that Pharaoh Ahmose ('the liberator') had swept through southern Canaan destroying all the Hyksos strongholds after their retreat from Avaris and the Egyptian delta. In the destruction of Jericho City IV (at the end of her Tomb Group V with its simultaneous burials) Kenyon envisaged just such an attack and brutal eradication by Egyptian forces under the founder of the 18th Dynasty.

> … this group of tombs belongs to the very end of the Middle Bronze Age, it might be tempting to associate the mass burials with the final destruction of the Middle Bronze Age town, probably to be ascribed to an Egyptian raid in the campaign which drove the Hyksos out of Egypt at the beginning of the 18th Dynasty …[28]

Thus the last graves at Jericho (including H13 with its Sheshi scarab) were dated to the very end of the Hyksos period and the start of the Egyptian New Kingdom. In fact, the New Kingdom was seen as the era of the Late Bronze Age, just as the Middle Kingdom and Second Intermediate Period represented the historical eras of the Middle Bronze

Age. This very neat picture remained the fashion for a generation after Kenyon's time. But recent and more accurate archaeological observations have revealed a much more complex picture. Today, few Egyptologists would argue for a destruction of Jericho by Egyptian forces, and the start of the Late Bronze Age has been pushed back into the Hyksos period. As a result, we can no longer be certain of the historical or archaeological date for Jericho's demise – and that goes for all the cities destroyed towards the end of the Middle Bronze Age.

Not one to sit on the fence, I am going to attempt to date these destructions to a somewhat earlier time than the era of the Hyksos expulsion as Kenyon and her colleagues believed. What evidence there is seems to point to the period immediately preceding the Greater Hyksos 15th Dynasty – and it all hinges on the date for Sheshi and his little scarab from tomb H13.

Chapter Two

THE HYKSOS KINGS

*Sheshi and Sheshai -- MB Scarabs -- The Early Hyksos
Kings -- Tell ed-Daba Stratigraphy -- Sheshi in the Royal
Canon of Turin*

e will now turn our focus onto the conundrum of the Hyksos kings of Egypt themselves, to learn more about them and to try to determine their ethnic origins. You can read pretty much all that has been written about these mysterious northerners and find yourself still perplexed by them. Scholars have puzzled and argued over who they were for decades – but with no clear-cut answers or any sort of consensus.

What language did they speak – West-Semitic or Indo-European or Hurrian? Where was their homeland – southern Canaan or much further north in Phoenicia or beyond? Were they chariot-riding warriors or seafarers or both? Egypt has produced no reliefs or sculptures depicting the Hyksos kings. Artefacts specifically relating to them are few and far between. Their hieroglyphic names are confusing – some clearly being Semitic (Aamu, Yakub-Har), others purely Egyptian (Apophis), and several of unknown or indeterminate linguistic origin (Sheshi, Salitis, Bnon, Khyan). How should we envisage them – barbarian warlords or sophisticated monarchs bearing the full panoply of kingship?

Manetho casts them as 'foreign kings and brothers from Phoenicia' – but what does that mean and was he right to describe the Hyksos invaders of Egypt in this way? Were they really vile oppressors of the native Egyptians or are the later Egyptian texts merely diatribes and propaganda on the part of the native pharaohs against a period of objectionable foreign rule in Lower Egypt? What really was their relationship with their contemporary Egyptian kings of Upper Egypt during the late Second Intermediate Period? Was it just a case of war, war, war, or were there other things going on which have been lost in the fragmentation of history and suppressed by that successful post-Hyksos Egyptian propaganda?

And who did they become? Were these foreign lords of Avaris removed entirely from history with their expulsion from Egypt – or should they be recast as the progenitors of Hesiod's Heroic Age, made famous by the Classical legends of Greece and Rome? You are about to find answers to these fascinating questions – once the latest archaeological discoveries and the New Chronology timeline have been applied to this greatest mystery of the ancient world.

In *Chapter One* I related the story of Kenyon's discovery of what can legitimately be described as one of the most important artefacts for biblical history to be unearthed in the last two hundred years of archaeological endeavour. Despite its tiny size and initial apparent insignificance, the scarab of Sheshi found in Jericho Tomb H13 holds the key to dating Joshua's conquest of the Promised Land and therefore the whole chronological framework of the early Old Testament. I have even previously proposed that this Sheshi may be mentioned in the biblical book of Numbers where the Israelite tribes, encamped in the wilderness of Paran (southern Negeb), send spies into the Promised Land, the southern part of which is ruled over by the

9. A sample of Sheshi scarabs (from over 500 recovered from his long reign). They originate from Egypt and all over southern Palestine.

Anakim – known as Sheshai and his two 'brother' kings, Ahiman and Talmai.

> So they (the Israelite spies) went up and explored the land from the Desert of Zin as far as Rehob, towards Lebo Hamath. They went up through the Negeb and came to Hebron, where Ahiman, Sheshai and Talmai, the descendants of Anak, lived. [Numbers 13:21-22]

Aaron KEMPINSKI, a leading Middle Bronze Age archaeologist and historian, also came to the conclusion that the Sheshai of Numbers 13:22 had somehow been based on the historical figure of the Hyksos ruler Maibre Sheshi. New Chronologists, on the other hand, would argue that Sheshai was not just 'based on' the historically attested Sheshi but is one and the same character. Kempinski was forced to separate these two identities because of the constraints placed upon him by the conventional chronology which places Sheshi in *circa* 1700 BC and the biblical Sheshai in *circa* 1200 BC. Thus orthodoxy prevents any conclusion other than that offered by Kempinski: the inclusion of the name Sheshai in the book of Judges can only represent some garbled memory of a distant figure in history, woven into the Old Testament narrative to add colour and (false) detail – even though that biblical story was first written down more than a thousand years later than the time of the Hyksos King Sheshi! Again credulity is stretched beyond reason and yet another proto-biblical character is added to our 'Proto-Joseph' and the 'Proto-Israelites'.

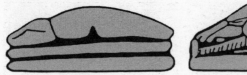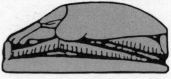

10. Scarab profiles, showing (left) sandwich style with plain legs and (right) notched-leg style.

Dating Sheshi

But how do we actually date Sheshi both in absolute terms (his New Chronology date BC) and relative terms (his archaeological context)? This is a complicated matter which requires me to put before you a series of interrelated pieces of evidence.

(A) Middle Bronze Age Scarab Design

In a detailed study of scarab types, Second-Intermediate-Period specialist Kim Ryholt has argued that Maibre Sheshi scarabs fall within a recognisable sequence of stylistic changes.[1] That sequence is best seen in the chart opposite. Specifically, a small percentage of Sheshi's scarabs have notched legs (see the profiles above) which otherwise occur (in higher proportions) during the reigns of Yakub-Har, Khyan and Apophis. Ryholt designates this early appearance of notched legs in the time of Sheshi as the 'Middle Phase' in Middle Bronze Age scarab design seriation. On the other hand, many of Sheshi's scarabs have plain legs which is a trait of earlier scarabs from the 13th Dynasty and the reigns of 'lesser' Hyksos kings such as Ya-Ammu, Yakebim, Kareh and Ammu. All these kings predate Khyan and Apophis (both kings of the 'Greater Hyksos' era, conventionally designated the 15th Dynasty).

Opposite: Chart showing the development of scarab styles through the late Second Intermediate Period. Note that the notched-leg style only begins with the reign of Sheshi.

Name of Hyksos King (prenomen & nomen)	Grooved Legs	Notched Legs	Plain Legs	Sandwich Profile	Triangular Head	Panels on Flanks
Nubuserre Ya-Ammu				■	■	■
Sekhaenre Yakebim			■	■	■	■
Khauserre Kareh			■		■	■
Ahotepre Ammu			■		■	■
Maibre Sheshi		■	■	■	■	■
Meruserre Yakub-Har	■	■				
Seuserenre Khyan	■					
Auserre Apophis	■					

Another significant development was that the sculpturing of the scarab became more complex with time. For dating purposes, one of the most important changes is the transition from the simple sandwich profile and plain legs to notched legs during the reign of Sheshi, and the increasing number of seals with grooved legs during the 15th Dynasty.[2]

So it seems that Sheshi's reign falls some time before Khyan's – at a point when the notched-leg style was beginning to come into use and at the end of the period when scarabs with plain legs predominated. We thus get a sequence of Hyksos rulers something on the following lines (but note that the interval between each king in this list is unknown).

Nubuserre Ya-Ammu	– scarabs with sandwich profile & plain legs
Sekhaenre Yakebim	– scarabs with sandwich profile & plain legs
Khauserre Kareh	– scarabs with sandwich profile & plain legs
Ahotepre Ammu	– scarabs with sandwich profile & plain legs
Maibre Sheshi	– scarabs with plain legs & notched legs
Meruserre Yakub-Har	– scarabs with notched legs
Seuserenre Khyan	– scarabs with notched & grooved legs
Auserre Apophis	– scarabs with notched & grooved legs

Unfortunately none of the names of the kings in this list appears on the surviving fragments of the Royal Canon of Turin (a king-list recorded on a papyrus document which we will be discussing in more detail later) so they do not help us to place Sheshi in anything other than a relative and general sense. However, there is a connection to another king of this era who *does* appear in the Royal Canon – a minor ruler whose name is found at the top of Column VIII of the Turin Museum papyrus and whose artefacts have been located at a number of sites in Egypt's eastern delta.

(B) The Archaeological Date for Nehesi

King Nehesi reigned for less than a year (according to the Royal Canon, VIII:1), but he is also attested by a number of monuments and scarabs as 'crown-prince' (prior to his accession). Unfortunately, it is nowhere stated who his royal father was. However, Kim Ryholt has come to the same conclusion as myself in proposing that Nehesi's father was none other than Maibre Sheshi. In particular he notes the significance of the fact that scarabs of Nehesi 'contain a range of attributes which correspond exclusively to that found on the seals of Sheshi' – indicating that these two kings were very close in time.[3] In fact, Nehesi's scarabs show the same notched-legs design as those of Sheshi (in addition to the other new features).

Moreover, another group of scarabs of identical design belongs to a Queen Tauti, whose name suggests she was of Kushite or Nubian origin. Ryholt proposes that Tauti was a wife (and possibly chief queen) of Sheshi and that the reason for Nehesi's unusual name (for a delta ruler) – the 'southerner' or 'black man' – could best be explained if he was the eldest son of the dark-skinned Tauti and crown-prince of the long-reigned Sheshi.[4] All three personalities were certainly near contemporaries if the closeness of their scarab designs is anything to go by.

> Queen Tauti is attested by eleven scarab-shaped seals of which two were found at Tell el-Yahudiya and one at Abydos. The use of both the sandwich profile, plain legs and notched legs dates this queen specifically to the reign of Sheshi when the transition from the two former to the latter took place. Accordingly, she may be regarded as the spouse of Sheshi.[5]

> While the few seals produced for Nehesi after he had become king can only be dated very

approximately, his date is firmly established by the numerous seals produced for him when he was still a prince.[6] ... Ipku (another prince and possible son of Sheshi) and Nehesi can be dated specifically to the reign of Sheshi since the attributes of the (scarab) seals of both princes include the sandwich profile, plain legs and notched legs, and thus reflect the transition from the two former to the latter which took place during the reign of this king.[7]

Now we can fix an archaeological date for Nehesi with reasonable certainty – thanks to a discovery made at Tell ed-Daba (ancient Avaris) by Professor Manfred Bietak and his team of Austrian and international archaeologists. When excavating the main settlement at Tell ed-Daba in the 1970s, they identified four early strata which appeared to cover the following historical periods:

(1) Stratum H (lowest level) covering the late 12th and early 13th Dynasties

(2) Stratum G/4 covering the mid-13th Dynasty

(3) Stratum G/1-3 covering the late 13th Dynasty

(4) Stratum F covering the beginning of what Bietak calls the 14th Dynasty

The archaeologists noted a break in occupation between the end of Stratum G/1-3 (which culminated in mass graves) and Stratum F. Bietak specifically refers to this interruption of activity in the main Asiatic settlement area (Tell A) with the expression '*kein Kontinuum zu Stratum G*'[8] which translates as 'no continuity from Stratum G'.[9] At the end of G, the town (occupying the main Tell A) was abandoned by its highly Egyptianised Asiatic (Semitic) population before a new group of non-Egyptianised Asiatics settled there and turned the place into a large sacred precinct with warrior graves, mortuary chapels and cult temples (beginning in Stratum F).

The Lesser Hyksos Arrival at Avaris

In *A Test of Time* I argued that the 'local' Asiatic population of Avaris which occupied the site from Stratum H through to Stratum G/1-3 represented the Israelites of the biblical tradition who, according to the Genesis and Exodus narratives, sojourned in Egypt from the arrival of Joseph and Jacob in Goshen down to their departure into Sinai under Moses – an interval of approximately 215 years. I also proposed that the newcomers of Stratum F, with their warlike characteristics, were invading nomadic groups from the Negeb – a disparate collection of militarised pastoralists collectively identified in the Bible as 'Amalekites' but known to the Egyptians as Aamu ('Asiatics') and Shosu ('shepherds'). These 'foreign' Asiatics, with such limited experience of Egyptian culture (confined to their ruling elite, perhaps from elsewhere, who used scarabs with hieroglyphic symbols), were also one and the same as the 'invaders of obscure race' who entered Egypt following a major disaster which struck pharaonic Egypt in the reign of a King Dudimose (Greek *Tutimaos*) according to Manetho.[10]

> Tutimaos. In his reign, for what cause I know not, a blast of God smote us (i.e. the Egyptians), and unexpectedly, from the regions of the east, invaders of obscure race marched in confidence of victory against our land. By main force they easily seized it without striking a blow ...

In his *Aegyptiaca*, Manetho states that these invaders devastated the land and brutalised the people before, eventually, one of their number – Salitis – founded the

Str D/2		
Str D/3	15th Dynasty	MB IIB (late)
Str E/1		
Str E/2		
Str E/3	14th Dynasty	MB IIB (early)
Str F		
Str G/1-3	13th Dynasty	MB IIA
Str G/4		
Str H	12th Dyn	

Historical chart of the Second Intermediate Period showing archaeological phases at Avaris in relationship to dynasties – as perceived in the conventional scheme adopted by most scholars.

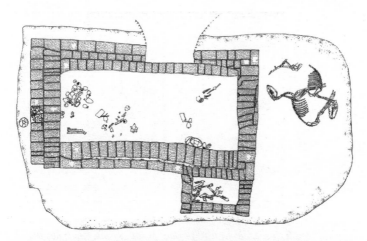

11. A typical Stratum F warrior grave (A/II-m/12:9) with mudbrick walls and vault (see plate 4). In front of the tomb lie the remains of sacrificed equids, whilst adjacent to the lower wall on the plan a small chamber has been added to house the remains of a female servant burial [courtesy of the Austrian Archaeological Institute, Cairo].

'Greater Hyksos' dynasty, continuing with Bnon (identity unknown), Apachnan (Khyan?), Ianass (Yanassi, son of Khyan), Apophis (Auserre Apopi) and Aseth (Asehre Khamudy?).

There is little doubt in my mind that a new group of foreigners did enter Egypt towards the end of the 13th Dynasty, not only because we see a break in occupation at the end of Stratum G at Tell ed-Daba but also because the excavators observed the subsequent establishment of an Asiatic culture which was non-Egyptianised compared to the 'highly Egyptianised' Asiatics of the preceding H and G strata. In addition, the warrior burials of these Strata F and E/3 newcomers included sacrificial female servant burials – a brutal practice entirely missing from the 'egalitarian' settlement remains of the earlier Asiatic population. Some graves have more than one body in them – a situation which also suggests simultaneous interment, probably family members or close retinue buried at the time of the master of the household. Again, this is not a practice observable in

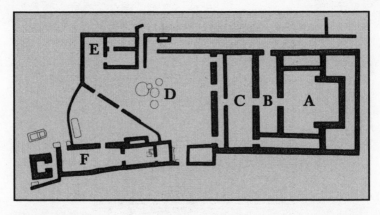

12. *Plan of the large Canaanite temple complex begun in Stratum F or E/3. The main temple, perhaps dedicated to Baal or his consort, Anat, has a wide cella (A) with large central niche. Two broad antechambers (B & C) give access to the holy of holies from an open court with oak trees (D) and an altar. What may be the priest's house (E) is located in the upper left corner of the courtyard. A smaller long-room temple (F) stands on the opposite side of the court with a tower to its left. This temple may be the shrine of Anat or Asherah/Astarte [after Bietak].*

the earlier Asiatic settlement of H and G. The burial rites of the two foreign groups were very different.

Most striking of all, Stratum E/3 (which immediately followed the transitional Stratum F at Tell ed-Daba/Avaris) contained 'one of the largest sanctuaries known from the Middle Bronze Age world', measuring 33.75 by 21.50 metres (Temple III).[11]

In precisely this location, near the temple entrance (but unfortunately found in the disturbed context of a later Ramesside pit), Bietak unearthed part of a limestone door-jamb bearing the badly preserved cartouches of Nehesi. A second fragmentary jamb was also located in the vicinity (but again not *in situ*) which appears to be the sister of the one found in front of the temple. These monumental stone blocks once decorated the entrance to an important building, whereas the only structure of this kind in the area was the large Canaanite temple. Bietak, therefore, logically (and correctly in my view) concluded that Nehesi was probably

Hyksos Expulsion
Stratum D/2

Stratum D/3

Stratum E/1
Greater Hyksos Dynasty Starts

Stratum E/2

Stratum E/3

Stratum F
Second Asiatic Settlement

Plague & Partial Abandonment
Stratum G/1-3

Stratum G/4

Stratum H
First Asiatic Settlement

A simplified chart of the Avaris stratigraphy with the three main occupation phases (A) the first Asiatic settlement, (B) the second Asiatic settlement and (C) the Greater Hyksos period.

13. Two fragments of door jambs, found within the Temple III precinct at Avaris, with enough hieroglyphs remaining to identify the prenomen and nomen of Pharaoh Nehesi [courtesy of the Austrian Institute of Archaeology, Cairo].

the king of Avaris when the temple was completed, making the following important comments.

(i) 'As Temple III is the only monumental building which dates approximately to this period, it seems likely that the jambs came from this temple, although we cannot be absolutely sure.[12] ... It is extremely tempting to bring this major temple into connection with the foundation of a new dynasty in Avaris under the father of Nehesi.'

We have now determined that, in all likelihood, the father of Nehesi was King Maibre Sheshi. So Sheshi becomes the putative founder of the Canaanite Temple III at Avaris.

(ii) 'It would also make Nehesi a direct ancestor of the Hyksos whereas his name points rather to the south, to Nubia.'

We have seen that a Queen Tauti, whose name appears to be Nubian or Kushite, had scarabs of identical style to both

Plate 1: View of the excavations at Ezbet Helmi showing the Hyksos fortification wall on the left and, inside that wall, the remains of tree-pits from the Hyksos garden and/or vineyard. The 'Minoan' frescoes were unearthed in this general area, adjacent to the platform palace situated under the camera position.

Plate 2: An Egyptian workman carefully removes the earth from a pile of Aegean fresco fragments at Ezbet Helmi in 1991.

Plate 3: Typical graves of the Asiatic population of Avaris during the late 12th and 13th Dynasties (Tell ed-Daba Strata H and G). These MB IIA graves are lined with mudbricks and have a mudbrick vaulted roof. The left grave has been excavated down to the burial whereas the right grave is yet to be opened by Professor Bietak's team [courtesy of the Austrian Archaeological Institute, Cairo].

Plate 4: An Early Hyksos warrior grave from Stratum F at Avaris. In the foreground a large pit containing sacrificed equids has been exposed by the archaeologists. To the left of the main chamber (upper half of photo) is a much smaller mudbrick compartment containing the remains of a single female servant burial which was undoubtedly contemporary with the funeral of the warrior chieftain [courtesy of the Austrian Archaeological Institute, Cairo].

Plate 5: Model made by the Austrian Archaeological Institute, Cairo, of the Ezbet Helmi Hyksos fortification wall running along the east bank of the Pelusiac branch of the Nile at Avaris. Beyond the wall is a fortress-palace first believed to be of Hyksos date but later re-assigned to the 18th Dynasty. To the left of this palace is a garden or vineyard (here represented by date-palms).

Plate 6: Foundations of the great Hyksos mudbrick fortress wall, measuring 6.2 metres thick in its initial D/3 phase before being widened to 8.5 metres in its second D/2 phase. At lower right, the angle of one of the massive outer buttresses can be seen.

Plate 7: The small workshop at Avaris in which the Theran pumice was found. This building was constructed in Helmi Stratum c (Daba = C/2). The discarded Aegean frescoes were discovered a short distance to the left of this mudbrick structure (beyond the wavy wall) but in the earlier Helmi Stratum d (Daba = C/3) [courtesy of the Austrian Archaeological Institute, Cairo].

Plate 8: A pile of Theran pumice collected from the small workshop or tannery at Helmi I, close to the find-spot of the Aegean frescoes but in a stratum higher than the dumped frescoes. This indicates that the final eruption of Thera occurred some considerable time after the Helmi I palace was stripped of its Aegean decoration.

Plate 9: The granite blocks of Pharaoh Amenemhat's doorway as they appear today, lying in the midst of the houses of Ezbet Helmi.

Plate 10: The top of Column VIII of the Royal Canon of Turin, showing the entry for King Nehesi (Turin Egyptological Museum).

Plate 11: The new Hyksos fragment 112 of the Turin Canon.

Plate 12: Golden pendant of antithetical dogs found in Stratum G at Avaris..

Plate 13: Egyptian marine Ahmose sa-Ibana from his tomb at el-Kab.

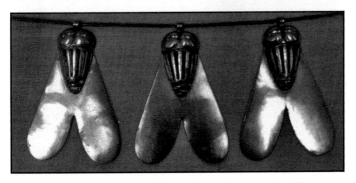

Plare 14: Ahhotep's three golden flies – medals of honour for a fighting queen [Luxor Museum].

Plate 15: The smaller golden coffin of the young Ahhotep made for her before she provided Sekenenre Taa with his male heir – Ahmose [Cairo Museum].

Plate 16: The mummy of Ahmose, son of Ahhotep, discovered amongst the re-buried kings of the Royal Cache near Deir el-Bahri.

Plate 17: The rock-cut temple of Hatshepsut, known as the Speos Artemidos and/or Stabl Antar. The pharaoh's proclamation is carved above the portico façcde.

Plate 18: *The Middle Bronze Age cemetery at Byblos viewed from the Roman colonnade. The sarcophagus extracted from the shaft of Tomb IV can be seen at the centre of the picture.*

Plate 19: *One of the most remarkable frescoes from the palace at Ezbet Helmi I is this fragment of a bull-grappling scene. It shows an Aegean youth clinging to the neck of a bull whilst trying to vault over its back. The background represents a labyrinthine maze. This image is partly restored by superimposing the artist's semi-transparent restoration (by Lyla Pinch-Brock) over the original plaster fragment in order to bring out the details of the scene [courtesy of the Austrian Archaeological Institute, Cairo]. Professor Bietak informs me that the excavation catalogue of the Ezbet Helmi frescoes (in full colour) has gone to press and should be available for study early in 2007.*

Sheshi and Nehesi, and, along with Ryholt, I suggest that Tauti (perhaps a Kushite princess) was Nehesi's mother and the wife of King Sheshi. This would explain how Nehesi could be both 'ancestor' of the Asiatic Hyksos and, at the same time, a 'southerner'.

(iii) 'The second major Canaanite incursion would have happened shortly before his reign.'

Bietak is here making it quite clear that he sees evidence of two distinct groups of Asiatics arriving in the delta and settling at Avaris. The first group is that represented by Stratum H through to Stratum G/1-3; the second group consists of newcomers who were responsible for building the Canaanite temple complex during the reigns of Nehesi and his father. The 'incursion' (I would call it an invasion) into the Egyptian delta would have taken place about a generation or so before Nehesi.

Professor Bietak's Comments on the Transition from Stratum G to Stratum F

Stratum F: A redistribution of the plots; the foundation of a sacred complex for Temples III and V surrounded by small family cemeteries in the west of the settlement, whereas in the east the area was left as fallow land. Donkey burials; servant burials; MB IIA-B culture. There is no continuation from Stratum G.[13]

A comparison of the occupational development between Stratum G and Stratum F is most revealing. In Area I and Area X and to the east – that is, for a short period, everywhere in the vicinity of the large sacred compound and its connected cemeteries – the construction of domestic dwellings ceased (in Stratum F). The sacred complex of Area III and the small cemeteries surrounding it (Areas I, II and possibly X) were established, whilst to the west of Area I the domestic settlement (of Stratum G) continued to expand (Area VII). So here there seems to have been a direct continuation from Stratum G to Stratum F. ... an explanation other than the decision to construct a necropolis and sacred temenos must be considered in order to explain the abandonment of the Stratum G settlement, because the different parts of the site were not simultaneously redeveloped after they had been vacated.[14]

Conclusion One

The Second Intermediate Period should be divided into three distinct historical phases. Phase One – the 'Proto-Israelite Period' – comprises a gradual and relatively peaceful incursion of Asiatics into the eastern delta during the late 12th Dynasty. It ends with the fall of the 13th Dynasty. These foreigners become Egyptianised and some serve in high office within the pharaonic state. In the second part of the era this Asiatic population is enslaved, becoming domestic servants to native Egyptian families. Phase Two – the 'Lesser Hyksos Period' – begins with an invasion of a second wave of Asiatics who are, by comparison, not Egyptianised. These folk are dominated by a warrior element. They overthrow native 13th-Dynasty rule in Lower Egypt. Phase Three – the 'Greater Hyksos Period' – is represented by an elite super-stratum of foreign kings and their retinue known as the 15th Dynasty. They rule over the Asiatic sub-stratum population of Phase Two. These rulers continue the push south, driving the native Egyptian pharaohs out of Middle Egypt beyond the new frontier at Cusae.

Let us look in a little more detail at the warrior chieftains of Phase Two. These 'ancestors of the Hyksos' are represented by the archaeological remains of Stratum F, Stratum E/3 and (according to the New Chronology) Strata E/2 and E/1. This clearly is a substantial period and makes the 'Early Hyksos' or 'Lesser Hyksos' dynasty a significant element in the history of the Second Intermediate Period. In the conventional scheme these kings are given little attention and are somehow either subsumed into the 13th Dynasty era as a parallel 14th Dynasty (as proposed by Ryholt) or act as a subservient vassal 16th Dynasty under their more powerful 'Greater Hyksos' 15th Dynasty neighbours (a view held by the majority of scholars). The New Chronology, on the other hand, assigns these 'Lesser Hyksos' or 'Early Hyksos' kings a time period entirely to themselves between the 13th Dynasty (ending soon after the reign of Dudimose) and the '15th Dynasty' founded by Salitis.

With Ryholt's scarab evidence and the findings of Bietak at Avaris, we are logically drawn to the conclusion that Sheshi, father of Nehesi, was an early Hyksos ruler and that he was the founder of the Canaanite temple constructed in Stratum F or E/3. The absolute or exact New Chronology date for the founding of Temple III can be determined using an important document from the 19th Dynasty known as the 'Year Four Hundred Stela' which I shall be dealing with in the next chapter. But, for now, I will attempt to reconstruct a history of Hyksos-period Avaris based on the stratigraphical evidence produced by the Austrian excavators and the application of the New Chronology to that evidence.

(C) The Hyksos Stratigraphy at Tell ed-Daba

We have seen that Stratum F was the fourth archaeological level of the Second Intermediate Period city at Avaris (following H, G/4 and G/1-3). But the site continued in use right up to the Hyksos expulsion in the reign of Ahmose, founder of the 18th Dynasty. This continuing stratigraphy adds a further five major levels which, with Stratum F, thus encompasses the entire Hyksos era:

(4)   Stratum F (short hiatus, arrival of the first 'Lesser Hyksos' chieftains/kings)

(5)   Stratum E/3 (early 'Lesser Hyksos' – including Sheshi and Nehesi)

(6) Stratum E/2 (middle 'Lesser Hyksos')

(7) Stratum E/1 (late 'Lesser Hyksos' including Yakub-Har)

(8) Stratum D/3 (early 'Greater Hyksos' starting with Salitis)

(9) Stratum D/2 (late 'Greater Hyksos' ending with the capture of Avaris by Ahmose)

It is obvious, even to the layman, that the interval of time between the start of Stratum F and the end of Stratum D/2 must have been considerable. The conventional dating scheme, used by the majority of Egyptologists, assigns 180 years to the whole era of Avaris' existence from the late 12th Dynasty to the end of the 15th Dynasty (c. 1710-1530 BC) and Professor Bietak assigns an average of thirty years per stratum. We will later conclude that the duration of the Hyksos period must be extended by a considerable number of years, based on the historical evidence, and that these six major strata must have lasted around three hundred years in total.

The Greater Hyksos Arrival at Avaris

Bietak begins the main Hyksos 15th Dynasty in Stratum E/1 (the first of the last three Middle Bronze Age strata) because he requires three thirty-year strata to make up the 108 years of the 'Greater Hyksos' dynasty of kings (as given in the Royal Canon of Turin). It has to be said that this schematic chronology is entirely arbitrary (as, no doubt, Bietak himself would admit) and there is no *specific* archaeological evidence to support it. No inscribed monuments from the 'Greater Hyksos' dynasty have ever been found in their original context – all, so far, were unearthed in later New Kingdom strata where they had been re-used. In terms of pottery, there was indeed a change or development within Stratum E/1 – but we have no way of telling if this change was instigated either by a new dynasty or even through any sort of cultural change. Pottery cultures can develop new shapes/fabrics/decoration as a consequence of many different influences and factors (trade/invention/popular taste). Rarely can we claim that a change in dynasty or royal bloodline brought about a marked change in the pottery culture of the sub-population ruled over by their elites.

Nothing in the archaeological record of Tell ed-Daba, as yet, permits us to pinpoint the exact stratigraphical era when Salitis and his dynasty arrived at Avaris. However, we do have to make some sort of attempt at doing this in order to construct our history of Avaris – but with the cautionary note that the basis of this chronological model for the late Second Intermediate Period is founded on meagre evidence.

The New Chronology places the entire 'Greater Hyksos' dynasty within Strata D/3 and D/2, in part because it is not restrained by any schematic stratigraphy which divides the nine strata of Avaris into thirty-year periods. It can therefore assign the full century of the 'Greater Hyksos' dynasty (108 years) to two strata. The clue which suggests that the 'Greater Hyksos' dynasty arrived in Egypt only shortly before the development of Stratum D/2 at Tell ed-Daba is the mention by Manetho of 'massive walls' built at Avaris by the dynasty founder, Salitis.[15]

> In the Saite [Sethroite] nome he (Salitis) found a city very favourably situated on the east of the Bubastite (Pelusiac) branch of the Nile, and called Auaris (Avaris) after an ancient religious tradition. **This place he rebuilt and fortified with massive walls, planting there a garrison of as many as two hundred and forty thousand heavily armed men to guard his frontier.** Here he would come in summertime, partly to serve out rations and pay his troops, partly to train them carefully in manoeuvres and so strike terror into foreign tribes.

As I explained in the *Preface*, just such a massive enclosure wall has been found at Avaris on the east bank of the Pelusiac branch of the Nile – and it has been dated by Bietak to the period of Strata D/3 and D/2 (see plate 6). Its first (and major) phase was constructed in D/3 and then later thickened at its base in D/2. Given that no earlier wall which might be assigned to Salitis has been found to date, it is tempting to accredit the building of the fortress wall to the founder of the 'Greater Hyksos' dynasty – after all it is the *only* massive bastion which *has* been found. There are no other candidates. And so, I have come to the conclusion that Stratum D/3 and the following Stratum D/2 must represent the entire line of Hyksos kings that succeeded Salitis. Thus the 'Lesser Hyksos' period which preceded the 'Greater Hyksos' dynasty is represented at Avaris by the four strata F through to E/1 lasting around two centuries.

Conclusion Two

The impressive mudbrick fortress wall of Strata D/3 and D/2, discovered at Ezbet Helmi, near Tell ed-Daba, was originally erected during the reign of Salitis (in Stratum D/3), founder of the Greater Hyksos dynasty. This was the wall, reinforced by Apophis (in Stratum D/2), which protected Avaris during the later sieges of Kamose and Ahmose prior to the expulsion of the Hyksos at the beginning of the New Kingdom.

(D) Sheshi's Position in the Royal Canon

As I stated earlier, the name of King Nehesi (along with his reign-length of less than a year) features in the Royal Canon of Turin and this is going to give us a relative chronological fix for Sheshi and therefore, through the evidence from

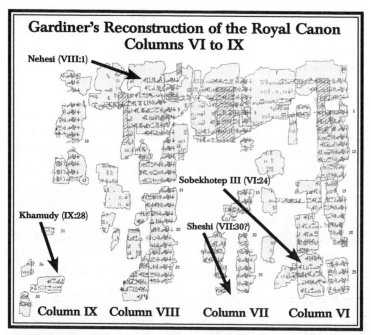

14. *Illustration showing the interval from Sobekhotep III to Nehesi, and Nehesi to Khamudy in the current mounting of the Royal Canon of Turin (after Gardiner, 1959).*

tomb H13, for the archaeological date of the destruction of Jericho by Joshua and the Israelites.

Whether Sheshi was the father and predecessor of Nehesi is not what matters here (although this seems likely). What really counts is (a) that we can date Sheshi's reign close to that of Nehesi, and (b) that Nehesi is found on the Turin Canon at the top of Column VIII (see plate 10) – well before the time of the 'Greater Hyksos' kings, the last of whom – Khamudy – is currently located towards the bottom of Column IX of the Canon (some fifty-eight places later).[16] Because the immediate successors of Nehesi are extant in Column VIII of the Canon and Sheshi is not amongst them, it is very likely that Sheshi's name would have been placed at the bottom of Column VII, which unfortunately no longer survives. This reasoning places Sheshi decades, and perhaps centuries, before the expulsion of the Hyksos kings at the beginning of the 18th Dynasty (the time of Khamudy more than fifty reigns later – though some of the lines of rulers would have been contemporary).

Conclusion Three

Maibre Sheshi was one of the early rulers of the 'Lesser Hyksos' dynasty which preceded the 'Greater Hyksos' dynasty founded by Salitis. Sheshi is therefore to be dated centuries before the expulsion of the Hyksos from Egypt in Year 11 of Ahmose, founder of the 18th Dynasty.

The implication of this is clear. If Sheshi was ruling long before the time of Ahmose and the Hyksos expulsion, then Jericho also fell and was destroyed long before that momentous date in Egyptian history because scarab 3281, carrying the cartouche of Sheshi and found in tomb H13, dates Jericho's demise approximately to his time. Thus Kenyon was completely wrong when she suggested that the destruction of Jericho City IV might be attributed to Egyptian forces under Ahmose. The fall of Jericho had nothing to do with events resulting from the Hyksos expulsion from Egypt.

Chapter Three

THE ROYAL CANON

*The Egyptian King-List –– A Misplaced Patch ––
Discovering the Hyksos Fragments*

s we have seen, the chronological position of kings
Sheshi and Nehesi is crucial for determining the
date of the fall of Jericho and therefore also of the
Israelite Conquest of the Promised Land.

It is now time to look in detail at the most important
document covering the Second Intermediate Period which
will enable us to pin down the history of this complex era.
The Royal Canon of Turin plays a major role in dating the
kings of ancient Egypt and can help us to resolve the issue
of the interval duration between Sheshi and the Greater
Hyksos. But first we need to correct a drastic mistake
made during the second restoration attempt of the Canon
fragments in 1930 by Hugo IBSCHER.

The story of how the Royal Canon ended up in scores
of tiny fragments when it arrived at the Turin Egyptological
Museum is enough to make one's toes curl. The virtually
intact papyrus was originally purchased for the collection of
the King of Sardinia. Bernardino DROVETTI then acquired
the Royal Canon on behalf of the museum in Turin and it
was duly despatched from Sardinia in 1823 – in a tin box,

making part of the journey on the back of a donkey! By the time the box was opened in Turin this most precious of artefacts had been shaken into tatters. Just imagine if we still had the Royal Canon in its original, almost pristine state. How much more would we know about Egyptian chronology and history if only it had been properly packed and despatched to its new home? As it is, we are left with a document whose fragmentary remains represent only about half the original contents – and there is much concern about the way the remaining pieces of the papyrus have been re-assembled.

The Turin Canon: A New Reconstruction

Back in 1987, during one afternoon spent undertaking research in the Amelia Edwards Library at University College London, I chanced to come across the original publication of *The Royal Canon of Turin* by the renowned Egyptologist and linguist, Sir Alan GARDINER.[1] I decided to thumb through the pages of this large-format volume, just to give my brain a rest from the long and somewhat dry tome that I had been studying for my degree in Egyptology. Almost at once I noticed something on Plate III that struck me as very odd.

In the middle of Column IX of the reconstructed papyrus (now numbered 1874 in the Turin catalogue), Ibscher[2] had placed a repair patch (fragment 41+42) bearing the names of what appeared to me to be primeval gods. These ancient repair patches – visibly darker than the rest of the papyrus – were otherwise consistently to be found at the top of the Canon's columns of cursive hieroglyphics. This got me thinking.

The most reasonable explanation I could come up with for the existence of these patches was that, after the original 19th Dynasty tax list on the recto was rolled up and put into store, the papyrus had been attacked by an insect – leaving a hole eaten right through the document, a couple

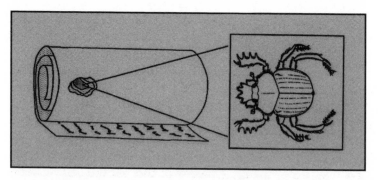

15. A studious beetle devours his way through the rolled-up tax account document during its period of storage. When subsequently opened for the recording of the king-list on the verso, *the resultant holes, positioned at intervals along the top of the scroll, were covered with darker papyrus patches.*

of centimetres from the top edge of the papyrus roll. When the papyrus was then reused to record a copy of the king-list (on the blank *verso*) it was necessary to stick small patches of papyrus over the holes that had been discovered upon unfurling the papyrus. The patches thus appear at intervals of roughly seventeen centimetres along the upper section of its length – that is, except for the patch currently mounted half-way down Column IX and one which remains in the collection of unplaced fragments.

What appeared quite obvious to me was the simple fact that in three places where one might have expected to find repair patches there were none – in the gaps at the top of Columns I and IV and the left side of Column IX. Why then hadn't someone suggested that the patch in the middle of Column IX (and that assigned to the fragments) belonged in one of the gaps at the top of these columns? Surely a closer scrutiny would reveal why those who had assembled the fragments had not taken this logical step? Subsequent investigation has, however, convinced me that a serious error was made in the second mounting attempt of the Turin Canon by Ibscher which was later retained by Gardiner in his publication (although, to be fair, he does mention in his notes considerable doubt about the fragment's placement).

This, in turn, has led to a number of false assumptions about the length of the Second Intermediate Period and the position of the main Hyksos dynasty within that period.

Looking in detail at the two patches of concern: the one mounted in Column IX (fragment 41+42) bears names that Gardiner describes as 'wholly fictitious beings' and 'fantastically named royalties'.[3] They include animal deities such as *hib* 'ibis' = Thoth? (IX:17), *iped* 'goose' = Geb? (IX:18) and *hapu* = Apis (IX:19), and the term *shemsu* 'Followers [of Horus]' – a designation for the semi-divine beings and supporters of the early kings of pre-dynastic Egypt. If any location on the papyrus were to suit these strange entries it must surely be in the space at the top of Column I where, at the bottom half of the column, we find the gods and demi-gods of the prehistoric era.[4] This would leave the patch from the unplaced fragments (containing only numerals of reign durations) to occupy either the top of Column IV or the left half of the top of Column IX.

By removing the rogue patch from Column IX we now find ourselves with a large gap in the middle of that column and an equally large question begging to be answered – why, in the first place, was the Canon reconstructed into eleven columns when all the pieces could have been mounted in ten columns? The small fragments in Column X could easily fit in the new space now made available in Column IX and, what is more, fragments 150 and 152 certainly do not belong at the top of Column X where they currently reside, as neither is a patch (on the arguments already aired above, a patch would have to stand here). The *recto* tax-list, on the back of the fragments placed in Columns IX to XI, is 'wholly chaotic' (in Gardiner's words), so is useless in determining any of the positions for the fragments of the last third of the document. Unfortunately, it seems that most historians in recent years have taken the order and position of these fragments to be established with some degree of certainty (with the exception, principally, of Kim Ryholt, see below), and have failed to take into consideration Gardiner's

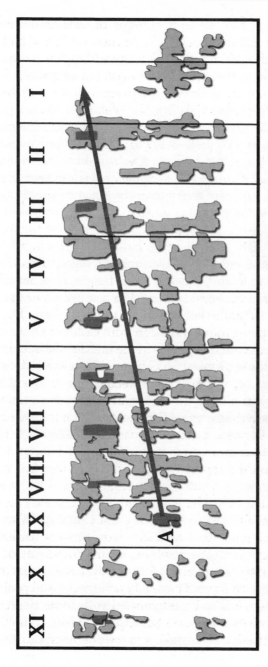

16. Simplified layout of the papyrus fragments belonging to the Turin Canon, indicating the positions of the patches in the current mounting and with the out-of-place patch (A) retained in the lower half of Column IX.

cautionary remarks found in the notes of his publication of the Turin Canon.[5]

It is thus difficult to understand why two important modern works on the chronology and sequence of reigns in the Second Intermediate Period – those of Jürgen von Beckerath (1964 & 1984[6]) and Jaromir Malek (1982[7]), have made use of the existing mounting of Columns IX and X to develop their arguments. However, in 1997, another Egyptologist – Danish scholar Kim Ryholt – finally recognised the problems of the inaccurate mounting of the patch and has come to a conclusion similar to mine, proposing the removal of the offending fragment from Column IX.

> The remainder of Gardiner's Column IX and the following Column X include a number of fragments which are evidently misplaced since they contain the names of gods and 'demi-gods'. … The position of fragment 41+42 could not be established through its fibres which are obscured by the thick patch. … Patches occur at intervals of about sixteen to seventeen centimetres (along the top of the papyrus) and it is therefore clear that the papyrus had been damaged while rolled up. A patch is expected seventeen centimetres to the right of the patch preserved on fragment 1, and it is in this position that fragment 41+42 belongs.[8]

The consequences of removing the patch fragment from Column IX are far-reaching. It is my contention that Ibscher's Column X now becomes superfluous, resulting in an artificial stretching of the Canon (and therefore the chronology of the SIP) by one column of approximately thirty kings. Column XI, containing some of the 17th Dynasty rulers, should be renamed as Column X and brought into contact with a reconstructed Column IX –

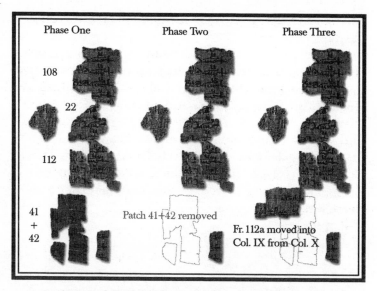

17. A step-by-step remounting of Column XI. Phase One: the fragments as currently mounted with patch 41+42 in the wrong place. Phase Two: removal of the incorrectly placed patch. Phase Three: with the newly created space it is possible to introduce fragment 112a from Column X (containing the name Khamudy and the Hyksos years total) locating it at the bottom of fragment 108, thus giving us six lines of the Greater Hyksos dynasty.

including some of the remaining fragments from Ibscher's defunct Column X.

The reconstruction of Column IX is best explained by reference to the illustration (above). The top two fragments (108 & 112) have been retained in their original position with fragment 22 from the old Column X placed between them. Patch fragment 41+42 has been removed, and, in its place, is positioned the un-numbered fragment bearing the name of the last Hyksos ruler, Khamudy, followed by the total line: 'six rulers of foreign lands for 100[+x years]' (this fragment, previously mounted in the defunct Column X, will be designated by the number 112a in order to simplify references to it in the following discussion). Now let us look at the results of this arrangement to see what information can be gleaned.

CHAPTER THREE

The Greater Hyksos Kings in the Turin Canon

The place to start is with the central fragments 112 (see plate 11) and 112a which form the focus of this new reconstruction. What we now have is the following:

[...]	– Line IX:14
Dual King [...]	– Line IX:15
Dual King Anak[...]	– Line IX:16
Dual King Ia[...]	– Line IX:17
Dual King Ap[...]	– Line IX:18
[...] Khamudy	– Line IX:19
6 [heka]-khasut for 100[+x years]	– Line IX:20

I would therefore like to tentatively propose that this constitutes the six kings of the Greater Hyksos '15th' Dynasty and that Manetho's list of Hyksos kings may be arranged as follows:

(1) Lost = Manetho's Salites/Saites
(2) Lost = Manetho's Bnon/Baion
(3) Anak[...] = Manetho's Apachnan = Anak-idbu (Khyan's Horus name)
(4) Ya[...] = Manetho's Iannas/Staan = Yanassi (son of Khyan)
(5) Ap[...] = Manetho's Apophis = Auserre Apophis
(6) Khamudy = Manetho's Assis/Archles = Asehre(?) Khamudy

Thus we have almost the entire Greater Hyksos dynasty partly preserved, sitting squarely in the middle of Column IX and separated from Nehesi by Column VIII (in its entirety) and the first thirteen kings of Column IX – a total of forty-three rulers. The entry bearing the name and reign-length of Sheshi (Nehesi's father and predecessor on the throne) would have originally resided at the bottom of the now destroyed lower part of Column VII. Thus

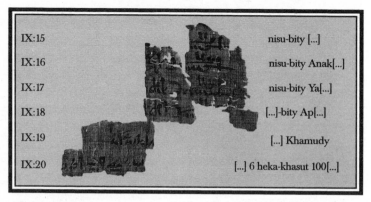

IX:15		nisu-bity [...]
IX:16		nisu-bity Anak[...]
IX:17		nisu-bity Ya[...]
IX:18		[...]-bity Ap[...]
IX:19		[...] Khamudy
IX:20		[...] 6 heka-khasut 100[...]

18. Close up of the new join between fragments 112 and 112a in Column IX.

we can state with some confidence that, according to the Royal Canon of Turin, Sheshi and his son Nehesi reigned many decades and perhaps centuries before the Greater Hyksos dynasty which, in turn, lasted over one hundred years before the establishment of the Egyptian New Kingdom in around Year 11 of Ahmose. By adopting this new proposal, a number of the riddles that have tended to confuse the chronology of the SIP have been solved and an opportunity exists to establish a clearer chronological framework for this fascinating period of Egyptian history.

Conclusion Four

Sheshi (whose scarab was found in one of the last tombs at Jericho before its destruction) does not date to the end of the Second Intermediate Period and the fall of the Greater Hyksos but rather to centuries earlier. Middle Bronze Age Jericho was therefore destroyed long before the beginning of the Egyptian New Kingdom.

Chapter Four

SETH'S KINGDOM

*Slavery in Egypt -- Sothic Dating -- Nehesi and the '14th'
Dynasty -- The Fortress Town of Zile -- Seth 'Lord of Ro-
Ikhte' -- The Year 400 Stela -- Speos Artemidos*

ntil recently much of what had been written on
the Second Intermediate Period revolved around
attempts to establish its chronology, both in relative
and absolute terms. Little monumental or settlement
archaeology had apparently survived upon which to
draw conclusions about the social and cultural history of
the period. Scholars were therefore dependent mainly on
later written sources to reconstruct any sort of history of
the era between the Middle and New Kingdoms. Some of
these sources were nearly contemporary, such as the Speos
Artemidos inscription (mid-18th Dynasty) – in which the
female pharaoh, Hatshepsut, proclaims her restoration of
monuments neglected by the Asiatics of an earlier time; the
Turin Canon (mid-19th Dynasty) – in part listing the kings
of the 13th to 17th Dynasties; and the Papyrus Sallier story
(late-19th Dynasty) of Sekenenre Taa-ken and Apophis – a
somewhat fantastical folk tale about the machinations of
a 17th Dynasty Theban king and his contemporary, the

'Hyksos' ruler of Avaris. From several centuries later we also have the Genealogy of the Memphite Priesthood – a large block from a tomb in the Sakkara necropolis containing a list of priests of Ptah (and, in some instances, the rulers under whom they served) extending back to Montuhotep II of the 11th Dynasty and therefore including the Second Intermediate Period. Finally, of course, considerable use had to be made of the history of Egypt recorded by the Ptolemaic priest, Manetho, as handed down to us in the writings of Africanus, Eusebius and, for this period in particular, Josephus.[1]

The only two major primary source documents – that is, contemporary with the period under discussion – are the Kamose victory inscription (recorded on a pair of stelae) describing the Theban king's war against Auserre Apophis (supplemented by the Carnarvon Tablet – a schoolboy copy of part of the first stela which has been severely damaged) and an autobiography from the el-Kab tomb of Ahmose, son of the lady Ibana,[2] who served in the army of Ahmose I (founder of the 18th Dynasty) and who had participated in the siege and capture of Avaris – the event which finally resulted in the Hyksos expulsion from Egypt. Both these texts deal with the end of Hyksos rule and so, as things stand at the moment, we possess no *contemporary* material which throws light on the events which led up to the rise of the Asiatic 'Hyksos' dynasties in Lower and Middle Egypt.

Recently, within the last forty years, historians have at last begun to receive data from settlement sites of the period, and the initial results are suggesting that a new approach is needed to aid both our understanding of the nature of 'Hyksos' culture and the historical events related to their occupation of Egypt. In this chapter we will review the corpus of material currently available to us (including recent archaeological discoveries in the eastern delta) and attempt to assimilate this material with our new reconstruction of the Turin Canon papyrus fragments.

The first of our tasks is to construct a picture of the

society that occupied Egypt (and in particular the delta) in the years following the 12th Dynasty and prior to the Hyksos dominance. In other words, we shall be discussing the archaeological and textual evidence for Manetho's 13th and 14th Dynasties.

Let us start with a new phenomenon that was apparently introduced for the first time (on a significant scale) into Egyptian society during the 13th Dynasty.

Evidence for Slavery in Egypt

The major document which has come to light concerning the Canaanite population of Egypt during the 13th Dynasty is Brooklyn Papyrus 35.1446,[3] but there are also several papyri from the pyramid town of Senuseret II at Kahun, known collectively as the Illahun Papyri.[4] In the case of the former, out of a total holding of one Theban estate amounting to seventy-nine domestic slaves, no fewer than forty-five bore Canaanite or Semitic names.[5] The fact that the household was located in Upper Egypt suggests that an even higher proportion of Asiatic servants might be expected for the eastern delta where Egypt adjoins Canaan. Thus it is reasonable to infer that between fifty and seventy-five per cent of the delta slave/servant population during the 13th Dynasty was of Asiatic/Canaanite origin.

The French Egyptologist, Georges POSENER, has noted that all the early references to Aamu living in Egypt date to the period from Amenemhat III down to the mid-13th Dynasty, around the time of Neferhotep I (Turin Canon VI:25).[6] The evidence further suggests that they were more numerous in the 13th Dynasty (in spite of the poverty of archaeological data for this period) compared to the relatively rich preceding dynasty.[7] In general, they seem to have assimilated well into the existing culture of Egypt. The surviving Aamu population records of the 13th Dynasty also suggest a greater proportion of female slaves to male slaves.[8]

Several texts have come to light which indicate that certain of these Aamu managed to reach high positions in the administration during the latter part of the 12th Dynasty (some also marrying Egyptian women), but that this state of affairs did not last long into the 13th Dynasty.

> The fact that important persons in the time of Amenemhat III felt free to designate themselves as *Aam* (Asiatic) or as born of an *Aamet* (female Asiatic) means that one can hardly consider them as slaves in the ordinary sense as in the Brooklyn Papyrus. One must therefore reckon with a deterioration in the status of Asiatics between the time of Amenemhat III and that of Neferhotep.[9]

John van Seters also compares the Aamu of the Middle Kingdom with the Habiru, referred to throughout the Levant from the Middle Kingdom to the el-Amarna period.[10]

This is all very interesting because, without realising it, he is describing, in precise and almost uncanny terms, the Israelites and mixed Asiatic multitude (Hebrews) of the Sojourn period as described in the books of Genesis and Exodus. Anyone who has read *A Test of Time* will know that I identify the Asiatic population of Avaris during the late 12th Dynasty and 13th Dynasty (up to the reign of Dudimose) with the Israelites of the Sojourn period (or 'proto-Israelites' if you are so minded).

In the New Chronology model, the era begins with Aamu – such as Joseph – rising to high office in the Egyptian administration [Genesis 41:38-49]; followed by the arrival of Asiatic tribal groups – such as Jacob's extended family – into the eastern delta as free immigrants [Genesis 46:1-7]; according to the book of Exodus these foreigners from Canaan are subsequently enslaved under a 'pharaoh who did not know Joseph' [Exodus 1:8-14].

To me the parallels are obvious. The archaeological picture and the biblical story correspond well and are worthy of equation on the basis of any normal historical criteria. However, the academic response has been less than enthusiastic – because of the chronological implications that arise out of such a radical proposition. The furthest any of the more open-minded scholars are prepared to go (in private but not in print!) is to accept the possibility that the Asiatic peoples of Avaris, as revealed by archaeology, formed the 'historical basis' for the tradition of 'Israelites' sojourning in Egypt at some distant time before the establishment of the Israelite state in Canaan. You may ask yourself 'So what's the difference between this and actually saying that the Second Intermediate Period Asiatic population *were* the Israelites of Genesis and Exodus?' Well, the distinction is important to the academics because, as we have seen, it allows them to retain the historical rise of the Israelite state during the Iron Age (that is, Iron Age I for the Judges period and Iron Age IIA for the Monarchy period) whilst, at the same time, giving themselves the manoeuvring space to concede the possibility of a 'folk memory' for an Israelite Sojourn based on the Asiatic population of the Second Intermediate Period (i.e. Middle Bronze II). If they were to accept, straightforwardly, the equation of the Israelite slaves with the 13th Dynasty Asiatic slaves – as I do – then the consequences would simply be too hard to swallow, for they would then have to concede that the Exodus must have taken place in the Middle Bronze II period, the Judges would have lived during the Late Bronze I, and the United Monarchy era would need to be placed in the Late Bronze II – in other words well before the Iron Age IIA of the conventional scheme. This is the chronological stumbling block that lies at the heart of the schism between New Chronologists and the establishment. It is the principal reason for the outright rejection of a direct link between the Israelites and the Asiatics of Avaris.

And why is it impossible to shift the Egyptian chronology downwards (along with the archaeological periods) to tie

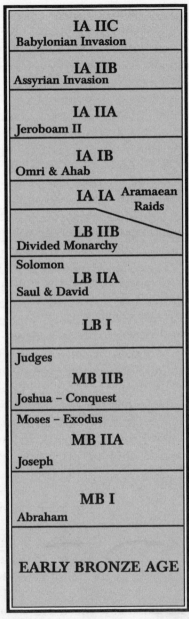

The Old Testament and Levantine stratigraphy in the New Chronology model.

everything in with biblical history as I have suggested? It seems that the main issue (though many would be reluctant to articulate it) is that old chestnut – Sothic dating.

Sothic Dating

For those who are unfamiliar with this purely Egyptological phenomenon, let me explain what Sothic dating is.

Put simply, the Egyptians began their calendar on the first day of the first month of Akhet (the inundation season) which, when the calendar was established, fell on the day that the Dog-Star (Greek *Sothis* = *Sirius*) rose heliacally – that is, just before sunrise – after its seventy-day disappearance (whilst the sun passed in front of the star in the annual solar cycle). If you observe this heliacal rising of Sirius today, you will see that the event occurs around 19/21 July every year, just before the beginning of the Nile flood. However, this apparent stability is because we have devised a leap-year system in which, every fourth year, we add an extra day to the month of February. We do this because the solar year (the time the Earth takes to complete its orbit of the Sun) is not 365 days but 365.25 days. So we need to add a day every fourth year to correct the quarter-day shift between our 365-day calendar and the actual solar cycle – otherwise that calendar would slip backwards against the solar year by a quarter-day every year. If we failed to make this correction, then, after 730 years, our New Year's Day (1 January) would be celebrated in midsummer! Clearly this would not be acceptable and so we have found a way to avoid such a situation. But what did the ancient Egyptians do?

According to the surviving textual evidence, they adopted a twelve-month calendar of thirty days – making a total of 360 days in their year. In order to stay in synchronisation with the longer solar year, they then added five festival (epagomenal) days at the end of the year to celebrate the birthdays of the main gods, bringing the total number of days in the calendar to 365 – just like us.

However, most Egyptologists believe that the ancient Egyptians never adjusted or corrected their calendar to compensate for the extra quarter-day shift which we allow for in our leap-year system. They actually argue that the otherwise astute Egyptians permitted this chaotic situation to persist for three thousand years with summer months falling in winter and festivals dated to the calendar occurring completely out of step with the seasons – except for the few years when the 1460-year Sothic cycle came back to its starting position again. To me this view of an unadjusted Egyptian Sothic calendar is untenable. Of course the Egyptians would have found a way to reset the calendar to the natural solar year. NC astronomer David Lappin has suggested that they achieved this by means of adding three months (i.e. ninety days) to a chosen year when the slippage had reached unmanageable proportions (i.e. after approximately 360 years).[11] I myself have proposed that these eras of calendrical adjustment should be recognised in the term 'Repeating of Births' (Egyptian *wehem mesut*) and in the pharaonic title 'Repeater of Births' which occasionally occur throughout Egyptian history. Those records which survive of this 'repetition' are dated to Amenemhat I, Seti I and Ramesses XI. Such a sequence would suggest that another calendrical reform had also taken place during the Hyksos period and this is indeed what Manetho records for the reign of Apophis. However, no contemporary document from his time survives which might have confirmed him as a 'Repeater of Births'.

Interestingly one specific attempt to make just such an adjustment to the calendar has come down to us in the Canopus Decree of 238 BC. The reform was proposed by the Macedonian pharaoh, Ptolemy III.

> It came about that the festivals which were celebrated in winter fell in the summer, and those celebrated in summer were instead in winter.

On this occasion the priests resisted the calendrical reform. This demonstrates that kings could propose such reforms but that they were not always approved by the clergy. However, this single instance of rejection certainly fails to prove that correction of the *annus vagus* had not taken place earlier – only that in the Ptolemaic period an adjustment to the calendar was resisted by the then conservative priesthood.

If the New Chronologists are right in assuming that the Egyptians were not remiss enough to allow their calendar to slip into complete chaos throughout all periods of their history, then the occasional but regular 'Repeating of Births' would be entirely consistent with a policy of ninety-day adjustments to the calendar in order to reset its synchronism with the solar year. This, then, is what I believe actually happened. But, for two centuries now, Egyptologists have tacitly accepted that no such reforms ever took place in ancient Egypt, permitting them to use the slippage of the natural year against the artificial year to calculate absolute dates for the framework of Egyptian chronology whenever a 'Sothic date' is recorded in a papyrus document.

Their starting point is the comment by CENSORINUS that the Sothic cycle was synchronised with the natural solar year in AD 139. Thus the previous occasion when this had happened was 1460 (i.e. 4 x 365) years earlier in 1321/22 BC (as the historians calculated[12]). THEON of Alexandria mentions an 'era of Menophres' (*apo Menophreos*) which began in 1321 BC, and this has been identified with the start of the Great Sothic Year which ended in AD 139.

Now, because Ramesses II has been dated to the thirteenth century BC by means of retro-calculation from the dates for Shoshenk I (identified as Shishak, plunderer of Solomon's Temple in 926 BC), this King Menophres had to be identified with one of Ramesses' immediate predecessors – either his father, Menmaatre Seti I, or his grandfather, Menpehtyre Ramesses I. The popular choice amongst scholars was to identify Menpehtyre with Menophres – even

115

though the two names are clearly not a convincing match (the middle elements *pehty* and *nophr* being completely different). Even so, at that time Ramesses II was dated to 1290 BC and so Ramesses I (in around 1320 BC) had to be Menophres.

However, times have changed. With Kenneth Kitchen's now widely accepted lower date of 1279 BC for the coronation of Ramesses II and the highest regnal date for Seti I recognised as Year 15, Ramesses I's single year of rule is currently set in 1295 BC – unfortunately some twenty-six years after Theon's date of 1321 BC for the 'era of Menophres'.

This name Menophres is almost certainly derived from Egyptian *Men-nofer-re* (written in the Egyptological literature as Menneferre). This prenomen was chosen by only one pharaoh in Egypt's entire history. The name occurs on a number of scarabs dating from the Second Intermediate Period and can be attributed to an obscure ruler of the little-known period from the end of the reign of Dudimose to the beginning of the Greater Hyksos Dynasty. In the New Chronology King Dudimose (identified as the Pharaoh of the Exodus) reigned around 1447 BC, whilst Salitis (first ruler of the Greater Hyksos dynasty) began his reign in *circa* 1288 BC. Thus the New Chronology window for the reign of Menneferre (between 1447 and 1288 BC) is entirely consistent with an 'era of Menophres' starting in 1321 BC. Both the name and date match – unlike the conventional scheme where neither the name nor the date matches.

Still, such problems have not concerned Egyptologists, being put to one side for the better good of establishing a chronology based on absolute dates derived from Sothic dating. They anchor this orthodox dating framework on two key presumed Sothic dates – one from the Middle Kingdom and one from the early New Kingdom.

(1) Year 7 of Senuseret III is dated to 1830 BC using the so-called Sothic date contained in an Illahun papyrus

and, thus, the end of the 12th Dynasty is placed in 1759 BC.[13] In recent years variations on this date based on different observation points for the heliacal rising have been proposed but they make only a few years' difference.

(2) Year 9 of Amenhotep I is dated to 1505 BC using the so-called Sothic date contained in Papyrus Ebers which results in a starting date for the New Kingdom of 1529 BC (Year 11 Ahmose = expulsion of the Hyksos from Avaris).

And so the Second Intermediate Period is restricted to just 230 years between 1759 and 1529 BC.[14] The settlement of Avaris would thus have been founded in around 1800 BC during the reign of Amenemhat III, giving a total duration of approximately 270 years for the Middle Bronze Age Asiatic occupation at the site. Professor Bietak then divides the nine strata (H to D/2) of MB II Avaris into this figure to arrive at thirty years per stratum (whilst acknowledging that this is no more than a schematic arrangement purely for the sake of convenience). Thus Stratum G/1-3 would come to an end in *circa* 1709 BC – a date which also heralds the beginning of Stratum F, which itself marks the start of Bietak's 14th Dynasty (see below).

A New Chronology Dating for the SIP

That is how the standard scheme works. But what happens in the New Chronology? Well, first the two so-called Sothic dates are abandoned as tools for fixing absolute dates because the proponents of the New Chronology simply do not accept that the Egyptians failed to undertake a single calendrical reform throughout their entire history. Any such reform during the New Kingdom would, of course, completely invalidate Sothic calculations worked backwards from the Censorinus AD 139 date. So, on this

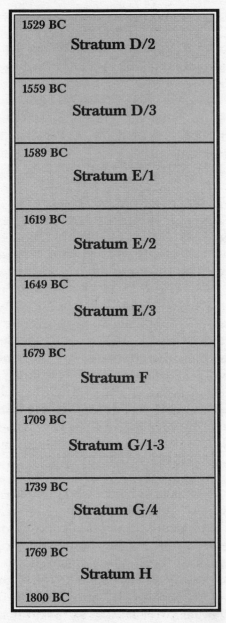

1529 BC

Stratum D/2

1559 BC

Stratum D/3

1589 BC

Stratum E/1

1619 BC

Stratum E/2

1649 BC

Stratum E/3

1679 BC

Stratum F

1709 BC

Stratum G/1-3

1739 BC

Stratum G/4

1769 BC

Stratum H

1800 BC

The schematic chronology of the Tell ed-Daba stratigraphy based on Sothic dating.

basis, we can ignore both of the Sothic dates of 1830 BC and 1505 BC.

Second, a chronological fixed point based on retro-calculations for a sequence of lunar month-lengths recorded in ancient documents is much more reliable for absolute dating as it would be entirely independent of Sothic chronology. New Chronology astronomer, David Lappin, has shown that the best match for the series of Egyptian Middle Kingdom lunar dates falls in the seventeenth century BC and results in a start-date for the 13th Dynasty of *circa* 1632 BC.[15] This is 127 years later than the conventional date based on Sothic chronology. Third, at the other end of the Second Intermediate Period, the New Chronology date for the start of the New Kingdom (in or soon after Year 11 Ahmose) is determined as *circa* 1181 BC – based on the highest regnal dates and Manethonian reign-lengths for the kings of the 18th and 19th Dynasties retro-calculated from the reign of Ramesses II whose New Chronology accession-year is currently fixed at 943 BC (via the lunar date of Year 52).[16]

These dates are supported by another astronomical event – the near-total solar eclipse of 30 April 984 BC that took place in Year 8 (previously thought to be Year 10[17]) of the Hittite king, Murshili II, whilst on campaign in north-east Anatolia. There are very few alternative candidates for this eclipse – especially within a revised chronology model such as that being proposed here.

The 1419 BC Venus Solution for Year 1 of Ammisaduga (tenth ruler of the Babylon I dynasty), as determined by astronomer Wayne Mitchell,[18] confirms an approximate date for the reign of his predecessor, Hammurabi (sixth ruler of Babylon I), and, via various synchronisms with Mari and Byblos, the dates for Neferhotep I of Egypt (NC – *c.* 1543-1533 BC), twenty-second ruler of the 13th Dynasty.

In the New Chronology, the start of the 13th Dynasty is dated to 1632 BC and Year 11 Ahmose to 1181 BC, giving us a total of 450 years for the Second Intermediate Period. This

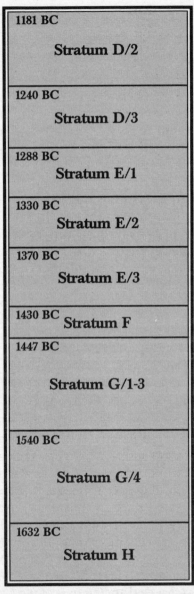

1181 BC

Stratum D/2

1240 BC

Stratum D/3

1288 BC

Stratum E/1

1330 BC

Stratum E/2

1370 BC

Stratum E/3

1430 BC **Stratum F**

1447 BC

Stratum G/1-3

1540 BC

Stratum G/4

1632 BC

Stratum H

The schematic chronology of the Tell ed-Daba stratigraphy based on New Chronology dating (using astronomical anchors and biblical dates retro-calculated from the founding of the Temple of Solomon in c. 967 BC).

is nearly double the 230 years of the orthodox chronology based on Sothic dating. Quite a difference! As a result, the nine major strata of Avaris cover a much greater interval of time and the start of Stratum F, marking the arrival of the '14th' Dynasty, is dated to 1445 BC (or thereabouts). The duration of this 'Lesser Hyksos' dynasty then works out at around 147 years before we arrive at the start of the succeeding 'Greater Hyksos' dynasty founded by Salitis in 1288 BC. Time then to take a look at this mysterious '14th' Dynasty in more detail.

The so-called '14th' Dynasty

An obelisk of a 'king's son' Nehesi found at Tanis[19] has been used to establish the relative date for the beginning of the new '14th' Dynasty in the eastern delta. This identification of the Nehesi dynasty as the '14th' is probably a misnomer; however, I have retained it here to avoid any confusion. In the box on page 122 I have attempted to reconstruct the sequence of Second Intermediate Period dynasties in the light of our fresh understanding of both the Turin Canon and the nomenclature of Manetho (Eusebius version).

It has been almost unanimously agreed that this new '14th' Dynasty arose some time during the second half of the 13th Dynasty, whilst the kings of the latter dynasty apparently still ruled from the old 12th Dynasty royal residence at Itj-tawy south of Memphis. The argument goes something on the following lines. As artefacts for the 13th Dynasty kings succeeding Khaneferre Sobekhotep IV (Turin Canon VI:27) have not been found in the delta, these kings must have lost control of Lower Egypt to a local dynasty which the archaeological evidence suggests was located at or near Avaris. In spite of the fact that it is an argument based on negative evidence from a region which had (until recently) rarely received the archaeologists' attention, this understanding of Second Intermediate Period history has remained the popular option. This is, in no small measure,

Rulers of Upper Egypt	Rulers of Lower Egypt	Tell ed-Daba Strata	Archaeological Periods
18th Dynasty Ahmose		Stratum C	LB I
		Stratum D/1	
Kamose 16th Dynasty (Thebes)	17th Dynasty Greater Hyksos Salitis	Stratum D/2	MB IIB (late)
		Stratum D/3	
15th Dynasty (Thebes)	Yakub-Har 14th Dynasty Lesser Hyksos Sheshi	Stratum E/1	MB IIB (early)
		Stratum E/2	
		Stratum E/3	
		Stratum F	
Dudimose Sobekhotep IV 13th Dynasty (Itj-tawy & Memphis)		Proto-Exodus	MB IIA
		Proto-Moses	
		Stratum G (Proto-Israelite)	
Amenemhat III 12th Dynasty (Itj-tawy & Memphis)		Proto-Joseph	
		Stratum H (Proto-Israelite)	

The New Chronology nomenclature of the Second Intermediate Period dynasties in relation to the stratigraphy of Tell ed-Daba/Avaris. This scheme uses the Eusebius and Scholia to Plato redactions of Manetho rather than that of Africanus. The latter is the only edition which identifies the 15th Dynasty with the Greater Hyksos. The rest give the dynasty founded by Salitis as the 17th. The former is now so well entrenched in the literature that it would be difficult to change the numbering. As a result, I have not given the Greater Hyksos dynasty the Manethonian label of the 17th Dynasty to avoid confusion with the Theban 17th Dynasty of the Egyptological literature. However, it is important to understand that the majority of Manethonian redactions separate the Greater Hyksos 17th Dynasty from the end of the native Egyptian 13th Dynasty.

due to the chronological restrictions that have been imposed upon the 13th to 17th Dynasties as a result of the two key Sothic dates. Given the minimum lengths attributable to both the 13th and '14th' Dynasties – as derived from the Turin Canon and Manetho – this must force an overlap between the two dynasties simply on chronological grounds. In essence the interval set for the period by Sothic dating is too short to accommodate both dynasties sequentially. However, in the New Chronology it is an entirely different matter because we have a Second Intermediate Period which is nearly twice as long as that in the conventional scheme. Thus we can have the '14th' Dynasty following on directly from the 13th Dynasty without any substantial overlap.

So, the revised chronological model of the SIP would envisage Strata H through to G/1-3 at Avaris as representing the 13th Dynasty hegemony over the delta, whilst Strata F (following the abandonment of eastern Avaris) through to E/1 would represent the Lesser Hyksos '14th' Dynasty founded by Sheshi and his son Nehesi. Strata D/3 and D/2 would then be left for the last century of the Second Intermediate Period and the Greater Hyksos '15th' Dynasty.

The Fortress of Zile

A newly discovered fortress town of both Ramesside and Second Intermediate Period date, located in northern Sinai east of the Suez Canal, may be the famous frontier town of ZILE, known to have been near the modern town of Kantara, and which was undoubtedly occupied throughout most of Egypt's history – given its strategic importance as the 'gateway' into the delta. The large four-hundred-metre by four-hundred-metre enclosure of Tell el-Hebua contains an Asiatic occupation level, beneath the New Kingdom structures, which would have been contemporary with the reigns of Sheshi, Nehesi and the Greater Hyksos pharaohs.

The site actually consists of three associated fortress structures, two of which lie on either side of a depression which may once have contained the Pelusiac branch of the Nile. Here the waterway breached a long sandy causeway, south-west to north-east, between what is now salt flats but which was once treacherous marsh with large tracts of open water. The Egyptians named the salt marshes on the north side of the sand spit, adjacent to the open sea, *Shi-Hor* ('Lake of Horus'), whilst the enclosed marshes to the south of the causeway were known as *Pa-Zufy* ('The Reeds') – in my view one and the same as *Yam Suph* ('Reed Sea') of the Exodus miracle. The Pelusiac channel (or perhaps an artificial canal) flowed from The Reeds marsh into Shi-Hor and on out to the Mediterranean, creating an impassable barrier infested with crocodiles. This waterway, cutting through the sandy causeway, acted as a frontier which could be crossed only via a wooden bridge that the Egyptians had built between the two main fortresses at Hebua. A representation of this amazing border-post is to be found amongst the war reliefs of Seti I at Karnak where the king is shown escorting prisoners back to Egypt across the bridge at Zile.

All this points clearly to Tell el-Hebua being one of the major fortress towns built to protect the principal eastern entrance into Egypt. Its dimensions (the largest Egyptian

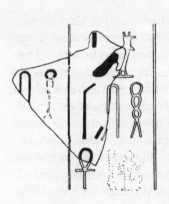

fort ever found) reduce the possibilities of identifying the site to just two – either Seti I's 'House of the Lion' (mentioned in the Karnak annals) or Zile (also, as we have seen, in the same annals), both of which lay at the western end of the line of Ramesside forts leading across northern Sinai to Canaan. The fact that the Hebua stronghold also existed in the Second

19. Fragmentary text from an obelisk set up by 'the king's son Nehesi', found at Tanis in the eastern delta but possibly originally from Avaris. The right column (with restorations) reads 'Nehesi, repeating life' [after Petrie: Tanis].

Intermediate Period would greatly favour its identification with Zile – the frontier fort whose history goes back to a time many centuries before Seti I and the Ramesside era – according to the Egyptian records.

Seth – Lord of Ro-Ikhte

Returning to Nehesi, we can make certain tentative assumptions about his era and geographical control based on eastern delta archaeology. As obelisks – such as those of this ruler found in secondary use in Tanis – are associated with temple façades, it would be reasonable to assume that Nehesi was involved in the construction of a temple, somewhere in the eastern delta or north-west Sinai; this is on the basis of the provenance of other Ramesside obelisks found at Tanis which originally came from the city of Pi-Ramesse, built at the site of the earlier city of Avaris. The Nehesi obelisk from Tanis is inscribed with the phrases 'eldest royal son, Nehesi, beloved of Seth, Lord of Ro-Ikhte' and 'beloved of Hery-sa.f' (Arsaphes). Montet has suggested that perhaps the origin of the name of the Sethroite (14th) nome is to be identified with the cult of 'Seth Ro-Ikhte'.[20]

Van Seters has persuasively argued that Ro-Ikhte, which means 'gateway' (literally 'mouth') 'of the cultivation' is to be located at Zile where cultivation and desert meet.[21] The phrase 'beloved of Arsaphes' gives us a further clue as to where the Nehesi obelisk may have been erected. Arsaphes was worshipped in later times at Heracleopolis Parva, capital of the 14th nome, and this too has been tentatively located at or near Zile. Thus we may postulate that Nehesi's obelisk, and therefore the temple that it adorned, was probably erected at the Tell el-Hebua fortress site where substantial remains of his time have been found. What is more, the only stelae recovered so far from el-Hebua are two bearing the name of Nehesi.[22] The implication of all this is that Nehesi, as a king's son and heir, was charged with the protection of

Egypt's eastern frontier and that he may have resided at Zile – at least for a time.

Soon after Nehesi became king, he established or enhanced the cult of 'Seth, Lord of Avaris' (a block of his bearing this epithet was found at Tell el-Mokdam – one of the two primary candidates, along with Tell er-Retaba, for the biblical Pithom). It has thus been suggested that Nehesi also built a temple to Seth at Avaris which in turn is perhaps to be identified with the Canaanite temple found by Bietak at Tell ed-Daba (built in Stratum F or E/3).[23]

We thus get a picture of the crown-prince (and then later king), Nehesi, as acting ruler in the north-east delta, appointed to administer military control over the border region on behalf of his (unfortunately) anonymous father, the Lesser Hyksos king (whom we have identified with Sheshi). The latter may therefore have been an absentee ruler – perhaps resident in Sharuhen in southern Canaan or occupied further south in military campaigns against the remnant 13th Dynasty based at Itj-tawy (in which case Nehesi's father was probably resident at Memphis) – leaving his son in charge of overseeing the construction of the two temples to Baal/Seth at Zile/Ro-Ikhte and Avaris.

The Year Four Hundred Stela

Hiding in one of the darker corners of the Cairo Museum is a large pink granite stela dated to the reign of Ramesses II. It is neither elegantly proportioned nor well carved, but it is of immense historical and chronological significance. This monument, unearthed at Tanis (and therefore almost certainly originating from Avaris), is known as the 'Year Four Hundred Stela'.

The upper section (or lunette) of the monument depicts Ramesses II making an offering to the god Seth of Avaris, but the deity is not shown in his normal guise as a hound or mythical hybrid creature. Here he is a human, king-like figure, wearing a tall crown. In fact he is represented as the storm-god Baal. Seth/Sutekh is thus clearly being identified here with the Canaanite god as originally worshipped in the Hyksos city of Avaris.

It has long been recognised that Ramesses II's dynasty originated from the north-east delta and that they were a military family whose home was almost certainly in Avaris. This is surely why Ramesses chose to build his new royal residence, Pi-Ramesse, at this same spot. Some scholars have gone even further by suggesting that Ramesses I and his successors were of Hyksos descent.

The hieroglyphic text below the lunette scene tells us that a vizier, Seti (the later Seti I, father of Ramesses II), celebrated the four-hundredth anniversary of the coronation of Seth as Lord of Avaris. In other words four hundred years had passed since the founding of Seth's temple at Avaris. Seti was undoubtedly vizier under Pharaoh Haremheb and possibly under Tutankhamun, so it was during this period that the fourth centenary occurred. In the New Chronology, Ramesses II ascended the throne in 943 BC. His father Seti's reign lasted a maximum of nineteen years and his grandfather Ramesses I's just over a year. Thus Haremheb's last regnal year fell in *circa* 962 BC and Tutankhamun's first year in *circa* 1007 BC. If we then, for the purpose of our calculations, place the Seth commemoration in the middle of this forty-five-year period – in 985 BC – we can fix the foundation of the Seth temple at Avaris to *circa* 1385 BC (plus or minus twenty years, depending on when Seti performed the ritual).

I would argue that the Seth temple which was founded four hundred years before Haremheb or Tutankhamun must have been the large Canaanite Temple III at Tell ed-Daba (Stratum F or E/3) built on behalf of his father by Crown-Prince Nehesi. This enables us to date the last years of Sheshi – whom we have identified as that royal father – to *circa* 1385 BC. That is twenty years after the Israelite Conquest of the Promised Land when Caleb and his Israelite troops fought against the Anakim ruler named Sheshai whom we have also identified as the long-reigned Hyksos king, Sheshi. So the Egyptian Year Four Hundred commemoration appears to fit neatly into our chronological scheme. The Lesser Hyksos ruler Sheshi was a Baal worshipper (possibly originating from the Phoenician north) whose son dedicated temples at Avaris to Baal (in the Egyptian form of Seth) and his consort Anat or Astarte/Asherah (no doubt in the Egyptian form of Nephthys). This female deity has been identified with Baalat-Gebel ('Lady of Byblos'), worshipped in Phoenician Byblos, whose temple there stood alongside that of the storm-god Baal-Shamem – ('Lord of the Heavens' = Amorite Hadad). Everything about the temple complex of Early Hyksos Avaris points us north to the area known in Classical times as Phoenicia. Manetho may have been correct when he stated that the Hyksos kings came 'from Phoenicia'. As Manetho's translator, William WADDELL, noted back in 1940:

> This statement of the Phoenician origin of the Hyksos kings has generally been discredited until recently: now the Ras esh-Shamra (Ugarit) tablets, which imply a pantheon strikingly similar to that of the Hyksos, have shown that the Hyksos were closely related to the Phoenicians.[24]

Ugarit (modern Ras Shamra) was one of the major coastal cities of northern Canaan/Phoenicia. The Lesser Hyksos rulers may have invaded Egypt from their bases further south (Sharuhen/Tell el-Ajjul in particular) but, as we will soon see, they were almost certainly northerners of mixed Anatolian and Amorite stock.

Shemau

Back in 1989, whilst completing my degree at University College London, I organised a students' study tour of Egypt. Because no student has more than a few quid to rub together, the trip was planned on a tight budget with what might be described as 'rustic accommodation' and a minibus capable of transporting twelve souls and luggage up and down the country. We certainly managed to investigate some out-of-the-way sites, right off the tourist route, as well as all the major attractions. One of those somewhat obscure monuments was the Speos Artemidos – a rock-cut temple carved out of the Eastern Desert mountains about ten kilometres south of Beni Hassan in Middle Egypt.

The dirt track which separates the cultivation zone from desert scarp at Beni Hassan took us past the Middle Kingdom tombs (including that of Khnumhotep, with its scene of Asiatics entering Egypt in their 'coats of many colours'); on past the abandoned smugglers' village of the Beni Hassan tribe, forlorn in its ruined mudbrick desolation; and finally to the village of Beni Hassan es-Sharruk. From there we left the comfort of our, by now, rather pungent minibus and set off on foot eastwards across the flat desert sands, heading for a great gouge in the high cliffs about three kilometres ahead of us. This was the territory of the mountain-lioness Pakhet – the ancient Egyptian deity of rock erosion who, over millennia, had carved and scratched the deep gullies and canyons of her desert domain. The temple we were heading for, cut into the cliff of a steep-sided wadi, was dedicated to her (see plate 17).

After about half an hour we found ourselves wandering through a vast cemetery of mummified cats which had been buried here as offerings to the lioness-goddess. Then we were there, standing before the much-damaged façade of Hatshepsut's temple from the mid-18th Dynasty. It was nestled beneath a high wall of limestone on the southern side of the wadi, deep in the shadow of the morning sun which had moved south behind the mountain.

We had collected the 'keeper of the keys' – a rather reluctant local villager charged with the guardianship of the temple on behalf of the Egyptian Antiquities Service – and he set about unlocking the heavy iron grille which barred our entry into the inner sanctum of the shrine. Ten minutes later he was still at it, having tried every large rusty key on his heavy belt chain. He eventually admitted defeat, turned to us rather sheepishly and shrugged his shoulders before settling down on a rock in the welcome shade. We were left to study the exterior of the monument, but that was not so bad, as this was what we had really come all this way to see. For here, above the entrance, was a long hieroglyphic inscription – a great proclamation dictated by Pharaoh Hatshepsut to adorn her most important surviving monument after the famous terraced mortuary temple at Deir el-Bahri in Thebes.

Unfortunately, being in the mountain shadow, the text was very hard to make out and therefore difficult to read. In our party were a couple of postgraduate students who have subsequently gone on to become 'leading lights' in Egyptological linguistics – Mark Collier and Bill Manley (authors of the best-selling book *How to Read Egyptian Hieroglyphs*). Eyes adjusted to the conditions, they began to read the text with some fluency.

> Hear you, all people and folk – as many as there may be. I have done these things through the counsel of my heart. I have not slept forgetfully, (but) I have restored that which had been ruined. I have raised up what had formerly decayed, since the **Aamu** (Asiatics) were in the midst of **Avaris of the Northland**, and the **Shemau** (aliens) were in the midst of them, overthrowing that which had been made. They (the Shemau?) ruled without Re, and he did not act by divine command down to (the reign of) my person.

> (Now) I am established upon the thrones of Re. I was foretold for the limits of the years as a born conqueror. I am come as the Uraeus-serpent of Horus, flaming against my enemies. I have made distant those whom the gods abominate and the earth has carried off their footprints.[25]

For me the fascination of this text lies in the first paragraph that gives a hint at the chaos and disorder which pertained (at least according to Hatshepsut) during the Hyksos age. Most specifically, I was intrigued by the reference to the Shemau – usually translated as 'wanderers' or 'vagabonds' but perhaps best thought of as 'immigrants' or 'aliens'. This was such a rare term in the Egyptian texts that its use here surely had to have had some historical significance.

Few Egyptologists have taken much notice of this detail and have signally failed to distinguish between the Asiatics (Aamu) and the 'aliens' (Shemau). But Hatshepsut is quite clear in making the Shemau a sub-group within the overall Asiatic population of Avaris. These Shemau lived 'in the midst' of the Asiatics – a fact which suggests a ruling elite residing at the heart of Avaris and controlling the Semites from Canaan. It seems from the subsequent sentence that it is the Shemau (not the Asiatics) who 'ruled without Re' – that is, without the approval or consent of the sun-god – and that it was this group which had been 'overthrowing that which had been made' – in other words systematically plundering the Egyptian state.

We are going to hear a great deal more about these aliens – singled out by Hatshepsut for particular disdain – as they loom large in our story. For they are the Lords of Avaris represented by the Greater Hyksos dynasty. But first we should complete the history of the Second Intermediate Period by dealing with the Egyptian war of independence and the end of Hyksos rule in Egypt.

20. The hieroglyphs which spell out 'Shemau' in the Speos Artemidos inscription.

131

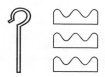

Chapter Five

THE HYKSOS EXPULSION

*The Theban Revival — Sekenenre Taa 'the brave' — Kamose
'the battler' — Ahmose 'the liberator' — Sharuhen — The
Jebusites*

ow did the indigenous Theban pharaohs eventually
relieve northern Egypt of its foreign occupation?
The answer turns out to be the stuff of Hollywood
epic.

The history of the expulsion of the Lords of Avaris has
been reconstructed from folktale (the story of Sekenenre
and Apophis), contemporary documents (victory stelae and
tomb biographies) and extracts from the narrative history
of Egypt written by Manetho (as quoted by Josephus). We
are even able to study the battle-scarred body of the Theban
king who began the great fight-back. The story involves
brave native pharaohs fighting heroic battles as they slowly
push north into enemy territory; a disastrous reverse; a
remarkable heroine who holds the country together in a time
of great crisis; the final siege of Avaris itself; and a surprising
negotiated withdrawal of the enemy to their foreign bases.

133

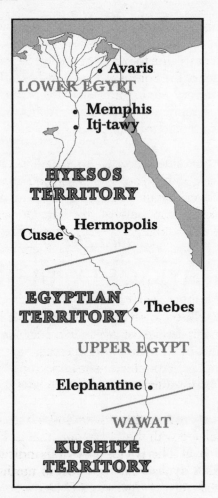

21. The division of Egypt during the Hyksos period.

Taa 'the brave'

Let us begin with the folktale that is the first sign of conflict between the Hyksos-dominated north and the Theban 17th Dynasty south. The text of Papyrus Sallier II tells the story of a quarrel between the Hyksos king, Apophis, and his Theban counterpart, Sekenenre Taa II.

Once upon a time the land of Egypt was in misery, for there was no lord (as sole) king. Then a day came to pass when King Sekenenre was ruler of the Southern City (Thebes). (To the north) misery was in the town of the Asiatics, for Prince Apophis was (ruling) in Avaris and the entire land paid tribute to him [...]

Clearly, by the late Second Intermediate Period, the Greater Hyksos 15th Dynasty had reached a point of total domination over Egypt with the exception of the now much shrunken rump state of the 17th Dynasty (that is, the remnant of the defunct 13th Dynasty) based south of Hermopolis and extending down to Elephantine/Syene (Aswan).

King Apophis personally adopted Seth as lord and he refused to serve any other god that was in the entire land except Seth. He built a temple of eternity made of fine workmanship next to the house of King Apophis and he appeared at dawn (there) in order to sacrifice daily to Seth [...]

The patron deity of Apophis was Seth who, at that time, was clearly assimilated with the Canaanite (that is, Phoenician) weather-god, Baal. This is a fairly obvious indicator that the Greater Hyksos dynasty had its roots in north-west Syria – in the coastal cities of Ugarit and Byblos where Baal was the principal deity.

Now King Apophis desired to send a provocative message (to) King Sekenenre, Prince of the Southern City. [...] he (Apophis) summoned the high officials of his palace and proposed to them that a messenger should be sent to the Prince of the Southern City (Sekenenre) with a complaint [...] However, he was unable to compose it

himself. Thereupon his scribes and wise men
[…] and high officials said: 'O sovereign, our
lord, you should demand that there be a removal
of hippopotami from the canal which lies at the
east of the (Southern) City because they prevent
sleep from coming to us either in the daytime or
at night, for the noise of them is (in) our citizens'
ear(s).' And King Apophis answered them
saying: 'I shall send to the Prince of the Southern
City […] a command […] so that we may assess
the power of the god who is his protector, for he
does not rely upon any god that is in the entire
land except Amun-Re, King of the Gods.'

Is there a clue here in the phrase 'However, he (Apophis)
was unable to compose it (the letter to Sekenenre) himself'
which might suggest that the Hyksos king was not a fluent
Egyptian speaker or writer? Was his inability to write
personally to his fellow Egyptian monarch due to the
fact that he could not physically do it? It is a well-known
tradition that, of the later Ptolemaic pharaohs, only the
infamous Cleopatra VII took the time to learn to speak and
write Egyptian. The rest of her line continued to speak their
native Greek in the Alexandrian court, leaving Egyptian
officials to deal directly with the indigenous population.
It would certainly fit into the picture we are painting of
the Hyksos aristocracy to imagine the Shemau ('aliens')
speaking in a foreign tongue. On the other hand, one might
argue that Apophis was simply stuck for words and could
not come up with an insult of his own without calling upon
his speech-writers to do the job for him. But how much
more interesting it would be if the problem of the tongue-
tied Lord of Avaris was a matter of language.

What is also fascinating is that the ridiculous demand
devised by the courtiers of Avaris involved noisy hippopotami
because, of course, the association of Seth and the dangerous
'river-horse' of Egypt's swamps and water channels would

have been obvious to all hearing the story. How then could Sekenenre kill or drive out the hippopotami without causing serious offence to Seth and therefore to his Hyksos worshippers? The demand from Avaris was tantamount to forcing the Thebans into a no-win situation. Whichever course Sekenenre took – comply or refuse – would drive him into war.

> Now after many days King Apophis then sent the complaint that his scribes and wise men had concocted for him to the Prince of the Southern City. And when the messenger of King Apophis reached the Prince of the Southern City he was taken into the presence of the Prince of the Southern City. Then His Majesty (Sekenenre) said to the messenger of King Apophis: 'Why have you been sent to the Southern City? For what reason have you come journeying here?' The messenger then told him: 'It is King Apophis who has sent (me) to you in order to say, "Remove the hippopotami from the canal which lies at the east of the (Southern) City, because they disturb my sleep both in the daytime and at night, for the noise of them is (in) his citizens' ear(s)".'
>
> The Prince of the Southern City was so taken aback that he was unable to reply to the messenger of King Apophis for some time. Finally the Prince of the Southern City said to him: 'Is it through this that your Lord would investigate matters regarding the canal of the hippopotami which lies at the east of the Southern City?' Then the messenger said to him: 'Comply with the command which he (Apophis) sent through me!' Then the Prince of the Southern City arranged for the messenger of King Apophis to be taken care of with good things: meat, cakes […] The

> Prince of the Southern City (finally) said to
> him: 'Go and tell your lord, "As for whatever
> you (Apophis) will order, he (Sekenenre) will
> comply" – so you shall tell him.' […] Then the
> messenger of King Apophis hastened to journey
> to where his lord was.

So, at this stage in the drama, the Theban monarch has
agreed to comply with the demands of his northern
neighbour, suggesting, if the language of his response to
the Hyksos herald is anything to go by, that his status is
that of subservient vassal of the Hyksos king, and that, as
the continuation of the text implies, he is attempting to
buy time in order to prepare for the inevitable, impending
confrontation.

> The Prince of the Southern City (Sekenenre)
> had his high officials summoned, as well as
> every ranking soldier of his, and he repeated
> to them every issue concerning (the message)
> which King Apophis had sent to him. They were
> uniformly silent for a long while, without being
> able to answer him, be it good or bad. Then King
> Apophis sent (a second message?) to […]

At this point, infuriatingly, the text breaks off, leaving us
hanging in mid-air. Was Apophis' second message (if that is
what it was) another insult intended to push Sekenenre into
war – in spite of the reluctance of his officials and military
commanders? If so, we can surely envisage the reaction of
the Theban monarch. The papyrus is an Egyptian folktale,
so one has to understand that its purpose was to extol the
bravery of Sekenenre. Something dramatic certainly did
happen at this time which we can assume involved a major
clash between the armies of the two factions. Sekenenre's
body (found in the Royal Cache at Deir el-Bahri – DB 320)
displays horrifying war wounds with several gaping holes

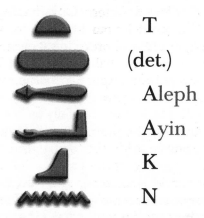

T

(det.)

Aleph

Ayin

K

N

22. The hieroglyphs which make up the name Taa-ken.

in his skull caused by axe, spear and mace strikes. One of the wounds is the exact dimensions and proportion of a typical Hyksos chisel-shaped axe blade.

The conclusion that King Sekenenre Taa II died in the thick of a ferocious battle appears inescapable. No wonder that, shortly after his demise, Sekenenre was honoured with a new epithet attached to his nomen. He became Sekenenre Taa-ken ('Taa the brave'). Perhaps, as with Lord Nelson at Trafalgar, an Egyptian victory was tainted by the death of the hero? A battle won but a terrible setback that must surely have triggered a crisis at Thebes. However, Sekenenre Taa-ken's brother and successor – Kamose – was ready to take up the campaign to rid Egypt of the occupiers.

Kamose 'the battler'

The story of Kamose's war against Apophis is narrated in the two great victory stelae of the king found at Karnak and is also partly preserved on a wooden writing board (now called the Carnarvon Tablet) from Thebes. The latter is a copy of the first victory stela which was unfortunately badly damaged when discovered, and so it contributes some important details concerning the beginning of Kamose's campaign. Presumably the original royal inscription had been chosen by a tutor for a child's writing exercise. Thus the first part of the Theban strike northwards is known to us through the chance find of a schoolboy's writing lesson. We can just picture him sitting cross-legged, with the writing board on his knees, looking carefully up at the great granite stela to make sure that every sign was in the right place in his 'exercise book' copy.

> Regnal Year 3 of the Horus (king), he who has appeared on his throne; the Two Ladies, 'repeating monuments'; the Horus of Gold, 'who pacifies the Two Lands'; the Dual King, Wadjkheperre; the Son of Re, Kamose, given life, beloved of Amun-Re, Lord of the Thrones of the Two Lands, like Re for ever and ever! A mighty king, a native of Waset (Thebes), Wadjkheperre, given life for ever, even a good king! It is Re who personally made him king and who authorised victory for him (Kamose) in very truth!
>
> His Majesty spoke in his palace to the council of nobles who were in his retinue: 'Let me understand what this (royal) strength of mine is for! (One) prince is in Avaris, another is in Kush, and (here) I sit between an Asiatic and a Kushite! Each man has his slice of Egypt, dividing up the land with me. No-one can journey as far as Memphis (even though it is) Egyptian water! See he (Apophis) even has (control of) Hermopolis! No man can settle down when (he is) oppressed by the taxes of the Asiatics. I will grapple with him (Apophis) so that I may rip open his belly! My desire is to save Egypt and to smite the Asiatic!'
>
> Then the magistrates of his council spoke: 'See, as far as Cusae it is Asiatic water and to a

man they are sticking their tongues out (at us). We
are doing all right with our (own part of) Egypt:
Elephantine is strong, and the heartland is with
us as far as Cusae. Their free land is cultivated
for us and our cattle graze in the delta fens, whilst
corn is sent for our pigs. Our cattle have not been
seized and have not been eaten. He (Apophis)
has the land of the Asiatics – we have Egypt.
Only when someone comes to act against us
should we act against him.'

It is almost as if we are picking up where Sekenenre's
conversation with the Theban courtiers came to an abrupt
end at the crumbled edge of Papyrus Sallier II. Those same,
weak-willed advisers of the new king are not just at a loss
for words but now unashamedly urge caution to the point
of capitulation. Better to kowtow to the high-king in the
north than to take on this Lord of Avaris in a war that they
could not win. Clearly there was no appetite or enthusiasm
for more conflict following the devastating death of the
previous pharaoh in what had ultimately been a failed war
of liberation. The brave and probably reckless younger
brother of Sekenenre was having none of this. He was
going to ensure that Thebes would take its bloody revenge
for the death of his predecessor.

But they (the nobles) troubled His Majesty's
heart: 'As for your counsel, it is anathema to
me. He who partitions the land (of Egypt) with
me will never respect me [...] the Asiatics who
[...] are with him. I shall sail north to engage the
Asiatics and success will come! If he intends to
be at ease in [...] his eyes weeping along with
the entire land!'

Here again, in the fragmentary phrase 'the Asiatics' (i.e.
Aamu) 'who [...] are with him' (i.e. Apophis), we get a hint

of a recognised distinction between the ruler of Avaris and the Semitic-speaking population over which he ruled. This may be a vital contemporary parallel to Hatshepsut's Speos Artemidos retrospective on Hyksos rule where she refers to the 'Aamu' (Asiatics) who were 'in the midst of Avaris of the Northland' and the 'Shemau' (aliens) who were 'in the midst of them' – an elite ruling class of unspecified, though distinctly alien, origin supported by a large population of Semitic-speaking vassals from Canaan.

> The mighty ruler in Thebes, Kamose the Strong, protector of Egypt: 'I went north because I was strong (enough) to attack the Asiatics through the command of Amun, just of counsels. My valiant army was in front of me like a blast of fire. The troops of the Medjai (Nubian mercenaries) were ahead of us, seeking out the Asiatics and pushing back their positions. East and west had their fat and the army foraged for supplies everywhere. I sent out a strong troop of the Medjai while I was on the day's patrol […] to him in […] Teti, the son of Pepi, within (the town of) Nefrusi. I would not let him escape while I held back the Asiatics who had withstood (the army of) Egypt. He had made Nefrusi the nest of the Asiatics. I spent the night in my boat with a contented heart. When day broke I was on him like a falcon. When the time of breakfast had come, I attacked him. I broke down his walls, I killed his people, and made his wife come down to the riverbank (to plead for mercy). My soldiers were like (ravenous) lions as they spoiled (the town), taking slaves, cattle, milk, fat and honey, dividing up property to their hearts' content.'

Eventually Kamose found himself standing on the deck of his flagship as he looked up at the great fortress wall of Avaris, having fought his way to the very threshold of Hyksos power. There he could spy the wives and princesses of Apophis' harem staring down at the Egyptian fleet in the midst of the Pelusiac branch of the Nile. An Egyptian victory and eradication of the hated Hyksos were close at hand.

The Egyptians ravaged the port and raided the vineyards of Avaris but Apophis and his entourage held out inside their impregnable fortress. Kamose hurled insults up at his former overlord, trapped like a bird in a cage, hoping to goad Apophis into sallying forth to the fight.

> I will drink the wine of your vineyard (grapes),
> which the Asiatics whom I have captured now
> press for me. I lay waste to your (royal) residence
> and I cut down your trees.

It appears that a small part of this very vineyard and the tree-pits of Apophis' garden have been unearthed by the Austrian mission at Ezbet Helmi, within the fortress wall and beside the great platform terrace. You can imagine the Hyksos king looking down from the inner stronghold to witness Kamose's troops ransacking his luxuriant garden with its shady vine stands.

It is a rare thing when archaeology and contemporary records from the past come together in such a specific and satisfying way, and Professor Bietak at first, and quite understandably, savoured the moment when his team appeared to 'have found these very gardens'.[1] However, later seasons of excavation now bring all this into question. I will deal with the issue of the date of the platform stronghold at Ezbet Helmi in the next chapter when we come to discuss who lived there and decorated it with lavish frescoes. In the meantime, back to the protracted war of liberation.

Kamose returned to Thebes to regroup, prepare for the next campaign and record his triumph on the two 'victory stelae' at Karnak. But then, once again, something terrible

143

happened. The Thebans seem to have suffered another reverse over which the official sources fall silent. All we know is that Pharaoh Kamose died suddenly in his third year, leaving a mere child to succeed to the throne. This boy (probably not much older than seven or eight) was Prince Ahmose, the son of Sekenenre Taa-ken and his widow, Queen Ahhotep. The new pharaoh was obviously too immature to take full control of the reins of power at such a critical moment.

It seems highly likely that his uncle, Kamose, just like his father, had died in battle, fighting against the Hyksos or their Kushite allies in the south. Complete victory had been snatched from his grasp just as the Egyptian army had fought its way to the stronghold of the northern enemy.

Kamose did not just have to contend with his erstwhile northern foe in Avaris. There was also a major threat from the south. There, in the region of northern Sudan, a powerful Kushite kingdom had allied itself with the Hyksos of Avaris. As we have seen, one of the early Hyksos rulers – Sheshi – may have married a Kushite princess. So Kamose was trapped 'between an Asiatic and an Kushite' pressing him from north and south. Either could have been the agent of the Theban pharaoh's demise. We do know – from the second Kamose stela – of an intercepted message sent by Apophis, via the Sahara oases, in which the Hyksos king commands his southern vassal to strike the Egyptian forces in the rear.

> Aauserre, the Son of Re, Apophis, sends greetings to my son, the ruler of Kush. Why do you arise as ruler without letting me know? Can you see what Egypt has done to me? The ruler there – Kamose the strong, given life – is attacking me on my own soil, although I have not attacked him ... Come north; do not falter. Look, he is here in my hand and there is no one who is waiting for you in this part of Egypt. See, I will not give

> him leave until you have arrived. Then we shall
> divide the towns of Egypt and our lands will be
> happy in joy.

This particular message may not have got through to the Kushite ruler – but perhaps others did? Interestingly, an actual invasion of Egypt by the Kushite army has recently come to light in a tomb biography at el-Kab (near Edfu) – and it took place around this time. In February 2003 the joint British Museum and Egyptian mission, under the directorship of Vivian Davies, had been cleaning and restoring the tomb of the 'Governor, Hereditary Prince of Nekheb, Sobeknakht' when a previously unknown hieroglyphic inscription of twenty-two lines, written in red paint, began to emerge out of the heavily sooted walls.

> Listen you, who are alive upon the Earth ... Kush
> came ... aroused along his length, having stirred
> up the tribes of Wawat (Nubia) ... the land of
> Punt and the Medjai.

It seems clear from this autobiographical text that the Kushite army, along with its allies from Nubia and Punt, had initially swept past the heavily fortified town of el-Kab (having perhaps looted the nearby tombs) heading for Thebes. Indeed, an alabaster vase intended for Sobeknakht's burial (inscribed with his name and titles) was found in the great tumulus-tomb of a Kushite king in Kerma, the capital of the African kingdom – no doubt booty from this raid. A potential invasion from the south during the Second Intermediate Period was no idle threat – the evidence from Sobeknakht's tomb inscription shows that it actually happened at least once (and almost certainly at least twice if we are to include the invasion recalled by Artapanus – in his 'History of the Jews' in Egypt – during the reign of a King Khenophres, that is, Khaneferre Sobekhotep IV of the 13th Dynasty).[2]

Was the Kushite attack in the time of Sobeknakht (late 17th Dynasty) a response to Apophis' call for help from his southern ally during the war against Kamose? Was it directly due to this massive assault from the rear, when the Kushites 'swept over the mountains and over the Nile, without limit',[3] that Kamose had to call off a second assault upon Avaris? If so, on this occasion he was successful in repelling the attack from the south because Sobeknakht recalls being rewarded by the (un-named) pharaoh for his stout defence of el-Kab and subsequent harassing of the retreating Kushite army.

Kamose must have spent his entire short reign of three years fighting on two fronts – north and south – and it is quite possible that an attack something like the Kushite raid brought down this last of the 17th Dynasty pharaohs, leaving a widowed mother and young boy to defend the rump Egyptian kingdom.

Ahhotep 'the steadfast'

Into the Theban crisis stepped one of the most remarkable females from Egyptian history. She is not as well known as Cleopatra or Nefertiti, but to the New Kingdom Egyptians she ranked as a genuine saviour – along with her son Ahmose – of the Black Land from the hated oppression of the Hyksos tyrants.

Queen Ahhotep held the country together whilst her son grew to maturity. For several years she ruled the land as regent and commander of the army which continued to hold off both Asiatics and Kushites on Upper Egypt's borders. She was clearly a woman of character and inner strength. Having lost her husband in war and then witnessed his brother and successor succumb to that same enemy, one might have expected her to have lost all hope. But Ahhotep picked up the pieces of her young son's shattered kingdom and rallied the Theban forces to her command. We know nothing of the trauma of this time – only its outcome – because contemporary documents have not survived. But we can imagine, in this silence, a grim struggle to hold the line against the pincer movement of two powerful enemies. The fact that Egypt would eventually be victorious is mute testimony to Ahhotep's success in keeping the kingdom intact. In the years of her regency the military became strong (expanding to some half a million troops) and growing in confidence as they watched their sovereign reach manhood. King Ahmose had been well trained in the arts of war and now gathered a competent and enthusiastic military command around him. No weak and indecisive advisers from the old regime were to be a part of this team of young Egyptian lions.

The caretaker queen had done her job with great skill and determination. She had probably fought defensive battles herself during the remaining years of Ahmose's childhood. In so doing, she had bought precious time for the Egyptian recovery following the deaths of the last two pharaohs of the 17th Dynasty. Lying within her coffin (dug up in Dra Abu el-Naga on the west bank of Luxor in 1859) were found a set of three large golden flies – the medals of honour awarded to the most valiant warriors of the Egyptian army.

The Egyptians of the late New Kingdom and Third Intermediate Period certainly held this lady in high esteem – one noble's tomb (TT 2, contemporary with the reign of Ramesses II) even depicting her as a pharaoh in her own right with suitable kingly titles.[4] Thus her regency was regarded as the period of her own kingship.

Ahmose 'the liberator'

So, finally, the day had come to exact Egypt's revenge for the deaths of Ahmose's father and uncle – and for all those years of despoiling and humiliation. It was time to take back the rich black earth of Egypt from the forces of chaos whose origins lay in the desert wastes of the north and south.

The expulsion of the Hyksos and Kushites from Egypt

proper is well documented through the autobiographical text of Ahmose sa-Ibana, inscribed in his tomb at el-Kab (see plate 13). From this text and, in particular, a passage from the Rhind Mathematical Papyrus, we can be fairly confident that the expulsion of the Hyksos took place in Year 11 of Ahmose[5] and that the fall of Sharuhen (here identified as Tell el-Ajjul), to which some of the Hyksos retreated, occurred around Year 15, following a three-year siege.[6] I will tell the story of the Hyksos withdrawal by quoting sections from these contemporary texts and from a fascinating 'extract' that has survived of Manetho's narrative history of Egypt.

Let us begin with that precious fragment which is 'quoted' in Josephus' *Contra Apionem* (bearing in mind that the Jewish historian has clearly indulged in some 'editing' so as to make the context more applicable to his own time – the first century AD – and readership). I have done something of the same kind by placing in round brackets a number of clarifications, based on what we now know about the Theban war of independence.

> ... there came a revolt of the kings of the Thebaid and the rest of Egypt against the Shepherds (i.e. the Hyksos), and a fierce and prolonged war broke out between them. The Shepherds, he (Manetho) says, were defeated and driven out of all the rest of Egypt by a king whose name was Misphragmuthosis (i.e. Kamose). They were confined in a region, measuring within its circumference 10,000 *arora* (2,000 hectares), by the name of Auaris (i.e. Avaris).
>
> According to Manetho, the Shepherds enclosed this whole area with a high, strong wall, in order to safeguard all their possessions and spoils. (This is the wall first built by Salitis in Stratum D/3 but then later strengthened by Apophis in Stratum D/2.) Thummosis (i.e. Ahmose), the son (rather the nephew and

successor) of Misphragmuthosis, attempted by siege to force them to surrender, blockading the fortress with an army of four hundred and eighty thousand men.

Finally, giving up the siege in despair, he concluded a treaty by which they (the Hyksos and their Asiatic vassals) should all depart from Egypt and go unmolested where they pleased. On these terms the Shepherds (i.e. the Asiatics), with their possessions and households complete – no fewer than two hundred and forty thousand people – left Egypt and journeyed over the desert into Syria (i.e. Canaan). There, dreading the power of the Assyrians (i.e. Mesopotamians) who were at that time masters of Asia, they built – in the land now called Judaea – a city large enough to hold all those thousands of people, and gave it the name of Jerusalem. [Josephus: *Contra Apionem*, Book I]

This is an astonishing story and almost too hard to believe. But elements of it have come to light in tantalising fragments from contemporary documents. Other aspects of the narrative may need to be reinterpreted in the light of Josephus' rather unhelpful rewriting of the Manethonian original.

First the names of the two Egyptian pharaohs require some discussion. It has long been argued that Misphragmuthosis represents a rather garbled Greek version of Menkheperre Thutmose III and that Thummosis is simply his second successor, Thutmose IV. All this is admittedly a bit of a stretch but might conceivably derive from a misinterpretation of Thutmose III's successful series of military campaigns into Palestine and Syria (against possible descendants of the Hyksos). When we compare the names Misphragmuthosis and Kamose (the first native Egyptian king to besiege Avaris) it is clear that there is no hope of reconciliation.

149

On the other hand, the switch from Ahmose to Thummosis is easier to account for, enabling us to reject this king's identification with Thutmose IV. Here one could argue for a rather different etymology by proposing an Egyptianising of the name of the moon – Yah – to the moon-deity, Thoth. Thus the name Yahmose ('Born of Yah' = Ahmose) would become Thutmose ('Born of Thoth') and so Greek Thummosis. Indeed, it is quite possible that the historical switch from early 18th Dynasty Yahmose to Thutmose I, II, III and IV was a deliberate Egyptianising of the original founder's royal nomen on the part of his successors who wished to be called 'born of the moon' but identified with the very Egyptian deity Thoth (Zehuti).

We can be even more confident that Ahmose is meant by Josephus' Thummosis because the Book of Sothis (a work of Pseudo-Manetho) places at position thirty-three in the king-list (marking the start of the 18th Dynasty) the entry 'Amosis, also called Tethmosis, (a reign of) 26 years'. Africanus, in his redaction of Manetho, also names the founder of the 18th Dynasty as 'Tethmosis' giving him 25 years and 4 months of reign. And, most telling of all, Josephus himself subsequently names the 18th Dynasty founder as Tethmosis – this time by directly quoting Manetho rather than paraphrasing him.

> For the present I am citing the Egyptians as witnesses to this antiquity of ours. I shall therefore resume my quotations from Manetho's works in their reference to chronology. His account is as follows: 'After the departure of the tribe of Shepherds from Egypt to Jerusalem, Tethmosis, the king who drove them out of Egypt, reigned for 25 years 4 months until his death ... [*Contra Apionem*, Book I]

So Thummosis/Tethmosis was a later corruption of Ahmose and, therefore, his predecessor named Misphragmuthosis, who besieged Avaris, can scarcely be identified with anyone other than Kamose. Whatever Misphra represents, we can probably take the central G of Misphra-g-muthosis as an Egyptian K to give us Kamuthos for Kamose.

Gmuthosis – Kamuthos – Kamashisha (ancient vocalisation) = Kamose

More important to our historical reconstruction is Josephus' statement that Ahmose's siege of Avaris did not end in a mass attack on the citadel but with an agreement that the beleaguered Hyksos should be allowed to depart unmolested. This is astonishing but nevertheless absolutely true – as another contemporary document attests.

The Climax of the War of Liberation

Manetho's tale of the assault upon Avaris, an assumed siege (of around two months), and a negotiated withdrawal of the Hyksos into southern Canaan is supported by two texts – the autobiography of a Crew Commander Ahmose, son of Lady Ibana, from el-Kab and three tantalising columns of text in the margin of the Rhind Mathematical Papyrus. First the autobiographical text:

> The Crew Commander, Ahmose son of Ibana, the justified. … He speaks as follows: I grew up in the town of Nekheb (el-Kab), my father being a soldier of the Dual King Sekenenre (Taa-ken), true of voice. Baba son of Reinet was his name. I became a soldier in his stead on the ship 'Wild Bull' in the time of the Lord of the Two Lands, Nebpehtyre (Ahmose), true of voice. I was a youth who had not married. I slept in a hammock of netting.
>
> Now, by the time I had established a household, I was assigned to the ship 'Northern' because I was brave. I followed the sovereign on foot when he rode about in his chariot. When

151

the town of Avaris was besieged, I fought bravely
on foot in His Majesty's presence. Thereupon I
was appointed to the ship 'Rising in Memphis'.
Subsequently there was fighting on the water in
Pa-Zedku of Avaris. I made a capture and carried
off a (severed) hand (as proof of my kill). When
it was reported to the royal herald, the gold of
valour was given to me. Then they fought again
in this place. I again made a capture there and
carried off a hand. I was given the gold of valour
once again.

Then there was fighting in Egypt to the south
of this town (of Avaris) and I carried off a man as
a living captive. I went down into the water – for
he was captured on the city side – and crossed
the water carrying him. When it was reported
to the royal herald I was rewarded with gold
once more.

These skirmishes – all in the vicinity of Avaris – suggest an
Egyptian army taking action wherever it can in order to
maintain the siege cordon. However, quite suddenly and
without further elaboration, Ahmose sa-Ibana states that
the Hyksos stronghold was taken.

Then Avaris was plundered and I brought spoil
from there: namely one man and three women
– a total of four people. His Majesty gave them
to me as slaves.

Hardly a huge number of captives for one of Pharaoh's
brave marines – and a pretty good indication that Avaris
was not exactly bursting at the seams with potential slaves
when it was seized by the Egyptian army. Had the city been
evacuated? The evidence for just such a mass evacuation
does exist in two source documents which I will turn to
shortly.

Then Sharuhen was besieged for three years. His
Majesty plundered it and I brought spoil from it:
namely two women and a hand. Then the gold
of valour was given to me, and my captives were
given to me as slaves.

Another small haul which may be explained by the fact that
Sharuhen – if correctly identified with Tell el-Ajjul south of
modern Gaza – was a port from which the Hyksos elites
could again escape the clutches of the vengeful Egyptians.

Now, when His Majesty had slain the nomads
of Asia, he sailed south to Khent-hen-nefer, to
destroy the Nubian bowmen. His Majesty made
a great slaughter among them, and I brought
spoil from there: namely two living men and
three hands. Then I was rewarded with gold once
again and two female slaves were given to me.
His Majesty journeyed north, his heart rejoicing
in valour and victory. He had conquered both
the southerners and the northerners.

King Ahmose, having pushed the Hyksos out of Egypt and
cleared out their stronghold in southern Canaan, had next
turned his attention to the south so that he could take long-
overdue revenge on the Kushites for invading Egypt fifteen
years earlier.

Then Aota came southward. His fate brought
on his doom. The gods of Upper Egypt grasped
him. He was found by His Majesty at Tent-Taa.
His Majesty carried him off as a living captive,
and all his people as booty. I brought two young
warriors as captives from the ship of Aota. Then
I was given five people and portions of land
amounting to five *arora* (one hectare) in my town.
The same was done for the whole crew.

> Then came that foe named Tetian. He had
> gathered the malcontents to himself. His Majesty
> slew him; his troop was wiped out. Then I was
> given three people and five *arora* of land in my
> town.

Towards the end of his twenty-six-year reign, Ahmose
had been forced to fight two more battles with northerners
before the soldier Ahmose sa-Ibana found himself serving
a new pharaoh – Ahmose's son, AMENHOTEP I.

> Then I conveyed King Djeserkare (Amenhotep
> I), true of voice, when he sailed south to Kush, to
> enlarge the borders of Egypt. His Majesty smote
> that Nubian bowman (chieftain) in the midst of
> his army. They were carried off in fetters, none
> escaping, the fleeing destroyed as if they had
> never existed. Now I was in the vanguard of
> our troops and I fought well. His Majesty saw
> my valour. I carried off two hands and presented
> them to His Majesty. Then his (the Kushite
> ruler's) people and his cattle were pursued, and
> I carried off a living captive and presented him
> to His Majesty. I brought His Majesty back to
> Egypt in two days from 'Upper Well' and was
> rewarded with gold. I brought back two female
> slaves as booty, apart from those that I had
> presented to His Majesty. Then they made me
> a 'Warrior of the Ruler'.

Amenhotep had returned to the task of clobbering the
Kushites but the failure to mention any war in Canaan at
this point in Ahmose sa-Ibana's autobiography suggests that
the new king contented himself with this single campaign
to the south. It was left to his successor, THUTMOSE I, to
turn his attention northwards – but then only after another
major assault upon Kush. Ahmose sa-Ibana continues:

Then I conveyed King Akheperkare (Thutmose I), true of voice, when he sailed south to Khent-hen-nefer in order to crush the rebellion throughout the lands and to repel the intruders from the desert region. I was brave in his presence in the rapids whilst towing the ship over the cataract. Thereupon I was made 'Crew Commander'. Then His Majesty [was informed that the Nubian ...] At this His Majesty became enraged like a leopard. His Majesty let loose (his bow) and his first arrow pierced the chest of that foe. Then those [enemies turned to flee], helpless before his Uraeus. A slaughter was made among them; their dependants were carried off as living captives. His Majesty journeyed north, all foreign lands in his grasp, with (the body of) that wretched Nubian bowman hanging head downward at the bow of His Majesty's ship 'Falcon'. They landed at Ipet-sut (Thebes).

With Kush tamed, Thutmose I prepared his army for a daring thrust into Asia – but not along the Via Maris (coastal road) leading up into southern Canaan. The people of the coastal plain had not witnessed an Egyptian army marching through their territory in thirty years and it appears that Thutmose did not bother them either.

After this (His Majesty) proceeded to Retenu (northern Canaan) to vent his wrath throughout the lands. When His Majesty reached Naharin (Mitanni), His Majesty found that foe marshalling troops. Then His Majesty made a great slaughter of them. Countless were the living captives which His Majesty brought back from his victories. Now I was in the vanguard of our troops and His Majesty saw my valour. I brought a chariot, its horse, and him who was on it as a living captive.

> When they were presented to His Majesty, I was
> rewarded with gold once again.

From what Egyptologists have gleaned in recent years about early New Kingdom military strategy, it seems that the Egyptian army did not march north through southern Canaan to Syria and northern Mesopotamia in order to confront the kingdom of Mitanni. Instead the troops and chariotry were transported up the coast by ship to the port of Simyra (between Byblos and Ugarit). There they were off-loaded to begin their march to the Euphrates, beyond which lay the land of Naharin ('twin rivers' = Mitanni). The assessment that the Egyptian expedition against Mitanni was partly undertaken by water is supported by the fact that the Crew Commander, Ahmose sa-Ibana, participated in this war. Egyptian marines went with Pharaoh on his campaign against the Mitannian kings.

But who provided the seagoing fleet which took the Egyptians to their new battleground? It may have been the Cretans because they possessed the only large maritime navy at the time. The Egyptian vessels were riverine and would have been incapable of such a journey. Besides, the Egyptians never saw themselves as great seafarers (especially in the often dangerous waters of the Mediterranean) and regularly hired foreign vessels and their crews for journeys across open sea. Navigating the Nile was a tricky business with its sandbanks and currents, but Homer's wine-dark sea which saw the end of many a Greek hero (cf. the *Odyssey*) was a very different kettle of fish. This was the domain of the three great seafaring nations – first the Minoans of Crete, then the Mycenaean Greeks and the Levantine Phoenicians.

And why did Pharaoh Thutmose I attack Mitanni – so far away to the north? Was it because this Hurrian kingdom, ruled over by Aryan kings, had something to do with the oppression of Egypt during the Greater Hyksos occupation? The heartland of Naharin was nearly one thousand kilometres north of Egypt. The pharaohs had never before gone so far out of their way to fight a war. So why? The Egyptian determination to seek out the distant Mitannian rulers for destruction only seems explicable to me if we assume that this expedition was an act of revenge.

The other question that has occurred to Egyptologists is why the Egyptian army of self-confessed landlubbers so purposefully avoided the march on dry land through southern Canaan (along the *Via Maris* or the coast road) and instead took to the unfamiliar sea? And why did a campaign into southern Canaan have to wait another twenty-five years, until the mid-reign of Thutmose III, before Egypt finally took control of the coastal plain of Canaan as far as Megiddo and then beyond? What took them so long to conquer the territory nearest to their own frontier? Could it have been because a terrible plague (the 'Canaanite Illness') was rife in the region, as some have thought,[7] requiring the Egyptians to stay well clear? Or did the Hyksos remnant remain a dominant force in the plain to the north of Sharuhen – in the area later known as Philistia? Or perhaps both? These are big questions – but I believe they can all be explained and accounted for within the New Chronology historical model being proposed here.

Having fought beside the first three warrior pharaohs of the 18th Dynasty, Ahmose sa-Ibana finally died in old age. He had seen his beloved Egypt recover its Lower Kingdom from the 'aliens' and had played his part in the expulsion of the hated Hyksos. Egypt's three-hundred-year nightmare, which began with the Exodus of the Israelites, was over and he could now rest in peace.

> I have grown old and reached the end. Favoured as before, and loved [by my lord], I [rest] in the tomb which I myself made ...

I have quoted this text of the Crew Commander, Ahmose, at length because it gives a real flavour of the ongoing conflict between the early 18th Dynasty pharaohs of Thebes and their Hyksos and Kushite enemies. The campaign to push these foreign invaders out of Egypt and pursue them, even to their homelands, lasted for decades and spanned a total of five reigns (from Sekenenre Taa-ken to Thutmose I). Thutmose III would complete the task by taking control of southern Canaan in the final decades of his kingship. But the seeds of the Egyptian New Kingdom empire were sown in that relentless half-century of conflict leading up to his reign. Not for another five hundred years would foreigners (in this case Libyans) occupy the Black Land and rule over its people. The New Kingdom pharaohs made sure that Egypt's borders were protected by the deep buffer zone of their northern empire in Canaan (including the lands of Lebanon, southern Syria, Philistia and Israel).

The Fall of Avaris

The autobiography of Ahmose sa-Ibana gives us the broad sweep of events during the Hyksos expulsion, but there is another tiny text which provides tantalising details completely absent from the Crew Commander's narrative, though easily accommodated 'between the lines'. The precise moment of Egypt's freedom is recorded in just three short columns of HIERATIC written in the margin of a papyrus dated to Year 33 of the Hyksos king, Auserre Apophis. The marginal note is clearly of a later date than the original text on the papyrus (a mathematical treatise) and, as Hans Goedicke recognised back in 1986, it is probably datable to the reign of Pharaoh Ahmose, founder of the 18th Dynasty.[8] The first line reads:

> Year 11, second month of Shemu (inundation
> season): His Majesty entered (the city of) Iunu.

Sailing (and fighting their way?) up from Thebes, Ahmose and his army had reached the ancient sun-worshipping city of Heliopolis (Iunu) where the north-east suburbs of Cairo stand today. They must therefore have taken Memphis, further south, and were now heading into the eastern delta to attack the Hyksos stronghold at Avaris, just as the king's brother had done a decade earlier. Remember how Ahmose sa-Ibana informs us that 'the town of Avaris was besieged' and then subsequently 'plundered'. However, Manetho reveals a far more complex and interesting picture. It appears that the Egyptians were forced to conclude terms with the Hyksos rulers before they could seize the fortified compound of the foreigners because the walls of Avaris were too strong to breach.

> Finally, giving up the siege in despair, he (Ahmose) concluded a treaty by which they (the Hyksos and their subjects) should all depart from Egypt and go unmolested where they pleased. On these terms the Shepherds, with their possessions and households complete – no fewer than two hundred and forty thousand people – left Egypt and journeyed over the desert into Syria (Canaan). [Josephus: *Contra Apionem*, Book I]

The second line of the Rhind Mathematical Papyrus marginal note seems to refer to this exodus of the Shepherds, with Ahmose and his army ensuring their rapid departure through Egypt's Sinai border-post at Zile.

> First month of Akhet (growing season), day 23: The King drove the one (i.e. leader) of the Shemau/Shepherds towards Zile.

Pharaoh's army was driving the enemy before it – not attacking, but ensuring that they reached the Egyptian border and kept going. The single hieratic sign which I have translated as Shemau ('aliens') – and which Professor Goedicke translates as 'Shepherds' – appears to be the

shema ('alien')

23. *The three columns of text written in the margin of the Rhind Mathematical Papyrus dated to Year 33 of Auserre Apophis. The first column is on the right and the third on the left. The determinative sign for 'shema [chieftain]' (a seated man carrying a pole with a sack tied to its end) is located within the white box. This figure appears to be a combination of the two determinatives (left) in the Speos Artemidos inscription of Hatshepsut. There we have a walking man carrying a sack on a pole and the seated man with plural strokes indicating a 'people' just as in the name of Israel on the Merenptah Stela.*

same hieroglyphic determinative used by Hatshepsut in her Speos Artemidos inscription where she refers to the Shemau living in the midst of the Aamu ('Asiatics') at Avaris. It is (in this case) a walking figure of a man carrying over his shoulder a pole to which a small bag is attached (the image of Dick Whittington comes to mind here). He is followed by a seated man with plural strokes representing 'people'. If the same word is being used both in the Rhind marginal note and Hatshepsut's decree, then this is surely significant because it would confirm that the contemporary Egyptian term for the foreign Lords of Avaris was Shemau 'aliens', as opposed to – and distinct from – the Aamu population over whom they ruled. This gives real credence to Manetho's etymology for the term 'Hyksos' as 'Shepherd Kings' – that is, Hykau-Shosu, literally 'Rulers of (i.e. over the) Shepherds'.

As both Ahmose sa-Ibana and Manetho inform us, King Ahmose kept his side of the terms of capitulation only as far as its literal wording went. Once the Hyksos were escorted out of Egyptian territory 'unmolested' the obligations of the treaty had been fulfilled. From that moment on, the retreating Hyksos were at the mercy of the pursuing Egyptian army. Some of the leaders of the foreign occupiers barricaded themselves in the fortified port of Sharuhen which was then 'besieged for three years' before 'His Majesty plundered it'.

According to Manetho, another major Hyksos group literally took to the hills and settled in the city of Jerusalem. In the New Chronology, these were the Jebusites of the Bible whose rulers bore names of Hurrian origin – for example, IR-HEBA, often mis-transcribed as Abdi-Heba of the el-Amarna letters or Araunah, the former Jebusite ruler (Hurrian *Aruwana*?) of Jerusalem mentioned in 2 Samuel 24:18-25. Josephus mistakenly understood Manetho to be referring here to the Israelite departure from Egypt and eventual occupation of Jerusalem but – as you will know from *A Test of Time* – that Exodus had taken place centuries earlier and had nothing to do with the Hurrian retreat to Jerusalem. Jebusite Zion (the Tian of the Amarna Letters) would finally succumb only with the rise of King David who seized the city in his seventh year as ruler of Hebron (in the New Chronology during the third regnal year of Tutankhamun *c.* 1005 BC). What is of considerable interest is the Hurrian element of Jebusite rule. If I am right to identify the Jebusite enclave of Jerusalem as one of the Hyksos post-expulsion refuges, then this would suggest a participation of the Hurrians in the foreign occupation of Egypt – just as a number of scholars have long suspected. But I contend that the Hurrians were not the only Shemau 'aliens' resident in the midst of the Aamu at Avaris.

A Possible Link with Thera

The main discussion concerning the role that the eruption of Thera/Santorini had to play in the New Chronology revised history of the ancient world will come later. But we need to begin thinking about this impending catastrophe here because of Hans Goedicke's controversial interpretation of the third column of hieratic found in the margin of the

Rhind Mathematical Papyrus. The text reads:

> Year 11, first month of Akhet (growing season),
> the birthday of Seth: the majesty of this god
> caused his voice to be heard. The birthday of
> Isis: the sky rained.

These last lines are critical to what happened during the expulsion of the Hyksos and have received considerable attention from scholars. Here I have produced my own translation based on the work of Professor Hans Goedicke who realised the potential significance of the short text back in 1986.[9] He controversially relates the 'voice of Seth' to something of a seismic nature, rather than a simple clap of thunder, because it seems extremely unlikely that such thunder could be separated from the thunderstorm itself (that is, the rain) by a full day. The birthday of Seth was succeeded directly by the birthday of Isis on the following day. These 'birthdays' belong within the five epagomenal days which preceded the first day of the new year (on day one of the first month of Akhet) and therefore precede the driving of the Shemau out of Egypt (1st Akhet, day 23) by just over three weeks.

Goedicke thus believes that we have a reference here to an initial eruption of Thera (heard in the Egyptian delta) followed by an ash fall over Avaris. The storm-god, Seth, had voiced his disapproval of Hyksos rule in Egypt from across the northern sea and Isis had rained tears of ash at the sorry plight of the Black Land. These were the great signs and portents which may have instigated the treaty of capitulation between the Egyptians and Shemau that resulted in the Hyksos withdrawal from Egypt.

However, this roaring of the 'voice of Seth' does not mark the *major* catastrophic eruption of Thera which we have all heard of, because Bietak's latest findings at Avaris indicate that that event took place later. A recent re-interpretation of the archaeology at Ezbet Helmi (west of Tell ed-Daba) now suggests a mid-18th Dynasty date for the first (and only) appearance of Theran pumice at the site – considerably more than a half-century after Goedicke's date in Year 11 of Ahmose. I would see Goedicke's earlier eruption of Thera as that which the excavators found evidence for early in Late Minoan IA. This preliminary blast caused considerable destruction in the town of Akrotiri, overthrowing houses. The people then simply rebuilt their homes and the LM IA settlement continued to flourish for a further seventy years or so before being completely buried in the ash and pumice fall of the final catastrophic eruption.

So, perhaps Seth did roar in the weeks before his Hyksos worshippers were finally expelled from Avaris. But he would make a far greater impact three generations later when, in his Aegean guise as the storm-god Zeus (the Greek version of Baal), he would bring the mighty Cretan THALASSOCRACY to its knees in the greatest catastrophe the ancient world had ever witnessed.

Part Two

Divine Pelasgians

Chapter Six

SONS OF ANAK

A Phoenician Origin for the Early Hyksos — The Byblos
Tombs — Rephaim and Anakim — The Original Philistines

ne great puzzle concerning the Hyksos period has always been the origins of the Hyksos kings themselves whom Hatshepsut refers to as Shemau ('aliens'). The grand old man of German Egyptology, Professor Wolfgang HELCK, originally proposed a Hurrian origin for the Greater Hyksos. However, this suggestion received little support from his colleagues, principally because of the huge influence that the Austrian excavations at Avaris have had on the matter over the last forty years. The fact that Second-Intermediate-Period Avaris was very much 'Western Asiatic' in character has convinced most scholars that the Hyksos kings themselves were of Canaanite origin and spoke West Semitic, not Hurrian or Indo-European. It was also noted that many of the Lesser Hyksos rulers bore obvious West Semitic/Amorite names.

However, now that it is clear that the Lesser Hyksos were a separate entity to the Greater Hyksos, we simply cannot assume direct continuity between the Asiatic (i.e. Canaanite) Lesser Hyksos and the mysterious Greater Hyksos rulers.

Some of the names of the latter are by no means obviously West Semitic and Helck may not have been that far from the historical truth when he identified them as Hurrian lords from the north. Indeed, following the criticisms offered by his colleagues, the great German professor subsequently amended his proposal and suggested Aegean (specifically Cretan) origins for the Greater Hyksos kings. I will take up the challenge of identifying the origins of the Greater Hyksos later in this chapter, but first we need to establish where the Canaanite Lesser Hyksos kings of the earlier period came from.

A Byblos Connection

During the course of Maurice DUNAND's excavations at Byblos (from 1928 to the outbreak of the Lebanese civil war in the 1970s) the French archaeologist uncovered a large fragment of a bas-relief bearing the following hieroglyphic inscription:[1]

> ... h3ty-ᶜ n Kpn Intn whm ᶜnh r n h3ty-ᶜ Ykn m3 hrw ...

> ... the governor of Byblos, Yantin, repeating life, son of the governor, Yakin, true of voice ...

The term *maa(t)-heru* ('true of voice' or 'justified') indicates that Yakin, father of Yantin, was deceased, whilst *wehem-ankh* ('repeating life') tells us that Yantin himself was very much alive at the time the inscription was cut. The importance of this relief lies in the fact that a second column of text is partially extant in which the latter part of the nomen of the Egyptian pharaoh Neferhotep I – the 21st ruler of the 13th Dynasty – can be discerned. William Foxwell ALBRIGHT identified the owner of Tomb IV at Byblos as this same Yantin[2] and he seems to have been correct in his attribution: a badly damaged vase inscription from the tomb does indeed appear to bear the name Yantin.[3] On the basis of the Dunand relief, the adjacent Tomb III has been attributed to Yantin's father, Yakin (probably the Yakin-El or Yakin-ili of the Carnarvon cylinder[4]).

André PARROT's excavations at Mari on the Euphrates (1934 to 1938) of the palace of Zimri-Lim unearthed a cuneiform archive, one document of which contained an inventory of gifts from the local Levantine rulers, including a gold vase from 'Yantin-Ammu, king of Byblos'.[5] The obvious step was to equate Dunand's Yantin with Parrot's Yantin-Ammu and thus provide an important synchronism between Mesopotamia and Egypt. As Zimri-Lim's palace was destroyed by Hammurabi of Babylon in the latter's thirty-second regnal year, it was possible to link Yantin with another astronomical date – that of Year 8 of Ammisaduga (penultimate ruler of the Babylon I dynasty), as calculated from the Venus observation recorded on Tablet EAE 63 of the Enuma Anu Enlil texts.

In *A Test of Time*, I introduced the work of astronomer Wayne Mitchell who re-examined the astronomical data used to establish the 'Venus Solution' dates employed by astronomers and historians to date Ammisaduga and, thus, Hammurabi of Babylon. By the matching of a sequence of regnally dated thirty-day month contracts from the Old Babylonian dynasty (Babylon I) to an actual astronomical sequence of thirty-day months (as calculated using lunar periodic tables) to the three Venus Solutions of 1702 BC, 1646 BC and 1582 BC (for Year 1 of Ammisaduga), a trio of chronologies was established. These alternative dating schemes became known as the 'High', 'Middle' and 'Low' chronologies which provided accession dates for Hammurabi of 1848 BC or 1792 BC or 1728 BC. With Zimri-Lim dated to around the same time as Hammurabi (remember the former's palace was destroyed in the latter's thirty-second regnal year), and Yantin of Byblos being a contemporary of Zimri-Lim (the gift of the gold cup), and Neferhotep of Egypt being the overlord of Yantin, scholars could then place the reign of the 13th Dynasty pharaoh in *circa* 1830 BC or 1770 BC or 1710 BC.

Venus Solution Candidates			
1702 BC	20 months of 30 days	5 months of 29 days	20 matches
1646 BC	14 months of 30 days	11 months of 29 days	14 matches
1582 BC	18 months of 30 days	7 months of 29 days	18 matches
1419 BC	23 months of 30 days	2 months of 29 days	23 matches

The High, Middle, Low and Ultra-Low (i.e. NC) dates for the Venus Solution (= Year 1 Ammisaduga).

What Wayne Mitchell did was to examine possible lunar sequence matches for *later* dates, in order to test out the New Chronology hypothesis which placed Hammurabi, and therefore Neferhotep, about two centuries later than the lowest of the three orthodox chronologies. Mitchell ran his computer programs and found that one sequence in particular outshone all the others – including the High, Middle and Low VS dates.[6] The table above shows the lunar-month-length matches for the four Venus Solution candidates. You will see that, of the twenty-five thirty-day lunar months recorded in the Babylonian contracts, the best of the three conventional chronologies (that is, the High Chronology, not favoured by most historians) gets an eighty per cent match in the sequence

24. The inventory of gifts found at Mari which includes mention of a gold cup given by Yantin-Ammu of Byblos.

with five mismatches. The Venus Solution of 1419 BC found by Mitchell (and therefore the New Chronology candidate) performs a great deal better with a ninety-two per cent success rate and only two mismatches.

So, back in 1995 it seemed that the New Chronology had acquired a fixed astronomical date of 1419 BC for Year 1 of Ammisaduga. Working back through the reigns of the Old Babylon dynasty we were then able to arrive at a date of 1565 BC for Year 1 of Hammurabi. The eleven-year reign of Neferhotep of Egypt would thus fall in around 1550 BC, with the synchronisms allowing us to place Yantin of Byblos and Zimri-Lim of Mari in that same era. This meant that the first twenty kings of the 13th Dynasty down to Neferhotep covered a period of eighty-two years as the end of the 12th Dynasty had been established at 1632 BC, the New Chronology dates for Amenemhat III having been set at 1682 to 1636 BC.

Then, in 2002, another astronomer, David Lappin, worked on the late 12th Dynasty lunar dates and confirmed that the NC dates for Amenemhat III were accurate to within three years of his astronomically derived dates for this king.[7] This was all very encouraging. But things have moved on since then and the dates for Neferhotep may have to be adjusted by a few years to accommodate the latest findings by Mitchell and Lappin, now working together on NC astronomical research. Any subsequent adjustment to the mid-13th Dynasty dating will not, however, require emendation of the late 12th Dynasty regnal dates (of Senuseret III and Amenemhat III) because they are fixed by the independent lunar month-length chronology established by Lappin.

The Tombs of Byblos

Reference to the map of the Middle Bronze Age section of the royal cemetery at Byblos (p. 172) shows that there are four known tombs. These are the earliest shaft tombs at the

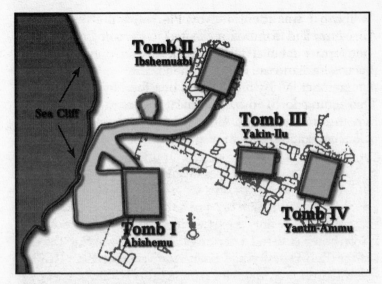

25. *The layout of the Byblos Middle Bronze Age cemetery. The first tomb to be found by Montet came to light when the cliff face subsided revealing the burial chamber of Abishemu in Tomb I.*

site and appear to run chronologically from west to east; thus Tomb I is the first of the series and Tomb IV the last.

I have already stated that Tomb IV probably belonged to Yantin and is to be dated to *circa* 1545 BC in the New Chronology. If we assume, with Kitchen,[8] that Tomb III belongs to Yakin-El who, according to Egyptian artefacts found in his tomb, is otherwise a contemporary of Sehetepibre (tenth king of the 13th Dynasty according to Ryholt[9]), then we have a two-generation sequence of funerary artefacts to analyse. We might take one further step and assume that Tombs I and II do not precede III by more than a couple of generations, given their close proximity to III and the absence of other tombs to fill the gap between the two tomb pairings. However, the cemetery does teeter on the edge of a cliff and there is the possibility that a part of the area has crumbled into the sea. So another group of tombs may have existed here and subsequently disappeared as a consequence of subsidence.

Tomb I was identified by Pierre Montet as that of Abishemu and Tomb II attributed to his son Ibshemuabi – the former datable, in Egyptian terms, to Amenemhat III (by an obsidian vase found in the tomb[10]) and the latter to Amenemhat IV (by an obsidian box found in his tomb[11]). This dating for Tombs I and II is consistent with the hypothesis that the Area A necropolis comprises a sequence of four generations of Byblite rulers from Abishemu to Yantin

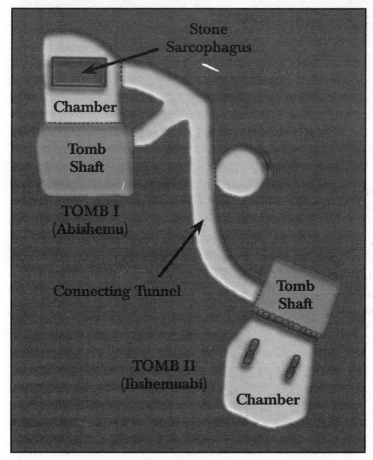

26. Plan of Byblos Tombs I and II showing the connecting passage between the shaft of Ibshemuabi and the shaft and chamber of Abishemu.

Egyptian-Byblite Synchronisms

Pharaoh Amenemhat III (NC – 1678-1634 BC)
contemporary of Abishemu of Byblos (NC – c. 1660-1645 BC)

Pharaoh Amenemhat IV (NC – 1649-1641 BC)
contemporary of Ibshemuabi of Byblos (NC – c. 1645-1605 BC)

Pharaoh Sehetepibre II (NC – 1594-1590 BC)
contemporary of Yakin-El of Byblos (NC – c. 1605-1570 BC)

Pharaoh Neferhotep I (NC – 1550-1540 BC)
contemporary of Yantin-Ammu of Byblos (NC – c. 1570-1545 BC)

– in the conventional Egyptian chronology the interval between Amenemhat III to Neferhotep I representing some seventy-six to one hundred years (according to Kitchen[12]) and therefore a reasonable generation of between twenty and twenty-five years.

In the New Chronology, the reign-lengths of the Byblite kings are longer, averaging just over thirty years. On the other hand, a shorter generation may be inferred if some tombs have been lost as a result of the collapsing cliff. However, given that we have no direct evidence for more than four rulers of Byblos for this period, we will assign the longer reign-lengths to the known kings which results in the chronological links in the table above between the Egyptian pharaohs and their Byblite vassals.

So, the sequence and chronology of the kings of Byblos during the Middle Bronze IIA period – in the NC contemporary with the Israelite Sojourn in Egypt – can be reasonably well established. These are rulers with good Canaanite West Semitic names who have strong links with Egypt. They even employ Egyptian titles (such as *h3ty-c* – 'governor' or 'mayor') and inscribe their possessions and monuments with Egyptian hieroglyphs. They use scarab seals – just like the Lesser Hyksos rulers who invaded Egypt within a century of Neferhotep and his contemporary Yantin.

Their names are also very similar. Remember Ya-Ammu and Yakub-Ammu – the predecessors of Sheshi? These names clearly belong in the same cultural and linguistic family as Yantin-Ammu. Indeed, that most famous of ancient names, Hammurabi, king of Babylon, carries the same theophoric element. Hammu was the Amorite sun-god and the dropping of the initial aspirant in the Byblite and Hyksos names to give Ammu is well attested. Thus Yantin-Ammu means '(H)ammu has given' whilst Hammurabi means 'Hammu is my Great One'. Yakin-El/ili, on the other hand, has the meaning 'El raises up' or 'God raises up' – a name which is entirely consistent with the Hyksos name Ili-Milku ('God is king'). These are all names which would be well at home in the West Semitic Amorite lands of coastal Canaan and in the major maritime cities of Byblos and Ugarit.

Given the clear parallels in names between the Byblite kings and the Lesser Hyksos rulers of Egypt plus the fact that the rulers of Byblos were highly Egyptianised – using hieroglyphic writing, scarabs, Egyptian titles and even, in a couple of instances, enclosing the royal name in a cartouche – it is extremely tempting to take Manetho's redactors at face value when they summarise Manetho's Hyksos dynasties as 'shepherds who were brothers from Phoenicia and foreign kings'. We could understand 'shepherds' as meaning Amorite pastoralists who migrated into coastal Phoenicia during the era of Amorite incursions at the beginning of the Middle Bronze Age (as attested in documents from the Ur III dynasty). The term 'brothers' might refer to tribal chieftains from the extended West Semitic clans. And they were certainly 'foreign kings'.

Archaeologically speaking, the evidence from the site of Tell ed-Daba (Avaris) is entirely consistent with the view that the early Hyksos culture originated from northern Canaan (i.e. Phoenicia). Indeed, Manfred Bietak has made the very same judgement following his international excavation team's careful and comprehensive study of the pottery and artefacts.[13]

175

> ## Conclusion Five
>
> The Lesser Hyksos kings of Avaris came originally from northern Canaan, perhaps from the cities of Byblos and Ugarit (Manetho's Phoenicians). They were themselves highly Egyptianised, whereas the Asiatic 'shepherd' (i.e. Amorite) population over which they ruled was initially far less Egyptianised. In later years (during MB IIB) the principal base of these Canaanite elites shifted to Tell el-Ajjul (Sharuhen) in southern coastal Canaan.

But this is not the complete story because there is evidence of another group of Hyksos rulers who seem not to have belonged within the Syrian/Amorite cultural sphere. They begin to appear in the Egyptian delta later than the initial invaders but subsequently rise to full dominance in the region. I believe that this is precisely what Hatshepsut is referring to when she describes Shemau 'aliens' living in the midst of the Aamu at Avaris. These foreigners may have had a connection (through trade and marriage) to the rulers at Byblos and Ugarit (and elsewhere) whose ancestors had been contemporaries of the 12th and 13th Dynasty pharaohs. In time the 'shepherd brothers' – that is, the Amorite Lesser Hyksos sub-dynasty (Ya-Ammu, Yakebim, Kareh and Ammu) – became vassals of the Shemau – first the Lesser Hyksos king, Sheshi, and then, later, the Greater Hyksos dynasty of Salitis – whose ethnic origins lay outside the Levant and the Semitic-speaking world.

Anakim in the Negeb

The Bible provides tantalising clues to the origins of an elite ruling class who appear in the Levant towards the end of the MB IIA period. The overall term for these rulers is

Rephaim (*Repa-im* = Repa+plural ending) or 'ancestors', and they are perceived as a race of giants [Genesis 14:5; Deuteronomy 2:11, 20, 3:11, 13; 2 Samuel 21:16, 18, 20 & 22]. They appear in the Amorite lands (such as Bashan) and, outside the Bible, in the texts from Ugarit, where, in the 'Legend of Aqhat', the hero's father is called a 'Rapa-man'.[14]

Within this broad designation of Rephaim is a sub-group called the 'Anakim' – descendants (or clan) of Anak – also men of great stature (described as 'mighty men' or 'giants'). This name Anak is simply the Indo-European word for 'ruler' (as in the term Homer uses for Agamemnon – the *wanax* or 'high-king' as compared to the *basileus* or 'lesser-king'), most at home in southern and western Anatolia. As we have seen, the three 'brother' rulers of southern Palestine at the time of the Israelite wanderings in the Negeb and Arabah were described as Anakim.

> They (the Israelite spies) went up by the way
> of the Negeb as far as Hebron, where Ahiman,
> Sheshai and Talmai – the Anakim – lived.
> [Numbers 13:22]

This passage is ambiguous and we do not simply have to understand that the three rulers ruled from the single town of Hebron. Rather we might interpret it to mean that the Anakim ruled in the region of the Negeb 'as far as Hebron'. This would allow us to place Sheshai (whom I have identified with the Lesser Hyksos king, Sheshi) in the western Negeb with his principal bases in the Wadi Ghazza at Tell el-Farah South and Tell el-Ajjul (Sharuhen). Ahiman and Talmai may then have ruled from Kiriath-Sepher (the later biblical Debir = Tell Beit Mersim) and Kiriath-Arba (the later biblical Hebron). The book of Joshua informs us that Arba was the ancestor of the Anakim and therefore probably the first of the foreign rulers to arrive in the Negeb region. This would place the appearance of the Anakim in southern Canaan during late MB IIA when the Middle Bronze II fortified strongholds of the region began to be constructed.

If I am right to interpret the biblical Anakim in this way, then we could view the later mention of Hebron in the time of Caleb (during the last years of the Conquest of the Promised Land = MB IIB) as the rallying place of the three Hyksos lords in defence of one of their kingdoms against the Israelite invaders from the east.

> Caleb son of Jephunneh was given a share within that (allotted territory) of the sons of Judah, in accordance with Yahweh's order to Joshua: Kiriath-Arba, the town of the father of Anak – that is, Hebron. Caleb drove out the three sons of Anak: Sheshai, Ahiman and Talmai, descended from Anak. From there he marched on the inhabitants of Debir; Debir in olden days was called Kiriath-Sepher. [Joshua 15:13-15]

With their initial defeat at Kiriath-Arba and subsequent over-running of a second stronghold at Kiriath-Sepher, the Lesser Hyksos Anakim would have retreated to the safety of Sharuhen, leaving their former territories in the hands of Caleb and the victorious tribe of Judah. This military reverse may not have been the disaster it sounds because Sheshi had by now expanded his domain across northern Sinai into the rich Egyptian delta. He could afford to leave the Israelite roughnecks to their own devices in the harsh environment of the interior hills and wadis of southern Canaan. After all he was not only the ruler of the wealthy port of Sharuhen but also the incumbent Lord of Avaris.

I have stated that these Anakim lords were not indigenous to southern Canaan. But what evidence is there for this? The name Sheshai/Sheshi and the names of his brother kings – Ahiman and Talmai – are not obviously Semitic and could be Indo-European/Anatolian. Their 'ancestor' – Anak – may certainly be viewed as an Anatolian. Indeed, the Greek traditions name just such a ruler – the giant Anax – king of Anactoria (coastal south-west Anatolia called Anaku in the epic of Sargon the Great).[15] This may well be the original homeland of the biblical Anakim who would then have spoken a dialect of Western Luwian before being assimilated into the Canaanite milieu. The 'founder' of Kiriath-Arba – Arba himself – bears a name that might have originated from any part of the ancient world. In addition we have the references to Rephaim at Ugarit and the abundant evidence of Indo-European and Hurrian settlers in northern Syria (especially at Alalakh and Ugarit) at this time. It then comes as no surprise to discover the three rulers of Ay-Anak – Erum, Abi-yaminu and Akirum – as enemies of Egypt listed in the 13th Dynasty Execration Texts. The Egyptians too knew of the Anakim.

It is therefore my contention that the books of Genesis, Deuteronomy and Joshua are recalling the presence of Indo-Europeans in southern Canaan (albeit bearing Semitic names) during the MB II period (contemporary with the Israelite Conquest of the Promised Land) represented by the mighty men of the Rephaim and Anakim. Other scholars have argued that there is fragmentary archaeological evidence which points to the appearance of Indo-European elements in the Levant as early as the beginning of the Middle Bronze Age (MB I).

The Arrival of the Anakim

To establish when this non-Semitic minority arrived in the Levant we must jump back several centuries to the transition between the Early Bronze Age and Middle Bronze Age – an archaeological era otherwise referred to as the MB I or EB-MB (depending on which school of archaeology you follow).

Returning to Byblos, we again find a synchronism with Egypt. During his excavations of the temple area in the

1920s, Pierre MONTET discovered a considerable quantity of scarabs bearing the prenomen Neferkare retrieved from a half-metre thick ash layer which marked the end of the Early Bronze city.[16] Their deposition was thus assumed to have taken place during the reign of the 6th Dynasty Pharaoh Neferkare PEPI II and this appears to be confirmed by a total of thirty-six inscriptions of this pharaoh found within the Byblos site. The ninety-four-year reign of Pepi II therefore coincided with the major series of destructions and conflagrations which brought the Early Bronze Age to an end across the Levant. This would mean around 2100 BC in the New Chronology.

Muntaha Saghieh, who specialises in Lebanese Bronze Age archaeology, has suggested that more than one population group occupied Palestine during the centuries which followed the collapse of the Early Bronze Age urban culture. At least two ethnic groups can be identified from the cultural remains – a Semitic/Amorite majority (what we might envisage as the indigenous population) alongside a non-Semitic/Anatolian minority centred on the coastal region and resident, in particular, at Byblos itself.[17] Through a detailed re-examination of third-millennium Byblos, Saghieh has shown that the burnt EB III town (phase KIV) was succeeded by an EB-MB town (phase JII) that was strongly influenced by Indo-European newcomers. Characteristic of this northern group are swollen-headed toggle pins[18] and metal torques[19] – both typical of the EB-MB but not attested in either the EB or MB.

Saghieh's Stratum JII thus appears to mark the arrival of a new group around the time of the long reign of Pepi II – evidenced by the appearance of this king's name associated with the construction of a MEGARON-type building by these 'Torque Wearers' as the archaeologists call them. Both the megaron architectural form and the bronze torque are typical of Anatolian culture.

If we regard the new group as the agents of destruction of the KIV town (which seems likely), then we can fix the arrival of our invading northerners to some time in the second half of the long reign of Pepi II. The characteristic group of artefacts which distinguishes this group from the indigenous Canaanites was also found by Claude Schaeffer at Ugarit, pointing, perhaps, to a seaborne link with their country of origin.[20] This non-Semitic group, who were skilled in metal-working and who have been equated with a proto-Hurrian[21] as well as an Anatolian element, may therefore be the first generation of Rephaim and Anakim who, centuries later, gave rise to the tradition that the Hyksos rulers originated from Phoenicia.

Jonathan Tubb of the British Museum has also recently identified a particular grave type from this period which he believes has its origins in Anatolia and even further north.[22] It consists of an oblong pit, cut into the ground, which is then lined with stone slabs. As a result, it has become known in the archaeological literature as the 'stone-lined' or 'stone-built' grave.

> The distribution of this grave type shows a broad arc stretching from Baghouz on the Euphrates, through central and coastal Syria and into Palestine as far as the Negeb, and into Transjordan as far as the southern Dead Sea plain.[23]

Tubb is also convinced that the appearance of this distinctive burial type is intrusive in the Levant and reflects the arrival of a foreign warrior elite through a process of infiltration that can be seen to begin already towards the end of the preceding Early Bronze period. Moreover:

> The stone-built grave is sometimes found in the Levant translated into mudbrick, as for example at Jericho. Most significantly, however, the mudbrick variant is found in Egypt at Tell ed-Daba (Avaris) where it characterises the graves

of the Hyksos, bringing into question once again their assumed Levantine origin.

This is astonishing stuff. A member of the British Museum Department for Western Asia and an experienced Levantine archaeologist is suggesting that the Hyksos mud-brick vaulted tombs at Avaris, and found elsewhere in southern Canaan where stone is not readily available, are the successors of the stone-lined graves of the early Middle Bronze Age which, in turn, appear to derive from Anatolian originals. Their arrival in the Levant also coincides with the destruction of EB III Byblos and the erection there of a megaron palace built by the wearers of torques. All this points to Indo-European origins for a new social stratum of Middle Bronze Age aristocrats who appear to have taken over the kingdoms of Early Bronze Age Canaan.

Conclusion Six

The first group of Indo-European migrants arrived in the Levant at the beginning of the Middle Bronze Age, their distinctive houses, graves and personal ornaments indicating an origin in Anatolia. These elite settlers, although a minority, took over the rule of the Early Bronze Age cities – especially the coastal ports – and grew wealthy through maritime trade. Eventually their descendants occupied Egypt as the Hyksos 'Shepherd Kings' ruling over the local Canaanite pastoralist population which arrived at Avaris in the century following the departure of the Proto-Israelites from that city towards the end of the 13th Dynasty.

So, in the historical model being developed here, we can pin down when the Rephaim arrived in the region (concentrating on the Phoenician coast) and be reasonably confident that they originated somewhere along the Anatolian seaboard. But were all the Hyksos rulers of the same origin? There now appears to be growing evidence that the final group of Greater Hyksos kings were from even further afield. This evidence is principally archaeological but we also have strong clues in the legendary stories of the region.

The Original Philistines

In the New Chronology the Proto-Israelite Exodus takes place at the end of the 13th Dynasty during the reign of Pharaoh Dudimose – archaeologically speaking, at the end of MB IIA. The Conquest of the Promised Land then falls approximately forty years into the period known as MB IIB (though I personally believe that MB IIB began earlier in Canaan than in Egypt, placing the Proto-Israelite Conquest as much as sixty years after the start of MB IIB in that region).

One of the criticisms often employed to challenge this new historical model has been what has become known as the 'Philistine Problem'. Put simply, in the Orthodox Chronology, the first archaeological appearance of the Philistines has been dated to the transition between the Late Bronze IIB (Greek LH IIIB) and Iron Age I (Greek LH IIIC). It is at this time, shortly after the Sea Peoples' invasion of the southern Levant in Year 8 of Ramesses III, that we first begin to see decorated pottery of Aegean stylistic origin (akin to LH IIIC:1b of Greece itself) in the Levantine archaeological record. The pottery has been dubbed 'Philistine ware' because of its approximate contemporaneity with the Peleset – one of the invading groups belonging to the Sea Peoples' confederacy – who have been equated with the biblical Pelishtim (or Pelishti).

In the Orthodox Chronology, the Israelite Conquest of the hill country of southern Canaan occurs prior to the time of Ramesses III, thus placing the first conflict between Israelites and Philistines in the subsequent Judges period, contemporary with the late 20th and early 21st Dynasties in Egypt. This is all very neat – but is it right?

Just because Peleset (almost certainly Philistines) appear in coastal Canaan during the 20th Dynasty, it does not necessarily follow that they were the *first* Philistines to arrive in the region. There may have been an earlier migration of these people into the Levant that would fit just as well with the New Chronology historical model. The case for an earlier occupation of southern Canaan by the Philistines at the start of the Late Bronze Age was brilliantly made back in 1990 by John Bimson.[24] Not only did he place Philistines in southern Canaan during the transition between the Hyksos period and the New Kingdom, but he reminded us that these people (or at least their ancestors) were already in the region at the beginning of the Middle Bronze Age – in the time of Abraham and Isaac, according to the Bible. I will briefly summarise his detailed arguments here, and add a few observations of my own, so that you can see how strong the circumstantial evidence is for this earlier movement of the Pelishtim.

(1) The Philistines of the Bible

First we should look at the earliest references to Philistines in the Old Testament tradition. The book of Genesis informs us that a group of Pelishtim already inhabited the territory around Gerar in the western Negeb during the lifetimes of the patriarchs. In any chronology this would be long before the Sea Peoples' invasion of the Levant in Year 8 of Ramesses III (OC – *c.* 1177 BC; NC – *c.* 856 BC). Whatever absolute date you choose for the appearance of the Philistine Sea Peoples, the relative date for the Patriarchal period of Abraham, Isaac and Jacob falls centuries earlier. So the Bible itself contradicts the conventional view that the Philistines first arrived during the post-Conquest era.

Plate 20: Professor Trevor Palmer provides the scale in this photograph of the ash and pumice deposit from the LM I eruption of Kalliste, exposed here in the quarry just to the south of Fira town, capital of Santorini/Thera.

Plate 21: A spectacular view from the terrace of the Congress Hall (home of the Third Thera and the Aegean World Conference and the Thera Foundation) on Santorini in the island's capital, Fira, perched high above the bay of the caldera. The LM I village of Akrotiri lies beyond the cliffs to the south (in the distance), facing towards Crete.

Plate 22: The earthquake-damaged staircase at Akrotiri.

Plate 23: Façade of the West House, facing onto Triangle Square, Akrotiri.

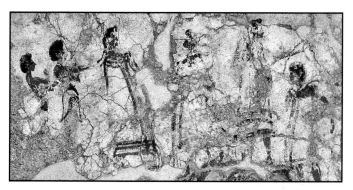

Plate 24: The meeting on a mountain peak [National Museum, Athens].

Plate 25: Following the shipwreck, the boar's-tusk helmeted warriors march off towards a city [National Museum, Athens].

Plates 26, 27 & 28: A griffin (above) depicted in the Nilotic scene of the West House Miniature Fresco [National Museum, Athens]. Compare this to fragments from the Tel Kabri fresco depicting a griffin in the 'flying-gallop' pose (below right) [Tel Aviv University] and the golden griffin (below left) from the shaft-graves at Mycenae [National Museum, Athens].

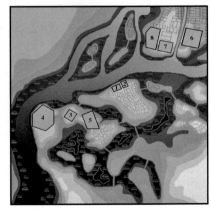

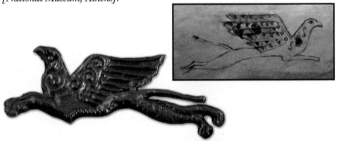

Plate 29: A map showing the topography of ancient Avaris as it has been reconstructed by surveyor Josef Dorner (of the Tell ed-Daba archaeological mission). Now compare this to the city (far right) from the West House Miniature Fresco set in a Nilotic landscape and with a river curving around its western side and dividing into two branches just as in the Avaris survey map. The Hyksos fortress is located at 4 on the map.

Plate 30: Another detail of the Nilotic scene with a wild cat chasing a goose amidst the papyrus plants and palms [National Museum, Athens].

Plate 31: The well preserved Town IV, located at the end of the Nilotic scene, with a river to its west dividing into two branches. The citizens of the town watch the departure of a large flotilla of ships, heading for Kalliste and the port of Akrotiri [National Museum, Athens].

Plate 32: The Pelasgian fleet heads across the sea to Kalliste with the chieftains seated in their palanquins at the stern of the vessels [National Museum, Athens].

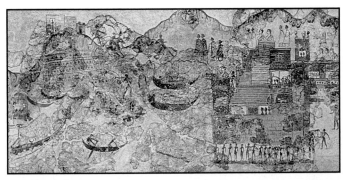

Plates 33 & 34: The return of the Pelasgian fleet to Kalliste [National Museum, Athens], compered to the fragmentary scene of the fleet's return from the Tel Kabri fresco [Tel Aviv University].

Plate 35 & 36: Detail from one of the main ships in the fleet's return to Kalliste, showing the captain in his palanquin, and (below) the large fresco of a palanquin from the West House with its undulating border [National Museum, Athens].

Plate 37: A life-size bronze statue of Poseidon in the National Museum, Athens.

It is not the Philistines who are the newcomers here but the Israelites. And it is their arrival which triggers hostilities with their neighbours on the coastal plain.

Both Genesis 26:1 and 26:8 specifically state that the ruler of Gerar at the time of Isaac's sojourn in southern Canaan was himself a 'Philistine king' who, however, bore a recognisably Semitic name – Abimelech ('father of the king'). This is very enlightening because it implies that the early Philistines had long been assimilated into the predominantly Amorite population of the Levant. Through intermarriage and acculturation these foreign lords had, in time, become almost indistinguishable from the native peoples of Canaan.

You might wish to question the notion that Indo-European rulers, having settled in Canaan, then chose to be known by West Semitic names – but is this really any different to the story of the current British royal dynasty founded in 1714 by George I (Georg Welf from Hanover) who could not speak a word of English? The Hanoverian monarchs of Great Britain then received the new German family name of Saxe-Coburg-Gotha with Victoria's marriage to Prince Albert. By the turn of the century and the onset of the Great War with his cousin the Kaiser, GEORGE V felt it prudent to adopt the quintessentially English surname 'Windsor'. When Elizabeth Windsor subsequently married Philip of Battenburg, the royal surname Windsor was retained. However, Princess Anne signed the register at her first marriage with the surname 'Mountbatten' – the Anglicised version of Battenburg. It took just two centuries for the Hanoverians to become Windsors (and it has to be added that, from the start, every one of those 'foreign' rulers of the British people bore traditional English or Anglicised names – George, William, Victoria and Edward). Why, then, should this type of recasting of such ruling aristocrats not have happened in a more distant past? In fact, this is precisely what Kenneth Kitchen himself argues for the biblical Philistines within his conventional scheme.

Thus, in many spheres acculturation was so great as to replace the original culture of the Philistines and their relatives almost completely in about two centuries.[25]

Such an Indo-European (Philistine) to Canaanite (Amorite) 'acculturation' would also explain why every Philistine deity mentioned in the Bible was well rooted in the indigenous West Semitic pantheon. Baal, Dagon, Anat and Astarte were all Syro-Canaanite deities with no obvious Indo-European links.

All this implies that the Philistines had been living in the Levant for decades by the time of the patriarch Isaac, and for centuries by the time of Shamgar ben Anath of the Judges period in whose 'judgeship' the first clash with the later Philistines is recorded [Judges 3:31].

On the other hand, one could take the view that the reference to Abimelech as 'the Philistine king at Gerar' is simply another example of those irritating and misleading anachronisms added by a later biblical redactor – just like the Israelites building the city of Raamses, as I myself argued earlier. Abimelech may have been a purely West Semitic king who was incorrectly transformed into a Philistine because he once ruled over the region that later became known as Philistia (Hebrew *Peleshet*). This is a perfectly reasonable stance to take – and, indeed, has been the majority position held within biblical scholarship – but it does not so easily explain the other references to Philistines in Genesis. One involves a dispute over watering rights between Isaac and the herdsmen of Gerar at the wells of Esek and Sitnah.

Isaac sowed his crops in that country (southwest Canaan), and in that year he reaped a hundredfold. Yahweh blessed him and the man became rich. He prospered more and more until he was very rich indeed. He acquired flocks and herds and a large retinue. **And the Philistines began to envy him.**

The Philistines had blocked up all the wells dug by his father's servants – in the days of his father Abraham – filling them in with earth. Then Abimelech said to Isaac, 'You must leave us, for you have become much more powerful than we are.' So Isaac left.

He pitched camp in the valley of Gerar and there he stayed. Isaac reopened the wells dug by the servants of his father, Abraham, and which had been blocked up by **the Philistines** after Abraham's death. And he gave them (the wells) the same names as his father had given them.

But when Isaac's servants, digging in the valley, found a well of spring-water there, the herdsmen of Gerar disputed it with Isaac's herdsmen saying, 'That water is ours!' So Isaac named the well Esek because they had disputed with him. They dug another well, and there was a dispute over that one also. So he named it Sitnah. Then he left there and dug another well and, since there was no dispute over this one, he named it Rehoboth saying, 'Now Yahweh has made room for us to thrive in the country.' [Genesis 26:12-22]

So the Genesis narrative concerning Isaac's settlement near Gerar is riddled with 'anachronistic' Philistines. Then there is the earlier passage from the time of Abraham that twice mentions 'Philistine territory'.

After they (Abraham and the king of Gerar) had made a covenant at Beersheba, Abimelech and Phichol, the commander of his army, left and **went back to Philistine territory**. And Abraham planted a tamarisk at Beersheba and

> there he invoked the name of Yahweh. Abraham
> stayed for a long while **in Philistine territory**.
> [Genesis 21:32-4]

So far we have half a dozen references to a Philistine
presence in southern Canaan hundreds of years before the
Judges period. But that is not the end of it. The narrative
which immediately follows Genesis – known today as the
book of Exodus – famously refers to both 'the way to the
land of the Philistines' [Exodus 13:17] and 'the Sea of the
Philistines' [Exodus 23:31] – again some considerable time
before the Sea Peoples' migration in the eighth year of
Ramesses III (within the OC scheme). These references are
found in the passages covering the departure of the Israelites
from Egypt and their stay at Mount Horeb in Sinai. The
events are therefore set during the reign of Ramesses II
– according to Kitchen's chronology – which places such
Philistine territorial designations (Erez Pelishtim/Peleshet)
more than eighty years before the Sea Peoples' settlement
in coastal Canaan.

If the mention of Peleset in Year 8 of Ramesses III and
the later appearance of so-called 'Philistine ware' really does
mark the first arrival of the Philistines in the Levant, then
the Bible has got it completely wrong. On the other hand,
we may have seriously misread the significance of the Sea
Peoples' invasion. Any biblical reference to Philistines or
Philistine territory prior to the 20th Dynasty undermines the
conventional view and supports the New Chronology – even
if that reference is only a few decades prior to the reign of
Ramesses III. After all, a miss is as good as a mile.

(2) Philistine Origins

Now we come to the question of the mysterious and
somewhat cryptic origins for the Philistines as given in
the Old Testament. First there is the association of the
Philistines with the 'island' or 'coastland' of Caphtor. In

the book of Amos, God reminds Israel that its origins were little different from those of the other peoples now settled in the region. They had all come from outside the Promised Land.

> Did I not raise up Israel from the land of Egypt, and the Philistines from Caphtor and the Amorites from Kir? [Amos 9:7]

Jeremiah [47:4] too refers to the Philistines as 'the remnant of the Isle of Caphtor'. However, the word here translated 'isle' (Hebrew *'iy*) has also been understood to mean 'coastland'. Incidentally, this is the same term used for the Ay-Anak of the Execration Texts which could therefore mean 'coastland of the Anakim'. Caphtor could therefore be either an island or a coastal region or both. On the other hand, the Table of Nations in Genesis 10 states the following:

> Mizraim (i.e. Misra/Egypt) fathered the Ludim, Anamim, Lehabim, Naptuhim, Pathrusim, Casluhim (whence came the Pelishtim) and Kaptorim. [Genesis 10:13-14]

This apparent disagreement between the origins for the Philistines in Caphtor (as given by Amos and Jeremiah) and their origins in Casluh (as given by Genesis) has been resolved to most scholars' satisfaction by proposing a scribal error which placed the phrase 'whence the Philistines came' after Casluhim rather than in its original and correct position after Kaptorim. In this way all the biblical references to the original homeland of the Philistines have them coming from Caphtor.

This then raises the issue as to whether other biblical references to the 'Kaptorim' can be equated with the Philistines. Was the term Kaptorim another, perhaps earlier, designation for Philistines? The amended statement found in the Table of Nations 'Mizraim fathered the ... Kaptorim, whence came (i.e. originated) the Philistines' appears to confirm this suspicion. If so, then we can add an important detail to the story of how the Philistines ended up in the Judges period as the dominant force on the coastal plain of southern Canaan. They were 'fathered' by the land of Egypt (biblical Mizraim).

What does this mean? How can the people of Caphtor be fathered by Egypt? You can take this two ways – either they came from Egypt to Caphtor, or they came from Caphtor to Egypt where they stayed for a period before entering Philistia as the Philistines. This last interpretation would be precisely like the tribe of Abraham who initially came from northern Mesopotamia/Syria to Egypt where they stayed for more than two centuries before entering the Promised Land as the Israelites: 'Did I not raise up Israel from the land of Egypt?'

This is where it gets exciting because we are finally getting close to an answer to the puzzle of the origins and racial identity of Sheshi and the subsequent Greater Hyksos Lords of Avaris. Could it be that the Bible has provided the crucial clue? Were the Kaptorim – fathered by Egypt – one and the same as the Hyksos Shemau? Was their expulsion into Palestine during Middle Bronze IIB the point at which they became the biblical Philistines?

I am imagining here a migration by sea, over centuries, from an island or coastal region (or perhaps both) called Caphtor to southern Canaan and Egypt, followed by a sojourn in the Land of the Pharaohs where they became Egyptianised, and a final resettlement in the region of Canaan later known as Philistia – 'the land of the Philistines'.

The biblical traditions are thus made to be consistent and are at the same time supported by the archaeological evidence. This is especially so when the island/coastland of Caphtor is identified not just with Crete but also the Aegean islands, Cyprus and the neighbouring coastland of southern Anatolia – in other words the entire coastal region of the Indo-European seafaring clans.

(3) Bichrome Ware

A new pottery class, known as 'Bichrome ware', appears in the Levant and Egypt at the beginning of LB I (that is roughly towards the end of the Greater Hyksos dynasty). It has strong Aegean characteristics with painted decoration in red and black on a buff background. One of the common painted images is of a backward-looking bird set in a metope (rectangular frame) – a typical Indo-European motif which then recurs in the so-called 'Philistine ware' of the Early Iron Age.

An examination of the clay used to make Bichrome ware (by means of neutron activation analysis) has demonstrated that much of it was manufactured in Cyprus. This Bichrome ware has been found by the Austrian excavators at Avaris in the final Hyksos stratum (D/2) and early 18th Dynasty levels at Ezbet Helmi. It is then found in quantity within the LB I strata of the coastal cities of southern Philistia and at major lowland centres of Canaan such as Megiddo. However, this distinctive pottery has not been found at any of the sites that the book of Joshua claims were destroyed by the Israelites during the Conquest and subsequently left unoccupied. This, of course, is what we would expect if these Proto-Israelite MB IIB destructions (*c.* 1407 BC) preceded the exodus of the

27. *Typical Bichrome ware vessels from the early LB I. Note the backward-looking bird on the far-right example.*

Hyksos out of Egypt and into lowland Canaan which took place some time after the start of LB I (c. 1200 BC).

(4) Other Cypriote LB I Pottery

Several other classes of Aegean and Cypriote pottery appear in the region at this time, including Monochrome ware (with similar decoration to the Bichrome ware but in a single, usually red, colour on the buff background), White Painted ware and Proto White Slip ware (especially milk bowls decorated with hatched patterns). In her famous book *Archaeology of the Holy Land*, Kenyon stresses the sudden flowering of Cypriote culture, made manifest in its pottery, throughout southern Canaan.

> Cypriote imports during the Middle Bronze Age are rare, though they begin to appear towards the end of that period. But in the transitional period … they become much more numerous until, during the Late Bronze Age, almost as much pottery of Cypriote connections is found as that in the native tradition.[26]

Yet, once again, none of this LC I (=LB I) Cypriote pottery has been found in the destruction levels of the cities of the hinterland – such as Jericho and Tell Beit Mersim (Debir), indicating that these classes of pottery did not arrive in the region until *after* the fall of the MB IIB cities. This is entirely consistent with the New Chronology model which has these cities being destroyed by Joshua's Israelite army some considerable time before the start of LB I.

Bietak's team has also recovered this whole range of Cypriote pottery in the early 18th Dynasty levels at Ezbet Helmi and in the last occupation levels of Hyksos Avaris indicating at least a strong trading connection between the Hyksos and Cyprus if not people of Cypriote origin living in Avaris.

> An enormous increase in Cypriote pottery (as containers for commodities the identity of which remains to be determined) can be observed in strata D/3-2 ... At Tell ed-Daba the whole spectrum of early types of Late Cypriote pottery appears: White Painted V, White Painted VI, Proto White Slip, probably White Slip I and Bichrome ware.[27]

This discovery has effectively pushed the start of the Late Bronze Age back into the Hyksos period because the arrival of Cypriote pottery (especially the distinctive Bichrome ware) has been adopted as the recognised marker for the start of LB I. Thus the Late Bronze Age did not begin with Ahmose's expulsion of the Hyksos from Avaris and subsequent destructions of the Middle Bronze Age cities by the Egyptian army as Kenyon proposed. Instead the appearance of early LB I foreign wares strongly argues for trading, and probably cultural, links between the Lords of Avaris, based in the Egyptian delta and southern Canaan, and the island of Cyprus.

(5) The Pelethites, Cherethites, Avvim and Hattim

We now come to yet more Indo-European conundrums thrown up by the biblical text. Four other 'peoples' occur in the narratives living in southern Canaan at this time – the Peletim, Keretim, Avvim and Hattim. The first two are later found in the military of David's Israel – no doubt foreign mercenaries. It has been argued that the Keretim are Cretans (Kreti) for obvious reasons and that the Peletim are Philistines (Peleset). This is not so obvious but most modern Bibles substitute 'Philistines' for the old 'Pelethites' of the King James translation. If the equation Pele[se]ti = Peleset[i] is correct, this clearly requires us to distinguish between the Philistines from Caphtor and Cretans. Ezekiel 25:16 makes the distinction quite clear.

> I will stretch out my hand against the Philistines
> (Pelishtim), and I will cut off the Cherethites
> (Keretim), and destroy the rest of the sea coast
> (or islands).

Zephaniah 2:5 separates the two groups in similar fashion.

> Woe to you inhabitants of the sea coast (or islands)
> – you nation of the Cherethites (Keretim)! The
> word of the Lord is against you, O Canaan – land
> of the Philistines (Pelishtim) …

Cretans were not Philistines. This strengthens the case for identifying Caphtor not just with Crete (as commonly held) but also with that other large island in the eastern Mediterranean – Cyprus ('Copper Land'). Indeed, the tribute bearers depicted in Theban tombs during the mid-18th Dynasty and described as Keftiu do not only bring fine pottery vessels with them but large hide-shaped ingots of copper.

There can be little doubt that the Egyptian designation 'Keftiu' is linguistically comparable to biblical Caphtor (Hebrew *Kaptor*) and Assyrian Kaptara. The earliest

hieroglyphic writing of the name is found in the Middle Kingdom where we find K-F-T-*3*-ω where the aleph (*3*) should be read as R and the wav (ω) as A, giving us Kaftara. There is no real issue regarding the variation of Egyptian F and Semitic P, so all three names are essentially the same.

28. A tribute-/gift-bearer from Keftiu comes to Egypt carrying an Aegean jug in his left hand and a large copper ingot on his shoulder [Tomb of Rekhmire, Thebes].

Conclusion Seven

The region of Caphtor/Keftiu/Kaftara/Kaptara encompasses much of the Aegean and southern Anatolian coastlands, as well as Cyprus and Crete. The early Caphtorim came to Egypt before finally settling in Philistia as the biblical Philistines. This movement from Egypt to Palestine is represented historically by the Hyksos expulsion from the eastern delta into southern Canaan at the beginning of the New Kingdom.

This leaves us to deal with the question of the Avvim and the Hattim. Joshua 13:2-3 tells us that the Avvim (Hebrew *Awim*) dwelt to the south of Gaza on the coastal plain down to the border with Sinai. They were then wiped out by the Kaptorim according to Deuteronomy 2:23.

> As for the Avvim, they occupied encampments as far as Gaza. The Kaptorim, who came from Caphtor, exterminated them and settled in their stead.

If our new historical model for the Hyksos period is correct, then we may also be able to identify these Avvim. They were settled in the area dominated by the Lesser Hyksos. Thus the Avvim may have been the 'shepherd' (Egyptian *Aamu* = Hebrew *Awim*?) population of the Negeb who moved into Egypt along with their Lesser Hyksos lords (Ya-Ammu, Yakebim, Kareh & Ammu) at the fall of the 13th Dynasty. It is interesting that Deuteronomy refers to these Avvim as occupying 'encampments' as this is precisely the time of the great 'Early Hyksos encampments' of the MB II with their large enclosures surrounded by glacis ramparts.

The Kaptorim who subsequently arrived in the region and 'exterminated' the Avvim, according to Deuteronomy, would then be the Greater Hyksos Indo-European-speaking elite from Caphtor (perhaps initially led by the 'son of Anak' Sheshi). We have seen how these last Hyksos oppressors of Egypt eventually occupied the whole of the southern coastal plain following their departure from Avaris at the beginning of the New Kingdom. The Bible then recasts these Shemau of Late Bronze Age Philistia as the *seranim* ('lords') of the Philistine Pentapolis – Gaza, Ashdod, Ashkelon, Gath and Ekron.

The Hattim are straightforwardly identified with the Hittites but as they appear in the story of Abraham's burial of Sarah at Kiriath-Arba (Hebron), this too is seen as anachronistic. In the New Chronology, with Indo-European elements moving south into the Fertile Crescent at the time we place Abraham's journey into Canaan, there is no problem in seeing Anatolian (early) Hittites ruling at Kiriath-Arba followed by Anakim from western Anatolia, along with early Philistines (Kaptorim) in Gerar, Avvim in the Gaza region, Kretim along the Canaanite coast, and Rephaim in Phoenicia.

Which brings me to a final thought for this chapter. We have seen that the Egyptian sign normally representing aleph in this period can be read as an R or an L when positioned adjacent to another aleph or ain. The Egyptians describe their northern neighbours as Aamu and scholars have identified these Aamu with the Amorites. I have just mentioned that Abraham 'the wandering Aramaean' (as the Bible calls him) is placed within this Middle Bronze I era in the New Chronology historical model – long before most scholars would be prepared to accept for the first attestation of Aramaeans in the historical records of the ancient Near East. Could we therefore cast Abraham as one of these MB I Aamu but read the name rather as Aramu – 'Aramaeans'? Perhaps the Bible was right all along.

Chapter Seven

THE REAL LORDS OF AVARIS

Aegeans at Avaris –– Dating the Aegean Presence –– The Legend of Io, Epaphus and Telegonus –– Inachus –– Queen Ahhotep

n the *Preface* to this book I told the story of the discovery of 'Minoan' frescoes at Ezbet Helmi/Avaris. Amongst these typically Aegean wall paintings are several remarkable images of bull-leaping – some miniature but others in partial raised relief (perhaps of bulls without leapers) of almost life-size dimensions. Such bull-leaping scenes have been found all over the eastern Mediterranean in areas closely associated with Indo-European-speaking cultures. I will be dealing with the origins and history of the bull-leaper culture when we journey to the island of Crete to investigate Arthur Evans' 'Minoan' civilisation. But, for now, we need to concentrate on the new evidence from Egypt which has set the bull in a china shop when it comes to the relationship between the Egyptian pharaohs of the early 18th Dynasty and the toreadors of the north.

The bull-leaping scenes from Avaris are pivotal in the evolutionary history of the ancient world because they apparently represent the first monumentally expressed depictions of this extraordinary contest between the power of the 'Earth-Shaker' and the guile, agility and cunning of humankind. This ritualised humiliation of the bull is Man's way of demonstrating his control over the wilder forces of nature. It is a sporting ceremonial to accompany the age-old iconic motif of the 'Master of Animals' depicted in so many artistic forms: controlling bulls, pairs of wild lions, and other beasts hazardous to existence (snakes, scorpions, crocodiles, hippos, etc.). And there is no doubt that 'controlling' the bull as fertility-king of the beasts (probably climaxing in the slaughter of the animal) was a dangerous business. There is so much material concerning this fascinating subject that an entire book has been dedicated to it – *The Power of the Bull* – by my colleague and fellow 'diffusionist', Michael Rice.[1] I can cover only a small part of the evidence for bull-worshipping and bull-contesting here, but can heartily recommend Michael's book to those who would like to delve into the subject on a much deeper level.

What we see in the Avaris frescoes are both bull-leapers and bull-grapplers. They are sometimes shown performing their deeds within a maze-pattern background which immediately transports us to the legend of Theseus and his battle with the Minotaur of Knossos in his labyrinthine lair. The word labyrinth comes from Minoan *labrys* which is the word for the double-axe of Aegean sacred ritual and it has been suggested that this was the weapon used to despatch the bull at the climax of the bull-leaping ritual. Equally the 'horns of consecration', so emblematic of Aegean palace culture, were representative of bovine horns.

The Egyptians do not appear to have indulged in the ritual humiliation of bulls in quite the same way. It is clear that pharaohs occasionally participated in wild bull hunts in Syria and temple scenes do depict pharaonic bull-lassoing scenes – but these appear to be royal activities designed to portray the king as a Master of Animals. Such activities were not for young male and female acrobats like those depicted in the Aegean bull-leaping scenes. In Egypt the relationship between man and bovid was that of worshipper and deity. The bull was the animal manifestation of the Memphite deity Ptah (Apis), as well as being associated with the solar cult of Heliopolis (Mnevis). The cow was the manifestation of Hathor (the fertility/nurturing goddess) and many female deities wore crowns with bulls' horns. Oxen were slaughtered for temple sacrifices but the bull was not an object for ritual humiliation. This was an alien cultural trait.

It then seems astonishing and quite bizarre to find such bull-leaping frescoes at Avaris in the Egyptian delta. These could not be the work of Egyptians. This typically Indo-European cultural imagery must have been the responsibility of Aegean artists commissioned by an Aegean/Cretan/Anatolian sovereign to decorate his or her royal residence. Manfred Bietak is clear on the matter.

> It is amazing that the technology, style and motifs of the frescoes are purely Minoan, with not a hint of an Egyptian emblem or royal symbol of power.[2]

Conclusion Eight

The palace at Ezbet Helmi I was built for a non-Egyptian royal figure of the early New Kingdom who was of Indo-European origin. The frescoes that once decorated this palace (including the bull-leaping scenes) were for state rooms and porticoes and must therefore reflect the cultural background and religion of their royal patron.

The Legend of Io

There are many different stories surrounding a certain Aegean princess of the Argolid named Io, daughter of the semi-mythical King Inachus. Io's adventures are described in several different forms – some more far-fetched and supernatural than others. In one case she is transformed into a beautiful heifer – a myth which scholars have suggested links her to Hera, the cow-goddess of Argos. But here we are going to concentrate principally on the story of Io as told by Herodotus.

In explaining the causes of the war between Hellas (Greece) and Persia (Iran), the celebrated Greek historian opens his long-famous book *Historia* with the tale of the abduction of Princess Io by Phoenician sea-traders who had arrived at Argos in the Peloponnese to barter their wares. However, they were not the Phoenicians of the Iron Age and late antiquity. These were the *earlier* Phoenicians of the Bronze Age – we would call them Canaanites in conformity with the Old Testament – who, according to ancient folklore, had, many generations earlier, journeyed from their original homeland on the twin islands of Dilmun (modern Bahrain, known as Tylos, and Muharrak, known as Aradus) in the Persian Gulf. The latter was then labelled the 'Lower Sea' which formed part of the greater 'Red Sea'. It is clear from the writings of Herodotus that in ancient times the whole of the Arabian Sea/Indian Ocean was named the Red Sea and that what we today call the Red Sea was merely one of its gulfs.

> There is in Arabia, not far from Egypt, a gulf of
> the sea entering in from the sea called Red; its
> length and narrowness are as I shall show. For
> length, if one begins a voyage from its inner
> end, to sail right through into the broad sea is
> a matter of forty days for a boat that is rowed.
> [Herodotus Book II]

The story of their migration was told in *Legend: The Genesis of Civilisation* (1998) where I attempted to piece together the evidence for contact between Mesopotamia and Egypt during the prehistoric age before the 1st Dynasty. Petrie was the first Egyptologist to articulate this picture of early Phoenician migration – a proposition which is virtually ignored in modern scholarship but which unquestionably has striking archaeological support (much of which was presented in *Legend*). Why is it ignored today? Perhaps because the 'Father of Egyptian Archaeology' was rash enough to suggest that the early pharaohs themselves were of the same origin.[3]

Petrie's hypothesis was based not only on artefactual evidence, which he had personally dug up during his wide-ranging excavations, but also on his knowledge of Classical literature such as STRABO of Amaseia's *Geographika* and Herodotus of Hallicarnassus' *Historia*. Before the age of fast-food education, most grammar school pupils studied the Classical languages – and Herodotus was the standard textbook for any student translating from Greek into English. So, virtually the first ancient Greek words a child read were Herodotus' story of the abduction of an Aegean princess by Phoenician traders.

The 'Father of History' was well aware of a Persian Gulf origin for the Phoenician seafaring nation as the opening chapter of *Historia* clearly shows and which neatly brings us back to the matter of Princess Io.

> The chroniclers among the Persians say that the Phoenicians were the cause of the feud (between the Greeks and the Persians). These (they say) came to our seas from the sea which is called Red, and having settled in the country which they still occupy, at once began to make long voyages. Among other places to which they carried Egyptian and Assyrian (i.e. Mesopotamian) merchandise, they came to Argos, which was at that time pre-eminent in every way among the people of what is now called Hellas (Greece). The Phoenicians then came, as I say, to Argos, and set out their cargo. On the fifth or sixth day

after their coming, their wares being now well-nigh all sold, there came to the seashore, among many other women, the king's daughter, whose name (according to Persians and Greeks alike) was Io, daughter of Inachus. They stood about the stern of the ship: and while they bargained for such wares as they fancied, the Phoenicians heartened each other to the deed, and rushed to take them. Most of the women escaped. Io, with others, was carried off. The men cast her into the ship and made sail away for Egypt. This, say the Persians (but not the Greeks), was how Io came to Egypt. [Herodotus, Book I][4]

But the Phoenicians do not tell the same story about Io as the Persians. They say that they did not carry her off to Egypt by force. She had intercourse in Argos with the captain of the ship. Then, perceiving herself to be with child, she was ashamed that her parents should learn of it, and so, lest they should discover her condition, she sailed away with the Phoenicians of her own accord. [Herodotus, Book I]

Whatever the truth as to the way in which Io left her home-land of the Argolid, all the sources agree that this Aegean princess from Argos ended up in Egypt. The sailing to Egypt strongly suggests that either the Nile delta was the home of these Phoenician traders or they were of a mind to sell female captives to the residents of that region.

When was this 'incident' in the long history of the pharaohs? Can we pin down the era and the actual pharaoh ruling at the time? Another edition of the Io legend gives us some further (though often contradictory) details.

Inachus, a son (i.e. descendant) of Iapetus (the biblical Japheth?), ruled over Argos, and founded

the city of Iopolis – for Io is the name by which
the moon was once worshipped at Argos – and
called his daughter Io in honour of the moon.
Zeus Picus (the woodpecker), King of the West,
sent his servants (the Phoenicians?) to carry off
Io, and outraged her as soon as she reached his
palace. After bearing him a daughter named
Libya, Io fled to Egypt ...[5]

Yet another version has Io giving birth not to Libya but
to 'Epaphus, who became the ancestor of Libya, Agenor,
Belus, Aegyptus, and Danaus'. Now Agenor was a
legendary king of the Phoenicians who left Egypt to found
his Canaanite dynasty, whilst Aegyptus and Danaus were
residents of Egypt.

Agenor, Libya's son by Poseidon and twin to
Belus, left Egypt to settle in the land of Canaan,
where he married Telephassa, otherwise called
Argiope, who bore him Cadmus, Phoenix, Cilix,
Thasus, Phineus, and one daughter, Europa.[6]

Here again we see legendary connections of an Egypt-
based dynasty of Phoenicians of Indo-European descent
to the great founders of Aegean countries – Cadmus who
founded Greek Thebes and brought writing to the Western
world; and Europa, the mother of Minos, king of Knossos
and supreme ruler of Crete. According to legend, this entire
line of Phoenician, Greek and Cretan rulers descended
from Io and her son Epaphus – presumably either the child
of the Phoenician sea captain (according to Herodotus) or
a Phoenician king (if we may be permitted to interpret the
alternative legend minus the supernatural element).

The legend then goes on to say that Io subsequently
married an Egyptian king named Telegonus (in the Greek
form of Herodotus' day). So the Egyptian connection
becomes even more intriguing. Not only is Io the 'great

mother' of several legendary monarchs whose ancestors came out of Egypt, but she also married into a native Egyptian dynasty of pharaohs.

You will recognise without much difficulty that the name of her first child, Epaphus, is a garbled version of the Hyksos royal name Apophis which immediately puts us in the time of the Greater Hyksos dynasty and their Theban contemporaries of the 17th Dynasty.

The name borne by Io's Egyptian husband is a little more tricky. First, we need to consider one or two linguistic peculiarities that scholars have come across – especially when dealing with Egyptian names transferred into foreign languages such as Greek.

(1) The Egyptians often failed to distinguish in their script between the letters R and L – both written with the mouth hieroglyph (sometimes the L takes the form of a recumbent lion). Thus, for example, the Lesser Hyksos royal name written I-**R**-I-M-I-**R**-K-U represents the original Canaanite Ili-Milku. And, of course, there is the famous Merenptah Stela bearing the signs Y-S-**R**-I-A-**R** for Israel where the first mouth sign represents R and the second L!

29. *The crude hieroglyphs which spell out the name Israel on the Merenptah Stela. From right to left: two reeds (Y or I); the bolt (S) above the mouth (R); a single reed (I); a vulture (A); another mouth (this time representing L) above a vertical stroke and a throw-stick (a determinative for Asiatic); and two seated figures (male and female) with plural strokes below (the determinative for 'people' or 'nation') [Cairo Museum].*

(2) During the Middle Kingdom and Second Intermediate Period the Egyptians often used the sign for *aleph* not just as the Semitic phonetic value aleph (a glottal stop vaguely similar to the short form of our letter A) but also to indicate the consonants R and L – especially when writing foreign names. This is most apparent when two alephs appear adjacent to each other in a name where one aleph must clearly be a consonantal L or R. This may also apply to the combination of aleph and *ayin* (the latter a guttural sound preceding a vowel, unknown in English). As examples of alephs representing L or R, here are some famous place-names as they appear in the earlier Middle Egyptian/Second Intermediate Period forms, as compared to the later New Kingdom versions; in transliteration the ᶜsymbol represents ayin (expressed as an A or I or E), the ω symbol a vowel marker (usually vocalised as A or O or U), and the 3 symbol the aleph (standing for either L or R) in Middle Kingdom texts:

Place	Middle Kingdom	New Kingdom
Ashkelon	ᶜsk3nnωn (AskeLannon)	ᶜsk3ln3 (Askalana)
Pella	pᶜh3ωm (PahiLim)	pᶜhl (Pahil)
Hazor	hzωᶜ3ᶜ (HazoaRa)	hᶜzr (Hazor)
Tyre/Tyrus	zᶜ3m (ZaRim)	tz3ωr (Zaur)
Ullaza	ωω3zᶜ (AuLaza)	ωlzω (Ulaza)
Kaptara	kft3ω (KaftaRa)	kftᶜω (Kaftara)
Alashiya	ᶜ3sy (ALasiy[a])	ᶜlsᶜ (Alasa)

(3) There is a fairly common interchange between the Egyptian letter K and the Canaanite and Greek letter G. For example, from the time of Ramesses III one of the Sea Peoples' groups is referred to as Shekelesh whom scholars have identified with the Sagalassans of the Anatolian and Phoenician coasts (see *Chapter Sixteen*).

CHAPTER SEVEN

Identifying Telegonus in Egyptian History

Armed with this knowledge, let us now tackle the name
Telegonus to see with which Egyptian ruler this Greek
name might be identified in the era of the late Hyksos
period and early New Kingdom. The initial point to make
is that very few of the Egyptian pharaohs' names actually
begin with the letter T. Those that do are:

  Teti (Old Kingdom 6th Dyn)
  Taa I and Taa II (Second Intermediate Period 17th Dyn)
  Tutankhamun (late 18th Dyn)
  The female pharaoh Tausert (late 19th Dyn)
  The three Takelots (Third Intermediate Period 22nd Dyn)

We can safely rule out most of these on chronological
grounds, as we are restricting our search to the approximate
time of the Epaphus/Apophis mentioned in the Io legend
– that is, the late Second Intermediate Period. This leaves
us with the two Taas – Senakhtenre Taa I and Sekenenre
Taa II – and I believe we can narrow our search down to
the second ruler to bear the Taa nomen (birth name).

Sekenenre Taa II of the 17th Dynasty was probably the
son of Taa I and almost certainly brother of his successor,
King Kamose. He was definitely the father of King Ahmose
(founder of the 18th Dynasty). As we have already seen
in *Chapter Five*, both of these warrior pharaohs (Kamose
and Ahmose) followed Sekenenre's example in their
determination to expel the Hyksos from Egypt. It seems
that Kamose died in the attempt – as had his predecessor
– before Ahmose finally succeeded in defeating the foreign
kings of Avaris with the help of his strong-willed mother
Ahhotep. This period of conflict was precisely the time
of the Hyksos king, Auserre Apophis, erstwhile enemy of
both Sekenenre and Kamose. So, Sekenenre Taa II has to
be our best candidate for the Egyptian King Telegonus of
the Io legend.

Let us now apply the linguistic rules we have observed to this pharaoh's full nomen *and* epithet to see where we get.

(1) Sekenenre died in battle fighting the Hyksos and was given the epithet 'the brave' (Egyptian *ken*) appended to his birth name or nomen which thus became Taa-ken. This happened very soon after his death according to the evidence of contemporary documents. Remember here that the vowel between the K and N is unknown, so Egyptologists interpolate an E purely for convenience.

(2) The nomen Taa includes the adjacent letter combination aleph and ayin (represented in scholarly literature by the symbols 3 and ^{c}). However, the aleph is very likely here a writing for R or L – a common practice in this era. If we substitute the letter L for the aleph and retain the A for the ayin, we get TELAKEN (for the moment marking other potential vowel positions with the letter E).

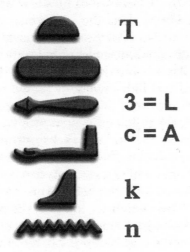

30. The hieroglyphic signs which spell out the royal nomen Taa-ken which may also be read as Tela-ken.

(3)   Exchange the Egyptian K for a Greek G and we arrive at TELAGEN.

(4)   Add the typical Aegean termination -US and we have TELAGENUS – close enough to the Telegonus of the Io legend!

This is not just a matter of linguistic conjuring, because the historical picture of this time strongly supports the equation.

Identifying Io in Egyptian History

Remember that, according to the Greek legend, Telegonus married Princess Io, daughter of Inachus, some time after she had given birth to Epaphus. If this Epaphus is the Hyksos king Apophis, then Io had been brought to the Egyptian delta and probably Avaris by the Phoenicians during the late Second Intermediate Period. This makes good sense because we have already determined that the Hyksos rulers (perhaps from Sheshi onwards) were themselves of 'Phoenician' stock (actually descended from Anatolians settled along the Phoenician seaboard). The seafarers who had arrived in the bay of Argolis to trade with the kingdom of Inachus must have been Hyksos from Avaris or at least Levantine traders with Avaris.

Trade was indeed the source of Hyksos wealth. These plunderers of Egypt had been exploiting the rich bounties of the Nile valley for the past two centuries by the time of Auserre Apophis, and their principal customers were Indo-European and Hurrian kinsmen of the Aegean and Phoenician coastal regions. Princess Io's 'importation' into Hyksos Egypt from Argos had merely been a part of that profitable commerce – whatever you make of the fanciful story behind her arrival as given in the various legends. She was subsequently passed on southwards into Upper Egypt in order to further the political aims of a Hyksos king in this world of barter and trade – the Aegean half of a marriage treaty with a native pharaoh which came about as a result of the vassalage of Upper Egypt to Avaris following Khyan's victories in the south.

Putting this to one side for a moment and concentrating on the internal picture in Egypt during the late Second Intermediate Period, we find that several Egyptologists have commented on the rather ambiguous nature of the relationship between the Theban 17th Dynasty and the Greater Hyksos 15th Dynasty: sometimes at war, sometimes at peace; often squabbling like sibling members of the same family, writing complaining letters to each other. This has raised the possibility, in some minds, of royal marriages between the two kingdoms. Howard Carter himself suggested something of the kind when he discovered the Theban tomb (Dra Abu el-Naga B) of Ahmose-Nefertari – the wife of Ahmose and mother of Amenhotep I. The tomb contained fragments of an alabaster vase inscribed with the name of a Princess Herit, daughter of Auserre Apophis. Finding such an object in the burial chamber of an 18th Dynasty Great Royal Wife led Carter to ask the question:

> Could the appearance of Apepi's name here indicate some kind of relationship between the Hyksos and Theban royal families?

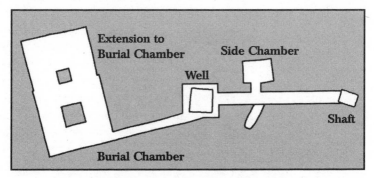

31. Plan of tomb Dra Abu el-Naga B showing the 'double' burial chamber.

209

The implication of the discovery of a Hyksos princess'
name in the tomb of Ahmose-Nefertari is precisely that
raised in Carter's question. It may well be that, prior to the
final protracted war of liberation which saw the Hyksos
depart from Egypt, Indo-European princesses were being
married off to the male royals of the native Egyptian 17th
Dynasty (and perhaps vice versa). This is the typical practice
of master and vassal where a vassal's loyalty is secured by
the obligations of a marriage treaty. Did this practice begin
with Io's betrothal to Sekenenre Taa-ken? The answer to
this startling question is, I believe, yes – the Io legend may
have a basis in history.

It is time to investigate one of Egypt's most renowned
queens – the celebrated Great Royal Wife Ahhotep, spouse
of Taa-ken and mother of Ahmose – and a heroine of the
war against the Hyksos of Avaris. So, could *this* lady be the
Aegean princess, daughter of Inachus, who came to Egypt
on a Phoenician ship and married an Egyptian pharaoh?
Let us, first of all, take a look at her name.

Ahhotep is a good Egyptian nomen with the meaning
'Yah is content'. You will immediately see that the name is
actually Yah-hotep, even though Egyptologists have become
accustomed to dropping the initial Y. Interestingly this also
goes for Ahmose, whose name is actually written Yah-mose
('Born of Yah' or 'Offspring of Yah'). Who or what is this
Yah? Well, the hieroglyphic sign used to represent the name

32. *The hieroglyphs which spell out the name Ahhotep. The first symbol – the
crescent moon – can also be represented in its inverted form, resembling a crescent-
shaped ship with central cabin.*

is a 'crescent-moon-with-rising-sun' motif – believed to be the symbol of an obscure 'Canaanite' moon-deity called Yah. However, it is nigh impossible to find anything in the Egyptological literature that actually informs us about this so-called deity. Otherwise it is simply the Egyptian word for 'moon'.

The main Egyptian moon-gods were Thoth (god of writing, represented by the ibis) and the child Khonsu (son of Amun). It is somewhat extraordinary, then, that this foreign god's name should form part of the nomen of a native Egyptian pharaoh and the name of his mother. Female moon-deities (associated with fertility) were Isis and Hathor. The theophoric royal birth-name 'Yahmose' is rare, occurring only at the beginning of the 18th Dynasty and at the end of the 26th Dynasty (c. 570 BC) when Pharaoh Amasis (Yahmose II) was named after his illustrious predecessor Yahmose I.

But there is another possible origin for this theophoric name which arises out of our investigation of the Io legend. Within the Semitic language groups of the Levant, and in Egypt itself, a person of Greek origin was (and still is) called a 'Yawani' – the equivalent of the Classical designation 'Ionian' (originally Iaones[7]). In ancient times the Aegean region as a whole was known as Yawan and only later became specifically identified with the land of Ionia on the western coast of Anatolia (by association with its settlers – the Ionian Greeks). The Bronze Age Greeks wrote the name in their Linear B script in the form *Ia-wo-ne*. In later times we find Persian *Yauna* and Egyptian Demotic *W-y-n-n* for Ionia.[8] The Old Testament also refers to Greece as Yawan in the Table of Nations, listing it amongst the Indo-European descendants of Japheth.

> These are the descendants of Noah's sons, Shem, Ham and Japheth, to whom sons were born after the flood: Japheth's sons were Gomer, Magog, the Medes, **Yawan**, Tubal, Meshech, Tiras. Gomer's

> sons were Ashkenaz, Riphath, Togarmah. Yawan's
> sons were **Elishah**, **Tarshish**, the **Kittim** and the
> **Dananites**. From these came the dispersal to the
> islands of the nations. [Genesis 10:1-5]

The penultimate sentence enumerates the tribal groups or clans that derived from Yawan – the islanders of Elishah (Alashiya on Cyprus), the people of Tarshish (Tarsus in Cilicia?), the Kittim (the people of Kition in eastern Cyprus) and the Dananites (the Danaioi of Homer and/or the Danuna/Dana of Adana in Cilicia).

From all this we can be confident that the legendary name Io (its Classical Greek form) was actually pronounced Ya in earlier times. Ya-hotep and Ya-mose could, therefore, be linked directly to the name carried by the legendary princess of the Aegean – the eponymous ancestor of the Ionian Greeks.

You may recall that earlier in this chapter I quoted from Robert Graves' famous book *The Greek Myths* where he states that the moon-goddess of the Pelasgians – that is, according to tradition, the indigenous, pre-Mycenaean people of the Aegean – was called Io (Ya).

> ... Inachus, a son of Iapetus, ruled over Argos, and
> founded the city of Iopolis – **for Io is the name
> by which the moon was once worshipped
> at Argos** – and called his daughter Io in honour
> of the moon.[9]

This Ya/Io was later assimilated with Hera Βουπισ ('cow-faced'), worshipped at the Argive Heraeum.[10] This lunar cow-goddess had crescent-shaped horns, just as the cow-goddess Hathor of Egypt was associated with the moon through her crescent horns. From this we may assume that Hera's earlier incarnation, Ya/Io, was also a lunar cow-goddess and, as the Greek myth informs us, Princess Io was herself transformed into a beautiful heifer by Zeus.

Coincidence? Hera, the wife of Zeus, was especially worshipped in the Argolid and was associated with the image of a cow. Coincidence? One of the iconographic motifs of Egyptian Hathor (*hwt-hr* – the 'House of Horus', i.e. the womb of the king's mother) was a pair of cow's horns with the sun rising up between them and this may be the origin of the hieroglyphic sign of the 'crescent-moon-with-rising-sun' which represents the sound Yah. Remember that Ahhotep, as the mother of Ahmose – founder of the 18th Dynasty – heroine of the Hyksos expulsion, was in effect the womb from which the New Kingdom pharaohs sprung. She was the true human manifestation of the goddess Hathor.

Ahhotep – The Warrior Queen

In the Cairo Museum there is a large stone slab numbered CG 34001 known as the 'Ahmose Stela'. The text found on this monument, discovered by George LEGRAIN at Karnak in 1900, is our major source for the status and titles of Queen Ahhotep, mother of Ahmose.

> Give praise to the Lady of the Land, the **Mistress of the Shores of the Hau-nebut**, whose name is raised over every foreign country, and who governs the people. **The Wife of the King**, the **Sister of the Lord** – life, prosperity, health! **Princess, King's Mother**, the noblewoman who knows things and takes care of Egypt. She looked after its (i.e. Egypt's) soldiers and protected them. She brought back its fugitives and gathered its dissidents together. She pacified Upper Egypt and expelled its rebels. The King's Wife, Ahhotep, may she live.

Professor Peter Jánosi of the Institute of Egyptology in Vienna notes how utterly unique these titles for a queen of Egypt really are.

The epithets given to Ahhotep are indeed remarkable, and it would be a mistake to treat them only as a venerated status for the queen honoured by her son, Ahmose. The epithets used for Ahhotep can be compared with similar titles and epithets that were normally given to the pharaoh. The king was the ruler of Egypt and all foreign lands. Besides this similarity to the titles of Pharaoh, another important fact has to be stressed: to our knowledge, no other queen or royal lady throughout Egyptian history ever possessed the title *hnwt idbw h3w-nbwt* ('Mistress of the Shores of the Hau-nebut'). Such a title would not have been bestowed without good reason. One is inclined, therefore, to believe that it relates to genuine historical events.[11]

The title 'Mistress of the Shores' (or Coastlands) 'of the Hau-nebut' is indeed an epithet requiring explanation. The Hau-nebut ('that which is beyond the islands') is considered by Gardiner and other authorities to be the Egyptian term for the lands bordering the Aegean Sea. The 'shores beyond the islands' would therefore be the coastlands of Greece and western Anatolia. If Ahhotep really is the legendary Io, then one could not choose a more appropriate epithet for Taa-ken's widow. As the daughter of a Pelasgian king – a princess of Aegean origin – she well merited the title 'Mistress of the Aegean'. There is no doubt in my mind that this unique title states plainly that Ahhotep was a foreigner. She was also the 'Wife of the King' – that is, the Great Royal Wife of Sekenenre Taa-ken – and a 'Princess' – as daughter of King Inachus (and not necessarily the blood daughter of Taa I as most scholars have previously assumed). The term 'Sister of the Lord' is often carried by wives of the early New Kingdom pharaohs and does not mean a literal blood-sister of the monarch (as many Egyptologists have realised). However, in our new historical model, Ahhotep, with her Aegean origins, might, in reality, be the actual sister (by blood) of a Hyksos Lord of Avaris. If, as the legend states, she was the mother of Epaphus – following this logic the king we know as Auserre Apophis – then Ahhotep would have been of the same generation as the Hyksos king, Yanassi (note the moon-deity Ya in his theophoric name), the predecessor of Apophis and son of the great Lord of Avaris, Khyan (according to the text of a door-jamb recently found at Avaris[12]). Khyan's Horus name was Anak-idbu – 'Embracer of the Coastlands' (of the Aegean?). It is tempting, therefore, to equate Anak-idbu Khyan with the Pelasgian King Inachus (Anak[us]) of the legend, making Ya/Io the sister of Yanassi – that is, 'Sister of the Lord' (of Avaris?). I would then initially reconstruct the Greater Hyksos dynasty in the following way.

The Six Kings of the Greater Hyksos Dynasty in the New Chronology

1. SALITIS (unidentified but perhaps Sakil-Har/Shalek with metathesis) – a 'Phoenician' or Hurrian
2. BNON – a 'Phoenician' or Hurrian
3. ANAK-IDBU KHYAN = Inachus 'Embracer of the Coastlands', father of Ahhotep – a Pelasgian
4. YANASSI, son of Khyan and the brother of Ahhotep – a Pelasgian
5. AUSERRE APOPHIS (Epaphus), son of Ahhotep and step-brother of Ahmose
6. ASEHRE KHAMUDY (as yet unidentified)

Inachus – A Hyksos King?

So, could Khyan really be the legendary Inachus, father of Io and formerly ruler of Argos according to the legend? Remove the early Greek termination -US and we are indeed left with the name ANAK – the Bronze Age Aegean word for 'high-king'. The legendary name Inachus may, therefore, be nothing more than a garbled version of the title 'ruler' or 'king' – just as the name of the Hittite founder-king 'Labarna' becomes the honorific title for kings of the later empire period, and the name 'Caesar' is borne by the emperors of Rome after their 'founder' Gaius Julius Caesar. There is no doubt as to the Greek and Anatolian origin for this term *anak* which appears in the *Iliad* in the form *wanax*, as borne by Agamemnon – high-king of the Greek confederacy of city-state rulers. We have also associated this title with the Anakim of the Bible and the early Hyksos king, Sheshi (biblical Sheshai), ruler of Sharuhen (Tell el-Ajjul and biblical Beth-Aglayim) and Avaris.

The extraordinary prospect that Inachus might be one and the same historical figure as Anak-idbu (Khyan) would certainly explain the international character of Khyan's reign with the appearance of his cartouche on artefacts ranging across the ancient political landscape. Such finds have turned up in Knossos (the royal palace of Minoan Crete), Boghazköy (the Hittite capital of Hattusha) and Baghdad (presumably originally from mighty Babylon).

Scholars have noted that the first three Greater Hyksos rulers (down to Khyan) did not employ their nomens in royal inscriptions but rather their Horus names. And so we should perhaps expect Khyan to be known (at least in his early years) as Anak – the hypocoristicon or shortened form of his Horus name Anak-idbu. I would interpret this name 'Embracer of the Coastlands' as 'he who is high-king over the sealand kingdoms'. He was 'the ruler' *par excellence* of the islands and coastlands of the eastern Mediterranean and arguably the greatest of the Hyksos kings.

The Treasure of Queen Ahhotep

Over the last two hundred years Egypt has gained a well-deserved reputation as *the* land of wondrous discoveries – so much so that some Egyptophiles can appear to get rather blasé about all its spectacular sites and artefacts. No other civilisation has come close to giving up such comparable wealth from its past. And what ancient culture has left us the bodies of its rulers – preserved intact – whose faces we can still look upon, thanks to the embalmer's art?

The coffins of the kings and queens of the New Kingdom were originally buried in the limestone hills of Western Thebes, but many were collected together towards the beginning of the Third Intermediate Period for safety, during a time of serious troubles and civil war which left the burial grounds vulnerable to plundering and desecration. As a result, the royal corpses were deposited in an unprepossessing shaft-tomb well hidden in the folds of the cliffs overlooking the Nile valley. When Émile BRUGSCH descended into the Royal Cache just south of Deir el-Bahri in 1881, he found scores of coffins containing the mummified remains of their royal occupants. These included Sekenenre Taa-ken and his son, Ahmose. But there was no Ahhotep – the Great Royal Wife of the former and King's Mother of the latter. This was in spite of the fact that other queens of this period were discovered in the Royal Cache. However, a coffin bearing the name of a Queen Ahhotep was found – but now carrying the body of Pinudjem I of the 21st Dynasty Theban line of kings. Clearly this was re-used.

Why was Queen Ahhotep not reburied with her husband and son in the hiding place of the New Kingdom pharaohs? Because her body had already been reburied elsewhere (close to that of Kamose) and subsequently left undisturbed when the rest of the royal mummies were being gathered together for reburial in the tenth year of King SIAMUN of the 21st Dynasty. When, prior to this, was she reburied? Probably not long before, in the reign of the Theban king PINUDJEM I who 'borrowed' her outermost coffin for his own funeral equipment.

In fact, the discovery of Ahhotep's reburial had already been made by workmen in the pay of Auguste MARIETTE in 1859 at Dra Abu el-Naga – the cemetery of the 17th Dynasty royal house on the slopes of a rocky hill just to the north of Ta-Djeser ('the Sacred Land' – the cliff bay of Deir el-Bahri).

Unfortunately, the 'excavation' was a minor disaster with the body of the queen being completely destroyed in the process. Today, only the magnificent golden coffin (see plate 15) and its contents (minus the body) can be studied in the Cairo and Luxor Museums. Even so, the find remains a landmark in Egyptology because the burial goods are truly extraordinary. They include a stunning ceremonial axe of solid gold, a number of beautifully crafted golden daggers and a set of giant-sized golden flies (see plate 14) – a symbol of military prowess akin to our military medals of honour.

Before we examine these objects in more detail, I need just to cover the thorny topic of whether there were two queens bearing the name Ahhotep rather than one. The issue revolves around the two coffins and the inscriptions with which they are decorated.

The text on the golden coffin found by Mariette's workers at Dra Abu el-Naga lacks the title 'King's Mother' whilst the coffin in the Royal Cache (reused for the burial of Pinudjem I) does indeed bear this title – as one would expect for the mother of Ahmose. It has therefore been proposed that the coffins were for two different queens: Ahhotep II (the mother of Ahmose whose coffin was found in the Cache) and a mysterious Ahhotep I (whose coffin was found at Dra Abu el-Naga). This latter Ahhotep was buried in the time of Ahmose, was honoured by the king with fine gifts of a distinctly military nature, happened to have the same name as his mother but was, in fact, somebody else – perhaps Ahmose's grandmother. This all sounds pretty incongruous to me. Beyond the fact that we have a coffin of Queen Ahhotep which does not carry the 'King's Mother' title, there is no unambiguous evidence for an earlier Ahhotep. As Marianne Eton-Kraus has, in my view, satisfactorily argued, the smaller coffin discovered by Mariette's men (and in which her body was found) may simply have been made soon after Ahhotep's marriage to Sekenenre Taa II, before she had provided the king with any offspring, whilst the larger coffin from the Royal Cache was made when she was much older, during the reign of her son. Whether the two coffins formed part of a nested pair at the original burial of the queen is a matter of conjecture. However, this does not affect the general premise that both could have been made for the same queen at different points in her career – first as 'Great Royal Wife' of Sekenenre Taa II and then as 'Mother of the King' in the reign of Ahmose. The mysterious and somewhat anomalous Ahhotep 'I' thus disappears and need not worry us.

The exotic royal objects interred with Ahhotep in the Dra Abu el-Naga golden coffin carry the cartouches of King Ahmose and, to a lesser extent, his uncle King Kamose. They were surely buried with her in recognition of the queen's undoubted contribution to the campaign against the Hyksos when her son was still a minor, in the decade before the expulsion dated to Year 11 of Ahmose.

These precious artefacts are remarkable not only on account of their exquisite craftsmanship and opulence but also for the peculiarity of their decoration.

> One piece in particular, the ceremonial axe of Ahmose, shows in its decoration some unusual features that have to be mentioned in detail. The inscriptions and depictions clearly express one thing: the king is represented as the victorious ruler over the Hyksos. On one side of the axe-blade a griffin is depicted. Griffins are known in Egyptian art from prehistory onwards, but this type shows interesting features that are found only in depictions of griffins from the Aegean. The outstanding characteristics are the beak of the vulture; the crested head; the upraised wing; and the spirals on the neck, shoulder, and wing. A similar creature is depicted in the throne room of the palace of Knossos. Although their postures are different, the shape of the heads and decoration on the shoulders are similar.[13]

33. Left: The golden axe-head found in Queen Ahhotep's coffin at Dra Abu el-Naga. It appears to have belonged to her son Ahmose who laid it in his mother's coffin at burial. On this face Pharaoh is portrayed as a recumbent sphinx grasping the severed head of an enemy in his human hand [Luxor Museum].

34. Right: The personal dagger of Ahhotep with four female heads decorating the pommel and a cow's head at the hilt with four phases of the moon on its forehead. In Pelasgian Argos the goddess Io/Ya (later given the name Hera) was represented by a heifer. The hieroglyphs on the blade are fairly crude imitations of good Egyptian text, suggesting a foreign craftsman at work.

35. Above Left: The line-drawing (top) shows the other face of Ahmose's axe with a typical 'Minoan' griffin – similar to the much larger griffin (bottom) from the priestess' throne-room at Knossos. This is just one of several images associated with the Ahhotep treasure which point to strong Aegean influence amongst her personal possessions. An Egyptian sphinx, representing Pharaoh Ahmose, on one side of the axe and a 'Minoan' griffin (a symbol of female power) on the other, perhaps representing a co-regent Queen Mother Ahhotep, princess of the Hau-nebut?

Likewise the dagger has a scene carved along its blade with a lion – in the pose known as the 'flying gallop' – chasing a fleeing calf. The rest of the same side of the blade is incised with a row of four grasshoppers whilst the other side has a line of hieroglyphs. This style of decoration is very reminiscent of the daggers found by Schliemann in the shaft graves at Mycenae in the Argolid. The handle of the dagger is also very interesting. It has what appears to be a Hathor-style cow's head (with protruding ears) at the joint with the blade. Four small round objects decorate the forehead and I would hazard a guess that they represent celestial objects – perhaps four phases of the moon. The cow's horns are crescent-shaped – a motif which, in similar examples of this type of iconography, has been associated with lunar imagery. At the other end of the hilt, the pommel is made up of four female heads, one on each side. To my mind this is clearly not a male dagger but one specially made for a female, perhaps associated with a cow-goddess and related lunar cult. This personal weapon of the queen fits perfectly into our scenario of Ya/Yahhotep as the priestess of the Pelasgian moon-goddess, Ya, and now wife of Pharaoh Telaken and mother of Yahmose.

The imagery on the golden axe and the Hathor (Pelasgian Ya) dagger with Aegean blade suggest foreign goldsmiths or artisans at work here. The pose of the king smiting a captive on one side of the axe-blade is a standard pharaonic motif, except that the king is not smiting at all because there is no pear-shaped mace or scimitar raised above his head – he is, in fact, apparently in the act of slitting the throat of his victim with a dagger. This is certainly not typical and suggests a battle scene rather than ritual slaying. The sphinx on the other side holds a severed head in its (human) left hand whereas, with similar iconography, the hand usually holds a vessel or cartouche. Such unusual variations indicate an integration of Egyptian motifs with foreign elements, resulting in a hybrid Egypto-Aegean form. Wolfgang Helck has rightly argued that even the hieroglyphs on the dagger blade were not made by a native Egyptian but rather a foreigner unfamiliar with the script.[14] All this suggests that Queen Ahhotep was not a native Egyptian.

Conclusion Nine

Queen Ahhotep, Great Royal Wife of Sekenenre Taa-ken and mother of Ahmose, was a Pelasgian princess, introduced into the 17th Dynasty royal family of Thebes probably by diplomatic marriage. The Greek tradition of Io and Telegonus may reflect this union and raises the intriguing possibility that Ahhotep was also the mother of the Hyksos king, Apophis. This would make Ahmose and Apophis half-brothers who fought for control of the delta in what was effectively an internal dynastic struggle between the ruling elites of the country.

Putting all this together we might postulate that these artefacts of Ahhotep and Ahmose, 'which show clear Aegean influence in their decoration', came from an Aegean workshop located in Egypt (probably in the delta) which had close connections with the early 18th Dynasty – in other words a royal workshop. This, for me, points us right back to Avaris and the remarkable discovery of 'Minoan' frescoes near the village of Ezbet Helmi. Was the palace at Avaris, from which this remarkable Aegean art originated, the residence of an Aegean queen of Egypt and her foreign entourage?

Chapter Eight

THE VOICE OF SETH

The Eruption of Thera — Ezbet Helmi — Perunefer
— Theran Pumice at Avaris — The Canaanite Illness
— The Theran Vulcanological Sequence

y now you will no doubt have the impression that a good deal of travelling has been necessary in order to piece together all the evidence for this story of the origins of Western Civilisation – and we are hardly a third of the way through our adventure. So far we have sailed up and down the Nile, scrambled across the fields of the Egyptian delta, explored the ruins of Phoenician Byblos, and tramped the sculpture galleries of museums in London, Cairo and Turin. Later we will be wandering through the Minoan palaces of Crete, climbing the cyclopean walls of the Mycenaean strongholds of the Peloponnese, exploring the landscape of the Trojan War, travelling the length and breadth of Anatolia (Turkey) and getting lost amongst the rolling hills of Etruria/Tuscany.

Our principal destination in this chapter is a stunning volcanic island which is the geological navel of the Aegean Sea. Of course, I am referring to Santorini – known in the Classical era as Thera but in the Bronze Age as Kalliste ('the most beautiful') or Strongyle ('the round one'). You will probably not need reminding that the reason we are all familiar with the name Thera is because of the famous eruption of its central volcano in the second millennium BC. This cataclysmic event has been linked to the legend of Atlantis, the extinction of Minoan civilisation, frost-signatures in Irish bog oaks and sulphuric acid peaks in the ice-cores of Greenland. Thera was perhaps the biggest bang in human history and it surely had a significant impact on the civilisations of the eastern Mediterranean. We will try to date the eruption archaeologically and compare that date to the scientists' favoured date for the event that has caused so

Cretan/Minoan Archaeological Periods in the Orthodox Chronology

MM IB	c. 1900-1800	–	Foundation of First Palaces (temp. 12th Dynasty)
MM II	c. 1800-1650	–	Kamares ware; destruction of First Palaces (temp. 13th Dynasty)
MM III	c. 1650-1540	–	Foundation of Second Palaces (temp. Hyksos Dynasties)
LM IA	c. 1540-1480	–	Floral Style; eruption of Thera (temp. early 18th Dynasty)
LM IB	c. 1480-1440	–	Marine Style; post eruption (temp. Hatshepsut & Thutmose III)
LM II	c. 1440-1400	–	Palace Style; Mycenaean takeover of Crete (temp. Amenhotep II & Thutmose IV)
LM IIIA	c. 1400-1330	–	(temp. Amenhotep III & Amarna period)
LM IIIB	c. 1330-1190	–	(temp. 19th Dynasty)

Abbreviations

MM =	Middle Minoan	LM =	Late Minoan
MH =	Middle Helladic (Mycenaean)	LH =	Late Helladic (Mycenaean)
MC =	Middle Cypriote	LC =	Late Cypriote
MB =	Middle Bronze (Levantine)	LB =	Late Bronze (Levantine)

MH contemporary with MM IB, MM II & MM III
LH I contemporary with LM IA
LH II contemporary with LM IB & LM II
LH IIIA contemporary with LM IIIA
LH IIIB contemporary with LM IIIB

much bitter dispute in recent years. Then I will introduce you to the fabulous artistic treasure buried beneath the pumice fall which, in turn, links us back to Egypt and the Greater Hyksos kings. For now, though, let us take a deep breath and dive into the foaming waters of 'scientific dating versus archaeology'.

Dating the Eruption of Thera

Over the past fifty years or so Aegean archaeologists have pretty much reached a consensus concerning the dates and durations of the archaeological periods in Greece, the Aegean islands, Cyprus and Crete. By cross-referencing the pottery found at the various sites throughout the region and then cross-dating the diagnostic ceramics to finds made by Petrie and, later, other archaeologists working in Egypt, the sequence on page 224 has been established within the conventional dating scheme.

For us, the crucial date is that for the transition from Late Minoan IA (LM IA) to Late Minoan IB (LM IB) which, according to most authorities, must be placed after the eruption of Thera since no LM IB pottery was found beneath the ash fall at Akrotiri. The name Akrotiri has been given to the buried town located on the south coast of Thera because it was discovered near to the modern village of Akrotiri. The ancient name of the place is unknown.

The discovery of the site was, as is often the case, a matter of local knowledge passed on to the professional archaeologists. A 'field guard' from Akrotiri, one Stathis Arvanitis, noticed that a hole in the ground had opened up within a shallow ravine at a place called Favatas, just south of the village. A thin layer of ashy soil had given way to reveal a hollow within which neatly cut stone blocks could be discerned. A large well-built house was buried here. Farmers had also experienced problems ploughing the adjacent field because of large stone blocks protruding out of the ground (these later proved to be from the upper floor of the West

House – see the next chapter). The archaeologists in Athens were duly notified.

When Professor Spiridon MARINATOS began to excavate the site in 1967, he discovered streets of wonderfully well-preserved houses beneath a thick deposit of ash and pumice. Huge quantities of large PITHOI and pots were decorated in the 'Floral Style' of LM IA with no 'Marine Style' decoration typical of the LM IB period at Knossos. Aegean specialists therefore concluded that Akrotiri must have been buried by the eruption before the LM IB styles came into fashion. In several parts of Crete a layer of Theran ash which had fallen on ancient settlements was found *beneath* the occupational

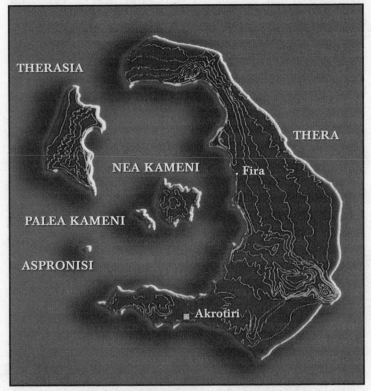

36. *The volcanic island of Kalliste/Thera shattered into fragments following the great eruption of the Late Minoan I period.*

levels containing LM IB pottery (that is, in LM IA), though there was also evidence of severe conflagration *at the end* of LM IB.

When it comes to discussing the dating controversy surrounding the eruption of Thera, it will be necessary (at least initially) to work within the conventional dating scheme – so as to avoid any confusion when dealing with published dates. Only after demonstrating that the scientific dating methods are wildly inaccurate (in respect of their interpretation) for the pre-1000 BC era, will I introduce the New Chronology date for the event. You will then see how this new eruption date, somewhat ironically, may be compatible with what is potentially the most reliable of the scientific dating techniques.

So when did the LM IB pottery style come into use? According to the archaeological evidence, its introduction is generally thought to have coincided with the middle years of the 18th Dynasty in Egypt – around the time of Hatshepsut, lasting through to the late reign of Thutmose III when LM II began and we see evidence that Minoan Crete had been taken over by Mycenaean Greeks. Thus, in the Orthodox Chronology, LM IB lasted from *circa* 1480 to 1440 BC (based on the Egyptian dating). The earlier LM IA – the period of the town of Akrotiri – must then be dated from *circa* 1540 to 1480 BC. As a result, the 'archaeological date' for the Theran eruption has been set towards the end of LM IA, in approximately 1500 BC – that is, the reign of Amenhotep I in Egyptian terms.

However, within the last couple of decades, the scientific disciplines have come up with several different ways to date the Theran eruption – principally by means of (a) narrow tree-rings in oaks and pines which grew (in Europe and the USA) during the BC era, (b) radiocarbon dating of seeds found in jars buried at Akrotiri by the volcanic ash, and (c) sulphuric acid layers found in cores drilled through the ice sheets of Greenland. These technologies have produced the following set of dates for the Thera event.

Scientific Methods for Dating the Theran Eruption	
Irish bog-oak frost signature (two narrow tree rings)	– 1628 BC
Bristlecone pines frost signature (two narrow tree rings)	– 1628 BC
Turkish pine tree rings (two wide tree rings!)	– 1628 BC
Akrotiri seed C-14 dates (immediate pre-eruption)	– 1619 BC
Dye 3 Greenland ice-core sulphuric acid peak	– 1644 BC
GRIP Greenland ice-core sulphuric acid peak	– 1636 BC
GISP 2 Greenland ice-core sulphuric acid peak	– 1623 BC

As you can see, the general date of *circa* 1630 BC arrived at for the Theran eruption by employing scientific techniques is around 130 years earlier than the date of *circa* 1500 BC determined by the archaeologists. One of the most vociferous advocates of the high scientific date amongst the archaeological community is Sturt Manning of Reading University who argues that the combined scientific evidence requires archaeologists to move their date for Thera and LM IA back into the Hyksos period.

> The main volcanic and climate (dendro) signal within the potential Thera date window lies in the mid to late seventeenth century BC. In each of the three ice-core records there is a significant volcanic eruption variously dated 1644 BC (Dye 3), 1636 BC (GRIP), or 1623 BC (GISP 2) … These ages are consistent with the radiocarbon evidence for the eruption of Thera and, in each case, a link with Thera has been proposed at some stage by the ice-core teams.[1]

The ice-core dates are grouped between 1644 and 1623 BC (possibly recording a single event, allowing for errors in reading the ice-cores) and appear to support the claim of the dendro-chronologists that a major volcanic event occurred around 1628 BC which caused a dramatic cooling of the climate, resulting in negligible growth in the trees of

California and Europe. So we are talking about a worldwide climatic event here which must have been caused by something very big. Ironically, Peter Kuniholm (who is currently preparing a dendro-chronology for Anatolia) has argued for increased growth in his trees caused by the same volcanic event! He suggested that the dust veil, which produced the marked cooling elsewhere on the globe, resulted in increased temperatures and humidity in Anatolia close to the point of cataclysm. This encouraged rapid growth in the local trees as observed in his tree-rings. In other words the effect upon Mediterranean trees was the opposite of that found in northern Europe and the USA! Of course, the event they are all proposing to link with the tree-ring evidence (both narrow and wide) is the massive eruption of Thera, because their date of 1628 BC generally ties in with the radiocarbon date for the seed from Akrotiri (1619 BC +/− 30 years). So one method of dating the Theran eruption (dendro-chronology) is, in reality, largely dependent on the other (radiocarbon dating).

However, this is not so in the case of the analysis of the Greenland ice-core acid peaks – a technology which has now become the 'silver bullet' for the Thera debate. This is because sulphuric acid layers from the various ice-cores contain tiny particles (shards) of volcanic pumice/glass which carry chemicals characteristic of the volcano from which the particles were ejected into the atmosphere before returning back to Earth in snowflakes falling on Greenland (or so the theory goes). The GISP 2 acid peak of 1623 BC, for example, holds the signature of a particular volcano. The dendro-chronologists (principally Mike Baillie of Queen's University in Belfast) and the scientist behind the original ice-core drilling project (Claus Hammer of Copenhagen University) claimed a Theran origin for the 1623 BC acid peak but, unfortunately, a recent thorough chemical analysis of the volcanic glass in the ice at this point in the core has resulted in a rejection of Thera as the source.[2] The pumice is, in fact, apparently from Aniakchak volcano in the Aleutian islands of Alaska. So the expected ice-core confirmation of the late-seventeenth-century eruption date for Thera has not materialised, leaving only the radiocarbon (C-14) evidence to support the 1628 BC dendro date.

Is the C-14 evidence sound? No, not really. There are a number of reasons to be wary of accepting the data at face value (see Appendix C in *A Test of Time* and the references there to other critiques[3]), not least of which is the reliability of the samples used for obtaining the C-14 dates.

Seeds grown in volcanic soil – especially when a nearby volcano is active – almost inevitably become contaminated by volcanic gases venting through the soil and from fissures in the ground. These gases contain 'old carbon' which, once absorbed by the living plant, can contaminate the seed samples. Thus grain grown in the fields of Thera and stored in the pithoi of Akrotiri following the harvest prior to the town's abandonment (some time before the great eruption) will certainly have been 'aged' by the absorption of old carbon, giving C-14 results several centuries older than the historical date when the grain grew and the volcano erupted. Interestingly, an experiment has already been undertaken in which modern seed samples from Santorini were submitted for C-14 analysis and, perhaps unsurprisingly, produced dates in the early Middle Ages, nearly one thousand years before the true date of the seed! So much for science – or at least our interpretation of the data produced by science.

In reality the archaeological date for the Theran eruption – placed some time in the first half of the Egyptian 18th Dynasty – remains secure, whatever the absolute dates for that dynasty actually are. Science has failed to push the date for Thera back into the Hyksos period as Manning and his colleagues would propose. However, the most recent findings from Avaris have actually forced us to consider moving the date of the eruption even lower than the early 18th Dynasty where it is usually put, placing it towards the middle of that dynasty. This would make the gap between the archaeological date and the scientific date for Thera even wider. Archaeology and science seem, in fact, to be travelling in opposite directions.[4]

The 18th Dynasty Palaces at Avaris

As I said in the *Introduction*, I travelled to Egypt in April 1991 to visit the Austrian dig at Tell ed-Daba/Avaris. There I witnessed the discovery of the now famous 'Minoan' frescoes which indicated the presence of Aegeans in the eastern delta during the late Hyksos period. That was the view of the excavators in 1991. Since then, Professor Bietak (Director of the excavations) has radically revised the dating of these frescoes – twice!

When the platform of the palace at Ezbet Helmi, a kilometre west of Tell ed-Daba, was first unearthed it was assumed that its construction and decoration were datable to the final years of the Greater Hyksos dynasty – probably during the reign of Auserre Apophis (OC – *c.* 1560 BC). This was partly because the building appeared to be associated with the great wall surrounding the fortified Hyksos stronghold of Avaris, mentioned in the second Kamose stela. However, further investigation revealed that the Helmi I (H/I) palace platform was cut into the Hyksos wall. The implication of this was that the palace must have been built during the reign of Ahmose after the Hyksos had left Avaris.

> At first, it seemed certain that the platform dated to the late Hyksos period. ... However, the results of further excavation have forced a reconsideration.[5]

Indeed, Bietak himself pointed out the similarity between the great casemate mudbrick platform of H/I and the palace platform at Deir el-Ballas, known as the 'southern palace', north of Luxor, which is known to have been occupied by Ahmose during his war against the Hyksos.

37. *The junction between the Hyksos wall and the early 18th Dynasty platform palace at Ezbet Helmi I. Bietak argues that the palace cannot be of the late Hyksos period (as previously believed) because the north-east corner of the palace cuts into the wall and must therefore post-date the latter's construction.*

So the date of the palace – and by implication the 'Minoan' frescoes – was lowered by thirty years to *circa* 1530 BC in the conventional chronology. This led to some very interesting discussions as to what might account for the Aegean presence in early 18th Dynasty Egypt. A foreign style of decoration in a palace of the Hyksos period might be expected – but in a New Kingdom Egyptian setting? That needed some explaining. Here were Aegean paintings on a royal scale – not only miniature bull-leaping scenes but pieces of plaster depicting much larger bovids.

> There were, however, also fragments of half life-size representations of bulls in stucco relief. They were found, like most of the wall-paintings, just east of the ramp which gives access from the north to the palatial platform-building ... As stucco reliefs were placed out of doors, their original location was probably near the northern entrance of the fortification wall, on one or both sides of the ramp. Such a situation would be very similar to that of the stucco relief-bulls at the northern entrance to the palace of Knossos.[6]

In addition, there were fragments containing paintings of typical Aegean flounced skirts which were scaled to fit almost life-sized 'Minoan' ladies, as well as decorative designs in the forms of labyrinthine patterns and half-rosette friezes. A tantalising fragment of a griffin wing and a leaping leopard were also found which have parallels in the Knossos and Akrotiri frescoes. The Avaris artwork pointed to state-room decor or colonnade-wall decoration (the miniature bull-leaping friezes, griffins, etc.) *and* a monumental ceremonial entrance (the large bovids and royal ladies).

> Representations of bull-leaping can be considered distinctive of royal art, as may also those of the half-rosette-triglyphic frieze, the griffins and the depiction of hierarchy in nature in the form of felines chasing other animals. Such symbolism shows clearly that the Minoan paintings at Tell ed-Daba/Avaris are to be seen in the context of a royal architecture that was of equal political importance to that of Knossos.[7]

Who ruled from here? Surely this grand building was not decorated to native Egyptian tastes? The art bore absolutely no resemblance to the rather rigid and formal Egyptian style. The H/I palace decoration flowed with effervescent life and originality. There was no mistaking its pedigree – this was full-blown Minoan/Aegean art in its most vivid form, painted by Aegean artists. Who commissioned the work? Surely not a native Egyptian pharaoh?

The remarkable discovery of 'Minoan' frescoes came hand in hand with an almost equally surprising find. Immediately adjacent to the north-east side of the H/I palace platform the archaeologists uncovered a courtyard enclosed by houses and workshops – all of which were constructed above the stratum containing the fresco fragments. By implication, this was later than Ahmose and the decorated

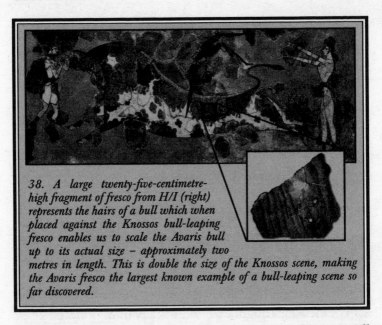

38. A large twenty-five-centimetre-high fragment of fresco from H/I (right) represents the hairs of a bull which when placed against the Knossos bull-leaping fresco enables us to scale the Avaris bull up to its actual size – approximately two metres in length. This is double the size of the Knossos scene, making the Avaris fresco the largest known example of a bull-leaping scene so far discovered.

palace built during his reign. In the corner of one small mudbrick room (see plate 7) Peter Jánosi found a pile of pumice (see plate 8) which appeared to have been collected with the intention of employing the pieces as abrasive tools. Other lumps of pumice were found in the area outside the workshop. During a subsequent visit to Tell ed-Daba in 1992, Professor Bietak asked me if I could arrange for the pumice to be analysed at the Institute of Archaeology in London, and so I took a piece back with me when I returned for the following term of study.

Unfortunately, the chemical analysis of the pumice was not undertaken by the Institute's archaeological scientists (wheels within wheels!) but Bietak managed to have the work done in Vienna a year later. His suspicions were confirmed by the results. The pumice had come from the Late Bronze Age eruption of Thera.[8] It had probably been gathered along the nearby shore of the Egyptian delta or perhaps outside the walls of Avaris – brought there by wave action following the collapse of the Theran caldera. Remember that the palace of H/I and the old Hyksos wall stood on the east bank of the Pelusiac branch of the Nile and so lumps of pumice may have been carried into the river mouth and up to the walls of Avaris. This suggested that the use of the pumice at Avaris could not have been long after the eruption, thus fixing the cataclysm to a definable archaeological and historical band, between the reigns of Ahmose I and Amenhotep II at its widest limits (a sequence of scarabs bearing the cartouches of the pharaohs between these two kings having been found in the two main H/I strata, rather neatly appearing in a stratified sequence). It is also important to stress that *no pumice has been discovered at Avaris either from strata before or after this period.* Whatever the means of its transportation to the delta, the Theran pumice appeared to be a single-period, first-half-of-the-18th-Dynasty phenomenon.

So, an archaeological date for the eruption was now finally confirmed in a datable Egyptian context – after the start of the New Kingdom and definitely not a hundred years

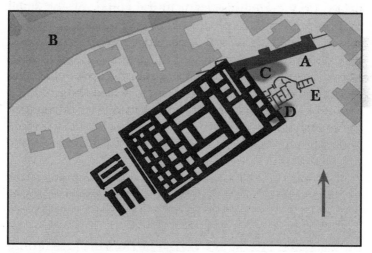

39. *The platform palace at H/1 in relation to the village houses of Ezbet Helmi, the Hyksos fortress wall (A) and the ancient course of the Nile (B). The two shaded areas (C & D) are the locations of the Aegean fresco dumps whilst the later workshop (E), in which the Theran pumice was found, is slightly further to the east.*

earlier during the Hyksos era. The date of the palace had been lowered by Bietak by more than a generation – from the late Hyksos period down into the early 18th Dynasty. Then came another shock to those of us studying the history of Avaris.

The Austrians had subsequently begun to dig about one hundred metres to the south-east of H/I (at a site close to the Didamun canal) which was designated H/II. Here they came upon another platform structure very similar to that found at H/I. This too was an 18th Dynasty palace – but the pottery from this royal building indicated that it had been built (or at least occupied) during the reign of Thutmose III (OC – *c*. 1479-1425 BC).

The archaeologists moved on, selecting a field slightly to the north-east of H/II and due east of H/I which they named H/III. Here they found the northern limit of the Thutmosid palace with its enclosure wall and entrance gateway. Digging deeper the excavators discovered that the part of the Thutmosid structure at H/III was overlying mudbrick magazines/platforms from the Hyksos period. It was here that they turned up a large limestone door-jamb carved with the cartouche of the Hyksos king, Sakil-Har. For the first time in archaeological discovery, a monumental hieroglyphic text included the title Heka-Khasut (literally 'Ruler of the Mountain Countries' but usually interpreted as 'Ruler of Foreign Lands') from which many scholars believe Manetho's term 'Hyksos' derives (although I have my doubts*).

---

* It seems to me that the term Hyksos is (as Manetho himself suggests) more likely derived from the Egyptian word for 'ruler' = Hyka, appended to the word the Egyptians used to describe the bedouin peoples of the Negeb desert in southern Palestine = Shosu, who first appear in the Egyptian texts in the early 18th Dynasty (immediately post the Hyksos period). Thus Hyka-Shosu (Graecised as Hyksos) would mean 'Ruler of the Shepherds' or 'Shepherd King'. This would be a very satisfactory etymology and entirely appropriate for the Shemau (Indo-European) rulers of the Aamu (Western Asiatic) pastoralists living in Avaris and the eastern delta.

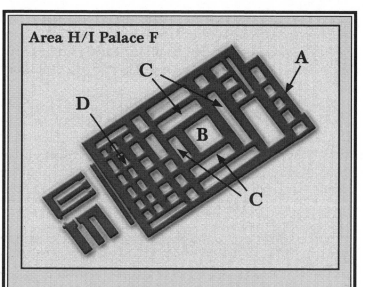

Area H/I Palace F

A
C
D
B
C

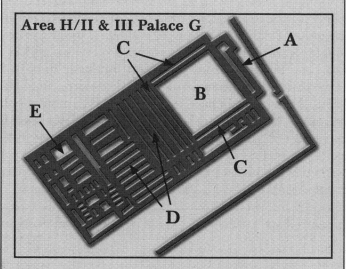

Area H/II & III Palace G

A
C
B
E
C
D

40. The two 18th Dynasty palace platforms of Ezbet Helmi. The casemate structures enable the archaeologists to visualise the walls of the palaces built on these foundations with entrance ramps (A), open courts (B), pillared porticos (C), state rooms (D) and private apartments (E). These plans are not to scale as Palace G is much bigger than Palace F.

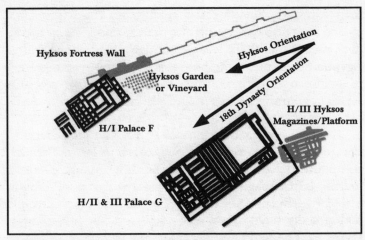

41. The alignment of the Hyksos and 18th Dynasty structures in the Ezbet Helmi environs.

So again, just as at H/I, an 18th Dynasty building was found on top of a Hyksos structure. Things became even more interesting when plans of the 18th Dynasty palaces and the earlier Hyksos constructions were set out on a single archaeological map of the Ezbet Helmi locality. It immediately became apparent that the Thutmosid palace of H/II and H/III (Palace G) was aligned in parallel with the palace at H/I (Palace F) across the fields. They seemed to be part of a grand scheme and must therefore have been built at the same time. This was confirmed when it was noted that the Hyksos fortress wall at H/I and the Hyksos magazines at H/III were also parallel but several degrees out of alignment with the 18th Dynasty structures. There were therefore two layouts to the fortified compound at Avaris – the earlier Hyksos layout and the later Thutmose III plan – but with quite different orientations.

The Port of Perunefer

Why does any of this matter? Well, because if the original Palace F at H/I belonged to the time of Thutmose III rather than Ahmose, then the Aegean frescoes decorating that palace must also date to the mid-18th Dynasty. And this, in turn, means that there was Aegean royalty residing in the Egyptian delta not at the beginning of the New Kingdom, as had been thought, but fifty years further down into the New Kingdom when Egypt was at its military zenith. And, of course, the Theran pumice would be even later.

Bietak has suggested that the New Kingdom riverine port of Perunefer was located at Avaris and that the palace compound of Ezbet Helmi – with its storage magazines and military barracks – was at the heart of that lost port.[9] This is a brilliant deduction and makes absolute sense. Egypt would undoubtedly have exploited Avaris' strategic advantages, just as the Shemau had done in the previous century. The second Kamose victory stela makes it clear that the Hyksos had established a large port on the Pelusiac branch of the Nile within easy access of the sea. From there they had sent out their vast fleet to trade the plundered wealth of Egypt with fellow Indo-European rulers in places like Sharuhen, Byblos, Ugarit, southern Anatolia, Cyprus, Crete and the Aegean islands. It was natural for the 18th Dynasty pharaohs to make use of those parts of the Hyksos maritime network that they had seized in the first fifty years of expansion under Ahmose, Amenhotep I and Thutmose I.

By the same reasoning, Bietak goes on to argue that the early 18th Dynasty pharaohs must have allied themselves with the Cretan thalassocracy in order to make use of the Minoan fleet to transport Egypt's land armies northwards in its war against the Indo-European rulers of Mitanni. Such Minoan allies would therefore have had a presence in Perunefer. This is certainly also possible and, in fact, highly probable. But we must remember that the palace at H/I was a royal establishment suggesting not merely an Aegean/Minoan naval presence in Perunefer but actual royalty. Did Thutmose III marry a Minoan princess? This seems unlikely to me. During the co-regency between Hatshepsut and Thutmose III (when Bietak now dates the first phase of the Helmi palaces), the male pharaoh was just a young boy. It is true that during the later years of Thutmose III's sole rule (nearly three decades) several Theban tombs were decorated with scenes of Keftiu delegations bearing gifts to the Egyptian court. However, close trading relations between the Aegean and Egypt – even royal gift exchange – do not have to imply marriage alliances. These same tombs show gifts being brought from Africa and Syria but nobody argues that Thutmose III married princesses from Punt or Amurru on that basis.

I am uneasy with the concept of a foreign palace in the Egyptian delta during the mid-18th Dynasty when the pharaonic empire was expanding to its limits under a series of strong militaristic pharaohs. Besides, surely Thutmose III was too young to have had an Aegean bride with her own palace, decorated in mature Minoan queenly style, during the era of Hatshepsut's dominance. So could the Austrian excavators perhaps be a little too precise in their dating? Or, put another way, might we interpret the evidence – both Egyptian and Aegean – differently?

Theran Pumice

Even more disturbing for Minoan and Mycenaean historians and archaeologists is the implication of Bietak's revised-revised dating of the Helmi palaces for the date of the Theran eruption. If the frescoed palaces belong to the time of the co-regency between Hatshepsut and Thutmose III, then the Theran pumice, found in a higher level at H/I (and subsequently at both H/II and H/III), must be later than the co-regency period. This, in turn, means that the massive Theran eruption occurred, not early in the 18th Dynasty but rather in the middle of that dynasty – at some time after the death of Hatshepsut and before the reign of Amenhotep II at which point LM II pottery was already established. However, what this does is to reduce the length of the LM IB period to virtually nothing.

Minoan Pottery and Egyptian Dating in the OC		
Start of Late Minoan IA	Late Hyksos period	(*c.* 1550 BC)
Destruction of Akrotiri	Sole reign of Thutmose III	(*c.* 1450 BC)
Start of Late Minoan IB	Late reign of Thutmose III	(*c.* 1440 BC)
Start of Late Minoan II	Last year of Thutmose III	(*c.* 1425 BC)

Such a reduction in LM IB (to around fifteen years) is at odds with the evidence from many Minoan sites (especially Mochlos) where this phase is regarded by the excavators as being of considerable duration.[10] This is therefore another good reason to re-examine Bietak's Thutmose III date for the Helmi frescoes or rethink the Aegean pottery chronologies. Both, at first glance, cannot be sustained in this new post-Helmi age.

Of Pots, Pharaohs and Precision Dating

So, how can we reconcile these historical and archaeological conflicts? Perhaps we should not so quickly abandon the original links to Ahmose. Remember that Bietak himself was quite convinced a few years ago that the platform palaces were typical of that era.

> The parallelism of platform H/I and the palace compound H/II, H/III (at Avaris) with the southern and northern palaces of the royal residence of Ahmose at Deir el-Ballas, called Sedjefa-tawy, as well as the monumental dimensions, **indicates a royal building compound which can only be associated with Ahmose.**[11]

Moreover, if – as is apparent from Bietak's public lectures and follow-up papers by his ceramic specialists[12] – the dating of the Helmi palaces is based on the associated pottery which is apparently typical of the Thutmose III era, then there is an obvious question to be asked. It is fairly well understood that a high percentage of pottery found in an excavated building derives from the very end of that building's life. This is because old pottery tends to be cleared during continuous occupation, so that only the latest pottery is left in the abandonment of a building. In the mid-1990s Bietak appeared to endorse this position based on the study of pottery found in a compound unearthed adjacent to the H/I palace.

> New excavations in 1995 have revealed to the west of platform H/I a part of a huge compound (H/V), which is without doubt another royal building project **of the first half of the 18th Dynasty**. ... The collected pottery from the corridor debris would suggest the middle of the 18th Dynasty as a *terminus ante quem* for the end of its functioning.[13]

The compound area thus ceased to function at around the time of Thutmose III or slightly later (Bietak's *terminus ante quem*), so its period of functioning must surely have been during the first half of the 18th Dynasty. This building's orientation – the same as palaces H/I and H/II – strongly suggests that the two palaces were of the same date and all could therefore have been constructed (first phase) towards the beginning of the 18th Dynasty.

In addition, given that (a) it is hard to differentiate between an early 18th Dynasty pot and a mid-18th Dynasty pot, and (b) no specific inscriptions have been found to date the palaces to Thutmose III, might we not consider moving the *construction* of the Helmi palaces back to the late reign of Ahmose where Bietak, until five years ago, thought they belonged? In 2000 he made the following firm and unequivocal statement.

> To sum up, there cannot now be any doubt that the paintings date to the early phase of the palace

of the early 18th Dynasty, and that they had
fallen off the walls before the period of Thutmose
III. This result is a conclusive one.[14]

That conclusive result lasted three years before a further
revision was instigated by the pottery specialists (in my
opinion unjustifiably so) – based on an overconfidence in
the precision of their dating techniques.

A good way to visualise the problems associated with
this new narrow dating window was offered to me by one
of the Tell ed-Daba pottery specialists, David Aston, who
explained that if two bags of Egyptian pottery sherds – one
from the early 18th Dynasty and the other from the mid-18th
Dynasty – were mixed together, the pottery specialists would
be hard pressed to separate out the two groups back into their
original bags. The reality is that archaeologists are, to a large
extent, dependent on the foreign imported pottery found
with the Egyptian material to date any early 18th Dynasty
stratigraphy bereft of monumental inscriptions. And that
(usually) means Cypriote or Cycladic wares which are not
common and come with their own dating issues.

> Absolute dating of these ceramic periods from
> artefactual evidence is far less precise than we
> would like.[15]

> ... each conventional archaeological datum at
> issue is contestable to varying degrees. Therefore,
> the conclusion must be that the ceramic evidence
> is *not* precise, only suggesting various wide
> chronological ranges, and, usually, merely a
> *terminus ante* or *post quem*.[16]

Let us consult another specialist, this time from the
discipline of Cypriote archaeology. Louise Maguire has
made the following statement in relation to the Cypriote
pottery found associated with the Ezbet Helmi palaces.

243

42. *Above left: Fragments of Cypriote pottery (Proto White Slip ware) excavated from the Tell ed-Daba late Hyksos strata [courtesy of the Austrian Archaeological Institute, Cairo].*

43. *Above right: Sherds of the distinctive Bichrome ware excavated from Tell ed-Daba Stratum D/2 (last Hyksos phase) [Cairo Museum].*

44. *Left: A Cypriote White Painted V ware bowl excavated from Tell ed-Daba Stratum D/2 [courtesy of the Austrian Archaeological Institute, Cairo].*

The Ezbet Helmi examples are in complete contrast to the Middle Bronze Age repertoire found on the main Tell (ed-Daba) area. Jugs and juglets predominate but the wares themselves are very different. From the earliest levels of the 18th Dynasty occupation we have Base Ring and White Slip wares, **which continue through to the reign of Thutmose III.** ... (However) **using Base Ring found at Ezbet Helmi to date sequences in Cyprus should not be attempted**. ... as with the White Painted ware sequence, the divisions place too much emphasis on chronological succession and the criteria originally used to define WP I and WP II are inadequate to establish a succession.[17]

So, if the Helmi Base Ring and White Slip wares found in Egypt cannot be employed to date Cypriote archaeology precisely, how can the reverse be true? How can one use the discovery of this imported pottery at Ezbet Helmi to date the palaces solely to the time of Thutmose III? Sturt Manning warns of the danger in trying to use limited quantities of Cypriote luxury wares to pin down strata in too precise a way.

> … it is very difficult, even dangerous, to reach any specific and precise chronological conclusions, and especially *phasal* correlations, from finds of a few 'exotic' traded items.[18]

Moreover, the actual chronological and stylistic development of Base Ring, White Slip and White Painted wares is also too vague to be chronologically useful. Robert Merrillees summed up the position as it stood in 2002.

> There is still no scholarly consensus on the absolute chronology of the Middle and Late Bronze Age in Cyprus.[19]

Moreover, other Cypriote pottery styles unearthed in the palace strata at Ezbet Helmi are also found in Canaan but associated with typical Middle Bronze Age artefacts.

> The characteristic wares – White Painted Pendent Line Style, White Painted Cross Line Style, White Painted V, Red on Black – are present at over forty sites in Syria and Palestine, deposited in classic MB/Hyksos assemblages – alongside toggle-pins, knives, daggers, jugs, jars, pithoi and scarabs – a standardised tomb package.[20]

Yet most scholars would be reluctant to accept a date as late as Thutmose III for the end of Middle Bronze II and the start of Late Bronze I. The usual view is that MB II ended and LB I began at the beginning of the 18th Dynasty (i.e. at the time of Ahmose). These observations made by Maguire, Manning and Merrillees might thus allow us to move the Helmi palaces back towards the beginning of the 18th Dynasty where Bietak had them in 1998.

Remember, also, that the fresco fragments were found in the garden area to the north-east of the H/I Palace F platform and *below* the courtyard, houses and workshop containing the Theran pumice. The fragments were also *below* the three sub-strata containing scarabs bearing cartouches of all the early 18th Dynasty pharaohs – *including* Ahmose. How can the frescoes date to Thutmose III if they lie below scarabs of Ahmose? Thutmose reigned half a century *after* Ahmose and so palace decoration of his reign cannot possibly predate scarabs belonging to the reign of his ancestor. Bietak's solution is to suggest that the scarabs were found associated with a workshop and may thus have been in the process of being reworked for re-use. However ingenious this idea is, it does not convince. Scarabs are simply too numerous and minuscule to make any such operation worthwhile. It is surely much easier to make new ones rather than fiddling around with these tiny second-hand sculptures. Besides, according to the findings at the time of the excavation of the courtyard and workshops adjacent to Palace F, the scarabs were in an historical sequence with those of Ahmose lower (that is, earlier) than those of Thutmose III in the stratum. This is confirmed by Bietak himself.

> Within the stratigraphy of this courtyard scarabs with the names of Ahmose, (Ahmose-)Nefertari, Amenhotep I, Thutmose III and Amenhotep II were found. Those with the names Ahmose and Amenhotep I were found immediately on a surface which may be attributed to the earliest construction phase. Those with the names of Ahmose-Nefertari and one of the scarabs with the

name of Thutmose III surfaced in a storeroom of the middle phase. From the same room several more plaques with the names Amenhotep and more than one hundred scarabs without names were found, as well as amulets, bronze objects, calcite vessels, shells and pottery which, after a preliminary analysis by Irmgard Hein, seem typical of the Thutmose III era (c. 1479-1425 BC). ... During the late phase the storeroom was finally abandoned and covered by another structure. A scarab of Amenhotep II also belongs to this phase.[21]

The royal scarabs were not all found together in the workshop but in different locations and separated by layers of deposit, indicating the passage of time between the scarab depositions. It therefore seems inescapable to me that the frescoes of the earliest phase of Palace F predate all the kings whose scarabs appear in the stratum above them and that the palace from which they came (in its initial phase) must also have been earlier than Thutmose III.

All this convinces me that there is no certainty, as yet, in determining the construction date of the first phase of the royal palaces at Ezbet Helmi, decorated with their Aegean frescoes. I believe that the known flexibility involved in dating pottery permits me to step back to the Austrian mission's original chronological placement of the construction of the 'Minoan' palaces at the time of Ahmose and Ahhotep. What I am going to propose is the following.

Phase I: The great Hyksos fortification wall of Stratum D/3 was built by Salitis at the beginning of the Greater Hyksos period (as according to Manetho). The wall was then widened and further fortified (in Stratum D/2) during the reign of Auserre Apophis (again as according to Manetho) in order further to protect Avaris from attack by the Theban 17th Dynasty warrior pharaohs.

Phase II: Following the departure of the Shemau from Avaris, Ahmose constructed a new royal compound in the original Hyksos precinct (in Stratum D/1), following a brief period of occupation by his Medjai (Nubian) mercenaries or perhaps Kushite troops stationed there in the very last years of Hyksos occupation. Their remains are represented by sub-strata D/1.2 (grain silos) and D/1.1 (graves). The H/I Palace F was built for the court of Ahmose's Pelasgian mother, Ahhotep, and decorated in Aegean style. Palace G at H/II was the king's royal residence in the north, from which he could launch military expeditions into Canaan (if required) or protect the eastern delta from any attempt at reconquest by the expelled Shemau. This was the residence of the whole royal family because Palace F was for ceremonial purposes only as, according to Bietak, it appears to have had no private apartments.[22]

Phase III: After the death of Ahhotep, in the closing years of Ahmose's reign, the Aegean frescoes were stripped from the walls and dumped in the garden area. Both palaces continued in use during the succeeding reigns of Amenhotep I, Thutmose I and II, Hatshepsut and Thutmose III (but decorated in a more traditional Egyptian style). This is the period of the deposited scarabs starting with Ahmose and extending down to the reign of Amenhotep II (Strata C/3 to C/1). The old port and military compound of Avaris was renamed Perunefer – the oft-mentioned New Kingdom riverine port with access to the Mediterranean but previously of unknown location.

Phase IV: The final eruption of Thera took place during the sole reign of Thutmose III after the death of Hatshepsut (Stratum C/3). The workshop (dated to the last decade of Thutmose III and early reign of Amenhotep II) – built above the stratum containing the frescoes – was used for light industry which included the employment of Theran pumice as an abrasive.

This historical scheme is, of course, entirely reliant on the original pre-2000 reports published by Bietak and his colleagues. If the detailed pottery evidence subsequently proves, without contest, a *construction* date in the time of Thutmose III, then this sequence will need to be revised downwards. However, as things stand at the time of writing, I believe the initial building of the twin royal palaces at H/I and H/II-III should, on historical and archaeological grounds, remain assigned to the late reign of Ahmose when Avaris had been seized from the Hyksos and his mother, Queen Ahhotep, was still alive.

The Theran Eruption in the New Chronology

So what about the New Chronology date for the eruption of Thera? Well, first I need to remind you that my position in regards to radiocarbon dating is that I can accept its use for relative dating (that is, establishing the period of time between two C-14 dated samples) but I cannot go along with this method for absolute dating (that is, establishing the period of time between a C-14 dated sample and the present). This is because I do not accept the calibration method bequeathed to the C-14 dating techniques by the dendro-chronologists. The reasons for this are too complex and voluminous to go into here, but suffice to say that many archaeologists are uncomfortable with the results produced by the calibrated radiocarbon method. A classic recent example is precisely the schism that has arisen over the dating of Thera where, even in the Orthodox Chronology, calibrated C-14 produces dates at least a century older than the archaeological and historical evidence would suggest. That is, of course, with a date for the Theran eruption in the reign of Amenhotep I (where most would set the event). However, with Bietak's new placement of the eruption in the reign of Thutmose III, the difference between the C-14-based eruption date of *circa* 1645 BC and mid-Thutmose III (OC – 1450 BC) stretches to nearly two hundred years!

I should also just point out that the *uncalibrated* C-14 dates obtained from samples dated to the BC historical period are generally about three hundred years younger than the Orthodox Chronology dates and therefore much closer to the dates calculated within the New Chronology. Perhaps we really do not need to apply the dendro calibration at all to make best use of the radiocarbon dating method!

Let me now explain my reasoning for following Bietak in placing the final cataclysmic eruption of Thera during the reign of Thutmose III. After this chronological outline I will then take you to Akrotiri – the ancient Aegean town buried under the ash-fall of Thera – in order to examine the archaeological evidence directly so that you can get to grips with the detail of the historical reconstruction.

The First Theran Event

As we saw in *Chapter Five*, Hans Goedicke has interpreted the marginal note in the Rhind Mathematical Papyrus as a reference to the effects of an eruption of Thera (but not the final cataclysm) as witnessed from the Egyptian delta. He dates this first event to Year 11 of Ahmose. I believe he is right in his interpretation of the text and have suggested that it was this ominous portent which persuaded the Hyksos to retreat from Avaris in *circa* 1181 BC (according to the NC).

Goedicke also notes another potential reference to this first Theran event in an incantation from the Hearst Medical Papyrus (of the early 18th Dynasty) which apparently describes a tsunami.

45. *The marginal text of the Rhind Mathematical Papyrus recording the activities of an Egyptian military campaign led by Ahmose (?) against the city of Avaris and one of its Shemau leaders.*

Who is wise like Re? Who knows the like of this God – when the body is coal-black with charcoal (spots) – to resist the High-God (of the northerners). **Just as Seth had banned the Great Green (Mediterranean sea)**, Seth will ban you likewise, O 'Canaanite Illness'! You shall not pass through the limbs of X, born of Y.[23]

It appears that the Black Death was introduced into Egypt by foreigners who had arrived from the north during the Hyksos era – a plague specifically associated with their high-god (presumably Baal/Hadda, weather deity and patron of sailors).

Ships' rats were the means of transporting the bubonic plague into Europe during the Middle Ages and this may have been the mechanism by which the plague entered Egypt in much earlier times. Vermin could have carried the deadly disease to the port of Avaris, in the holds of the Hyksos trading vessels, from where it spread throughout the city. By the time of Ahmose's revolt, the Hyksos elites were so weakened by the Black Death that they were in no position to resist the Egyptian pressure for long.

With Ahmose besieging Avaris, the plague rampant in the city, the voice of Seth and the tears of Isis descending from the darkened skies, all appeared lost for the Shemau and their Asiatic vassals.

Year 11, first month of Akhet, the birthday of Seth: the majesty of this god had caused his voice to be heard. (The next day,) the birthday of Isis: the sky had rained. [Rhind Mathematical Papyrus, marginal note, 3rd column]

A little over three weeks later, the Hyksos departed from Egypt *en masse*, taking the deadly plague with them, Pharaoh and his troops finally pushing the foreign occupiers out of Egyptian territory (from a safe distance).

> First month of Akhet, day 23: the King (Ahmose)
> drove the one (i.e. leader) of the Shemau/
> Shepherds towards Zile. [Rhind Mathematical
> Papyrus, marginal note, 2nd column]

This appearance of the Black Death may also explain the
reluctance of Amenhotep I and his successors to campaign
in southern Canaan to where the Hyksos enemy had
fled. The early 18th Dynasty pharaohs concentrated their
military efforts in the African south (against the Kushites)
precisely because they so feared the plague which was
rife in the Asiatic north. This first recorded reference to
bubonic plague and its effect upon historical events is
fascinating enough, but the crucial phrase for us in the
Hearst Medical Papyrus incantation is the banishing of the
Mediterranean sea by Seth – something which certainly
requires explanation. Goedicke has the answer:

> When Seth in this capacity successfully ban-
> ished the Mediterranean sea, this can only be
> understood as a reference to an intrusion of the
> sea into the delta where it came to a halt at or
> near Avaris. Needless to say, Avaris is far beyond
> the normal reach of the sea, even during the
> severe winter storms. This makes it necessary to
> see in the alluded advance of the Mediterranean
> sea, which Seth halted, a flood-wave caused
> by a natural catastrophe. There is only one
> conceivable cause for such a penetrating flood-
> wave in the eastern Mediterranean sea, namely
> seismic activity in connection with the volcanic
> island of Thera.[24]

The tidal wave dissipated just outside the walls of Avaris
having swept inland for fifty kilometres across the northern
delta. Seth was not only the god of Avaris but Egypt's
primary storm-god. Plutarch states that Seth was regarded

46. Impression from a cylinder seal excavated from Tell ed-Daba Stratum G. It depicts: the Phoenician weather-god Baal (?) or Amorite Hadda (?) standing on two mountain peaks; a bull standing on waves (?) perhaps representing the Ugaritic god El; a ship with mast; a lion and a snake (Yam?). The glyptic art of this seal suggests that the owner was from coastal Syria and had strong connections with the sea. Trade with the eastern Mediterranean was therefore already in existence in the earliest settlement at Avaris [courtesy of the Austrian Archaeological Institute, Cairo].

as a sea-god in Classical times, but this association goes back to much earlier periods. In the Ramesside era he was clearly linked with the sea, and it seems likely that this association originated in the Hyksos era when sea-trade was so prevalent during the rule of the Shemau aliens at Avaris. In effect, Seth's identification with Baal was as a protector of sailors. He was probably a sea-god in the time of Sheshi – the Anakim formerly from coastal Phoenicia. Sheshi's southern capital was the port of Sharuhen. The temple this Hyksos king (and his son Nehesi) built for Seth/ Baal at Avaris was painted blue. This may be the colour of the sky – but it is also that of the sea and most appropriate for a storm-god of both sky and sea. In this capacity Seth was clearly the god capable of banning the encroachment of the waters of chaos into Egypt beyond Avaris where he had his temple home.

The implications of this Egyptian textual evidence for the sequence of events at Akrotiri are also important. I would suggest that the initial Late Bronze Age earthquake and eruption of Thera (witnessed at the time of the Hyksos expulsion and recorded in the margin of the Rhind Papyrus) produced a tsunami which reached the Egyptian delta (referred to in the Hearst Papyrus incantation). The Egyptian storm-god (in his guise as Baal of the sea) may have 'banned the primeval waters' from reaching the temple of Seth 'Lord of Avaris', thereby saving the Hyksos city but, back at the source of the wave, the violent earthquake had resulted in the first (early LM IA) destruction of Akrotiri (*c*. 1181 BC). The town was then rebuilt and flourished for three generations (during the rest of LM IA).

The Second Theran Event

Another piece of evidence marshalled by Goedicke for his Theran hypothesis is a somewhat cryptic reference in the Speos Artemidos decree to a flooding by the 'waters of Nun' (or chaos) and a glow on the horizon (according to Goedicke's translation) during the reign of Hatshepsut.

> This was the directive of the Father of Fathers
> (i.e. Nun – the primeval waters), who came at
> his time! ... The Lord [of the glow] was over
> the coastline – although his flames were beyond
> the horizon – braziers were distributed, which
> enlarged the shrines into favoured places.

The primeval waters came in Hatshepsut's time; there was a glow beyond the horizon over the sea; and darkness came so that the people huddled in the shrines of the gods. Was this another eruption of Thera and a second tsunami? Goedicke thinks that it was the final catastrophic eruption but I believe this was the event which led to the abandonment of the town of Akrotiri prior to the big bang which tore the heart out of the island of Kalliste. That final event was to still to come, some twenty-five years later.

An earthquake more powerful than the previous one had shaken the town once again (*c*. 1120 BC). The people abandoned their homes. Akrotiri lay a shattered wreck as pumice began to rain down upon the empty ruins. The glow from this powerful eruption is what was seen in Egypt during the reign of Hatshepsut near the end of the Cretan pottery period known as Late Minoan IB. Some considerable time after (perhaps as much as two decades), a group of Therans returned to the island in an attempt to repair the damage by clearing the streets of pumice and begin anew. But the volcano soon let them know that it really was time to leave and seek permanent refuge elsewhere. A thin layer of ash was deposited on the ruins of Akrotiri which turned yellow with oxidation as time passed in the re-abandoned town.

The Third and Final Theran Event

According to the pumice evidence found at Ezbet Helmi/Avaris/Perunefer, the final blow-out of Thera and the collapse of the island could not have occurred before the reign of Thutmose III. I would more narrowly date the event to the years of Thutmose III's sole rule following the demise of his aunt, Hatshepsut. Indeed, because the pumice was found in a stratum dated by scarabs to late Thutmose III and Amenhotep II, I believe we can date the appearance of Theran pumice within the last decade of Thutmose's reign – say in or around his Year 44. This places the final cataclysmic eruption of Thera a further generation after the earthquake and eruption which occurred in Hatshepsut's reign (the second event). Bietak's pumice evidence (mid-18th Dynasty) would fit neatly into this picture.

If all the above proves to be generally on the right lines, then the massive sulphuric acid peak identified in the Greenland Dye 3 ice-core at *circa* 1090 BC would be the key scientific fingerprint we are searching for to pin down Thera. In other words, if a test were to be run to analyse the microscopic shards of volcanic glass in this acid peak (if they can be found) and the chemical breakdown shows Thera to be the cause of the acid horizon, then the debate would be over. The conventional date for Year 44 of Thutmose III is 1435 BC but the New Chronology date is currently some 335 years later in *circa* 1100 BC – within a decade of this massive Greenland spike of *circa* 1090 BC.

> ## Conclusion Ten
> The final cataclysmic eruption of LBA Thera occurred during the late reign of Thutmose III in *circa* 1100 BC. The signature of this eruption may be represented by the large sulphuric acid peak in the Dye 3 Greenland ice-core which is dated to 1090 BC +/− 20 years.

Deucalion's Flood

All the evidence for the mid-18th Dynasty Theran eruption I have put to you so far has been based on Minoan and Egyptian archaeology. But there is also an Indo-European legend originating from Classical Greece which has come down to us in the great poem of OVID entitled *Metamorphoses*. This includes the dramatic cataclysmic event known as Deucalion's Flood which drowned the world. It has often been equated with the biblical flood of Noah, clothed in Greek attire, but the event remembered in Greek legend apparently occurred much later – in Hesiod's Silver Age. Of course, we can simply dismiss this as poetic fantasy slipped into an era of prehistoric myth – but why then did Manetho (Africanus' redaction) recall that Deucalion's Flood took place in the time of Thutmose III?

47. Keftiu gift-bearers from the tomb of Rekhmire, vizier to Pharaohs Thutmose III and Amenhotep II.

> The sixth king (of the 18th Dynasty) – Misphrag-
> muthosis – (reigned) for 26 years. In his reign the
> flood of Deucalion's time occurred. [*Aegyptiaca*,
> Fr. 52]

The position of this Misphragmuthosis in the middle of the dynasty puts us in the time of Menkheperre Thutmose III (twenty-six years sole rule following Hatshepsut's death who began her reign in Year 7 of the young Thutmose III) and there is a consensus amongst Egyptologists that the Manethonian (that is Greek) name Misphragmuthosis is simply a corruption of Thutmose III's combined prenomen and nomen. According to this evidence, the great flood of Greek legend occurred in the middle years of the 18th Dynasty when Thutmose III sat on the throne of the pharaohs – precisely the time that the archaeology of Avaris pinpoints the eruption of Thera with its tsunami drowning the lands bordering the eastern Mediterranean.

Chapter Nine

A LOST EPIC

Santorini -- Akrotiri -- Thera and the End of Minoan
Crete -- The West House Miniature Fresco

n May 1999 I flew out to Athens with a group of fellow travellers to undertake a study tour of the Mycenaean and Minoan sites of the Aegean. In truth I have been very fortunate to have a number of major tour operators willing to put together trips to places I want to explore, on the basis that I accompany the tours as 'guest historian'. I get to design the itineraries and choose the sites to be visited – often going to places rarely seen by archaeologists and historians, let alone ordinary tourists. Those of you who have spent a fortnight hacking your way through undergrowth or clambering up mountains and across deserts with me, will know what it is like to join a 'David Rohl special' – not exactly a beach holiday but certainly an experience not quickly forgotten (hopefully for the right reasons). I always feel sorry for the poor local tour operators and land agents who have to work out the logistics for such expeditions. But it is all in a good cause (research and photography) and we do get to explore some of the most extraordinary places in the ancient world.

Ring of Fire

Santorini is not difficult to reach – indeed you will find it as a tourist destination in many brochures. However, few visitors either examine the geology or understand the history of this fascinating and beautiful island. Our group had spent the previous week at the Mycenaean sites of the Peloponnese before boarding the Piraeus ferry to Santorini. The sailing had already been delayed by twenty-four hours due to a violent storm blowing out to sea. Eventually we got under way with the tempest unabated, the large ship being tossed about like flotsam and jetsam in the huge swell. We were having a hard enough time enduring the wrath of Poseidon in this big tin tub; how terrifying, then, for the likes of Odysseus in his tiny wooden ship, blown across the Mediterranean in just such a storm, three thousand years earlier, on his return from the Trojan War.

> This was a man of wide-ranging spirit who had sacked the sacred town of Troy and who wandered afterwards long and far. Many were those whose cities he viewed and whose minds he came to know; many the troubles that vexed his heart as he sailed the seas, labouring to save himself and to bring his comrades home. ... For though all the gods had compassion on him, Poseidon's anger was unabated against the hero until he returned to his own land.[1]

Eventually we reached the haven of Santorini's vast caldera surrounded by towering cliffs of ash and tephra. At the centre of the circular bay was Nea Kameni – the new volcano gradually rising out of the shell of Bronze Age Kalliste. The ferry anchored in front of the main island of the broken ring and our party went ashore to spend the night in Fira (the island's capital named after ancient Thera), perched high on the edge of the cliffs (see plate 21).

The next morning we headed to the southern, outer shore of the main island to explore the buried town of Akrotiri, swathed in its blanket of ash and pumice. After the initial excavations, the Greek authorities covered the excavated area with a roof fixed on iron girders. So you enter a giant hangar of a building to walk the streets of ancient Akrotiri.

The first thing you see is the building complex named Xeste 3 and immediately come upon a score of handsomely decorated pithoi of the LM IA period. Then the path follows an anti-clockwise route up hill and down dale as you wind your way between the excavated buildings. On the left is a group of attached houses (Complex Delta) with more storage jars (once containing seeds used for radiocarbon tests) set on and in benches. A little further on from the storage jars and around the corner is a stone staircase cracked along its length by the second earthquake which preceded the major eruption of the central volcano (see plate 22).

The archaeological evidence which determines the chronology of the cataclysm has revealed the following sequence.

(1) An initial earthquake caused the collapse of many buildings. The late MM III/early LM IA town was then rebuilt and flourished during the following decades in which buildings such as the West House and the House of the Ladies were decorated with the famous Akrotiri frescoes.

(2) A second earthquake then struck – this time associated with major volcanic activity – at which point staircases cracked and buildings were overthrown. After a period of abandonment, some Therans returned to demolish the ruins and clear the streets of pumice in an attempt to rebuild. But then they completely deserted the town (due to further signs of impending disaster), settling on Crete and other islands of refuge.

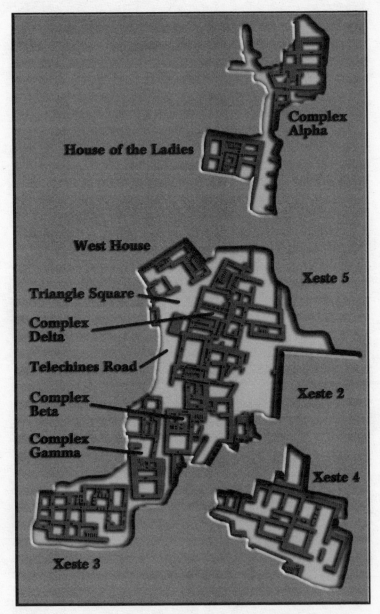

48. Plan of the excavations of Akrotiri showing the main structures so far relieved of their mantle of ash and pumice.

(3) This second earthquake was followed by two periods of abandonment of unknown length – but possibly of years rather than months. The first came immediately after the earthquake and before the attempt at demolition and rebuilding. This is demonstrated by the fact that there is evidence (admittedly contested by some) of soil deposition on top of the crumbled walls. Professor Peter Warren had been shown this layer of earth by Christos Doumas in 1970 but it was not analysed until 1972.

> Dr I. W. Cornwall analysed four samples taken from this layer and identified humus in all of them.[2] Two of them he judged to be soil *in situ* **requiring 'probably several decades' for its development**. ... It remains certain that the interval between earthquake and eruption was long enough to allow humus to develop 'probably for several decades' along the upper surface of a wall.[3]

Obviously the time taken for soil to form is considerable and, as Denys Page argues, may indicate decades between the abandonment of the town and the final catastrophic explosion (see (4) below).

The second phase of abandonment came after the short-lived and failed attempt at rebuilding. In support of a fairly long interval between the demolition phase and final eruption is the geological observation that during this second period of abandonment, a thin layer of ash fell across the island. This thin layer has a bright yellow encrustation which vulcanologists argue indicates oxidation.

> The earliest stratigraphic evidence of the (final) eruption is a very thin layer of fine pumice about 2-3 cm thick. ... Marinatos describes this layer as 'hardened like some

sort of plaster'. In fact it has an encrustation on top, and due to oxidation it has a yellow-ish appearance. **The oxidation suggests that this layer of pumice was exposed to the air for some time before it was covered by the next pumice fall.**[4]

As Doumas states, this yellowing can only be caused by exposure of the layer to the atmosphere, probably following rainfall onto the exposed surface which caused the encrustation. The fact that the yellow colouring permeates the entire layer suggests to me that the exposure period (before being buried by the main deposit) could have lasted several years.

(4) Finally, there was the massive eruption which com-pletely buried the site in a layer of pumice followed by fine volcanic ash and large basalt boulders ejected violently from the core. This event was relatively short in duration – perhaps a week at most. It is likely that it was at this time that the magma chamber collapsed and the caldera you see today was formed. It appears that Strongyle/Kalliste was already doughnut shaped (with an internal lake/bay and central volcanic island) as the consequence of a previous explosion (many centuries earlier) but it was during the final eruption that the outer ring was further broken in several places and the salt sea rushed in, causing a tidal wave which devastated the northern coastline of Crete and elsewhere.

So, Akrotiri had been unoccupied for some years *before* the major eruption. This sequence of events is very helpful for the LM IB duration debate. If the evidence of soil formation and the yellow ash layer is reliable and correctly interpreted, then the last pottery to be made or imported into Akrotiri must be dated perhaps as much as twenty years before the final eruption.

It is also worth mentioning here that the settlements of eastern Crete produced LM IA style pottery well into the LM IB period initiated at Knossos. Thus, if Akrotiri was culturally connected to the east Cretan population rather than the royal palaces in central Crete, the last pottery phase at Akrotiri may, in fact, have been influenced by the eastern part of the island where the LM IA style continued to be manufactured.[5] This would mean that the final eruption of Thera did not occur in the late LM IA but some period of time into the LM IB period at Knossos. The start of the Knossian LM IB Marine Style (the second phase of MB IB) might thus fall within the early co-regency between Hatshepsut and Thutmose III whilst Akrotiri was abandoned a decade or so later (at the time of the Theran event recorded in the Speos Artemidos decree). The dates in the New Chronology would then be as follows.

LM IA:1	c. 1210-1181	–	Akrotiri destroyed by first earthquake/volcanic eruption (Year 11 Ahmose)
LM IA:2	c. 1181-1120	–	The town rebuilt but destroyed by second earthquake/eruption (early reign of Hatshepsut)
	c. 1120-1100	–	The town abandoned; soil deposition followed by main eruption (late reign Thutmose III)
LM IB:1	c. 1130-1120	–	Continuation of Floral Style developing out of LM IA in eastern Crete
LM IB:2	c. 1120-1095	–	Knossos Marine Style (late co-regency of Hatshepsut & Thutmose III)
LM II	c. 1095-1050	–	Greek takeover of Crete (last years of Thutmose III down to Thutmose IV)

This then allows us to retain the eruption date in the time of Thutmose III (as Bietak's pumice evidence requires) whilst, at the same time, providing reasonable durations for LM IA (ninety years) and LM IB (thirty-five years) as suggested by the Aegean and Cretan archaeological evidence. But it would also help to resolve one of the great arguments amongst Minoan scholars.

The LM IB Destruction Debate

One of the most contentious debates of the last fifty years or so has been the issue of what caused the massive destructions on Crete which mark the end of LM IB. In the succeeding LM II we find nine thousand Linear B tablets at Knossos, indicating that Mycenaean Greeks had taken over from the indigenous Minoan rulers of central Crete. Prior to Michael Ventris' decipherment of Linear B – that is, before it was realised that the language of the tablets was Bronze Age Greek – it had been believed that the LM IB destructions had been caused by the Theran eruption. There was no reason to envisage a Greek invasion followed by widespread human destruction and occupation.

Towns had been wrecked and heavily burned; ash was in evidence along with signs of seismic activity; all the palaces (with the exception of Knossos) lay destroyed and abandoned. Why? How? Those were the big questions – and initially Thera seemed to provide all the answers. If the cataclysmic eruption had been the agent of the LM IB destructions on Crete, as Marinatos and others believed, then this might be the historical event behind the Atlantis legend – a sophisticated and dynamic civilisation brought down by an exploding volcano. The idea seemed attractive and plausible. Marinatos persuaded many scholars that the Atlantis legend was not merely the invention of popular culture but had a basis in real historical events. The Minoans were the Atlantean culture which oppressed and fought a war with the Greeks of Athens before being destroyed by a cataclysmic eruption of their island (Thera) which disappeared beneath the sea.

But then, as we have seen, in recent years, thanks to the excavations at Akrotiri, the date of the Theran eruption has been moved back into the LM IA period and therefore separated from the destructions on Crete at the end of LM IB by about half a century. Even so, some scholars continue to cling on to the original theory by suggesting that Thera

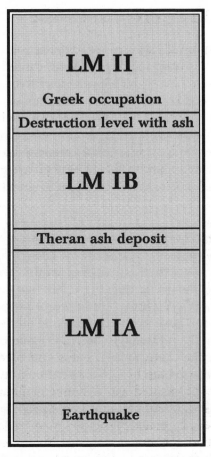

Simplified stratigraphic diagram showing the main destruction levels on Crete during the LM IA and IB periods.

laid Crete so low with its devastating effects that Mycenaean Greeks were eventually able to successfully invade and conquer the indigenous Minoans. The problem is that the 'eventually' lasted too long to make historical sense.

And, of course, there is another puzzle. If Thera's final eruption had taken place during LM IA, what volcano was responsible for the apparent ash-fall associated with the LM IB strata reported at several dig sites?

It was in this (LM IB) period that the fourth, and greatest, catastrophe occurred, a devastating disaster of enormous proportions. A tremendous wave of destruction – earthquakes, followed by fires, rains of volcanic ashes – swept over eastern Crete and buried its palaces and towns, killing a great part of the population and, of course, of the livestock, spoiling the crops and making the farmlands sterile for a considerable time. The greater part of the island was lying waste, crippled and defenceless, and was an easy prey for invaders.[6]

Surely a disaster on this scale, apparently of natural causes, had to have originated from nearby Thera. Yet Thera had apparently blown itself out at least half a century earlier, according to the latest thinking. This really makes little sense, and perhaps what we should be considering is how to reconcile the new archaeological evidence from eastern Crete, Akrotiri and Avaris with the vulcanological data from Thera. On Crete, at sites such as Zakro, volcanic ash has been found in both LM IA (sealed in the layer) and LM IB horizons. At Mochlos ash lies directly under an LM IB house. But at Pyrgos, Gournia, Mallia and Vathypetro the tephra ash was apparently found in the LM IB destruction level.[7]

It seems obvious to me that we are looking at *three* eruption events – the first (in the time of Ahmose) fairly big and causing the initial LM IA destructions at Akrotiri; the second much bigger and resulting in the abandonment of the destroyed town (during the reign of Hatshepsut); and the third massive eruption which blew out the centre of the island (in the late reign of Thutmose III). The downward shift of the final eruption from the early 18th Dynasty to the reign of Thutmose III, with a series of lesser seismic and volcanic events preceding the final LM IB catastrophe at intervals of several decades, would provide a plausible working hypothesis and explain the Egyptian records noted by Goedicke (in Year 11 Ahmose and some time in the reign of Hatshepsut). The New Chronology sequence, laid out in the previous chapter, would seem to provide a framework to accommodate all the data supplied by archaeology and the contemporary texts. We now have the final cataclysm of Thera's explosion and collapsing caldera in Year 44 of Thutmose III (NC – c. 1100 BC). The start of LM II and the arrival of the Mycenaeans at Knossos then takes place just five years later, in the closing years of Thutmose's reign (c. Year 49; NC – 1095 BC).

The Fall of Minoan Civilisation

Picture the mighty Minoan fleet hauled up on the beaches of the north Cretan shore at Katsambas and Amnissos (the ports of Knossos) and Mallia (they apparently had no stone-built harbours in those days[8]). Suddenly there is an almighty roar as the island of Thera tears itself apart. From the brightly painted palace terraces at Knossos a huge mushroom cloud is seen looming on the horizon. Within minutes, as darkness descends, a giant wave sweeps across the one hundred kilometres of sea separating Crete from Thera. The tsunami crushes the wooden ships into splinters.

The power of the Minoan thalassocracy is wiped out in a few terrifying heartbeats. The surviving Cretans try to recover but their enemies are well aware of their weaknesses – the palaces and towns, dependent on the fleet for protection, are unwalled. The Mycenaeans prepare their own ships for invasion. A decade later the Greeks are in residence at Knossos, having devastated what was left of the Minoan towns, the indigenous population retreating into the mountains of eastern Crete. The palace of Knossos is now decorated in Aegean style (a mixture of Pelasgian and Minoan elements and what the visitor sees today), ruled over by a Greek King Minos.

> ## Conclusion Eleven
>
> The final eruption of Thera was directly responsible for the collapse of the Minoan thalassocracy towards the end of LM IB. With the Cretan fleet destroyed in the Theran tsunami which struck the north coast of the island, the Minoan civilisation became vulnerable to attack from across the sea and subsequently, at the beginning LM II, the palace elites of Crete were replaced by Pelasgian overlords from the Greek mainland.

It was not just in the story of Atlantis that the ancients held some memory of the fall of Minoan Crete and the sudden death of a volcanic island. Homer may also have left us a tantalising fragment of oral memory handed down to his own time from the Brazen Age of Man.

Alkinoos, the king of the Phaiakes (the Homeric name for a people who once lived on a magical, long-lost island), having returned Odysseus to Ithaca after his years of wandering, recalled with great sadness a prediction concerning the impending doom of his people. As with most 'prophecies', the story may stem from past legendary events which, according to the principles of omen interpretation, repeat themselves in cyclical fashion. What happened in the past will happen again when the heavenly portents return. If the future is destined to replicate the past, then the Phaiakes, once living peacefully on their magic island (Kalliste?), were devastated by the wrath of Poseidon, their fleet annihilated and their city (Akrotiri?) buried in mountains of ash.[9]

> Alas! Now I remember the age-old prophecy told by my father; he said that Poseidon was once angry with us ... that Poseidon the Earth-Shaker would some day (once more) destroy the

fine ships of the Phaiakes in the misty deep, and
raise huge mountains around their city and bury
it. [*Odyssey*, Book VIII]

The West House

I left you some time ago standing in front of the cracked
staircase of Complex Delta at Akrotiri as I went off on one
of my frequent diversions. Sorry for that, but it is the nature
of the beast we are tracking in this labyrinthine quest. Let
us now continue on our walk through the ruins of the town
to see what else we can find.

About fifty metres further on, the path curves around
and down into a small triangular piazza which is at the north
end of the 'Telechines Road'. Marinatos named it 'Triangle
Square' – a geometrical contradiction if ever there was one.
Taking up the whole of the west side of this open area is
an impressive two-storeyed residence known as the 'West
House' (see plate 23).

In its heyday, you would have entered the building
through the doorway at the right side of the façade. This led
to the downstairs rooms (probably used for storage) and a
staircase leading to the upper floor where the owners of the
house once lived and slept. It was here that Marinatos found
some of the most beautiful and extraordinary frescoes which
now adorn the Theran rooms at the National Archaeological
Museum in Athens. I am going to show you around a
very special room in this house. We will have to do this in
our minds because access is not possible today and, more
importantly, because I want you to imagine the place not
only as the archaeologists found it in the 1960s but also as
it was three thousand years ago, before the earthquake and
eruption.

We are going to head straight to the largest of the upper-
storey rooms (Room 3) which in turn leads, through a door
in its north-west corner, into another large, almost square
room (Room 5) covered in plaster, vibrant with richly

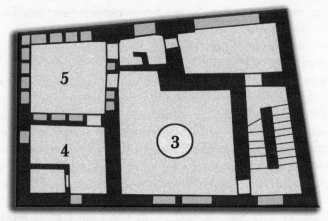

49. The upper floor of the West House at Akrotiri.

coloured frescoes. Here there are deep niches around the walls (probably cupboards and windows), set above dado panels painted to look like veined marble. In the two wall spaces not taken up by the 'cupboards' and doorways are panels depicting young, naked fishermen with their catches. On the jamb of a door leading into Room 4 (which contains a latrine) there is a fresco depicting a 'priestess' carrying a bowl of hot charcoal (almost certainly an incense burner).

Back in Room 5, above all the cupboards and middle zone frescoes, just below the beamed ceiling, there is a stunning miniature frieze which sweeps around all four walls. This long fresco (just 45 centimetres high at its maximum) is described in the official publication of the Akrotiri art – *The Wall Paintings of Thera* (published in 1992 by the current excavator, Christos Doumas, on behalf of the Thera Foundation) – as 'one of the most important monuments in Aegean art'. This statement is absolutely right on several counts.

The 'West House Miniature Fresco' or 'Frieze' (as it is now known) represents the first surviving example of recognisable narrative art in the history of European civilisation. Each element/episode in the story follows in a linear, clockwise direction around the room and, as Doumas (along with many other experts) argues, 'it is almost certain that this frieze actually represents different events in a single tale'.[10]

With the aid of photographic details (see plates 24 to 33) and a plan of the room, I am going to describe the narrative first in its visual form, then tell the story from an historical standpoint, because I believe that we have here something rather extraordinary – a famous ancient epic, the narrative of which has been lost in its literary form but which survives here at Akrotiri in its illustrative form. What I mean by this is perhaps best explained by drawing a parallel with the much later black- and red-figure ware from Corinth, which ended up in the tombs of Etruscan nobility in Italy (*c.* 600 BC), and which is decorated with selected scenes from legend – especially the Trojan War. These painted pots are the visual representations of Homer's story. But just imagine trying to interpret them if the great poet's literary works (the *Iliad* and the *Odyssey*) had not survived to the present day. Would we be in any position to understand this mysterious legend, well known to the ancients but lost to us today? The West House Miniature Fresco seems to be just such a visual of a lost legend.

I have come to this conclusion because fresco fragments of what appear to be the same or a similar story were found at three other locations in the eastern Mediterranean – on the nearby Aegean island of Kea, at Miletus in Turkey and at Tel Kabri in northern Israel. I came across the latter in a

50. *An artist's reconstruction of Room 5 in the West House with the Miniature Fresco running around the room above the niches.*

glass display case in the corridor of Tel Aviv's Department of Archaeology back in early 1995. Tim Copestake, the Director of the TV series 'Pharaohs and Kings' had taken me to Israel to meet Professor Israel Finkelstein with a view to having a 'pre-discussion' about my New Chronology theory, prior to coming back out to Israel with the camera crew to shoot the formal interviews for the programmes that summer. This sort of pre-filming visit is called a recce in the TV jargon. The two-hour discussion with Israel's leading archaeologist was fascinating but draining – it is not often that I get to be interrogated by such a sharp mind. However, the material we ranged across concerned the intricacies of Levantine archaeology and is for another time.

It was only upon leaving Finkelstein's office that I noticed the display case containing the tiny fragments of fresco. They had been set in a larger slab of modern plaster which positioned them in relation to each other. In between the restorers had outline-painted the reconstructed scene, joining lines from fragment to fragment. It was fairly clear, as Bietak later confirmed to me, that the restoration is itself based on the West House Miniature Fresco. That more complete version had been used as a guide to reconstructing the Tel Kabri pieces. Even so, there is no doubt in my mind that the tiny original fragments in Tel Aviv do represent the remains of a copy of the last scene/tableau in the Akrotiri frieze.

I took a rather poor photo of the fresco fragments from Tel Kabri, mounted in the glass case, and made a mental note of their importance. Even then, back in 1995, I was thinking about the subject matter of this book. I just did not envisage it taking ten years to write! That photograph is reproduced alongside the West House fresco (see plates) for comparison.

I have not seen the Miletus fragments at first hand but have been informed that they too closely parallel the Akrotiri scenes. Three such similar paintings, so widely dispersed around the eastern Mediterranean, clearly point to a common tradition. The original epic represented by these frescoes became a 'decorative theme' not just on Thera but in other places where the Bronze Age Indo-European elites resided. This is surely strong evidence for a bardic tale about a famous adventure in the Homeric mould – but from a much earlier age.

An Epic Adventure

The Miniature Fresco from the West House has been studied by the experts in narrative art and the consensus is that it follows a chronological sequence starting in the south-west corner, running along the west wall, turning onto the north wall, then the east wall and finally the south wall before reaching its original starting point. As we shall see, the circular nature of the narrative, which starts and ends in the south-west corner, is well suited to the upper decoration zone of the room.

Much of the west panel and the middle of the north panel have been lost because they were attached to outer walls of the house which collapsed during the second LM IA earthquake. However, a detailed study of the unmounted fresco fragments was undertaken by Christina Televantou who was able to reconstruct the scenes in convincing order. The sections which survive on the north wall make it clear that we are dealing with an epic journey, almost certainly undertaken by a fleet of ships sailing from Kalliste itself.

> From the restoration and completion of this wall-painting it is clear that the painter of the Miniature Frieze sought to tell the story of a major overseas voyage, in the course of which the fleet visited several harbours and cities, five in all, which the artist successfully depicted on the four walls of Room 5. The narrative evidently begins and ends at the south-west corner of the room, since the very few surviving fragments with representation of a town (Town I) seem to

belong at the southernmost end of the west wall, exactly above the fisherman. If, as it is logical to assume, the voyage immortalized in the wall-painting was a Theran expedition, then Town I could be identified with Akrotiri itself, the harbour from which the fleet set sail.[11]

Doumas' summary thus describes the departure *and return* to Town I which he (surely correctly) identifies with Akrotiri where the West House is located. But because almost identical fragmentary frescoes of this story have been found as far afield as Turkey and Israel, it cannot simply be a personal journey made by the owner of the West House – perceived, on account of the Miniature Fresco and other fresco clues, to have been a sea captain.

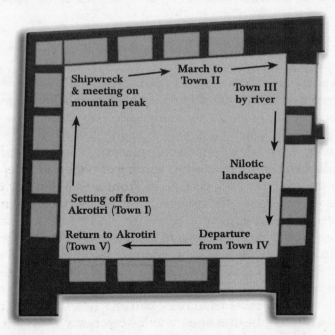

51. *Position and narrative direction of the Miniature Fresco in Room 5 of the West House at Akrotiri.*

The epic was common currency. We will return to this issue later, but first the story itself.

As I said, most of the first panel above the west wall has disappeared. There are just a few unassembled fragments to show that the ships set out across the sea from Akrotiri (Town I) and, by the end of the panel, were approaching land in a mountainous region. Here, in the lower part of the next (north) panel, we see the fleet reaching a rocky shoreline with men drowning in the turbulent sea. The narrative is telling us that part of the fleet was destroyed in a storm before it made landfall.

It is important to stress the point here that we are not dealing with a fictitious journey to imaginary destinations – this is the record of an actual voyage to specific geographical locations in the eastern Mediterranean. And I am not alone in taking this view, as these words from Professor Doumas make clear.

> The harbours illustrated in this miniature frieze are not figments of the artist's imagination; they are actual places. ... Indeed, this wall-painting may be considered as a primitive maritime chart ...[12]

On the coast (above the storm scene) there are buildings and agricultural activities (the herding of cattle and sheep). To the left, women gather water from a well. Further to the left, a separate scene shows two men of noble stature meeting on the summit of a nearby mountain. Both men are wrapped in white cloaks with red trim around the edge. The leader on the right is attended by followers dressed in similar garb whilst the leader on the left has a line of bare-chested servants behind him, wearing typical Aegean short kilts. All the figures have black hair shaped in the form of what can only be described as teddy-boy quiffs. Everything about this scene suggests a parley or meeting between two rulers of the same cultural background. Is this a formal treaty ceremony between the leader of the shipwrecked fleet and the local ruler of the mountain country (perhaps an Aryan lord of the Hurrians) cast in typical Homeric and Virgilian mould?

To the right of the buildings and below the cattle scene we see a line of soldiers marching off. They are leading us down the north panel towards the north-east corner of the chamber. Unfortunately the fresco breaks off at this point, but from unmounted fragments Televantou has been able to restore a large city (Town II) towards which the troops are heading. We then reach the beginning of the east panel where a few restored fragments depict another city (Town III) at the mouth of a river.

Returning to the marching soldiers for a moment, for they are well worth a more detailed look. The warriors carry huge rectangular shields of hide – as described by Homer for the Achaean warriors fighting in the Trojan War.

> Ajax came nearer, carrying like a tower his body-shield of seven ox-hides sheathed in bronze – a work done for him by the leather-master Tychius in Hyle: Tychius made the glittering shield with seven skins of ox-hide and an eighth of plated bronze. Holding this bulk before him Ajax Telamonius came on toward Hector and stood before him. [*Iliad*, Book VII]

The soldiers are also armed with long thrusting spears and what appear to be sword scabbards, jutting out from behind the tower shields. But, most interesting of all, each warrior sports a boar's-tusk helmet surmounted by plumes. This again is typical Aegean Bronze Age armour exactly as worn by the Cretan warrior, Meriones, and Odysseus in the *Iliad*.

> And he set on his head a leather helmet; on the inside it was drawn tight by many thongs, and

on the outside the white tusks of a gleaming-toothed boar were set well and with skill, this way and that, and in the middle a felt cap was fitted. [*Iliad*, Book X]

Having turned the corner onto the east panel we come to Town III beside a river mouth. This is the start of a fabulous frieze, occupied in its entire length by an exotic river. This scene has often been described by scholars as a 'Nilotic landscape' – without actually saying that it is the Nile itself that is depicted. But let us not play with words here. This *is* the Nile and our journeymen have reached their target destination – Egypt.

The various elements of the Nilotic landscape leave little room for doubt. The river is bounded by date-palms growing in a sandy terrain; papyrus plants shoot up from its banks; a wild cat chases a goose; a winged griffin is depicted (in the flying-gallop pose) – all elements (perhaps with the exception of the fantastical griffin) perfectly at home in the exotic and mysterious Land of the Pharaohs. What other river could it be if not the Nile?

The riverine scene is not just a decorative fresco panel (though it is a beautiful piece of art in its own right) but a clear memory of a real river perhaps visualised by the artist from personal experience. The content is informative and accurate. What is more, as Doumas notes, 'the representation is entirely cartographic (seen from above)'. In other words it is visualised as a map – a point which is all the more important when we come to discuss the city on the left side of the south wall towards which the flowing river leads us.

Christos Doumas suggests that there is one further function that must be accorded to the Nilotic river scene.

With the representation of the river on the east frieze the artist temporarily interrupts the narration of the seashore episodes and, much in the manner of the Homeric poems, inserts in the

> lay a description of the hinterland in great detail.
> ... Perhaps by interpolating this episode the
> painter wished to show the fleet's long sojourn
> in the river delta ...[13]

So time is also an element in the story. Having journeyed
across the sea and marched on land to reach a country with
a Nilotic river, the well-armed adventurers remained in this
exotic country for some considerable time. How long is, of
course, indeterminable. Doumas elaborates upon his case
for a long sojourn by suggesting that we should identify the
cities at either end of the river panel as one and the same
port – the place to which the Indo-Europeans came (Town
III) and the place from which they eventually left (Town
IV) to return to their homeland in the Aegean (Town V).

> Town IV is, like Town III, at once coastal and
> riverine, being located on the delta and it is not
> impossible that they are in fact the same place.
> Indeed through their repetition on the frieze,
> the artist perhaps sought to pick up the thread
> of the story of the fleet, after the interpolation of
> the description of the exotic land.[14]

Finally, we turn to the last (southern) wall of Room 5.
Here, at its left side, the panel of the Miniature Fresco
depicts a large city (Town IV) bordering the river. Two
men, clad in sheepskin cloaks, are talking to each other
across the river channel. Others (both men and women
– the latter represented as pale-skinned) look out from the
ramparts towards the right where we see a large fleet of
finely decorated ships setting off across the sea. These are
elaborate vessels compared with the ships which originally
set out from Town I (Akrotiri) all those months or even
years ago. They are colourfully ornamented with images
of doves and dolphins. The sterns are carved into leopards
and lions. They are large vessels with as many as forty oars.

Noblemen sit under awnings, dressed in their white, blue and red robes. Above their heads hang boar's-tusk helmets and long spears, held horizontally under the canopy by brackets. These are elite warriors heading home after their epic adventure. One smaller ten-oared boat transports a man of high rank out to the departing fleet. Doumas suggests that this is the most important figure in the scene.

> A small rowing boat in front of Town IV, with five oarsmen [actually representing only a half of the crew in this flat, single-dimension perspective] and a helmsman, seems to be carrying an important person, whose head projects above the throne-like structure on the stern. Perhaps it is a local dignitary who is accompanying the departing fleet as it leaves the harbour.[15]

This high-ranking dignitary is not the only leader in the fleet. Each of the large ships has a 'sea captain' seated within a palanquin at the stern of the vessel, next to the steersman, from where he can view the course ahead. We will take a closer look at these strange palanquins shortly, but let us return to the city of departure (Town IV) to make some important observations.

First, I want you to look closely at the river channel between the two men clad in sheepskin (see left side of plate 31). You will see that it does not, in fact, flow into the sea. The artist has intentionally painted a coastal bank between the two waters. A similar situation applies to the main river flowing from right to left on the east wall. Following it upstream around the south-east corner it merges into the background countryside and, again, does not join the river flowing to the left side of the town. Thus, although the artist cleverly blends each scene together with his brush so as not to interrupt the flow of the frieze, there is no doubting that the geography/topography of Town IV is to be treated separately from the riverine scene and the ship departure scene – even though the latter is related by proximity and by the people on the rooftops watching the leaving fleet. We must not forget that this is narrative art. Scene element A flows seamlessly into B and B flows into C within the story-telling process – both chronologically and pictographically – so there are no hard boundaries between the scenes. Televantou is clear on this point: 'there is no direct iconographical relationship between the sea of the South Frieze and the river of the East Frieze'[16] and this concept must also apply to Town IV which is separate from both.

Let us also recall what Doumas said about the Nilotic scene. It is 'cartographic', to be 'seen from above'. In other words, the artist is representing the landscape as a sort of map. If we view Town IV in the same way, we see a city boarded on its western side by a river which divides into two as it flows northwards (remember that we are looking at a topographic scene where north is up). Now compare this to the map of Avaris as determined by Josef Dorner's drill-core project undertaken on behalf of the Austrian mission at Tell ed-Daba (see plates 29 & 31). Avaris was boarded on its west by the Pelusiac branch of the Nile which divided into two channels at this point (perhaps explaining its earliest name of Rowaty – 'Mouth of the Two Ways'). Avaris is also a delta site just as Doumas argues for Town IV. The Hyksos Shemau 'foreign' elites remained in Egypt for several generations. Our Indo-European adventurers of the West House fresco sojourned in the Nilotic land for some length of time, again according to Doumas' interpretation of the frieze.

There is no doubt in my mind that the town from which the fleet is departing must be Egyptian Avaris and that the noble warriors of the Miniature Fresco are the Shemau who 'dwelt amidst the Aamu at Avaris' according to Hatshepsut's Speos Artemidos inscription.

The last part of the Miniature Fresco depicts the arrival of the fleet back at its starting point – the rocky landscape upon which the town of Akrotiri sits. Small fishing boats welcome the fleet's arrival (this in both the Akrotiri and Tel Kabri versions). The townsfolk gather on their rooftops to witness the return of their cousins from Avaris. The town of Akrotiri is bustling with life. It is a vision of Pelasgian civilisation at its peak – a civilisation made wealthy by its exploitation of Egypt's plundered treasures and natural resources. Within a few years that vibrant metropolis would be destroyed by the Earth-Shaker, its houses – resplendent in their frescoed walls – abandoned by their terrified owners. Decades later the great eruption of Thera would seal the town's fate in metres of pumice and ash, awaiting discovery by Marinatos some three millennia later.

Conclusion Twelve

The West House Miniature Fresco at Akrotiri depicts a genuine historical event in which a fleet of Indo-Europeans set out from Thera and made landfall on the Levantine coast. There they made a treaty with the local Aryan or Hurrian ruler before together setting off south towards Egypt by land and sea. Upon arrival in the Egyptian delta, the Shemau allies established themselves at Avaris, living amongst the existing Asiatic people of the late Hyksos period. The Theran contingent eventually left by sea, returning to their homeland in the Aegean islands.

Our epic legend is therefore not entirely lost to us if we piece it together from both the archaeological and pictorial remains. And we have the following Egyptian sources to illuminate our pictorial evidence from Akrotiri.

(1)   The Speos Artemidos inscription informs us that the Shemau were distinct foreigners from the Asiatic population of Avaris. They exploited the wealth of Egypt without the divine approval of the sun-god Re.

(2)   The Carnarvon Tablet and Kamose Stelae tell us of a war of liberation in which Pharaoh Kamose besieged Avaris and burnt part of the heavily laden Hyksos fleet moored in its harbour.

(3)   The biographies of Ahmose sa-Ibana and Ahmose pen-Nekhbet describe the culmination of the war of liberation under Kamose's successor, Ahmose, when the Rhind Mathematical Papyrus marginal note informs us that the Asiatics (led by a Hyksos chieftain) fled across Sinai to Sharuhen. The el-Kab tomb biographies record that the southern Levantine port fell after a three-year siege.

(4)   Manetho crucially tells us that Avaris did not fall by means of direct military assault but rather through a negotiated withdrawal of the Hyksos occupants. This, I believe, is partly what we are witnessing in the departure scene in the West House Miniature Fresco, where the fleet is carrying the Shemau warrior nobility back to their homeland after their long Egyptian adventure, to be greeted by their kinfolk on Kalliste (some eighty years before the final eruption of the volcano).

So, the master of the West House had perhaps experienced at least part of this epic journey – almost certainly the last chapter. I am sure that scholars are right to identify him as one of the sea captains of the returning fleet. That would make very good sense. He would naturally take great pride in his adventure and wish to record it (along with the events which led up to the finale) on the walls of his home. Our West House sea captain decided to settle in Akrotiri after guiding his vessel across the sea, carrying his precious cargo of noblemen from Avaris. Others, as we shall see, journeyed on to other destinations and formed the historical core for another great Helladic tradition – the legend of Danaus and Aegyptus. That story rightly belongs to the next chapter when we go in search of the origins of Mycenaean civilisation.

Our sea captain from Akrotiri surrounded himself with the memorabilia and iconography of the Hyksos adventure in Egypt – one of the most significant symbols of which was the sea captain's palanquin illustrated at the stern of every ship returning from Avaris (see plates 32 & 35). Room 4 in the West House is decorated with large frescoes of these different palanquins, showing how important they were to the captain and perhaps indicating that the individual designs were akin to heraldic emblems. Each captain had his own distinctive decoration – a different plant motif at the top of the supporting poles or a particular pattern to the bull's hide which surrounded the lower half of the palanquin.

To me, the most intriguing aspect of the palanquin design is the shape of the hide dado. In every example the upper edge is portrayed with an undulating profile – a central 'hill' and outer 'half-hills' (see plate 36). I may be fantasising here, but is this not the Egyptian hieroglyphic symbol for 'foreign lands' (Egyptian *khasut*)? The image of the aristocrat sitting in his palanquin decorated with the 'foreign-lands' symbol may surely be understood as a 'sportive writing' spelling out the title 'Heka-Khasut' – 'Ruler of Foreign Lands' – the title of the Hyksos rulers of Egypt.

It is no easy task to get one's bearings in a problem where most of the proposed solutions show a remarkable ability to be dismembered and securely entombed in one generation only to rise again to haunt later scholars. One does not ask 'where is the Indo-European homeland?' but rather where do they put it *now*?

[J. P. Mallory: *In Search of the Indo-Europeans* (London, 1989)]

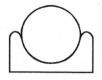

Chapter Ten

ORIGINS

Homeland of the Indo-Europeans -- The Early Hittites
-- The Arrival of the Greeks -- Keret -- Interim Summary

here did the INDO-EUROPEAN speakers come from? Where was their original homeland? When did they first 'arrive' onto the stage of history? What archaeological period marks 'the coming of the Greeks' into the Aegean? These are the questions which we will try to address in this chapter. Such enquiries necessitate briefly delving into the complex and very specialist world of Indo-European studies where comparative linguistics play such a major role. However, with all due respect to decades of scholarship, I will try to keep things fairly simple. First the 'where'.

The Indo-European Homeland

In the eighteenth century, as Europe's trading horizons stretched further around the globe, Western scholars began to study the relationship between different languages displaying elements of commonality. Contact with Persia/ Iran and the Indian sub-continent revealed remarkable linguistic parallels between Persian, the old Indic languages,

German, English and the Latin languages of the northern Mediterranean. It was realised that both vocabulary (words) and grammar (language structure) were related by descent from a common source. Back in 1786, the English poet and Justice of the High Court in Bengal, Sir William JONES, made the following statement which effectively kick-started the scholarly discipline of Indo-European studies.

> The Sanskrit language whatever be its antiquity, is of a wonderful structure; more perfect than the Greek, more copious than the Latin, and more exquisitely refined than either – yet bearing to both of them a stronger affinity, both in the roots of verbs and in the forms of grammar, than could possibly have been produced by accident; so strong, indeed, that no philosopher could examine all three without believing them to have sprung from some common source which, perhaps, no longer exists.[1]

So the ancient language of the Indus and Punjab (Pakistan and north-west India) had developed from an original mother-tongue which was also the mother-tongue of Greek and Latin and, as a consequence, the European languages. Just to give a few examples of Sanskrit and Latin cognates:

Sanskrit	Latin	Meaning
devas = deus	= 'deity' or 'god'	
pitr = pater	= 'father' (from which 'paternity' derives)	
matri = mater	= 'mother' (from which 'maternity' derives)	
ajras = ager	= 'field' (from which 'agriculture' derives)	
agni = ignis	= 'fire' (from which 'ignite' derives)	
ratha = rota	= 'chariot' (from which 'rotation' derives)	
asti = est	= 'is'	
dvau = duo	= 'two' (from which 'dual' derives)	
trya = tria	= 'three' (from which 'triple' derives)	
ecatur = quattuor	= 'four' (from which 'quarter' derives)	
sapta = septem	= 'seven' (from which 'September'* derives)	
nava = novem	= 'nine' (from which 'November'* derives)	

It was quickly accepted that the languages of Europe and parts of the East must have had a common origin. Most striking was the relationship between Persian and the Vedic hymns of India, written in Sanskrit but apparently transmitted from the distant past through oral recitation.

It was that well-known polymath, Thomas YOUNG, who first coined the term 'Indo-European' in 1816 to cover this over-arching language group and the ancient mother-tongue was soon dubbed 'Proto-Indo-European'. The people who carried the earliest manifestation of our common language out from its heartland (presumably located somewhere between East and West) thus became known as Proto-Indo-Europeans or simply the PIE people. In *The Lords of Avaris* we are specifically interested in tracing the origins of the PIE people who moved into Anatolia and the Aegean, so we need not involve ourselves here in the Germanic, Slavic or Celtic branches of the Indo-European language family. What concerns us is the initial contact between the PIE or 'Japhetic' people and the Semitic and Hamitic civilisations of the ancient world (to use their biblical nomenclature).

In the early days of Indo-European studies the general belief was that the people carrying the Proto-Indo-European mother-tongue descended into the eastern Mediterranean coastal regions from the Eurasian steppe-lands – that is, the rolling plains to the north of the Black Sea and Caucasus mountains. There, in southern Russia and the Ukraine, archaeologists would soon be unearthing an Early Bronze Age, semi-nomadic, horse-breeding culture – as evidenced by the artefacts found in low tumulus burial mounds or barrows scattered across the region.

The Proto-Indo-European tribes have long been recognised as the people who introduced both the horse and chariot into the ancient world towards the end of the

---

* Before the introduction of the months of July and August, named after Julius Caesar and Augustus, there were ten months in the Indo-European calendar of which September was the seventh and November the ninth.

third millennium BC (at the beginning of the Middle Bronze Age) and so it was only natural to identify these newcomers, bringing their revolutionary *blitzkrieg* weapons of war, with the descendants of the Early Bronze Age Aryan horsemen from southern Russia. Vere Gordon CHILDE's influential book *The Aryans*, published in 1926, was the culmination of the 'southern-Russia hypothesis'.[2] There Childe confidently asserted that the horse was 'a specifically Aryan animal' and 'the Aryan animal *par excellence*'.[3] The spoked-wheel, horse-drawn chariot was an Indo-European trademark and wherever/whenever it first appeared in a region it signified the arrival of the Aryans.

The image of a mighty horde of chariot-driving Aryans bursting upon the incumbent Bronze Age cultures, sweeping all before them, was very much to the fore in the days of nineteenth-century empire when European seafaring nations were the masters of the world. The Indo-European speakers were seen as the natural leaders of men during the Victorian Age, just as they had been thousands of years earlier when our ancestors had come from eastern Europe to conquer the Fertile Crescent, the Indian sub-continent, Anatolia and the Aegean. It was typical of nineteenth-century scholarship to perceive the 'Aryan' spirit of Western Civilisation, reinforced by 'social Darwinism', as a gift – almost by divine right – of both past and present.

> In a period before all historical knowledge, which is lost in the darkness of time, a whole race, destined by Providence to reign one day supreme over the entire Earth, grew up slowly in the primitive cradle, preparing for a brilliant future. Favoured above all others by nobility of blood and the gift of intelligence, in a natural setting which was beautiful but harsh and which yielded up its riches without lavishing them, this race was destined from the outset to create by its labours the basis of a lasting industrial

organisation, which would raise it above the
elementary necessities of life. ... this was the
race of the Aryas, who were endowed from
the beginning with the very qualities which the
Hebrews lacked, to become the civilisers of the
world ...[4]

The Greeks and Romans were our cultural ancestors, the
Germanic tribes our genetic strength and vigour – and all
were the distant progeny of the chariot-riders of the Eurasian
steppes and quite separate, ethically and genetically, from
the Semites of the Middle East. The 'Aryan Myth' and the
doctrine of Aryanism had been born.

In the 1930s such ideas were, of course, at the heart of
European nationalism which spawned Heinrich Himmler's
AHNENERBE – a state-sponsored group of academics set
the task of revealing Europe's Aryan origins (amongst
other ridiculous things). German SS archaeologists were
despatched to the east, into Romania, Poland, Greece and
occupied Russia – even into the Himalayas – in order to
dig for our ancestors and to undertake anthropological
surveys.

The southern-Russia hypothesis held sway until the post-
war years when a new theory began to take root – one less
encumbered by colonial and nationalistic sentiments. It was
first propagated a decade earlier, right at the height of the
Nazi era, by a German woman – Gertrud Hermes – whose
study of bronze bits demonstrated that this essential tool for
controlling the horse came late to eastern Europe.[5] Horse bits
first appeared south of the Caucasus mountains in the region
of eastern Anatolia and western Iran – a place which the
Classical authors came to know as the land of Armenia.

This was a mountainous zone broken by large valleys
and plains, amply supplied with several varieties of wood
from which to make spoked wheels and light chariot wagons.
This locality was also ideally situated to obtain horses from
the Eurasian steppes. A small-scale but advanced bronze

industry soon developed in the Kuro and Araxes valleys so that horse and chariot equipment could be sourced locally. The Kuro-Araxes Culture (as it is now known) of the third millennium BC was perfectly placed in geography and time to be the inventor of chariot warfare. Hermes concluded that the fast horse-drawn chariot (quite distinct from the slow oxen- or donkey-drawn solid-wheeled wagon of the Sumerians) originated in the Kura and Araxes valleys, as well as the plains around the great lakes of Sevan, Van and Urumia.[6]

The debate then switched, once more, back across the Caucasus mountains as Lithuanian scholar, Marija GIMBUTAS of Harvard University, published her theory in 1956, proposing that the now much better understood archaeology of the southern-Eurasian steppes and advanced linguistic studies proved a Proto-Indo-European *Urheimat* or 'homeland' in the tumulus burial grounds of that region.[7] The horse-breeding, nomadic peoples of the Pontic steppe thus became known as the 'Kurgan Culture' (after the Russian word for burial mound) and Gimbutas' theory was labelled the 'Kurgan Hypothesis'. She argued for tribes of semi-nomadic horsemen striking out in all directions on a mission to conquer by plunder and pillage. The linguistically based southern-Russia hypothesis was back in vogue – renamed and now supported by archaeological remains. The focus of the Kurgan Culture appeared to be in the region immediately to the north of the Black Sea at the beginning of the third millennium BC, specifically named the Yamna Culture (Kurgan IV phase). This study by Gimbutas still holds sway today but was recently challenged (in 1987) by one of the great figures in British archaeology – Lord Renfrew of Cambridge University.

Colin Renfrew has sent us heading southwards once more, across the Caucasus mountains, arguing that Proto-Indo-European origins are to be found in the Neolithic population of eastern Anatolia. The Indo-Europeans were indigenous Stone Age pastoralists and early agriculturalists who, from 7000 BC onwards, gradually spread into Europe from Anatolia, bringing the new farming techniques of the Neolithic Revolution with them (the 'Wave of Advance' theory).[8]

Professor Renfrew's hypothesis brings us right back to the area proposed by Gertrud Hermes (although extending further westwards) but to a much earlier period – thousands of years before the invention of the chariot or any Aryan military migration. In effect, Hermes' charioteers, sweeping across Europe and the Middle East at the turn of the third millennium, as envisaged by Gimbutas, were not the bringers of Indo-European language to Europe. That honour, Renfrew argues, must be accorded to the Neolithic farmers of the seventh millennium who first communicated in the Indo-European mother-tongue within the lush valleys and rolling plains of eastern Anatolia and western Iran.

Return to Eden

Those of you who read *Legend: The Genesis of Civilisation* (the second volume in the *A Test of Time* series) will immediately recognise that this is precisely where (and when) I placed the biblical Eden. It was from this legendary land that the book of Genesis claims origins for the three great linguistic groups named after the sons of Noah – Ham (the Hamitic speakers including the Egyptians and Kushites), Shem (the Semitic speakers of Mesopotamia and the Levant, including the Israelites), and Japheth (the Japhetic Indo-European speakers of Anatolia and the Aegean, including the Hittites and Greeks). Whatever you make of this story, it is the Bible's way of explaining the division of the three great language families of the ancient world from an original *Urheimat* in Eden.

In *Legend* I argued that the civilisations of Mesopotamia and Egypt were born out of a series of early migration movements that began in the mountainous region north of the Fertile Crescent. It was in the rich-soiled and well-protected upland valleys of the Zagros and Taurus ranges that agriculture and animal husbandry first took hold. Some of the tribal groupings of this land of Eden moved southwards into the broad valley of the Tigris and Euphrates to found the Mesopotamian civilisations familiar to us today – Sumer, Agade, Assyria and Babylonia. I also proposed that Pharaonic Civilisation had its roots in southern Mesopotamia and Susiana (south-west Iran) from where a secondary wave of migrants sailed to the Nile valley via the Persian Gulf and Red Sea. None of this, of course, is the subject of this book, but the legendary origins of these peoples are worth recalling in the context of our search for the legendary origins of their close neighbours – the Proto-Indo-Europeans.

The latter were the last of the Edenic tribal groups to look beyond their mountain homeland. They were still very much a part of the northern uplands in the time of Abraham when he migrated from Harran, in northern Syria, down into southern Canaan at the beginning of the Middle Bronze Age (EB-MB/MB I, NC – *c.* 1860 BC). I identified the Hurrian ruler, Tishdal, from the Zagros mountains, as the biblical Tidal, 'king of the Goiim' ('the nations'; i.e. overall leader of the mountain tribes) – one of the four Mesopotamian kings who invaded Canaan in Abraham's time [Genesis 14]. The book of Genesis calls the greatest of the four monarchs Amraphel ('voice from the mouth of the moon-god El'), king of Shinar (Sumer), whom I proposed was one and the same as Amar-Sin ('voice of the moon-god Sin'), king of Kish in Sumer (NC – *c.* 1834-1825 BC).

The Hurrians were based in the mountains north of upper Mesopotamia and Syria in the land called Subartu by the Assyrians. They did not speak an Indo-European language but were closely allied with (and subservient to) their Indo-European-speaking lords throughout history. These elite Aryan rulers were a minority in the Hurrian lands but somehow controlled the indigenous population to such a degree that, in time, they were able to establish the powerful military kingdom of Mitanni, dominating northern Mesopotamia. When these Mitannian kings began to surface in the excavated tablets of the ancient Near East (first in the Amarna Letters) it was quickly realised that their names showed remarkable connections with the heroes of the Indian RIG VEDA. In particular the names of the Mitannian rulers often included the Vedic word for chariot within them.[9]

Mitannian		Vedic		Meaning
Artatama	=	rta-dhaman	=	'whose abode is the chariot'
Tushratta	=	tvesa-ratha	=	'possessing a chariot of terror'
Sattiwaza	=	sati-vaja	=	'acquisition of booty'
Zuratta	=	su-ratha	=	'owner of a good chariot'

In addition, a treaty between a Mitannian ruler, Matiwaza, and the Hittite emperor, SHUPPILULIUMA I, was sworn in the name of several Indic deities – *Mi-it-ra* (Mitra), *Aru-na* (Varuna), *In-da-ra* (Indra) and *Na-sa-at-tiya* (Nasatya). Clearly these deities were also the gods of the Mitannian lords. What is more, the Mitannian word for 'nobleman warrior' – *marya* – is exactly the same in Vedic.[10]

I am drawn to the idea that this Aryan chariot-riding aristocracy from Mitanni (or thereabouts) are represented in the West House epic from Akrotiri, Thera, as one of the parties engaged in treaty talks atop the mountain peak. I think that this was a meeting of fellow Indo-European kings – one from the west arriving by sea, the other from the north-east arriving by land. The treaty location was probably in coastal north Syria, not far from the city of Ugarit. Just fifty kilometres north of that city is the holy mountain of northern Canaan – Mount Sapan ('Mount of Victory') or Zaphon. This 1,900-metre peak (known to the Greeks as Mount Casius, modern Gebel el-Akra) was the traditional high throne of Baal-Zaphon – Lord of the North – and, of course, he was the Hyksos supreme deity associated with Egyptian Seth. What better place to convene a meeting between two kings for the purposes of sealing a sacred covenant of conquest.

Both the epic and history suggest an alliance between the Hyksos Shemau and the Hurrians, led by their Aryan warlords. The Shemau of the Aegean, with their fleet of ships, and the Hurrians, with their fast-moving chariots, would have represented an overwhelming military force quite capable of seizing Egypt from the Anakim already ensconced there following the destruction of the Egyptian army during the Exodus catastrophe. Centuries later some of those Indo-European and Hurrian peoples were forced to leave Egypt and, according to Manetho, settle in Jerusalem. I have argued that this element of the Hyksos group are the biblical Jebusites who named their fortified city 'Mount Zion' – and which was identified as the new Mount Zaphon. This otherwise strange association of Mount Zaphon near Ugarit with Mount Zion in Jerusalem has a satisfactory explanation once we realise that the Jebusites were Baal-worshipping Hyksos from the north. It would also explain the Ugaritic myth in which Baal, god of the sea and storms, took over from El as supreme deity in northern Syria. The change from Amorite El to the mysterious new 'Lord' may reflect a change in rule at Ugarit from Semitic-speaking Canaanites to Indo-European seafarers.

This all happened during the Middle Bronze Age when the Indo-Europeans became the third great force in the political landscape of the ancient world.

The Coming of the Hittites

We have seen how the Indo-European *Urheimat* has been located in the Caucasus region with some theories placing its heart north of the mountains which lie between the Black Sea and Caspian Sea, whilst others prefer an Edenic location in eastern Anatolia/western Iran to the south of the Caucasus mountains. The recent monolithic work by the Russian linguists Tomas Gamkrelidze and Vyachislav Ivanov has strongly supported the latter view that the Proto-Indo-European language was 'initially' spoken south

52. Seal impression from the city of Kanesh (Kültepe Level II) showing a ruler riding in his chariot with two horses looking distinctly like dogs (with hooves). It has been suggested that this is because the horse was a new phenomenon in the artistic tradition of the times and the seal cutter had little idea how to represent this new form of transport with its strange horse-power.

of the Caucasus – based on their exhaustive study of Indo-European linguistics.[11]

So, I am myself going to propose that the PIE people originated in the region of Lake Van and Lake Sevan during the Neolithic period, with other linguistic groups neighbouring them to the east and south. These included:

(1) the pre-Sumerian immigrants to southern Mesopotamia who originated in the region around Lake Urumia and Sahand volcano;

(2) the Semitic-speaking tribal groups who moved down from the northern Zagros mountains (the biblical land of Havilah) to occupy northern Mesopotamia;

(3) the Kassites who eventually moved into southern Mesopotamia from their homeland in the Gaihun–Araxes valley below Savalan volcano (the land of Kush adjacent to Eden according to Genesis 2).

The PIE tribes almost certainly would have made contact with the horse-breeders of the northern Caucasus region with their kurgan burials but also, in due course, with the eastern Anatolians who had, by the end of the third millennium, secured a lucrative trading network with the

Assyrians in northern Mesopotamia. This trade principally involved Assyrian woven fabrics and tin (the source of which is unknown) for Anatolian silver and gold, and it is in the *karu* (trading posts) of eastern Anatolia that we first begin to see evidence of Indo-Europeans in the local population – but, more importantly, amongst the local city rulers.

The best known of the *karum* cities was Kanesh (modern Kültepe) over which a dynasty of kings from Kushara ruled during the OLD ASSYRIAN PERIOD. Unfortunately, we do not know where the city of Kushara was located, but these first attested Indo-European kings were the ancestors of the great Hittite empire. The tablets from Karum Kanesh are mainly letters and contracts mentioning both Semites and Indo-Europeans (the great majority[12]), but one or two other artefacts from the upper citadel of Kanesh carry the names of Indo-European kings. Most notable is a dagger blade inscribed with the words '(property of) the palace of Anitta, the king'. Anitta was the son of Pithana – the king of Kushara who conquered Kanesh. Amongst the seal impressions found in the karum below the Kanesh citadel, one depicts a chariot. This is our earliest evidence of chariot warfare in the ancient world.[13]

An ancestral King Anitta is recorded in the Hittite archives as attacking and burning the city of Hattush – capital of Pijusti, king of the Hattians. Hattush was another of the Assyrian trading centres with a colony of Assyrian merchants in residence there. The Hattians were the indigenous population of central Anatolia who spoke Hattic (a non-Indo-European language). In the Old Hittite cuneiform texts, Anitta is called 'king of Kushara and Nesha'. Scholars recognise that Nesha is the Hittite hypocoristic name for Kanesh and so we can be confident that Anitta of Kanesh, found on the dagger blade, is one and the same as Anitta of Nesha, destroyer of Hattian Hattush. According to the Hittite legend, Anitta sacked and cursed the city, before leaving it in ruins and abandoned.

It was centuries before the city was re-occupied by the first historically attested great king of the Hittites – HATTUSHILI I. The old Hattian city of Hattush was renamed Hattusha and became the capital of the Hittite kingdom. On re-occupying the city, the king took the name 'Man of Hattusha' – we do not know his original name. Late in his reign Hattushili attacked and destroyed Alalakh on the Orontes in north Syria and tried to do the same to Aleppo, capital of the kingdom of Yamkhad. In this he failed but his successor, MURSHILI I, returned to the task and successfully burnt Aleppo to finish off Yamkhad. Amazingly, the Hittite king then went on a daring *razzia* southwards along the Euphrates and sacked Babylon in 1362 BC (NC), bringing an end to the dynasty of Hammurabi. This sudden and dramatic raid proved to be a pivotal moment in Mesopotamian history since the vacuum left by the fall of the First Dynasty of Babylon was quickly filled by the Kassites, arriving in their chariots from the north. These foreigners were to rule in Babylon for the next four hundred years.

Chieftain of the Umman Manda

In the Orthodox Chronology, the reigns of Hattushili I and Murshili I fall roughly at the time of the first Hyksos kings of the 15th Dynasty in Egypt (OC – c. 1648-1590 BC). Babylon was sacked by Murshili in 1595 BC (roughly contemporary with the rule of Khyan at Avaris). However, in the New Chronology model, the situation is rather different. With a Venus Solution of 1419 BC for Year 1 of Ammisaduga of Babylon and the end of the First Dynasty of Babylon coming just fifty-seven years later we discover that the fall of Babylon in Year 37 of Samsuditana (NC – 1362 BC) took place more than half a century *before* the arrival in Egypt of Salitis – the first of the Greater Hyksos kings (NC – c. 1288 BC). Thus the collapse of mighty Babylon I could have been the initial stimulus which led to the rise of the Indo-European Greater Hyksos rulers of Avaris.

It is then surely intriguing to note that one possible etymology for Salitis (Manetho's Greek spelling) comes from the early Hittite records, where we find mention of a chieftain of the Umman Manda named Caluti.[14] The gentilic Umman Manda was used to describe the chariot aristocracy of the Hurrian and Aryan tribes. Did this Caluti/Salitis and his warriors eventually occupy the vacuum created by the Hittite raids which brought about the collapse of the powerful kingdom of Yamkhad? Did the Greater Hyksos Shemau ('aliens') take advantage of the burning of Aleppo and Alalakh by Hattushili and Murshili to first invade the coastal region of northern Syria/Phoenicia (just as the Kassites moved into Babylonia following the burning of Babylon) before moving on south, a few decades later, to Avaris?

The Indo-European Incursion

The tablets from Hattusha detailing the victories of Hattushili I and Murshili I represent the first textual evidence for the dominance of Indo-Europeans in the Middle East, but we have seen that their cousins – the Anakim from southern Anatolia – had already established themselves in the Levant by the late MB IIA (or earlier) where they had become the ruling elites of the Middle Bronze Age city-states. We see evidence of them in the new glacis-rampart defensive systems which suggest that chariots, battering-rams and composite bows were already in use at this time. The arrival of the Anakim had changed the political and military landscape utterly. However, they were illiterate and so left us no tablets to tell of their achievements. The Hittites who came from Kushara to take over Kanesh (Anitta and Pithana) were contemporaries of these early Anakim. We then have a fairly long period before the rise of Hattushili and Murshili who destroyed the kingdoms of Yamkhad and Babylon in the thirteenth century BC (in the NC). Thus the OLD HITTITE PERIOD was inaugurated at precisely the time the Israelites were seizing the Promised

Land and the Lesser Hyksos Sheshi was ruling from
Sharuhen, Memphis and Avaris.

A century later the political picture had moved on. The
Shemau were now dominating northern Egypt with their
Aryan/Hurrian chariots; the remnant Anakim remained
ensconced in the cities of the Levantine coastal plains; the
Hittites were well established in Anatolia whilst the Mitanni
(with their Hurrian army) dominated Upper Mesopotamia.
The Kassites (though not Indo-European speakers) had
occupied Babylonia; and more Aryan warlords (long
celebrated in the Rig Veda legends as the chariot aristocracy
led by Lord Indra) were heading east with the intention of
putting an end to the Indus valley civilisation of Mohenjo
Daro and Harrapa. By the close of the Middle Bronze Age
the Indo-European elites and their allies had become the
masters of the ancient world.

The Legend of Keret

There is a strange and semi-mythical tale which comes
from the archive of tablets found in the ruins of Bronze
Age Ugarit (modern Ras Shamra on the north-west coast
of Syria). It tells of a King Keret who has suffered a great
tragedy, having lost his beloved wife and several sons to
disease and war.

> (So) he enters his cubicle (and) weeps, ... His
> bed is soaked by his weeping, and he falls asleep
> as he cries. Sleep prevails over him, and he lies;
> slumber, and he reclines. And in his dreams El
> descends, in his vision the Father of Adam.[15]

The dispirited ruler is comforted by the god El who, in the
dream, tells Keret to launch a campaign against the city
of Udum in the land of Gari. This is probably Adamah
in Ga[shu]ri – biblical Geshur around the Sea of Galilee
– because, according to the Keret narrative, it takes four

days' march beyond the cities of Tyre and Sidon on the Levantine coast to reach Gari. El tells Keret that he will then be offered surrender terms by Pabel, the ruler of Udum, and he should ask only for the hand in marriage of the Princess Hurriya who will bear him several new sons and daughters. All this duly comes to pass and the king is once more content with life.

The text of the legend informs us that the capital of Keret's kingdom is Bet Khubur ('House of Khubur') in Khubur the Great which may be identified with the region of the Khabur triangle between the rivers Euphrates and Khabur. This was the heart of the Hurrian kingdom of Mitanni, ruled over by chariot-riding Aryan lords. So was Keret an early Indo-European ruler – one of the legendary Rephaim of the Ugarit texts? His military activities in Gari (part of Bashan) place him where the Ugaritic texts locate Rephaim. His second wife, Princess Hurriya, bears a name strongly suggestive of a Hurrian background. So was her father, King Pabel, another of those legendary Rephaim?

The epic of Keret is not just significant in respect of

53. *A Middle Bronze Age cylinder seal impression from north-west Syria depicting a ruler before his god (left) and with two acrobats vaulting a bull (right) – one of the earliest precursors of the sport which culminated in the famous 'Minoan' bull-leaping frescoes of Avaris and Knossos.*

Indo-European activities in the Levant but the king's very name might well also impinge on the origins of the so-called Minoan civilisation. Scholarly opinion has suggested that the Cretans who built the Old Palaces at Knossos and Phaistos may have come to the island from north-west Syria where the earliest bull-leaping iconography has its origins. If Keret was an early Aryan lord ruling over the lands of north-west Syria, then he is perfectly placed to be the eponymous ancestor of those Indo-Europeans who settled on Crete during the Middle Bronze Age – the Kretim of the Bible – who gave their name to the island of Kreta (Crete).

Interim Summary

We are about halfway into our story of the origins of Western Civilisation. We have also moved from the Middle Bronze Age (Hesiod's 'Silver Age') into a new era which Hesiod called the 'Brazen Age' – the time of the great New Kingdom empires of Egypt, Hatti and Achaean Greece, and what archaeologists refer to as the Late Bronze Age. Perhaps, then, this is an appropriate moment to summarise what we have learnt so far and to present what has to be a simplified overview of the rise of Indo-European culture.

The Arrival

One of the great historical and archaeological horizons in human history occurred at the beginning of the second millennium BC (in the NC) when most of the great Early Bronze Age cities of the civilised world collapsed into rubble and flame. This 'global' catastrophe – probably caused partly by a natural disaster involving earthquake and sudden climate change – heralds the arrival into the Levant of northerners from Anatolia and perhaps further afield who appear in the archaeological record at around the time of the transition from the Early to the Middle Bronze Ages.

In the coastal city of Byblos these newcomers build a 'palace' in the architectural style we later recognise as the Anatolian/Greek megaron. Associated with the clothing of the dead are bronze torques. These people are expert metallurgists. This suggests that they have come from the great bronze-working centre of Anaku (otherwise known as Anactoria) – a large region in western Anatolia which would later comprise the kingdoms of Lydia, Caria and Lycia [Pausanias, Book VII]. Its royal capital might have been the city of Purushanda mentioned in the Old Kingdom Hittite texts. This is the area where the champion of the Philistines in David's time may have originated. The name Goliath (Hebrew *glyt*) has long been considered to be a biblical version of the Lydian prototype Alyat (*'lyt*), recently found written in Proto-Canaanite script on an Iron Age IIA sherd excavated from the mound of Tell es-Safi – proposed as the site of biblical Gath, stronghold of the Philistines.[16]

At the same time, during the Old Assyrian period, the rulers of Ashur are encouraging trading contact between Mesopotamia and eastern Anatolia. At cities such as Kanesh – which is part of the trading network connected to Anaku – large karu (market centres) are set up. Here archaeologists have uncovered archives of cuneiform tablets associated with the Old Assyrian trading network. In these documents we begin to find, for the first time, Indo-European and Hurrian names. The local king of Kanesh – Anitta – bears just such a 'foreign' name. His city, Kanesh, gives its name to the language of the Hittite kings which was known as Nesite (*Nesili*). Anitta, king of Kanesh and

54. Seal impression of a chariot from the Old Assyrian period showing the use of nose-rings to control the chariot horses.

Kushara, is the ancestor of the first historically attested Hittite monarch, Hattushili I, who takes over the land of Hatti, beyond the River Halys in central Anatolia, and incorporates the name of the city of the Hattians into his own coronation name. Hattushili means 'Man of Hattusha'. The city of Hattusha would remain the centre of Hittite political power in the region for the next four hundred years.

Also found amongst the cuneiform tablets of the Assyrian traders based at Kanesh are a few cylinder seals depicting chariots. The horses are shown with nose-rings which are attached to reins in order to control the horse teams.

In northern Syria the Indo-Europeans are integrating with the local Amorite population, their names beginning to appear in documents from that region. By the time the Middle Kingdom pharaohs Senuseret III and Amenemhat III occupy the throne of Egypt, the Indo-European foreigners are well established in the Levant – especially along the coastal zone at cities such as Alalakh, Ugarit and Byblos.

We see them for the first time in the Bible during the wanderings of Abraham and Isaac when the ruler of Gerar is called 'king of the Philistines', even though he bears a Semitic name (Abimelek – 'father of the king'). Either he is an Amorite king ruling over a Philistine population or he has adopted an Amorite name through intermarriage and assimilation.

These early 'Philistines' (Pelastoi –ΠΕΛΑΣΤΟΙ)– that is, Anatolian Pelasgians (Pelasgoi – ΠΕΛΑΣΓΟΙ) – form a super-stratum elite, superimposed (probably by means of military superiority) upon the local Canaanite population. They are the new political and cultural force in the region, bringing with them more advanced technologies and military innovation. Their super-weapon is the horse-drawn battle-wagon or chariot driven by a specialist military elite known as the *maryanu* (an Indo-European word for 'noble warriors'). With their arrival the tactics of warfare have changed utterly. Soon they are ensconced in southern Canaan on the borders of Egypt.

The Horse

The introduction of the horse is itself a pointer to the Indo-European north as the homeland of the *maryanu* and their royal masters. The wild horse originated in the temperate steppe lands of central Europe and western Asia north of the Caucasus. The climate in the Middle East is simply too warm an environment for such animals to breed and survive naturally, so they have to be specially bred and nurtured – there being no well-watered grazing grounds for them. The domestication and use of the horse as a means of transport is detected in the archaeology of the Early Bronze Age in Europe and Asia, but we find no evidence of horses in the Fertile Crescent before the Middle Bronze Age – no bones, no horse-related artefacts, no mention of horses in the texts. However, within a relatively short period horses are everywhere in the ancient world. The horse is therefore an import into the Levant at this time – along with those who could breed, train and ride horses.

During the UR III era we hear of the *anshe.kur* (Sumerian 'ass from the mountains') distinguished from the indigenous ONAGER. This new, sleeker equid is also called *anshe.zi.zi* (Sumerian 'speedy ass').[17] This is certainly the horse which receives its name by reference to the much slower (and temperamental) *anshe*-donkey/ass. This is the speedy equid from the mountains of the north.

It is not long before this innovation becomes the preferred mode of transport for Middle Eastern royalty – always, as you might expect, the first to seize upon new technology. So we find King SHULGI of Ur III riding a horse from one city to another, much to the astonishment and delight of his subjects. The horse was so new to the region that this was akin to Queen Victoria appearing at a function in one of those new-fangled 'horseless carriages' we now call cars.

Horse bones first appear in 'exceptional quantity'[18] at 'horse-breeding' Troy in western Anatolia following the destruction of the city labelled Troy V when the

55. Stela of Prince Khonsuemwaset (son of Dudimose) and wife, seated together along with objects associated with their lives illustrated below the bench. The King's Son and Army Commander of Edfu has a pair of gloves displayed as his career motif which strongly suggests that he was a charioteer.

archaeological evidence suggests a new people took over the settlement and began to expand the place out of all recognition. The succeeding Troy VI would be the city which eventually fell to the Mycenaean Greeks many generations later after a siege of ten long years according to Homer.

In Egypt there is tantalising evidence for the use of horses in the 13th Dynasty which comes in the form of bones found at the fortress of Buhen in Nubia, prior to its fall to Kushites during the early Hyksos period. We also find illustrations of chariot gloves in the time of Dudimose – the Pharaoh of the Exodus in the New Chronology.[19] So, although relatively new to the Nile valley, the horse and chariot were apparently deployed in the pharaonic army of early Second-Intermediate-Period Egypt.

Of course, the light chariot could not have been pulled too effectively by a team of horses without that essential piece of equestrian equipment – the bit. This too was a northern invention from outside the Fertile Crescent. It was introduced soon after the Old Assyrian period and transformed military tactics, permitting the light two-wheeled chariot to be driven at great speed and with better manoeuvrability.

Hand in hand with these new military realities, brought about by the introduction of chariot warfare, comes a new kind of city defence which archaeologists have called the 'glacis rampart' – a steeply sloping bank, sometimes covered in lime plaster, separating the town walls on top of the glacis from attackers below. Examples of such defence systems are to be found in southern Canaan at Hazor, Jericho, Tell el-

Farah South and Tell el-Ajjul (Sharuhen). In several of these towns a new type of building has been discovered, dubbed the 'patrician's house'. These spacious villas may be the residences of the local Indo-European or Hurrian rulers.

New tomb architecture, in the form of stone-lined pit graves, also appears. This type of grave is otherwise attested in Anatolia – another clue as to the origins of these newcomers. By the time of the Middle Bronze IIB period, the fortified cities of the Anakim (as the Bible calls them) are prosperous trading centres enjoying close contact with Egypt. Their rulers – now completely assimilated into the Canaanite milieu – write their names in crude hieroglyphs on scarab seals. These have been found at several of the MB II settlements – especially in the cities of the coastal plain such as Sharuhen. It is from these strongholds that the first wave of Hyksos invaders seizes Egypt's eastern delta from the last pharaohs of the 13th Dynasty at the start of MB IIB.

Indo-Europeans in the Bible

In the meantime, a hundred years before that traumatic event, Asiatic groups are migrating into the Egyptian delta with the approval of the last kings of the 12th Dynasty. Among them is Jacob with his twelve sons – the eponymous ancestors of the Israelite tribes. They settle in the region around Avaris and prosper during the early years of the 13th Dynasty. Then, in the reign of Sobekhotep III, the Asiatic population is enslaved by a new sub-dynasty of pharaohs whose principal rulers are the two brothers, Neferhotep and Sobekhotep IV. It is at this difficult time for the Israelites that Moses is born.

In the reign of Dudimose (38th ruler of the 13th Dynasty) another disaster hits the eastern Mediterranean. A massive earthquake demolishes the Old Palaces on Crete (at the end of Middle Minoan II) and Egypt is 'smitten by God' as Manetho puts it. Evidence of a virulent plague has been unearthed at Avaris, represented in the archaeological record by a series of mass graves. The Asiatic population abandons the city and departs into Sinai under the charismatic leadership of Moses. At the same time the nomadic warriors of the Negeb are moving across Sinai to take advantage of a weakened Egyptian state. The Land of the Pharaohs is ripe for plunder.

The invaders – the Egyptians first call them Aamu ('Asiatics') and then later Shosu ('shepherds') – are led by the Awim and Anakim (the latter's distant origins in Anatolia). They are the Lesser Hyksos kings of Sharuhen and Avaris, the greatest of whom is Sheshi. He rules at the time of the Israelite Conquest of the Promised Land – his scarab worn by one of the last residents of Jericho before its destruction. Caleb clashes with Sheshi and his brother rulers in a series of battles during the final stage of the Conquest as the tribes of Judah and Simeon try to secure their 'inheritance' in the southern highlands and the Negeb desert. These Indo-European rulers are the descendants of the 'Philistines' of Abraham and Isaac's days, still living in the same area of southern Canaan. They have been there now for more than two centuries.

The Early Hyksos Milieu

The Indo-European phenomenon is no simple affair. It is hard to disentangle all the threads of their contact with the Levant and Egypt. A general movement of peoples, speaking different dialects of a single language group, does not necessarily stand out archaeologically in an era when the written sources are thin on the ground. Archaeologists sometimes unearth a splendid archive in their excavations – but this is rare. On the whole, the Middle Bronze Age is linguistically mute except for the names of rulers which occasionally turn up in Egyptian or Mesopotamian documents. No Indo-European archives have been found in Canaan – and one should not really expect them. If any Middle Bronze Age archive were to turn up from a

Canaanite city (Hazor comes to mind here as the most likely candidate), then it would almost certainly be in the form of cuneiform tablets. After all, it is extremely likely that the politics of the day would have been administered by indigenous scribes trained in the languages of Egypt and Mesopotamia. The Anakim from the north almost certainly came to Canaan with a language but without a developed script – something only invented in the two great centres of civilisation in the Middle East. Just as it appears that the Anakim adopted Canaanite names, so they will have adopted the method of transferring words to documents such as tablets (cuneiform) and scarab seals (hieroglyphs). There is nothing strange in this. The illiterate Indo-Europeans were skilled in warfare, not writing.

Bull-Leapers

What they did bring with them was bull-leaping and grappling. This ritualised sport almost certainly originated in the region of south-eastern Anatolia and northern Syria. It is attested during the Hyksos period at Alalakh – probably the summer residence of the king of Yamkhad whose capital was at Aleppo. And it is here that we find Indo-Europeans and Hurrians living alongside the local Amorite population. Just to the north-east of Aleppo, across the Euphrates is the region the Egyptians call Naharin which soon becomes the heartland of the Aryan kingdom of Mitanni – Egypt's great enemy for the next century.

Part Three

The Coming of the Greeks

Chapter Eleven

MINOS AND THE MINOTAUR

*Arrival of the Greeks in Crete — King Minos — Dating
the End of the Labyrinth — The Pelasgians — Bull Cults
— Human Sacrifice*

he legend of Keret has brought us across 'the wine-
dark sea' to Crete and to Arthur Evans' Minoans (as
the discoverer of Knossos dubbed the extraordinary
civilisation he revealed). The beautiful island of Crete is
scattered with fine palaces, royal villas and their associated
settlements – none of which was enclosed by fortifications.
It appears that the 'Minoans' were dependent on a powerful fleet both for their wealth and protection. The traditions
confirm this Cretan thalassocracy (empire of the sea).

In discussing the frescoes from Avaris you may have
noticed that I chose to describe them as 'Minoan' – enclosed
in quotation marks – or Aegean. The reason for this is that
I have never been entirely convinced that the so-called
Late Bronze Age 'Minoan civilisation' was either centred
on Crete or indigenous to that island. The legendary King
Minos himself was probably an amalgam of two rulers
from different time periods – one soon after the takeover
of the island by 'Greeks' in the Late Minoan II (LM II), the

other during the Heroic Age leading up to the Trojan War (LM IIIB). For purposes of identification we will call these (as historians have done in the past) 'Minos the Elder' and 'Minos the Younger' – although there may well have been a number of kings called Minos, as this famous eponym could simply be a title rather than a personal name.

Seeing Double

The traditions point to the origins of our eponymous Minos in a Late Bronze Age Pelasgian world – as the son of Europa and therefore the great-great-great-grandson of the Pelasgian princess, Io. At the same time, there is straightforward archaeological evidence (in the form of some nine thousand Linear B tablets) to indicate that Greek speakers were ruling at Knossos from LM II onwards – that is, about one hundred years or four/five generations after the Hyksos expulsion from Egypt. This Linear B Greek appears to be an early form of the AEOLIAN dialect.

So the legendary genealogies link King Minos to the Pelasgian aristocracy and place him just a few generations after the Hyksos departure from Avaris. At the same time, however, these same legends inform us that Minos was a contemporary of Theseus, future king of Athens, who killed the Minotaur in Minos' Labyrinth; and Theseus was succeeded by Menestheus who led the Athenian contingent in the war against Troy. This presents us with a real problem – well recognised by the ancient historians – and it comes down, once again, to a matter of chronology. If Minos lived three generations before Agamemnon (the son of the daughter of Catreus, son of Minos), he could not, at the same time, belong to the fourth generation after the Hyksos period. Seven generations is simply insufficient to stretch back from the Trojan War to the time of the expulsion of the Hyksos – on any chronology. So it is impossible to reconcile the interval between the two eras with a single Minos at its centre.

It seems to me that the least problematic solution is to accept Plutarch's assertion (enthusiastically supported by DIODORUS SICULUS) that there were two kings named Minos – 'the Elder' and 'the Younger' ('grandson' of the former). Plutarch had learnt this from the people of Naxos, whilst the Parian Marble, outlining a chronology for early Greece, gives a period of more than one hundred years between two kings named Minos. This allows us to connect Minos the Elder (grandson of Agenor and descendant of Epaphus) with the Hyksos, whilst Minos the Younger (great-grandfather of Agamemnon) remains firmly linked to the Trojan War heroes.

However, there still remains a serious problem with the second Minos whom legend portrays as king of Knossos with a large maritime fleet. He was the father of Princess Ariadne (Theseus' lover). His architect, Daedalus, 'built' the Labyrinth (Cretan *Labyrinthos* – 'House of the Double-Axe'). This King Minos was a contemporary of Laius and Oedipus of Cadmaean Thebes and of Aegeus, king of Athens. Aegeus' son, Theseus, fought the Minotaur in the Labyrinth. Later Minos died during an expedition to Sicily where the Knossian fleet was destroyed, allowing the Achaeans and Carians to become the new masters of the sea – again all according to legend.

Clearly the great palace of Knossos – the legendary Labyrinth – plays a major role in this story. Archaeology, on the other hand, has the palace destroyed during early LM IIIA:1 and not rebuilt on any significant scale. This is around a century before Theseus' *floruit* (LM IIIB) and therefore the time of Minos the Younger. So the conventional view is that Knossos lay in ruins when legend says that Theseus fought the Minotaur and later seized the palace of Knossos! Of course, we can simply put this down to the perils of trying to make history out of legend, but that is what we are attempting to do here and it would make no sense to have a powerful King Minos ruling at Knossos when Knossos no longer existed as a royal residence.

We will try to resolve this conundrum shortly. In the meantime I need to return to the question of the Greek takeover of central Crete and the reigns of the four (or more) Pelasgian rulers of Knossos who reigned there before Minos the Younger.

The Greeks of Knossos

As we have witnessed, at the end of Late Minoan IB (following the Theran eruption) the palace of Knossos was occupied by a new culture with clear connections to the Greek mainland. The new ceramic repertoire is classified as 'Palace Style' Late Minoan II but it is characteristic of Helladic ware from the mainland, with new pottery shapes typical of the Late Helladic IIB period. Bronze Age Greeks appear to have controlled Crete from LM II onwards until the arrival of the Dorian Greeks at the beginning of the Iron Age.

Thus the palace at Knossos, excavated and 'restored' by Arthur Evans (and what the visitor sees today) is a 'mainland Greek' rather than 'Minoan' royal residence. The construction itself is not Mycenaean as the layout and architectural style are Cretan (much having been built a century earlier during the LM I period). The wall decorations are a mixture of Mycenaean and Minoan art-forms. However, the tell-tale signs of foreign occupation are (a) the pottery found in the LM II palace at Knossos which is certainly characteristic of

56. Right: Keftiu gift-bearers from the tomb of Senenmut, Thebes; Left: the Vaphio gold cup from Bronze Age Greece [National Museum, Athens]. Note the similarity of the single-handled cups.

Helladic shapes, and (b) the appearance of Linear B tablets which Michael Ventris deciphered in 1951 and which proved to be Late Bronze Age Greek. The earlier Linear A script has not been deciphered but scholars regard it as the script of the original language spoken on Minoan Crete (possibly a dialect of Luwian from Anatolia).

Evidence from Egypt

There are other clues, this time from Egyptian Thebes, which support the Knossian evidence for a Greek occupation of central Crete in LM II. These also tell us when, in Egyptian terms, it happened.

Keftiu in the Theban Tombs

During the reigns of the pharaohs Hatshepsut, Thutmose III and Amenhotep II emissaries and offering bearers labelled 'Keftiu' (probably pronounced Kaftara) are depicted in the tombs of Theban nobles bringing gifts from the royal houses of Crete to Pharaoh's court. These envoys are at first typical of what we have come to recognise as 'Minoan' with long black hair, thin waists and colourful kilts (e.g. as portrayed in the tomb of Senenmut). They bring fabulous gifts, including single-handled cups with bull's crania decoration, similar to the famous Vapheio Cup (left) from LACEDAEMON Greece; bull's-head rhytons identical to the magnificent example from Knossos; and rhytons like the harvester's libation vessel and the conical black steatite 'Sports Rhyton' from Aghia Triada (the royal villa of Phaistos).

Anyone examining the scenes in the Theban tombs would not hesitate in labelling these Keftiu as Minoans. But in the tomb of Rekhmire an important detail appears to confirm the transition from Cretan dominance of the region to that of the Greeks. The kilts of the offering bearers were initially illustrated with typical Minoan (i.e. Cretan)

57. Detail from one of the kilts of the original 'Minoan' envoys represented in the tomb of Rekhmire. It is clear that the 'Minoan' short kilts with cod-pieces or phallus sheaths were the first garments worn by the envoys. Then, a subsequent alteration was made to paint these Cretan features out and replace them with Mycenaean/mainland Greek kilts (minus cod-pieces). The tomb owner served both Thutmose III and Amenhotep II and so it has been argued that a Mycenaean takeover of Cretan trade (contemporary with the LM II takeover at Knossos by mainland Greeks) occurred during the early reign of Amenhotep II.

cod-pieces or phallus sheaths. However, these were then painted over in order to represent standard Greek kilts (which did not include cod-pieces). Rekhmire was vizier of Egypt during the latter years of Thutmose III and the early years of Amenhotep II, and so this must have been when the Greeks arrived in Crete and usurped power from the Minoan lords of Knossos.

The Tomb of Maket at Kahun

Do you remember, right at the beginning of this book, how I described Petrie's discovery of Aegean pottery in the Tomb of Maket at Kahun? The scarabs found with the coffins ranged from Thutmose I to Thutmose III when the tomb was in use (presumably for the multiple burials of a single family). This means that the imported Aegean and Cypriote pottery associated with the burials is datable to this seventy-year period. One particular vessel – an alabastron (squat jar) decorated with ivy leaves – has been recognised as typical Mycenaean LH IIB style (contemporary with LM II). It was found in Coffin Nine which also contained a large scarab of Thutmose III (stylistically late in his reign), suggesting that LH IIB/LM II had begun before the death of this pharaoh. Aegean pottery specialist Vronwy Hankey, and scarab expert Olga Tufnell, discussed this jar in an

58. *Above: Detail from the Harvester's Rhyton; Left: The conical Sports Rhyton [Iraklion Museum].*

59. *Tribute from the Keftiu as depicted in the tomb of Rekhmire: a jar with antelope's head, a bull's-head rhyton and three copper ingots.*

important paper published in 1973 entitled: 'The Tomb of Maket and its Mycenaean Import'.

> In shape and decoration the Maket jar fits well into the LH IIB period, early rather than late. ... Coffin Nine also contained a scarab with the name of Thutmose III. ... As we have shown above, a larger scarab may point to a late date in

60. The Maket LH IIB squat jar.

the reign of Thutmose III. We therefore suggest
that the LH IIB jar was made late in that reign,
and that it was deposited in the Tomb of Maket
soon after its importation into Egypt … The
presence of an LH IIB pot in one of the latest
burials is the first support from an excavated site
in Egypt for the generally accepted view that the
Late Helladic IIB period began at the end of the
reign of Thutmose III …[1]

So, just like the Theban tomb paintings, the evidence
from the Tomb of Maket indicates that the transition from
Minoan LM IB to Greek LM II (= LH IIB) took place
late in the reign of Thutmose III. Moreover, two pieces
of pumice were found in a corner of this tomb (possibly
a burial offering made soon after the eruption of Thera)
which tends to support the archaeological evidence from
Avaris for a date during the reign of Thutmose III (rather
than at the beginning of the 18th Dynasty or earlier) for the
Theran catastrophe.

Everything points to the collapse of Minoan sea power
shortly after the final eruption of Thera in LM IB (not LM
IA), soon followed by an invasion of Crete by Greeks
marking the beginning of LM II. The so-called 'Minoan
thalassocracy' which subsequently dominated the eastern
Mediterranean for the next 170 years was therefore a Greek
affair ruled over by Greek kings resident at Knossos. The

ruler of Crete who sent eighty ships to Troy was Greek-speaking Idomeneus, grandson of Minos the Younger.

King Minos the Elder

So it seems that around the time of Thutmose III's last years on the throne of Egypt, the island of Crete was taken over by Greeks who produced their own pottery and kept palace records in their own language and script. In the New Chronology the approximate date would be 1090 BC (OC – c. 1435 BC). The takeover is confirmed by Diodorus Siculus who states that the Greek warrior Tectamus, son of Dorus, had colonised Crete with his mixed group of Aeolian and Pelasgian settlers.[2] This Tectamus was the father of Asterius, the king of Knossos who married Europa, daughter of Agenor of Tyre (descendant of Epaphus/ Apophis of Egypt). Europa gave birth to Minos the Elder who thus was the third ruler of the 'Greek' dynasty of Knossos. We would then place Tectamus and Asterius in the relatively short LM II and have them succeeded by Minos, son of Europa, in the prosperous LM IIIA (c. 1060 BC).

As we have seen, it is not just the archaeological evidence but also the Greek traditions which make King Minos the Elder a Pelasgian Greek rather than an indigenous Cretan ruler. His 'heroic' genealogy reflects this.

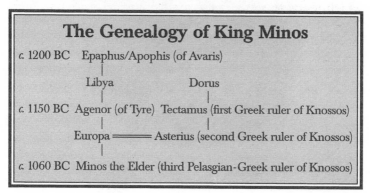

The Genealogy of King Minos

c. 1200 BC   Epaphus/Apophis (of Avaris)

Libya   Dorus

c. 1150 BC   Agenor (of Tyre)   Tectamus (first Greek ruler of Knossos)

Europa ══════ Asterius (second Greek ruler of Knossos)

c. 1060 BC   Minos the Elder (third Pelasgian-Greek ruler of Knossos)

According to legend, this Minos was the son of Europa (after whom the continent is named), the daughter of King Agenor of Phoenicia and sister of Cadmus who founded Cadmaean Thebes in central Greece. Agenor had left Egypt where his brother Belus/Baal ruled as king. Baal, of course, was represented in Egypt by Seth and Manetho tells us that the last Hyksos ruler of Avaris was named Aseth. Both Agenor and Belus were sons of Libya, daughter of Epaphus, who was the son of Io. So, according to legend, Minos the Elder was the 'fifth-generation' descendant of Io and the 'fourth-generation' offspring of a Hyksos king (Auserre Apophis) – if we have interpreted the legend correctly.

King Minos the Younger

Herodotus states that 'in the third generation after the death of Minos came the Trojan War'[3] which puts this Minos' demise (apparently in a naval campaign against Sicily) around sixty to seventy years before the fall of Troy. In *Chapter Thirteen* you will discover that the New Chronology places the start of the Trojan War in *circa* 874 BC, so the

61. Seal impression from Knossos, possibly of a ruler – perhaps Minos the Younger himself?

death of Minos the Younger should be set in *circa* 935 BC –
long after the time of Minos the Elder, son of the Pelasgian
Queen Europa.

We can therefore begin to put some approximate dates
to the legendary genealogy of the Inachus line.

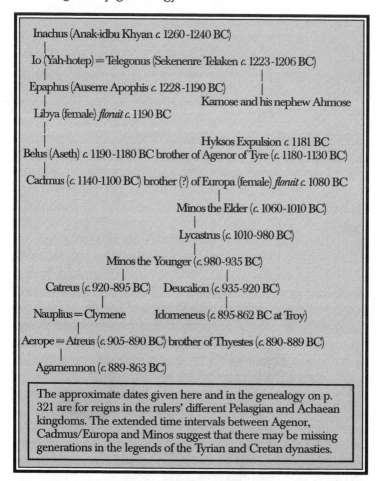

Inachus (Anak-idbu Khyan *c.* 1260-1240 BC)

Io (Yah-hotep) = Telegonus (Sekenenre Telaken *c.* 1223-1206 BC)

Epaphus (Auserre Apophis *c.* 1228-1190 BC)

Kamose and his nephew Ahmose

Libya (female) *floruit c.* 1190 BC

Hyksos Expulsion *c.* 1181 BC

Belus (Aseth) *c.* 1190-1180 BC brother of Agenor of Tyre (*c.* 1180-1130 BC)

Cadmus (*c.* 1140-1100 BC) brother (?) of Europa (female) *floruit c.* 1080 BC

Minos the Elder (*c.* 1060-1010 BC)

Lycastrus (*c.* 1010-980 BC)

Minos the Younger (*c.* 980-935 BC)

Catreus (*c.* 920-895 BC)   Deucalion (*c.* 935-920 BC)

Nauplius = Clymene   Idomeneus (*c.* 895-862 BC at Troy)

Aerope = Atreus (*c.* 905-890 BC) brother of Thyestes (*c.* 890-889 BC)

Agamemnon (*c.* 889-863 BC)

The approximate dates given here and in the genealogy on p.
321 are for reigns in the rulers' different Pelasgian and Achaean
kingdoms. The extended time intervals between Agenor,
Cadmus/Europa and Minos suggest that there may be missing
generations in the legends of the Tyrian and Cretan dynasties.

You will also discover, in *Chapter Thirteen*, that Atreus was
a contemporary of the Hittite emperor Tudhaliya IV and
therefore Ramesses II (late reign NC – *c.* 890 BC). So
Minos the Younger would have ruled in Knossos when

Haremheb and Seti I reigned in Egypt and therefore at the beginning of the pottery period known as LM IIIB (starting *c.* 980 BC). If LM II began in the last decade of Thutmose III's reign (*c.* 1090 BC), as we have determined, then a gap of roughly a century for LM IIIA is left in which to place the long-reigned Minos the Elder and his son Lycastrus. It would be consistent with our working historical model to place the reigns of Tectamus and Asterius in LM II, followed by that of Minos the Elder in LM IIIA:1, and with the reign of Lycastrus falling in LM IIIA:2. Thus we are able to put legendary names to archaeological periods in our reconstructed history of 'pre-historical' Crete.

The Late Minoan Pottery Sequence in the NC		
LM IA	*c.* 1210-1130	– Final eruption of Thera in Year 44 Thutmose III (*c.* 1100 BC)
LM IB	*c.* 1130-1090	– Marine Style at Knossos but Floral Style continuing in east Crete and Thera
LM II	*c.* 1090-1060	– Greek takeover at Knossos; the reigns of Tectamus and Asterius
LM IIIA:1	*c.* 1060-1010	– The reign of Minos the Elder
LM IIIA:2	*c.* 1010-980	– The reign of Lycastrus
LM IIIB	*c.* 980-860	– Starts with Minos the Younger and ends with Idomeneus who fought at Troy
LM IIIC	*c.* 860-815	– Ends with the Dorian occupation of Crete

The era of LM IIIA would be the perfect time to place Minos the Elder with his 'Minoan thalassocracy'. As Philip Betancourt acknowledges, this is when Crete reaches a pinnacle of wealth and population density.

> Economic prosperity increases, and the number of tombs and settlements suggests a large population during LM IIIA and IIIB. Trade

and manufacturing flourishes, but occasional setbacks like the destruction of the Knossian palace at the beginning of LM IIIA:2 interrupt the development.[4] ... The third Late Minoan period is a time of increased production and expanded commercial enterprise. Mycenaean pottery reaches both the Near East and the West in increasing quantities, vivid testimony to the thriving Aegean economy. Crete, well within the Mycenaean sphere, has a good share in this profitable trade. ... The period to the end of LM IIIB is long and stable, allowing for a considerable development. It is economically successful, and Crete supports a sizeable population.[5]

The archaeological unity of LM IIIA on Crete appropriately reflects the legendary era of the three 'brothers' Minos the Elder, Rhadamanthys and Sarpedon ruling from the royal centres of Knossos, Phaistos (Aghia Triada royal villa) and possibly Kydonia (Khania). The LM IIIB with its further expansion of trade suggests a wealthy Crete perfectly compatible with an historical Minos the Younger with a maritime hold over the eastern Mediterranean prior to his death in Sicily. However, the questionable destruction and dereliction of the palace of Knossos towards the end of LM IIIA:1 is a thorny topic which now needs to be addressed.

The Destruction of the Palace at Knossos

Clearly the royal palace of Knossos had to have been in existence and flourishing during the Late Minoan IIIB if we are to maintain a wealthy King Minos the Younger in that era (equivalent to Late Bronze IIB). After all, how can we have Theseus leaping bulls or wrestling champions within the environs of Minos' Labyrinth if that palace of the double-axe had lain in ruins for a century?

In most general history books on Minoan civilisation you will read that the Knossian palace was destroyed during or towards the end of LM IIIA:1 – that is, roughly contemporary with the Amarna period in Egypt – and not rebuilt on any major scale. Evans refers to the subsequent LM IIIB occupiers of Knossos as 'squatters'. A legendary King Minos ruling from the Knossos Labyrinth can hardly be described as a 'squatter' and must therefore have pre-dated the fall of the Egyptian 18th Dynasty according to archaeology. On the other hand, the genealogical evidence from Classical Greece places Minos the Younger just three

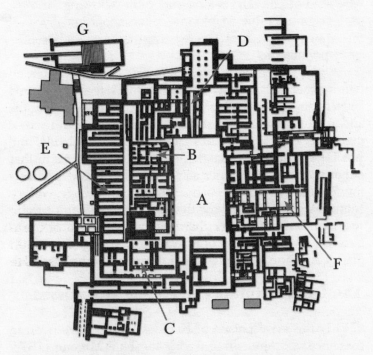

62. Plan of the vast complex of the Knossos palace with (A) the central court where the bull-leaping contests may have taken place; (B) the throne room of the high-priestess with its griffin decoration; (C) the South Propylaeum area where the first tablets were found in a larnax; (D) the north entrance flanked by a portico decorated with a raised relief bull scene; (E) the storage magazine area; (F) the Queen's Megaron; and (G) the theatre.

generations before the Trojan War, which puts him squarely in the LM IIIB – contemporary with the 19th Dynasty in Egypt. Which of these views – modern or ancient – is correct?

I believe the answer to this question lies in siding with the minority view in one of Aegean scholarship's greatest debates – what Philip Betancourt calls 'one of the most hotly contested points in Minoan archaeology' and Oliver Dickinson regards as 'one of the most important unresolved questions in Aegean prehistory'.[6] The minority opinion, first voiced by Blegen, is regularly ignored in popular books which tend to favour the consensus, but I believe the logic of the non-orthodox argument is convincing and resolves the Minos problem at a stroke. Let me first explain the archaeological issues.

When Arthur Evans excavated Knossos in the 1900s he found a dramatic destruction layer in which were unearthed large quantities of Linear B tablets (in different locations) and various deposits of pottery. He determined – based on the appearance of a collection of fine LM II (and some LM IIIA:1) vessels – that the palace was destroyed in that pottery period and only partially reoccupied in LM IIIB on a much less significant scale – hardly suitable for the legendary Minos. And so this became the standard view.

However, in 1960, Leonard Palmer, Professor of Comparative Philology at Oxford, restudied the excavation notes and came to the view that this was not the case.[7] He found that Evans and his assistant Duncan Mackenzie had described the tablets as being in a destruction layer which contained three types of pottery – two of which belonged to LM IIIB – that is, later than LM IIIA:1. He therefore concluded that the palace was destroyed at the end of LM IIIB rather than two centuries earlier in LM II (later revised to LM IIIA:1).

> The detailed scrutiny of the source material has shown that no deposit of tablets or sealings was

found associated with a cache of LM II vessels or sherds. On the other hand, we have a most striking instance of the contrary – the 'great deposit' (of Linear B tablets) entangled with a large hoard of intact LM IIIB double-amphorae.[8]

... masses of whole LM III pots were found, in many parts of the palace, juxtaposed with massive deposits of tablets, but in no single case a whole LM II vessel.[9]

One of the main caches of tablets was unearthed within the South Propylaeum area, in a small room containing a *larnax* (clay bath-tub). Evans' personal note-book, used to record the finds as they were excavated in 1900, describes the discovery.

6 April 1900: The clearing of the cement flooring adjacent to the column base still continues today. The contiguous corridor running NS to the W of the portico with the column bases was also this morning being further cleared down to the floor

63. *A typical larnax 'bath-tub' from the Late Minoan III period [Ayios Nikolaos Archaeological Museum].*

Plate 38: The Horns of Consecration at Knossos palace.

Plate 39: Portico of the north entrance to the palace of Knossos decorated with the painted relief of a charging bull set in a natural landscape (restoration).

Plate 40: The hill-top sanctuary of Anemospilia, overlooking the plain of Knossos, near Arkhanes, where the scene of ritual sacrifice of a young man was discovered by I. and E. Sakellarakis in 1979. The shrine had collapsed in an earthquake (the same event that destroyed the Old Palaces at the end of the MM II period), burying the players of this macabre drama in its final act. The tripartite sanctuary, positioned just below the summit of Mount Juktas, has a wide antechamber with three entrances opposite the three inner chambers. The central chamber housed the statue of the deity (probably Zeus). To its left was a storeroom and to its right the chamber where the ritual sacrifice took place.

Plate 41: One of the western storage magazines of Knossos with some of the large pithoi still in situ and the stone-lined cists running down the centre of the magazine exposed.

Plate 42: The snake-goddess of Knossos [Iraklion Museum].

Plate 43: The intimidating Cyclopaean entrance to the Mycenaean citadel.

Plate 44: Mycenae Grave Circle A with the plain of the Argolid beyond.

Plate 45: Entrance to the Treasury of Atreus outside the Mycenaean citadel.

Plates 46 & 47: The famous golden mask usually, but incorrectly, claimed as the one Schliemann dubbed the 'face of Agamemnon' and (left) the Warrior Vase from Mycenae [National Museum, Athens].

Plate 48: The plaster head of a Mycenaean female or possibly the head of a sphinx. This rare example of monumental sculpture is dated to the LH IIIA or IIIB.

Plate 49: The great portal to the tholos chamber traditionally known as the 'Tomb of Clytemnestra' but probably originally built for her murdered husband Agamemnon. This spectacular tomb lies close to tha Cyclopean wall of Mycenae but, like the other tholos tombs, is located outside the citadel.

He stands in the morning twilight of Greek history and looks back to a preceding age which, according to him, was an age of much more brilliant glory and valiant men than the age in which he himself lived.

[M. P. Nilsson: *Homer and Mycenae* (New York, 1968)]

Plate 50: The poet Homer as perceived by the sculptors of the Classical world [Capitoline Museum, Rome].

level. On the level of the floor as reckoned from the cement flooring of the portico having been reached [the cup-bearer fresco was found]. … In the next space to the E is the large gypsum block I worked so as to look like the E side of a doorway opening in S. Immediately N of this block we came on a deposit largely mixed with charred wood and gradually the outline, fragmented at the rim all round, of an oval terracotta bath came into view. The black wood deposit in it was found to contain a large hoard of Mycenaean inscription tablets like those previously discovered, but this time several were found whole or complete in fragments. They were found packed together in rows in the deposit of the bath so that the latter may have been used for holding them.

This larnax, according to Palmer, stood on a floor level dating to LM IIIB and above the plastered floor level of LM II. The bath appears to have been used to store the Linear B tablets and was associated with charred timber ash which must have fallen from an upper storey during the conflagration which brought an end to the royal palace. The tablets thus appear to have been placed there after the LM IIIB floor was established and not during the LM II era.

Moreover, the large magazine storage area in the western part of the palace was paved with stone slabs under which, according to Palmer, the excavators turned up LH IIIB pottery sherds, indicating that the large *pithoi* (storage jars) found sitting on the floor and the cist depositories running down the centre of the magazines (see plate 41) were still in use during the LM IIIB era. This is clear proof that the palace was functioning as an elite residence during that time and was not occupied by mere squatters. It was also above this floor that several Linear B tablets were found. In addition, Palmer makes the more general point that the tablets found at Knossos were consistently associated with typical Mycenaean stirrup jars which are part of the classic LM III repertoire and rarely found within an earlier archaeological context.

All this made perfect sense to Palmer as he had already taken the view that the Greek language contained in the Knossian Linear B tablets was later than that unearthed at Mycenae and Pylos – both of which dated from towards the end of LH IIIB. Although other philologists have subsequently disagreed with Palmer's linguistic arguments, it is disconcerting to me that some scholars are comfortable with the idea that the Knossos tablets are separated from the other Linear B texts of the mainland by considerably more than a century. Where are the tablets in-between? Even the discovery of texts at Cadmaean Thebes (perhaps dated to a couple of generations before those from Pylos) does not permit us to push the date of mainland (LH IIIB) Linear B back to Knossian (LM II) Linear B times. The recently discovered tablets from Kydonia (Khania) on Crete in an LM IIIB archaeological context support the view that the Knossian LM II tablets are 'out of time' with all the other Linear B archives. As Dickinson sees it: 'the demonstration of clear links between the Linear B texts of Khania and Knossos would inevitably argue for dating the last palace at Knossos to LM IIIB'.[10] All this suggests that Palmer was on the right track when he questioned Evans' LM II (actually LM IIIA:1) date for the final destruction of the Mycenaean palace at Knossos.

The chronological gap is either a problem to be resolved by future discovery (in my view unlikely) or we should definitely reconsider lowering the date of the Knossos destruction and therefore the majority of the so-called LM II tablets down into LM IIIB as Palmer and, subsequently, Erik Hallager[11] and Wolf-Dietrich Niemeier[12] have argued. Such a move would place all the Linear B tablets into the same general era and we could then reinstate a wealthy administration of King Minos operating within a royal palace at Knossos when the genealogies say that Minos and Theseus lived.

> ## Conclusion Thirteen
> The royal palace at Knossos, known to legend as the Labyrinth, was not finally destroyed in LM IIIA:1 but rather some time during the LM IIIB. It was in this LM IIIB pottery period that King Minos of the Minotaur legend ruled in Crete and when, following his death during an expedition to Crete, Homer's Achaeans of mainland Greece succeeded to the maritime domination of the Aegean, just sixty years before the Trojan War.

The Pelasgians

You may have noticed that I have intentionally continued to mix my terminologies for the last pharaohs of the Greater Hyksos dynasty (from Khyan onwards) and now the kings of Crete from LM II onwards. They were both Pelasgians *and* Bronze Age Greeks, the latter writing their documents at Knossos in an early form of the Greek language. Was this legendary ethnicon 'Pelasgian' simply a term used by the later historians for pre-Mycenaean Greeks? And what does the modern term 'Mycenaean Greek' mean anyway? Homer calls the latter 'Achaeans' (*Achaoi*) and 'Danaeans' (*Danaioi*). So our historical term Mycenaeans is a little misleading. It derives from the fact that the dynasty of Atreus and his son Agamemnon ruled from Mycenae when the ruler of that fortified palace was high-king (*wanax*) of the Greek mainland and Aegean islands. The Greeks never called themselves Mycenaeans and neither did their neighbours. The Hittites referred to them as men of Akhiyawa (i.e. Achaiwoi = Achaeans) and the Egyptians knew a people called Akawasha (believed to be the hieroglyphic writing for Achaiwoi). Another scholarly term for this dynasty is the 'Pelopids', as Pelops was the father of Atreus and a foreigner who came from Anatolia to seize the kingship from the old Perseid dynasty which began with Perseus, son of Danae, grand-daughter of Danaus.

Homer's term 'Danaeans' originates with Danaus, the legendary founder of the whole line who, legend has it, came to the Argolid from Egypt, at which point the indigenous Pelasgian population were ordered to call themselves *Danaioi* in honour of their new king.

> Danaus, the father of fifty daughters, on coming
> to Argos took up his abode in the city of Inachus
> and throughout Greece he laid down the law that
> all people hitherto named Pelasgians were to be
> named Danaeans.[13]

The Bronze Age Greek legends will be covered in the next chapter when we cross the Aegean Sea from Crete to the Peloponnese, but here the point to make is that these early Greek rulers, whatever their dynastic names, were of Pelasgian descent – until, that is, the time of the Pelopids who originated in Anatolia. So the early Greeks who invaded Crete and occupied Knossos during the LM II were pre-Pelopid Pelasgians just as Diodorus Siculus claims.

So the original rulers of Knossos were replaced by Pelasgian Greeks, most likely at the transition between LM IB and LM II, shortly after the final Theran eruption. It was these mainlanders who destroyed the Cretan palaces and towns brought to a low point by the cataclysm of a few years earlier. We have assigned the legendary name Tectamus – the grandfather of Minos the Elder – to the archaeologically anonymous leader of those Greek invaders.

The Indo-European legends tend to emphasise a different origin for this Minos and his descendants – through the female line. These traditions claim that Europa, daughter of Agenor of Tyre, came from Phoenicia to Crete where she gave birth to Minos the Elder. If we filter out the miraculous fathering of Minos by Zeus, we may perhaps see in this tale a marriage alliance between the Pelasgian ruler of Tyre (Agenor descendant of Epaphus/Apophis) and the Pelasgian Greek ruler of Knossos (Asterius son of Tectamus).

On the other hand, we could take the alternative non-supernatural traditions seriously and have Europa abducted from Phoenicia by Taurus, admiral of the Cretan fleet during the rule of Asterius. In this case she would have been brought to Knossos against her will. The Bronze Age Aegeans were notorious abductors of women, as attested in legend, Homer and the Linear B tablets (with their lists of foreign female slaves).

Did this new and powerful king, Minos the Elder, with strong ties to the Greek mainland through his Pelasgian heritage, choose to employ Aeolian Greek scribes to administer the Knossian palace records? After all, according to tradition, his grandfather (on his supposed father's side) brought both Pelasgians and Aeolians with him when he occupied Crete. His uncle (on his mother's side), Cadmus, was famous throughout the Classical world as the 'bringer of writing' to Greece, whilst cuneiform texts (on seals) were indeed found in Cadmaea along with a (later) collection of Linear B tablets. And Aeolian was a dialect of Greek originating in the region of central Greece where Cadmaean Thebes was located.

All the ancient writers saw the Pelasgians as an early population of the Aegean. They were given epithets like 'divine' and 'earth-born'. Whatever their prehistoric beginnings may have been, I would argue that they are the great ancestors of Western Civilisation. And it is these *Pelasgoi* who are the key to understanding the origins of the Indo-European super-elites who took over the Middle Bronze Age coastal ports of the northern Levant and became the Greater Hyksos lords of Avaris. Their extended adventure in the Levant and Egypt, where they ruled over the indigenous Asiatic populations, was epic in every sense. Their exploits and familial relationships were legendary to the later Greeks. They are Hesiod's generations of the First Brazen Age which preceded the Age of Heroes – the latter being the era of Helladic kings and supermen who fought first for Cadmaean Thebes and then at Troy.

These Greek mainland Pelasgians who also 'colonised' central Crete at the beginning of the Late Minoan II pottery period were traditionally identified with the ancestors of the Philistines (Egyptian Peleset) who first settled in Cilicia and then later moved into Canaan along with the other Sea Peoples. This famous invasion is recorded amongst the reliefs of Ramesses III's mortuary temple in Thebes and dated to his eighth regnal year (NC – c. 856 BC; OC – c. 1176 BC). The great dictionary of Hesychius (fifth century AD) has a reference to both Pelasgikon (derived from Pelasgoi) and Pelastikon (derived from Pelastoi/Peleset) where it can be surmised that ΠΕΛΑΣΓΙΚΟΝ has been confused with ΠΕΛΑΣΤΙΚΟΝ. The Greek letters Γ (G) and T (T) could easily be misread.[14]

When Tectamus invaded Crete at the beginning of LM II he brought with him both 'Pelasgians and Aeolians'. Scholars have determined that the Aeolian dialect came from north-central Greece whilst the dialect known as Ionian predominated in south-central Greece and the Peloponnese. The traditions held that these Ionian-speakers, who later migrated to Ionia in western Anatolia, were originally Pelasgians. In effect, Tectamus brought with him mainland Greeks from both north and south.

> The Ionians ... according to the Greek account, as long as they lived in what is now known as Achaea in the Peloponnese, before the coming of Danaus and Xuthus, were called Pelasgians of the coast. ... The Islanders too ... are a Pelasgian people: they were later known as the Ionians.[15]

I would argue that the Ionians were named after the Pelasgian Princess Io or Ya – hence the term 'Yawani' used by the Levantine nations to describe the Greeks of Yawan. So far we know of three ancient names for Greece – Akhiya (Homer's Achaea and the Hittite Akhiyawa), Yawan and Hellas (the name the later Greeks gave to their country). In the next chapter you will discover that the Classical Greek historians knew of an even earlier name for the region – Pelasgiotis (land of the Pelasgoi).

The Kretim

It is equally apparent that the Cretans (biblical Kretim) are distinct from the Keftiu (biblical Kaptorim) even though modern scholars tend to identify the Keftiu/Caphtorim with the Minoans of Crete. The book of Genesis lists both peoples which surely requires us to maintain a distinction. Homer refers to Eteo-Cretans ('original Cretans') as the indigenous population of the island and I would consider their kings to be the 'Minoan' ruling elites of the Middle and Late Minoan I periods at Knossos, Mallia, Phaistos and Kato Zakros. With the arrival of Pelasgian Greeks in LM II the indigenous Minoans moved into eastern Crete, leaving Knossos and the surrounding region to the newcomers from the mainland. The characteristically Greek LM II pottery initially tends to be restricted to Knossos and does not play a part in the culture of eastern Crete where the LM IB styles continue in use. Only in LM IIIA does the ceramic repertoire reach across the whole island, indicating a unified or more encompassing rule. This is when we have placed Minos the Elder in our historical reconstruction.

What this means is that the biblical Kaptorim (Anglicised as Caphtorim) can be identified with the legendary Pelasgians who are to be found all over the Aegean during the Late Bronze Age – in Greece, the Cyclades (including Thera), central Crete, Cyprus and coastal Anatolia (west and south) – whilst the biblical Kretim ('sons of Keret'?)

were the original Eteo-Cretans of eastern Crete and parts of the south Canaan coast during this same period. In effect, the term Keftiu or Kaptorim referred to the people of the Aegean (both islands and coastal regions) as a whole rather than just Crete.

> ## Conclusion Fourteen
>
> **The people the Egyptians referred to as Keftiu (Kaftara), as well as the region of Kaptara mentioned in the Assyrian sources (described as 'beyond the Upper Sea') and the biblical Caphtorim are to be recognised as the legendary Pelasgians of the north-eastern Mediterranean littoral and islands. They include the last rulers of the Greater Hyksos dynasty in Egypt. The Kretim of the Bible were one and the same as the Eteo-Cretans who dominated Crete prior to the Greek invasion at the end of LM IB.**

Black Athena

In 1987, Professor Martin Bernal published a famous book entitled *Black Athena: The Afroasiatic Roots of Classical Civilization* in which he proposed an Egyptian origin for Western Civilisation.[16] The material sources for his thesis were much the same as those I am using to construct this history, yet he reached a very different conclusion – as his sub-title suggests. Bernal took the view that the direction of the cultural and creative movement was from east to west – in other words from Africa and the Levant to Greece (and therefore Europe). *Black Athena* caused huge controversy because it upset centuries of scholarship which had come to the collective conclusion that the roots of Western Civilisation were to be found in Indo-European culture, even though there had been some oriental influence from the Levant and Egypt. Bernal simply took the legendary sources from the Classical writings and argued for a genuine historical migration of people – carrying their distinctive culture from the south and east – which did much more to mould Greek civilisation than previously believed.

Certain radical African-Americans took these arguments even further, arguing a black African origin for Egyptian civilisation and therefore (linking to Bernal's work) Classical civilisation via their distant ancestors who migrated to Greece during the Hyksos period. These 'black' pharaonic migrants thus brought with them north-east African culture which formed the foundation of Western culture. University departments were set up in black universities in the USA to teach and propagate these views.

However, this Afro-centric perspective and Bernal's original, less radical, position are both wrong because they fail to take into consideration the origins of the Hyksos kings whose descendants left Egypt for the Aegean. Their homeland was not in Africa or Egypt or the Levant. They came not from the south or east but from the Pelasgian north – as migrants (probably as military conquerors) who took over dominion of the Levant and Egypt in the Middle Bronze Age. During that era they sojourned in the region for at least three centuries, identified in the Bible as Rephaim, Anakim and Caphtorim, and in the Egyptian tradition as Hyksos. They were then pushed out of Egypt by the

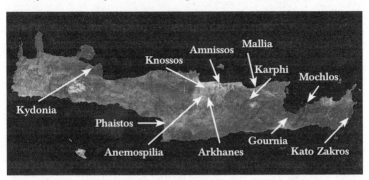

64. Satellite image of Crete showing the principal palace centres and sites discussed in this book [photo courtesy of NASA].

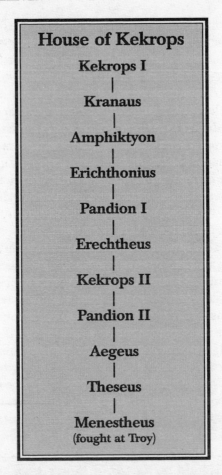

House of Kekrops

Kekrops I
|
Kranaus
|
Amphiktyon
|
Erichthonius
|
Pandion I
|
Erechtheus
|
Kekrops II
|
Pandion II
|
Aegeus
|
Theseus
|
Menestheus
(fought at Troy)

native Egyptians (the rulers of whom were themselves part Pelasgian through dynastic marriage) and returned to their original homeland in the Aegean.

Others of their kin remained in southern Canaan – the Bible knows them as Philistines and Jebusites – whilst their Aryan allies in the north took on the guise of the Mitannian rulers of the Late Bronze Age.

There were no major African influences going out of Egypt to the Aegean beyond those acquired during the Hyksos period from pharaonic (Nilotic) culture which was itself predominantly influenced by the ancient Near East and not black Africa beyond the Second Cataract of the Nile.

Theseus and the Labyrinth

I hardly think you will need reminding of the story of Theseus and the Minotaur, but perhaps it would be a good idea just to run through it, picking out one or two salient points in an attempt to offer rational explanations for the stranger aspects of the tale. More importantly, I want to make you aware of an alternative Theseus tradition which is much more 'credible' than the 'incredible' story we were all introduced to as children. But first the incredible version with its half-man-half-bull, a magic ball of string, a contest to the death in the bowels of the Labyrinth and an architect of that Labyrinth who escapes from Crete on wings of feather and wax.

The story begins with Minos the Younger established on the throne of Knossos. He has a powerful fleet which dominates the Mediterranean. His son Androgeus is treacherously slain whilst visiting Attica (the territory of Athens) and Minos exacts his revenge by conquering Megara and harassing Athens. Aegeus, king of the Athenians, succumbs to the pressure and offers reparation for the death of Minos' son. The penalty in requital of the crime is a cruel tribute which Athens must pay every nine years. Seven boys and seven girls must be sent from Athens to Knossos as a sacrifice to the Minotaur of the Labyrinth.

In the third draft of Athenian youth (that is, after twenty-seven years) Aegeus' own son, Theseus (Linear B *te-se-u*), is chosen by lot to go to Knossos. With the help of Minos' daughter, the priestess Ariadne, who has fallen in love with the young prince from Athens, Theseus manages to penetrate the Labyrinth and slay the Minotaur. He is able to do this because Ariadne presents him with a magic ball of string, given to her by Daedalus – the architect of the Labyrinth who had fled from Minos (following an accusation of betrayal) and sought refuge on the island of Sicily. This is the mythical 'flight', on wings of feather and wax, made by Daedalus and Icarus (the son who flew too near to the sun and fell to Earth when the wax holding his wings together melted).

Back in Knossos, Theseus uses the string to find his way in and out of the Labyrinth to confront the Minotaur in his lair. Having despatched the bull-man, Theseus departs from Crete, taking Ariadne with him. The daughter of Minos is then heartlessly abandoned on an Aegean island and Theseus returns to Athens alone where he is crowned king following the death of Aegeus (after whom the Aegean sea is named).

Minos sets out in his fleet to find and punish Daedalus but is murdered whilst taking a bath in the palace of Cocalus, king of Sicilian Camicus, where Daedalus is hiding. The Cretan fleet is destroyed and its crews forced to settle on Sicily where they build the city of Minoa. That, in a nutshell, is the basic story, but it is worth looking at a few details.

The extraordinary thing about this legend is that one of the supernatural elements – the sacrifice of the Athenian youths to the Minotaur – actually has an historical explanation. As I have argued from the beginning, rational explanations can often be found in the most obscure or incredible tales – and this is a case in point. Probably the most famous aspect of Cretan culture is the bull-leaping ritual of Knossos (and now Avaris). We find frescoes of young men performing acrobatic somersaults over bulls or even grappling with the fearsome animals. Surely this is where we will find a reasonable explanation for the tale of the Minotaur.

The Athenian youths were sent to Knossos not to be thrown into the Minotaur's deep lair for sacrifice but to perform a sporting feat laced with religious ritual – an adversarial contest between Man and the animal manifestation of the storm-god[17] and old Earth-Shaker himself.[18] Most, if not all, of the Athenian acrobats would have been killed in their attempts to complete the challenge but any survivor may have been entitled to slaughter the bull with the Minoan double-axe and receive the plaudits of the Knossian audience, perhaps garlanded in the fashion of the remarkable fresco of the so-called 'priest-king' from Knossos.

A fascinating detail from the Greek legend of Theseus and the Minotaur is the part played by two 'effeminate boys' chosen by Theseus to replace two of the girls sent to Knossos. These, what we would today call 'gay' teenagers, were instructed to wear pale makeup and dress like females. What is quite extraordinary is that the sole surviving bull-leaping fresco from Knossos shows two pale-skinned youths in support of the principal jumper who is depicted with darker skin. Scholars have suggested that the two pale-skinned figures are female – but they have no breasts and wear the same type of kilt as the male leaper. Nanno Marinatos (daughter of the famous excavator of Akrotiri), herself an expert in Aegean art, is in no doubt as to their gender.

> That they are not female is shown by the fact that they have distinct male anatomy: broad torsos, articulated muscles shown as striations in the legs, no breasts. ... these are the *conventions for male anatomy* in Minoan art. ... Given the above observations, it is difficult to believe that the white colour is an indication of the female sex in this case. Some other distinction is operative here which has to do with the youth of the acrobats. Thus, white acrobats are younger and less skilled, brown ones have attained the desired degree of skill.[19]

Marinatos' explanation for the pale colour of the young male athletes is not entirely convincing. By not paying due attention to the detail of the Minotaur legend, she has missed a trick here. Given the strange tradition about the effeminate youths in Theseus' draft of Minotaur victims, it is tempting to relate the bull-leaping fresco from Knossos directly with Theseus' victory over the Minotaur. We might even see Theseus himself as the successful leaper (helped by his two pale-skinned companions) – which would then make this famous fresco a specific piece of narrative art.

Was this the historical reality behind Theseus' victory over the Minotaur? Perhaps. But there is an alternative version of the legend which is very different from the Athenian tale and much more believable.

According to the Cretan tradition (quoted by Plutarch from Philochorus), Theseus came to Knossos to participate in the funeral games held in memory of the murdered Androgeus. These games may indeed have included bull-leaping but the Cretans claimed that Theseus was involved in another contest. Knossos had a champion named Taurus (perhaps the grandson of the Taurus who had abducted Europa from Phoenicia?) who had never been beaten in a wrestling match. However, the powerful Theseus was able to throw him three times and claim the wrestling championship. In doing so he won the heart of Ariadne. Taurus is, of course, the word for bull (and forms the second part of Minotaurus – 'Bull of Minos') but it is also a personal name. So was the legendary bull-man simply a wrestling champion? Either way – by bull-leaping and slaying the bull, or by defeating Taurus in a wrestling match – Theseus was able to return to Athens having cancelled the blood-debt with his victory.

According to the same Cretan tradition, King Minos himself, not overly enamoured with arrogant Taurus (who he believed was having an affair with his wife Pasiphae), was delighted with Theseus' victory and offered his daughter's hand in marriage.

The Cypriotes had yet another story (quoted by Plutarch from Cleidemus) which has Theseus invading Crete after the death of Minos on Sicily. With the Cretan fleet destroyed and Minos dead, the throne of Knossos falls to Deucalion. He gathers a second Minoan fleet (perhaps taking several years to build new ships) and dispatches it to Sicily to exact revenge for the murder of his father. This second fleet is also destroyed – this time by Poseidon. In the meantime Theseus, now king in Athens, secretly builds his own fleet to invade Crete. With the destruction of the Minoan navy, he is able to sail unhindered to Knossos where he kills Deucalion during a pitched battle within the Labyrinth. The palace of the Pelasgian kings of Knossos is then put to the torch. This could conceivably be the destruction unearthed by Evans in which the Linear B archive was found and which we have dated to some time within the LM IIIB. Thus the Linear B deposits at Knossos would be roughly contemporary with those from Cadmaean Thebes, perhaps associated with Laius and Oedipus whose palace was subsequently destroyed by the EPIGONOI just a generation before the Trojan War.

Theseus then marries Ariadne, the Knossian heiress, whilst the hostages tied to the blood-debt of Androgeus are returned to Athens, and a peace accord is made between the two states which puts an end to the Athenian tribute. The couple then sets sail for Athens but the fleet is driven by stormy seas to Cyprus where Ariadne, now heavily pregnant, asks to be let ashore for fear of a miscarriage. The Athenian fleet is then, once again, driven from the island by strong winds, leaving Theseus' pregnant bride behind. Ariadne dies in childbirth and is buried on the island where her tomb at Amathus is still known in Classical times.

Whichever story one chooses to accept, they all have the Cretan navy wiped out on the expedition to Sicily. With Minos' death at Camicus and his fleet destroyed, the domination of Pelasgian Knossos over the mainland was broken and the era of Achaean power over the Aegean, culminating in the Trojan War, had begun.

The Power of the Bull

The contest between Man and bull stretches back into the mists of time. It begins with the search for food during the early Stone Age and develops into the domestication and breeding of the wild cattle herds in the late Stone Age (start of the sixth millennium).

The oldest bull-hunting scene we know of comes from the Neolithic settlement of Chatal Hüyük (Level VIII) in south-central Anatolia (OC – c. 6280 BC). It depicts scores of men chasing down and distracting a large bull so that one of their number can strike the animal behind the neck in its most vulnerable spot – a deadly contest that would manifest itself, thousands of years later, in the form of the bull-leaping festivals of Minoan/Aegean civilisation. Unfortunately it is impossible to say whether these Neolithic peoples of the seventh and sixth millennia BC spoke an ancestral language of the Indo-Europeans because Chatal Hüyük existed and died out long before the invention of writing. Bulls' heads were also used at Chatal Hüyük to decorate what appear to be cultic rooms.

In Egypt's Eastern Desert the archaeological survey teams which I led in the late 1990s discovered literally thousands of rock carvings depicting bull-lassoing which appear to be either bull-catching or herding scenes. Many of these seem to date from the predynastic era or Egypt's Neolithic Age (though the herding rock-art does continue throughout the pharaonic era and beyond – differentiated from the predynastic art by lighter PATINATION and a more sophisticated carving technique).

The 1st Dynasty mastaba tombs at Sakkara were surrounded by bulls' heads, set in plaster on a low plinth, indicating a strong affinity between this animal and the human occupants of the tombs. The bull was not just a powerful fertility symbol to the elites of early Egypt but was also directly assimilated with kingship itself, as is made abundantly clear by the iconography of the Narmer Palette.

But this association between bull and man was not just an Egyptian phenomenon. It had as big an impact on both Mesopotamian and Indo-European cultures. Numerous cylinder seals from Sumer and Agade depict a bull-man (Sumerian *gud-alim*, Babylonian *kusarikku*) and bull-fighting imagery (traditionally associated with Gilgamesh and Enkidu).

These scenes touch upon one of the great themes of early civilisation – the mastery of nature. The motif of the 'Master of Animals' is the symbol of Man's control over nature's wilder aspects. Man (in the form of the semi-divine hero or ruler) is thus seen as the conqueror of the wild beasts – and the bull was the epitome of wild nature.

The Indo-Europeans took this idea in an extraordinary direction. They invented a ritualised sport to re-enact this contest on a regular basis – the bull-leaping festival. It is first represented on cylinder-seal impressions discovered by Sir Leonard Woolley at Alalakh (Tell Atchana Level VII) in northern Syria – a stronghold of Indo-European culture during the Middle Bronze Age (contemporary with the Hyksos period[20]). The line-drawing of the seal (below) depicts two acrobats (with the familiar tight waist of Minoan art) performing somersaults (in antithetical pose) on the back of a bull.[21] According to Dominique Collon – a world-renowned expert on glyptic art – this seal, and another similar to it from the same region, 'provide the earliest representations of bull-leaping as a highly skilled and fully developed athletic feat'. It is therefore, in a material sense, our first piece of recognisable Indo-European art.

Next in the sequence come the 'Minoan' bull-leaping frescoes of Avaris which appear to precede those of Knossos (by how much is at present contentious). These are the most free-flowing and naturalistic

65. *Detail from the Alalakh seal showing two antithetical bull-leapers performing hand-stands on the back of a bull with an ankh symbol between them.*

representations discovered so far – not large but exquisitely rendered. Much bigger fragments of a bull (including elements in raised relief plaster) were possibly associated with a ceremonial ramp to the Helmi I palace, something akin to the great bull of Knossos represented above the north entrance ramp to that palace.

Then we have the most famous of all bull-leaping images – that found in the palace of Knossos and now on display in the Iraklion Museum. As Nanno Marinatos points out, bull-leaping and hunting were elite or royal activities performed within the environs of the palaces and their estates.

> ... both hunting and jumping appear on media of official art only: frescoes, rings, bronze figurines, ivory pieces, gold cups. All these items are costly and could only have been possessed by an elite. No modest clay offerings have been found in nature sanctuaries where we see the offerings of the common man. From this alone we would be entitled to say that the activities were connected with the aristocracy of Minoan society.[22]

Then, beyond the Aegean islands to the north-west, we have the Helladic culture where 'scenes depicting bull-games are numerous'.[23] Here we find bull-tethering scenes

66. *Charging bull in an open countryside setting – very similar to the bull of the north portico at Knossos, only here found in the Treasury of Atreus at Mycenae.*

67. Ambassadors from Keftiu/Kaftara (left) and Kheta/Hatti (right) depicted in the tomb of Menkheperre-seneb (temp. Thutmose III).

(the Vapheio Cup); seal-stones, frescoes and painted sarcophagi, all depicting various bull-sports; the bull's-head rhyton from Grave Circle A at Mycenae; and, of course, the Athenian legend of Theseus and the Minotaur played out in the Knossian Labyrinth.

So the sport of bull-leaping and bull-grappling was not specifically or exclusively a Minoan affair. Indeed, as early as 1930 Arthur Evans himself postulated that the activity had originated in Anatolia.[24] Dominique Collon recently suggested that we should look for the immediate antecedents of Minoan bull-leaping in Syria,[25] whilst Nanno Marinatos argues that 'bulls and bull games were associated with Minoans *consistently outside* Crete in the eastern Mediterranean'.[26] This is hardly surprising given that the isolated island of Crete could never have had an indigenous population of wild bulls and that *Bos primigenius* must therefore have been imported from the continental mainland by ship.[27] The acrobats depicted on seals from Syria (specifically Atchana) wear what we think of as 'Minoan-style' garb, whilst one Egyptian tomb painting from the 18th Dynasty (above) shows a typically Syrian looking figure labelled as a 'Chieftain of the Keftiu'. Perhaps we would be better-off calling all these bull-leapers 'Caphtorim' or even 'Pelasgians' rather than the more narrow term 'Minoan' – after all, the Minoans were only one part of a much greater family of Indo-Europeans stretching from Hyksos Avaris to Pelasgian Argos to Anatolian Arzawa and Hattusha to Canaanite Ugarit and Alalakh.

We have seen that many of the citizens of Alalakh/Atchana bore Hurrian names during the Hyksos era and that Hurrians were closely associated with the Aryan elites of the Middle and Late Bronze Ages. It is tempting, therefore, to see bull-leaping as an Indo-European sport introduced from southern Anatolia and northern Syria when northerners swept across the eastern Mediterranean, settling in coastal cities and on the major islands. This would be consistent with the tradition of Keret, hero of Ugaritic legend, who originated in Syria but perhaps gave his name to the island of Crete (Kreti or Kreta). If Keret was the eponymous ancestor of the Eteo-Cretans who built the first palaces at Knossos and Phaistos, then the first bull-contests on Crete may date to their time. A stunning image of a bull made to function as a libation vessel has two tiny human figures grasping its mighty horns. This earliest bull-rhyton dates to the beginning of the Middle Bronze Age (MM IA) and was found in the Mesara plain near the palace of Phaistos.

Finally, leaping across the centuries, we witness, all over south-western Europe, the modern, but no doubt anciently practised, bull-running (southern France and Spain), bull-leaping (Portugal and Spain) and bull-fighting (Spain) sporting rituals. Dominique Collon draws attention to the Roman attraction to bull-sports introduced into the arena at the beginning of the empire period (towards the end of the first century BC).

> Julius Caesar is supposed to have introduced the *taurokathápsia* into Italy where 'it appealed to the sensation-loving Romans, and ultimately gave rise to the bullfights of Spain and France'.[28]

However, I am not convinced that bull-leaping was specifically exported to the Iberian peninsula by Rome but suggest that Phoenician and Aegean migrants into the western Mediterranean, during the so-called colonisation period of the first millennium BC, were responsible for the cultural phenomenon. All down the Spanish coast are the remains of ancient cities colonised by 'Phoenicians' (see *Chapter Seventeen*) and it would hardly be surprising if these descendants of Canaanites, ruled over by a Pelasgian aristocracy, brought with them sporting rituals such as bull-leaping which have survived through to modern times.

I have personally witnessed bull-leaping in the ancient Plaza de Toros in Ondara (near Denia – named after the goddess Diana) and, believe me, it is a thrilling spectacle – dangerous for the young men who leap the animals but harmless for the bulls themselves. These black bulls are young and fast (with sharp horns) whereas the Minoan frescoes depict much larger mottle-hide bovids. Excavations in the ruins of a house at Knossos unearthed two huge skulls of bovids whose horns measured thirty centimetres in circumference.[29] Amazingly, just such gigantic animals are used by the bull-master of the leaping contest in Ondara to herd the young black bulls from the arena after their contests. To give you an idea of how the modern equivalent of the ancient sporting ritual is performed, I have included photographs of a leap and those amazing giant bulls. But nothing compares to the real thing. The ancient sport, with all its spectacle, colour and drama, must have been one of the greatest sights witnessed by our ancestors – worthy of legend.

Ritual Human Sacrifice

High up on the slopes of Mount Juktas, looking down onto the northern coastal plain, the palace of Knossos, and beyond across the sea to Thera, is a tiny stone sanctuary (see plate 40). It consists of a broad antechamber leading to a central shrine and two flanking chambers, the lower rear walls of which are formed by the natural rock. This is probably a sanctuary of the Cretan Zeus (Zeus Cretagenus) whose burial, legend has it, took place on Mount Juktas. The ruin is today called Anemospilia ('Cave of the Winds').

When the Greek archaeologists excavated this isolated site in 1979, they made one of the most astonishing and disturbing discoveries in the history of Cretan archaeology. The sanctuary had been destroyed in a violent earthquake, at the end of the Middle Minoan II period, which tore down the first Minoan palaces. This was some considerable time before the eruption of Thera but contemporary with the Exodus from Egypt in the New Chronology (therefore *c.* 1447 BC). New palaces were constructed over the ruins of the old and these residences lasted through to the Mycenaean occupation of Crete (LM II) and beyond.

What the archaeologists found under the collapsed roof of the sanctuary at Anemospilia was evidence of ritual sacrifice – perhaps an act of placation to Zeus and his brother, Poseidon, intended to calm the violent earth. It did not succeed. Buried under the rubble were four bodies. In the antechamber lay a figure whose gender could not be determined, beside him/her a vessel that, almost certainly, had contained the blood of the sacrifice. The vessel was an example of the type of Kamares ware pitcher used for gathering blood from sacrificed bulls as can be seen on the Aghia Triada painted sarcophagus.

The priest/priestess was on his/her way from the right-hand side-chamber into the central room which contained a wooden effigy of the shrine's deity (only the large life-size clay feet remaining when the room was cleared by the excavators).

In the sacrificial chamber, to the right of the central chapel, lay the skeletons of a priestess and the high-priest, of tall and slender build, wearing his gold signet-ring. At the heart of the room was a low altar, just centimetres above the floor, on which lay the pitiful remains of a youth, his hands and feet originally bound. Beside the boy was the long bronze knife which had been used to slit the jugular and end his life. Here was no ordinary sacrifice of a lamb or goat, not even a bull, but a human, offered up to placate an angry god.

Was this the hidden face of Minoan Crete? Many Greek scholars baulk at the idea – but this darker aspect of Minoan life is hard to deny, given the evidence from Anemospilia and, even more recently, from Knossos.

Child Sacrifice at Knossos

This macabre discovery was a great embarrassment to all those archaeologists and historians who had proclaimed the peace-loving nature of Minoan society. The image of elegance, free-flowing art and unwalled population centres remained to conjure up this hippy idyll – but here was a dark side to the upper echelons of Minoan society which had previously been unknown and unanticipated. But should it have been? The legends had told us of the sacrifice of young men to placate the violent nature gods of Crete. Everybody knew the story of the Minotaur and his youthful victims. And then came a second, even more disturbing discovery – this time from the Labyrinth itself.

On 24 July 1999, Peter Warren (Bristol University) and Nicholas Coldstream (UCL) jointly delivered the first Vronwy Hankey Memorial Lecture entitled 'The Excavation of Knossos' at the Institute of Archaeology, London, to the members of ISIS.

The professor and renowned archaeologist from Bristol presented the results of his recent excavation work at Knossos, including the story of how he had uncovered a series of rooms in which there were the scattered remains of several children. Their bones were disarticulated and, upon closer examination, appeared to have multiple laceration marks made by a straight-edged implement. The flesh of these children had been cut from their bones with a sharp knife. This was hardly the practice for normal burial and not even for ritual sacrifice where the cutting of arteries for blood-letting was sometimes the norm. Here the bodies of the children had been butchered.

There was only one conclusion to be drawn from this discovery: human sacrifice and cannibalism were practised in the palace of Knossos during Late Minoan times. The awful reality of the Minotaur legend had struck home. Like their Pelasgian cousins in Phoenicia, the Pelasgian Greeks and Cretans were child sacrificers. But the Pelasgians were not alone in this terrible practice. The gods required the gift of your most precious possession – a first-born child – in order to demonstrate your total devotion (just as El required of Abraham). The ancient world could be a cruel and bloody place in which to be born.

The Bible tells of Canaanite parents offering up their children to Molech (fire sacrifice), and a vast cemetery of immolated children at Phoenician Carthage is grim testimony to this dreadful ritual. The origin of the word Molech is Phoenician and means 'king' (originally *melek* – where the biblical redactor has substituted the vowels of *boshet* 'shame'). The Israelites of the Northern Kingdom practised Molech sacrifice before their deportation to Assyria in 722 BC. Eventually the people of Jerusalem also succumbed to the influences of Canaanite religion and set up a tophet (place of ritual burning) in the Hinnom valley where even the sons and daughters of kings 'were made to pass through the fire of sacrifice'.

> They have set up their horrors in the temple that bears my name, to defile it, and have built the high places of tophet in the Valley of Ben-Hinnom, to burn their sons and daughters. [Jeremiah 7:30-31]

Chapter Twelve

DANAUS AND AEGYPTUS

Mycenaean Shaft Graves -- The Last of the Shemau --
Hesiod's Races of Men -- The Atreid Dynasty of Mycenae

I have proposed that the Greater Hyksos kings of Egypt, ruling from Memphis and Avaris, were one of the last elements of a great movement of northerners into the Fertile Crescent which began at the end of the Early Bronze Age (NC – *c.* 2100 BC) and ended during the last phase of the Middle Bronze Age (NC – *c.* 1200 BC). These Greater Hyksos were of Hurrian and Indo-European stock. Salitis and Bnon may have been leaders of the Aryan Umman Manda of northern Mesopotamia and the Zagros mountains, their successors – Khyan, Yanassi, Apophis and Khamudy – of Aegean origin, more specifically the people Homer called 'Divine Pelasgians'. The original homeland of these Pelasgians was the northern shore of the Black Sea before they moved into mainland Greece (focused on the Plain of Argolis) at the beginning of the Middle Bronze Age. They then spread throughout the Aegean and along the Anatolian and Phoenician coasts.

Herodotus [Book I] tells us that these original Pelasgians did not speak Greek and it is my view that the language spoken by Khyan and his line was an early branch of

Indo-European using the distinctive locative suffix endings, including -sos, -ndos and -ntha/-nthos, reflected in names such as Knossos, Amnissos, Lindos, Tirynthos (Tiryns), and words such as kissos (ivy), kyparissos (cypress tree), olynthos (wild fig), plinthos (brick). This Pelasgian linguistic trait is found in Greece, Crete and Anatolia – associated with the Western Luwian speakers of the latter region. In the earliest Hittite texts we hear of the land of Luwili from where the Luwian language originated. This part of western Anatolia was later known as Arzawa – a general term which included (from north to south) the kingdoms of Wilusa, the Seha River Lands, Mira and Haballa. It seems very likely that the aristocracy of Wilusa/Ilios were Luwian-speakers because a seal was recently found at Hissarlik by Donald Easton which is claimed to be 'the first attested prehistoric inscription from Troy'.[1] The script on the seal is in Luwian.

This group of Luwian-speakers had crossed the Hellespont and Bosporus from Europe to settle in north-western Anatolia. Their descendants were the Dardanians and Trojans of Wilusa (Ilios) and Arzawans of Sardis (in the land of Mira, later known as Lydia) and Epasa (Ephesus). Other Indo-European speakers moved down from the Caucasus region and occupied the uplands of eastern Anatolia (the Hittites), northern Mesopotamia (the Aryans) and southern Anatolia, centred on the major trading and metal-working city-states such as Purushanda (probably Kara Hüyük near modern Konya, Classical Iconium). From the coastal areas these Indo-Europeans expanded onto the eastern Mediterranean islands – especially Cyprus, Crete and Thera – and, of course, mainland Greece.

68. The small round two-sided seal found in the Troy VIIa level at Hissarlik by Donald Easton during the recent German excavations led by Manfred Korfmann. The language of the text is Luwian [after Latacz, 2004, p. 50].

Herodotus claims that the people of the Peloponnese were descendants of the Pelasgians and the people of Attica descendants of the Hellenic (Greek-speaking) peoples.

> ... the Lacedaemons (of the Peloponnese) are of the Doric race, the Athenians (of Attica) of the Ionic. For these had been the outstanding races from the olden time – the one Pelasgian and the other Hellenic. [Book I]

Those Peloponnesians who settled on the coast of western Anatolia at the end of the Bronze Age, during the Ionian migrations, were also of Pelasgian descent.

> The Ionians were called Aegialian Pelasgians (say the Greeks) for the entire time they lived in the Peloponnese, in what is called Achaea, and before Danaus and Xuthus came to the Peloponnese. [Book VII]

At the beginning of the Middle Bronze Age several south-western Anatolian chieftains became rulers of the major ports of northern Canaan (Classical Phoenicia) enabling their trading fleets to gain access to the city-states of the Levantine interior. These Indo-European warrior elites intermarried with the local Amorites and, in due course, took West Semitic names. The Bible and the legends of Ugarit refer to them as the Rephaim ('ancestors') – men of giant stature who ruled the world in a time of distant memory. Centuries later (during the MB IIA) a group of these Rephaim moved further south into Canaan where they rebuilt the destroyed Early Bronze Age towns, fortifying them with strong walls and glacis ramparts. The Bible knows this sub-group of Canaanite lords as the Anakim. The Greek tradition has these 'giants' or 'men of great stature' originating in the land of Anactoria located in south-west Anatolia (the region later known as Lycia).

CHAPTER TWELVE

Sargon the Great of Agade (NC – *c.* 2117-2061 BC) refers to the lands of Kaptara and Anaku 'which lie beyond the Upper Sea' (i.e. the eastern Mediterranean).

With the collapse of the 13th Dynasty in Egypt following the Israelite Exodus, the Anakim seized the moment and invaded the eastern delta. We have identified them with the Lesser Hyksos 'Shepherd Kings' of Manetho who plundered Egypt in the era following the reign of Tutimaos (Dudimose). The arrival of Joshua and the tribes in the hill country of Canaan, forty years later, forced the Anakim to concentrate their rule in the coastal plain of southern Canaan and the Egyptian delta, leaving the deserts and hills of the interior to the Israelites.

A further century passed before a new dynasty of Indo-European rulers from the north established themselves in Egypt towards the end of the Second Intermediate Period. Scholars know them as the 15th Dynasty Hyksos kings but I have termed these 'aliens' the Greater Hyksos to distinguish them from their predecessors – the Lesser Hyksos of mixed Anatolian-Canaanite origin. These Greater Hyksos – the first two perhaps being Aryans (Umman Manda), the remainder Pelasgians – are the Shemau of the Speos Artemidos inscription. According to the imaginative history being constructed here, these were the two aristocratic groups which met on Mount Zaphon near Ugarit to form an alliance for the purposes of invading southern Canaan and Egypt. Their story is told in the West House Miniature Fresco at Akrotiri.

Over time the Aegean Pelasgoi were transformed, subsumed and diluted – evolving into new branches of the original stem and taking their names from eponymous founders. One of those branches was known to Homer as the Danaoi or Danaeans, named after the legendary Danaus – a Hyksos refugee from Egypt.

Heinrich Schliemann arrived at Mycenae on the morning of 7 August 1876. He was already a celebrity – fêted (though not without dissenters) as the man who discovered Homer's Troy at the little mound of Hissarlik in north-west Turkey. Now he was about to prove that the 'Age of Heroes' described in the Classical literature was supported by tangible Bronze Age cultural remains as he began to excavate the legendary citadel of 'Golden Mycenae'.

> For my part, I have always firmly believed in the Trojan War; my full faith in Homer and in the tradition has never been shaken by modern criticism, and to this faith of mine I am indebted for the discovery of Troy and its treasures. … I never doubted that a king of Mycenae, by the name of Agamemnon … had been treacherously murdered … and I firmly believed in the statement of Pausanias, that the murdered persons had been interred in the acropolis (of Mycenae).[2]

Always a committed believer in the historicity of the Homeric legends, and with the Classical texts as his guide, Schliemann was almost single-handedly bringing the world of Priam, Hector, Achilles and Agamemnon to light. Following his successes at Hissarlik, the citadel of Mycenae – home of Agamemnon in the Peloponnese – was the obvious place to continue his archaeological adventure. With Pausanias' book *A Guide to Greece* (*c.* AD 260) in his hand he stood at the main gate to the fortress, its majestic heraldic carving of a sacred column flanked by twin lions looming up before him. Turning to Book II, chapter 16, he read the ancient Greek traveller's description of the Mycenaean ruins.

> Some parts of the circuit-wall are still to be seen, including the gate with lions standing over it.

357

69. One of the stelae from Grave Circle A with its chariot scene [National Museum, Athens].

This, they say, is the work of the Cyclopes who built the walls of Tiryns for Proetus. In the ruins of Mycenae are a water-source called Pershia, and the underground chambers of Atreus and his sons, where they kept the treasure-houses of their wealth. Here is the tomb of Atreus and the graves of those who came home from Troy only to be cut down by Aigisthus at his supper-party. ... There is also the tomb of Agamemnon and that of Eurymedon the charioteer. A single grave holds Teledamos and Pelops – Cassandra's twin children whom Aigisthus slaughtered along with their parents whilst still mere infants. ... Clytemnestra and Aigisthus were buried a little further from the wall, as they were not fit to lie inside (the wall) where Agamemnon and the men who were murdered with him rest. [Pausanias, Book II]

This last sentence was the key to finding the grave of Agamemnon. Schliemann knew what he must do. He scrambled through the rubble-filled Lion Gate, turned immediately to the right and ordered his workmen (fifty-five in all) to make the first break in the dry earth. Before the end of August the wealthy German businessman, turned adventurer, had uncovered stone stelae carved in low relief depicting chariots, warfare and hunting scenes, framed with decorative spirals. These were grave-markers, erected above rectangular shafts which filled a circular area bounded by a double wall of orthostat slabs. 'Grave Circle A' (see plate 44) appeared to be a burial ground of the early kings of Mycenae and its discovery would be recognised as Heinrich Schliemann's greatest achievement.

Golden Mycenae

Over the next two months Schliemann and his men opened up five shaft-graves (a sixth was found later) to discover in each several bodies lying amongst a confused mass of exotic objects, many made of fine sheet gold. The death masks of the kings were truly outstanding and have become the iconographic symbols of Mycenaean Greece. The most evocative of these faces of the dead was found in shaft-grave V, depicting a mature man with beard and moustache of regal proportions. Its discovery has been immortalised in Schliemann's legendary remark as he stood over the burial: 'I have looked upon the face of wide-ruling Agamemnon.' In fact, it was another body from shaft-grave V which instigated these famous words (sent by telegram to a Greek newspaper), and what he actually said was rather less awe-inspiring: 'This corpse very much resembles the image which my imagination formed long ago of wide-ruling Agamemnon.' Once again, the succinctness of legend had outdone cumbersome reality.

There were many puzzles resulting from the haphazard and hasty clearance of the tombs. The excavator believed that

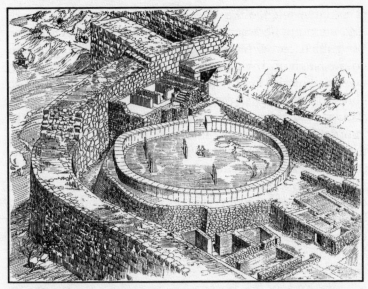

70. *Archaeological reconstruction of Grave Circle A with the 'Granary', attached to the circuit wall, immediately beyond, and the rear of the Lion Gate beyond that. The 'House of the Warrior Vase' (see plate 47) is at the bottom of the drawing.*

the multiple burials in each pit were simultaneous because it appeared that the shafts had been filled directly over the grave in a single operation with no apparent disturbance of the covering. It was highly unlikely that several metres of fill would have been regularly removed from the shafts in order to inter future burials subsequent to the original inhumations. Of course, Schliemann was completely convinced that these graves represented the burials of Agamemnon and his companions who, upon their return from Troy, had been murdered by Clytemnestra (Agamemnon's queen) and her lover Aigisthus. Obviously they would have all been buried in a single operation. And this is precisely what Schliemann believed he had found in Grave Circle A 'within the wall of Mycenae' just as Pausanias had described it. Moreover, the site had been a place of special reverence in late Mycenaean times when its ring of orthostats was constructed to protect the sacred area and the carved tombstones were re-erected at a higher level. Who else could it have been for if not Agamemnon, hero of the Trojan War?

Years later, Dörpfeld – Schliemann's loyal colleague and co-excavator of Troy – carefully re-examined the excavation notes and diaries from Mycenae after his patron's death and concluded that the tombs had, in fact, been sealed with stone slabs resting on wooden beams positioned across the shafts in order to create a cavity above the burials. The earth was then piled over this roof to fill the rest of the shaft up to the surface. As a result of this new and undoubtedly correct re-interpretation, some scholars argued that the construction technique permitted the regular re-opening of the tomb for burials of the additional bodies found in each shaft. This explanation has been tacitly accepted ever since. However, I am not so sure that such an interpretation satisfactorily accounts for the evidence.

The burials do appear to be contemporaneous as Schliemann believed. The bodies were laid out in a fashion which would suggest simultaneous interment with no brushing aside of old burials to accommodate new – a standard practice in family sepulchres such as the great tholos or beehive tombs of later Mycenae and in the slightly earlier and contemporary shaft-tombs of Grave Circle B (see later).

> Many of the graves in Grave Circle B at Mycenae
> have multiple burials, the early ones having been
> brushed to one side for the later interment. …
> Of the time of the shaft-graves there is no extant
> or surviving building structures such as palace or
> town at Mycenae.[3]

No occupational remains contemporary with Grave Circles A or B have ever been found at Mycenae. It seems that the site for the royal cemetery was chosen *long before* the first palace was constructed on the summit of the hill and that the contents of the shaft-graves pre-date the establishment

of Mycenae as a royal citadel (traditionally in the reign of
Perseus). What I mean by this is that the artefacts found
with the burials predate artefacts excavated from the first
palace and that, consequently, the royal corpses must
belong to the century prior to the foundation of Mycenae
as a royal citadel.

Alan Wace, who excavated Mycenae in the 1920s on
behalf of the British School in Athens, was convinced that
the positions of the bodies pointed to a single act of burial
– at least for each tomb.

> ... from Schliemann's account of his excavations
> it is clear that the bodies had not been moved
> since they were first laid in the grave, for the
> bones and gear were all in order. Only in grave
> VI was a secondary interment noticed. There the
> remains of the first skeleton had been collected in
> one corner when the second was laid out in the
> centre of the grave. This recalls the procedure
> in chamber tombs.[4]

Burnt offerings were discovered in the Grave Circle A
shafts in a single pile of ashen remains – one ritual for all
the burials in each shaft. Tombstones were erected over the
burials (both at the original shaft-opening level and at the
surface of the raised terrace created by the later reorganising
of the site). Would these have been removed for every
reopening of the shaft? In spite of Dörpfeld's undoubtedly
correct reinterpretation of the construction methods used
to roof the graves, there is no clear-cut evidence that these
sepulchres were ever reopened for a sequence of burials
(apart from the one exception found in shaft-grave VI
noted by Wace). The bodies in each tomb do appear to
have been placed there in a single operation as Schliemann
claimed.

In addition, it seems that the male royal burials were
generally kept separate from the females in Grave Circle

A. Shaft-graves II (one body) and V (three bodies) both
housed males, the last marked by the carved stelae of
warrior activities (war and hunting). These male burials
were accompanied by large amounts of weaponry, including
spears, swords and daggers. The faces of the corpses were
also covered by the golden masks mentioned above. Shaft-
graves I (three bodies) and III (three bodies), on the other
hand, held the remains of females and were marked by a
plain, uncarved stela. These burials were not accompanied
by weapons and had no golden face-masks. Instead, the
ornaments included spectacular golden diadems. Shaft-
grave IV (five bodies) was the only tomb found with a mix
of males and females. Here were found two men lying side
by side, and a second group of one man and two women
lying next to each other at right angles to the other pair of
males. Presumably, as a result of this mixture of sexes, the
grave marker above the tomb was not carved with a war
or hunting scene. A sixth tomb was found after Schliemann

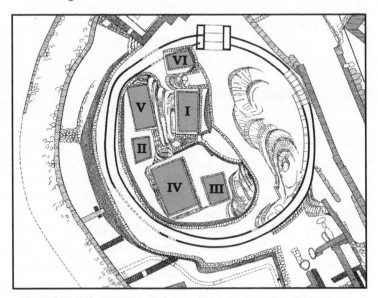

*71. Plan of Grave Circle A with the shafts of graves I to VI within the
enclosure.*

halted his own excavations at Mycenae and this contained two bodies – both male. This was the grave that had been reopened for the introduction of a second body.

In spite of the evidence outlined above, as I have said, the scholarly consensus tends towards a rejection of Schliemann's single-interment hypothesis, preferring to envisage a sequence of burials in the same shaft-graves. But is it really likely that tomb shafts were regularly being dug out over a century-long period to inter the male and female royals of Mycenae in segregated burial vaults? The reason why it is believed that the time-span of the whole tomb group is around a hundred years is that there appears to be two main styles of burial goods – fairly plain and much more elaborate – the argument being that the former must have preceded the latter. It is then estimated that such changes would take two to three generations to develop. So, if there are three generations or more of burials in the six shaft-graves, then the burials could not have been simultaneous. This is a reasonable position to hold, but it does not take into account the historical scenario which I think we can now propose, based on the evidence and arguments I have put before you in the previous chapters.

Mummies on the Move

A few years ago it was realised that an Egyptian mummy on exhibition in the Niagara Falls Daredevil Museum was laid out in the characteristic pose of a New Kingdom pharaoh, with arms crossed above his chest as if holding crook and flail. The mummy had been brought to the USA in around 1860 by an adventurer named James Douglas. This was two decades before the sensational discovery of the Royal Cache at Deir el-Bahri in 1881. However, the Cache was in fact found *at least* ten years earlier and only revealed to the authorities in 1881.

In August 2000, I wrote an article for the *Daily Express* (for which I was Archaeology Correspondent at the time) proposing that the Niagara Falls mummy was none other than Ramesses I (grandfather of Ramesses II and founder of the 19th Dynasty) whose coffin had been found in the Cache but whose body appeared to be missing from the collection of royal mummies. At the same time, my colleague, Aidan Dodson, was himself on the case, visiting the mummy and checking out its pedigree. You may have seen the subsequent television programme in which Egyptological opinion was that the pharaonic corpse was most likely to have come from the Royal Cache, before its official discovery, and been sold to Douglas who then brought it to America. Although not the only candidate for identification, it was concluded that the Niagara mummy was probably the missing Ramesses I and, following a thorough examination and clean-up at the Michael C. Carlos Museum in Atlanta, the Egyptian pharaoh was duly flown back to Cairo for a royal welcome worthy of a great Ramesside ruler. 'Ramesses I' now resides back in Thebes whence he came over a hundred years ago, reverently displayed in the new extension to the Luxor Museum.

As you might imagine, examples of deceased pharaohs travelling abroad are rather rare. Ramesses I was the first and his grandson, Ramesses II, the second and last to require a passport when he went for a clean-up in Paris. The spirits of the dead kings of Egypt were believed to journey through the underworld towards the 'Isle of Flame', beyond the eastern horizon, where they were united with the rising sun. But the body was decidedly not expected to accompany the spirit on this mysterious journey, and the royal mummies remained sealed within their sarcophagi, buried deep in their sepulchres in the Valley of the Kings. Ramesses I and Ramesses II were therefore the exception … or were they?

In some respects we are extremely fortunate in Egyptology to have more than twenty mummies of the kings of Egypt. It is often overlooked that ninety-nine per cent of the kingly remains from the ancient world have been lost

– destroyed through tomb-robbery, decay or cremation. The Hittite kings were cremated – just as Homer describes for the Trojans and their Greek attackers, who adopted the practice for their slain heroes whilst away from home at the long siege of Troy. The kings of Mesopotamia (Sumerians, Assyrians and Babylonians) have long rotted into the damp ground of the Euphrates and Tigris valleys. The tombs of the Israelite kings remain unknown, even though they 'slept with their ancestors' within the walls of the City of David. And the royal sepulchres of the flamboyant Minoans have never been identified in or near their Cretan palaces (perhaps with the exception of the so-called Temple-Tomb at Knossos, which may have been constructed for either of the legendary kings called Minos, and a few other chamber tombs, all found empty). Only in Egypt *and at Mycenae* are royal tombs of the Late Bronze Age preserved with their owners' bodies and grave goods intact.

In Schliemann's own report concerning one of the corpses in shaft-grave V at Mycenae, he mentions something which may also link the Grave Circle A burials with Egypt.

> Of the third body, which lay at the north end of the tomb, the round face, with all its flesh, had been wonderfully preserved under its ponderous golden mask; there was no vestige of hair, but both eyes were perfectly visible, also the mouth, which, owing to the enormous weight that had pressed upon it, was wide open, and showed thirty-two beautiful teeth. From these, all the physicians who came to see the body were led to believe that the man must have died at the early age of thirty-five. The nose was entirely gone. ... The colour of the body resembled very much that of an Egyptian mummy.[5]

Other comments scattered throughout Schliemann's publications suggest that several of the bodies (if not all) had been embalmed or mummified in some way. The respected Greek archaeologist, Chestos Tsountas, who followed Schliemann at Mycenae and uncovered the royal palace there, believed that his predecessor's account of the state of preservation of more than one body from Grave Circle A had to be taken seriously and that mummification must have been employed to preserve the deceased.[6] Yet the bodies themselves were clearly not Egyptian but Caucasian.

Mummification was an Egyptian practice and was surely, in the case of the Mycenaean royal 'mummies', introduced as a result of direct contact with, or residence in, the Land of the Pharaohs. Were the bodies in Grave Circle A brought to the site *en masse* from somewhere else, along with their exotic burial paraphernalia? This might explain the multiple, simultaneous burials and the fact that the human remains which Schliemann found appear to have been embalmed. Could that somewhere else have been Egypt – the land of mummification? Perhaps Ramesses I and Ramesses II were not the only pharaohs to have journeyed abroad after they had died.

Wealth Beyond Reason

The other big question which arose from Schliemann's discovery of Grave Circle A has challenged the experts for generations. In the early 1950s archaeologists found a second grave circle, just outside the walls of the citadel at Mycenae, that turned out to be slightly older than Grave Circle A. The twenty-four tombs in this Grave Circle B were nowhere near as richly endowed as those from Schliemann's excavations with their 'gold, silver, ostrich eggs from Nubia, lapis lazuli from Afganistan, alabaster and faience from Crete, ivory from Syria and amber from the Baltic'.[7] Something had happened to the rulers buried at Mycenae which, in the space of a couple of generations, radically changed their fortunes.

There is little to prepare us for the sudden out-
burst of power and luxury which is displayed
by the shaft-graves (of Grave Circle A). The five
hundred years down to 1600 BC (in the OC) were
comparatively poverty stricken, the inhabitants
of mainland Greece subsisting with meagre
bronze tools in small, huddled communities,
usually unfortified and entirely lacking palatial
buildings.[8]

The early, pre-palatial Mycenaean necropolis thus centred
around two grave circles – one relatively poor and typical
of the Bronze Age Greek world (Middle Helladic III)
and the other fabulously wealthy with exotic, exquisitely
crafted, cosmopolitan treasures (Late Helladic I). As David
Trail, author of *Schliemann of Troy*, put it in 1995:

This brings us to what is perhaps the most
fundamental puzzle of the shaft-graves. It was
succinctly posed thirty years ago by one of the
leading experts on Mycenaean art: 'How did the
princes of the shaft-graves get so rich?' It has never
been satisfactorily answered.

The evidence for the foreign nature of the Grave Circle
A royals is striking. The earlier bodies of Grave Circle B
were found in contracted or semi-foetal position whereas
the Grave Circle A bodies lay in extended posture just
like Egyptian mummies. And the grave goods were truly
international in character, many originating in Crete
or the Nile valley – with the glint of Egyptian (?) gold
everywhere.

The profusion of gold is startling, especially
in contrast with the poverty of earlier Middle
Helladic remains. … Whether this collective
use of a tomb is by itself a seriously significant

departure from the Middle Helladic practice
of single burial is debatable ... the change
from contracted to extended posture ... the
excess of grandeur, the prodigal use of hitherto
unparalleled riches, has to be explained; and in
the grave-goods themselves there are numerous
innovations of form and decoration that hardly
allow us to regard these burials as a natural
development and elaboration of Middle Helladic
practice.[9]

Even though there appear to be characteristically 'Minoan'
artefacts included with the burial goods, the occupants of
the tombs themselves were clearly not typically Cretan.

The manner of the burials is not Minoan; the
tenants of the graves, to judge from the broad,
bearded faces of the gold masks, are quite
unlike the elegant, smooth-chinned Minoans;
their bones show a 'champion's physique' ...
and their prodigal ostentation in grave-gifts has
something barbarous about it by comparison
with anything known from Crete. Again, the
emphasis in their *objets d'art* on scenes of fighting
and hunting is alien to the spirit of Minoan art.
The rulers of Mycenae at this time cannot be
Minoan. ... Several objects among their contents
– a crystal bowl in the form of a duck, a box of
Egyptian sycamore with appliqué ivory figures of
dogs – are imports from Egypt; the influence of
Egyptian mummy-casings has been suggested to
account for the gold masks; the Nilotic scene on
one of the daggers has already been mentioned.
Further, the carved grave stelae have no
precedents (or immediate successors) in Greece,
and no parallels in Crete; but monuments of
carved stone had long been usual in Egypt. The

reliefs are our earliest evidence for the horse-drawn chariot in Greece; and it may have been introduced from Egypt, where it first appears under the Hyksos rulers.[10]

I am sure you can see where this is leading. The occupants of Grave Circle A were neither from the Middle Helladic mainland culture of Greece, nor from the Middle Minoan Cretan culture. These chariot-riding warriors were 'men of great stature' who appear to have been influenced by Egyptian culture.

> It is clear that the rulers of Mycenae who were buried in these graves moved in a larger world than their predecessors, a world that stretched at least to Egypt; but what events caused this widening of horizons is still difficult to explain. ... One scholar has even surmised that the reliefs on the silver vessel from shaft-grave IV known as the 'Siege Rhyton' actually depict a scene from some such campaign in the Egyptian delta.[11]

The solution to this puzzle may finally be in sight with the latest discoveries at Ezbet Helmi and a recognition that the Shemau of Avaris were a distinct group from the Aamu Asiatics who had lived in the eastern delta for several generations prior to the arrival of the 'immigrant' Greater Hyksos kings.

To what period do the experts date the royal burials at Mycenae? The answer is approximately to the beginning of the Late Bronze Age (Late Helladic I) and therefore contemporary with the end of the Second Intermediate Period and the rise of the New Kingdom in Egypt. In other words, the men and women represented by the Mycenaean mummies, with their rich grave goods, were contemporary with the late Hyksos kings and the first pharaohs of the 18th Dynasty. This is entirely consistent with the foundation legend of the Mycenaean royal dynasty which was established with the arrival of Danaus in the Argolid following his expulsion from Egypt.

Conclusion Fifteen

The shaft-graves from Grave Circle A at Mycenae may include the re-burials of the Greater Hyksos Pelasgian rulers of Avaris, brought to Greece by Danaus following the expulsion of the Hyksos Shemau from the Egyptian delta at the beginning of the New Kingdom.

The Legend of Danaus and Aegyptus

In addition to the Io legend, which brought the Pelasgian Greeks of the Argolid to Egypt, there is a second well-known tradition which links the Peloponnese to the Nile delta. The story, epitomised in Aeschylus' drama *Supplices*, describes the flight of Danaus and his family from Egypt to the Argolid where he founded a new royal dynasty known as the Danaeids. Danaus, as begetter of the line, gave his eponym to the Pelasgian Greeks – the Danaio of Homer. Danaus was the fourth-generation ancestor of Danae – the mother of Perseus who, according to Pausanias, founded the royal citadel at Mycenae as is 'known to any Greek' [Book II:1]. Perseus was the third-generation ancestor of Heracles and Eurystheus, the latter succeeded by his uncle, Atreus son of Pelops. And Atreus, in turn, was the father of Agamemnon and Menelaus. Altogether, according to legend, there were roughly ten generations between Danaus (founder of the dynasty) and Agamemnon (the Pelopid leader of the expedition against Troy).

Danaus had fled from his brother Aegyptus (surely a clear reference to a native Egyptian pharaoh) and arrived by ship on the shores of the Argive plain. There he challenged the local ruler, Gelanor, for the throne and was subsequently crowned king by the population. The *Supplices* gives him claim to the sovereignty of Argos through his descent from Io. So Danaus was not a native Egyptian but of Argolid Pelasgian descent. However, from this point in Greek history, the people of Hellas began to call themselves Danaoi (one of Homer's names for the Bronze Age Greeks) after the new dynasty founder.

> Danaus ... became so powerful a ruler that
> all the Pelasgians of Greece called themselves
> Danaeans.[12]

Having already delved deeply into the Hyksos era and the war of liberation which resulted in the overthrow and expulsion of the foreigners, I am sure you will be thinking (as I and several scholars in the past have done) that the Danaus and Aegyptus story has to be a garbled version of the Hyksos expulsion, personified in the tale of two quarrelling brothers. This is surely right, in spite of the fact that Manetho inserts the tradition not at the end of the Hyksos period but between the 18th and 19th Dynasties where we read:

> Armais, also called Danaus, [reigned] for five
> years. Thereafter, he was banished from Egypt
> and, fleeing from his brother Aegyptus, he
> arrived in Greece, and, seizing Argos, ruled over
> the Argives.

Identifying Danaus with Harmais (apparently a Greek version of Haremheb) and Aegyptus with Sethos (Seti I) makes little historical sense and, as we will see in the next chapter, such a chronological setting is far too late for the Argive dynasty of Danaus, whose founder ruled ten generations before the Trojan War according to Greek tradition. The time of the Hyksos expulsion is a much more convincing era to place the story and, as I have postulated, the Lords of Avaris did indeed flee across the sea to their kindred lands following the siege of their delta stronghold by Ahmose (whom we can identify with Aegyptus – the native pharaoh of Egypt who banished his 'brother' king).

So, was Danaus the last Hyksos ruler of Avaris? The original name of the sixth Greater Hyksos king in the Turin Canon is given as Khamudy – a name, in fact, closer to Cadmus – the 'Phoenician' ruler who sailed to Greek Thebes and brought 'writing' to the West according to tradition. I cannot be the first person to envisage here a simple case of metathesis where an original KHADMUY has become KHAMUDY in the 19th Dynasty Royal Canon (copied centuries after the fall of the Hyksos). It is therefore intriguing to note that, in the genealogies of later tradition, Danaus is identified as the nephew of the Phoenician king Agenor, father of Cadmus. Thus, in legend at least, Danaus and Cadmus were contemporaries. Were they both Hyksos 'rulers of foreign countries' (Egyptian *hekau-khasut*)

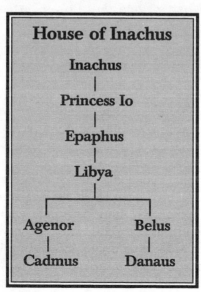

House of Inachus

Inachus
|
Princess Io
|
Epaphus
|
Libya
|
Agenor — Belus
| |
Cadmus   Danaus

– one of Pelasgian stock through Io, the other of mixed Phoenician stock through Agenor? As you will see later, this attractive possibility may be prevented by the constraints of chronology.

However, putting genealogical chronology aside for the moment, this makes the statement by Herodotus that Cadmus sailed to the island of Kalliste (Thera) on his way to Euboea on mainland Greece all the more intriguing.

> There were in the island that is now called Thera (but in those former times was called Kalliste) descendants of Membliarus, the son of Poeciles, a Phoenician. For Cadmus, son of Agenor, searching for Europa, had put in at the island now called Thera; and when he put in there, the place pleased him so much (or he may have had some other personal reason) that he left in it, along with other Phoenicians, one of his own kinsfolk – Membliarus. These occupied this island, Kalliste, for eight generations before ever Theras came there from Lacedaemon. [Book IV]

Theras takes us down into the early Iron Age era of the Dorian invasion when he set out to colonise Kalliste which was then renamed 'Thera' after him, but here, back at the start of the Late Bronze Age, just let fantasy fly for a moment and imagine with me that it is the very journey of legendary Cadmus which is depicted in the West House Miniature Fresco from Akrotiri. I have already suggested that the last scene represents the return of the Shemau from Avaris to Akrotiri. So, could the high-ranking young man in the flagship be none other than Cadmus himself, setting out for Greece via Kalliste?

The Parian Marble tells us that Danaus made his voyage from Egypt to the Argolid eight years after Cadmus arrived in Greek Thebes. So Danaus would have been the very last foreign ruler of Avaris following the departure of Khadmuy/ Cadmus. And he would then be the anonymous Hyksos ruler who negotiated the final withdrawal of his kin from Avaris in the eleventh year of Ahmose – in the same year that Thera erupted for the first time in the LM IA–LM IB sequence.

Danaus was therefore a Shemau chieftain – a royal descendant of Inachus through Io and her son Apophis – just as the traditions state. If Ahhotep is the legendary Io, as I have argued, then, as the mother of both Apophis and Ahmose, she would be the Aegean gene-source for both the Greater Hyksos *and* the 18th Dynasty royal lines. Any Hyksos child of hers (before her marriage to Sekenenre Telaken or Telegonus) would rightly have been a half-brother of Ahmose/Aegyptus.

All this, of course, is pure speculation – but there is certainly some support within Egyptology for intermarriage between the Hyksos kings of Avaris and the pharaohs of the Theban 17th Dynasty. There is a strong suspicion – reading between the lines of the Kamose texts – that, prior to the war of liberation, cordial (perhaps familial) relations existed between the Avaris/Memphite and Theban royal courts. When the rift came it was prolonged and bloody – as wars between members of the same extended family often are. The First World War predominantly fought between Kaiser Wilhelm II's *Reich* and the kingdom of Britain, ruled over by George Windsor (né Saxe-Coburg-Gotha), readily springs to mind. Kaiser Bill, King George V and Tsar Nicholas of Russia were all cousins. A similar state of affairs may well have pertained in Second Intermediate Period Egypt where, in later eras, intermarriage between the great royal families of the ancient world was commonplace.

This might also provide an explanation for the discovery of alabaster jars, bearing the cartouches of Apophis and his daughter, Princess Herit, in the tomb of Ahmose-Nefertari (Pharaoh Ahmose's Great Royal Wife). These objects cannot simply be 'booty' from Hyksos Avaris but may be evidence of a marriage between Apophis' daughter and Ahmose. The burial chamber of tomb Dra Abu el-Naga B was enlarged in order to accommodate a second burial and it is my contention that both Ahmose-Nefertari and Herit were originally buried there by Ahmose's successor, Amenhotep I. Perhaps one of Ahhotep's strategies to avoid her kingdom being overrun by Hyksos or Kushites during the period of her regency (when Ahmose was still young) was to agree to a marriage alliance between her young son and Apophis' daughter. This would have bought her valuable time (around ten years) to prepare for Ahmose's final assault on the Hyksos following the death of Apophis.

The 17th/18th Dynasty Theban branch of the family (of part native bloodline) was eventually victorious and succeeded in negotiating a withdrawal of their Hyksos cousins from the delta. The main body of the Aamu population of Avaris, led by some of their Hyksos lords, departed for the coastal plain of southern Canaan where they re-established themselves at Sharuhen.

Others went into the hill country (of later Judah) and established the Jebusite enclave at Jerusalem. Manetho refers to the people of Jerusalem as Solymites – an ethnic term which has nothing to do with Solomon or the Israelites but more likely is a direct reference to the Solymi of Anatolia.[13] These Solymi appear to have originated in the region of Anactoria/Anaku (later Lycia) which would then make them one of the Indo-European clans belonging to the overall tribal designations of Anakim and Rephaim used in the Old Testament.

The main extended Greater Hyksos royal family surely left by sea in the ships belonging to their powerful merchant fleet and we can conclude that these Hyksos royals were widely dispersed throughout their trading empire following the expulsion from Egypt. It seems entirely likely, therefore, that one group (perhaps the core royal family – Danaus and his fifty daughters, whatever their true number) departed for their ancestral homelands in the Peloponnese.

> ## Conclusion Sixteen
> The catalyst for the rise of the wealthy Late Bronze Age dynasties of Greece, Crete and western Anatolia was the dispersion of the Greater Hyksos ruling elite from Avaris out of whom such legendary figures as Agenor (of Tyre), Cadmus (of Thebes), Danaus (of Argos), Minos (of Knossos) and Perseus (of Mycenae) were descended.

Time then to attempt an historical reconstruction of pre-Classical Greece, from the arrival of the Hyksos refugee Danaus down to Agamemnon and the Trojan War. This is going to involve considerable reliance on the core genealogical frameworks provided by the later Greek literature – something which most scholars would consider an unreliable methodology.

But my position is very simple: I take the view that Strabo was right when he argued that, once the mythological and fanciful elements surrounding the Greek heroes are filtered out of the tales, the basic stories are essentially true. What I think we can take from this is that the personalities in the tales are probably based on real characters and events (after all, these stories can be classified as legends rather than myths) and that their legendary relationships to each other and to their ancestors and descendants are reasonably accurate. In other words the genealogies and wars between city-states are historical – once we have dispatched the interfering gods back to Mount Olympus. There is nothing inherently wrong in taking this position as a starting point. It has been demonstrated over and over again that genuine aspects of history can be exaggerated and embellished over time into legend and folklore.

There are unfortunately no contemporary documents (beyond the Linear B non-literary administrative texts) that we can employ to support our reconstruction. We only have the traditions to work with and they are complex and multi-faceted – as a glance through Robert Graves' famous volume *The Greek Myths* soon makes abundantly clear. On top of that you will have to cope with another collection of nearly unpronounceable names for our Greek personalities, many of whom may not be familiar to you – given the failure of our modern education system to cover the Classics in any serious way these days. Graves was bemoaning just this situation when he began his book back in the 1950s.

> ... the Classics have lately lost so much ground in schools and universities that an educated person is now no longer expected to know (for instance) who Deucalion, Pelops, Daedalus, Oenone, Laocoön, or Antigone may have been. ... at first sight this does not seem to matter much, because for the last two thousand years it has been the fashion to dismiss the myths as bizarre and chimerical fancies – a charming legacy from the childhood of the Greek intelligence, which the Church naturally deprecates in order to emphasise the greater spiritual importance of the Bible. Yet it is difficult to overestimate their value in the study of early European history, religion, and sociology.[14]

How many of the six legendary figures mentioned by Graves have you heard of? Do you know their stories? I have to confess that, without looking them up, only five out of the six are familiar to me. Deucalion the flood hero – yes, no problem; Pelops the son of Tantalus and founder of the Pelopid line of kings at Mycenae (including Atreus and Agamemnon) – that one is straightforward, after all the Peloponnese ('island of Pelops') is named after him; Daedalus – of course, he was the designer of the famous Labyrinth on Crete (home of the Minotaur) and the first human to fly 'on the wings of Daedalus'; Oenone – I haven't got a clue; Laocoön – Troy's prophet of doom, swallowed up by a great sea-serpent, is easy because I have just recently stood before his famous statue in the Vatican Museum; Antigone – I seem to recall that she was the daughter of King Oedipus who accompanied her blind father into exile following the disgrace of his incestuous relationship with his mother. How did you do? Congratulations if you did better than me, but don't worry if you struggled a bit – just remember that Robert Graves was the leading authority of his day on the Greek legends and so he is bound to know more than either of us!

Graves was also quite right to be concerned at the shift in emphasis from our Indo-European cultural origins to Christianity-based teaching which tends to deny, or push to one side, the great wealth of literature from the pre-Christian 'pagan' world. Whatever its failings from a religious perspective, the cultural aspects of early Indo-European civilisation should not be denied to its ethnic descendants, whatever their spiritual background. That was one of the considered reasons for writing this book, especially in the light of so many new archaeological findings. Such a history has been attempted before – but not since the amazing discoveries of Tell ed-Daba, Akrotiri, Troy and, of course, the emergence of the New Chronology.

The Five Great Races of Man

This seems the appropriate time to deal with Hesiod – an approximate contemporary of Homer – and his famous fivefold division of human history. The Boeotian poet divided human existence into 'metallic' eras or ages. First came the Golden Age, then the Silver Age, then two phases of the Brazen (i.e. Bronze) Age before the final Iron Age of his own days. The first 'Golden Age' clearly reflects what we would regard as the pre-agricultural era of the Palaeolithic and Mesolithic when hunter-gatherers roamed the Earth.

According to Hesiod these were the earliest humans:

> ... who lived without cares or labour, eating
> only acorns, wild fruit, and honey that dripped
> from the trees, drinking the milk of sheep and
> goats, never growing old, dancing, and laughing
> much. Death, to them, was no more terrible
> than sleep.[15]

This epoch was followed by the 'Silver Age' of the Neolithic period and what we call the Early Bronze Age when crop-planting (grain and vegetables), animal husbandry and pastoralism became the norms. Archaeological discoveries in Anatolia have shown that this was the era of the great Earth-Goddess.

> Next came a Silver Race, eaters of bread, likewise
> divinely created. The men were utterly subject
> to their mothers and dared not disobey them,
> although they might live to be a hundred years
> old. They were quarrelsome and ignorant, and
> never sacrificed to the gods but, at least, did
> not make war on one another. Zeus destroyed
> them all.[16]

The Silver Age ended with the collapse and destruction (by some unknown natural catastrophe) of the Early Bronze Age city-states in the Fertile Crescent when the Zeus-worshipping (that is storm-god-worshipping) Indo-Europeans arrived in the Middle East. All was overthrown in *circa* 2100 BC (OC – *c.* 2300 BC) with the cataclysmic events of EB III followed by the arrival of the Rephaim and Anakim from the north. In biblical terms this was the age of long-lived patriarchs (of the post-flood era) culminating in the Amorite chieftains, Abraham, Isaac and Jacob, who settled in Canaan during MB I. So the momentous Silver Age ended in the birth of Middle Bronze Age Pelasgiotis

(Greece) – when we enter Hesiod's 'Brazen Age' – which included the extraordinary final 'Age of the Heroes'.

> Next came a Brazen Race, who fell like fruits
> from the ash-trees, and were armed with brazen
> weapons. They ate flesh as well as bread, and
> delighted in war, being insolent and pitiless men.
> Black Death has seized them all.[17]

It seems to me that there is a reference here to northerners from the forested Indo-European homelands of the Caucasus region, arriving in their ash-wood chariots, armed to the teeth with weapons of bronze. Their skills in warfare enabled them to conquer the old Early Bronze Age world before the 'Canaanite Illness' (bubonic plague = Black Death) decimated their ranks at the end of the Middle Bronze Age (as witnessed in the early New Kingdom papyri of Egypt).

> The fourth race of man was brazen too, but
> nobler and more generous, being begotten by the
> gods on mortal mothers. They fought gloriously
> in the siege of Thebes, the expedition of the
> Argonauts, and the Trojan War. These became
> heroes, and dwell in the Elysian Fields.[18]

Here, of course, we are on familiar territory with the likes of Perseus, Oedipus, the Seven Against Thebes, the Epigonoi, Heracles, Jason and the Argonauts, Achilles, Agamemnon and Odysseus. And the transition from the third to the fourth race (the second of brazen-clad warriors) appears to have been the 'divine born' Perseus.

So far in this book we have been concentrating on the earlier of Hesiod's two 'brazen' races – the Lords of Avaris who plundered Egypt and returned to their Aegean homelands laden with the wealth of Egypt stashed in the holds of their ships. They were the ancestors of Hesiod's fourth race whose time we are now entering in our reconstructed history of the Greek Bronze Age.

Danaus and the Flight from Egypt

With the Egyptian army of Ahmose (Aegyptus) besieging Avaris, Danaus, perhaps like Cadmus, departed from the Hyksos stronghold by sea and, having followed the anticlockwise currents of the eastern Mediterranean, arrived at the island of Rhodes. He then sailed on to the Peloponnese to land near Lerna on the southern shore of the Bay of Argolis. From there he rode to Argos to claim the throne as the descendant of Inachus (through Io). Gelanor, the incumbent ruler, was forced to abdicate and a new dynasty of Pelasgian rulers was established with the coronation of Danaus. The people of the Argolid, though themselves indigenous Pelasgoi, were henceforth known as Danaoi after their new ruler.[19]

This appears to be confirmed by the Egyptians who record the receipt of a gift from the 'prince of Danaya' of 'a silver flagon in Kaftara-work' (i.e. made by the Caphtorim/Keftiu) in Year 42 of Thutmose III.[20] Then, two generations later, we find a statue base of Amenhotep III recording toponyms in the territories of Kaftara and Danaya, including *Amnisa* (Amnissos), *Bayasta* (Phaistos) and *Kanusa* (Knossos) on Crete and *Mukana* (Mycenae), *Thegwais* (Thebes), *Misane* (Messenia), *Napliya* (Nauplion), *Weliya* (Elis) and *Amakla* (Amyclae) in Greece.[21]

Danaus had a daughter named Hypermestra who married Lynceus. The latter succeeded Danaus (by murdering him) and was the father of Abas, the third king of Danaeid Argos. This Abas had two sons who divided the kingdom between them following an internecine war – one, Acrisius, ruling from Argos, the other, Proetus, ruling from Tiryns. Acrisius had a daughter named Danae who married Polydectes, king of the small Aegean island of Seriphos where she gave birth to a son (by Zeus or Polydectes) – the famous Perseus who,

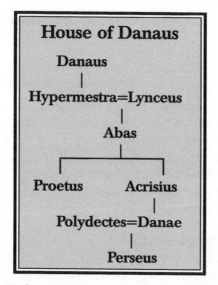

House of Danaus

Danaus
|
Hypermestra=Lynceus
|
Abas
|
Proetus   Acrisius
|
Polydectes=Danae
|
Perseus

having killed his grandfather Acrisius, ruled the Argolid and built the citadel of Mycenae. Thus King Perseus of Mycenae was the fifth-generation descendant of Danaus.

The New Chronology date for the fall of Avaris and the Hyksos departure from Egypt is *circa* 1181 BC. This, then, would be the approximate date of Danaus' journey to Greece. If we round the figure down to 1180 BC for this Hyksos lord's accession to the throne of Argolis, and then allow one hundred and thirty years for the reigns of Danaus and his three successors (the last, Acrisius, ruling for two generations), we would find Perseus building the citadel at Mycenae in the second half of the eleventh century.

The building of Mycenae may mark the arrival of non-Pelasgian Greeks into the Peloponnese, represented by Perseus' rule in the Argolid. With him may have come Greek-speaking forces from the islands which, though led by a man of Pelasgian (Danaean) descent, were not part of the 'divine Pelasgian' elite world. Perseus' name is properly Pterseus, which means 'destroyer', perhaps reflecting his role in the overthrow of the Pelasgian Danaeid rulers of Argos. Perseus marks the transition into Hesiod's second Brazen

Age which culminates in the Trojan War. This is followed by the poet's own race of lacklustre men of the impoverished Early Iron Age.

> The fifth race is the present Race of Iron, un-worthy descendants of the fourth. They are degenerate, cruel, unjust, malicious, libidinous, unfilial and treacherous.

The age of heroic men had passed and both Hesiod and Homer looked back to the glories of Man's recent Bronze Age past for their inspiration.

The House of Atreus

The final transformation of Bronze Age Greek culture comes with the arrival of Pelops, grandfather of Agamemnon. According to tradition, he was the son of Tantalus, a 'Phrygian' or 'Lydian' ruler of the kingdom of Paphlagonia near Mount Sipylus (the later land of Lydia) in western Anatolia.[22] On succeeding to the throne, Pelops found himself being harassed by King Ilus of Troy (after whom Ilios is named) and chose to flee to Greece, landing in ELIS, later home of the Olympic Games which were inaugurated in memory of Pelops. He is aided in his conquest by the charioteer, Myrsilus, clearly a Greek version of the Hittite name Murshili(sh).[23] This story no doubt reflects an actual invasion of the Greek mainland by Achaean warriors from Anatolia because Pelops had soon subjugated virtually the whole of the Peloponnese which, from this time onward, was known to the Hittites as Akhiyawa – 'land of the Akhaiwoi' (i.e. Homer's Achaeans). In fact, the large landmass to the south of the Gulf of Corinth (and attached to Europe by the slender Isthmus of Corinth) was, according to tradition, originally called Pelasgiotis ('land of the Pelasgians') and only renamed the Peloponnese after Pelops' successful takeover.[24]

With the conquest of Danaya ('land of the Danaoi') by the son of Tantalus, the multi-faceted civilisation of Bronze Age Greece took its final form with the Achaean leaders of the Trojan War claiming their descent from Pelops. It is from this point on that we find references in 19th Dynasty Egyptian monumental inscriptions to Akawasha (i.e. Achaiwoi/Achaeans) and in Empire-period Hittite records to Akhiyawa (i.e. Achaea) 'across the sea'.

Pelops was a contemporary of Laius, king of Thebes and father of Oedipus. He had several sons – including Chrysippus, Thyestes and Atreus. The latter fled from Pisa, capital of Elis, following the death of Chrysippus (who had been abducted by Laius to serve as his young male concubine in Thebes). It seems that Atreus may have been implicated in the boy's murder, otherwise it is difficult to explain why he needed to seek refuge in the court of Eurystheus (third successor of Perseus) at Mycenae. This Eurystheus was the king who set the labours of Heracles and, following the famous hero's death, went to war against the Heracleidae ('sons of Heracles').

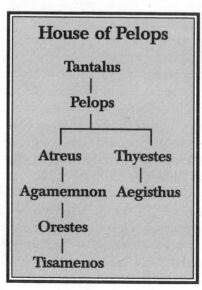

385

As he marched off to Athens in order to do battle with his enemies, Eurystheus appointed his uncle Atreus as regent in his stead. The king was then killed by Hyllus, the eldest son of Heracles, and, in the absence of an heir, Atreus was chosen as the new ruler of Mycenae. So began the Pelopid Dynasty which ended with the Dorian invasion and the 'Return of the Heracleidae' eighty years later. This was one of the bloodiest eras in Greek history when virtually every member of the royal line was murdered by a family member. The internecine blood-letting began with the quarrel for succession between Pelops' two sons.

Atreus took Aerope, daughter of King Catreus (the son of Minos the Younger of Crete), as his wife and she bore him Agamemnon and Menelaus. Atreus threw his surviving brother into prison because he perceived him as a rival to power. In this he was soon proved right when Thyestes persuaded his son, Aegisthus, to murder Atreus. Once the deed was done Thyestes seized the throne of Mycenae for a brief time before Agamemnon, raising an army in Sparta with the support of King Tyndareus, wrested the sceptre from Thyestes and banished his uncle from the kingdom. Agamemnon then forcibly married Clytemnestra, daughter of Tyndareus, having killed her first husband, Tantalus of Pisa, in battle. This brought the famous Dioscuri – the twins CASTOR AND POLLUX – to the gates of Mycenae. Being the brothers of Clytemnestra they intended to seek revenge for the death of her husband and abduction of Tyndareus' eldest daughter. However, Agamemnon fled to Sparta and succeeded in gaining forgiveness from the old Spartan king. As a result, he was able to return to Mycenae and continue his rule.

It is not made clear in the traditions if the army of the Dioscuri destroyed or burnt the palace of Mycenae in Agamemnon's absence – but a destruction has been found by the archaeologists towards the end of the Late Helladic IIIB period. As we shall soon see, this was the era when the Trojan War was fought, and the attack of Castor and Pollux,

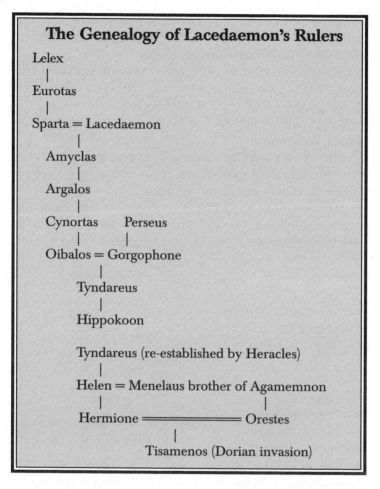

The Genealogy of Lacedaemon's Rulers

Lelex
|
Eurotas
|
Sparta = Lacedaemon
|
   Amyclas
   |
   Argalos
   |
   Cynortas   Perseus
   | |
   Oibalos = Gorgophone
        |
        Tyndareus
        |
        Hippokoon

        Tyndareus (re-established by Heracles)
        |
        Helen = Menelaus brother of Agamemnon
        | |
        Hermione ============ Orestes
                |
                Tisamenos (Dorian invasion)

a few years prior to the Trojan expedition, may provide an historical setting for the otherwise unexplained burning of the palace at Mycenae.

The Mycenaean House of Pelops grew wealthier and more powerful as the years went by. The Dioscuri passed away leaving Agamemnon as undisputed high-king (*wanax*). His brother, Menelaus, married Tyndareus' second daughter, the beautiful Helen, and the Spartan king was persuaded to abdicate in favour of his daughter's new husband. So

Menelaus became king of Lacedaemon and the Pelopids gained control of most of the Peloponnese. But all was not well in the citadel palace of Mycenae.

A seething hatred lingered in the breast of Agamemnon's queen. She had witnessed the slaying of her first husband and now she had to endure the sacrifice of her beloved daughter Iphigenia as a blood offering to inaugurate the expedition against Troy. During the ten-year absence of her husband, fighting his war with the Trojans, Clytemnestra plotted her revenge. She took Aegisthus, son of Atreus' brother Thyestes and the former's assassin, as her lover. The two awaited the king's return. The day of his arrival back in Mycenae was Agamemnon's last. He was murdered as he took a bath to soak away the stains of his bloody victory in far-off Troy.

Chapter Thirteen

THE TROJAN WAR

The City of Ilios --Troy VI or VII? -- LH IIIB and
LH IIIC -- Eteocles and Atreus -- Hittites at Troy --
Manetho's Date for the Trojan War

as the Trojan War a genuine historical event? The
Greeks themselves believed without question
that it was – and that is good enough for me
and many authorities who have studied the controversial
question.

> Indeed the fact that the Trojan War was accepted
> as historical by all the ancient Greek world, and
> that no writer in all that nation of sceptics ever
> questioned its historicity, is the most compelling
> evidence that it really did take place.[1]

It has been a long voyage to reach what is to many (and
certainly to the Greeks and Romans) one of the great
turning points in human history. We have arrived with
Agamemnon's Achaeans as they beach their 1,186 black-
hulled ships on the sandy shores of what is today called
Besik Bay, just eight kilometres from the high walls of sacred

Ilios. The ten-year siege of Troy is about to begin and the world is destined to change for ever as a consequence of that terrible folly.

The year is 874 BC (in the NC) and Ramesses the Great has been resting in his tomb in the Valley of the Kings for the past four years. Following the great pharaoh's death, after a sixty-six-year reign, Egypt has descended into civil war with Ramesses II's thirteenth son, the aged Merenptah, struggling to hold on to power as rivals to the Egyptian throne rise from amidst the ranks of his father's copious offspring.

In Israel the descendants of Jacob have been divided into two kingdoms for nearly sixty years, following the Schism upon the death of Solomon in 932 BC. The Northern Kingdom is now ruled by Ahab son of Omri, with the rival Southern Kingdom of Judah under the rule of the powerful and long-lived Asa.

In Mesopotamia the Assyrian despot, Ashurnasirpal II (who liked to decorate his palace with scenes of rebels being impaled and flayed alive), is in his tenth year as absolute monarch over an ever-expanding domain.

In Anatolia the mighty Hittite empire has recently collapsed – humbled by plague, famine and marauding tribes from the north. The last emperor, Shuppiluliuma II, had desperately tried to defend his capital at Hattusha from the Kaskan tribes of the Pontus region (southern Black Sea coast) and hordes of newcomers from the north-west – comprising the Mushki (Phrygian) and Tabal clans of the Danube basin. In the end he failed. Shuppiluliuma also failed to hold on to the kingdom of Alashiya (part of Cyprus), with its rich copper mines, which had been under constant pressure from piratical Aegean adventurers.

The Hittite emperor's military failures had left his allies in the west vulnerable to raids from across the Aegean Sea. Wilusa – Homer's Ilios* (originally Mycenaean Greek Wilios

---

* In the *Iliad* the name Ilios appears a total of 106 times, whereas the name Troy occurs only 50 times.

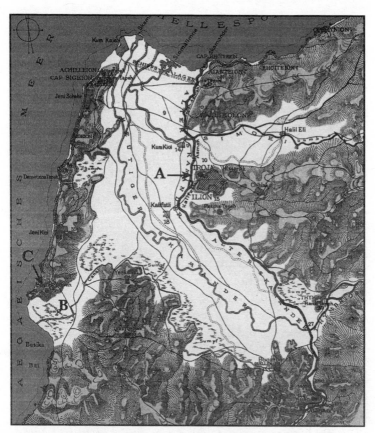

72. *An original map of the Troad by T. Spratt (1894) with Troy/Hissarlik (A) and the Greek camp at Besik Bay (B) separated from each other by the valley of the Scamander river. The tumulus of Achilles is located above the Greek camp at Besik Tepe (C).*

written with an initial archaic digamma[2]) – in north-west Anatolia could no longer rely on Hittite support to protect its territory from 'the men of Akhiyawa' as they called them – Homer's *Achaiwoi* (Achaeans) – led by the ambitious Agamemnon of Mycenae.

The bronze-clad Greeks were now encamped on the western coast of Anatolia, ready to exploit the power vacuum left by the Hittite collapse.

Lofty Towers at Windy Troy

The great city of Troy had stood in its commanding position overlooking the plain of the Scamander flowing into the Hellespont, for more than a thousand years. The walls which enclosed and protected the sacred acropolis of Ilios (known as the Pergamos), where the royal family held court and worshipped in the shrines of Zeus, Athena and Apollo(n) – the Anatolian deity Apaliuna – had been standing proud and erect for centuries. Below the Scaean Gate, which guarded the road leading up through the royal quarter to Priam's palace, sprawled a vast lower city (of some two hundred thousand square metres), teeming with mercantile life. The population has been estimated at between five and ten thousand (excluding those living in the countryside of the Troad outside the city) – many times the size of Joshua's Jericho.

> In haste the old king (Priam) boarded his bright car (chariot) and clattered out of the echoing colonnade. In front the mule-team drew the four-wheeled wagon ... through the town. Family and friends all followed, weeping as though for Priam's last and deathward ride. Into the lower town they passed, and reached the plain of Troy.
> [*Iliad*, Book XXIV]

This lower city was, in turn, enclosed by a stone and mudbrick fortification wall on the inner edge of a rock-cut trench – a barrier deep and wide enough to prevent any assault by chariot or battering-ram.

Buried under the Late Bronze Age ramparts and megaron palaces of Troy VI were five earlier cities – one of which (Troy II) produced the magnificent golden treasure unearthed by Schliemann, now in the Pushkin Museum in Moscow. But none of these earlier cities compared to the spectacular fortified stronghold of Troy VI. The city of Ilios (founded by [W]Ilus, after whom the Anatolian kingdom of Wilusa was named) was the wonder of its age. The walls of the Pergamos (inner city) were constructed of massive stone foundations (four-and-a-half metres thick) made up of ASHLAR blocks woven into panels eight metres in length and four metres high, each slightly offset from its neighbour to produce the sweeping curve of the wall and protect against earth movement in this land of the Earth-Shaker (see plate 52). Atop the gently battered stone base rose a broad mudbrick rampart reaching to a total height of around nine metres from the ground. Along the length of this massive wall were positioned huge square towers, protecting the various entrances to the upper city. In the sixth book of the *Iliad* Homer describes the vivid scene of Hector's wife, the Princess Andromache, standing with child in arms on the topmost level of the 'Great Tower of Ilion' from where she could survey the bloody conflict being fought out for possession of her beloved city.

> He (Hector) turned away and quickly entered his own hall, but found Princess Andromache was not at home. With one nursemaid and her small child, she stood upon the Tower of Ilium in tears, bemoaning what she saw. ... Up to **the great Tower of Ilium** she had taken her way, because she had heard that our men were spent in battle by Achaean power. [*Iliad*, Book VI]

It was from the mighty walls of Troy that her little son, Astyanax, heir to the Trojan throne, would be cast down to his death during the sacking of Troy at the hands of the Achaean butchers.

On the south-west side of the great circuit wall was a section much thinner and less well built than the rest. The legends of Troy held that, whilst the majority of the Pergamos wall was built by Poseidon (with the help of Apollo), this inferior section had been constructed by Aeacus of the Leleges (the old name for the Carians) in the fourth generation before the Trojan War. This was the place which Andromache had advised Hector to guard as it was the most vulnerable part of Troy's defences.

> Draw up your troops by the rocky mound of the wild fig-tree; that way the city lies most open, men most easily could swarm the wall where it is low: three times, at least, their best men tried it there in the company of the two called Ajax, with Idomeneus (the Cretan king), the Atreidae (Agamemnon and Menelaus), and Diomedes.
> [*Iliad*, Book VI]

Later, perhaps at this same spot, Patroclus would thrice attempt to scale the wall only to be cast down by Apollo.

> Troy of the towering gates was on the verge of being taken by the Achaeans under Patroclus' drive: he raced with blooded spear ahead and around it. On the massive tower Phoebus Apollo stood as Troy's defender, deadly toward him. Now three times Patroclus assaulted **the high wall at the tower joint**, and three times Lord Apollo threw him back with counterblows of his immortal hands against the resplendent shield.
> [*Iliad*, Book XVI]

Where Aeacus' weak wall abutted the much more substantial defences on its eastern side, stood a gate protected by a strong bastion. If you are inclined to accept the legend, it was through this portal – dismantled and widened – that the Trojan Horse was dragged into the city and up into the temple courtyard of the Pergamos.

> 'Bring the horse to Minerva's (Greek Athena's) shrine! Pray for her goodwill!' All of our people

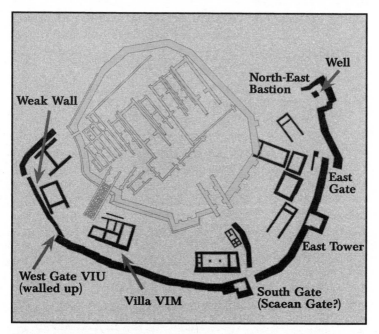

73. Plan of the Troy VI (black) superimposed over the smaller citadel of Troy II (grey) at its centre. Schliemann continued to believe that Troy II was the city of Priam until shortly before his death when he came to realise that he had dug through the real Troy of the Trojan War mistakenly thinking that the fine blocks of Troy VI represented the remains of a Lydian city.

> shouted. **We cut into our walls, laid open the heart of the city.** Everyone set about the task: we inserted rollers under its hooves, put hawsers of hemp around its neck, and strained. The disastrous engine was jockeyed over the walls – an army in its womb. [*Aeneid*, Book II]

Following the sack of Troy the survivors blocked up the gaping hole in Troy's defences that had led to their fall (see plate 53). In the later Archaic period (around 700 BC) the new Greek colonisers of Ilion (Troy VIII) built a shrine with altars in front of this part of the wall in remembrance of its role in the taking of Troy by their ancestors.

The layout and character of Troy which I have just described (and interpreted) have all been revealed through archaeology:

(1) First with Schliemann's massive gouging through the mound (seven campaigns, on and off, from 1870 to 1890) to the lowest levels of the Early Bronze Age (Troy I and Troy II), completely failing to recognise the true city of the *Iliad* (which he ploughed up thinking that its fine masonry could only belong to later Lydian times); just a couple of months before his death on 9 October 1890, he reluctantly accepted (in a letter sent to Richard Schöne of the Berlin Museum) that Homer's Troy was not City II but City VI;[3]

(2) Then with Wilhelm Dörpfeld's careful re-examining of the site (in 1890 and 1893-94) to reveal the walls of Troy City VI of the Late Bronze Age which he associated with Homeric Troy sacked by the Achaeans, stating

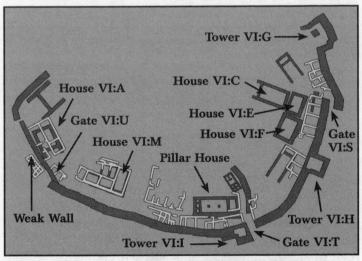

74. *The complex relationship between Troy VI (dark grey) and Troy VII (light grey) with its shanty-town houses built into the ruins of Troy VI whilst retaining the use of the City VI wall for protection against further assault.*

in 1902: 'The citadel was completely destroyed by enemy action. ... We distinguished traces of a great fire in many places';[4]

(3) Then Carl Blegen's discovery (excavating annually from 1932 to 1938 under the general direction of Professor W. T. Semple of Cincinnati University) of the last phases of City VI – which he renumbered VIIa and VIIb – identifying the first of these sub-periods as Priam's Troy;

(4) And finally the ongoing excavations of the German mission originally led by Professor Manfred KORFMANN of Tübingen University (1988 onwards) which are revealing the huge lower city of Troy VI-VII (beneath the Roman city) with the aid of sophisticated ground-penetrating radar.

Which Troy?

Whether Troy VI (final phase h) was the city of the great war, as Dörpfeld believed, or Blegen's Troy VIIa, with clear signs of human destruction following siege conditions within its walls, is difficult to determine with any certainty. The issue is still a matter of fierce debate with advocates of both positions. For decades Blegen's arguments held sway amongst the majority of historians. However, more recently, there has been a swing back in favour of Dörpfeld's view. I will give my reasons for also favouring Troy VIh over VIIa shortly – but, first, here is Blegen's description of the archaeological character of the two candidate cities.

> Troy VI came to its end in a tremendous catastrophe which has left abundant testimony in many places ... The upper part of the fortification wall toppled over, some of it outwards, but more inwards ... The superstructures of the large

houses that stood inside the fortress on the lower ring of terracing were also hurled down …

… in the succeeding period, Troy VIIa, we see that the fortification walls were immediately repaired and supplemented; some of the old houses were also reconstructed and reoccupied and many new ones built, filling almost all the available space inside the stronghold.[5]

They (the Troy VII houses) differ conspicuously from the imposing freestanding manorial houses of Troy VI. The walls, though thick and sturdy, were roughly built of heterogeneous material, including a great many squared blocks that were recovered from the debris heaped up by the earthquake (of Troy VI). No real effort seems to have been made to render the structures handsome: the work was probably done in the haste born of emergency. These small houses were crowded closely together, often being separated only by party walls, a device which seems not to have been used in Troy VI.[6]

Blegen believed that Troy VIh was destroyed by earthquake but there is nothing in the evidence to demonstrate this unequivocally. We cannot discount the possibility that some (at least) of the overthrown walls were the result of human agency. Indeed, this is exactly what is described in Virgil's *Aeneid* as the hero, Aeneas, tells of the last hours of mighty Troy's existence. He explains that it was the Trojans themselves who first began to hurl the stones and mudbricks of the parapets down upon the invading enemy.

The Trojans, for their part, are stripping the turrets and roof-tops, ready (since now the end is in sight) to use the material for missiles, to put up a stern defence – though death is upon them.

75. *One of the giant pithoi from Troy discovered by Schliemann and later attributed to the City VII shanty-town [after Schliemann:* Ilios, *p. 589].*

... A tower stood over the sheer of the wall, its apex soaring skyward. The tower commanded a long-familiar prospect across the Troad to the Greek ships and the Achaean lines. This we (the Trojans) attacked with crowbars all around, where the weak joints of its flooring offered a purchase, prised it off from its deep bed and pushed hard at it: the tower tottered and fell full length with a sudden crash, bursting all over the massed attackers. [*Aeneid*, Book II]

... the gods, I tell you, are hostile. It is they who have undermined Troy's power and sent it tumbling ... look at that litter of masonry there, huge blocks, stone torn from stone, and the dust-laden smoke billowing up from the debris – it is Neptune's work: he gores and tosses the walls,

the foundations, with his great trident until the
whole city is disembowelled. [*Aeneid*, Book II]

Unambiguous literary (albeit late) evidence here, then, of
human destruction by the defenders in the first passage,
but also a definite suggestion in the second of Poseidon's
(Roman Neptune's) wrath – as epitomised in the mighty
bull Earth-Shaker tossing the walls with his horns. If you
are not, therefore, entirely convinced by the Trojan Horse
story, you could interpret the episode of the horse as
reflecting an earthquake which provided the Achaeans
with the opportunity to breach the walls of Troy and enter
the city. After all, Poseidon was not just personified in the
bull but possessed the horse as a sacred animal.

So was Troy VI destroyed both by human demolition and
earthquake? This is entirely within the bounds of possibility
and, indeed, is mirrored in the story of Jericho whose walls
came tumbling down, allowing Joshua and the Israelites to
capture and destroy the city. However, the order of events
at Troy – an earthquake followed by, or contemporary with,
the sack – is laid open to doubt by an often overlooked detail
found in the final scene of Euripides' play *The Trojan Women*.
The Greeks certainly held that Troy was battered down by
the Achaean sackers but here, in this tradition, the sound of
the crashing walls is once again likened to the rumble of an
earthquake – only this time clearly *after* the seizing of the
city by the Greeks.

Troy blazes. The buildings of Pergamum and
the city and the tops of its walls are consumed
with fire. ... The flame of destruction and the
spear-point have you in their power. You will
soon fall upon the dear earth into anonymity.
The dust winging its way to the sky like smoke
will mask the house which I (Queen Hecuba,
wife of Priam) shall see no more. The name of
our land will go into oblivion. All is scattered and

gone, and unhappy Troy is no more. Did you
understand? Did you hear? Yes, the crashing as
the citadel tumbles. An earthquake over all of
Troy, an earthquake overwhelms the city.[7]

Was this just dramatic metaphor or a real earthquake? If
the latter, then the seizing of Troy by the Greeks must have
taken place *before* the earthquake which did so much to bring
down the walls of Troy VIh. This is because Euripides' play
is set in the aftermath of the fall of Troy when the Trojan
women are being led off to the Greek ships and into slavery.
It is only then, when they are beyond the Scamander river
and some distance from their beloved city, that the pitiful
women of Priam's royal household hear the sound of the
tumbling citadel as Neptune buries the remains of Troy's
last stand.

Tantalising evidence of human conflict has indeed
been unearthed in the archaeological remains of Troy VI's
destruction. Several Late Bronze Age weapons were found
by Schliemann, Dörpfeld and Blegen in the upper city
ruins (even though the latter failed to see any connection

76. *Reconstruction of one of the fine villas of Troy VI in which the sons of Priam
and his courtiers lived.*

with the famous Achaean assault). These early excavations of Troy VI produced: several barbed arrow-heads, two stemmed arrow-heads, a riveted dagger with flanged haft, two lance-heads, five double-headed bronze axes, masses of terracotta sling-shots, three bronze sickle-shaped blades, and several other knives – all of which were of Mycenaean type and which have been paralleled in finds from excavations undertaken on the Greek mainland.[8] Korfmann's team have also recovered sling-shots, bronze spear-heads and arrow-heads, the latter lodged in the joints between the blocks of the Pergamos fortress wall.[9] Just imagine how many arrows would have struck and bounced off the stones of this wall if several managed to find their way into the narrow joints.

Troy VI also conforms so well to the grand image of Priam's Ilios as described in the *Iliad* with its broad streets and grand houses. Troy VIIa, on the other hand, is a miserable place with shanty-town constructions packed inside the walls of the destroyed City VI. Still, it could just as well be argued that this is precisely the picture one might expect for a city under siege for ten long years as the tradition requires.

Two historical models therefore remain which can be constructed, one way or another, to fit the archaeological evidence.

(1) The Troy VI Model

If we assume that Troy City VIh was the place destroyed by Agamemnon's Achaeans, then the collapsed blocks from the houses and fortification walls, found by both Dörpfeld and Blegen, were overthrown partly by the defending Trojans as a last desperate attempt to crush their enemies but, in addition, by the Greeks themselves as they sacked and burnt the city. Earthquake might also have been involved. Then the shanty-town of Troy VIIa, with numerous storage jars set into the floors of houses, would be the post-war refugee city of the Trojan survivors,

77. An example of 'knobbed ware' excavated by Schliemann from the Troy VII city [after Schliemann: Ilios, p. 591].

led, according to tradition, by Aeneas. This city was also destroyed by an unknown enemy. The succeeding phase VIIb eventually saw newcomers arriving at Troy – people who had migrated from Thrace (and the Danube basin) bringing with them a distinctive form of pottery known as 'Bückelkeramik' or 'knobbed ware'. These migrants would be the Phrygians (Mushki) and Mysians of the Greek tradition.

We can illustrate this historical synthesis of Troy's archaeological sequence in simplified tabular form:

Troy VIh	–	reign of Priam, destroyed by Achaeans under the leadership of Agamemnon
Troy VIIa	–	reign of Aeneas (before leaving for Italy) and his successors, perhaps destroyed by Mysians
Troy VIIb	–	arrival of Phrygian settlers in the Troad with their distinctive knobbed ware
Troy VIII	–	arrival of Aeolian Greeks to found Archaic Ilion with its altars outside the old walls

(2) The Troy VII Model

If, on the other hand, we assume that Troy VIIa was the city destroyed by Agamemnon's army, then Troy VI may have indeed been severely damaged by earthquake, prior to the time of Priam and the Greek siege. Tradition does, however, require an earlier war against Troy, 'when Heracles, the prodigious son of Zeus, had plundered Ilion'[10] in the time of Priam's father, King Laomedon, which might reflect a previous Achaean conflict in the Troad and a possible sacking of the city as witnessed in the destruction of Troy VIh. The Hittites do refer to a conflict over Wilusa. In the 'Tawagalawas Letter', written to the anonymous Akhiyawan ruler by Hattushili III (a contemporary of Ramesses II), the Hittite emperor tantalisingly states: 'Now, as we have come to an agreement on Wilusa, over which we went to war …'.

Whatever the cause of Troy VI's demise, this then leaves us with a rather impoverished picture of Priam's Troy – City VIIa – which was attacked and burnt to the ground, just as described in the Homerica and in Virgil's *Aeneid*. The subsequent Troy VIIb:1 would then be the refugee city of Aeneas, prior to its abandonment (traditionally with Aeneas' departure for Italy) and before the arrival of the Phrygian settlers with their knobbed-ware ceramic culture (Troy VIIb:2). The archaeo-historical sequence would then look like this:

Troy VIh	–	reign of Laomedon, destroyed by an earthquake or Achaeans at the time of Heracles (?)
Troy VIIa	–	reign of Priam, destroyed by Achaeans under the leadership of Agamemnon
Troy VIIb:1	–	reign of Aeneas, abandoned in search of a new home in Hesperia (Italy)
Troy VIIb:2	–	arrival of Phrygian settlers in the Troad
Troy VIII	–	arrival of Aeolian Greeks to found Archaic Ilion

As with many modern scholars, I have difficulties in associating Homer's grandiose Troy with the beleaguered City VIIa and see this shanty-town much more as Aeneas' refugee settlement following the Achaean *nostoi* or 'returns' to the Greek homeland.

One further clue to support Troy VIh over Troy VIIa as the city of the war is to be found back at that weak part of the wall near the south-west gate. The most recent excavations have revealed two new pieces of information. First, the gate had been approached by a wide paved road rising up from the plain. This makes the south-west gate (VI:U) the principal entrance into the Pergamos. Second, the gate was blocked up at the beginning of Troy VIIa. If the Trojan Horse story has any element of truth to it – and there seems no reason in my view to disbelieve it – then there may be something in the passage quoted above from Virgil that describes the Trojans widening a gate in order to bring the great wooden offering into the temple court of the Pergamos.

I can certainly picture the wooden horse being hauled up the paved road from the plain to the principal gate of Troy. Finding it too narrow for Poseidon's great symbol to enter, the Trojans dismantled the gate buttresses on either side. Following the fall of Troy VI the surviving Trojans could no longer live in the lower city which had been razed to the ground and lay buried deep in ash. So they made their homes in the ruins of the upper city, building a shanty-town from the stones of Troy VI's fallen walls. To afford some protection against further attack they then blocked up the gate by which the Trojan Horse had entered the city, using the Scaean (central southern) Gate (VI:T) as the main entrance to their refuge. The blocking of the main south-west gate at the end of Troy VIh only makes sense if we see it as the place which afforded the Greeks access to the citadel – a stable-door closed only after the horse had bolted. I also think that Troy VIh must have been the Troy of the *Iliad* purely on chronological grounds as I will now attempt to demonstrate.

Clues from the Aegean

The pottery found scattered in the ruins of Troy VIh included a limited amount of typical Late Helladic IIIB ware (ninety per cent being local Grey Minyan pottery). According to Blegen, the succeeding Troy VIIa contained no LH IIIC pottery, indicating that this phase of the city had come to an end before IIIC developed out of IIIB. However, more recent studies of the Hissarlik pottery corpus have contradicted Blegen's position, demonstrating that LH IIIC pottery was already being produced in the time of Troy VIIa. Hittitologist, Trevor Bryce, comments:

> ... new ceramic evidence and analysis associate Troy VIIa with the LH IIIC era, and Troy VIIb now appears Sub-Mycenaean, eliminating phases of the citadel later than Troy VI from the Homeric experience.[11]

Donald Easton (one of the archaeologists working at Hissarlik with Professor Korfmann) agrees with this view, pointing out that a huge military expedition against Troy would hardly have been possible in the era of LH IIIC when Mycenaean power had already begun to wane on the Greek mainland.

> Late Helladic IIIC sherds among the deposits of Troy VIIa suggest that the destruction took place at a date later than that of the Mycenaean palaces, when the Mycenaeans ought not to have been able to muster a coalition of the sort described by Homer.[12]

Thus Troy VIh would have come to an end within the last stages of LH IIIB whilst Troy VIIa was certainly in existence during the transition from LH IIIB to LH IIIC and was therefore destroyed during LH IIIC. What this means historically we will attempt to unravel shortly.

It has been established that LH IIIB represents the pottery of the high Late Bronze Age in the Helladic world (contemporary with Mycenae at its zenith – the

Troy VIII	MG
	EG
Troy VIIb	SM/PG **Mainland Destructions**
Troy VIIa 20th Dynasty in Egypt	LH IIIC
	Mainland Destructions
Troy VI 19th Dynasty in Egypt	LH IIIB
Amarna Period in Egypt	LH IIIA

The Greek archaeological/pottery phases in relation to the settlements at Troy, the destructions on the Greek mainland and the contemporary Egyptian dynasties. Note: LH = Late Helladic/Mycenaean; SM = Sub-Mycenaean; PG = Proto-Geometric; EG = Early Geometric; MG = Middle Geometric.

Lion Gate, Treasury of Atreus, etc.) whereas LH IIIC was contemporaneous with the decline of Helladic culture at the very end of the Bronze Age. This was the era of what scholars call the Mycenaean 'systems collapse' and subsequent migration from the Greek mainland, with groups of refugees sailing eastwards from their mustering points within Attica (mainly Athens) in search of new homes on the coast of Anatolia (principally Ionia and Aeolia).

According to the ancient literary tradition, this Achaean departure from the Peloponnese and Attica was triggered by an incursion of Dorian Greeks from the north. These invaders overcame the incumbent Achaean rulers prior to settling in the region. Indeed, excavations at Mycenae and other Late Bronze Age sites on the Greek mainland have revealed that some of these Achaean strongholds *were* destroyed *twice* – first near the end of LH IIIB, roughly contemporary with the last phase of Troy VI, and then again towards the end of LH IIIC and therefore approximately at the same time as the end of Troy VII.

Archaeologists have found conclusive evidence that the palace at Mycenae was rebuilt after the first LH IIIB destruction and reoccupied by an identical Mycenaean elite culture. It was only after the LH IIIC destructions that this palace was abandoned and never reoccupied.

So, if we accept Blegen's argument that the end of Troy VIIa (now associated with LH IIIC pottery) marks the fall of Priam's Troy, it would require a complete rejection of the Heroic Age literary tradition which has the Mycenaean palaces overturned by the Dorian invaders some considerable time (two generations) *after* the fall of Troy. Blegen himself admitted that LH IIIC could not be the time of the Trojan War.

> The period when pottery in the style of LH IIIC was being made and was in general use was one of poverty and decay, and the great days of Mycenaean glory were only a memory. That was not the time when a mighty coalition of Mycenaean kings and princes could be formed to undertake an ambitious and risky overseas war of conquest.[13]

> ## Conclusion Seventeen
> The Trojan War took place towards the end of Late Helladic IIIB and is recognised in the destruction of Troy VI. Troy VIIa thus becomes the city of the Trojan refugees, led by Aeneas, following the Greek sack of Troy VIh. Troy VIIb is then a settlement of the Phrygians (Mushki) from the Danube region.

The End of Mycenae

This alternative model (with Troy VI as the city of the Trojan War and the end of LH IIIC marking the Dorian invasion) is best illustrated by looking at the archaeology of Mycenae itself – the home of Agamemnon. Here Christos Tsountas excavated the royal palace on top of the rocky summit between 1884 and 1902, revealing the LH IIIB megaron and sacred compound with an open court in between. On top of this he found a large Archaic/Hellenistic temple (probably dedicated to Hera), unusually orientated north–south, almost at right angles to the Mycenaean palace. If we are correct in the chronological placement of Atreus and Agamemnon during the late LH IIIB – and assign to them the construction of the Lion Gate, the 'Treasury of Atreus' and the great palace megaron – then it was probably Atreus' royal residence that was destroyed towards the end of LH IIIB. All the evidence points to this destruction being caused by a severe earthquake, though, just as with Troy VI, human activity cannot be ruled out. In the previous chapter I suggested that this destruction may have been the work of the Dioscuri, Castor and Pollux, but it is just as likely that Poseidon was the perpetrator.

> During the last quarter of the thirteenth century BC a violent earthquake, signs of which have been noticed both inside and outside the citadel,

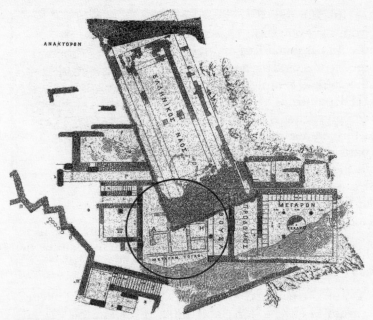

78. *Plan of the palace area at Mycenae made by Dörpfeld for Tsountas, showing a series of rooms (ringed) under the Temple of Hera (of Archaic to Hellenistic date) but above the ruins of the LH IIIB megaron. This complex likely belongs to the palace of LH IIIC.*

overthrew the palace and many other buildings and started fires which caused the total destruction of several of them. Immediately afterwards they were all repaired and set to rights. The Great Ramp was broadened, House M and the storerooms in the cyclopean wall were built, the Grand Staircase was erected at the south side of the palace and the north-east extension with its houses and with the underground cistern added to the enceinte. For the first time the citadel was made really impregnable ...[14]

This repair-work and large-scale rebuilding would be the work of Agamemnon in the historical model I am proposing.

In addition, it seems clear from his excavation plan of the site that Tsountas had exposed a set of walls sandwiched between the Archaic temple and the LH IIIB palace. This was almost certainly another royal residence which, by associating it with other parts of the citadel, can be dated to the LH IIIC pottery period. I say this because considerable amounts of LH IIIC 'Close Style' and 'Granary Style' pottery were found in the building known as

79. An LH IIIC Close Style stirrup jar with intricate and dense decoration, from the Granary deposit at Mycenae.

the 'Granary', located beside the Lion Gate, in a context later than LH IIIB. So, these fine-quality wares demonstrate a continuity from LH IIIB to LH IIIC with all the trappings of palace culture. Tsountas' LH IIIC palace would then be the royal quarter of post-Trojan-War Mycenae occupied by Agamemnon's successors.[15]

According to legend, Agamemnon was murdered in his bathroom immediately upon the king's return to Mycenae from Troy. The assassins were his wife, Clytemnestra, and her lover, Aegisthus (son of Agamemnon's predecessor, Thyestes). They, in turn, were killed, less than a decade later, by Orestes (son of Agamemnon) and with this act of revenge the blood-letting, so characteristic of the House of Pelops, was finally brought to an end. It was therefore King Orestes and his successor Tisamenos (the last ruler of Mycenae) who must have occupied the LH IIIC palace which was sacked by the Dorians two generations after the Trojan War.

80. Plan of the Granary between the Lion Gate and Grave Circle A.

81. More examples of LH IIIC Close Style pots from the Granary at Mycenae.

It remains to account for the final destruction of the earlier palace by earthquake at the very end of LH IIIB in the history we are constructing. The timing of this collapse and burning of the Mycenaean palace may be the same as the destruction of Troy VIh. From an archaeological standpoint it is hard to pin these events down precisely, but they are both late in the LH IIIB pottery period. Perhaps we are dealing here with a major earthquake across the entire Aegean. Our own recent history provides clear and dramatic evidence that natural disasters can devastate whole regions in a single day – even if those regions are thousands of kilometres apart and on different continents. A major earth movement (or perhaps a series of high-level tremors) centred on the Aegean area may well have affected both Greece and coastal Anatolia during the last century of the Late Bronze Age.

If we place such an earthquake at the end of LH IIIB, then Agamemnon's Mycenaean palace may have been toppling at the very moment of his greatest triumph on the shores of Wilusa. At least it would be some sort of poetic justice to imagine his royal residence – a metaphor for the Greek king's bloody dynasty – being destroyed by the same earthquake that brought down the walls of Troy.

The Post-War Era

The years following the Trojan War saw an inexorable decline in the fortunes of the Achaeans. Internecine conflicts and dynastic turmoil weakened the Mycenaean power base to such an extent that it became ripe for takeover by outsiders – and the Heracleidae ('sons of Heracles') were waiting in the wings. Since the death of Heracles (grandson of Perseus) these legitimate Pelasgian descendants of the Perseid line had been exiled from the Peloponnese. When Hyllus, son of Heracles, had tried to retake his father's inheritance by force during the reign of Eurystheus, plague and misfortune had struck the invading army. Hyllus was then killed three years later following the Delphic Oracle's decree that the Heracleidae must not return to claim their rights until three generations had come and gone. Hyllus' invasion was in 890 BC (in the NC) and his death followed in 886 BC. It was now 820 BC. The three generations of exile were past and their moment had finally come.

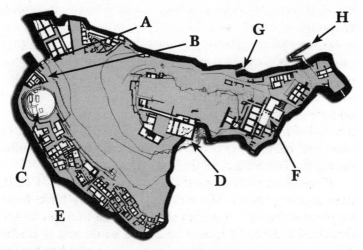

82. *Plan of the Mycenae citadel with the Lion Gate (A), the Granary (B), Grave Circle A (C), the palace quarter (D), the House of the Warrior Vase (E), the Artisan Quarter (F), the Postern Gate (G) and the underground Water Cistern (H).*

Allied with the Dorian tribes of Thrace, the Heracleidae swept into the Peloponnese and destroyed the Achaean strongholds. Mycenae and Sparta fell and were burnt to the ground. Tisamenos, the last ruler of Mycenae, fled with his followers into the central mountains of the Peloponnese – a wild and inhospitable region that would be named Achaea after these Mycenaean refugees.

Others (including the ruler of Pylos) sailed from their harbours to seek refuge in Achaean Attica which had not succumbed to the Dorian assault. Within a year the Dorians and their Heraclid leaders had seized great swathes of the Peloponnese. The Achaean refugees no longer had a homeland. And so Athens became the setting-off point for a great migration from the Greek mainland to new settlements on the western seaboard of Anatolia. All these dramatic events are part and parcel of the Classical Greek perception of how the Heroic Age came to an end.

These traditions, reported by both Strabo and Pausanias, claim that Achaean refugees, having first sought sanctuary in Athenian Attica, fled to Anatolia as a direct result of this aggressive incursion of northern Greeks into the Peloponnese.

As we will see, such a scenario is only really possible within a revised chronology model, such as proposed here, which greatly reduces the intervals between (a) the end of the Trojan War, (b) the final collapse of Mycenaean civilisation with the successful Dorian invasion and (c) the migrations to Ionia and Aeolia in western Anatolia. In the New Chronology these events directly follow on from each other – all within the period of seventy years subsequent to the sack of Troy. In the Orthodox Chronology the collapse, invasion and migration are separated from each other by centuries, making any causal relationship between them difficult to sustain.

> This conclusion has profound consequences
> when one considers the chronology of the many

movements of population. It affects the whole question of the arrival of the Dorians in the Peloponnese. The balance of probability must be that they were in no way connected either with any of the disasters of the end of the thirteenth century or with the further decline in the twelfth (in the OC model).[16]

It is easy to see the problem when we compare the New Chronology and Orthodox Chronology dates for these major turning points in Greek history.

Event	Pottery Period	NC Date	OC Date
End of the Trojan War	LH IIIB (near end)	c. 864 BC	c. 1184 BC
Dorian Invasion	LH IIIC (near end)	c. 820 BC	c. 1050 BC
Ionian Migration	Proto-Geometric	c. 800 BC	c. 900 BC

Thus in the Orthodox Chronology the interval between each of the three major events is approximately one-and-a-half centuries, which means that they can hardly have been interconnected with each other in any historically meaningful way. The ancient Greek literary traditions must therefore be wrong when they say that the Trojan War was followed by two generations of internecine conflict before the Dorian invasion which then triggered the migration of the Achaeans and their Pelasgian allies to Ionia.

In the New Chronology, however, we can reinstate the early history of Hellas as described by the Greek historians because the revised dating is entirely consistent with a fairly rapid decline in Mycenaean civilisation (during the reigns of Aegisthus, Orestes and Tisamenos), followed by the Dorian invasion and, then, within a couple of decades, the start of the Ionian migration (marked by the appearance of Proto-Geometric ware in the Greek foundation cities of the Anatolian/Ionian coast).

Conclusion Eighteen

The Dorian invasion took place sometime towards the end of Late Helladic IIIC, approximately forty-five years after the fall of Troy, and is recognised in the destruction and abandonment of Mycenae which took place at the end of this pottery period.

This is all very neat then ... but history does not really work that way. There are always added complications. In this case we have the persistent traditions that several of the Greek heroes of the Trojan expedition did not return directly home from the war but spent many years wandering around the Mediterranean.

We all know about the adventures of Odysseus, as described in Homer's *Odyssey* (including a raid on the Egyptian coast), but there are a great many more legends concerning the *nostoi*. Menelaus was also purported to have visited Egypt in the time of a King Polybus (also called Thuoris) and the Greek archer Teucer (eponymous ancestor of the Teucrians?) sailed to Cyprus where he founded the Greek city of Salamis.

We will hear more of these wandering Mycenaean Greeks and Late Bronze Age Anatolians in *Chapter Sixteen*. For now, though, we have simply to envisage a movement of Aegean warrior groups that *preceded* the migration of Mycenaean refugees from Attica to Ionia in around 800 BC.

This military sweep through southern Anatolia, taking in Alashiya (a kingdom on Cyprus) and pushing southwards into the Levant is known to Egyptologists as the invasion of the Sea Peoples (dated to Year 8 of Ramesses III = NC – *c.* 855 BC) and in the New Chronology it took place within a decade of the sack of Troy – that is, half a century *before* the main Ionian migration.

Clues from Egypt

In Egyptian terms, the beginning of the Late Helladic IIIC pottery phase – our approximate date for the end of the Trojan War – seems to have been contemporary with the start of the 20th Dynasty or thereabouts. This is just before the Sea Peoples' invasion of the Levant and their attempted incursion into Egypt during Ramesses III's eighth regnal year. In my opinion, such a mass migration of Achaean and Anatolian clans really only fits the post-Trojan-War era when Greek warriors and their Anatolian counterparts were rampaging around the Mediterranean (as described in the *Odyssey* and the traditions of the *nostoi*). As archaeology has shown, by the time of LH IIIC, Mycenaean civilisation was in decline and could not possibly have mounted the sort of spectacular expedition to Troy described in Homer's *Iliad*. However, we might justly equate the Sea Peoples' movement of Ramesses III's Medinet Habu reliefs with the maraudings of the remnant Achaean fleet, in combination with the refugees of the Anatolian kingdoms which they overran. The whole of the Aegean and Anatolian seaboard seems to have been on the move in the disturbed conditions which followed the sack of Troy.

Moreover, the Egyptian texts provide further clues to help us date the demise of the Trojans and their allies. There were two previous occasions in which Anatolian troops confronted Egyptian pharaohs in battle.

The first came in Year 5 of Ramesses II when the Hittite emperor, Muwattali, fought with the Egyptians at the Battle of Kadesh (NC – *c*. 939 BC). The Hittite confederacy included warriors from Dardany. These people have been universally identified as Dardanians (Homer's *Dardanoi*) – the Trojan allies from the Dardanelles represented in the *Iliad* by Aeneas and his men.

The second conflict took place in the western delta when the Libyans attacked Egypt in the reign of Ramesses' successor, Merenptah. According to the king's great Karnak inscription, dated to Year 5, the Teresh or Tursha 'of the sea' were allies of the Libu (Libyan) invaders. During the battle 742 of the Tursha were killed. They were therefore no token force but a major element of the invading army. So who were these Tursha of the sea? They have been identified by many experts with the Classical Tursenoi of the Troad (i.e. the Trojans) and their counterparts in Arzawa (later Lydia) – a people who would eventually turn up in western Italy as the Tyrsenoi or Etruscans of Tuscany.

So, in the reigns of Ramesses II and Merenptah we find the mention of two major allies on the Trojan side of the war against Agamemnon's Achaeans – the Tursenoi/Trojans themselves and the Dardanians. However, they had both disappeared entirely from the list of Sea Peoples by the time of the much bigger invasion of northerners in Year 8 of Ramesses III. This suggests to me that Tursha and Dardany were no longer around to participate in the Sea Peoples' activities by the beginning of the 20th Dynasty. Equally, it seems highly improbable that Trojans/Tursha would be sailing off in support of a Libyan invasion of Egypt if Troy was engaged in a life-and-death struggle with Agamemnon's Achaeans at this time. Therefore, in terms of the Egyptian inscriptions, the only window of opportunity in which to place the Trojan War lies between Year 5 of Merenptah and the Sea Peoples' invasion in the first decade of Ramesses III's reign.

Clues from Anatolia

So, Homer's Troy must have fallen *before* Year 8 of Ramesses III according to the Late Helladic pottery chronology and the contemporary textual evidence from Egypt. On the other hand, at the opposite boundary of our window of opportunity, the closing years of the Hittite empire provide documentary evidence which appears to confirm that the Achaean siege of Troy took place *after* the reign of Ramesses II.

In the archives of Hattusha (modern Boghazköy) two clay tablets were discovered which belonged to the international correspondence of King Tudhaliya IV (I do not follow the attribution of these texts to Tudhaliya I/II, as is currently the fashion, for sound historical reasons[17]). The documents concern a troublesome western vassal of the Hittites named Madduwattash who was constantly in conflict with the ruler of Milawatta (Greek Miletus on the western coast of Anatolia, also referred to as Milawanda). The king of Milawatta had an ally – 'Attarisiyas, the man of Akhiya' – who was raiding the neighbouring settlements along the coast and making military incursions (with one hundred chariots) into the 'Lukka Lands' (Lycia in south-west Anatolia). In the reign of Arnuwanda III (Tudhaliya IV's successor) Madduwattash turned against his Hittite overlord and allied himself with Attarisiyas. Together they invaded Alashiya (Cyprus) by sea.

So the career of both Madduwattash and Attarisiyas extended from the last years of Tudhaliya IV down into the early reign of Arnuwanda III (the penultimate ruler of the Hittite empire) who was a contemporary of Merenptah of Egypt. Arnuwanda was succeeded by Shuppiluliuma II at around the time of the Libyan and Tursha incursions into Egypt's western delta. Merenptah's Karnak inscription informs us that the Hittites were apparently in dire need of Egyptian grain to stave off a severe famine at the beginning of Shuppiluliuma's reign. The Egyptian pharaoh duly despatched the grain supplies by ship 'to keep alive the land of Hatti'. Things were not going well for the mighty Hittite empire which showed every sign of crumbling at its edges.

Attarisiyas of Akhiya

As has often been noted by Helladic scholars, this name 'Attarisiyas' bears a remarkable resemblance to what would have been the Helladic (i.e. Linear B) vocalisation/ writing of Atreus, king of Mycenae. If Attarisiyas 'the man of Akhiya' (i.e. Homer's Achae[w]a as first noted by the Swiss Hittitologist Emil Forrer in 1924) is indeed the historical Atreus, then the reign of his son and successor, Agamemnon, must have begun some time subsequent to the Madduwattash era and therefore during the reign of Merenptah – in other words during the period of the 19th Dynasty collapse which led to the foundation of the 20th Dynasty. This fits neatly with our *termini post quem* and *ante quem* for the Trojan War and therefore gives us a twenty-five-year window for the ten-year-long *Iliad* event between, say, Year 5 of Merenptah (i.e. the Libyan war, NC – *c.* 880 BC) and Year 8 of Ramesses III (i.e. the Sea Peoples' war, NC – *c.* 855 BC).

Event	Regnal Year	NC Date	OC Date
Libyan/Tursha War	Yr 5 Merenptah	*c.* 880 BC	*c.* 1209 BC
Start of Trojan War	To be determined	*c.* 874 BC	*c.* 1194 BC
End of Trojan War	To be determined	*c.* 864 BC	*c.* 1184 BC
Sea Peoples' Invasion	Yr 8 Ramesses III	*c.* 855 BC	*c.* 1177 BC

Alaksandu of Wilusa

There is other evidence, also derived from the Hittite records, which precludes an *earlier* date for the Trojan War. In the *Iliad*, the king of Ilios is named as Priamos (Priam) and he is the last ruler of his line. Following Priam's slaying by PYRRHUS at the fall of Troy, the survivors of the Achaean onslaught re-establish themselves for a period in the ruined city under the leadership of Aeneas of Scepsis, a prince of Dardanus on the southern shore of the Dardanelles (near the modern town of Chanakkale).

A treaty from the reign of Muwattali (NC – *c.* 966-937 BC) – the Hittite adversary of Ramesses II at the Battle of Kadesh – records that the king of Wilusa at that time was named Alaksandu.

Thus says Muwattali, Great King of Hatti, beloved of the Storm-god of Lightning, son of

Murshili (II), Great King and Hero.

Formerly, when my forefather, Labarna, had conquered all the lands of Arzawa and the land of Wilusa, thereafter the land of Arzawa began war, and the land of Wilusa defected from Hatti – however, the matter is long past. ... When Tudhaliya (II) came [up] against the land of Arzawa, he did not enter [the land of Wilusa as it was] at peace [with him] and regularly sent [him messengers]. ...

[When your] day of death arrives, Alaksandu, then [...]. In regard to any [son] of yours whom you designate for kingship – [whether he is by] your wife or by your concubine, and even if he is still a child – if the population of the land refuses him and says as follows: 'He is the progeny [...]' – I will not agree. ... And as I protected you, Alaksandu, in goodwill because of the word of your father, and came to your aid, and killed your enemy for you, in the future my sons and my grandsons will certainly protect your descendants for you, to the first and second generation. If some enemy arises against you, I will not abandon you, just as I have not now abandoned you. I will kill your enemy for you. But if your brother or someone of your family revolts against you, Alaksandu, or later someone revolts against your son or your grandsons, and they seek the kingship of the land of Wilusa, I will absolutely not allow them to depose you, Alaksandu.[18]

Here then we see that, from at least the reign of Tudhaliya II, Wilusa was an ally of the Hittite empire and under its protection. The treaty also promised ongoing military support from the time of Muwattali for at least a further two generations. It is therefore significant to note that Hittite forces do not obviously appear in the *Iliad* as allies of the Trojans of Ilios, indicating that the Hittites were in no position to fulfil their treaty obligations by the reign of Priam of Troy (but see later). Interestingly, Priam's son Paris was also known as Alexandros, but he was never the *ruler* of Ilios in the Homeric tradition, merely a prince who died in the war against the Greeks. So this Alaksandu of the Wilusa treaty must have been an earlier king of Ilios – perhaps Priam's grandfather and Paris/Alaksandu's like-named great-grandfather.

There was no need to invoke the guarantees of the treaty in the time of Hattushili III (NC – *c.* 931-912 BC) – the Hittite emperor who signed the peace treaty with Ramesses II in the latter's twenty-first year and who subsequently brought his daughter to Egypt as a bride for the pharaoh in Year 34. A letter sent by this Hittite emperor to the Akhiyawan king refers to a former conflict over Wilusa between Hatti and Akhiyawa – a conflict that no longer pertained since peace had broken out between the two nations. Wilusa/Ilios was not under threat from the Achaeans at this time – that is, up until the date of the writing of the letter.

However, another document, from the reign of Tudhaliya IV (Hattushili's son and successor, NC – *c.* 912-890 BC), records that a ruler of Wilusa – by the name of Walma – was ousted from power during the latter years of Hattushili III's reign. Walma was still in exile from his kingdom by the reign of Tudhaliya who ordered him to be reinstated.

We do not know the identity of the new occupant of Walma's throne in Wilusa from the Hittite records. However, we might speculate in identifying this Walma with King Laomedon of Ilios, the father of Priam, in whose time, according to Homer, Troy fell to Heracles and his Achaean troops. In that case his successor would be none other than Priam who was established on the throne of Ilios by Heracles.

But (I hear you say), the names Walma and Laomedon are completely different. How can they be the same king? This could be because many of the characters, places and peoples in Homer's epic carry more than one name (e.g. Priam formerly known as Podarces, Paris also called Alexandros, Wilios/Troy, Palaemon/Heracles, Pyrrhus/Neoptolemos, Danaoi/Achaewoi, etc.). This practice of giving characters dual names (known as diglossia) is typical of the legendary tradition.

Or perhaps I could propose how the two names might be reconciled. This requires four linguistic steps.

(1)   The Anglicised versions of the Ionic Greek vocalisations found in Homer and other traditions are somewhat different to those same names found in the Linear B tablets from Bronze Age Greece, Crete and the Hittite cuneiform texts. Thus we find Linear B *to-ro-ya* for 'Trojan (female slave?)', *pu-ru* for 'Pylos', and *e-te-wo-kle-wes* for 'Eteocles', whilst the Hittites have 'Wilusa' for 'Ilios', 'Taruisa' for 'Troia' (Troy), 'Milawatta' for 'Miletus', 'Alaksandu' for 'Alexandros' and 'Attarisiyas' for 'Atreus'. Note that in the case of Pylos the Linear B has an R for later Greek L – this will be important for a subsequent point in this chapter.

(2)   Ionic Greek (in which Homer composed) characteristically vocalises the Bronze Age Greek letter A (alpha) as E. Moreover, Greek O (omega) is equivalent to the Linear B/Hittite W. Thus we might imagine the Anglicised Greek name Laomedon would have originally been something like *la-wo-ma-du* or Lawmadu in Linear B.

(3)   The next stage of our phonetic juggling involves what is known as 'metathesis' – the switching of syllables or consonants so that they appear in a different order. For example, a West Indian will often say 'aks' for 'ask'. There are just such examples of this phenomenon in the ancient world (e.g. Ushpilulume for Shuppiluliuma) and, though not common, could

provide the explanation we need to turn an original Luwian Walmadu into Linear B Lawmadu or later Greek Laomedon.

(4) Finally, personal names in the ancient texts were often shortened into more familiar forms (what we might call nicknames based on a fuller version). We all have such 'hypocoristicons'; for example, Beth for Elizabeth, Lady Di for Princess Diana, Fred for Frederick, etc. The kings of the ancient world were no exception. We know, for instance, that the Egyptian name Amenemhat was abbreviated to Ameni, that Ramesses II (pronounced Riamashisha) was known as Shisha in Canaan, and that Tiglath-pileser III of Assyria was called Pul in the Bible. Scholars have also suspected that the name Priam(os) itself may be a shortened form of an historically attested name such as Pariyamuwa (Luwian for 'exceptionally courageous'[19]). So, could Priam's father also have possessed a hypocoristicon something on the lines of Walma, derived from a longer Anatolian Walmadu?

Thus we would have the following transmission path:

Luwian WALMADU (hypocoristic WALMA) = Linear B LAWMADU = Homeric LAOMEDON

Whether this explanation is valid or we simply accept that Walma was another (hypocoristic) name for Lawmadu, the historical picture for this king of Wilusa could fit the story of the assault of Heracles on Laomedon's Troy. The Hittite records make it clear that Walma was exiled from Wilusa – a situation which may have pertained when Heracles launched his raid and sacked Troy in the time of Hattushili III, though legend has it that Laomedon was killed and replaced by Priam. I believe he did not die but fled into exile and was succeeded by his long-reigned son, Pariyamuwa/Priam, early in Tudhaliya IV's reign. Thus we would have the following sequence of rulers for Wilusa/Ilios:

KUKUNNIS	a predecessor of Alaksandu but not his father (according to Hittite records)
ALAKSANDU	a contemporary of Muwattali and therefore early Ramesses II
WALMADU/LAOMEDON	a contemporary of Hattushili III and therefore mid-reign of Ramesses II
PARIYAMUWA/PRIAM	a contemporary of Tudhaliya IV, Arnuwanda III & Shuppiluliuma II and therefore late Ramesses II, Merenptah, Seti II, Siptah & Tausert
AENEAS	a contemporary of Ramesses III

Of course there may have been other rulers in the early part of this list for whom we have no contemporary references, but this sequence would seem to mitigate against any placement of the Trojan War during the reign of Ramesses II and places the Greek siege at the very end of the 19th Dynasty. Given that the destruction of Troy VIh cannot be earlier than the reign of Ramesses II, the only time to place Priam in the list of Wilusan rulers is after Walma.

Eteocles and the Epigonoi

Another tantalising piece of evidence to shed light on the general history of the Heroic Age that led up to the Trojan War is to be found in the diplomatic correspondence of the Hittite emperor, Hattushili III, and this too points to the general correctness of our historical reconstruction. Hattushili sent a letter to the king of Akhiyawa (whose name is unfortunately lost). The Hittite emperor mentions a certain Tawagalawas, the brother of the ruler of Akhiyawa, who had been involved in an uprising in the Lukka lands. The rebels were about to be crushed by a Hittite expeditionary force when they sought asylum with the Akhiyawans. The king's brother, Tawagalawas, had sailed for Anatolia to intervene.

Now in the Greek tradition there is another epic tale known as 'The Seven Against Thebes' (as performed in the Aeschylus theatrical drama and referred to in Sophocles' play *Oedipus at Colonus*). The story, regarded by Pausanias [Book IX] as the most significant internal Greek conflict during the whole of the Heroic Age, concerns an alliance of seven Achaean rulers who launched an ill-advised military campaign against the pre-eminent city of Thebes in the region of Boeotia (a kingdom then known as Cadmaea after King Cadmus). To avoid confusion with Egyptian Thebes I will simply refer to Cadmaean Thebes as Cadmaea. This conflict took place two generations before the Trojan War. The seven failed in their ambitions, with only one of their number – Adrastos of Argos – returning from the siege. However, the enterprise was then taken up by their offspring or *Epigonoi* ('sons of the seven') in the following generation, one of whom – Diomedes – later fought alongside Achilles in the Trojan War. On this second occasion Cadmaea fell to the Epigonoi and was duly sacked. This is consistent with the results of archaeological excavation which found that the acropolis of Bronze Age Thebes had been burnt and abandoned during the Late Helladic IIIB pottery phase. It is perhaps also significant that no Cadmaean contingent played a part in the Trojan campaign according to the Catalogue of Ships listed in Book II of the *Iliad*.[20]

It seems clear that, prior to the rise of Mycenae, Cadmaean Thebes held the supreme kingship amongst the Bronze Age Pelasgian Greeks. Linear B tablets recently found in the burnt citadel demonstrate that the king of Cadmaea ruled over 'a large kingdom which included the island of Euboia and had a harbour in Aulis' and that his palace 'could have been a hub, perhaps even *the* hub, of the empire'.[21] As if to confirm the tradition that the Theban royal house was founded by the legendary Cadmus, the only letter so far discovered which was sent by the high-king of Akhiyawa to the Hittite court (as opposed to the other way around) makes reference to a forebear who gave his daughter

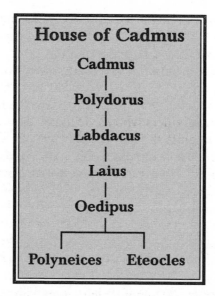

in marriage to the Anatolian ruler of Assuwa.[22] The name of that ancestor, mentioned in the letter, was Cadmus.

The king of Cadmaea at the time of the first expedition of the 'Seven Against Thebes' was Eteocles, son of the legendary King Oedipus. Eteocles had a brother named Polyneices who had co-ruled in Cadmaea. At this time Cadmaean Thebes was pre-eminent in Greece and so the two co-regents were the high-kings of the mainland Greeks. Polyneices was then overthrown by Eteocles and exiled to Argos where he persuaded King Adrastos to mount a military expedition against his brother in Cadmaea. According to legend, in the battle that ensued, the two brothers both fell in a duel to the death. This Classical Greek name Eteocles has been found in the Mycenaean Linear B tablets recovered from the palace of Pylos in its Bronze Age form – Etewoklewes.

Now, I am not for one minute arguing that we should accept the Greek legends at face value and treat every aspect of them as pure history. But I do take the view that genuine historical figures from the Late Bronze Age had legendary stories woven around them which were based loosely on actual historical events. So I have no difficulty in identifying the legend of the Epigonoi with the archaeologically verified destruction of Cadmaea in the LH IIIB. And I see no reason to doubt that there were two brother kings of Cadmaea at the time bearing the names Polunikes and Etewoklewes. A system of dual kingship was fairly common in Greece – a sacral king and a tanist or administrator king ruling side by side. This may have been the method of dual monarchy practised by the Spartans in later generations. With the caveat in mind that we are dealing with legendary material here which may not be accurate in all its detail, we will now return to what Michael Wood refers to as 'one of the most fascinating documents from the ancient Near East'.[23]

In the Hittite archive found at Boghazköy (Hattusha) the German archaeologists found a tablet that has become known as the 'Tawagalawas Letter'. As we have seen, it was written by Hattushili III and deals with the activities of a foreign prince from Akhiyawa called 'Tawagalawas' who is helping Lukkan rebels and causing trouble for the city of Milawanda (Miletus) on the coast of Anatolia. This Hittite writing of the name Tawagalawas appears to be very close to Linear B *e-te-wo-kle-wes* – the original form of Eteocles. If I just add a prothetic aleph to the beginning of the cuneiform Hittite version and exchange Anatolian letters G, W and A for Greek K, O and E respectively (both recognised linguistic procedures) you will see what I mean.

(A)tawagalawas = Atawakalawas = Etewoklewes = Eteocles

This similarity has been observed by many philologists of both Bronze Age Greek and Anatolian Hittite. But can we go further than this and argue that this Akhiyan ruler who appears in the correspondence of Hattushili III is actually the legendary Eteocles son of Oedipus? The chronological position of the 'Tawagalawas Letter' fits perfectly into the picture we have constructed, with an Achaean sacral king of Cadmaea (Polunikes) actively supporting disruptive elements on the fringes of the Hittite empire through his

brother (and tanist co-ruler of Cadmaea), Tawagalawas/
Etewoklewes. The extended sequence of events leading up
to the Trojan War and beyond would now be as follows:

c. 943 BC	Alaksandu of Wilusa Treaty (Year 24 Muwattali) (Year 1 Ramesses II)
c. 939 BC	Battle of Kadesh with Tursha (Trojan) and Dardany (Dardanian) forces in the army of Hatti (Year 28 Muwattali) (Year 5 of Ramesses II) under the above treaty obligation
c. 923 BC	Peace treaty between Egypt and Hatti (Year 21 of Ramesses II) (Year 9 of Hattushili III)
c. 920 BC	Accession of Polyneices and Eteocles at Cadmaea/ Thebes (Year 12 of Hattushili III)
c. 919 BC	Eteocles/Tawagalawas active in Arzawa and Lukka (Year 13 of Hattushili III)
c. 918 BC	Usurpation of the Cadmaean throne by Eteocles (Year 14 of Hattushili III)
c. 916 BC	First campaign against Cadmaean Thebes; the deaths of Polyneices and Eteocles (Year 16 of Hattushili III)
c. 910 BC	Sack of Troy by Heracles; Walma/Laomedon exiled to Milawatta/Miletus (Year 3 of Tudhaliya IV)
c. 909 BC	Accession of Pariyamua/Priam at Wilusa/Ilios/Troy (Year 4 of Tudhaliya IV)
c. 907 BC	Sack of Cadmaea by the Epigonoi (Year 6 of Tudhaliya IV)
c. 891 BC	Attarisiyas/Atreus of Mycenae raiding the Lukka lands (Lycia) (Year 22 of Tudhaliya IV)
c. 890 BC	First failed invasion of the Heracleidae and their Dorian allies (Year 23 of Tudhaliya IV)
c. 886 BC	Accession of Agamemnon at Mycenae; Mycenae now the dominant kingship following the fall of Cadmaea and the demise of Cadmus' royal line (Year 4 of Arnuwanda III)
c. 881 BC	Expedition of the Greeks, led by Achilles, against the Anatolian Seha River Land (Homer's Teuthrania in the Kaikos valley, *Odyssey* Book XI), repulsed by Telephus, king of the Mysians, eight years before the Trojan War (Year 1 Shuppiluliuma II)
c. 875 BC	Fall of the Hittite empire; the Kaska tribes destroy Hattusha (Year 7 of Shuppiluliuma II)
c. 874 BC	Start of the ten-year siege of Wilusa/Ilios; Agamemnon takes advantage of the collapse of the Hittite empire which has left Wilusa without superpower protection
c. 864 BC	The fall of Troy (during late LH IIIB); the death of Priam aged around seventy (Year 7 Tausert = Year 1 Setnakht)

c. 863 BC	Aeneas establishes refugee Troy (City VIIa) before sailing for Hesperia (Italy)
c. 820 BC	The Dorian invasion of the Peloponnese (destruction of Troy VIIa towards the end of late LH IIIC)
c. 805 BC	Birth of Homer
c. 800 BC	The start of the Ionian migration from Attica (beginning of the Proto-Geometric period)
c. 750 BC	Homer composes the *Iliad* in oral form (Middle Geometric period)
c. 725 BC	The *Iliad* is first written down by the Homeridae of Chios; the Greek colony of Ilion is founded on the ruins of Troy/Ilios (Late Geometric period)

Hittites in the Homeric Tradition

I stated earlier that there is no obvious mention of Hittites in the conflict over Troy as narrated in the *Iliad* and *Odyssey*. This might be explained, in the New Chronology, by the fact that the Hittite empire had collapsed just prior to the start of the Trojan War. However, there are a couple of incidents in the supplementary Homeric traditions which hint at Hittite involvement – though such an interpretation requires more linguistic conjuring. Hittite rulers seem to feature in the earlier attack of Achilles (really Akhilleus, Linear B *a-ki-re-u*) and the Achaeans on western Anatolia, eight years before the start of the Trojan War proper, and they may turn up again in the last days of that war only to fall victim to the final assault by the Achaeans.

The story goes that Helen was abducted by Paris and Aeneas some ten years before the Greeks finally set sail to seek revenge on Troy. This was not the first attempt to mount a naval campaign against Wilusa. In the second year after Helen's abduction a fleet, under the command of Achilles, set sail for the Troad [Appianus: *Mythographus*, Book III] but came ashore too far south in the Gulf of Adramyttion and found themselves ravaging the country of Teuthrania (named after King Teuthras) [Strabo: *Geographus*, Book XIII]. This place has been identified with the Seha River Land (a part of Arzawa mentioned in the Hittite texts) centred on the Kaikos valley where Classical Pergamon stands today.

There the Bronze Age Greeks met stubborn resistance from the local ruler who, in spite of his wounds, drove the invaders back onto their ships [Pindar: *Olympia*, Book IX]. Achilles then sailed for the island of Lesbos (Hittite *Lazpas*) which he sacked instead. Evidence of the destruction of Thermi on Lesbos has been found within the LH IIIB pottery period (dated to the reign of Ramesses II). The Greek fleet then returned home to its anchorage at Aulis where the ships languished for another eight years before Agamemnon launched his much more famous campaign against Troy.

The brave opponent of Achilles in the repulse of the Achaeans from Teuthrania, was Telephus, son of King Teuthras. The earliest form of his name in the Greek language is Telephanes ('he who shines afar') but I think this older name may represent a garbled version of the Hittite name Telepinu(sh) borne by an early Hittite king of the Old Kingdom period. His father's name, Teuthras, may also be Hittite.

83. *The two Achaean expeditions to western Anatolia. First the failed attempt of Achilles who landed at the shores of Teuthrania (the Seha River Land), was repulsed by the local ruler, Telephus, and expressed his pique by raiding Lesbos (Lazpas). Second, eight years later, Agamemnon's Trojan War which successfully reached the shores of Wilusa/Wilios.*

431

We have seen how Linear B Greek fails to distinguish between the letters R and L (*pu-ru* for Pylos, *a-ki-re-u* for Akhilleus/Achilles, etc.). Greek TH would also equate to Anatolian DH. Thus we might transcribe Teuthras in Hittite as Tudhalas – in other words the well-known royal name Tudhaliya(sh). Could it be that Telepinu(sh) (the legendary Telephus), ruler of the Seha River Land, was a son of the Hittite Great King, Tudhaliya IV? If so, then it has to be of considerable interest that a fragmentary Hittite tablet from the Late Hittite period refers to an attack upon the Seha River Land by a 'King of Akhiyawa' who then 'withdrew'. Is this a contemporary reference to the Achaean assault upon Teuthrania and the retreat of Agamemnon's forces under the command of Achilles?[24]

Telephus himself had a son named Eurypylus (Hittite *Urpaliya* or *Warpalawash*) who succeeded him and was the leader of the *Keteioi* – surely a reference to Kheta or Hittites – at the time of the Trojan War. At first the Keteioi refused to fight on behalf of the Trojans, in spite of Priam's pleas for help. But Eurypylus' mother was bribed by the king of Troy and instructed her son to lead a contingent of *Keteioi* warriors in the defence of Troy in the final year of the war. They were Troy's 'last hope' after the death of Hector, and initially succeeded in repulsing the Achaeans, but the Greeks were yet to play their hand with the deception of the wooden horse. Eurypylus died in the last terrible battle within the walls of Troy by the sword of Achilles' son, Pyrrhus (also known as Neoptolemus), who went on to slay Priam at the altar of Athena and cast his heir, Astyanax son of Hector, down from the walls of sacred Ilios.

> Many were those he killed in the grim encounter,
> nor can I now recount by name all the host of those
> who fell to him as he championed the Achaeans.
> But one above all was a worthy foe – Eurypylus son
> of Telephus. Of all men that ever I saw (with the
> exception of Memnon whose mother was a goddess)

this man was the most handsome. He was slain by
the sword of Neoptolemus, and round him his band
of Keteian (Hittite) comrades – all dead through the
bribing of a woman. [*Odyssey*, Book XI]

In the New Chronology the reign of the Hittite emperor,
Tudhaliya IV, comes to an end around 890 BC – just
nine years before Achilles' attack upon the kingdom of
Teuthrania, ruled at the time by Teuthras' successor,
Telephus. So this new chronological setting allows us to
postulate that the Achaean Greeks knew the region as
the land of Teuthras/Tudhaliya(sh) because of the Hittite
presence in western Anatolia during Tudhaliya IV's reign.
The Hittite records show that the Hittite emperor marched
west into Arzawa and Assuwa, seizing the Seha River Land.
Perhaps, then, he established his son, Telepinu, there as the
founder of a new ruling house within the expanded borders
of the Hittite empire in the west.

The traditions [*Scholium Lycophron*: 1249] also identify
Telephus as the father of Tyrsenus – the eponymous ancestor
of the Tyrsenoi. He was remembered as the Lydian hero
who led the Tyrsenians/Tyrrhenians on their migration
to Italy where they became known as the Etruscans. This
appears to place the departure of the Tyrsenians from
western Anatolia and their arrival in Italy during the decade
before the Trojan War – again in accordance with the
traditions (see *Chapter Seventeen*).

Manetho's Date for the Trojan War

We finally turn to the history of Egypt written by Manetho
(handed down to us in the writings of the early church
fathers) to seek confirmation of our placement of the
Trojan War during the final decade of 19th Dynasty Egypt.
We have seen that the placement of events in Manetho's
redactions is not always reliable but, in the case of the
Trojan War, we seem to be on firmer ground.

433

Let me first list the names and reign-lengths of the 19th Dynasty as they appear in Manetho's various redactions. This is a composite list of names and reign-lengths which I will then try to link with the known historical kings by comparing the names and regnal data from the period. You will immediately see that there are a number of serious copying errors which have crept into the redactions and which need to be corrected.

Manetho's Royal Names	Africanus	Eusebius	Eusebius (Armenian)
1. Sethos	51 years	55 years	55 years
2. Rampses/Rapsaces	61 years	66 years	66 years
3. Amenophthis	20 years	40 years	8 years
4. Ammenemes	5 years	26 years	26 years
5. Ramesses	60 years	—	—
6. Thuoris, by Homer called the active and gallant Polybus, the husband of Alcandra, in whose time Troy was taken, reigned for 7 years			

What can we make of this? Well, first we must identify the kings.

1. Sethos is clearly Seti I whose highest regnal date is Year 11, so we could amend Manetho to either eleven or fifteen years (rather than Africanus' '51' or Eusebius' '55' years).

2. Rampses/Rapsaces is equally clearly Ramesses II whose highest regnal date is Year 67 (i.e. 66 complete years of rule). In this case Manetho, according to the Eusebius redaction, is spot on.

3. Amenophthis must be Merenptah (or Merneptah) whose name was probably pronounced something like Menophta. The Greek version of this name, with a prothetic alpha, would give us the path 'Amenophta' to Amenophthis. Merenptah's highest regnal date is

Year 8, so the Armenian version of Eusebius would be accurate here.

4. Ammenemes is undoubtedly the usurper Amenmesse whose highest regnal date is Year 4. In this case we would amend Eusebius' '26' years to six years and give the Africanus redaction of 'five' years top marks for accuracy.

5. The name Ramesses appears only in the Africanus version and this king may be identified with Ramesses-Siptah – the co-regent of number six below – whose highest regnal date is Year 6. We must then amend Africanus' 'sixty' years to six years.[25]

6. Finally, Thuoris sounds like a garbled Greek version of the female pharaoh Tausert whose name was probably pronounced something like Tawosri. Her highest regnal date is Year 8, so Manetho's 'seven' years (all three versions) is close to the truth.

The problem is that Homer's 'active and gallant' Polybus – a resident of Egyptian Thebes – was a male ruler who, according to legend, acted as host to Menelaus and Helen following the sack of Troy when they visited Egypt on their return journey to Sparta. Tausert was, of course, female and so hardly fits the role of an 'active and gallant' male pharaoh of Egypt.

We may be able to resolve this confusion by suggesting that Polybus (also known as Proteus) was not simply another name for Thuoris but rather the Homeric name of a contemporary of Queen Tausert. And I would suggest that this brave Theban is none other than Pharaoh Setnakht, founder of the 20th Dynasty and father of Ramesses III, who was indeed militarily 'active and gallant'. According to a stela recently found at Aswan and the introduction of the Great Papyrus Harris, during the first year of his reign Setnakht expelled foreign mercenaries from Egypt in the pay of a Canaanite despot named Arsu who had taken control of Egypt during the final strife-torn years of the 19th Dynasty. The identification of Polybus/Proteus with Setnakht seems to be confirmed by Schliemann's observation that Proteus was succeeded by a pharaoh named Rhampsinitus who certainly sounds very much like Ramesses III (Ramessu-pa-netjer – 'Ramesses the god').[26]

So, if this interpretation of Manetho is right, we can place Menelaus' journey to Egypt in Tausert's eighth year (NC – *c.* 863 BC) after Setnakht had risen to power and was in his second year. This date fits very snugly into the window of opportunity which we established from both the Egyptian international correspondence and war reliefs, as well as the evidence provided by the Hittite annals mentioning Akhiyawa 'across the sea' and its unruly kings.

Conclusion Nineteen

The Trojan War began in the year following the fall of the Hittite empire and during the Egyptian civil war at the end of the 19th Dynasty. In the New Chronology the ten-year siege of Troy took place between *circa* 874 BC and 864 BC. This is approximately three centuries later than the conventional date for the Trojan War.

In Greek archaeological terms this places us in the final years of the Late Helladic IIIB when Troy VIh came to a disastrous end. So, to summarise why I would prefer to identify this Troy as King Priam's city rather than the succeeding Troy VIIa:

(1) The wide streets and fine detached megaron villas of Troy VIh fit well with Homer's picture of Priam's prosperous city.

(2) The LH IIIC pottery which has now been identified in Troy VIIa places that settlement in the period of Mycenaean decline when the Bronze Age Greeks would have been incapable of mounting an expedition to Anatolia on the scale described by Homer.

(3) Now that Troy/Ilios has been conclusively identified with Anatolian Wilusa, the historical evidence which was gathered from the Hittite archives referring to that kingdom and its kings places the fall of Troy at the end of the empire period.

(4) Likewise, the Egyptian records indicate that Trojan and Dardanian forces were active on the international stage up to the time of Merenptah, but no longer in evidence by the early years of Ramesses III (Sea Peoples' invasion).

(5) The Egyptian traditions (as passed down to us through the writings of Manetho) place the fall of Troy at the very end of the 19th Dynasty. This is consistent with (2), (3) and (4) above.

(6) The dismantling and subsequent blocking-up of the south-west gate (VI:U) of the Troy VIh Pergamos fortification wall not only uncannily fits the Trojan Horse story, but is best interpreted as the understandable reaction of Troy's few remaining post-war survivors who, having retreated into the citadel, continued to eke out an existence in the difficult years following the destruction of their city.

(7) Given all the above, the squalid nature of Troy VIIa, with its shanty-town dwellings built out of the fallen blocks of Troy VI, does not fit Homer's description of Priam's Troy but would be consistent with a refugee settlement following the sack of mighty Troy.

I once attended a conference on Troy at which some forty papers were presented, many of them addressing one or more of three fundamental questions: Was there an actual poet called Homer? Did Troy exist? Was there really a Trojan War? The line-up of speakers constituted a kind of *Who's Who* of Homeric scholarship and Bronze Age archaeology. ... The historical authenticity of the war and its participants, and the poet most famously associated with it, continues to be widely debated. At one end of the spectrum of opinion is the conviction that there was indeed such a war and that it was pretty much as the poet described it. From that we pass through varying degrees of scepticism and agnosticism to the other end of the spectrum where the tradition is consigned wholly to the realm of fantasy. ... In other words, the *Iliad* is a story about a war that never took place, fought between peoples who never lived, who used a form of Greek that no one ever spoke and belonged to a society that was no more than a figment of the imagination of a poet who never existed.

[Trevor Bryce: *The Trojans and their Neighbours* (2006)]

Chapter Fourteen

HOMER AND THE DARK AGE

Dark Age Anomalies –– Pottery Chronology –– Homer's Place in History

If ever there was a topic to generate passion and controversy in the study of ancient history it must surely be the question of the historical reality behind the epic traditions that the Greeks attributed to a poet called Homer.

The Birth of the Dark Age

As I explained in the *Introduction*, this most hotly contested of debates began with a number of important discoveries at the end of the nineteenth century which instigated a major rethink over the chronology of Greece for the pre-Classical era. The principal discovery came not from Greece or the Aegean but rather from Egypt, where, in the 1880s, William Matthew Flinders Petrie began to turn up Cretan and Greek pottery at the sites of Kahun, Gurob and Tell el-Amarna. At these sites Petrie found sherds with typical Late Helladic decoration which, with reconstruction, took on the familiar shapes of the stirrup jars, pilgrim flasks and alabastrons, characteristic of the era which has become known as the Mycenaean period. The imported pottery from el-Amarna was found in an archaeological context which dated it to the end of the 18th Dynasty (around 1350 BC in the OC) and later work showed that the pottery phases concerned (LH IIIA to IIIB) predominated for more than two centuries, before the final collapse of the Mycenaean culture of central and southern Greece at the end of the Late Bronze Age (LH IIIC).

The true significance of this discovery was clear and undeniable – the Heroic Age would have to be pushed backwards in time in order for its end to fall within the time-span of the 20th Dynasty in Egypt *circa* 1200-1070 BC rather than its previously assumed end at around 900-800 BC. This, of course, resulted in a major rewriting of early Greek history and the introduction of the three-century-long Dark Age, with all the problematical implications that this held for the Greek historian. Even so, this Greek Dark Age has gradually become 'an article of orthodox dogma'.

Petrie announced his dramatic conclusions in an article entitled 'The Egyptian Bases of Greek History' which included the following somewhat condescending statement.

> ... now the main light on the chronology of the civilisations of the Aegean comes from Egypt; and it is Egyptian sources that must be thanked by Classical scholars for revealing the real standing of the antiquities of Greece. Without the foreign (Greek) colonies on the Nile, they would still be groping in speechless remains, which might cover either a century or a thousand years, for aught that could be determined in Greek excavations.[1]

This typical attitude of nineteenth-century Egyptology towards the cultures existing outside Egypt belies the problems in early Greek history, for, as I have stressed over and over again, since Petrie's day it has been taken for granted that Egyptian New Kingdom chronology is fixed and secure (within a decade or so) and that the chronologies of much of the rest of the ancient world must be dependent on Egypt for their dating. The question must therefore be asked as to why this should be the case when the literary and archaeological evidence from Greece seems to point us in a different direction.

It is easy to forget that, previous to Petrie's announcement, the world of Greek scholarship had assumed continuity between the Heroic Age and the following historical age of Classical Greece. Prior to Petrie's discoveries at Kahun, Gurob and Amarna, Greek scholars simply followed the Classical historians in seeing the invasion of the Dorians as the reason for the sudden collapse in Greek Bronze Age civilisation and thinking that this invasion was followed by a relatively brief period of decline brought about by the arrival of a less cultured population. This original view of events was not really surprising. After all, the ancient Greeks themselves believed it and had given very little impression in their own writings of a long period of abandonment, interruption, recession, stagnation and slow recovery following the Heroic Age. Indeed, Homer himself seems to have been quite unaware that he was living in, or looking back across, a prolonged dark age.

> ... a reading of the Homeric poems is not enough to suggest either that a dark age had descended on, and still enveloped, the world in which the poems were shaped; or that such an age had come and gone in the interval since the Heroic Age.[2]

Similarly, Thucydides implies a continuity which 'would be quite unacceptable to modern minds'.[3] As the renowned Hellenist and arch sceptic, Moses Finley, noted in the 1970s:

The Greek antiquarians who put the story into writing more than five hundred years afterwards had no notion of the great breakdown of about 1200 BC, no idea of a Bronze Age, and therefore no sense of the very considerable time-span of the Dark Age.[4]

In his *Works and Days*, the poet Hesiod of Boeotia (a near contemporary of Homer) *does* complain of an inexorable decline of civilisation since the Heroic Age – but not of a sudden catastrophe from which Greece was gradually pulling itself out into the daylight.

... it has been well observed that for Hesiod there had been a gradual deterioration of the state of affairs from the earliest times, with no conception of a Dark Age from which there had by his time been a considerable recovery – for him, matters were still in process of going from bad to worse.[5]

It was only with the advent of archaeology that this lacuna in Greek history was to appear in the text books.

Dark Age Consequences

The theoretical chasm of the Greek Dark Age soon became self-fulfilling as archaeology delved deeper into the Greek soil. It was noted that there were hardly any physical remains to span the great gap. The archaeological pottery periods of the Dark Age – the Sub-Mycenaean and Proto-Geometric phases – were recognised as 'the poorest and darkest of all in the history of Greek civilisation except, perhaps, for the Stone Age'.[6] Moreover, in the generations which followed the Heroic Age, virtually every art and craft synonymous with civilisation seemed to have disappeared completely – only to return centuries later.

During these generations the changes that came about are little short of fantastic. The craftsmen and artists seem to vanish almost without trace: there is very little new stone construction of any sort, far less any massive edifices; the metal-worker's technique reverts to the primitive, and the potter, except in the early stages, loses his purpose and inspiration; and the art of writing is forgotten. But the outstanding feature is that by the end of the twelfth century the population appears to have dwindled to about one-tenth of what it had been little over a century before. This is no normal decline, and the circumstances and events obviously have a considerable bearing on the nature of the subsequent Dark Ages, and must be in part at least a cause of its existence.[7]

The reason why Vincent Desborough and others came to believe that there had been a dramatic change in the Greek world was that so few dwellings and graves belonging to the surviving population had been unearthed. Virtually all that did survive came from cemeteries and not properly stratified settlements. And what little there was in these burial grounds had to be spread over the whole era. How, then, to account for this paucity of graves spanning over three hundred years? The answer had to be some sort of massive depopulation, leaving tiny numbers of survivors in the impoverished settlements to eke out a living.

The importance of this aspect of the archaeological picture needs no emphasis; its fragmentary and unsatisfactory nature during the Dark Ages is, therefore, extremely depressing. ... Over the whole of Greece and the Aegean there are fewer than thirty sites on which settlement material has been recognised. For the most part our only evidence of such is a deposit of pottery

... There were, however, a number of instances
(about a dozen) where some construction was
associated with the pottery – houses or house
walls, circular pits and wells, hearths and ovens,
for instance. But in only one case was there
a complete settlement, Karphi (on Crete, see
Chapter Seventeen) – and that owed its unchanged
survival until modern times to the fact that few
in their right senses would ever dream of living
there. ... one speaks of a 'settlement', but in fact
what one means is that two or three houses have
been uncovered, or a scatter of unrelated house
walls, or a hearth – the almost wholly obliterated
debris of a forgotten age.[8]

Was this really a 'forgotten age' lasting centuries? Were
its settlements really 'obliterated' or had they, in fact,
never existed? As we have seen, one scholar was forced
to conclude that the post-Mycenaean era was 'the poorest
and darkest epoch in all Greek history except for the Stone
Age'.[9] In 1971 Professor Anthony Snodgrass of Cambridge
University finally gave voice to collective scholarly
frustration over the lack of archaeological material in the
centuries following the Mycenaean collapse.

... explanations on a profound level would
still be needed to account for this drastic
impoverishment in the archaeological record;
above all, for the *quantitative* impoverishment
which, along with others, I attribute primarily
to depopulation. Here, nothing in the past three
decades has served to bring about a change in
this quantitative picture, relative to the periods
before and after, except to reinforce it.[10]

Needless to say, if the Dark Age is a phantom of the
Orthodox Chronology, then the duration of the cemeteries

would be much shorter – just three generations or approximately seventy years – so the burial density would be greater, suggesting a less radical depopulation. But the Dark Age is now an historical certainty and this massive 'depopulation' appears to confirm that 'fact'.

> It is now clear that the 'Dark Age', at any rate in terms of the simple lapse of time, will not go away. It must be either radically reinterpreted, or explained as it is.[11]

Continuity Across the Dark Age

As Desborough noted above, there is another extraordinary consequence of the Dark Age theory which is hard to explain – the obvious cultural and technical continuity between two eras separated by a three-hundred-year gap. In the conventional scheme the skills, artistic motifs, manufacturing techniques and administrative practices (including writing) all have to bridge the void from the end of the Mycenaean period down to the Archaic period when a miraculous recovery of all these skills takes place. It is as if a Greek Rip van Winkle had suddenly woken after a centuries-long slumber and picked up his daily life exactly where he had left off. The situation is best summed up by the authors of *Centuries of Darkness* published in 1988.

> According to the generally accepted scheme, Mycenaean civilisation collapsed *circa* 1200 BC, after which literacy and the arts of ivory working, painting, metalworking, jewellery manufacture, relief sculpture and architecture largely disappeared until the renaissance of Greek civilisation around 800 BC. Population is thought to have sharply declined, as the evidence for settlements during this period becomes scarce.

Practically the only craft of which there is any continuous evidence from 1200 to 800 BC is pottery, most of which, however, is represented by tomb finds rather than stratified deposits ... The scenario just described is rendered even stranger by the fact that Mycenaean forms and traditions frequently reappear after the hiatus. Moreover, they generally recur in material of a luxury character, the kind of goods which one would have expected to disappear during the cultural 'Dark Age' generally envisaged ...

The disappearance of a wide range of skills (from literacy and ivory-working to building in stone) needs to be considered in the context of the contraction of economy and settlement following the collapse of Mycenaean civilisation. However, their reappearance (as yet unsatisfactorily explained), when taken in conjunction with the patchy nature of the stratigraphy for the Greek 'Dark Age', provides circumstantial evidence suggesting that our present chronology may be overstretched. Proto-Geometric and later buildings and occupational remains frequently occur immediately above Mycenaean structures with no intervening strata. What makes these instances puzzling is not so much the absence of occupational debris but the lack of any natural accumulation of sediment or silt over the centuries.[12]

Such problems started to surface almost as soon as the excavators began to familiarise themselves with the new Dark Age model. However, most scholars working in the field quietly ignored the implications of such difficulties.

I will cite three anomalies here – two from Troy and one from Tiryns – but there are many more.

Trouble at Troy

> There is nothing at Troy to fill this huge (Dark
> Age) lacuna. For two thousand years men had
> left traces of their living there; some chapters
> were brief and obscure, but there was never yet
> a chapter left wholly blank. Now at last there
> is silence, profound and prolonged for four
> hundred years; we are asked, surely not in vain,
> to believe that Troy lay 'virtually unoccupied'
> for this long period of time.[13]

Blegen's excavations at Troy had revealed a puzzle which
did not conform to this new Dark Age hypothesis. He noted
that in the last Bronze Age city of Hissarlik – Troy VII
– the citizens continued to manufacture the Grey Minyan
ware (now more often called Grey Anatolian ware) which
had been in use for centuries (all through the long era
of Troy VI). Then, according to the Dark Age scenario,
the site of Troy was abandoned for nearly four centuries
before being re-settled towards the end of the Geometric
period by Aeolian Greeks. Blegen's problem was that in
this new city of Ilion (Troy VIII) he also found copious
amounts of the same Grey Minyan ware. How could this
be after such a long period of abandonment? Were these
new settlers simply descendants of the old Troy VI/VII
culture, returning to the destroyed city after so many lost
generations?

> Whoever they were, these people carried with
> them the tradition of making Grey Minyan
> pottery and maintained it (elsewhere) down to the
> eighth century ... in the seventh century BC the
> Trojan citadel, which had been virtually deserted
> for some four centuries, suddenly blossomed into
> life once more with occupants who were still able
> to make Grey Minyan pottery.[14]

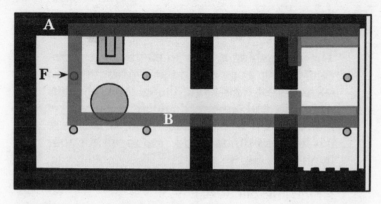

84. Plan of the great megaron at Tiryns (black) with the Archaic temple of Hera (grey) re-employing the foundations of the eastern wall of the Bronze Age building (A) and adding a new wall (B) to form the narrow cella of the new temple. The position of the camera in Plate 58 is marked by the letter F looking along the axis of the temple from its rear towards the entrance.

The excavator was puzzled. Where had these Grey Minyan potters gone off to for all that time? Was it really credible that they had abandoned Troy VII, disappeared from archaeology for fifteen generations, and then reappeared to begin making the same pots in Troy VIII as if nothing had happened to them in the interim?

The archaeological evidence, if taken at face value, suggested that City VIII had immediately followed City VII with no significant break between the two levels. According to the pottery evidence, the natural understanding any archaeologist might reach about the transition from Troy VII to VIII would be occupational and cultural continuity – but this is impossible within a Dark Age chronological framework.

The Dark Age model was dealt another blow when Geometric pottery was found by Blegen on the floor of House 814 – supposedly abandoned at the end of Troy VII. Could this Late Bronze Age house have really remained occupied throughout the Dark Age in order for Geometric pottery to be deposited there in the eighth century? This seemed highly unlikely.

It has been argued that Troy VIIb came to its end about 1100 BC. Generally considered, our evidence leads us to believe that a gap of four hundred years exists between the end of Troy VIIb and the beginning of Troy VIII, but **the possibility of a contrary view** is established by the evidence of several successive floors of House 814, and also by the presence of Geometric sherds in a context of Troy VIIb.[15]

The logical conclusion (Blegen's 'contrary view') was that the time interval between Troy VIIb (LH IIIC or slightly later) and the Middle Geometric had to be a great deal shorter – perhaps no more than fifty years (accounting for the 'successive floors'). Troy VIIb appeared to have come to an end during the eighth century.

These two specific examples from Hissarlik are symptomatic of a general malaise in the Dark Age pottery seriation: the sequence is imbued with uncomfortable chronological anomalies brought about by over-stretching. But there are also architectural puzzles.

I will just give one famous example of this last phenomenon – the case of the Tiryns megaron. Figures 363 and 364 show the Late Bronze Age megaron palace of the citadel at Tiryns on the shore of the Gulf of Argos. Tradition has it that this was the residence of Heracles. Superimposed on the plan of the large megaron you will see a much narrower structure which uses the walls of the earlier megaron as its foundations on the east side. This second building takes the form of a typical Archaic temple (usually dedicated in this area to the goddess Hera). We see many such sanctuaries in the post-Dark Age era of Geometric Greece – one being the temple built over the palace of Mycenae as discussed in the previous chapter.

The puzzle here for the Dark Age model is similar to that of the Late Bronze Age House 814 in Troy VIIb, on the floor of which Blegen found Geometric pottery. In the

Tiryns case it is hard to explain how a building seemingly from the eighth century (the Hera temple) could have utilised walls and column bases from four hundred years earlier (the Heracles megaron) which must surely have been long buried by the time the temple was conceived. As a result, there is considerable doubt about the later structure's true date, with some archaeologists wanting to push the temple back several centuries – even though it is clearly of a type well represented in the Archaic period.

> Some doubt also surrounds the date of a narrow megaron (the Hera temple) on the acropolis of Tiryns (20.90 x 6.90 metres), overlying part of the megaron in the Mycenaean palace. It shares the same floor level, and its central axis coincides with two of the Mycenaean column bases, which were re-used *in situ*. The excavators saw here the Geometric temple of Hera, whose offerings were found twenty-two metres away in a *bothros* deposit of *c.* 750-650 BC. Other scholars, disturbed by the implication that the Mycenaean megaron's plan was still known in the eighth century, prefer to assign the later megaron to a twelfth-century rebuilding of the palace.[16]

Setting the Greek Dark Age Boundaries

The recognised end of the Greek Dark Age comes with the appearance of Late Geometric pottery (conventionally established at *c.* 750-700 BC) when 'we enter the full daylight' of Archaic Greece as Professor Nicholas Coldstream puts it.

> This period is often called 'the Greek Renaissance', and with good reason. It witnessed the recovery of a prosperity unknown since Mycenaean times; it saw the rebirth of skills forgotten during the

Dark Ages; meanwhile, the diffusion of epic poetry inspired all Greeks with a pride in their heroic past.[17]

This was the time of Homer and the creation of the Heroic Age in the minds of the Greeks. The great tholos tombs of the Mycenaean era were being opened up and votive offerings placed inside to honour the ancestors – the Achaean warriors of the Trojan War and their kings.

> Excavators of Mycenaean tombs have often found small clusters of later material, either in the chamber or in the dromos. ... The offerings begin soon after 750 BC and indicate a new respect for the Mycenaean dead at about the time when knowledge of the *Iliad* was beginning to spread across to the Greek mainland. Copious deposits, going back to Late Geometric times, have come to light in the tholos and chamber tombs of Mycenae ...[18]

> In the eighth century the hero Agamemnon was also honoured at Mycenae with a hero cult, while his brother Menelaus was worshipped at Therapne (Sparta) along with Helen, a goddess known in pre-Archaic times.[19]

This was the era of seafaring trade and colonisation; the age of the birth of Western writing in the alphabetic script; the time of the inauguration of the Olympic Games in honour of the hero Pelops, founder of the Achaean dynasties in the Peloponnese.

> The Geometric period began in darkness, but the eighth century witnessed remarkable advances. With the renewal of eastward commerce and the foundation of colonies in the west, Greece

emerged from her isolation. Exchanges with the Near East brought the beginning of prosperity, the mastery of some skilled techniques, and knowledge of alphabetic writing; thus the darkness of illiteracy was finally dispelled. Figured art, almost forgotten during the Dark Ages, flourished once again; and an Ionic school of epic poetry reached its culmination with the composition of the Homeric poems. ... A fifth-century scholar, Hippias of Elis, calculated that the quadrennial games at Olympia were first celebrated in 776 BC.[20]

Small wonder that scholars have dubbed the mid-eighth century a 'renaissance' – a rebirth after four centuries of darkness and impoverishment, of emptiness and stagnation.

The Sub-Mycenaean and Proto-Geometric eras in the Orthodox Chronology currently span a massive three centuries of time, yet the pottery itself is spread very thinly on the ground.

In Athens the Proto-Geometric period is represented by less than a hundred graves, scattered across sites such as the Kerameikos. In Argos there is no Sub-Mycenaean phase between Late Helladic IIIC and the earliest Geometric pottery. This has led some scholars to propose that the Sub-Mycenaean and Proto-Geometric pottery styles were, in fact, contemporary regional variations, with the Sub-Mycenaean confined to western Attica.

... in 1964 Desborough put forward strong arguments for the view that the 'Sub-Mycenaean' pottery did not after all represent a separate chronological entity, so much as a geographical variant. It was, he showed, suspiciously narrow in its distribution, being largely confined, in its fully characterised form, to two excavated cemeteries, on the island of Salamis and in the Kerameikos at Athens. ... most significantly, in the still quite well-populated Argolid, there was a supposed chronological gap, with little or no 'Sub-Mycenaean' available to fill it, between the latest Mycenaean (FURUMARK's IIIC:1c) and the earliest Proto-Geometric material. Yet there were apparent signs of a direct connection between these two phases at Argos. These and other considerations led Desborough to conclude that the 'gap' in the series at Argos might after all be non-existent; that something approaching continuity between the latest Mycenaean and the earliest Proto-Geometric may have existed, not only in Argos but in several other regions where Sub-Mycenaean material was barely represented, but where the other two phases were found.[21]

Under normal circumstances an archaeologist would be reluctant to assign more than fifty years to such material remains, yet here the Greek Dark Age, created by William Matthew Flinders-Petrie and his Egyptologist colleagues, requires this meagre assemblage to bridge a huge void of two-and-a-half centuries between the last Bronze Age Mycenaean culture and the Early Geometric culture of the Archaic period.

The long time-span created by the Orthodox Chronology between the end of the Bronze Age (dated by the Egyptian evidence to *c.* 1125 BC) and the Greek 'renaissance' in the eighth century (fixed by Thucydides' dates for the foundations of the Greek colonies), has made many pottery specialists rather uncomfortable. They note that there is simply too much time for the pottery development they observe – but their hands are tied. They cannot shorten the duration of the sequence because the Egyptologists will not let them.

The Pottery Periods

As most of the ceramic material comes from the limited number of burials unearthed for the Dark Age era, there is very little pottery to spread throughout this extremely long period of time and hardly any associated settlements from which it has been unearthed.

> The implications for the general level of population at this period are obvious: not only is the number of sites known to be in occupation remarkably low, as was already clear; but the quantity of material in the sites that *were* inhabited is nearly always overshadowed by that from the Bronze Age or the Archaic period.[22]

The established pottery phases – Sub-Mycenaean, Proto-Geometric, Early Geometric and Middle Geometric – have to be stretched inordinately beyond their logical time-spans to fill the gap between Mycenaean LH IIIC (ending *c.* 1125 BC) and Late Geometric (starting *c.* 750 BC). Archaeologists have had to accept that there is no way around this 'archaeological fact' – the length of the era (as set by Egyptian chronology) means that everything has to be stretched and pulled within its temporal limits.

> We are faced with this conclusion: the middle and later phases of Mycenaean IIIC ... the Proto-Geometric, Early and Middle Geometric phases at Athens, which all together are represented by some ninety graves in the Kerameikos cemetery: **this brief sequence of periods must be extended over probably about four hundred years or more**. It is clear that we are dealing with a **very slow rate of development in the potter's art in Greece**. If we make a provisional hypothesis as to the duration of the styles, and

assume about one hundred and fifty years for the residue of Mycenaean IIIC, one hundred and fifty years for Attic (Athenian) Proto-Geometric, and fifty years each for Attic Early and Middle Geometric, we shall be taking a wholly arbitrary step; but we shall arrive at approximately the right total, without unduly straining credulity in any one case. We can also be virtually certain that **no reduction in any one of these figures is possible without a compensatory lengthening elsewhere** ...[23]

This is the real dilemma of Dark Age archaeology. Because 'no reduction' is possible without adjustments to other elements in this 'brief sequence' of pottery periods, we are forced to concede 'a very slow rate of development in the potter's art'. The 'approximate and notional' pottery chronology which has been devised to bridge the Dark Age chasm is as follows.

c. 1200 to 1125 BC	The Late Helladic IIIC Period (spanning 75 years)
c. 1125 to 1050 BC	The Sub-Mycenaean Period (spanning 75 years)
c. 1050 to 900 BC	The Proto-Geometric Period (spanning 150 years)
c. 900 to 850 BC	The Early Geometric Period (spanning 50 years)
c. 850 to 750 BC	The Middle Geometric Period (spanning 100 years)
c. 750 to 700 BC	The Late Geometric Period (spanning 50 years)

Snodgrass laments this awkward position over and over again in his classic reference work *The Dark Age of Greece*.

If Attic Late Geometric ended by *circa* 700 BC ... and Attic Middle Geometric began by *circa* 850 (Megiddo), then we have some one hundred and fifty years to apportion between these two phases. **We have the assurance of those who have studied the individual workshops of Late Geometric that this phase can barely be extended over much more than fifty years**; it is difficult to go against expert judgment ... If therefore the Late Geometric is to be concentrated in a span of, say, fifty to sixty years, then **Middle Geometric must cover ninety to one hundred years. This may seem excessively long** ...[24]

So, the approximately 150 years assigned to the Middle and Late Geometric together at Athens appears to be 'excessively long' in the view of both the pottery specialists and the man who wrote the book on the Greek Dark Age! But this only serves to highlight the even greater insecurity of the earlier pottery periods where we are expected to believe that Proto-Geometric also lasted a staggering 150 years. The same goes for that part of the Late Helladic III phase which preceded the beginning of the Dark Age. We have assigned forty years for the whole of LH IIIC in the New Chronology but some versions of the conventional scheme require that the second half of LH IIIC (from the Granary pottery style down to the start of the Sub-Mycenaean) must span in excess of a century.

... we have to allow perhaps one hundred and twenty-five years or more (!) for the duration of the Granary Class, and for the degeneration of Furumark's LH IIICic. This seems quite long enough, for **the material is hardly very plentiful** ...[25]

Needless to say, if Mycenae fell to the Dorians in *circa* 820 BC (as in the NC), then the end of LH IIIC would be dated close to that time. Thus all of the Sub-Mycenaean, Proto-Geometric and Geometric pottery phases would only be required to fill the interval down to 700 BC – a period of just 120 years compared to the 425 years of the conventional scheme. This is a 'radical re-interpretation' indeed of the Dark Age, and a proposition which would certainly qualify for Professor Snodgrass' 'explanation on a profound level'. But such an historical model is entirely consistent with the quantity of ceramic material and the limited artistic development of the Sub-Mycenaean and Geometric styles.

Middle Geometric Pottery at Megiddo

It is worth repeating here that the Greek Dark Age is not an historically recognised era, the events and details of which have been handed down to us by the ancients. It is undeniably a modern construct born almost entirely out of the necessities of a chronology bequeathed to Greece by Egypt.

> … the explicit concept of a 'dark age' was unknown to the Greeks of historical times, and is essentially a finding of early twentieth-century scholarship: only the implicit argument, from the silence and apparent ignorance of the Greeks of any names or episodes which we would date between the eleventh and the eighth centuries, can be cited as ancient support for this modern construct.[26]

The Greek Dark Age is, in reality, a theory based entirely on a potentially corrupt Egyptian THIRD INTERMEDIATE PERIOD chronology (as demonstrated in *A Test of Time*, Volume One) and on the highly dubious argument of 'silence and ignorance' presumed of the Greek historical records. The New Chronology does away with this unsatisfactory theory by unshackling the terminus for the Late Bronze Age in Egypt and the Levant from *circa* 1125 BC and allowing it to slip down to its much more natural chronological position

at around 820 BC. This is entirely in tune with a number
of recent discoveries and reinterpretations of the existing
evidence.

Two Attic Middle Geometric sherds were found in
Stratum VA/IVB at Megiddo – the level once thought
to belong to the time of Solomon (*c.* 970-931 BC), ending
sometime after his reign but 'no later than 850 BC'.[27] As a
result, Nicholas Coldstream's placement of the beginning
of Middle Geometric in 850 BC had to be the *terminus ante
quem* (latest starting date) for this pottery style. However, the
current excavators of Megiddo – Professors Israel Finkelstein
and David Ussishkin – are convinced that Stratum VA/IVB
is later than Solomon and most likely the city of Omri and
Ahab (*c.* 886-852 BC) continuing down, perhaps, for as much
as another fifty years to about 800 BC. Moreover, as Peter
James *et al.* noted:

> ... it was later stated by Hoerth that the
> provenance of the sherds had been incorrectly
> reported: 'at least one of the fragments was
> unearthed in Stratum IV, in the periphery of
> the town, near the fortification', the second
> piece in question probably coming from the
> same stratum.[28]

Hoerth's Megiddo Stratum IV is now designated Stratum
IVA and lies above (i.e. after) Stratum VA/IVB. So, if
Finkelstein and Ussishkin are correct in attributing VA/
IVB to the Omrid dynasty, the two Middle Geometric
sherds appear to come from a city level which post-dates
King Ahab of Israel – in other words *after* 850 BC. It is
generally thought that Megiddo IVA was destroyed by the
Assyrian king, Tiglath-pileser III, in 733 BC. This would
allow us to lower the date for the start of Middle Geometric
by as much as a century. As a result, the New Chronology
postulates a starting date for Middle Geometric – within its
schematised pottery sequence – in *circa* 760 BC.

In fact, each phase of the Geometric is given thirty years or less in the NC, the whole era spanning one hundred years (from *c.* 800 to *c.* 700 BC). This picture of much more rapid stylistic development is perfectly consistent with what one might expect from the Attic workshops producing the vessels – especially in the early phases – as scholars like Jean Davison have concluded, based on detailed studies of the development of the pottery styles.[29] A single generation of potters for each of the Geometric phases is adequate and, indeed, would be far less problematic.

The Demise of the Dark Age

If we now apply the New Chronology dating scheme to the Aegean pottery sequence, we get a very different picture. The archaeological void between the last Bronze Age Mycenaean period and the first appearance of Geometric pottery disappears. The 'Dark Age' – if we can still call it that – lasts less than three generations – at most sixty years (represented by the Sub-Mycenaean, partly contemporary Proto-Geometric and Early Geometric periods). In round figures the pottery scheme would be as follows:

Late Helladic IIIB   950 to 860 BC = 90 years
    (High Mycenaean palatial culture to Fall of Troy)
Late Helladic IIIC   860 to 815 BC = 45 years
    (Mycenaean decline)
Sub-Mycenaean   815 to 790 BC = 25 years
    (Post-Dorian Invasion Attic Mycenaean)
Proto-Geometric   800 to 780 BC = 20 years
    (Overlapping earliest Attic, Ionian Migration)
Early Geometric   780 to 760 BC = 20 years
    (Developing Early Attic)
Middle Geometric   760 to 730 BC = 30 years
    (Developing Middle Attic)
Late Geometric   730 to 700 BC = 30 years
    (Archaic Renaissance era)

> ## Conclusion Twenty
>
> The excessively long pottery periods which span the Bronze to Iron Age transition in Greece (from the start of Sub-Mycenaean down to the end of Late Geometric) can be reduced from a total of 425 years to just 115 years once the New Chronology dating is applied to the Aegean region.

Issues of pottery chronology are not the only difficulties with which scholars of the Greek world are confronted. They also have to deal with the 'Homeric Question' – another child of the Dark Age.

Homerica in a Dark Age

The Greeks themselves believed that Homer was raised or lived in Smyrna (modern Izmir in western Turkey), born to parents who were of that generation which migrated to Ionia from the Greek mainland as a consequence of the Dorian invasion. And so, in the New Chronology, this would place the great poet's *floruit* in Ionia just over a century after the Trojan War about which he sang. Ironically, this is precisely what Eratosthenes himself believed.[30]

Homer's name (*Homeros*) means 'hostage' or 'captive' which may reflect the circumstances in which his parents found themselves when they named their child.[31] Given that (according to Aristarchus) Homer the child participated in the refugee movement triggered by Dorian hostility in the homeland, perhaps his parents had initially been taken captive before escaping to Attica to board ships heading across the Aegean for western Anatolia.

So, if Homer lived in the eighth century BC, might he be both poet *and* author of the *Iliad* – Europe's first work of literature? It is obvious that the earliest *written* compositions of the celebrated poem (15,693 lines divided into twenty-four books) could not have existed before the appearance of alphabetic writing in the Archaic Greek world – and that event has been dated, on archaeological grounds, to the mid-eighth century BC.

> No aspect of the Greek Dark Ages is more poignant than illiteracy. The syllabic writing of Linear B, which had served the needs of Mycenaean palatial administration, was forgotten in Greece after the destruction of the Mycenaean palaces. Thereafter we know of no inscriptions in the Greek language until the earliest alphabetic graffiti on Geometric pottery, none of which is older than 750 BC.[32]

Thus Homer himself was certainly alive (about fifty years old if he was born *c.* 800 BC) at the time writing was introduced and could have been in a position to dictate the epic poems to literate associates prior to his death (aged about eighty) in around 720 BC.[33] However, things are far more complicated in the Orthodox Chronology model which either detaches Homer from the Trojan War by centuries (placing him in the eighth century) or has him singing his epics (in the tenth century) over two hundred years before the *Iliad* and *Odyssey* were finally written down.

One of the most obvious ways Petrie's revision of Greek chronology affected our understanding of Greek history was that it completely changed our thinking about the Homeric epic traditions and the date of Homer himself. Whereas prior to Petrie, Homer was seen to be a near contemporary of the events of the Trojan War and originator of the narratives, now, in the view of a number of eminent scholars, the final version of the epics had to be relegated to the status of a late eighth-century redaction of an oral tradition collated from a variety of earlier sources. This flew in the face of the direct evidence of the poetry itself which showed a continuity of style indicative of a single author of some genius.

Hesiod too was brought down into the late eighth century even though, in his *Theogony* (Greek creation myth), he was heavily influenced by the Hittite *Epic of Kumarbi* which could not reasonably have survived the end of the Bronze Age and the collapse of the Hittite empire.[34]

> ... the primitive Hesiodic story of how Cronos, at the prompting of his mother the Earth, castrated his father Ouranos, resembles the epic of Kumarbi which had been translated or freely adapted from Hurrian by the Hittites. ... Moreover, an alternative Greek version actually sites the conflict between Ouranos and Cronos at Mount Casius beside the Amik valley just to the south of the Orontes mouth; and that neo-Hittite territory is precisely where the Hurrian-Hittite epic had deliberately located the story.[35]

The writings of both Homer and Hesiod seem to have been heavily influenced by Bronze Age Aegean and Anatolian culture which, under normal circumstances, would logically place these authors in that era or very soon afterwards. There was, however, little choice in the matter as to when their works were written down because it had become clear from the archaeological evidence that the Greeks did not adopt the alphabetic script until the beginning of the eighth century at the very earliest. So the poems and narratives could not have been written down in their developed scriptural form until 'at the widest limits between 800 and 680 BC'.[36] All these factors were brought together in a new hypothesis summed up by my own tutor in Mycenaean archaeology, Professor Nicholas Coldstream.

> ... these sagas – and especially the saga of Troy – were elaborated in hexameter verse by many

generations of Ionian bards, until Homer himself gave them monumental expression.[37]

So there were now two points of view:

(1) either Homer lived in the eighth century (some four hundred years after the Trojan War) and collated the oral poetry in written form, or

(2) he must be placed vaguely somewhere in the eleventh-to-ninth-century Dark Age period as an oral poet whose works were later to be transcribed in the newly developed Greek script of the eighth century by a scribal school.

This latter view would require a Greek oral tradition of some sophistication capable of maintaining the works of Homer intact for at least the last two centuries of the Dark Age. On the other hand, if Homer himself was responsible for gathering the material for his *Iliad* from earlier oral sources, the latter themselves, as Martin Nilsson points out, could not really have preceded Homer by more than four to five generations.

> The unavoidable consequence is that the earliest poems incorporated by Homer and utilised in the composition of his poems cannot be more than, say, a century older than the Homeric poems themselves. This is the limit beyond which literary analysis is unable to transgress.[38]

Few scholars were prepared to place Homer any earlier than 1000 BC at the very earliest and so the great poet had to relinquish his previously assumed place as a near contemporary of the events about which he sang to become a phantom-like figure floating aimlessly in the Dark Age void of history. And yet, now we can be confident that

Hissarlik is the site of ancient Wilusa/Ilios, there is no doubt that 'the landscape of the *Iliad* is the landscape of Troy' and the Homeric descriptions appear to be 'drawn from the knowledge of an eye-witness'.[39]

A further possibility, perhaps less well supported, has been coupled to the late-date hypothesis for the *floruit* of Homer which even goes as far as to suggest a style and content for the narratives influenced almost entirely by the eighth-century environment. Michel Austin and Pierre Vidal-Naquet are forced by the many Homeric narrative anachronisms to ask the question:

> Should one consider the Homeric poems to reflect primarily the time in which they were composed, that is to say (according to the chronology most widely accepted at the moment) the eighth century, with the *Iliad* coming at the beginning of the century or slightly earlier, and the *Odyssey* in the second half?[40]

All this speculation as to the historical position of Homer – and even the question as to who he was (a single genius or a collection of bards edited together into a single composition) – has led to two schools of opinion. These have been dubbed the 'Unitarians' (Homer was one poet) and the 'Separatists' or 'Analysts' (Homer was an amalgam of poets and not a single individual). A slightly modified view of the Analyst school is that Homer was a late eighth-century editor who redacted the amalgam to turn the disparate sources into a single work. This whole complex and convoluted set of issues – virtually all born out of the long Dark Age chronology – has become known as the 'Homeric Question'.

> One must concede to the Analysts that many Homeric phrases, lines, similes and descriptions are of high antiquity, and must have been

current far earlier than any date at which one can reasonably place Homer. One must further allow that many of the scenes and incidents that occur in the poems must have been shaped for poetic purposes well before the time when the epics crystallised in the form we know. On the other hand, the Unitarians are on strong ground when they appeal to our aesthetic reactions to a reading of the *Iliad* and the *Odyssey*. Do you not feel, they will ask, that a mind of great sensitivity and creative power has shaped the phrasing, vivified the characters, and co-ordinated the incidents into a narrative of compelling interest, vigour and dignity? In short, can you fail to believe in Homer when confronted with the evidence of such poetic genius?[41]

The date for Homer, and by implication the Homeric epic poetry (with all its early 'phrases, lines, similes and descriptions'), had been removed from its secure, pre-Petrie, Bronze (i.e. Heroic) Age setting and released to wander around in the twilight of the new Dark Age unable, any longer, to hold on to a firm chronological anchor point. A number of major historical questions grew out of all this uncertainty.

On Homer's knowledge of the Late Bronze Age:

(1)   How did he know of so many social and cultural aspects of Mycenaean/Achaean civilisation if he lived anything up to four centuries after the end of the Bronze Age and following, at best, a good part of the Dark Age in which most of what had gone before must surely have been forgotten?

(2)   How is it possible that archaeological excavations at the site of Hissarlik have shown that Homer was

able to correctly and accurately describe a number of architectural features of the Trojan citadel even though the Late Bronze site would have been covered in debris and sedimentation by the poet's own time? Two such examples are found in *Iliad*, Book VI – the weak part of Troy's wall later found by Dörpfeld – and Book VI where Homer indicates the emplacement of a shrine outside the 'Scaean Gate', just as was found at the foot of the south gate at Troy by the archaeologists (see plate 51).[42] This shrine, with its podium of standing stones, was undoubtedly dedicated to *Apollon Agyieus* – the Greek Apollo of the Gates associated with a stone pillar cult. This aspect of the god was seen as a protector of the entrances and streets of the city. How could Homer have known that such an emplacement stood at the foot of the 'divine tower' [*Iliad*, Book XXI] adjacent to the south gate? In both instances the poet shows a familiarity with the walls of Troy that can only come from either visiting the site and seeing the exposed ramparts for himself or from talking to Achaeans with very long and detailed cultural memories (an obvious requirement of the centuries-long Dark Age).

> In these passages we seem to have a memory of actual fighting round a particular set of walls. There is nothing generalised about the incidents. Once Troy had been ruined and deserted, these features of its walls would have become hard to discern. Greek knowledge of them can best be explained as deriving ultimately from Achaeans who took part in the siege.[43]

(3) How could he have known the names of so many Mycenaean population centres on the Greek mainland when a great number had been abandoned, covered over and forgotten by the eighth century?

Although some scholars attribute the 'Catalogue of Ships' (*Iliad*, Book II) to another source, the mere fact that it is included in the Homeric narrative allows this anomaly to stand.[44]

On Homer's knowledge of the early Iron Age:

(4) Why is it that Homer introduces a mix of both Bronze and Iron Age armour and weaponry into the *Iliad*, suggesting that he could not have died before the introduction of iron into the battle equipment of the Greeks? This would anchor his *floruit* to the eighth century at the earliest.

(5) Why does he describe the Achaeans of the Trojan War burning the bodies of their slain nobility on funeral pyres when cremation did not become the common practice of the Greeks until one hundred years after the events described in the *Iliad*? Moses Finley points to this anomaly when he tells us that 'by about 1050 BC cremation of adults had become universal in most of the Greek world' but that previously 'the Mycenaean world buried its dead'. Thus he concludes that 'the *Iliad* and the *Odyssey* remain firmly anchored in the earlier Dark Age on this point ...'[45]

It was questions like these which led Finley to postulate that the Homeric tradition was a child of the Dark Age and that only an orator of that transitional period could have retained knowledge of both the Bronze and Iron Age cultures of Greece. This hypothesis certainly has its attractions but, in itself, is born purely out of necessity, resulting directly from the 'Dark Age Problem' – in reality one and the same as the 'Homeric Question'. Finley is correct in assigning the poems to the Late-Bronze-to-Iron-Age transition but he was unable to see that this transition was, in fact, very short and fell entirely within the first fifty years of the Archaic period (*c.* 800 to *c.* 750 BC), there being no extended Dark Age between it and the earlier Heroic Age.

Conclusion Twenty-One

Homer began to compose the *Iliad* within a century of the Trojan War, with the transition from the Heroic Age (Late Bronze Age) to the Archaic period (Iron Age) occurring in *circa* 800 BC at about the time when Homer was born.

Restoring a Ninth-Century *Iliad*

In the second part of this chapter we have principally dealt with just one aspect of the New Chronology – the effect such a revision would have on our understanding of the Homeric traditions – and, if we are allowed to adopt this scheme for a moment in order to assess the consequences, we can see some immediate and obvious benefits.

(1) Homer is now singing his epic poetry to audiences whose fathers witnessed the disturbances at the end of the Bronze Age. It is only around a hundred years since the fall of Troy. This is perfectly consistent with the requirement of Martin Nilsson (page 463 above) who argues that 'the earliest poems incorporated by Homer and utilised in the composition of his poems cannot be more than, say, a century older than the Homeric poems themselves'.

(2) At the same time, the Homeric Question can be satisfactorily resolved. Homer is now capable of being not only the 'singer' (or composer) of the *Iliad* but also the 'writer' (or dictator) of the canonical version of the poem because he was alive both in the era shortly

after the war, when place-names and events were still well known, and during the time when writing had been established in Ionia.

(3) Details of the siege, the armour and social structure of Mycenaean civilisation are also still fresh in the memory.

(4) The ruins of Bronze Age Troy remain unburied in Homer's time. He (or, if blind, his guide/informer) was able to see for himself the weak part of the citadel wall and the altar of monoliths at the Scaean Gate.

(5) Iron Age anomalies interspersed into the narratives are now explainable because there are no centuries of total impoverishment and loss of craftsmanship separating the two ages. The use of limited amounts of iron and the wearing of greaves is indicative of an intermediate phase in the practice of warfare – a practice which would make the full transition to the HOPLITE system within a century.[46]

(6) Cremation can now be seen in its proper context. The Achaeans, as a necessity of warfare undertaken a long way from their homeland, adopted cremation for their war casualties from the Anatolians, with the practice being maintained in the following century when the Mycenaean population was forced to emigrate to the Aegean islands and the far west as a result of the Dorian invasion. So, for example, we find tholos tombs with cremation burials at Salamis on Cyprus which are datable to the early Iron Age, and Euboean colonists at Pithecusae in Italy (c. 770 BC) quenching funeral pyres with wine as described in the *Iliad*.[47]

(7) The archaeology of Troy itself is relieved of its anomalies. The local Grey Minyan ware of City VII

now has a continuity with the identical ware of the subsequent City VIII (Archaic Ilion), whereas in the OC it was necessary to suggest that the site was abandoned for four hundred years and that, as a result, the technology of Grey Minyan pottery manufacture was re-exported to the site fifteen generations later.

These are just a few of the consequences for Homerica and early Greek studies which come readily to mind. If the new hypothesis opens up such rich potential for further study of this very interesting period in Greek history, then proper consideration of the scheme should be given by the recognised experts in the field to test further the potential of this simple but attractive alternative. It may yet hold the answers to many of the problems which beset the study of our surviving corpus of Homeric poetry and resolve at least some of the disagreements that have preoccupied Homeric scholars over the last hundred years.

Chapter Fifteen

THE SONS OF HERACLES

*The Arrival of the Dorians -- Eratosthenes' Error -- The
First and Second Dorian Invasions -- Calculating
Generation Lengths -- The Spartan Royal Genealogies
-- Other Greek Genealogies*

We now come to the story of how the famous militaristic state of Sparta came into being. In the orthodox chronology the Spartans surface in history and archaeology several centuries after the fall of the Mycenaean kingdoms of Greece, separated from them by the Dark Age. The traditions, however, paint a different picture with the Spartans identified with the Dorian invaders who entered the Peloponnese two generations after the Trojan War. I will attempt to show here that, with the New Chronology applied, the traditions are absolutely correct and that the Greek genealogies support the NC dates for the Dorian invasion.

The development of Sparta as a major power in Archaic Greece has been a subject of considerable interest to scholars, not only because of the unusual society which evolved but also because so little can be gleaned from the available evidence as to the origins of that famous sixth- and fifth-century Spartan culture. What is therefore crucial to our understanding of the rise to power of the Spartan state is to trace the origins of Spartan militarism and its connection, if any, with the arrival of the Dorians into the Peloponnese at the beginning of the Iron Age.

It would be logical, as a first step in this process, to place the events of the early period in relation to the low-chronology model already postulated, to observe its effect on the available evidence. At the same time, this will show that the dynasties of kings themselves, as handed down to us by the later writers, indicate a Dorian invasion just prior to the beginning of the eighth century rather than the mid-eleventh century BC.

The Coming of the Dorians

All the Greek historians claimed that the Achaean collapse culminated in a Dorian invasion from the north, traditionally associated with the 'Return of the Heracleidae' – exiles from the Greek mainland three generations earlier after a failed initial incursion of the Dorians led by Heracles' son Hyllus. The story of that first invasion is fascinating in its own right and beautifully sets up the legendary foundation of the Dorian kingdoms, explaining the nature of the future Spartan military state.

The brutish hero Heracles – a man of little charm or intelligence but huge strength and mindless violence – had been the vassal ruler of Tiryns under his overlord, King Eurystheus of Mycenae. Our 'hero' then set off on a long campaign of mayhem around the Mediterranean which culminated in the sacking of Troy during the reign of Priam's father, Laomedon. After Heracles had died, his mother, Alcmene, and those of his sons not already living in Boeotian Thebes, were exiled from Tiryns and sought asylum in Athens where Theseus (of Minotaur fame) ruled. Eurystheus then invaded Attica but met his death at the hands of Heracles' eldest son, Hyllus. The Mycenaeans were defeated and retreated southwards.

Plate 51: The altar stones in front of the South Gate tower at Troy (commonly thought to be the Scaean Gate) with a shrine to Apollo at its base.

Plate 52: The best preserved section of the Troy VI wall in the south-east sector of the citadel, with its distinctive offset panelling.

Plate 53: The main south-west gate of Troy VI which was walled up in the rebuilding of Troy VII. Was this gate dismantled and widened just before the final destruction of Troy VI? The left join of the blocking is indicated by the arrows.

Plate 54: The imposing Lion Gate at Hattusha with its heavy cyclopean walls.

Plate 55: The god Sharruma protects King Tudhaliya IV in the rock-cut sanctuary of Yazilikaya, near Hattusha.

Plate 56: The warrior god of the King's Gate at Hattusha.

Plate 57: The tumulus of Gordias viewed from the city mound of Gordion.

Plate 58: The great megaron at Tiryns (A – left and far right) with the Archaic temple re-employing the left wall of the LBA building and adding a new wall (B) to form the narrow cella of the new temple. The outlines of the Bronze Age hearth (C), column bases (D) and throne dais (E) are marked out on the modern floor.

Plate 59: Ruins of a bygone age of heroes. Tiryns – home of Heracles.

Plate 60: The crumbling ruins of Karphi, scattered over the rocky crag and in the little valley below, with the north coast of Crete in the far distance looking west.

Plate 61: Apollo of Didyma, western Anatolia's ancient sun-god.

Plate 62: Dagger with Nilotic scene from Mycenae [National Museum, Athens].

Plate 63: Ramesses III's mortuary temple at Medinet Habu, western Thebes.

Plate 64: The Second Pylon of Ramesses III's mortuary temple. On the right side of the doorway is the long text which tells the story of the Sea Peoples battles.

Plate 65: The captured leaders of the Peleset invaders.

Plate 66: King Azatiwatas seated on his throne at Karatepe (south gate).

Plate 67: A goddess suckles a child, perhaps representing the ruler of Karatepe. Although the art is very un-Egyptian, the motif is the same as Pharaoh being suckled by Hathor/Isis.

Plate 68: Another relief from the citadel of Karatepe depicting a Bess-like figure – perhaps another Egyptian influence introduced into the Anatolian land of Kode/Que/Cilicia via Phoenicia.

After a number of years had passed, Hyllus, resident in Thebes, then attempted to retake his father's throne in the Peloponnese and exact revenge on the incumbent Pelopids of Mycenae – now represented by Atreus, father of Agamemnon. Hyllus found support for his venture amongst the northern Greek tribes – especially from the king of the Dorians, whose daughter he had married. Together they invaded the south and wrought terrible havoc across the Peloponnese in *circa* 890 BC (according to the NC). They slaughtered the eleven brothers of the Pylian ruler, Nestor, and burnt the palace of Pylos to the ground (possibly the LH IIIB destruction).

In the second year of the invasion a terrible plague hit the region, laying low the combatants from both sides. An oracular decree was sought from the shrine of Apollo at Delphi to explain why the gods were displeased. The answer came back: 'The Heraclids have returned before their due time!' Taking heed of the oracle, Hyllus withdrew to Marathon and went to seek further advice from Delphic Apollo. He was then told that the Heracleidae must 'wait for the third crop' before they would be allowed by the gods to succeed in their aim of conquering the Peloponnese. Hyllus

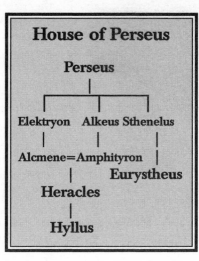

493

took this to mean three harvests and set off once again, three years later (NC – *c.* 887 BC), to seize his lost heritage. However, the Oracle of Apollo had meant three generations – not three harvests – and Hyllus met his end almost before the re-invasion had begun.

North of the Isthmus of Corinth – the narrow strip of land which joins the Peloponnese to the Greek peninsula – the army of Atreus, now high-king of the Achaeans, met the Dorians led by Hyllus. In order to avoid mass slaughter it was agreed that single combat between two champions (on the Homeric model) should settle the question. Hyllus was matched against King Echemos of Tegea. If the Heraclid won the contest, he would take the kingdom of Mycenae, but if the Achaean champion won, then the 'sons of Heracles' would agree to retreat back to Boeotia. Hyllus was killed and the Dorians returned northwards.[1]

The destructions witnessed by archaeology across the Peloponnese towards the end of the Late Helladic IIIB correspond remarkably well with the story of Hyllus, son of Heracles, and the first Dorian invasion, as Desborough observes.

> The various known factors, the destructions
> – especially of certain important citadels – the
> wholesale desertion of great tracts of mainland
> Greece, the consequent flight by land to remote
> and isolated districts or sites on the mainland
> ... all these suggest that there was an invasion,
> or a series of invasions, affecting the central
> and southern mainland ... If, however, there
> was an invasion, one would naturally expect
> the invaders to take over the country they had
> overrun. Of this there is no sign whatever. ... in
> spite of the losses discussed above, what remains
> is, so far as one can tell, purely Mycenaean. ...
> One would then have to assume that the invaders
> went on elsewhere, or retreated.[2]

This is precisely what the Greek traditions tell us. The Heracleidae and their Dorian allies, having desolated the Peloponnesian kingdoms, retreated to their home territories in northern Greece and Boeotia to await the allotted time for their prophesied successful conquest of the Achaean lands in the south. The Achaeans of the Peloponnese made preparation for the future Dorian assault by building a fortification wall at the Isthmus of Corinth across which the invasion would surely come. This wall has been dated 'to the latter half of the Late Helladic IIIB period'.[3]

Conclusion Twenty-Two

The initial invasion of the Heracleidae, led by Hyllus son of Heracles, was responsible for the widespread destruction found throughout the Peloponnese during the LH IIIB. The date of this event in the New Chronology is *circa* 890 BC, seventy years before the final destruction of Mycenaean culture at the end of LH IIIC (*c.* 820 BC).

Atreus was now left secure in the knowledge that no trouble would come from that direction to endanger his throne for many years. He therefore turned his attention to the east and the Anatolian kingdoms of Arzawa and Lukka (Lycia). As we have seen, Atreus appears in the Hittite royal archives as Attarisiyas 'the man of Akhiya', stirring up trouble in the time of the Hittite emperors Tudhaliya IV and Arnuwanda III.

Atreus was succeeded by his sons – Agamemnon in Mycenae and Menelaus in Laconia/Sparta. These rulers were therefore of the first generation following the initial Dorian assault led by Hyllus, leaving two more generations still to come and go before the Return of the Heracleidae. The Trojan War marks the end of the generation of

Agamemnon and Menelaus, thus giving two generations between the fall of Troy and the final Dorian invasion. Thucydides allots eighty years to this period.

> Even after the Trojan War Hellas (Greece) was in a state of ferment ... There was party strife in nearly all the cities, and those who were driven into exile founded new cities. Sixty years after the fall of Troy, the modern Boeotians were driven out of Arne by the Thessalians and settled in what is now Boeotia ... twenty years later the Dorians with the descendants of Heracles made themselves masters of the Peloponnese.[4]

In the historical model being proposed here, the final demise of Mycenaean power – at the end of LH IIIC – occurred within forty-five years of the fall of Troy VIh (which itself took place just before the end of LH IIIB). However, this interval is obviously not consistent with the above statement by Thucydides. There is a good reason for this.

Diodorus Siculus, following the Athenian historian, Apollodorus (second century BC, who himself used the chronology of Eratosthenes, third century BC) accepted this same time-interval between the Trojan conflict and the second Dorian invasion.

> ... from the Trojan War we follow Apollodorus of Athens in setting the interval from then to the Return of the Heracleidae as eighty years ...[5]

This round figure of eighty years appears rather suspicious and, indeed, we should be wary of it. Scholars have long recognised that the later Greek historians and chronographers – especially ERATOSTHENES of Cyrene (Resident in Alexandria) – used genealogies of the royal dynasties and great households as a means of establishing time-periods. As I will explain shortly, there is considerable evidence that the generation-length used by these early Greek historians was forty years – much too high for most modern historians to accept. In addition, these genealogical retro-calculations were themselves anchored to the traditional date of the First Olympiad, established as 776 BC by the fifth-century sophist, HIPPIAS of Elis – a date which itself has not gone unquestioned. Andrew Burn long ago recognised that Hippias' list of Olympic victors which forms the basis of the chronology of the early Olympiads was compiled 'on no very secure evidence'.[6]

> The establishment, or re-establishment, of the Olympic Games is traditionally dated 776 BC; but only by a much later calculation. Hippias, a scholar of Elis, some three hundred and fifty years later, collected all the names of traditional victors in the games which he could find, arranged them in a reasonable order and found they extended so far; but we cannot be sure that the list is complete, or that all are genuine, or that the festival was originally (as it was in Classical times) four-yearly. Hippias did his best with what material he had; later people 'canonised' his results.[7]

Archaeology Versus Genealogy

Doubts about the historical usefulness of the Greek genealogies were reinforced as the Dark Age model took hold within academia.

> ... it is clear that the method of chronography by pedigree (i.e. genealogy) in Greece particularly failed to illuminate the long period of twilight at and after the fall of Mycenae, the twelfth and eleventh centuries BC.[8]

Archaeology had shown that there must have been a very long interval from the Late Bronze Age, when Homer's heroes had supposedly lived, down to the Classical era and the time of the families claiming descent from those heroes. The number of generations given in the genealogies simply did not reach back far enough. This was especially true of the Spartan royal lines which claimed their foundation from the Heracleidae at the time of the second Dorian invasion.

Moreover, the extended early Dark Age chronology had forced archaeologists to separate the fall of Mycenaean civilisation from the arrival of the Dorians in the Peloponnese. The modern view concerning the disappearing role of the Dorians in the collapse of the Mycenaean world at the end of the Bronze Age was aptly summed up by Pavel Oliva in 1981.

> Earlier scholars tended to link the end of this (Mycenaean) civilisation with the 'Dorian invasion', that is to say, with the arrival on the Greek mainland of the last wave of Greek-speaking invaders. More recent archaeological research, however, has shown the Dorian settlement of the Peloponnese to be of more recent date; it can thus hardly have anything to do with the catastrophe that befell the Late Helladic centres, upset their economic stability and broke the political power of the Mycenaean rulers.[9]

The newly discovered Dark Age had been directly responsible for disconnecting the traditional agents of the sudden collapse at the end of the Heroic Age – the Dorians – from that collapse, leaving scholars to search for other explanations for the Mycenaean demise.

Modern scholarship has decided that the historical material handed down to us by the Greek historians has proved unreliable for this period – suspecting that the 'framework of early Greek history' had been constructed 'by feats of chronological carpentry'.[10] However, they were happy to accept a high chronology for the Trojan War such as that given by Eratosthenes of Cyrene – who proposed a date for the fall of Troy in 1184 BC because it coincided with the new high dates for the Trojan War. John Luce, in his much-read book *Homer and the Heroic Age*, gratefully embraced the ancient calculations.

> It is interesting to note how closely these estimates (of Eratosthenes) agree with the range of modern estimates based mainly on archaeological data.[11]

But the reality is that this was nothing more than a happy coincidence because scholars were well aware of the fact that Eratosthenes had used those same short genealogies for his chronological calculations – assigning to each a quite unrealistic forty years.

> Genealogical chronology is the oldest method of reckoning historical time and the most inexact. … the method is misleading in that it appears to be more precise than it is in fact. Thus, by using an exact number of years – say eight hundred – derived by multiplying a certain number of generations – say twenty – by another number representing the length of a so-called average generation – say forty – one implies a precision impossible to achieve. The method is therefore insidious.[12]

With a generation-length of between twenty and twenty-five years (the modern estimate) these same genealogies simply cannot reach back to the end of the Bronze Age within the conventional scheme, making the whole process a nonsense. Dark Age specialist Vincent Desborough wryly comments:

So, it seems, there is good reason to reject all or most accounts of links with Mycenaean Greece, together with the high chronology of the movements of peoples, and the venerable ancestry of the royal families.[13]

'Historical Greece' of the Iron Age had become completely detached from 'Heroic Greece' of the Bronze Age by a chronological chasm centuries wide.

Eratosthenes and the Spartan Royal Lineages

It is time then to take a look in greater depth at the mechanism which established such high dates for the Trojan War and Dorian invasion in the writings of the later Classical historians. How could they not have been aware of a long Dark Age and yet still placed the Heroic Age so far back in time as the twelfth century BC? The answer is that they all appear to have employed the chronological calculations of the mathematician Eratosthenes of Cyrene who, though famed in later generations as the man who correctly calculated the circumference of the Earth (to within ten per cent), was called *beta* ('second best') by his contemporaries because he was competent in many disciplines but not outstanding in any of them. It was this Alexandrian scholar of doubtful repute who seems to have been responsible for the widely accepted Classical date for the Trojan War and all that followed from it.

Modern scholars are well aware of the fact that the length of a generation used by the early Greek chronographers was set at a completely unreasonable forty years – a figure which made such calculations quite unrealistic. This is certainly the case with Eratosthenes' date of 1184 BC for the end of the Trojan War and, as a consequence, the Dorian invasion eighty years (or two forty-year 'generations') later.

The results are clear for all to see. For example, as Anthony Snodgrass points out, each ruler of the dynasty of

Spartan kings is required to have reigned for nearly forty years in order for the line to reach back to the established date of the Dorian invasion when the Spartan state was founded.

> ... the *average* length of generation on which the Spartan genealogies were based must have been forty years – an impossibly high figure which the Greeks (including Herodotus when he thought about it [Book II]) soon came to reject.[14]

The death of the Spartan hero Leonidas, who perished at the Battle of Thermopylae, is dated to 480 BC. There were sixteen 'generations' of kings back from Leonidas to the dynasty founder, Eurysthenes, one of the Heracleidae who led the Dorian military incursion into the Peloponnese. The number of years from 480 BC to the Eratosthenes-based date of 1104 BC for the Return of the Heracleidae amounts to 624. Thus each ruler of Sparta must have reigned, on average, for about forty years – a ludicrous figure given that the average reign-length in the ancient world was just seventeen years.

Professor Snodgrass is not the only scholar to make this point – it has been widely accepted for decades, as the following statement from Burn (writing in the 1930s) makes clear.

> It cannot be too strongly emphasised that the traditional date of the Trojan War, 1194 to 1184, adopted by Eratosthenes and more or less tentatively accepted in so many modern books, is absolutely worthless.[15]

That the ancient Greeks themselves became sceptical about Eratosthenes' high generation figure is well illustrated by the fact that Strabo [Book XIII] allotted the two-generation period from the fall of Troy to the second

Dorian invasion just sixty years – that is, of course, two thirty-year generations. Modern estimates for a generation-length would be even lower.

We will return to the Spartan royal genealogies later. For now, we need to pin down the length of time which must be allotted to the interval between the fall of Troy VIh, at the hands of Agamemnon, and the fall of Mycenae during the reign of his grandson, Tisamenos, at the hands of the Dorians.

You have seen that the period had been calculated by Eratosthenes as eighty years but that this figure is almost certainly based on assigning the two generations of Orestes and Tisamenos forty years each. We know that such a generation-length is unrealistic (as noted by Herodotus, Strabo and all modern historians) and so we should really allot each king something close to the average reign-length of seventeen years. However, the Spartan kings of later times seem to have enjoyed a slightly higher average reign-length of 19.6 years and this may be true of the Indo-European elites as a whole. The Hyksos emperors were long-reigned, as were Priam and Nestor according to Homer. It is entirely possible, then, that climate, diet or genes were responsible for Indo-European kings ruling longer than their Asiatic counterparts. So I have chosen to allot the last two Mycenaean kings reigns of twenty-two and fifteen years respectively as a working hypothesis (given that Tisamenos lost his throne prematurely).

Orestes (Linear B *o-re-ta*) did not immediately follow his father on the throne because Agamemnon was murdered by his wife, Clytemnestra, and her lover, Aegisthus, who ruled at Mycenae for a time before they too were killed by Orestes. Homer gives eight years between Agamemnon's homecoming/murder and the accession of Orestes [*Odyssey*, Book III], so a period of around forty-five years (8 + 22 + 15 = 45) seems appropriate for the era from the sack of Troy to the fall of Mycenae, which we have approximately equated with the pottery period known as Late Helladic IIIC.

We now refocus on the earlier Delphic Oracle, which forbade the original Heracleidae (led by Hyllus) from returning to their conquest of Greece for 'three crops' – a prophecy which was then later clarified by the Oracle to mean that a successful invasion would only be possible in the third generation after Hyllus. Herodotus confirms that the second Dorian invasion took place four generations after Heracles (Hyllus' father). We can therefore extend our overview backwards by another generation to reconstruct a simple but reasonably sound chronological framework for the closing years of Mycenaean rule.

The first (failed) Dorian invasion led by Hyllus took place in *circa* 890 BC (a few years after the death of Eurystheus of Mycenae) and around fifteen years before the start of the Trojan War; that war lasted ten years according to Homer; the subsequent era from the fall of Troy to the completion of the second (successful) Dorian invasion we have estimated at forty-five years. These three periods between the first and second Dorian invasions thus add up to approximately seventy years – that is, three generations/reigns of twenty-three years which is much closer to our modern understanding of the length of a generation (between twenty and twenty-five years). At Mycenae the four reigns following the death of Eurystheus are those of Atreus (the former's uncle and therefore of the previous generation), Agamemnon, Orestes and Tisamenos in whose time the final Dorian invasion occurred.

Event	Pottery Period	NC Date	OC Date
First Dorian Invasion	LH IIIB (mid)	*c.* 890 BC	*c.* 1210 BC
Start of the Trojan War	LH IIIB (late)	*c.* 874 BC	*c.* 1194 BC
End of the Trojan War	LH IIIB (end)	*c.* 864 BC	*c.* 1184 BC
Second Dorian Invasion	LH IIIC (end)	*c.* 820 BC	*c.* 1050 BC*
Ionian Migration	Proto-Geometric	*c.* 800 BC	*c.* 900 BC

* Note that, on archaeological grounds, the OC does not accept Eratosthenes' 1104 BC date for the second Dorian invasion but prefers a date some fifty years later.

> ## Conclusion Twenty-Three
> The final Dorian invasion took place in the last quarter of the ninth century BC (NC – *c.* 820 BC) and was the driving force behind the Ionian migration, as the Greek tradition suggests. There were no extended intervals of time between the Trojan War, the Dorian invasion and the Ionian migration, all of which occurred within a period of seventy years.

The Generation Game

So, scholars have seen Eratosthenes' date for the Trojan War (1194-1184 BC) as a typical Greek historian's chronological calculation – based on allotting forty years to each generation of the twin Spartan royal genealogies extending back from the first Olympic Games in 776 BC or the death of Leonidas in 480 BC to the time of Heracles, the eponymous ancestor of the Heracleidae and the Agiad and Eurypontid dynasties. These two contemporary royal lines were founded at the time of the Dorian invasion.

Prior to the Classical era there seems to have been no regnal chronology as such – or at least none that survived in documented form down into the Archaic period. Professor Snodgrass, one of the world's leading authorities on the Greek Dark Age (whom I have been quoting at length), summarises the position, writing of 'the genealogies of the Spartan kings, which were preserved down to Classical times and are detailed by Herodotus':

> Their importance lies in the fact that orthodox early Greek chronology seems to have been very largely founded upon them. King Leonidas, who succeeded his brother Cleomenes and fell at Thermopylae in 480 BC, was reckoned

twentieth in line of descent from Heracles – son having succeeded father in every case except the last. Since the orthodox dating for Heracles – also supported by Herodotus [Book II:145] – was at the end of the fourteenth century, the *average* length of generation on which the Spartan genealogies were based must have been forty years – an impossibly high figure which the Greeks (including Herodotus when he thought about it [Book II:142]) soon came to reject.[16]

So it seems that the later chronographers were entirely reliant on genealogies to reconstruct their chronologies for the Bronze Age. Today's historians studying the Old World would, of course, as Snodgrass concedes, assign a much lower figure to a generation – usually between twenty and twenty-five years. This sort of figure is clearly supported by the estimated life-expectancy of the period.

> ... it is sobering to reflect that from the evidence of skeletal remains of the early Iron Age it seems that the odds were against any baby surviving to the age of fifteen, and that it was a lucky Greek teenage male who saw forty, and girl who saw thirty.[17]

This is entirely consistent with other regions where such statistics have been gathered. For example, we know from the anthropological examinations of the Austrian archaeological mission at Tell ed-Daba (Avaris) that life-expectancy there was around thirty-four years. Couples would hardly have chosen to have their first children (amongst them the male heir) as late as thirty, or even twenty-five, if they had little expectation of living beyond forty. The age of forty was not the length of a generation but rather the length of life itself to the average Iron Age Greek.

Such anthropological data were not known in the early days of archaeology but academics were well aware of the fact that their own generation-length was considerably less than forty years. Even so, nineteenth- and early-twentieth-century scholars continued to use Eratosthenes to support the high chronology simply because it appeared to fit the growing archaeological evidence produced by the likes of Petrie (based on the established Egyptian chronology). Burn was one of the first scholars to expose this underlying methodological flaw:

> It is an indubitable fact that Eratosthenes' computation of the date of the Trojan War, which most recent writers, amazingly, treat with respect, is based on a wild over-estimate of the average length of a generation.[18]

I have come to the conclusion that an average generation-length was about twenty-one years in the hotter climates of Egypt and Mesopotamia but a little higher in the more temperate climates of Anatolia and Greece (perhaps up to twenty-five years). The typical reign-length appears to have been between fifteen and twenty years in the ancient world. This is based on research I undertook at university (and which was incorporated into *A Test of Time*) averaging the reign-lengths of 329 kings belonging to nineteen dynastic lines representing 5,511 years in total (the actual average being 16.75 years). Most of these dynasties are either from the much-better-known historical period of the seventh to first centuries before the Christian era or are taken from the king-lists and highest regnal dates of the rulers of both Assyrian and Egyptian civilisations.[19] However, as I have already noted, the later Spartan dynasties (from Leonidas and Leotichidas II on) seem to have benefited from slightly longer reign-lengths (19.6 years) and so I will favour the upper limit of our average range in the case of calculations based on the Spartan royal genealogies.[20]

We will now revise Eratosthenes' chronology for early Greece using a twenty-year average reign-length for the Dorian kings of Sparta to arrive at what should be a more accurate (though still approximate) date for the second Dorian invasion derived from the twin genealogies.

The Spartan Genealogies

The Spartan state had a system of two contemporary and parallel royal households or dynasties – the Agiads and Eurypontids. Agis I and Eurypon were the sons of the two leaders of the Heracleidae (Eurysthenes and Proclus) who seized Laconia (the territory of Menelaus' Sparta) two generations after the Trojan War. At the other end of the dynasty we have the historical date of 480 BC for the Battle of Thermopylae when three hundred Spartans fell in a heroic last stand against the massive invading Persian army. The Spartan leader, from the Agiad line, was Leonidas who came to the throne in 488 BC. He will be the starting-point for our calculation back to Agis I and the start of his Agiad Dynasty. The contemporary of Leonidas in the Eurypontid line was Leotichidas II who succeeded to the throne in 491 BC, and so we can work backwards through his dynasty to Eurypon in a similar fashion. However, this line of kings is less secure because several of the kings bear names which give all the appearance of being invented: for example, Prytanis ('president') and Eunomus ('law-abiding').[21] On the other hand, the Agiad line was pretty much unvarying in the different literary sources, so we may treat this dynasty as reasonably accurate (as most scholars do). We then need to add one further generation (for the fathers of the two dynasty founders) to arrive at our approximate date for the Return of the Heracleidae. However, this last generation would have been longer because tradition has it that the twins Agis and Eurypon were not born until after the Dorian invasion. Thus we need to add, say, fifteen years for them to reach the potential age of fatherhood.

Agiads		Eurypontids		
Eurysthenes	823	Proclus	826	– Dorian Invasion & Return of the Heracleidae
Agis	788	Eurypon	791	– Formation of the Spartan state
Echestratus	768	Prytanis	771	
Leobotas	748	Polydectes	751	– Lycurgus as Regent for Leobotas
Doryssus	728	Eunomus	731	
Agesilaus I	708	Charilaus	711	– The Laws of Lycurgus introduced
Archelaus	688	Nicander	691	
Teleclus	668	Theopompus	671	– Capture of Amyclae; First Messenian War
Alcamenes	648	Anaxandrides I	651	
Polydorus	628	Archidamus I	631	– Second Messenian War
Eurycrates I	608	Anaxilaus	611	
Anaxander I	588	Leotichidas I	591	
Eurycrates II	568	Hippocratidas	571	
Leon	548	Agasicles	551	
Anaxandrides II	528	Ariston	531	
Cleomenes I	508	Demaratus	511	– Attack upon Athens
Leonidas	488	Leotichidas II	491	– Persian Invasion of Greece

Although this is only a very generalised method of determining the starting-date for the two dynasties, it is encouraging that both lines have their beginnings within a few years of the date we had already arrived at for the Dorian invasion – that is, *circa* 820 BC. So it looks as if the Spartan genealogies generally confirm our chronology for the Trojan War and the Return of the Heracleidae whilst, at the same time, enabling us to reject, without reservation, the dates calculated by Eratosthenes – as most scholars (including Herodotus!), aware of his faulty methodology, must do.

> ## Conclusion Twenty-Four
> The royal genealogies of Sparta indicate that the two parallel dynasties began in the last quarter of the ninth century BC and that this was therefore the time of the Return of the Heracleidae and Dorian settlement in the Peloponnese.

The Greek Generations

The Spartan royal houses were not the only Greeks from the Classical era to trace their family trees back to the Heroic Age. And these other dynastic families produce a similar chronological picture to that of the more famous Spartan genealogies. Snodgrass argues that – within the conventional historical model – these 'pedigrees ... must remain chronologically valueless' because they imply a very high generation-length of forty years. With a more anthropologically realistic generation of twenty to twenty-five years, they cannot possibly span the Dark Age to reach back into the Heroic Age as they claim. But this is, of course, *within the conventional historical model.* If we apply the New Chronology model things are very different.

The celebrated Athenian house of the Philaidae recorded fifteen generations from Miltiades, victor of the Battle of Marathon in 490 BC, back to Ajax of Salamis, son of Telamon. This is the famous Ajax (Linear B *ai-wa*) of the Trojan War with his great club of meteoritic iron. Miltiades' *floruit* would have been around 520 BC, so fifteen generations of twenty-three years place Ajax in *circa* 865 BC – the time that we have set the Trojan War. However, in order for this genealogy to conform to the conventional dating of the Mycenaean expedition against Troy in around 1200 BC, the length of a generation would have to be raised to an incredible forty-five years!

King Pyrrhus II, the late fourth-century ruler of Epirus (and a cousin of ALEXANDER THE GREAT), claimed to be the twentieth-generation descendant of Achilles. The latter's son, Pyrrhus I, slew King Priam and cast Hector's son, Astyanax, down from the walls at the sack of Troy before founding the Molossian Dynasty at Epirus.[22] The later Pyrrhus (he of the 'Pyrrhic victory') ruled from 319 to 272 BC, and so his ancestor, Achilles, would be dated to *circa* 820 BC based on a twenty-five-year generation – still several decades after the Trojan War but within the sort of error margins which are possible when using genealogical data (actually requiring a twenty-seven-year generation). If, on the other hand, we require an early twelfth-century Mycenaean campaign against Troy (consistent with Eratosthenes' dates of 1194-1185 BC), the generation-length would have to be raised to forty-three years – again completely unrealistic.

The royal lineages of both Arcadia and Messenia also support a low date for the Trojan War and Dorian invasion. Hippothous became king of Arcadia when Agepenor, leader of the Arcadian forces at the Trojan War, failed to return home but instead sailed to Cyprus where he founded Paphos. Hippothous would therefore be dated to *circa* 864-844 BC in the NC. Reference to the chronological table opposite shows that Aristocrates, his twelfth successor to the throne in Arcadia, ruled in the last quarter of the seventh century BC. With an average reign-length (as opposed to generation) of twenty years for the Arcadian kings (in line with the Spartan dynasties) this would take us back to *circa* 868 BC for Hippothous (*c.* 628 BC + 12 reigns x 20 years = 868 BC) – within four years of the approximate New Chronology date for this king.

The line of Messenian rulers presents us with a very similar picture. Aristomenes, last king of Messenia, was a contemporary of ARDYS, king of Lydia (the son of GYGES) and

Opposite: Genealogical table comparing the ancestral lines of Aristocrates of Arcadia and Aristomenes of Messenia with the royal dynasties of Sparta.

Sparta

		Arcadia	Messenia	Agiads	Eurypontids
1	868 BC	Hippothous (immediate post-Trojan War)		Eurysthenes	Proclus
2	848 BC	Aipytos		Agis	Eurypon
3	828 BC	Cypselos		Echestratus	Prytanis
4	808 BC	Boukolion	Cresphontes	Leobotas	Polydectes
5	788 BC	Phialos	Aipytos	Doryssus	Eunomus
6	768 BC	Simos	Glaucos	Agesilaus I	Charilaus
7	748 BC	Pompos	Isthmios	Archelaus	Nicander
8	728 BC	Aiginetes	Dotadas	Teleclus (Amyclae)	Theopompus (Messenian War)
9	708 BC	Polymastor	Phintas	Alcamenes	Anaxandrides I
10	688 BC	Aichmis	Antiochos	Polydorus	Archidamus I
11	668 BC	Aristocrates	Euphaes (Messenian War)	Eurycrates I	Anaxilaus
12	648 BC	Hiketas	Aristodemos	Anaxander I	Leotichidas I
13	628 BC	Aristocrates	Aristomenes (temp. Ardys)	Eurycrates II	Hippocratidas
14	608 BC			Leon	Agasicles
15	588 BC			Anaxander I	Ariston
16	568 BC			Eurycrates II	Demaratus
17	548 BC			Leon	Leotichidas II
18	528 BC			Anaxandrides II	
19	508 BC			Cleomenes I	
20	488 BC			Leonidas	

PHRAORTES, king of Media – according to Pausanias [Book VI:24].[23] The Greek historian and geographer gives just nine reigns back to the first king of Messenia – Cresphontes – which totals around 180 years for the dynasty (assigning an average reign-length of twenty years). Ardys of Lydia is dated to the second half of the seventh century BC as was his contemporary Aristomenes of Messenia. Cresphontes must therefore have ruled at the very end of the ninth century BC (c. 628 BC + 180 = 808 BC). This is entirely consistent with the dates which we have estimated for the other royal lines of the Peloponnese. Cypselos of Arcadia was Cresphontes' father-in-law, and so he would have ruled some years before his son-in-law acceded to the throne in Messenia. As you can see from the chronological table, this is very much the case with Cypselos beginning his reign *circa* 828 BC in Arcadia and Cresphontes *circa* 808 BC in Messenia.

So all these genealogies and royal lines (and others like them) point not to the twelfth century for the Trojan War but rather to the ninth century, precisely as we have determined on historical grounds assessed within a revised chronological model. In fact, there are no Greek genealogies or royal dynasties, to my knowledge, which extend back to the twelfth century using a generation-length of thirty years or less. They all point to an Heroic Age spanning the tenth and ninth centuries BC.

Conclusion Twenty-Five

The traditional genealogies of Classical Greece do not support the conventional dating of the Trojan War, established by Eratosthenes at *circa* 1194 to 1184 BC, as they would require an impossibly long generation-length of at least forty years. These genealogies rather suggest a Trojan War dated to the ninth century BC.

A New History for Archaic Sparta

Having established what I believe to be a more reasonable time-span for the period leading up to the Persian war we can now introduce the historical events, handed down to us in the ancient literature, into this new chronological framework, to see how they might have influenced Spartan military and economic development during the period from *circa* 820 BC (the rough new date for the Dorian invasion) to *circa* 500 BC (the Persian war).

In the new condensed sequence of events it is no longer necessary to reject the information given by the ancient writers. The major argument for treating this material with extreme caution has been based almost entirely on the belief that it contains fundamental contradictions within a Dark Age chronological framework. Because of the interpolation of this Dark Age the current basic historical scenario for the ninth to seventh centuries is usually set out on the following lines, as summarised by Louise Fitzhardinge.

> When in the ninth century the Dorians, part of the last wave of Greek-speaking migrants to enter the peninsula, reached Laconia they found only a sparse and scattered population with no organised centres. ... The process of settlement, which occupied something like a century, was peaceful, except perhaps for some skirmishes around shrines like Amyclae; there were no successive conquests such as those imagined by Hellenistic scholars to flesh out the bare lists of kings, and no marked racial or cultural differences. So much we can infer from the archaeological remains. The historical record proper begins with the conquest of the upper Messenian plain in the third quarter of the eighth century, when the settlement of Laconia was complete ... The war, which lasted twenty years,

had been one of the heroic type, and the chief beneficiaries were the nobles of the plain ...[24]

However, the historical picture for early Sparta which would result from a non-Dark Age model could be envisaged along somewhat different lines.

After the Trojan War there was a forty-year period in which Thucydides tells us that the Achaean settlements and cities fought amongst each other whilst gradually slipping into decline.[25] There is evidence to suggest that the migrations known to have taken place in the eastern Mediterranean at this time may have been initiated by land hunger brought about by dramatic climate change. This could also have been the true motivation behind the arrival of the Dorians in the Peloponnese where they destroyed the Mycenaean citadels of the Argolid and entered into the rich valley of the Eurotas river (the heartland of Laconia) where they occupied the northern part, around the Mycenaean palace at Therapne, and enslaved the indigenous population. There they established the four (later five) settlements which were to become the principal population centres of the Spartan state.

Eight kilometres to the south, at Amyclae, the remnant Achaean nobility held out, preventing Dorian expansion to the south and into the plain of Helos for some considerable time. In the conventional historical model, however, archaeology has produced yet another chronological puzzle.

> ... at Amyclae near Sparta, a stratified deposit was found below the sanctuary area, and it was this that produced the bulk of our evidence for Laconian Proto-Geometric pottery, and though much of it must fall within the ninth century, it is reasonable to assign some to the tenth; and its votive character appears to be clear. So far, the material shows that there was some religious

cult in the Dark Ages, but no more. In the deposit mentioned, however, there were also a few Mycenaean sherds, a terracotta 'goddess' figurine and fragments of a votive animal, both Mycenaean; and other parts of the site produced many more figurines of these types, mostly datable to the twelfth century. ... However, there is no continuity between the two periods of offerings – this is absolutely clear from the fundamental difference between the two styles of pottery, and the virtual impossibility of dating either the Dark Age material earlier than 1000 BC or the Mycenaean later than 1100 BC. So we seem once again to be faced with the same problem, lack of evidence for the early Dark Age.[26]

This mix of Mycenaean and Proto-Geometric ceramics is impossible within the Orthodox Chronology which separates the two styles by more than a century. But in the New Chronology, the Proto-Geometric follows directly on from the LH IIIC and must represent the Achaean remnant of Laconia which held out at Amyclae against the Dorians/ Spartans for more than a century. Then, in around 665 BC, the Spartan warrior-king, Teleclus of the Agiad dynasty, overcame Amyclae (according to Pausanias) and was able to penetrate into the plain of Helos where the Spartans once more enslaved the local population. This group were later to give their name to the serf population of the whole of Spartan Laconia in the guise of the helot sub-class.

The same generation saw another warrior-king, Theopompus, from the Eurypontid line taking Spartan expansion even further with an invasion of Messenia via the Langadha pass and the capture of the fortress of Ithome. This first Messenian war lasted twenty years but eventually the rich valley to the west was taken and came under the sphere of Spartan influence by around 640 BC. At this stage warfare was still basically in the Heroic/Bronze Age mould, but lessons were being learnt by the Spartans during the protracted war and a new tactical system began to be employed thereafter.

When the second Messenian war got under way, two generations later, the Spartan hoplite army was beginning to take on the familiar appearance of later battles. After another prolonged campaign the Messenians were once more defeated and their land re-allocated to the expanding Spartan population. From then onwards Spartan power continued to grow in the years leading up to the Persian war of the fifth century.

Accepting the Traditions at Face Value?

The rather simplistic history outlined above agrees well with the ancient writers' perceptions of events and does not contradict them in any way. John BURY, however, is quite convinced that, in terms of the traditional literature, 'The story is too tidy to fit the archaeological evidence'.[27] Why? Because the standard chronology of the ancient world requires that the transition between the Bronze and Iron Age eras must have lasted well over three hundred years. So the 'neat' and 'tidy' scenario appears to fly in the face of the Egyptology-based chronology, according to which this sequence of events is greatly drawn out. Indeed, at a number of points, as a consequence of this stretching, the agents of the archaeologically traced events apparently must have been unconnected to each other. Thus the destruction of the Achaean/Mycenaean settlements at the end of LH IIIC is attributed to unknown assailants.

> In the present state of our knowledge we cannot reliably say how the Dorian tribes arrived in the Peloponnese. ... The palace of Therapne, standing on a hill not far from the left bank of the middle reaches of this river, **fell to unknown assailants**

who were probably the men who overthrew Mycenae, Tiryns and Pylos about this time. It was not until the end of the eighth century BC that attention was again drawn to the region, for it was then that the Dorian Spartans took up the ancient traditions of Laconia.[28]

In fact, Vincent Desborough, one of our leading Dark Age specialists, demonstrated that not only was there 'no positive evidence for a new population in the twelfth-century Peloponnese, but there was good reason to think that many parts of the Peloponnese and Central Greece had almost no population at all at the end of the second millennium. ... The "Dorian invasion" could only have been an infiltration into a half-empty land. In other words, the Dorians came not as destroyers and conquerors but as squatters.'[29]

Thus the destroyers of the Mycenaean palaces were separated from the first Spartans of Laconia by at least a century. Everything about this period is extended, painfully slow and uneventful – a very uncharacteristic interlude in the historical development of Greece and, in particular, of the Eurotas valley.

... for a century and a half or two centuries the evidence suggests that the area was virtually with-out people and certainly without any organised community. When the valley was settled again, the newcomers used a completely different type of pottery and generally, as at Sparta, chose new sites for their settlements ... Whether the newcomers brought the style with them or developed it after arriving we do not know, nor when it began, but it ended about the middle of the eighth century, and may perhaps have lasted for as much as two centuries. Throughout this time the style shows little change and no outside influence, suggesting an isolated people wholly absorbed in the arduous task of pioneering the resettlement of the long-desolate countryside.[30]

Early and Middle Geometric pottery development is here given an inordinate duration of two centuries, so much so that the development was more of a stagnation – all this based on the fact that the material remains which were discovered were so limited for such a long time period. The Spartans could not have been the agent of destruction of the Mycenaean civilisation because the archaeology implies an abandonment of the region by the Achaean population at the end of the Bronze Age. The so-called 'evidence' for depopulation is again the apparent lack of archaeological remains and stratigraphy. Both these phenomena disappear with the removal of what I and the *Centuries of Darkness* team contend to be a phantom Dark Age.

> In the survey of the early Dark Ages it was unfortunately necessary to admit that there was no material of any sort, from settlement, tomb, or sanctuary, or even from surface investigation, from anywhere within its district. ... In Laconia itself, in fact, there is the site of Amyclae where we know from the literary sources that the earlier god Hyacinthos continued to be worshipped into historical times; and yet there is no archaeological evidence between LH IIIC material of the twelfth century and the later artefacts which, as we shall see, can hardly precede 1000 B.C. As there was continuity of worship, what has happened to the offerings of the early Dark Ages?[31]

Precisely because of this extended chronology Moses Finley is forced to abandon all hope of establishing a clear picture of the history of Sparta in this period and, at the same time, is prepared to throw out the traditions which recur so persistently in the later Classical era.

Our ignorance of Dark Age Sparta extends still further, to the whole of its early institutional development. Archaeology has been even less helpful than usual here. The only prudent course, therefore, is to turn immediately to the Archaic period, from the early seventh century, putting aside all the efforts to reconstruct something coherent out of the blatant fictions permeating later traditions ...[32]

The consequences of this attitude are fundamental to the modern view of early Greek history and affect not only Sparta but also our basic faith in the veracity of the major literary sources of the period. How entirely different our history of Greece would be if it were not for the all-pervading darkness that supposedly engulfed the eastern Mediterranean between 1200 and 800 BC.

The Greek antiquarians who put the story into writing more than five hundred years afterwards had no notion of the great breakdown of about 1200 BC, no idea of a Bronze Age, and therefore no sense of the very considerable time-span of the Dark Age. They did not, and could not, know that there had been a gap of perhaps one hundred and fifty years between the destruction of Pylos (which was not the work of the 'Dorians') and the earliest movements across the Aegean, far too long for a crowd of Pylian refugees to wait in Athens, an inherently improbable situation anyway. ... It is fruitless to pursue in detail the later Greek traditions about the Dark Age in Asia Minor.[33]

Fruitless? Only in the Orthodox Chronology! Placing the Trojan War and Dorian invasion in the ninth century would solve, in an instance, the major problems of Homeric scholarship, return the Dorians to their original role as the overthrowers of the Achaean civilisation, eliminate the depopulation theory of the Dark Age, rehabilitate the Ionian migration as a reaction to the Dorian invasion, dramatically revise our view of the reasons for the population increase which initiated the subsequent colonisation movement, and eradicate the multiplicity of problems surrounding the loss of skills and craftsmanship at the end of the Bronze Age and their sudden reappearance four centuries later in the early years of the Archaic period. Removing the Dark Age by means of a revised Egyptian chronology is the solution.

Conclusion Twenty-Six

The Spartan kings were directly descended from the Heracleidae and their Dorian allies. There was no extended Dark Age between the Dorian invasion and the rise of the Spartan state. The militaristic character of that state came directly from the warrior culture and ethos of the Heroic Age.

I hope that I have been able to show that it is possible to 'reconstruct something coherent' from the later traditional literature for the origins of Spartan culture and its development in the period leading up to the Persian war. The reason why ninth- to sixth-century Spartan history is virtually a blank in the works of Herodotus and others is simply because the time between the Dorian invasion and the appearance of the Spartan state was no more than a couple of generations at most.

I have tried to demonstrate that the political structure of Sparta differed only slightly from the earlier Bronze Age model as transmitted by Homer. However, the characteristics of the Spartan socio/geographic structure tend towards the *ethnos* type of organisation with Spartan society paying only a sort of 'lip-service' to the political ideas associated with the *polis*. The *ethnos* social group is very much a characteristic of non-Achaean Greek society (such as in the north-western parts of Greece) and is therefore a further indication of the differences between Sparta and the other Greek states which tended to develop along Athenian lines. These states were mainly in the east, in areas that the Dorians did not penetrate – areas that became refuges for the Mycenaean peoples displaced by the invading northerners. This would be a further factor to account for the early Attic migrations across the Aegean to the west coast of Anatolia, which may in turn be evidence of a remnant Mycenaean/Achaean Peloponnesian population moving away to escape Dorian domination. In all the regions where the Dorian peoples settled we have native slave populations on the helot model: the *Penestai* of Thessaly; the *Klarotai* of Crete; the *Gymnetai* of Argos; and the *Woikiatai* of Locris. This strongly suggests that the Dorians and hence the Spartans were indeed a warrior class who did not slowly evolve out of an empty Dark Age Laconia but came into the region with a rush, led by their allies – the ousted Pelasgian sons of Heracles.

There is no mystery in the Spartan rise to power – they came as invaders and subjugated the region, expanding their hold on the Peloponnese in a single continuous process over a short period of time. However, with a small warrior group at the centre of its army, there was little chance that Sparta would then be able to sustain its initial military success for an indefinite period. The inevitable consequence of the long series of fifth-century conflicts, first against the Persians and then against Sparta's old enemy, Athens, was the depletion of the Spartiate population and a resultant loss of power and influence in the Greek world, from which the Spartan state was never to recover.

Part Four

The Great Migration

Chapter Sixteen

MOPSUS AND THE SEA PEOPLES

Karatepe -- The Sea Peoples -- Mopsus

The road into the mountains of south-eastern Turkey winds up from Adana through the valley of the River Pyramus (the modern Ceyhan) until, after eighty-four kilometres, it reaches the pine-forested crag of Karatepe. Today this rarely visited site is perched high above an azure lake created by the Ataturk Dam where the Pyramus once flowed.

The city of Adana (the fourth largest in Turkey) lies just south of the Taurus foothills, in the lower plain of the land anciently known as Cilicia and, before that, Kue (in the Neo-Assyrian period), Kode (by the Egyptians) and Kizzuwatna (in the Hittite New Kingdom period). This location was of considerable strategic importance because it lay on the navigable River Sarus (the modern Seyhan) flowing into the Mediterranean – making Adana a riverine port – and, at the same time, just twenty-five kilometres from the entrance to the deep gorge of the Cilician Gates which led up through the Taurus mountains onto the Anatolian plateau and the Hittite heartland beyond. Though little remains of the ancient city today, buried beneath the modern bustling metropolis, it is clear from ancient documents that Adana's history goes back at least to the second millennium BC and that it is almost certainly named after a mysterious people called the Danana or Dananayim. We will learn more about these Danana and their legendary leader shortly.

In the Footsteps of a Legend

The afternoon of 4 October 2003 was a good moment in my ten-year search for the lost history of the Homeric heroes. It had taken eight arduous days of travelling around the Anatolian coast from our setting-off point of Troy to reach the isolated archaeological site of Karatepe ('Black Hill'). My stalwart companions and I had come all this way to see one of Turkey's hidden secrets – and one particular monument which had not only unlocked the meaning of the Hittite hieroglyphic inscriptions but had also confirmed the historical existence of a mighty hero of Greek and Lydian legend. Unless you happen to be a scholar of Classical Greek literature, it is unlikely that you will have heard of him, but his role in the dramatic events which brought about the collapse of the great empires of the Bronze Age cannot be underestimated. In a sense he symbolises the new age which began following the sack of Troy and enables us to put a name to the great movement of peoples into the Levant at the start of the Iron Age.

Leaving our transport below the summit, we trudged up through the forest and found ourselves standing before a great stone gateway covered in finely carved bas-reliefs. The late afternoon sunlight raked through the pines to illuminate the orthostats of figures and hieroglyphs, bathing them in a warm glow. Just inside the gate stood a colossal statue of the storm-god, carved – like the rest of the sculptures – in typical NEO-HITTITE style. This half-smiling deity was a Baal figure in very human guise – a god to warm to rather than fear. In the little notebook I keep for logging the photographs taken on my travels I wrote one word – 'fabulous'.

It felt as if I was at the entrance to the fabled kingdom of the Fisher King of Arthurian legend. Our band of determined adventurers had chanced upon the hidden castle of the Holy Grail, buried deep in the forests of a distant, mountainous land, far from Camelot. Our path lay ahead, beckoning us through the mottled shadows to the place where a magnificent prize awaited the pure of heart. But this Grail was neither sacred cup nor philosopher's stone. The narrow path led us over the summit to the far side of Karatepe where an even more spectacular gate awaited us. This one was absolutely teeming with exotic life, delicately cut into the grey slabs of stone that lined the entrance to the citadel. And there it was, nestled between the carvings, on four finely cut basalt orthostats – a Phoenician text which represented the speech of a long-dead king of Cilicia.

> Azatiwatas speaks: I am indeed Azatiwatas, the blessed of the Sun, the servant of the Storm-God, whom Awarkus, king of Adanawa, raised up. The Storm-God made me father and mother to the city of Adana, and I developed the city of Adana, and I enlarged the land of Adana, both to the west and to the east. And in my days the city of Adana had prosperity, satiety and comfort. ... I built mighty fortresses on all my borders – on the borders where there had been bad men, leaders of gangs, none of whom had been subservient to the House of Mopsus. ... And in my days there was plenty, satiety, comfort and peace. And Adana and the land of Adana lived in peace and plenty. And I built this citadel, and I gave it the name of Azatiwadaya, because the Storm-God and the (other) gods directed me towards this, so that this citadel might protect the plain of Adana and the House of Mopsus. ... Here I settled the Storm-God and made sacrifices to him. ... I sanctified the Storm-God and he granted me long days, countless

years and great strength above all kings. And the
people who dwell in this land became owners
of cattle, herds, plenty (of food) and wine. Their
offspring was copious. By the grace of the Storm-
God and gods they rendered service to Azatiwatas
and to the House of Mopsus.

This is what I had come all this way to see – my personal Holy
Grail – the culmination of a 2,500-kilometre-long journey
from the desolate mound of Hissarlik with its crumbling
and bedraggled walls. I had finally fulfilled a long-held
ambition to stand before these rather unprepossessing
blocks – far less imposing than all that surrounded them
– to search out three tiny Phoenician signs which spelt out
a name.

When the site of Karatepe was first discovered in 1946
by the German archaeologist Helmuth Bossert, it was
quickly realised that the Azatiwatas Decree was recorded in
two languages and two very different scripts. One was the
Phoenician text before me, the other the Neo-Hittite (Luwian)
hieroglyphic text which adorned the spaces between all the
carved figures covering the gate itself. Back in the 1940s the
Phoenician text – being very similar to ancient Hebrew – was
easily read. This proved to be the crucial key in deciphering
the mysterious script and language of the Neo-Hittites. Just
as with Egypt's Rosetta Stone or Persia's Behistun relief of
Darius I, the Karatepe glyphs were compared to the known
Phoenician – the longest text in that language ever found
– and the Hittite symbols unlocked. Azatiwatas had spoken
in his native Luwian tongue for the first time in nearly three
thousand years. The Hittite monuments were no longer
mute and scholars could finally read the royal inscriptions
of Anatolia and north-west Syria.

This was all remarkable and certainly worthy of a visit
to Karatepe in its own right, but I had come to find one
particular group of signs hidden in the Phoenician text which
I knew recorded the name of a warrior from the time of

the Trojan War. This was the legendary hero who founded a dynasty at the city of Adana and who, according to the Lydian historian Xanthus, marched an army to the borders of Egypt where he died.

This man had been a great sage and ruler of Colophon in Ionia. He had founded many of the cities of Pamphylia and Cilicia, visited each summer by thousands of tourists on holiday in southern Turkey who head inland for respite from their beaches to explore these majestic ruins. Our hero's name was celebrated in all parts of southern Anatolia during the Hellenistic Age. But, most important from an historian's perspective, he appears to have been the ruler of the Danana warriors who had attempted to invade Egypt in the eighth year of Pharaoh Ramesses III. His name is written three times on the Karatepe inscription with three signs – M-P-SH – spelling out in Phoenician 'Mopshu' – the legendary Mopsus of the Greek literary tradition. The eighth-century kings of Adana – Arikkus and Azatiwatas – claimed their descent from this ancestral founder. They were of the 'House of Mopsus' and their ancestor was very real – no illusory legend of Greek myth. In fact, Mopsus is the first and, so far, only hero of the Trojan War era to step confidently onto the stage of real history. The traditions, contemporary documents and monumental inscriptions all place the mighty seer and war-leader in southern Anatolia – in the land of the Danana – in the years immediately following the siege of Troy. There is no question that in Mopsus we have a genuine historical figure whom legend proclaims as a contemporary of the Trojan War.

The Invasion of the Sea Peoples

One of the most dramatic monumental texts from the Land of the Pharaohs (and on a rather different scale to the Karatepe inscription) is to be found on the second pylon of the mortuary temple of Ramesses III at Medinet Habu in Thebes (see plate 64). It deals with an attempted invasion of

Egypt by a confederacy of northerners, collectively referred to, in the academic literature, as the 'peoples of the sea' or Sea Peoples. Major sections of this long text are worth quoting in order to get the fullest sense of the momentous events taking place at the close of the Bronze Age. It begins with the regnal year and titles of the pharaoh.

> Year 8 under the majesty of (Ramesses III) the Horus: Mighty Bull, the Strong Lion, mighty of arm, possessor of a strong arm, taking captive the Asiatics; … The terror of him is as great as a flame reaching to the ends of the Earth, causing the Asiatics to turn back (by) fighting on the [battlefield].[1]

In the New Chronology, the eighth year of Pharaoh Ramesses III is 855 BC. It is Year 20 of King Ahab of Israel and Year 17 of King Jehoshaphat in Judah. Ramesses describes how the crisis began.

> The foreign countries made a conspiracy in their islands. All at once the nations were removed and scattered in the fray. No country could stand before their arms – from Hatti (central Anatolia), Kode (south-east Anatolia), Carchemish (on the Euphrates), Arzawa (west-central Anatolia) and Alashiya (Cyprus) – all being cut off at once.
> A camp [was set up] in one place in Amurru (Syria). They desolated its people, and its land was like that which has never come into being. They were coming forward towards Egypt, while the flame was prepared before them.
> Their confederation was the Peleset, Tjekker, Shekelesh, Danana and Weshesh – all countries united. They laid their hands upon the territories as far as the circuit of the Earth, their hearts confident and trusting 'Our plans will succeed!'

It appears that this movement of Sea Peoples from the islands and coastlands of the Aegean and Anatolia was no small affair – in spite of what some modern scholars seem to think. The country of Hatti (the kingdom of the mighty Hittites) was unable to halt them; Kode (later known as Cilicia) and the city state of Carchemish could not prevent their violent progress into northern Syria; Alashiya (Cyprus, Egyptian *Yalasi*) appears to have fallen to their fleet; whilst Arzawa (Egyptian *Yarza*) in the west of central Anatolia was not spared.

Ramesses waited with his massive defence force as messengers arrived from the north to report on the Sea Peoples' devastating march southward through those vassal kingdoms of Canaan which had been under Egyptian hegemony for generations.

> Now the heart of this god (Amun-Re), the Lord of the Gods, was prepared and ready to ensnare them like birds. ... I (Ramesses) organized my frontier in Djahi (Canaan), prepared in anticipation of them (with) princes, garrison commanders and *maryanu* (foreign charioteers). I had the river-mouths (of the Nile) prepared, like a strong wall, with warships, galleys and coasters, fully equipped – for they were manned completely from bow to stern with valiant warriors carrying their weapons.
>
> The troops consisted of every picked man of Egypt. They were like lions roaring upon the mountain tops. The chariotry consisted of runners, of chosen men, of every good and capable chariot-warrior. The horses were quivering in every part of their bodies, prepared to crush the foreign countries under their hooves. I was the valiant (god) Montu, standing fast at their head, so that they might gaze upon the capturing of my hands.

Ramesses III marched his army into Canaan to meet the invaders. The estuaries of the different Nile branches of the delta were sealed and defended to stop the invading fleet from attacking Egypt whilst Ramesses was fighting his land battle on the coastal plain. This was the first major assault upon Egypt from the northlands since those terrible days of Pharaoh Dudimose and the invading Shosu ('shepherds') led by their Lesser Hyksos overlords (*c.* 1445 BC). But Ramesses was not about to let Egypt suffer a similar fate.

> Those who reached my frontier, their seed is not, their heart and their soul are finished for ever and ever.
> Those who came forward together on the sea, the full flame was in front of them at the river-mouths, whilst a stockade of lances surrounded them on the shore. They were dragged in, enclosed, and prostrated on the beach – killed and made into heaps from tail to head. ...
> The northern countries quivered in their bodies – the Peleset, Tjekker, and [...]. They were cut off (from) their (own) land and were coming (towards Egypt), their soul finished. They were *teher*-warriors on land; another (group) was on the sea. Those who came on [land were overthrown and killed ...]. Amon-Re was after them – destroying them. Those who entered the river-mouths were like birds ensnared in the net.
> ... Their leaders were carried off and slain.

Although we might expect an Egyptian pharaoh to boast of his overwhelming victory, we should not underestimate the importance of this turning back of the Sea Peoples' tide by Ramesses III.

The marauders – perhaps following several years of migration – had finally been halted at the Egyptian frontier after their four-thousand-kilometre trek of terror through the lands of Anatolia and Canaan, plundering and burning as they went. For a while, at least, Egypt would be secure from invasion – even if its northern empire was finally crumbling under a quite exceptional series of interrelated events.

Unfortunately, only a few decades passed before Egypt also began to see the effects of this world crisis amongst its own people. It is clear from documents dating towards the end of Ramesses III's reign and to the later pharaohs of the 20th Dynasty that the mighty civilisation of the Nile valley had begun to suffer a series of both natural and political disasters (the latter perhaps instigated by unrest created by the former) – but they were nothing compared to what was happening beyond Egypt's borders where the whole world appeared to have gone mad.

Archaeology has shown that the end of the Bronze Age was marked by a wave of destruction across the ancient world. The rich trading city of Ugarit was burnt and abandoned, never to be rebuilt; the coastal cities of Tell Sukas and Sidon were also attacked and destroyed; Hamath on the Orontes was captured and the vast Tyrian city of Salmon (Tell Abu Hawwam near Haifa) likewise fell to unknown assailants. The empire of the Hittites had already collapsed, its capital ransacked and abandoned; the kingdom of Arzawa passed into oblivion; Enkomi on Cyprus burnt; Homer's Troy (ancient Wilusa – Ilios) had been besieged and overthrown by Agamemnon's Achaeans a decade or so earlier, its men massacred, the women led off into slavery. That sacking of Troy marked the beginning of it all in poetry and song.

Not long after this most celebrated legend of Classical tradition, the Achaeans had begun to migrate eastwards, establishing new cities on the coasts of Anatolia and the Levant (as testified by locally made Mycenaean pottery found at various sites). Other peoples, indigenous to mainland Anatolia, were also on the move, heading south along the coastal Levant in search of new places to settle.

What was causing all this upheaval? A number of scholars are now convinced that it had something to do with a marked change in the global climate which brought severe drought for decades to the northern lands of the eastern Mediterranean. People were literally being forced south – domino fashion – in order to find refuge from famine and political unrest in their northern homelands. And the Nile delta, with its bountiful river and rich, deep soil, was well known in the ancient Near East as a haven in times of crisis. As a result, the thrust of this desperate tide of humanity was south, towards Egypt.

The movement of the Sea Peoples by land and sea, as recorded in Ramesses III's Medinet Habu inscriptions, was a major part of this migration. We can also see the Dorian invasion of Greece as another symptom of the dramatic change in climate with the tribes of the Danube basin first moving south into Thrace and then, led by the Heracleidae, through Euboea and on across the Gulf of Corinth into the Peloponnese. From there the Dorians pushed out into the southern islands of the Aegean (including Crete) forcing the Achaeans further east along the Anatolian coast and into the Levant. The whole ancient world of the eastern Mediterranean was on the move as a result of famine, over-population (created by the influx of newcomers from the north) and land hunger.

The problem is that climatologists have dated this sudden change in temperature and consequent disturbed weather patterns to the ninth century BC. So it is rather difficult to argue (as some have done) that the massive population movements, conventionally dated to the twelfth century, could have been the response to a marked climatological shift which took place some three hundred years later. As I argued in the three previous chapters, the revised chronology places the post-Trojan War wanderings, the Dorian invasion and the Achaean migrations not between 1200 and 1000 BC but rather in the ninth century – and thus these disturbances can be linked without special pleading to the dramatic climate change of that same century. The New Chronology of Egypt also places Ramesses III in the mid-ninth century and so the Sea Peoples' movement is clearly contemporary with this same climatological phenomenon.

> ## Conclusion Twenty-Seven
>
> The major climate shift which took place in the ninth century BC (according to the scientific evidence) was the trigger for a massive migration from central and southern continental Europe into the coastal Mediterranean and beyond through the Levant towards Egypt. This movement is reflected in the historical records by the invasion of the Sea Peoples (NC – *c.* 855 BC) and in the Classical literary traditions of the *Nostoi* (post-Trojan War wanderings) as well as the slightly later Dorian invasion of Greece.

Identifying the Sea Peoples

In Ramesses' Medinet Habu proclamation he lists the invading Sea Peoples' groups as Peleset, Tjekker, Shekelesh, Denyen (or Danuna) and Weshesh. I have written these names as they usually appear in the scholarly literature, but you have to remember that Egyptologists always interpolate the letter 'e' where a vowel of unknown value is likely to have been positioned in a word. Moreover, it has become customary to vocalise vowel markers (such as omega = ω, represented by the chick-bird or rope-coil in the hieroglyphs) as the letter U (as, for example, in $h\omega t$ = 'temple/house', vocalised by Egyptologists as *hoot*), whereas, on many occasions, it has been demonstrated that the vowel concerned was actually a letter A (as, for example, in $h\omega t$-ωrt= Hutwaret, the name of Avaris which must have been vocalised by the Egyptians something like *Haware* with silent Ts representing feminine endings). The ancient Egyptian language was written employing only consonantal signs – there were no hieroglyphic symbols for proper vowels. Thus the Sea Peoples' names are actually recorded in the glyphs as *p-l-s-t*, *tj-k-r*, *sh-k-l-sh*, *d-ny-n* (or *d-nw-n*) and *w-sh-sh*.

In an earlier skirmish with the northerners, dated to Year 5 of Merenptah (OC – *c.* 1209 BC but NC – *c.* 881 BC) other Sea Peoples are mentioned: the Ekwesh (*'-kw-sh*), Teresh (*t-r-sh*), Lukka (*l-k*), Sherden (*sh-r-d-n*) and, once again, the Shekelesh (*sh-k-l-sh*). These Sea Peoples are described as 'northerners coming from all lands'. We will now attempt to determine who these people (from both campaign-lists) really were by adding what I believe to have been the original vowels of the names in order to get close to their historical vocalisation.

(1) The Peleset

The Peleset (*p-l-s-t*) have long been identified with the Philistines of the Bible. The original Egyptian vocalisation may have been Pelasta, with which it is straightforward to compare the Greek *Pelastoi*, the Hebrew *Pilishtim* and the geographical names Philistia and Palestine.

This identification of the Pelasta with the Philistines is certainly correct. But, as we saw in *Chapter Six*, these Philistines were not the *first* Philistines to arrive in southern Canaan. An earlier wave formed part of the Indo-European migration at the beginning of the Middle Bronze Age represented by the Philistines of Gerar in Abraham's days, the biblical Anakim and, later, the Hyksos of Egypt's Second Intermediate Period. Now, towards the end of the Late Bronze Age, this second wave of Pelasta were moving out of troubled Crete and Anatolia as a militarised refugee movement seeking help from their kin in the Canaanite strongholds of the Pentapolis – the existing cities of coastal

Philistia. The Greek traditions have Puresati first departing from Crete and heading for the shores of Cilicia (whose capital was Adana of the House of Mopsus). From there they marched south into Canaan as the Peleset element of the Sea Peoples' movement.

On the other hand, according to the fifth-century Lydian historian Xanthus, a group of people from the Lydian lands, bordering the River Hermus (the modern Gediz north of Izmir), were called Pelasgians. As we have seen, this name is well known from Classical

85. The Pelest chieftain from a statue base at Medinet Habu.

literature and seems to represent an ancient name for the people of the Aegean region (although the various traditions are very confused). These Pelasgians may have been recent settlers to coastal Anatolia from the Mycenaean west – a proposition confirmed by the Lydians themselves who, claiming their own Cretan origins, regarded the Pelasgians as former colonists of their land and not indigenous to the region. An etymological link between Pelasgoi (Pelasgians) and Pelastoi (Philistines) is confirmed by the ancient variant writings Pelasgikon and Pelastikon. Homer describes 'spear-brandishing Pelasgians' of the southern Troad (considerably further north of Lydia)[2] whilst Herodotus – a citizen of Halicarnassus (modern Bodrum) – proposed Pelasgian origins for both the Ionian and Aeolian settlers in western Anatolia (which the Greeks themselves renamed Ionia and Aeolis). He also states that the 'Coastal Pelasgians' of Ionia originally heralded from the Peloponnese – the heartland of Mycenaean territory – and that Greece itself was once called Pelasgia.[3]

So the Pelasgians were regarded by the Greeks of the post-Heroic Age as the ancestral civilisation of Hellas (the Classical name for Greece) whose descendants colonised several regions including Ionia, Caria and Cilicia on the Anatolian coast. These ancient people of the Peloponnese represent the principal substratum of the Bronze Age population, ruled over by Mycenaean (i.e. Achaean) lords such as Agamemnon and Menelaus, whose ancestor – Pelops – had overthrown the dynasty of Perseus. The ousted Perseids (personified in the exiled figure of Heracles), and their descendants – the Heracleidae – who led the Dorian invasion were therefore themselves Pelasgoi, returning to the Peloponnese in order to take back their homeland from the usurpers. They, after all, were the 'original' people of the land who had lived in Greece and the Aegean since the reign of Danaus (and even further back to the time of Inachus). It is perhaps in this light that we should understand Homer's rather surprising epithet 'the Divine Pelasgians'.[4]

Onomastic evidence from the ancient Near East suggests that the Pelasgians may have spoken a dialect of Luwian – one of the oldest languages of Anatolia.[5] This would link them linguistically and perhaps culturally to the rulers of Wilusa/Ilios who, according to the latest evidence from Korfmann's excavations at Troy, employed Luwian hieroglyphs for their seals. If this is correct, we would envisage Agamemnon's Achaeans as Greek-speaking usurpers in an otherwise Pelasgian world.

We can summarise that the Peleset were Aegean Pelasgians who had settled in western and southern Anatolia during the Mycenaean period (LH II to LH III). Some migrated from Crete, in the aftermath of the Achaean invasion of that island (LM II), to settle in Cilicia; others headed from the Peloponnese to western Anatolia to occupy Milawatta (Miletus), Epasa (Ephesus) and the Hermus valley (later known as Lydia). During the turmoil of the post-Trojan War era these Pelasgoi/Pelastoi became one of the leading groups of the Sea Peoples' movement into the Levant.

(2) The Teresh, Taruisha or Trusha

The Teresh seem to be a people from north-western Anatolia. They appear in Classical Greek tradition as the Tursenoi who, legend has it, migrated westwards to become the Etruscans of Italy (after whom Tuscany is named). The common Anatolian ending '-enos' in the name Tursenos denotes ethnicity (i.e. 'a person of Tursha') in a similar fashion to the Hebrew ethnic plural ending '-im' as in Mizraim ('people of Mizra', i.e. the Egyptians). Several scholars have suggested that this group may well be the same as the inhabitants of Taruisha mentioned in the Hittite texts and equated them with Homer's Trojans. The final '-sha' in the Hittite and Egyptian versions (the latter taken from the former) of this name represents another Anatolian ethnic ending or Indo-European nominative.[6] The original place-name stem would therefore be something like Tarui – very close to Homer's Troia. The word to-ro-ya (female slave from Troy) appears on a Linear B tablet found at Pylos, home of old King Nestor who accompanied Agamemnon to Troy. We might then best pronounce the name of these Sea Peoples in the Egyptian form as 'Tarui-sha'. On the other hand, the Greek tradition (as expressed in Herodotus) would identify the Tursenoi as a people of 'Lydia' – that is, Bronze Age central Arzawa. If this tradition is accurate then we might envisage a tribal group closely related to the Shardana (see below) bearing an ethnicon something like 'Trusha' (from which the later Etrusci derives). Of course both traditions could be correct with two branches of the same clan.

(3) The Ekwesh or Akawasha

In recent years it has become generally accepted that the Ekwesh or Akawasha (*'-k-w-sh*) are to be identified with the people of Akhiyawa mentioned in Hittite documents of the period. In turn the Akhiyawa are now universally equated with the Akhaiwoi of Homer – in other words the Achaeans from the Greek mainland, otherwise known in the literature as the Mycenaeans. Again, the final '-sha' is a nominative ending. We would then pronounce the name of these Sea Peoples something like 'Akaiwa-sha'.

(4) The Tjekker

This group are almost certainly the Teukeroi of Greek tradition – the followers or clan of the Greek hero Teuker, legendary founder of Olba (Ura) in Cilicia and Salamis (near Enkomi) on Cyprus. The archaeological record from Enkomi suggests that the Teukrians were newcomers or colonists to Cyprus, their homeland being further west amongst the islands of the Aegean or Greek mainland. However, Herodotus [Book II:118] suggests that the Trojans were themselves of Teukrian stock and that Dardanus (after whom the Dardanelles are named) migrated from the island of Samothrace to western Anatolia where King Teuker (Greek Τευκροσ) ruled (and after whom the people were named Teukrians). Strabo, on the other hand, says that the Teukrians originally migrated from Crete into the Troad where they named a local peak as Mount Ida after the original mountain of that name on Crete. We would then have a complex sequence of migrations of these people, first from Crete, then to the land of Wilusa, before moving on once more to Cyprus and beyond. The Greek sources tell us that the Teukrians settled in Cyprus soon after the Trojan War.

So we have two possibilities for these people – they are either (a) a tribe from the Troad region (named after an earlier King Teuker) who migrated south following the sack of Troy, or (b) followers of the Mycenaean archer, Teuker, who fought in the Trojan War and subsequently led his warriors to Cyprus where they founded the Mycenaean IIIC settlement at Enkomi. Either way, I think we can confidently identify the Tjekker of the Medinet Habu reliefs as the

Teukrians of Greek tradition. We would then pronounce the name of these Sea Peoples something like 'Tjukera'.

(5) The Weshesh or Washesha

There are two possible Anatolian homelands for the Weshesh. We could identify this group with a region of Caria (south-western Anatolia) known as Ouassos (modern Iassos, south of Miletus). We would then pronounce the name of these Sea Peoples something like 'Washosha'. Alternatively, this name may derive from the region to the south of the Troad called Assuwa, and known in later Classical times as Asia – subsequently a Roman designation for the whole of Anatolia in the form 'Asia Minor'. The name is found in the form of *as-wi-ya* (female slave from Asia) on Linear B tablets from Pylos, Mycenae and Knossos. Again the Egyptian name has the nominative ending '-sha'. In this case the Egyptian pronunciation might be 'Washwa-sha'.

(6) The Shekelesh of Shakalasha

This is a much more difficult group to identify. We can be reasonably confident that they are the Sikels of later tradition (the Homeric *Sikeloi*), after whom Sicily was named – but that was only because this island, off the coast of southern Italy, became their homeland during the great migration period that brought the Heroic Age to an end. However, Sicily was not their *original* homeland any more than Carthage was the original homeland of the Carthaginian Phoenicians who founded that famous colony between 825 and 814 BC (depending on which Classical authority you accept).

It is possible that they are one and the same as the Sagalassan pirates active along the Levantine coast. Otherwise their homeland remains a mystery. One possibility is that they heralded from southern Anatolia where the later city of Sagalassa was located (in the region the Greeks called Pamphylia/Pisidia). We might then vocalise the name of this group of Sea Peoples as 'Shakala-sha' (again with the Indo-European nominative added).

(7) The Sherden or Shardana

The Shardana are a little easier to locate. They are probably the Arzawan warriors of Sardis in the region later to be known as Lydia but originally called Mysia (focused on the valley of the Hermus river in central western Anatolia). This was the heart of greater Arzawa known to both the Hittites and Egyptian rulers as the seat of a 'Great King' like themselves. Shardana mercenaries, with their distinctive horned helmets and round shields, had been employed in the Egyptian army from as early as the reign of Ramesses II (Battle of Kadesh) and are depicted on both sides in the Sea Peoples' battles of Ramesses III. Just like the Shakalasha, they ended up settling in the western Mediterranean, first on the Italian coastal plain west of the Apennines and then in Sardinia – which is, of course, named after them – and Corsica. Their name was clearly pronounced 'Shardana'.

(8) The Lukka

This group is universally acknowledged to be the same people as the Classical Lycians (Greek *Lykioi*) whose territory was in south-western Anatolia, based around the capital city of Xanthus (Luwian Awarna & Lycian Arñna). The Hittites referred to their region as the Lukka lands. The Egyptian pronunciation was probably also 'Lukka'.

(9) The Denyen or Danuna/Danana

This group deserve considerable discussion, for, as I have already hinted, they possess a rich legendary tradition connected to one of the great figures from the last days

86. Possible homelands of the Sea Peoples confederacy in western and southern Anatolia.

of the Heroic Age. In fact, the rest of this chapter will be devoted to exploring the history of this group who appear to have settled principally in eastern Cilicia, around the city of Adana, and on the island of Cyprus. The name of Cyprus in eighth-century Assyrian texts is given as Yadnana which must surely be interpreted as 'Isle of the Danana' (Ia-Danana) or, in its Greek guise, 'Isle of the Danaoi'.[7] The Egyptian vocalisation would have been 'Danana' or simply 'Dana'.

We can tabulate the results of this analysis of the names in the Egyptian inscriptions as follows.

Egyptian	Greek	Hittite	Modern Name
Pelasta	Pelastoi		Philistines/Pelasgian Anatolians
Taruisha	Troia	Taruisha	Trojans/Tyrsenians/Etruscans
Akawasha	Akhaiwoi	Akhiyawa	Achaeans/Mycenaean Greeks
Tjukera	Teukeroi		Teukrians (of Cyprus)
Washuasha	Ashiyoi	Ashuwa	Asians (of Asia Minor)
Shakalasha	Sikeloi		Cilicians/Sicilians
Shardana	Sardanoi		Lydians of Sardis/Sardinians
Lukka	Likkioi	Lukka	Lycians
Dana	Danaoi		Danaans/Pelasgian Greeks
Khara	Karioi	Karkisha	Carians
Dardany	Dardanoi		Dardanians/Trojans

Conclusion Twenty-Eight

The northerners of Merenptah's Libyan war and Ramesses III's Sea Peoples' war originated from Greece, Anatolia and Cyprus. Their dramatic movement southwards into the Levant in Year 8 of Ramesses III was triggered by the fall of Troy which itself created an unstable political situation in the region. Simultaneously the Phrygian and Mysian tribes moved into central Anatolia following (or resulting in) the collapse of the Hittite empire. The Dorian invasion of the Peloponnese was itself a consequence of worsening climatic conditions and the opportunity afforded by the long and debilitating campaign against Troy which left the Mycenaean homeland open to attack from the northern tribal groups.

The Legend of Mopsus

According to the literary traditions, one of the key figures in the great migration at the end of the Heroic Age was a sage and military leader named Mopsus, son of Rakius of Claros and Manto, daughter of Teiresias – the blind seer of the Oedipus cycle. Teiresias was killed during the campaign of the Epigonoi against Thebes and his daughter Manto had fled, with her followers, to Caria. There she married Rakius, apparently a Cretan (Pelasgian?) ruler in Caria and gave birth to Mopsus. Our hero was therefore half-Pelasgian Greek and half-Pelasgian Cretan/Anatolian. Xanthus regarded him as a Lydian but we do not know from where the Lydians of the seventh century BC originated – perhaps migrating Leleges (an old name for Carians) from ninth-century Crete?

... when Polyneices' son Thersander and the Argives (Epigonoi) captured Thebes, Manto was brought with the other prisoners to Apollo at Delphi, though her father Teiresias met his fate on the journey at Haliartia. The god sent them out to found a colony, so they crossed over by ship to Asia, and when they reached Claros the Cretans came out against them under arms and brought them before Rakius. Rakius found out from Manto who they were and why they had come, and took her for his wife, accepting her people as citizens of the colony. It was Mopsus the son of Rakius and Manto who completely expelled the Carians from the country. [Pausanias, Book VII]

We have dated the sack of Cadmaean Thebes by the Epigonoi to *circa* 907 BC, so we can place the birth of Mopsus in around 906 BC. He would then have grown to maturity during the thirty-two years leading up to the Trojan War (starting in *c.* 874 BC), bringing him to his *floruit* during the decade leading up to the Sea Peoples' invasion of the Levant (*c.* 855 BC). He can hardly have been born later than 906 BC because he was militarily active during the time of the Hittite emperor Arnuwanda III (NC – *c.* 889-881 BC).

The legends say that Mopsus first ruled in Colophon, close to the Carian coast of western Anatolia (north of Miletus) where he also established an oracular centre dedicated to Apollo at nearby Claros. It is interesting therefore that Late Helladic III pottery has been found in typical Mycenaean tombs at Colophon, demonstrating that a settlement was in existence there at the end of the Late Bronze Age.[8]

The Classical Greek name Mopsus has an earlier variant where the P is represented by K. Thus in Mycenaean Linear B we find *mo-ko-so*, whilst the Lydian Xanthus calls him

Muksus. In the Luwian hieroglyphic version of the Karatepe inscription Mopsus also appears as Muksas. So only the late Greek and Phoenician traditions call him Mopsus.

Amazingly, the name Mukshush appears in the Hattusha archive where he is mentioned in the Madduwattash Indictment. This makes him a youthful contemporary of Arnuwanda III – the penultimate ruler of the Hittite empire. In this Hittite document, Mukshush is portrayed as another of those trouble-making freebooters based on the western frontier of Hatti around Miletus, precisely where Mopsus is traditionally located. It is also interesting to note that his contemporary – the troublesome Madduwattash – was almost certainly himself of Lydian (i.e. Arzawan) stock as his name closely resembles the type given to the later Lydian royalty such as kings Sadyattes and Alyattes. We might therefore read the Hittite writing of Madduwattash as Lydian Madyattes. It would then make sense to see Mukshush as the son of a Lydian (ethnically Pelasgian) father (hence the tradition handed down in the writings of Xanthus) and a Pelasgian Greek mother (Manto of Thebes). As a consequence, several scholars have proposed to identify this Mukshush of the late Hittite New Kingdom with the Mopsus of Greek legend. The mention of Mukshush in the reign of Arnuwanda places his activities in Caria just a quarter of a century before the Sea Peoples' invasion of *circa* 855 BC which gives us good cause to study the traditions surrounding him with added interest.

The Composite Literary Tradition

According to legend, in the ninth year of the Trojan War a group of warriors sailed from Troy to Caria, led by Amphilochus of Mycenaean Argos. With them came Calchas – the Trojan seer who had turned traitor to his own people and aided the Greeks in their attack upon Troy. He was the evil soothsayer who had commanded Agamemnon to sacrifice his own daughter, princess Iphigenia, at Aulis

87. A bronze mirror engraved with the image of the seer Calchas performing a divination over the entrails of a sacrificed animal.

in order to placate a goddess and deliver a wind for the Mycenaean fleet setting out from the mainland for Troy.

> Letting fall her saffron robe to earth, she (Iphigenia) turned and looked upon those who would kill her. She smote each one with a piteous glance of her eyes. ... For the rest, as I saw it not, neither do I speak of it, but the arts of Calchas were fulfilled.[9]

Whilst the fleet lay becalmed at Aulis near the island of Euboea, the army of Agamemnon had witnessed two eagles devouring a pregnant hare and Calchas was summoned to interpret the omen. He predicted that this was a sign from the gods that the Achaeans would one day capture Troy. However, the lack of a fair wind continued to prevent the fleet from sailing. The men began to starve whilst their ships rotted in the bay. Calchas was again summoned by the king and this time he gave instructions that Agamemnon must sacrifice his own daughter to appease the goddess Artemis who was holding back the winds. Thus Calchas played

529

his part in the terrible blood-letting of the Pelopid dynasty which had begun with the murder by Atreus of his brother's children (whose flesh was offered to their unwitting father, Thyestes, in a banquet) and continued with the murder of Agamemnon himself before finally coming to an end with the killing of his assassin-wife, Clytemnestra, at the hands of Agamemnon's heir, Orestes.[10]

Following the Trojan War, in which Calchas makes an appearance on a number of occasions to administer his evil 'art', the Greek warriors disperse. One group, led by Amphilochus and including Calchas, headed south along the Anatolian seaboard in search of adventure. This is how they met up with Mopsus and how Amphilochus and the king of Colophon became allies in a great expedition eastwards into Pamphylia and Cilicia along the southern shores of Anatolia.[11] However, before that – according to one legend – Calchas met his end at the hands of the grandson of Teiresias who proved more than a match for Agamemnon's evil soothsayer in a contest of wills.

This tradition (preserved by Strabo, quoting a lost work of Hesiod) relates how Calchas and Mopsus of Colophon went head to head at Claros in a contest of divination. Mopsus won the challenge by out-soothsaying his challenger and thus founded the famous sanctuary of Apollo there, whilst the despondent Calchas committed suicide. This is a strange story, perhaps woven around some historical reality, though the death of Calchas at Claros seems premature given that he was regarded as the co-founder, with Mopsus, of Aspendos and Perge in southern Anatolia.

But this was just the start of the Mopsus legend. According to several sources (including Strabo, Herodotus and Xanthus), Mopsus and Amphilochus then led 'the people' eastwards across the mountains of Azarwa (the event referred to in the Sea Peoples' text?), through Pamphylia and Cilicia (Kode of the same text), founding settlements as they went. Some of Anatolia's greatest Hellenistic and Roman cities recognised Mopsus and Amphilochus (and Calchas) as their founding fathers. At the heart of the city of Perge, for example, stands a great gateway of Hellenistic date. This portal leads to a semicircular court once surrounded by statues of the city founders. Sadly the statues are long gone – but the plinths remain, with their dedicatory inscriptions, where the names of both Mopsus and Calchas survive.

Mopsus was also associated with the foundations of Syllium (where another statue-base inscribed with his name has recently been found), Phaselis, Mopsu-hestia and Mallus, the last two in Cilicia. Indeed, the very name Mopsu-hestia – 'hearth of Mopsus' – implies foundation, because every Greek city had a sacred fire or eternal flame burning in a special hearth (Greek *hestia*) near the council chamber (Greek *bouleterion*) which was purportedly lit by the founder of the original settlement. The practice was continued by the Romans who, claiming descent from the Trojans, built their own Temple of Vesta – goddess of the hearth – whose sacred fire was famously tended by the Vestal Virgins.

It is clear from the later Greek sources that there were indeed Helladic peoples living along the coast of southern Anatolia who had settled there in some earlier era. They had intermarried with the local Pamphylians and Cilicians and were subsequently known to Herodotus as 'sub-Achaeans' (Greek *Hypachaioi*) suggesting their ancestry in the Achaean world from which Mopsus' companions, Amphilochus and his warriors, originated.[12] The very name Pamphylia means 'mixed tribes' and there is a tradition that Mopsus himself married a woman named Pamphyle, daughter of Kabderus – clearly an aetiological story to account for the multi-ethnic society of the region where Pamphyle's father, Kabderus, represents the region of Kaptara/Caphtor – in this case southern Anatolia (Classical Cappadocia).

However, the Achaeans did not content themselves merely with the conquest of southern Anatolia. According to Xanthus, the mighty hero Mopsus marched his army south along the Levantine coast and reached Ashkelon, not far from the Egyptian border. There he cast the statue of the goddess Astarte into the sacred lake of her temple before finally dying, far from home, in the land which was later to be known as Philistia – the land of the Philistines.[13]

Could there be a connection here between this legend of Mopsus' great march to Ashkelon and the Sea Peoples' migration to Philistia? That link may well be found in the name of one of the confederate nations which attempted to invade Egypt in Year 8 of Ramesses III – the Danana or, more simply, Dana. It was long assumed that these Dana were one and the same as Homer's Dana-oi – another name for the Mycenaean Greeks who went to war against Troy (the '-oi' being the Greek plural ending). However, a more recent opinion (which is now gaining support) proposes that the Danana were the Danana-im of Adana – capital city of Cilicia known to the Egyptians as Kode (the '-im' being the Semitic plural ending). The name of Adana itself may simply represent an original Dana ('city of the Dana') with a prothetic aleph added – thus A-Dana.

We have seen that the House of Mopsus ruled at Adana and Karatepe and that the legend of Mopsus takes him to the borders of Egypt. His Danaoi/Dana were a part of the Sea Peoples' confederacy – led by a flesh-and-blood hero who lived at the time of the great war against Troy.

Conclusion Twenty-Nine

The Danana of the Medinet Habu reliefs were Danaoi/Mycenaean warriors of the post-Trojan War era who had initially invaded Pamphylia and Cilicia before marching south into southern Canaan in Year 8 of Ramesses III. Their principal leader was the legendary Mopsus, king of Colophon.

Chapter Seventeen

FROM THE ASHES OF TROY

*Neo-Hittites — Phrygians — Cretan Refugees —
Phoenicians in the West — Carthage — Wenamon and
Zikarbaal — Sardinians — Etruscans — The Greek
Colonisation Movement*

et us just recap, for a moment, where this non-Dark
Age history and archaeology of the Late Bronze
Age Aegean world has taken us. The end of the
Late Bronze II (= Late Helladic III) now falls in around
800 BC and the 'Greek Renaissance' is well under way by
750 BC (Middle Geometric). The Helladic decline (we can
hardly call it a dark age) and recovery has lasted just half a
century. The Classical sources' failure to acknowledge any
prolonged dark age turns out to be because there was no
dark age to report on. The ancient authors were telling the
truth all along and the consequences for our interpretation
of Aegean and Anatolian archaeology – and therefore
our understanding of early Western history – are highly
significant.

(1) The genealogies of the Greeks themselves are now
shown to be reasonably accurate and not compressed
as is currently argued.

(2) The initial migration (of Achaeans and Pelasgians to Ionia) occurs because an influx of a new people from the north (the Dorians) has resulted in over-population in the old Mycenaean homelands – just as the historical sources imply. The shortage of food and the threat from invading northerners force the indigenous population to seek new homes on the islands and in recently explored coastal regions of the eastern Mediterranean.

(3) The colonisation of the Black Sea coast and western Mediterranean is not separated from the Ionian migration by more than a century but rather follows on in one continuous movement, triggered by the Dorian invasion and culminating in the founding of Rome.

(4) As we shall see in *Chapter Eighteen*, the story of Aeneas, refugee from the Trojan War, travelling to Carthage to meet the city's founder, Dido, can now have some basis in reality as the various dates for the founding of Carthage (earliest 825 BC, latest 814 BC) fall just forty to fifty years after the Trojan War (ending in 864 BC).

It is not just Greece which suffers from a phantom dark age with all its consequences. The same problem is found all across the Indo-European-speaking world. And in every case the question is of a similar nature. Why is there an apparent chronological gap between the twelfth-century collapse of the Bronze Age civilisations and the eighth-century 'revival' in the ancient world of the early Iron Age, yet in so many ways there appears to be cultural continuity in the archaeological record?

A Neo-Hittite Dark Age

The celebrated bi-lingual text from Karatepe carved on the citadel gateway in both Hittite hieroglyphic (Luwian) and Phoenician tells us that the ruler of that fortress – one

Azatiwatas – was both of the Dananayim and of the 'House of Mopsus'.

It seems clear from the inscription that Azatiwatas was the contemporary of a king of Adana named Awarkus who had 'raised him up'. Specialists in Anatolian studies have suggested that Azatiwatas was a junior co-ruler of Cilicia. I would suggest that he is the tanist (or military ruler) of Cilicia during the reign of the sacral king, Awarkus, responsible for defending the kingdom. This type of dual monarchy goes back a long way to the Sumerian era when a *lugal* (literally 'big man') was administrator king and warrior whilst the *ensi* was the priest-king responsible for ritual.[1] In Egypt the pharaoh held both roles in the guise of the *bity* (worldly ruler) and the *nisu* (spiritual ruler). The dual-name *nisu-bity* does not mean 'King of Upper and Lower Egypt' as so many books state.

As with Mopsus/Mukshush, Awarkus 'king of Adana' in Kue (Kode/Cilicia) appears in datable documents from another civilisation – this time the eighth-century Assyrians. He is mentioned in the records of TIGLATH-PILESER III where his name is written in the East Semitic form, Urikki.

> I received the tribute of Kushtashpi of Kummuhu, Rasunnu (Rezin) of Aram (Damascus), Menihimmu (Menahem) of Samerina (Samaria), Hirummu (Hiram) of Tyre, Sibittibili (Shipitbaal) of Gubla (Byblos), **Urikki (Awarkus) of Kue (Cilicia)**, Pisiris of Carchemish, Enilu of Hamath, Panammu of Samal, Tarhulara of Gurgum, Sulumal of Melid, Dadilu of Kaska, Uassurme of Tabal ...[2]

As you can see, Urikki was a contemporary of REZIN of Damascus and MENAHEM of Israel/Samaria, who both appear in the second book of Kings [2 Kings 15:17ff. and 16:5-9]. In addition we find Sibittibili/Shipitbaal of Byblos as a vassal of Tiglath-pileser and from inscriptions found at Byblos we can determine that he was a contemporary of OSORKON II and TAKELOT II in Egypt (NC – c. 784-735 BC).[3] Scholars accept that this Urikki of Kue is one and the same as Awarkus of Adana mentioned in the Karatepe inscription. We can therefore date Awarkus and Azatiwatas of the House of Mopsus to the second half of the eighth century BC. However, this dating presents the Orthodox Chronology with a problem. The orthostat reliefs appear to have been influenced by the art-style and iconography of the late Hittite empire era conventionally dated at the latest to the early twelfth century.

Moreover, it seems extremely unlikely that a dynasty founded by a twelfth-century Mopsus would still be in existence four centuries after its foundation. This would make the dynasty of Adana one of the longest in human history. Such difficulties evaporate once the New Chronology is applied and the date for Mopsus is set to the time of a Trojan War and fall of Hatti in around 875 BC. This would place Awarkus and Azatiwatas just five generations (around 115 years) after the founder of the dynasty and bring the Hittite-style sculptures of the two Karatepe gates within reach of the immediate post-Hittite New Kingdom era, thus solving one of the many controversial aspects of the Neo-Hittite dark age.

The Neo-Hittite Art Problem

You see, it is not just the site of Karatepe which has an art-historical problem. That same Hittite sculptural tradition is found at north-Syrian Carchemish and Melid (modern Malatya). At both these Neo-Hittite sites the inscriptions of local rulers, linked to Assyrian kings of the late-ninth and eighth centuries, are associated with Neo-Hittite sculptures which would otherwise certainly be dated prior to the tenth century. The reason they are dated, at the latest, to the tenth century is that they appear very close in style to reliefs and sculptures of the Hittite empire period. Indeed, Sir Leonard WOOLLEY, one of the excavators at Carchemish between

1911 and 1920, maintained that the orthostat reliefs of the 'Herald's Wall' actually belonged to the empire period. On the other hand, art-historian, Henri FRANKFORT, identified clear Assyrian artistic traits in the Malatyan sculptures and took the view that at least some of the reliefs belonged firmly in the ninth to eighth centuries. Scholars have therefore been reluctant to place these masterpieces of Neo-Hittite art in either era.

> The chronology and sequence dating of the rich series of sculptures discovered at Carchemish remains a problem, even after sixty years of investigation, but it is generally recognised that Leonard Woolley exaggerated the antiquity of some of the orthostats and it is no longer possible to assign any of them to the second millennium BC. On the contrary, many critics will now support Frankfort's view that none of this particular series of sculptures could have been executed without an awareness of Neo-Assyrian art.[4]

As a result, many of the Neo-Hittite reliefs of Carchemish and Malatya have been relocated to the 'chronological vacuum'[5] of the Anatolian dark age – two centuries after the collapse of the Hittite New Kingdom and more than a century before the conquest of the region by the Neo-Assyrian rulers ASHURNASIRPAL II and SHALMANESER III. This has been an uncomfortable remedy which has been forced upon specialists working within an Anatolian dark-age world created by the orthodox chronology.

The elegant solution, of course, is to eliminate the dark age entirely and have Shuppiluliuma II (the last Hittite emperor) reigning in the early ninth century (c. 885-875 BC) rather than the early twelfth. With the Assyrian domination beginning in the second half of the ninth century, the period of artistic transition thus amounts to just fifty years, in which time – over the reigns of just two or three Neo-Hittite rulers – the style of the orthostat reliefs rapidly changed from Hittite empire influences to Neo-Assyrian influences. In the New Chronology the reliefs from Carchemish and Malatya are both immediate post-Hittite empire and early Neo-Assyrian. They belong stratigraphically and historically to the mid-ninth century – a brief era of Neo-Hittite 'afterglow' immediately before and during the rise of Iron Age Assyria.

Conclusion Thirty

The Neo-Hittite dark age is an artificial construct with no historical basis. The sculptural tradition of the post-Hittite empire is not dated to the tenth century BC but rather to the ninth and eighth centuries BC, bringing it into the same era as the annals of Assyrian kings mentioning the Neo-Hittite rulers associated with those sculptures.

Midas and the Mushki

In the conventional chronological scheme which places the collapse of the Hittite empire in the late thirteenth century we find references to a King Midas (written Mitash) of Pakhuwa ruling in northern Anatolia, whilst five hundred years later another King Midas (written Mita) of Mushki (the tribal name of a major element of the Phrygian confederacy) is at war with the Assyrian king SARGON II and subsequently defending his Phrygian kingdom from the incursions of the Cimmerians (c. 680 BC). This second Mita is the legendary King Midas whose touch turned everything to gold.

These two benchmarks encompass the era of the Phrygian dominance of northern and central Anatolia. Let us first deal with the earlier Midas whom we shall refer to as

Midas the Elder and the arrival of the Phrygians. Professor Ronald Crossland states the position in the Orthodox Chronology model.

> The obliteration of the Hittite empire in Anatolia certainly seems to have been the work of immigrants from Thrace, probably the ancestors of the Phrygians who occupied the central part of the Anatolian plateau in early Classical times, or a closely related people. Hattusha itself was sacked *c.* 1200 BC; its archives broke off abruptly and it ceased to exist as a Hittite city. The next settlement on the site has been defined as Phrygian on the basis of its pottery. The latest Hittite texts say nothing about the events which led to the final disaster, but they record that a chieftain with the name Mitash or Midash was giving trouble on the north-eastern frontier, in Pontus, *c.* 1230 BC. His name may have been identical with that of Midas, the legendary early Phrygian king who in the Greek story was so ludicrously punished for his lust for gold.[6]

More recent scholarly opinion (e.g. Kenneth Kitchen) would put the OC date for the fall of Hattusha about twenty years later in 1178 BC (a couple of years before the invasion of the Sea Peoples in Year 8 of Ramesses III). So, Midas the Elder was active at the end of the thirteenth century BC in the latest OC model – that is, during the reign of Arnuwanda III who, according to the contemporary records, attempted to curb his activities.[7] The trouble is that when we look at recognisable Phrygian occupational remains in Anatolia – such as the famous city of Gordion where Midas the Younger buried his father, Gordias, in a mighty tumulus – there is a puzzling gap because 'no Phrygian settlement has been identified which is certainly older than the ninth century'.[8]

Thus Midas the Elder of the Hittite texts is detached from the archaeology of Phrygia by three centuries. What is more, Midas the Younger is dated a further two centuries later than this according to the annals of Sargon of Assyria. Midas the Younger was the *last* king of the Mushki who, according to legend, committed suicide as Gordion was being plundered by the invading Cimmerians in around 675 BC.

The earlier Midas was not the first of the Phrygian kings. The Homeric traditions state that the original hero who led the Phrygian migration into Anatolia was a King Mygdon. His arrival was dated to the time of King Priam (in his younger years) who took a Trojan army eastwards into the territory of the River Sangarius (modern Sakariya), where Gordion is located, to support the Phrygians in their fight against the Amazons [*Iliad*, Book III]. This suggests that the Phrygian arrival in Anatolia (NC – *c.* 900 BC) predates the fall of the Hittite empire by at least a couple of decades – that is in the time of the Assyrian kings, TUKULTI-NINURTA II and Ashurnasirpal II whose annals are the *first* to refer to the activities of the Mushki. Within a conventional chronological framework in which Mygdon and Priam campaigned in Anatolia during the late thirteenth century BC there is the disconcerting fact that the Phrygians only get their first mention in Assyrian records some three hundred years later.

As we have determined that Priam was alive in the first half of the ninth century BC (the time of Tudhaliya IV, Arnuwanda III and Shuppiluliuma II in Hatti), the contemporary Hittite references to a Midas the Elder of Pakhuwa and the Assyrian reports on the Mushki neatly fit into the archaeological record which places the first Phrygian occupation level at Gordion also in the ninth century. In the NC the Phrygian occupation immediately follows on from the last independent Hittite level without the phantom three-century lacuna of the OC. Indeed, the last Hittite and first Phrygian cultures appear to have co-existed at the site according to the pottery evidence. This is in stark contrast to the conventional dark age model for which, leading

Anatolian specialist Ekrem AKURGAL observes, there is no archaeological evidence:

> ... in central Anatolia up to now neither Phrygian nor indeed any cultural remains of any people have come to light which might be dated between 1200 and 800 BC.[9]

A similar situation pertains at the Hittite capital of Hattusha (modern Boghazköy). The excavator Kurt BITTEL revealed a destruction level marking the fall of the city at the end of Shuppiluliuma II's reign (conventionally dated *c.* 1200 BC). Then immediately on top came the late-ninth-century Phrygian occupation level with no intervening sedimentation to represent a three-hundred-year abandonment of the site. The archaeological evidence suggested no gap between the Hittite empire and the Phrygian occupation of Level II.

> The earliest (Phrygian) constructions were undertaken at a time when Hittite ruins still lay visible above the surface. On top of them there is no trace of a sterile stratum as would have been formed by natural sedimentation. This stratigraphic observation as such does not give a measure of time, but it tends to limit the interval between the end of the Hittite citadel and the beginning of Level II. ... It has to be admitted that thus far Boghazköy has contributed little to the illumination of what we call the Dark Age. Not a single find has turned up which can be attributed safely to the centuries immediately following the fall of the Hittite capital.[10]

Herodotus mentions two kings of Phrygia named Midas – one the father of Gordias, the other his son. 'Midas', then, may well be a dynastic name carried by a number of Phrygian rulers (we know of at least three). In the New

Chronology (just as in the OC), Herodotus' second Midas (he of the golden touch) is dated from *circa* 725 to *circa* 680 BC.[11] The reign of his father, Gordias (see plate 57), can thus be established between around 765 and 725 BC. If Midas the Elder (of the time of Arnuwanda III) reigned in Pakhuwa around 885 BC he could not possibly be the same Midas who was the father of Gordias because of the substantial time-interval down to 765 BC (when Gordias' reign would have begun) – but he could be his like-named ancestor back three generations (around seventy years), giving us the following dynastic sequence.

c. 900-885 BC Mygdon campaigns with Priam of Wilusa against the Amazons (the Hittites?)
c. 885-855 BC Midas I of Pakhuwa overthrows the Hittite empire with the assistance of the Kaskans
c. 855-785 BC Three or more unknown rulers for seventy years
c. 785-765 BC Midas II (referred to by Herodotus as the father of Gordias)
c. 765-725 BC Gordias rules and is buried in the Great Tumulus at Gordion by his son Midas III
c. 725-675 BC Midas III of legend who committed suicide in the Cimmerian assault upon Gordion

Conclusion Thirty-One

The Phrygian arrival in western Anatolia took place one generation before the Trojan War in *circa* 900 BC. Their eventual takeover of the Hittite Kingdom in central Anatolia took place in *circa* 875 BC when they burnt Hattusha (with the help of the Kaskans) and occupied Gordion, which Midas the Elder made his new capital. There was no occupation gap at this city (as required in the OC) because the Phrygians took control immediately after the collapse of the Hittite empire. This is entirely consistent with the pottery evidence from the site.

The 'Nail'

Eastern Crete is separated from the central part of the island by a high plain ringed by mountains – a hidden place with its deep soil and lush vegetation known as the Lasithi plateau. Here in the northern face of Mount Dikte is the sacred cave where Cretan Zeus was purported to have been born. Bus-loads of tourists and school-kids visit Zeus' birthplace each year but hardly anyone climbs to the mountain ridge on the far side of Lasithi plateau to explore the ruins of Crete's most dramatic settlement – the refuge of Karphi ('the nail').

To reach this isolated mountaintop refuge you must first ascend to Lasithi via the Seli Ambelou pass, a thousand metres above the coast; then, having reached the village of Tzermiado, take a track leading northwards into the hills. After a good hour of hiking you will reach the small plateau of Nissimos where a tiny white chapel stands at the foot of a steep path heading up the side of a gorge. A further hour of puffing and panting takes you to a rocky saddle between two peaks … and there it is – a higgledy-piggledy mass of stone ruins perched precariously on the edge of Lasithi's encircling mountains, looking down directly onto the northern coastal plain of Crete (see plate 60). This situation is truly dramatic with stunning views, but hardly a place one would choose to make a home. Not only is the climb difficult and exhausting but the climate in the winter, at nearly two thousand metres, is appalling – bitterly cold, wet and windy. Why would anyone decide to build a community up here? The answer is that these Cretans were in fear for their lives.

Desperate people will go to the ends of the Earth and put up with tremendous hardship to avoid enemies who are intent on killing them. The enemies of these Cretan refugees were the Dorians who had recently swept through mainland Greece, slaughtering the Achaean rulers and their Pelasgian subject populations as they went. Many of the survivors took to the sea and fled across the Aegean to the western coast of Anatolia where they set up new Ionian settlements away from the marauding Dorian Greeks. On Crete the indigenous people (Eteo-Cretans) had no fleet in which to escape and so chose instead to move into the eastern part of the island and upwards into the mountains, leaving the lowland coastal regions to the northern occupiers.

The settlement of Karphi epitomises this desperate flight which took place at the end of the Bronze Age. It is probably the most significant 'dark age' site on the island because it appears to have been a specially built refuge for Minoans/Pelasgians fleeing from the Dorian invaders. This occupation of Crete by three Dorian tribes followed their conquest of the Peloponnese in the second generation after the Trojan War (that is, towards the end of LH IIIC) when they destroyed the Mycenaean citadels and palaces. Here, then, is that rare beast – a settlement site which was actually occupied during the transition from the last phase of the Late Bronze Age to the early Iron Age. Karphi is the crown jewel of Cretan dark-age archaeology.

> This is the sort of site that the archaeologist would ardently desire to find and excavate in many parts of Greece and the Aegean, in order to obtain any sort of true picture of the dark ages: there are just a few slightly comparable ones, but this is the best.[12]

From the pottery excavated by John PENDLEBURY in 1937-39, it seems that the site was first occupied at the very end of the Late Bronze Age – in the last phase of LM IIIC (known as Sub-Minoan). It then endured through to the end of the Proto-Geometric (at the very latest) – roughly a period of one hundred and fifty years in the conventional chronology. However, the site produced no rebuilding phases or multiple floors as would be expected for a settlement which lasted for such a time-period – especially one perched on a high ridge with ferocious weather conditions in the winter months. Reconstruction and repair work would have been necessary and commonplace in such an environment.

> ... it may be added that, as no significant re-building or succession of superimposed floors was found, the total time of occupation may perhaps not have been more than a hundred years, a hundred and fifty at the most, from about the middle of the twelfth century down to the later part of the eleventh (in the OC).[13]

When I stood on that ridge looking down the precipitous slopes towards Knossos on the distant horizon, I could not but think of those poor people forced to endure such hardships to preserve their miserable lives. They must have been desperate and ready to seek any alternative existence as soon as was humanly possible. Indeed, the subsequent 'broader and more comfortable' settlement of Ayiou Georgious Papoura is located beside the plain and is 'twice the size of Karphi, which it replaced'.[14] The archaeological evidence suggests that the occupation of the site of 'the nail' lasted little more than a generation (not Desborough's 150 years which is quite unrealistic) – any longer than that and new floors would have been laid over the floors made during the initial construction of the houses. Indeed, the pottery evidence suggests that the site did not continue long into the Proto-Geometric as inferred by Desborough but was abandoned near the beginning of that period. Karphi is predominantly a Sub-Minoan settlement 'with a slight scattering of Proto-Geometric'.[15]

In my view Karphi was short-lived – and that would certainly have been the case if we apply the lower dates of the NC rather than the high dates of the OC. Now we have LM IIIC reaching its end in *circa* 800 BC and Proto-Geometric lasting until about 780 BC, thus giving a single generation time-span of twenty to thirty years for the existence of Karphi.

The Western Phoenix

The main thrust of the latter part of this book has been focused on how to reconcile the fundamental differences between the information provided by the ancient historians of the Classical Greek, Hellenistic and Roman eras and the data provided by modern archaeological investigation. On one side we have the short traditional genealogies stretching back from Classical Greece to the Heroic Age (ending with the Dorian invasion – which we have determined could not have taken place much before 820 BC) and, on the other, a high historical date for the end of the Late Bronze Age (of *c.* 1100 BC) based on the conventional Egyptian chronology. My solution has been to lower the date for the end of the Late Bronze Age to *circa* 800 BC – based on a reassessment and downward revision of Egyptian chronology.

A classic example of the type of historical and archaeological conundrum that such a New Chronology is able to resolve comes in the form of the 'Phoenician problem' – a puzzle which has challenged all those who have specialised in western Mediterranean archaeology for the past century.

The most famous Phoenician colonies in the West are Kart-hadasht (Carthage) on the north African coast of Tunisia and Gadir (Cadiz) on the Atlantic coast of Spain beyond the Straits of Gibraltar. We will be looking at Carthage shortly when investigating the chronology of the kings of Tyre. Here I want to focus on the Phoenician colony of Gadir, the founding of which the Roman historian, VELLEIUS PATERCULUS, claims to have taken place eighty years after the Trojan War. Velleius was followed in his dating by many of the better-known ancient writers, including Strabo and Pliny.

As Phoenician expert Maria Aubet notes, eighty years later than the OC date of 1184 BC for the sack of Troy would bring us down to 1104 (still just within the twelfth century BC).[16] Yet, by the end of the nineteenth century of the modern era, it was becoming clear that no archaeological evidence had come to light which confirmed Phoenician activity in the West before the eighth century BC.[17] Hence the 'Phoenician problem' was born.

> The profound divergences between the archaeological record and the dates attributed by Classical historians to the founding of Gadir (Cadiz), Lixus (on the Atlantic coast of Morocco) and Utica (an early Phoenician settlement west of Carthage) have long fostered a search for compromise solutions to reconcile two almost irreconcilable types of dates. These have moved from exaggerated defence of a horizon of pre-colonial activity in the West during the twelfth to eighth centuries BC, characterised by 'silent' trade or simple barter, which would have left hardly any archaeological traces, to claiming an ancient chronology for certain archaeological materials, most of them isolated and out of context, which would demonstrate the presence of Phoenician peoples in the western Mediterranean from the beginning of the First Millennium. ... we cannot dodge the question of chronology. On it depends the objectivity or otherwise of the analysis of the meaning and character of the Phoenician settlements in the West.[18]

This debate has gone on for over a century and remains unresolved – that is, until now. The New Chronology places the end of the Trojan War in 864 BC. Some eighty years later brings us to 784 BC when, according to Velleius, the foundation of Gadir took place. And this is precisely the date archaeology provides for evidence of early Phoenician activity in the West.

A similar case can be made for the Phoenician colonies of Mediterranean coastal Spain stretching from Gibraltar up to Almeria. Here the settlements of Cerro del Prado, Cerro

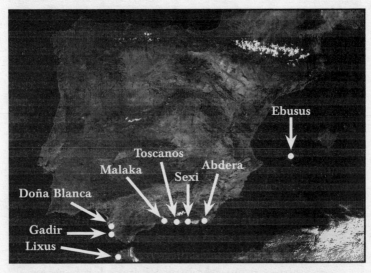

88. The Iberian peninsula with the principal Phoenician settlements [NASA].

del Villar, Malaka (Malaga), Toscanos, Sexi (Almuñecar) and Abdera (Adra) all produce typical late eighth to late seventh century pottery but nothing earlier. Yet 'Homer's repeated mention of the Phoenicians, especially in the *Odyssey*, therefore inevitably led to the belief that the Phoenicians were active in these waters from heroic times on'.[19] If the Phoenicians were 'active in these waters' of the western Mediterranean in the generations after the Trojan War (twelfth century), how was it that the earliest archaeological evidence at the Spanish colony sites was no earlier than the eighth century?

Excavations at the cemetery of Sexi have produced alabaster jars from Egypt bearing the cartouches of the 22nd Dynasty pharaohs, Osorkon II, Takelot II and SHOSHENK III, employed as cinerary urns. Kenneth Kitchen places these Libyan kings between 874 and 773 BC, yet their archaeological context dates the burials in which the jars were found from 770 to 700 BC.[20] In other words, the date of the jars in Spain is later than the pharaohs whose names decorate the vessels. In the conventional chronology these alabasters are required to have been 'venerable antiques' or 'plunder' from ninth and eighth century Egypt. On the other hand, in the New Chronology the dates for Osorkon II through to Shoshenk III extend from *circa* 784 BC to 720 BC – once again precisely when the cemetery was in use. This makes the manufacture of the Egyptian jars (along with their royal cartouches) contemporary with the colony and its burials. No need then for convoluted theories about venerable antiques or Phoenician plunder taken from Egypt.

Conclusion Thirty-Two

According to tradition, the first Phoenician colonies in the western Mediterranean were founded within a century of the Trojan War. However, in the Orthodox Chronology there is an interval of more than three centuries between Homer's Phoenicians active in the West – by implication founding colonies – and the archaeological dates for those foundations in the eighth century BC. In the New Chronology, with the end of the Trojan War dated to 864 BC, the Phoenician western colonies were founded in the mid-eighth century BC when the first settlements of those colonies are attested in the archaeological record.

Carthage and its Foundress

The legend of Dido is perhaps the most famous of the Phoenician traditions. Her original name was Elissa but the people of north Africa, where she founded Carthage, dubbed her Dido ('the wandering one') and this was how the Romans referred to the legendary queen. Elissa was the daughter of the Tyrian king, Mattan I, and the wife of her uncle, Sicharbas – almost certainly a corruption of Semitic Zikarbaal familiar from the Egyptian Tale of Wenamon where this name is carried by the ruler of Byblos.[21] Sicharbas, the high-priest, is murdered by Pygmalion, the succeeding king of Tyre, who is Elissa's brother. The name Pygmalion has been identified with Canaanite Pumayaton. In fear for her own life, Elissa and her entourage flee to Cyprus where they gather more followers before sailing for the coast of north Africa where they establish the 'New City' (Phoenician *Kart-hadasht* = Carthage) on the hill of Byrsa.

The Greek historian TIMAEUS of Tauromenium calculated that the foundation of Carthage took place thirty-eight years before the First Olympiad and therefore in 814 BC (776 + 38 = 814). Today virtually every historian accepts this date (though archaeologists are still unconvinced that the earliest material culture goes back quite so early). However, another ancient writer, POMPIUS TROGUS (according to JUSTINUS), argued for a foundation date about a decade earlier in 825 BC (seventy-two years before the founding of Rome in 753 BC).[22] This date, on the other hand, is consistent with both the Tyrian records of the ruling dynasty and the Old Testament which mentions two Phoenician kings during the reigns of Solomon (Hiram) and Ahab (Ithobaal).

Josephus [*Against Apion* I:18] gives a list of rulers and their reigns from Hiram to Pygmalion, referring to the now lost writings of Menander of Ephesus. Though there are a few discrepancies in the surviving manuscripts of Josephus, we can assemble an historically consistent sequence on the lines tabled opposite.[23]

As you can see, this list corresponds well with the chronology of the kings of Israel (determined from the books of Kings) and Israelite synchronisms with Assyria. So, Hiram's reign of 979-945 BC spans the reigns of David and Solomon with whom he had treaties according to 1 Kings 5:12. Ithobaal of Tyre gave his daughter to Ahab as the Israelite king's chief queen [1 Kings 16:31]. The reign

The Kings of Tyre According to Menander

Hiram (34 years)	– 979-945 BC	– attested in late reign of David and early reign of Solomon
Baalazar I (17 years)	– 945-928 BC	
Abdastart (9 years)	– 928-919 BC	
Astart (12 years)	– 919-907 BC	
Astartram (9 years)	– 907-898 BC	
Ittobaal I (32 years)	– 898-866 BC	– father of Jezebel, queen of Ahab (874-852 BC)
Baalazar II (6 years)	– 866-860 BC	
Mattan I (29 years)	– 860-831 BC	
Pygmalion (47 years)	– 831-785 BC	– Carthage founded in his 7th year = 825 BC

of Ahab falls during the latter half of the reign of Ittobaal of Tyre, according to Menander's list, which fits perfectly with the biblical picture of the Israelite king as the son-in-law of the older Tyrian ruler. The Phoenician tradition portrays Ittobaal as a usurper who rose from the ranks of the priesthood. In the New Chronology, Ittobaal of Tyre is taken to be one and the same as Itbaal-ramagu (Ittobaal 'the Priest') of Tyre attested in the records of Pharaoh Merenptah (NC – *c.* 884-876 BC).[24] In the Orthodox Chronology this is quite impossible with Merenptah reigning centuries earlier (in 1213-1203 BC according to Kitchen).

All this suggests that the Tyrian chronology of Menander is historically accurate and that Year 7 of Pygmalion fell in 825 BC (as according to Pompius) and not 814 BC (as according to Timaeus). So Carthage was founded by Dido/Elissa in 825 BC – eleven years earlier than you will read in most books on the Phoenician colonisation of the West.

In the Dido tradition the queen is aided in the foundation of Carthage by the people of Utica (modern Utique) – a Phoenician colony founded some forty kilometres to the west of Byrsa in the generation before Dido. This is one of the earliest Phoenician settlements on the north African coast and would place Phoenician ships in the western

Mediterranean within the general time-period that Homer has Phoenician seafarers 'active in these waters' (as described in the *Odyssey*). With a Trojan war ending in 864 BC we would have the Odysseus wanderings set between 864 and 844 BC, some twenty years before the founding of Carthage in 825 BC when Utica was already established according to Phoenician tradition.

Wenamon and Zikarbaal

I mentioned earlier that the name of Elissa's husband was Sicharbas (also written [Z]Acherbas) and that this name has been equated with Canaanite Zikarbaal or Zakarbaal. In Egyptological circles Zakarbaal is well known as the king of Byblos mentioned in the Tale of Wenamon – a papyrus which tells the story of an envoy of Karnak sent on a mission to obtain wood to build or repair the ceremonial bark of Amun. He reaches Byblos where he is eventually permitted to enter the palace of Zakarbaal, overlooking the sea, to request cedars of Lebanon from the Byblian ruler.

> When morning arrived, he (Zakarbaal) sent for me and bade me go up (from the port) ... (to the palace) on the seashore. And I found him seated [in] his high room, with his back turned to a window, so that the waves of the great Syrian sea were breaking against the back of his head.[25]

In the Orthodox Chronology it is unthinkable for this Zakarbaal to be the husband of Elissa as in the legend because Wenamon's journey is dated to the fifth year of the 'Repeating of Births' – an era at the end of the 20th Dynasty which Kitchen places between 1080 and 1070 BC. This is two hundred and fifty years before the founding of Carthage – the era of Sicharbas and Elissa. In the New Chronology, however, it just so happens that Year 5 of the Repeating of Births is dated to 826 BC – just one year before Elissa's departure for north Africa. So it suddenly becomes possible to identify Zakarbaal of Wenamon with Sicharbas/Zikarbaal of the Elissa/Dido tradition, murdered by Pygmalion.

In Virgil's *Aeneid*, Sicharbas is described as the high-priest of the Phoenician Heracles, identified with the god Melkart ('king of the city'), and therefore a resident of Tyre where the high-god of the city had his temple. This could be a problem for our proposed synchronism because Wenamon describes his Zakarbaal as the ruler of Byblos. On the other hand, the Phoenician kings were traditionally the high-priests of their cities, so Zakarbaal of Byblos would certainly have been the high-priest of that city's deities – Baalat-Gebel ('Lady of Byblos') and Baal-Shamem ('Lord of the Heavens'). Baal-Shamem is also identified with the Phoenician Heracles and he too had a prominent temple at Tyre.[26] So Zakarbaal of Byblos may have been high-priest of both sanctuaries dedicated to Baal-Shamem/Heracles. It could therefore be that Pygmalion did away with a rival city-ruler – Zikarbaal, his father's brother, rather than simply the high-priest of Tyre.

Maria Aubet describes Zikarbaal as 'occupying the second position in rank after the king of Tyre' and 'a powerful personage, rich and apparently a direct rival to the king'.[27] If Zakarbaal of Byblos was the brother of Mattan I of Tyre and uncle of Pygmalion, then he certainly would have been a potential threat to Pygmalion's ambitions. He married Mattan's daughter and tradition has it that Mattan's dying wish was for his two children to rule the country jointly. However, the people chose instead to be ruled by the male heir alone.

Elissa was almost certainly the older of Mattan's two offspring because Pygmalion came to the throne at the age of eleven when Elissa was (presumably) already married to her father's brother. As a result, it is entirely possible that Zikarbaal and Elissa acted as regents (or at least had royal authority) until the young king of Tyre reached an age when he could rule in his own right. Legend has it that Pygmalion's first attested deed was to order the assassination of his uncle, Sicharbas, in his seventh year on the throne – at the ripe old age of eighteen.

The Shardana of Sardinia

The evidence from Sardinia reveals a familiar story. Here we find a bronze-working culture which builds round stone towers known locally as *nuraghi*. The people responsible for them are thus known as the Nuraghic culture. They produced fine bronzes of their warriors (or gods) wearing horned helmets and carrying round shields and long spears. Their appearance thus bears striking comparison to the depictions of Shardana in the Egyptian reliefs from the time of both Ramesses II and Ramesses III.

Scholars have long been aware of the parallel but equally puzzled by the fact that the two peoples – the Bronze Age Shardana of Anatolia and the Iron Age Sardinians – are separated in time by several centuries.[28] The associated finds of the Iron Age Sardinians are dated through European (i.e. Greek pottery) archaeology to the ninth century BC.

The oldest inscription found on the island of Sardinia – the Nora Stone (written in Phoenician script) – is also dated to the ninth century BC and gives us the earliest known name of the island – *bet-shardan* ('House of Shardan') therefore confirming the link with the Shardana of the Egyptian reliefs.[29]

So here is the same basic chronological problem we have already witnessed, this time between twelfth-century Egyptian depictions of Shardana and ninth-century archaeology on Sardinia – a three-hundred-year gap that is not bridged by any sort of archaeological or historical data. The Sea Peoples' invasion of Egypt is dated in the New Chronology to *circa* 855 BC – that is, the mid-ninth century when the Sardinian Iron Age archaeology and the Nora Stone are also dated.

> ## Conclusion Thirty-Three
> The ninth-century Nuraghic Iron Age culture was established on Sardinia by Shardana from Anatolia following the failed invasion of the Sea Peoples in Ramesses III's eighth regnal year (NC – c. 855 BC). These Shardana migrated westwards as part of a general displacement of peoples in the aftermath of the Hittite collapse, the ensuing Trojan War and the main Phrygian invasion of central Anatolia at the end of LB IIB (= LH IIIB) dated to *circa* 860 BC in the New Chronology.

There is also growing archaeological and historical evidence to support the traditions of the eastern origins of the first Romans and their Etruscan neighbours. Herodotus claimed an original homeland for the Etruscans in Lydia (part of north-west Anatolia) whilst the later Romans always clung to the belief that they were descended from Aeneas and his band of men, exiled from the Anatolian Troad following the fall of Ilios as described in the *Iliad*. Indeed, as we have noted, the very name Julius, carried by the first Caesar, supposedly originated from his eponymous ancestor, King Iulus (Ascanius), son of Aeneas, who, in turn, was named after the ancestral homeland of Wilusa – the Anatolian eponym for Homer's Ilios/Troy. The city was, according to legend, named after Ascanius' great ancestor Iulus I – one of the legendary builders of Troy's mighty walls.

The Tursenoi of Lydia

According to Herodotus, the early inhabitants of Lydia were afflicted by eighteen years of severe famine which finally forced them to abandon their homeland and seek a better life overseas.[30] This happened in the general era of the Trojan War. They sailed west to Italy where they settled in the region north of the Tiber river – the land of Etruria, home of the Etruscan civilisation.

If this story holds true – and the archaeology does appear to support the legend – then we may identify the Anatolian Teresh/Trusha of the Sea Peoples' reliefs at Medinet Habu with the Tursenoi of Greek tradition, claimed as the founding fathers of the Etruscan civilisation. The Etruscan legend, as related through Herodotus, has it that these Tursenoi or Tyrrhenoi (as Herodotus has them) were named after Tyrrhenus (a mis-writing of Tyrshenus?), son of Atys, king of Lydia.

> The Lydians ... also colonised Etruria – and this is how it happened. In the time of King Atys, the son of Manes, there was a severe famine throughout all Lydia. The Lydians bore it at first with patience, but thereafter, when it did not cease ... the king at last divided all the people of Lydia into two halves and cast lots, for the one half that should remain in the homeland and the other to emigrate. For the part that should draw the lot to remain, he appointed himself to be king; but for the one that should leave the country, he appointed his son, whose name was Tyrrhenus. Now the part that was chosen by lot to leave the country came down to Smyrna and built boats for themselves, and into them they threw everything useful that would go aboard ship, and they sailed away in quest of a country and a livelihood. They passed many nations by in their progress and came to the Umbrians. There they established cities, and there they live until this day. From being called Lydians they changed their name in honour of that son of their king who led them out: they called themselves after him, Tyrrhenians.[31]

So it seems that the Tursenoi of Etruria and the Tyrrhenoi of Tuscany and Umbria are to be equated and identified as part of the pre-Lydian population of Arzawa, along with the Shardana of Sardis who also moved west to establish themselves on the islands of Sardinia and Corsica. Likewise, the Shakalasha of western Anatolia settled on the island of Sicily where they were known as the Sikeloi. You will no doubt have immediately seen that both Sardinia and Sicily are named after the Shardana and Shakalasha respectively.

So we can amalgamate several elements that made up the Sea Peoples' confederacy into a single geographical group of tribes originating out of the land of Arzawa. All this is very satisfying, until we recognise the same problem which has confronted us in other traditions (such as the Greek Dark Age, Mopsus, etc.) – that is, the chronological gap between the Late Bronze Age Sea Peoples' movement and the arrival of the Iron Age Anatolians on the shores of the western Mediterranean.

This is the principal reason why the obvious links between Shardana and Sardinians or Tursha and Tursenoi are often dismissed by scholars. The historical gap is simply too great to bridge. The ninth-century proto-Etruscans cannot be migrants from twelfth-century Sardis or Arzawa, otherwise where did they disappear to for the three centuries in between? So the origins of the Etruscan civilisation remain one of the great mysteries of ancient history.

Yet, the cultural similarities between the Late Bronze Age Anatolians of Azarwa and the Iron Age Etruscans have often been highlighted by modern historians. Both societies buried the remains of their noble dead in great tumuli (usually after cremation). Both constructed houses in a common design, originating in Anatolia.[32] And there is no doubt that the ancient Greek and Roman historians believed that they came to Italy from Lydia (the classical name for central Arzawa) – with the notable exception of DIONYSIUS of Halicarnassus who claimed an indigenous Italian origin for the Etruscans. VIRGIL calls them 'the elect manhood of Lydia'. HORACE refers to Emperor Augustus' counsellor, Maecanas, descended from a well-known Etruscan family, as 'the Lydian'. And, of course, Herodotus himself is our main source for the Lydian origins of the Etruscans.

A Foreign Tongue

Another mystery has been the language of the Etruscans which appears not to be Indo-European yet has affinities with the Luwian language-group of western Anatolia.

> It is known that Etruscan was not an Indo-European language. Nor was it Semitic or related to any known living or dead language. It seems to have certain grammatical features which occur in dialects of western Asia Minor, such as Lycian, Carian, and Lydian. But so far only one discovery outside Italy has suggested any definite clue. This is a grave stela of the sixth century BC found on the island of Lemnos in the Aegean. It contains two inscriptions in a language which has several remarkable similarities with Etruscan.[33]

The large island of Lemnos is close to the coast of northwest Anatolia and it may have had a part to play in the migration of the Tursenoi. The fleet which set out from Smyrna in Lydia could well have stopped there on the journey to Italy, which makes the fact that an inscription in 'Etruscan' has turned up on the island a remarkable confirmation of the legend that the Etruscans came from western Anatolia.

Perhaps the most impressive general point about Etruscan culture is the strong 'orientalising' influence in its art. These people looked east for their cultural heritage which makes Dionysius' arguments for an indigenous Italian origin somewhat hard to sustain.

The truth is that the origin and language of the Etruscans are still a mystery. But one thing seems undeniable – their close, direct dependence on the east, by which they were profoundly influenced. Many discoveries point to this conclusion. They suggest that Herodotus' account of a migration from the east, **even if his date for it is much too early**, contains a core of historical truth, and that Seneca was quite right when he said: '*Tuscos Asia sibi vindicat*' ('Asia claims the Tuscans as her own').[34]

Here Werner Keller brings us back to the core issue. In the conventional chronology the migration of the Sea Peoples (that is, the Trusha, Shakalasha and Shardana), as reflected in the records of Ramesses III (OC – *c*. 1176 BC) is far too early for the archaeological evidence of newcomers from the east in Italy and neighbouring islands which has been dated only after 850 BC.[35] You will note that the difference between these two dates is roughly three centuries – close to the number of years that I have lowered the reign of Ramesses III in the New Chronology. This is no coincidence. With the Sea Peoples' abortive invasion of Egypt in Year 8 Ramesses III dated to *circa* 855 BC, we would then have the founding of the Tursenoi settlements in Italy, the Shakalasha in Sicily and the Shardana in Sardinia at around the middle of the ninth century.

This brings us back to the alternative tradition which makes Tyrrhenus (after whom the Tyrrhenian sea was named) and his brother, Tarchon (after whom the Etruscan city of Tarquinia was named), the sons of Telephus who fought against Achilles to defend Teuthrania eight years before the Trojan War. We have seen that Herodotus names King Atys as the father of Tyrrhenus so we appear to have a contradiction here. It is, of course, possible that this is another of those situations where we have more than one name for a hero of the Heroic Age, but what really matters is that both fathers ruled prior to the Trojan War and their migrating sons left Anatolia for Italy not long before the start of that war, with others (the Trusha of the Sea Peoples) following on in subsequent decades. Thus the traditions and New Chronology would place the earliest arrival of the Proto-Etruscans in Etruria between 860 and 850 BC.

The Arrival of the Etruscans

The archaeology of Italy presents a similar picture. The Late Bronze Age Apennine culture appears to have been an indigenous population living in rather primitive conditions. They buried their dead by inhumation. Then a new and distinctive type of burial practice suddenly appears where the ashes of the cremated dead are buried in urns placed in shafts. These people performed the funeral rite of burning their dead on pyres. Before this sudden change cremation was unknown in Italy. The new 'urn-field' culture has been called Villanovan after the site, near Bologna, in which the first cemetery of cremation urns was unearthed in 1853. Associated with these new shaft burials are new forms of pottery. It is quite clear that this 'Villanovan' culture evolves directly into the Etruscan civilisation.

> Many of the large Villanovan settlements developed
> in the Archaic period into the city-states of Etruria,
> all of which can be shown to have had Villanovan
> antecedents.[36]

It is therefore my view that the first appearance of cremation burials in Italy marks the arrival of the Tursenoi from their homeland in Anatolia where cremation was the common rite of the warrior dead (in the mould of the Trojan and Mycenaean heroes of Homer).

But here again the conventional chronology hits the same obstacle – two centuries of interminable stagnation between Proto-Villanovan beginnings (Phase I, *c.* 1000 BC) and the full-blown Villanovan/Proto-Etruscan period (Phase IIB, *c.* 830-770 BC) when things really start to happen. In the New Chronology, on the other hand, the Proto-Villanovan period begins in *circa* 860 BC and the early Villanovan (Phase IIA, pre-urban) in *circa* 800 BC. By 750 BC we reach the traditional date for the founding of Rome (Phase III, proto-urban) and a little over a century later we find the Etruscan Tarquins reigning from a fully urbanised capital city during the last part of the regal period (Phase IVA), within a few decades of the start of the Roman republic (in 609 BC). In this model the whole process is considerably more rapid, with the founding of Rome coming just one hundred years after the fall of Troy.

> ## Conclusion Thirty-Four
>
> **The Etruscan civilisation, which contributed so much to the establishment of early Rome, originated in western Anatolia, the founders having migrated from Arzawa in the decade before the Trojan War and during its aftermath as part of the Sea Peoples' movement. They are represented in the Ramesses III reliefs by the Shardana (of Sardis in Lydia) and the Trusha (later known as the Tyrsenoi or Etrusci).**

The Greek Colonisation Movement

Having put forward the proposal (as others have done in the past[37]) that the Greek Dark Age may, in fact, be a scholarly invention and that the interval of time between the collapse of Mycenaean culture and the Archaic revival was relatively short, I now propose to consider what effect such a reduction in the chronology would have on the causes of Greek expansion in the Mediterranean. At the same time I will endeavour to give a brief summary of the archaeological evidence for continuity of occupation between the Bronze and Iron Age stratigraphy found at the principal colonisation sites under discussion. This will demonstrate that there are good reasons to suggest that the colonisation movement began with Homer's Achaeans and that the subsequent Archaic expansion directly followed the earlier founding of cities on the coasts of Sicily, Italy, Anatolia and the Levant by those Achaeans, thus avoiding the requirement of a two-phase colonisation hypothesis.

The standard view as to why the Greeks decided to found new trading-posts (*emporion*) and colonies (*apoikia*) around the Mediterranean is that the homeland had become too densely populated to sustain itself.

> Many parts of the Greek world seem to have suffered from the eighth century onwards from over-population, attested to indirectly by the considerable increase in the size and numbers of settlements revealed by archaeology.[38]

As we have seen, the conventional scenario was developed on the following basic lines. Approximately one hundred years after the Trojan War (*c.* 1100 BC), the Mycenaean Bronze Age came to an end and Greece plunged headlong into a dark age. Along with this Greek Dark Age came a severe depopulation as evidenced in the archaeological remains for the period.

> The substantial reduction in the number and size of occupied sites is proof of widespread depopulation: indeed some areas of the Aegean have so far produced no evidence of habitation during this period. Depopulation was accompanied by regional fragmentation and isolation, as communications ceased not only within the Aegean but also with areas beyond. A significant feature of the Dark Age is the scarcity of architectural remains at most sites.[39]

Some time in that historical void there may have been a movement of peoples, known by the later Greek writers as the Dorians, into the Peloponnese but the effect of this movement is not clear in the archaeological record. Then, around 1000 BC, the coast of western Anatolia was colonised by the Ionians – this is regarded as the first phase of colonisation by Greek-speaking peoples but not the last.

Two centuries or so later, without any obvious explanation, the population of Greece rose sharply, resulting in the failure of the agriculturally-based society to support itself. The mountainous terrain of the Greek mainland afforded little room for agricultural expansion to cope with the crisis, and so the Greeks chose a policy of emigration for a part of the population as a solution to their dilemma. Thus at around 800-750 BC we find the second Greek colonisation movement getting under way. These two phases of colonisation are regarded as quite separate in terms of both chronology and causality.

> One major gap in our knowledge concerns the situation in the Greek settlements of Asia Minor, the foundation of which goes back to the Dark Age and which do not belong to the same movement as the colonisation of the eighth century and after.[40]

Going hand in hand with this policy was the natural development of maritime trade brought about by improvements in shipbuilding technology and the need to find grain supplies from other regions to help feed the population which remained at home.

There is no doubt that over-population was a major factor in the Greeks going overseas, but an explanation for that population increase must be readily identifiable in the historical evidence (both written and archaeological) for any hypothesis to carry weight. In the New Chronology model, the decrease in population, brought about by the Dark Age

Classical Foundation Dates of Greek Colonies

Pithecusae (in the Bay of Naples, Italy)	–	c. 775 BC
Cumae (in western Italy)	–	c. 750 BC
al-Mina (on the northern coast of Syria)	–	c. 750 BC
Naxos (on the eastern coast of Sicily)	–	c. 734 BC
Syracuse (on the eastern coast of Sicily)	–	c. 733 BC
Leontini (on the eastern coast of Sicily)	–	c. 729 BC
Megara (on the eastern coast of Sicily)	–	c. 728 BC
Sybaris (in southern Italy)	–	c. 720 BC
Croton (in southern Italy)	–	c. 708 BC
Taras/Tarentum (in southern Italy)	–	c. 706 BC
Gela (on the southern coast of Sicily)	–	c. 688 BC
Byzantium (in the Propontis, Turkey)	–	c. 660 BC
Cyrene (on the northern coast of Africa)	–	c. 630 BC
Massalia (Marseilles in southern France)	–	c. 600 BC

recession, does not occur at all, precisely because there is no long Dark Age in which to dilute the remains.

This alternative scenario goes as follows. Not long after the Trojan War the Mycenaean Bronze Age culture degenerates through infighting amongst its aristocracy.

> Even after the Trojan War Hellas was in a state of ferment … There was party strife in nearly all the cities, and those who were driven into exile founded new cities. Sixty years after the fall of Troy, the modern Boeotians were driven out of Arne by the Thessalians and settled in what is now Boeotia … Twenty years later the Dorians with the descendants of Heracles made themselves masters of the Peloponnese. Thus many years passed by and many difficulties were encountered before Hellas could enjoy any peace or stability, and before the period of shifting populations ended. Then came the period of colonisation. Ionia and most of the islands were colonised by the Athenians. The Peloponnesians founded most of the colonies

in Italy and Sicily, and some in other parts of Hellas. All of them were founded after the Trojan War.[41]

Thus the 'many years' envisaged by Thucydides for the collapse of the Heroic Age and the interval of time between the fall of Troy and the colonisation period amounted to eighty years at most (I have suggested sixty-five years). The population did not decrease because the period between the return from Troy and the Dorian invasion was a mere two generations, and it was precisely this invasion from the north which created the sudden rise in the population in southern Greece. The influx of this new group was the very stimulus that forced the indigenous Achaean/Pelasgian population into their new adventures overseas.

> ## Conclusion Thirty-Five
> The Greek colonisation movement of the eighth century BC followed on almost directly from the Ionian migration at the end of the Bronze Age, which itself was triggered by over-population created by the influx of Dorian tribes from the north.

The above version of events is in almost complete agreement with the ancient writers themselves who stress that it was Achaeans (not Iron Age Greeks) who initiated the colonisation movement. In other words the early foundations occurred in the eighth century (according to Thucydides), yet the founders were Bronze Age Greeks. For example, Strabo on the founding of Croton (Italy) and Syracuse (Sicily):

> ... Antiochus says that when the god directed the **Achaeans** by oracle to found Croton, Myskellos departed to examine the site. ... He returned and

> founded Croton. Archias the founder (*oikistes*) of
> Syracuse also shared in the task, having sailed
> up by chance, when he was setting out upon the
> establishment of Syracuse.[42]

And Strabo on the founding of Tarentum (south-east Italy):

> They (the Partheniae/Spartan youths) were
> sent out and came upon the *Achaeans*, who were
> fighting with the barbarians. Sharing in the
> danger they founded Tarentum.[43]

Thucydides informs us that the Trojans were also heading for the western Mediterranean:

> After the fall of Troy, some of the Trojans escaped
> from the Achaeans and came in ships to Sicily,
> where they settled next to the Sicanians and were
> all called by the name of Elymi.[44]

It is, of course, one of the more persistent traditions that the Etruscans of northern and central Italy – the Early Iron Age Villanovan culture – were refugees from Anatolia (originating in Lydia), but it also seems likely that another Villanovan group in the neighbouring region of Emilia were these Elymi from the Troad described by Thucydides.

Archaeological Continuity

The archaeology from a number of the above sites argues in favour of the later Greek historians' views on Achaean colonisation. In southern Italy, at the sites of Porto Perone and Scoglio del Tonno (Tarentum), excavation has revealed Mycenaean pottery in the same archaeological context as both Sub-Apennine (Bronze Age) and Proto-Villanovan (Iron Age) wares. Indeed, in the case of Scoglio, the excavator, Quintino Quagliati, unearthed a house with an earlier stratum containing Sub-Apennine material and then a *later* stratum represented by both Mycenaean and Proto-Corinthian ware together *in the same deposit*.[45] The archaeology therefore appears to confirm Strabo's statement that Homer's Achaeans colonised southern Italy and that this was certainly not a considerable time (that is, centuries) before the main colonisation period of 750-650 BC.

The Pantalica North cemetery in eastern Sicily contained violin-bow and simple FIBULAE characteristic of the late Mycenaean age and an LH IIIC vase, indicating some contact with Late Bronze Age Greece. After the earlier Bronze Age Thapsos culture the archaeological record shows a long interval without settlements (exactly on the Greek Dark Age model) until the colonisation period at around 730 BC. Only evidence of cemeteries remains. In the words of Bernarbo Brea:

> ... a real Dark Age set in, only to be brought to an end five centuries later with the Greek colonisation of Sicily.[46]

What is really meant here is that there is practically no evidence of settlement in Sicily between the rich Thapsos culture (presumed to have ended *c.* 1250 BC) and the Finocchito phase (*c.* 730-650 BC) other than the cemeteries of the so-called Pantalican culture which appear to have almost no identifiable settlements. The implication is reasonably clear.

As in Greece, the chronology of the Pantalican phase must be dramatically compressed in order to explain the lack of material culture in Sicily for the Early Iron Age and, indeed, the Pantalican cemetery material itself may rather reflect the end phase of the Thapsos culture, contemporary with the Mycenaeans, or perhaps a short transition into the Late Geometric Finocchito phase.

A Connection with the Sea Peoples

In Homer's *Odyssey* we have glimpses of the period of Achaean colonisation in its earliest phase – a phase not far removed from an era of brigandry and piracy. Two examples from the exploits of Odysseus will suffice to create a picture of Greek seafaring activity at this time.

> ... before the sons of the Achaeans ever set foot on the land of Troy, nine times I had under my command men and swift ships to sail against foreign shores, and hence much booty reached my hands ...[47]

> From Ilion the wind drove me along and brought me to Ismaros, in the land of the Ciconians. There I sacked the city and put the men to death. We captured from the city their wives and much treasure, and divided it all among us, in such a way that no one went away deprived of his fair share through me.[48]

The marauding Achaean fleet described here brings to mind the threat posed by the Akawasha of Merenptah's Year 5 and the ships attacking Ugarit described in the archive of Hammurabi (last ruler of the city),[49] conventionally dated to *circa* 1180 BC but on the revised model to *circa* 860 BC.

One is also reminded of the story in the *Odyssey* where the Greeks ravage the delta of Egypt before being put to flight by the Egyptian army – a remarkable parallel to the maritime battle described in the Sea Peoples' reliefs at Medinet Habu. Clearly there were Mycenaean/Achaean expeditions to the east coast of the Mediterranean at this time, as evidenced by a quantity of LH IIIC ware found near al-Mina on the coast of Syria. We also have the Mopsus tradition, now confirmed to a degree by Neo-Hittite records. All this led John Boardman to suggest the very idea that this was a colonisation movement – but he was unable to go further than recognise the similarities with the eighth-century undertakings.

At the end of the Late Bronze Age, when Mycenaean Greeks had won ascendancy over the Aegean and succeeded to the Minoan 'empire', there are more **clear indications of what can almost be called colonising by Mycenaean Greeks** in the Near East, although the establishments may have been no more than trading-posts admitted under treaty with local kingdoms. ... On eastern shores, as on the western coastline of Asia Minor, **it was to the same areas and cities that the Greeks returned after the Dark Ages**, to found new settlements or open new markets, but here there was clearly a complete break in the continuity of Greek occupation, despite the survival or memory of names like Mopsus or the Danaans.[50]

Needless to say, the dramatic break in continuity Boardman refers to is not an archaeological fact but a requirement of the Dark Age chronology currently in use. With a date at the turn of the twelfth century for the Sea Peoples' invasions in the Orthodox Chronology, contact with Egypt also appears to cease for an astonishing five centuries.

In the Dark Age the Greeks lost all touch with Egypt, and contact was not resumed until *circa* 650, appreciably after the period when the Homeric poems took their present shape.[51]

The New Chronology only has a maximum period of around two hundred years between the large-scale movements by sea at the end of the Bronze Age and the establishment in the delta of the Greek city of Naucratis ('the camps') in *circa* 650 BC. Indeed, Herodotus tells us that it was bronze-helmeted, marauding Ionian Greeks and Carians who arrived on the shores of the Egyptian delta to aid Psamtek I (the Greeks called him Psammetichus) of the 26th Dynasty in his war to wrest control of Egypt from the other eleven regional pharaohs and unify the country in around 650 BC. This era of several kings ruling Egypt at the same time is set during the final years of the Third Intermediate Period when the Orthodox Chronology has the 26th Dynasty taking over from the Kushite 25th Dynasty as the sole rulers of all Egypt. The New Chronology, on the other hand, has several lines of kings belonging to the 22nd and 23rd Dynasties (as well as the early 26th) ruling from different capitals alongside the 25th Dynasty, just as Herodotus describes.

> So these twelve kings (of Egypt) lived in justice. A time came when they were all sacrificing on the last day of the festival in the temple of Hephaestus (Ptah) and they were about to pour the libation. The high-priest brought them golden vessels with which to pour the libation but he miscounted and brought out only eleven for the kings who were twelve in total. Then, when Psammetichus – he who stood last amongst them – had no vessel, he took off his helmet, which was made of bronze, and held it out and poured the libation with it. ... the other kings, grasping what Psammetichus had done and recalling the prophecy that he amongst them who should pour a libation with a vessel of bronze would become sole king of Egypt ... resolved to chase him away into the marshes, having stripped him of most of his power. And from these marshes he was never to issue forth or have anything to do with the rest of Egypt. ... Psammetichus believed that there was indeed great insolence in the way he had been treated by the eleven, and he resolved to be avenged on his pursuers. He sent to the oracle of Leto in the city of Buto ... and there came an oracle in answer to the effect that his revenge would

If you make no error you cannot recognise the truth. This is what scholarship is all about.

[M. Bietak: 'Rich Beyond the Dreams of Avaris: Tell el-Daba and the Aegean World – A Guide for the Perplexed' in *ABSA* 93 (1998)]

Plate 69: The celebrated statue of Laocoön and his sons being overcome by a sea-serpent on the beach of Troy [Vatican Museum, Rome].

Plate 70: Yes, it is as difficult and dangerous as it looks [photo by Ditas Rohl].

Plate 71: Clay funerary statuettes of an Etruscan couple [British Museum].

Plate 72: A mosaic depicting Aeneas departing from Troy for Hesperia [Gaziantep Archaeological Museum, eastern Turkey].

Plate 73: View into the building which protects the Thirteen Altars of Lavinium.

Plate 74: A tarpaulin covers the remains of the Heroon of Aeneas at Lavinium.

Plate 75: The great tumulus cemetery of Etruscan Caere.

Plate 76: The temple of Romulus in the Forum Romanum.

Plate 77: The temple of the Vestal Virgins in the Forum Romanum.

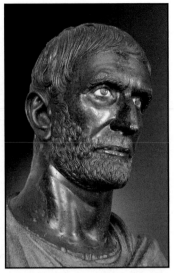

Plate 78: A small Egyptian faience vase found in a tomb at Tarquinia. It carries the cartouche of Pharaoh Bakenranef of the 24th Dynasty [Tarquinia Cultural Museum].

Plate 79: Junius Brutus, first Consul of Republican Rome following the Regal period. He was the illustrious ancestor of the assassin of Julius Caesar whose actions brought about the Imperial era.

Plate 80: The Forum Romanum with the three remaining columns of the temple of Castor and Pollux on the right and the temple of Vesta at the end of the paved way, behind which stands the Arch of Titus on the brow of the hill. The round building on the left side of the Forum is the temple of Romulus.

Plate 81: Bronze statue of Augustus Caesar which stands beside the Via del Fori Imperiali, Rome.

It was night, and sleep enfolded all denizens of the Earth. As I lay asleep, the sacred images of the gods – the Trojan home-gods which I had carried with me from out of the blazing heart of Troy – their images appeared before my eyes, revealed in a fullness of light, where the full moon's radiance was flooding through the windows of my room. They spoke to me, and their words relieved my anxious heart: … 'This is not the land which Delian Apollo oracled for you; it was not in Crete he bade you settle. There is a place which the Greeks call Hesperia – an antique land, well warded, possessed of rich soil. Oenotrians colonised it, whose heirs (so rumour says) have named it after their founder, Italy. There is our real home. There was Dardanus born and old Iasius too. There did our line begin.'

[Virgil: *Aeneid,* Book III]

Plate 82: The Middle Bronze II 'Temple of the Obelisks' at Byblos.

come in the shape of men of bronze emerging from the sea. A flood of doubt enfolded Psammetichus himself that bronze men would ever come to his rescue but, not long after, necessity constrained some Ionians and Carians, who were sailing about as pirates, to put into Egypt and come ashore. They came all clad in bronze armour. Now one of the Egyptians who had never before seen men armed in bronze came to the marshes to Psammetichus and told him that bronze men had arrived from the sea and were ravaging the plain. Psammetichus understood that the oracle was being fulfilled and made friends with the Ionians and Carians, promising them great things. And so he persuaded them to fight for him. With the help of those of the Egyptians who were his supporters, and along with these (foreign) allies, he put down the (other eleven) kings. ... To the Ionians and the Carians, who had taken his side, Psammetichus gave lands which lie on opposite (sides of the river) to one another for them to dwell in. Their name is 'The Camps' (*Naucratis*) ... [Book II]

Aeneas and the Trojan Refugees

We have seen how both the Greeks and (slightly earlier) the Phoenicians were setting out to found new cities in the western Mediterranean during the eighth century BC and, as I have argued, this process of colonisation followed directly on from the Achaean migration to Ionia on the coast of western Anatolia at the end of the ninth century. Troy had fallen in around 864 BC; the Dorians had invaded southern Greece forty-five years later in *circa* 820 BC; and the Ionian migration had begun soon after (becoming a formal colonisation movement in around 775 BC). The massive disturbances witnessed during the ninth century were probably caused by climate change which drove people to seek new ways of surviving the harsher conditions – wars of conquest to secure new land and wealth (particularly slaves), as well as the new idea of founding colonies to provide grain and metals (particularly iron) for the mother cities back in the homelands.

And there was one people more deserving of a fresh start than most. The Trojans – their city in ruins (Troy VI) and struggling to survive – chose to head west in search of a new beginning. The shanty-town of Troy VIIA had been constructed out of the tumbled blocks of Priam's Wilusa. The old king's successor, Aeneas, had walled up the gaping hole in the city wall where the Trojan Horse had been dragged into the Pergamos and brought the survivors of the Achaean sack inside the citadel where they built stone shacks against the walls and megarons of the royal quarter. In the months that followed, a plan was formed for some of the survivors to leave behind this city of death and destruction and head west to the new promised land of Hesperia.

Aeneas and his men spent some time constructing a fleet to carry the citizens of Troy on their journey. Now that fleet was ready to sail and the people went on board. As the Trojan ships rounded the off-shore island of Tenedos (behind which the Greeks had hidden their fleet before the sack of Troy), Aeneas looked back for a last glimpse of the once majestic city of Wilusa – the poignant symbol of a dying era. The Bronze Age had come to a violent end and the future now lay west, across the wine-dark sea and away from the ravages of the old eastern world. The rolling plains of Lavinium and the seven hills of Rome awaited on the distant shores of Hesperia.

Chapter Eighteen

THE FOUNDING OF ROME

*Lavinium --The Federal Altars of Latium -- The Penates
-- Dating the Roman Republic -- Dating the Regal Period
-- Dating the Foundation Period*

he sun was nearing the end of its descent towards the horizon out to sea as we clambered through a small hole in the fence beside the padlocked gates. Beyond was a dirt track heading over the brow of a low hill. With the light fading rapidly, I was not entirely confident that we would find anything in the fields beyond – but we had to try before beginning the more mundane search for a local hotel in which to spend the night. So on we marched into the open countryside, not really knowing what to look for.

My wife Ditas and I had driven directly from the Forum in Rome to Pratica di Mare on the coast of the Tyrrhenian sea just south of Ostia – Rome's ancient port. For the past week we had been exploring the archaeological sites of early Roman and Etruscan civilisation and had taken many of the photos you will see in the Italian section of this book. The stunning Roman statuary and exquisite red-on-black and black-figure imported Greek pottery depicting heroes from the Trojan War are principally to be found in the Vatican and Capitoline Museums, many of the latter recovered from Etruscan tombs in Tuscany. I had come to Italy (Hesperia) in search of the last great hero of the Trojan War – Aeneas – and his descendant, Romulus, but there was frustratingly little tangible evidence for either of them in Rome itself. The 'House of Romulus' – in reality a series of post-holes cut into the rock on the Palatine Hill – was 'closed for archaeological restoration'; the little Forum museum, containing an intriguing relief of Aeneas 'founding' Rome, was simply closed (no reason given by the over-zealous guardian). Excavations of early Iron Age huts in the Forum beside the later Temple of Romulus (see plate 76) had long been covered over. Not much to see of early Rome, then, in this great capital of the Roman empire.

We *had* seen the famous she-wolf in the Capitoline (site of the great temple of Jupiter looking down onto the Forum from the heights of the Capitol Hill). This fabulous life-size bronze was certainly of great antiquity – probably dating from the sixth century BC and therefore suggesting that the legend of Romulus and Remus was already current within a couple of centuries of the traditional founding date of Rome. But a tradition alone – no matter how tenacious or close in time to the event it purports to portray – is not in itself proof of the historicity of that event. Many Italian scholars are happy to accept the reports by Rome's Classical historians that a 'House of Romulus' (*casa Romuli*) was found on the Palatine Hill in the era of the Roman republic and that it was restored and rebuilt on several occasions during the Empire period. They see a vindication of their position in the discovery, in the 1940s, of three Iron Age (Archaic) wattle-and-daub huts near to the residence of Augustus Caesar, citing these eighth-century-BC structures as proof of the Romulus settlement on the Palatine just as the tradition states.

So there is something 'archaeological', at least, to support the Romulus foundation tradition (even though I was prevented from seeing the evidence directly for myself because of current restoration work) – but nothing in Rome to make Aeneas any more tangible than King Arthur. This is perhaps hardly surprising since the traditions themselves (with the odd exception) do not specifically make the Trojan hero the founder of the Roman capital. Popular legend only brought Aeneas to the coast of Latium, to the south-west of the Tiber valley, and it was here, the story goes, that he founded his new capital of Lavinium (named after Lavinia, the daughter of Latinus, king of the local Latins, whom Aeneas married). So it was to the site of ancient Lavinium we had to journey in order to get closer to an historical Aeneas.

The Thirteen Altars

The tramp up to the brow of the hill just south of Pratica di Mare involved considerable effort as we waded ankle-deep in pools of muddy water and sludged our way across furrowed fields of reddish-brown clay. At the crest was a lozenge-shaped mound – clearly an overgrown excavation dump for nearby trenches. I climbed up to the top to find out if I could see any evidence of those excavations in the diminishing light. The sun was now just above the sea and we had less than thirty minutes before darkness descended upon our search for the altars of Aeneas. Both beside and behind the dump were large square soundings covered in straggly weeds and half submerged in ground-water. These did not look very inviting or promising. Surely the altars were not going to be here. Looking out west towards the coast, the land sloped down in a great sweep and there, about half a kilometre away, I could just make out what appeared to be a metal shelter covering another archaeological trench.

So on we went, down an embankment, across two irrigation channels, along another muddy track, past a long cow-shed and left into another field. Available photography light was almost gone and so I ran on ahead to the metal awning.

Reaching the shelter only led to more disappointment. Yes, it was a fairly recent excavation site – but the low walls of the archaeological remains were covered in tarpaulins leaving little to view (see plate 74). In spite of the protective covering, it was at least possible to determine that the shape of the structure did not resemble a row of stone altars – so this was not the place we were searching for either. However, what I did notice was that the low walls at the centre of the site were surrounded by a circular ring of stones about ten metres in diameter. More on that later.

As I turned back, thinking that it was time to concede defeat and give up the quest, I could see Ditas waving at me down the track and pointing to the cow-shed. What I had missed in my blind rush to the shelter was a sign on the door of the long brick building which read:

Lavori di sistemazioni dell'area dell 13 are e dell'heroon di Enea a Pratica di Mare

With only rudimentary Italian, I understood this to mean 'The systematic work in the area of the thirteen altars and the Heroon of Aeneas at Pratica di Mare'. The Greek term *heroon* has a meaning something like 'cenotaph' or 'memorial' or simply 'shrine' of the hero. We went around to the west side of the building to find a long wall of glass facing the sun, now setting over the Tyrrhenian sea. And there they were, on the other side of the window, out of reach, inside the locked magazine – thirteen low podiums of stone, much bigger than I had imagined them to be. We had finally found Lavinium's altars set up to commemorate the confederation of the indigenous Latin communities of Italy and their union with the Trojan migrants led by Aeneas. Here, too, according to Timaeus (third century BC), stood (perhaps on the central altar) a large earthenware jar from Troy containing the Penates – the sacred symbols of Roman heritage – the original holy relics of Ilium brought by Aeneas to Hesperia after the sack of Troy.

With the blood-red reflection of the sun-disc glowing in the panes I cranked up the film-speed rating in the digital camera to 800 ASA and took my pictures as best I could through the dusty glass (see plate 73). We then headed back across the fields in the dwindling twilight.

That night, having found refuge in the soulless surroundings of the Holiday Inn in Pomezia (110 Euros for a double room and 14 Euros apiece for six square centimetres of lasagne!), I tried to sum up in my mind what we had seen in the mud of Pratica di Mare. Here was the city of Lavinium, buried beneath rolling agricultural fields, hardly scratched by the archaeologist's trowel. The shrine of the Thirteen Altars was discovered (in 1955) during the main Italian excavations (sponsored by the University of Rome) which had taken place throughout the 1950s and 1960s. The altars themselves (more than a metre square and nearly a metre high) show clear Greek architectural influence. Each is different and may have been contributed to the federal sanctuary by different communities in the area surrounding Rome at different times. The worship of Aeneas and the Penates was common to all the people of Latium.

What stood on each of the altars remains a mystery. Nor do we know precisely what was in the jar of the Penates. The ancient writings suggest that these Penates or 'home-gods' (from Latin *penus* – 'cupboard') were believed to be the sacred cult objects from Troy's royal palace. Virgil describes how, at the fall of Troy, Aeneas was instructed by the ghost of Hector to take the domestic gods of Troy to a new homeland far from Priam's ravaged city.

> The enemy is within the gates. Troy's tower is falling, falling. You (Aeneas) owe no more to your country or to Priam. If strong right hands could save our town, this hand of mine would have saved it long ago. Her holy things, her home-gods, Troy commends to your keeping. Take these as partners in your fate, for these

shall search out the walls you are destined to build after long roaming across the sea. [*Aeneid*, Book II:290]

I was in tears as I left my country's coast, the harbour, the plain where Troy had stood. Homeless, I took to the deep sea with my friends, my son, my home-gods and the great gods (of Troy). [*Aeneid*, Book III:10]

With Roman claims of descent from the Trojans, these mysterious symbols (perhaps statuettes of deities) were wholeheartedly adopted as the ancestral relics of Roman civilisation (later linked to the divine twins Castor and Pollux). Even after Rome had become a powerful city during the regal period and the later republic, and on into the empire period, the chief priests and magistrates were obliged to make an annual pilgrimage to the religious centre of Lavinium in order to perform rituals before the Penates. This celebration of the cult of the Trojan relics goes back at least to 300 BC and is probably much older.

Here, then, is tangible evidence that the Romans and Latins had strongly held beliefs in a close religious and cultural connection with Troy going back to Aeneas' arrival at Lavinium, when the hero brought with him the holy objects which symbolised the sanctity of once-great Wilusa.

Oh yes, and what about that strange circular structure under the shelter just one hundred metres behind the open-air sanctuary of the Thirteen Altars? All I can say is, at the time, it did cross my mind that the stone circle might be the exterior ring of a tumulus. Then, when we returned from our March 2005 'Italian expedition', a little further research revealed all. In 1968 a team led by Professor Paulo Sommella uncovered the circular structure with inner walls which I had come across under the shelter. The Italians believe they have uncovered the actual tumulus traditionally identified as the shrine of Aeneas himself, as described by Dionysius of

Halicarnassos in his *Roman Antiquities*. This humble earthen cenotaph and subsequent tiny shrine was the site of the Heroon of Aeneas – last hero of Troy.

> ... in the fourth year (after his arrival in Latium) – Latinus having died – he (Aeneas) succeeded to his kingdom, not only because of his relationship by marriage to Lavinia (she being the heiress after the death of Latinus) but also because he was commander in the war against the neighbouring tribes. ... Thereupon Aeneas succeeded to the kingdom of his father-in-law; but when he had reigned three years after the death of Latinus, he lost his life in battle during the fourth year. ... A severe battle took place not far from Lavinium and many were slain on both sides, but when night descended the armies separated. When the body of Aeneas was nowhere to be seen, some concluded that it had been translated to the gods and others that it had perished in the river beside which the battle was fought. And the Latins built a hero-shrine (heroon) to him with this inscription: 'To the father and god of this place, who presides over the waters of the River Numicius.' ... It is a small mound, around which has been set out trees (in regular rows) that are well worth seeing. [Dionysius, Book I:64]

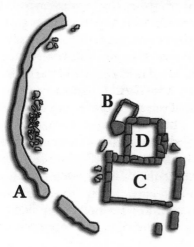

89. Archaeologist's plan of the Heroon of Aeneas with (A) the tumulus ring of the original tomb; (B) the original seventh-century burial chamber; (C) the fourth-century porch and (D) sealed shrine.

The excavations revealed a richly endowed tumulus of the seventh century BC with a fourth-century-BC shrine built into it (presumably the tarpaulin-covered walls I had seen at the centre of the stone circle). The original mound seems a little late to be contemporary with the death of Aeneas in the New Chronology (*c.* 820 BC or earlier, see below) but, nevertheless, it does at least appear likely that the people of Lavinium and their Roman kin believed that this was indeed the cenotaph of their great ancestor and chose to venerate the spot for centuries afterwards. A cult of *Pater/ Jupiter Indiges* ('Father of the Indigenous People') was established at the shrine and Aeneas, hero of the Trojan War and founder of Roman civilisation, became a god.

So, it seems, at first glance, that these traditions of a Roman ancestral connection to Troy are not only plausible from an historical perspective but also current from an early date in Rome's history, giving such stories added credibility. However, once again we find ourselves confronted by another chronological chasm which calls this link to Aeneas and Troy into question. Put simply, the 'canonical' date for the fall of Troy of 1184 BC (established by Eratosthenes) places Aeneas in the twelfth century, whereas Lavinium and Rome were founded four hundred years later according to both Roman chronography (Romulus settling on the Palatine Hill in 753 BC) and archaeology (Palatine Iron Age huts constructed in the eighth century BC). As a result, yet another 'raging controversy'[1] surrounds the origins of early Roman civilisation and the foundation of Rome itself. The traditions simply do not tally with the archaeological evidence – and, once again, dates are behind most of the contentious issues.

The later Roman historians themselves were aware of the difficulties resulting from Eratosthenes' Greek chronology and tried to resolve their Roman dilemma by inventing a dynasty of mythical kings ruling from the city of Alba Longa (in the hills south of Rome). These kings were placed between Aeneas (*c.* 1150 BC) and Romulus (*c.*

750 BC), even though the earliest legend (recorded by the poets Naevius and Ennius) made Romulus the *grandson* of Aeneas. However, this uncomfortable tradition was ignored in favour of interpolating the long dynasty of Alba Longa which helped to push Aeneas back into the twelfth century. Let us develop all these arguments in a little more detail.

The Roman Problem

The establishment of the Greek and Trojan settlements in Italy was ascribed in Roman tradition to the Homeric heroes wandering around the Mediterranean in search of new lands to settle following the destruction of Troy and subsequent upheavals throughout the eastern Mediterranean.[2] This tradition was regarded as unquestioned fact in the ancient world, so much so that the later leaders of Rome – such as Julius Caesar – claimed an ancestry going back to the Trojan heroes.[3] Roman writers composed stories and poetry based on the adventures of the Trojan founders of Roman civilisation, most famously Virgil's *Aeneid* which recalls the trials and tribulations of Rome's legendary ancestor and refugee from Troy – Aeneas.

> From the fair seed of Troy there shall be born a Caesar – Julius his name, derived from great Iulus (son of Aeneas) – whose empire shall reach to the ocean's limits, whose fame shall end in the stars. [*Aeneid,* Book I:286]

However, the date for the founding of Rome by Romulus and Remus is put at around 753/751 BC, according to those traditions. Prior to that, *The Early History of Rome* (as compiled by LIVY but probably heavily influenced by Cato's *Origines*) interpolates fifteen predecessor kings of Alba Longa who succeeded Aeneas following his founding of Lavinium on the west coast of Italy (at modern Pratica di Mare).

In the *Aeneid* Virgil gives the dynasty of Alba a duration of three hundred years, thus attributing a reasonable twenty-year reign-length to each of the fifteen kings. This would take us back to roughly 1053 BC for the first regnal year of Aeneas' son Ascanius (also known as Iulus, founder of the Alban dynasty). Livy [Book I:3] has a thirty-year interval between the founding of Lavinium by Aeneas and the founding of Alba Longa by Ascanius. We do not know when in Ascanius' reign he moved to Alba Longa, but adding say fifteen yearss to 1053 BC brings us to *circa* 1068 BC for the foundation of Lavinium which occurred in the year Aeneas landed in Italy. According to Virgil, the period of Aeneas' years in Italy amounted to four under King Latinus and then just three 'winters' of his own rule as king of the Latins before his death (which therefore fell in 1075 BC). With the seven 'summers' of wandering which preceded Aeneas' arrival in Italy, the date for Troy's fall would thus be set at *circa* 1082 BC – still more than a century from Eratosthenes' date of 1184 BC, calculated by counting forty-year generations

The Legendary Kings of Alba Longa

1. Ascanius (also called Iulus) (son of Aeneas founded the town of Alba Longa)
2. Silvius
3. Aeneas (II) Silvius
4. Latinius Silvius (founded several towns)
5. Alba Silvius
6. Atys Silvius
7. Capys Silvius
8. Capetus Silvius
9. Tiberinus Silvius (drowned in the River Albula which as a result was renamed the Tiber)
10. Agrippa Silvius
11. Romus Silvius (Romulus I) (killed by a lightning strike)
12. Aventinus Silvius
13. Proca Silvius
14. Amulius Silvius (assassinated by Romulus who founds Rome)
15. Numitor Silvius (grandfather and contemporary of Romulus)

back from the first Olympiad (estimated at 776 BC). It then becomes rather difficult to envisage Queen Dido of Carthage falling passionately for a centenarian (actually a *circa* 125-year-old) Trojan hero. Virgil does not appear to recognise his chronological difficulties.

In fact the chronology is immeasurably more problematical than Virgil's one-hundred-year gap suggests. This is because there is actually no evidence that the kings of Alba Longa ever existed. Nor, for that matter, does there appear to have been any such town or capital city from which they might have ruled.[4] These kings and their city appear to be pure fiction – an invention of the second- and first-century-BC Roman historians trying to reconcile the chronology of their legendary past. According to many specialists in early Italian history, the very names of the rulers of Alba Longa appear to be literary inventions and unlikely to be real historical characters. As a former tutor of mine at UCL, Professor Tim Cornell, told me over lunch at Manchester Museum in May 2004 'the dynasty of Alba Longa is manifestly a bogus list of rulers which cannot be treated as genuine history'. Coming from the leading British specialist on early Rome, such views have to be taken seriously and I understand that they are widely held amongst today's Roman historians.

A telling clue to the fabricated nature of the three-hundred-year Alban dynasty – which separates Aeneas from Romulus – is to be found in a paragraph where Virgil summarises the chronology of the foundation period.

> Aeneas, mightily warring in Italy, shall crush proud tribes, to establish city walls and a way of life, until a **third summer** has seen him reigning in Latium and **winter thrice passed** over his camp in the conquered land. His son Ascanius, whose surname is now Iulus – Ilus it was before the realm of Ilium fell – his reign shall have a full **thirty years** with all their wheeling months. He shall move the kingdom

> from Lavinium and make Alba Longa his sure
> stronghold. Here for **three hundred years** shall
> rule the dynasty of Hector, until a priestess and
> queen of Trojan blood, with child by Mars, shall
> presently give birth to twin sons. Romulus, then, gay
> in the coat of the tawny she-wolf which suckled him,
> shall succeed to power and found the city of Mars
> and with his own name endow the Roman nation.
> [*Aeneid*, Book I:262]

Seen in this context, the three years for Aeneas' reign in
Lavinium, followed by the thirty years of Ascanius, followed
by the three hundred years of the Alba Longa Dynasty are
to be understood as a poetical device emphasising growing
greatness in years (3, then ten times $3 = 30$, then ten times
$30 = 300$). Thus the only possible true time-period is the
one which starts the multiplier – that is, the three years
of Aeneas' life spent ruling at Lavinium before his death
fighting against the Etruscans of Caere. The other figures of
thirty and three hundred years are entirely fictitious.

As we have seen, all modern scholars acknowledge that
Eratosthenes' forty-year generation-length is also completely
unrealistic and, as a result, his calculations cannot be
trusted either. Even so, whilst continuing to work within
the conventional scheme (which also places the Trojan War
near the start of the twelfth century), historians openly admit
the chronological difficulties in linking the beginning of the
regal period, in *circa* 753 BC, with a Bronze Age hero from
the *Iliad* dated to 1184 BC. This, of course, is precisely why
those same historians have so much trouble in accepting the
Roman historical tradition, and the principal reason why
the ancestry of Roman civilisation through Trojan Aeneas
is regarded as nothing more than an elaborate mythology
borrowed from the Homeric epics.

> The literary tradition of the period before the
> foundation of the city is entirely legendary. This

was a pre-literate age, and cannot therefore have been documented in any way. It was also **too remote** for oral tradition to have any serious chance of surviving to historical times. It is worth saying that oral traditions about the origins of Rome can hardly have existed before the formation of a self-conscious political community – that is, before the formation of the city. It is unlikely, therefore, that the legends of the pre-Romulean period contain any vestige of historical fact.[5]

But what if the New Chronology is right in its placement of the Trojan War in *circa* 870 BC? What if Romulus was indeed the grandson (or near contemporary) of Aeneas as the much earlier traditions claim? Then the chronological sums add up to a much more promising synthesis between archaeology, history and legend, though still not entirely satisfying.

c. 864	BC	–	Fall of Troy VI (Aeneas rules over the shanty-town of Troy VIIA for thirty-two years)
c. 832	BC	–	Aeneas and followers begin their seven-year journey to Hesperia
c. 825	BC	–	Dido founds Carthage and Aeneas meets the Carthaginian queen
c. 824	BC	–	Aeneas founds Lavinium
c. 818	BC	–	Aeneas dies fighting the Etruscans of Caere
c. 803	BC	–	Ascanius (Iulus) founds Alba Longa (if it existed)
c. 788	BC	–	Ascanius dies
c. 753	BC	–	Romulus (great-grandson of Aeneas?) founds Rome (start of the regal period)
c. 509	BC	–	The Roman republic is established

Whatever you make of this idealistic timeline, it should at least be readily apparent that the New Chronology is the only historical model which offers a Trojan War followed by a founding of Lavinium by a refugee from that war

– and with chronological parameters which would even allow for a liaison between the queen of Carthage and the legendary father of Roman civilisation. The problem, however, remains the age of Aeneas who, according to Homeric tradition, aided Paris in his abduction of Helen ten years before the start of the Trojan War. This would surely put him in his late thirties at the fall of Troy in 864 BC and the ripe old age of seventy-seven at the earliest date he could have visited Carthage (in 825 BC).

On the other hand, the Dido romance element of Virgil's story may simply have been borrowed from an older tradition concerning the queen's death by self-immolation. This legend, which comes from Timaeus through Dionysius, and is therefore outside the Virgilian tradition, apparently has nothing to do with Aeneas but concerns the amorous advances of the native king, Hiarbas, in whose land the 'New City' was established. Hiarbas attempts to force Dido into marriage but, ever faithful to her murdered husband Sicharbas (Zakarbaal), the queen of Carthage throws herself onto a funeral pyre whereupon she is instantly deified by her subjects.[6] As a result, we do not have to accept or envisage a seventy-seven-year-old Trojan hero inflaming the passions of the Carthaginian queen if that seems improbable. It has also been argued that the motivation for including the Dido story in Virgil's *Aeneid* was to account for the long-standing animosity between Carthaginians and Romans which brought about the Punic wars of the third and second centuries BC: the age-old motif of a woman scorned leading to a tragic death and generations of enmity between two nations.

So perhaps the historical Aeneas never visited Carthage after all but went directly to Sicily and on to Italy – just as Dionysius of Halicarnassos describes.[7] This would allow us to abandon the link between Aeneas and Dido – putting it down to a touch of Virgilian poetic licence – and have Aeneas leaving Troy within a few years or even months of the fall of the city. Thus there would be no need to have him hanging around in Troy for decades until Carthage is founded in 825 BC. Dionysius proposes that Aeneas left his homeland almost immediately and founded Lavinium within two years of Troy's sacking. His own rule at Lavinium, following the death of Latinus, began in the sixth year following the departure from Troy and this lasted for three years. So Aeneas died nine years after the fall of Troy according to Dionysius. If he departed from the Troad in 863 BC (within the NC model) he would then have died in 855 BC – the date which would mark the accession year of Ascanius and give us just over a century down to the foundation of Rome by Romulus. The alternative schematic timeline would then be as follows:

c. 905	BC	–	Birth of Aeneas
c. 864	BC	–	Fall of Troy VI (Aeneas rules over Troy VIIA for one year whilst a fleet is built)
c. 863	BC	–	Aeneas and followers begin their journey to Hesperia
c. 862	BC	–	Aeneas founds Lavinium (aged about forty-three years)
c. 855	BC	–	Aeneas dies fighting the Etruscans of Caere (aged about fifty years)
c. 840	BC	–	Ascanius (Iulus) founds the (four-generation?) dynasty of Alba Longa (if it existed)
c. 753	BC	–	Romulus (great-grandson of Aeneas?) founds Rome (start of the regal period)
c. 509	BC	–	The Roman republic is established

Conclusion Thirty-Six

The foundation of Lavinium in *circa* 862 BC – the precursor to the founding of Rome – could well have been the act of Aeneas, a hero of the *Iliad*, once it is realised that the Trojan War took place in the ninth century (as in the New Chronology) rather than in the twelfth (as in the Orthodox Chronology).

Of course, as we have just seen, we need to be cautious in taking these stories or traditions too much at face value. As Professor Robert Ogilvie – author of an authoritative commentary on the Roman historian Livy – observes, it is abundantly clear that many of the early stories concerning the founding of Rome 'are not really Roman but Greek stories re-clothed in Roman dress'.[8] What he means by this is that the legendary elements and personal details surrounding the early kings of Latium (the region around Rome) are borrowings from Greek mythological tradition. This is perhaps best typified by the famous story of Romulus and Remus, the legendary founders of the city of ancient Rome itself.

Romulus and Remus

A brief recounting of the story goes as follows. Prince Numitor, eldest son and heir of King Proca of Alba Longa, is driven out by his younger brother, Amulius, who seizes the throne upon the death of the old king. The ruthless Amulius murders Numitor's sons and has his brother's only daughter despatched to the temple of the Vestal Virgins (see plate 77). Her obligatory virginity, Amulius reasons, will prevent Rhea from bearing any grandchildren to challenge his illegitimate rule. However, twins are born to the Vestal Virgin, who, tradition asserts, has been raped by the god Mars. On the orders of King Amulius, the baby boys are placed in a basket and cast into the flood-waters of the River Tiber to perish. However, they are saved by fate when the waters subside. A she-wolf nurtures the infants until they are discovered and cared for by the royal herdsman Faustulus. Romus (later known as Romulus) and Remus grow to adulthood and, upon finding out their true lineage, assassinate King Amulius before declaring their exiled grandfather, Numitor, as the true king of Alba.

Having set things aright in Alba, the twins then decide to found a new settlement on the Tiber. But conflict arises between their followers on the matter of who should be named as the founder and first ruler of the new city. Remus is killed in the subsequent fracas (either by the supporters of Romus or by his brother directly) and so it is King Romus who becomes the eponymous founder of the city of Rome. The name Romulus simply means 'the Roman' (as Diodorus Siculus similarly means Diodorus the Sicel, i.e. the Sicilian). As we have seen, the date of the founding is usually given as 753 or 751 BC based on the reign-lengths of the seven subsequently elected kings of Rome (totalling 244 years) added to the two most popular dates of 509 or 507 BC for the establishment of the Roman republic.

I am sure you can recognise a number of elements of much older stories in here from the legendary heroic motifs of the ancient Near East – the stories of Sargon the Great of Akkad and Prince Moses of Egypt, both cast into the river in baskets, for example. But the Romulus and Remus tradition is perhaps most closely mirrored in several Greek legends such as the birth-legends of Neleus and Pelias (sons of the god Poseidon) who were exposed on the River Enipeus and suckled by a bitch and a mare; or the story of Miletos, founder of Miletus in Ionia, suckled as an abandoned infant by wolves. It is clear that Greek mythological tradition permeates the Roman legends and, as such, the latter appear to borrow heavily from stories already circulating in the Hellenic world.

The History in Legend

So, it seems highly likely that much of what we find in Livy's tale of the Alban kings and seven Roman kings of the regal period (beginning with Romulus) may have been 'coloured' by existing heroic metaphor in order to give his history a narrative content beyond that of the circumspect priestly records and senate documents from which he (or his predecessors) may have obtained some of the names of those early rulers. It is entirely another matter as to where he learnt details of their reign-lengths and one should certainly question the reliability of his sources in this respect.

So there is reason to doubt the historicity of the three-hundred-year Alban monarchy period between Aeneas and Romulus. In reality it may not have existed or could have been much shorter (thus eliminating many of the spurious-sounding rulers of the dynasty). Things are rather different for the following era – that of the so-called regal period – when seven kings (some Latin and Sabine, others Etruscan) ruled over the rapidly expanding city of Rome. Here, I think, we should at least regard the major events and personalities described in Livy's story as genuinely historical. Even Roman scholar Professor Robert Ogilvie – who has a rather sceptical view of any attempt to use Livy in too much detail for historical reconstruction – concedes: 'the fact that most of the flesh and blood of Livy's narrative is fictitious should not lead one to doubt the bare bones'.[9] In other words, she-wolves suckling twin boys aside, we could consider Livy's basic chronography of the seven reigns as reliable and accept (with some reservations) the traditional foundation date for Rome as given by Terentius VARRO and Porcius CATO (Year 1 Romulus = 753 or 751 BC).

The timeline gets even more reliable with the following era of the Roman republic when a number of chronological tools become available to the historians of the following empire period endeavouring to construct their nation's past. This, then, would be a good point to begin a new construction of Roman history within the New Chronology model. As I have already hinted, the traditional history of early Rome is fraught with difficulties which the likes of Livy, Dionysius, Marcus Porcius Cato and the famous antiquarian Marcus Terentius Varro have all bequeathed to modern scholarship. But can we do any better some two millennia later? The answer is probably yes – with the help of archaeological discovery (unavailable to the first-century-BC Roman antiquarians and historians) and, above all, with the framework of the New Chronology to guide us.

Early Roman Chronology in Detail

So, let us attempt to work out a reasonable starting date for Rome and then, further back, the arrival of Trojan colonisers in western Italy, based on both the literary material and the more recent archaeological data. What you will see is that, if anything, the chronology for these events may need to be lowered by around a century for Rome's foundation and by as much as four centuries for the arrival of the Trojan refugees. As always, it is essential to work from the known towards the unknown – that is, from a well-established date, in this case the sack of Rome by the Galatian Celts in 386 BC, moving backwards in time to the legendary period of Rome's beginnings. The Celtic rampage through Rome was a pivotal point in early Roman history.

> ... no mercy was shown; houses were ransacked and the empty shells set on fire. ... For the Romans, beleaguered in the citadel, the full horror was almost too great to realise; they could hardly believe their eyes or ears as they looked down on the barbaric foe roaming in hordes through the familiar streets ... the yells of triumph, women's screams or the crying of children, the roar of flames or the long rumbling crash of falling masonry forced them to turn unwilling eyes upon some fresh calamity, as if fate had made them spectators of the nightmare stage-scene of their country's ruin ...[10]

The burning of the city by the Celts occurred, according to Polybius [Book I:6], in the same year as the siege of Rhegium by Dionysius I of Syracuse, known from independent sources to have taken place in 387 or 386 BC. This traumatic event in early Roman history is universally recognised as the severe destruction level found in the Roman Forum represented by a dark layer of burnt ash throughout the site. It falls within the historical period of the Roman republic, during the exile and subsequent emergency dictatorship of the great military general, Camillus.

The Roman Republic

When did the Roman republic begin? According to the Roman historians writing in the Augustan age (63 BC-AD 14) the republic came into being in the same year as (or perhaps within a year of) the inauguration of the Temple of Jupiter on the Capitoline hill above the Forum. The absolute date of this pivotal year was determined in at least three ways.

First, an often referenced archival list of annual dual-consuls (chief magistrates) known as the *Fasti Capitolini* ('list of the Capitol') must have been called upon by the later historians, as is readily apparent in their works. Each year of the republic was named after the two serving consuls. The different historical accounts, bearing the annual consular name-years, correspond closely (with minor differences) in those various histories, suggesting a common source document. This reconstructed list takes us back to the appointment of the first joint consuls – Junius Brutus (see plate 79) and Lucius Tarquinius Collatinus – following the expulsion of the last Roman king – Tarquin II (ending the regal period). The *Fasti*, which forms the chronological framework of the early Roman histories, is regarded by most scholars as a genuine list and unlikely to have been the invention of later antiquarians.

Second, the *Fasti* was supplemented by the *annales maximi* – a year-by-year chronicle of public events kept by the *pontifex maximus* (high-priest) – which listed those annual events according to the names of the dual-consuls of the year. According to Cicero these annals were also a prime source for the later Roman historians.[11]

Third, a document from the early republic still existed

in Livy's time which recorded an ancient law stating that a single nail had to be hammered into the wall of the temple of Jupiter to commemorate the passing of another year in the temple's existence and, it has been suggested, probably to ward off plague.[12] Livy quotes the decree thus:

> He who is the *praetor maximus* (chief magistrate) on the Ides of September (the anniversary of the temple's dedication) shall hammer a nail. [Book VII:3]

So, by counting the number of nails, it was possible for any historian to determine the date of the temple's dedication and therefore the inaugural year of the republic. The first consul to perform the task of hammering the nail must have been Marcus Horatius Pulvillus – chosen to dedicate the temple – who succeeded Brutus following the latter's death in battle against the exiled Tarquin II during that initial year of the republic's existence.

All three methods of counting back to the beginning of the Roman republic led to a date in the last decade of the sixth century BC according to the majority of our later Roman sources. Polybius even tells us that the dedication of the temple of Jupiter Capitolinus took place twenty-eight years before the Persian emperor Xerxes invaded Greece – a date well established at 480 BC (when the Spartans made their heroic stand at Thermopylae). Twenty-eight years earlier would bring us to 508 BC for the inauguration of the temple on the Capitoline. And so a date of around 508 BC can be reasonably established for the foundation of the Roman republic. In fact, the two most popular calculations using the *Fasti* were 507 and 509 BC.

Even though some modern scholars have attempted to lower the date by a few decades, it seems, therefore, that the foundation of the republic can also be treated as a reasonably secure fixed date – in fact, the earliest chronological anchor point in Roman history.

The Regal Period

Prior to 508 BC we have the so-called 'regal period' when Rome was ruled by elected kings (and the occasional usurper). Livy gives the following sequence of seven kings of Rome from the city's foundation by Romulus in *circa* 751 BC (according to Cato's reckoning) or *circa* 753 BC (according to Varro) down to the start of the republic in 507 or 509 BC. I have used Varro's dates as they have been adopted as the canonical version.

(1) Romus (Romulus) (II) (Roman)	– 753-716 BC
– 37 years (disappeared)	
(2) Numa Pompilius (Sabean)	– 716-673 BC
– 43 years (died)	
(3) Tullus Hostilius (Roman)	– 673-641 BC
– 32 years (killed in a palace fire)	
(4) Ancus Marcius (Sabean)	– 641-617 BC
– 24 years (died)	
(5) Lucius Tarquinius Priscus (Tarquin I) (Etruscan)	– 617-578 BC
– 39 years (assassinated)	
(6) Servius Tullius (Etruscan)	– 578-534 BC
– 44 years (assassinated)	
(7) Tarquinius Superbus (Tarquin II) (Etruscan)	– 534-509 BC
– 25 years (exiled)	

However, it has to be stated right away that, with this era, the dates are far less certain. First the duration of the seven reigns – according to Livy they totalled 244 years – seems impossibly long at an average of thirty-five years apiece. This would give the Roman dynasty the longest average reign-length in the ancient world where the typical duration of a king's reign is half that figure, at seventeen years.

> Such longevity is hard to believe for antiquity. For instance, the emperor Augustus had the longest reign at forty-one years, and the next longest is thirty-seven (Tiberius). Most are much shorter and it is unbelievable that the

early Roman king could have maintained such longevity.[13]

Not only is this general problem disconcerting but there are specific examples within the historical narrative itself where the sums simply do not add up. For instance:

> The fifth and seventh kings are L. Tarquinius Priscus and L. Tarquinius Superbus. By the traditional (incorrect) dating, Priscus came to the throne as an adult in 617. His son Superbus came to the throne in 534 and died in 495, respectively eighty-three and one hundred and twenty-two years after his father came to the throne. This is manifestly impossible.[14]

It has been suggested that this problem could be solved simply by making Tarquinius II the grandson of Tarquinius I (rather than his son) but such issues do highlight the type of difficulties we face with a set of such consistently long reigns. So, scepticism about Livy's individual reign-lengths of the Roman kings is certainly called for, and lower dates should be sought for at least some of the seven elected monarchs. This would inevitably lower the traditional foundation date from its high perch of 753 BC.

> ... we do not know why the Romans chose to date the foundation to the mid-eighth century, and there is a strong suspicion that their reasoning may have been arbitrary. ... It seems clear that the various dates given by historians for the foundation (Fabius placed it in 748 BC, Cincius in 728, Cato in 751 and Varro in 753) were linked to estimates of the length of the regal period as a whole, and to calculations of the date of the beginning of the republic, which could be established (within reasonable limits)

with the help of the *Fasti*. Most probably the date was fixed simply by counting back seven generations of thirty-five years: thus, 509 + (7 x 35) gives the Varronian date of 753. ... it seems likely that the foundation date was fixed by some kind of mechanical calculation.[15]

It is possible that Cornell's suspicions are correct and we should consider the likelihood that the duration of the regal period has been over-extended by a century (at Professor Cornell's suggestion[16]). This would bring Romulus (or more correctly the foundation of the city of Rome) down to around 650 BC. The dates of the kings of Rome would then work out very approximately as follows (in this case using an average reign-length of twenty years):

(1)	Romulus	–	c. 650-630 BC
(2)	Numa	–	c. 630-610 BC
(3)	Tullus	–	c. 610-590 BC
(4)	Ancus	–	c. 590-570 BC
(5)	Tarquinius I	–	c. 570-550 BC
(6)	Servius	–	c. 550-530 BC
(7)	Tarquinius II	–	c. 530-509 BC

This foundation date of *circa* 650 BC would require a down-dating of the corresponding archaeological periods with the proto-urbanisation of the Roman hills during the Latial III phase, conventionally dated from *circa* 770 to 720 BC, being lowered in the New Chronology to between *circa* 650 and 600 BC. The Latial (Iron Age) Phase III wattle-and-daub houses recently excavated on the Germalus summit of the Palatine hill – traditional site of Romulus' first settlement – are certainly consistent with the traditions. Latial III houses on the Palatine mark the beginning of Rome as a settlement and so, if the legends are historical, should be the dwellings of Romulus and his people.

With devastating incidents such as the sack of Rome by the Celts in 386 BC probably destroying much of the city's archives, we must assume that most of the original material which might have been used for the construction of pre-Republic Roman history was not available to Livy or his sources in written form. Only records of the annual consulship during the years of the Roman republic appear to have been readily accessible. Livy (and the earlier chroniclers Cato and Varro, and the second-century-BC historians Valerius Antias and Licinius Macer, the last two of whom appear to have been Livy's main sources) must have had to rely heavily on tradition rather than accurate and well-documented regnal data, thus opening up the possibility of invented or exaggerated reign-lengths for the early rulers of the city. Professor Cornell speaks for the majority of scholars when he states:

> That the famous legends of early Rome were handed down orally is not only inherently probable, but virtually guaranteed by the absence of any serious alternative. It is also likely enough that many of them go back a long way. The most outstanding example is the foundation legend itself; that the story was already well known in the archaic period is proved by the famous bronze statue of a she-wolf, an archaic masterpiece which may be earlier than 500 BC.[17]

So, evidence like the archaic bronze statue of the she-wolf pushes the traditions back by several centuries and much closer to the events upon which such legends have been grafted. This makes it inherently more likely that the core 'historical' (i.e. non-mythological) events are genuine traditions from the distant past. However, some have been embellished by layers of mythological motif and pseudo-chronological antiquity to make the telling of these stories (in oral recitation) seem more heroic and the participants more super-human or semi-divine – hence the tradition of Romulus' departure from the living world in a mysterious cloud which descended from heaven leaving an empty throne once the mist had cleared. In this world of legendary heroes and deeds it is the basic chronology that is most likely to suffer from exaggeration, making reigns longer and events older than the historical reality. But the people and events themselves are less likely to be inventions – once the stories are stripped of their mythological clutter.

> It is likely enough that many of the stories preserved in the literary tradition were handed down by word of mouth in the fifth and fourth centuries, and that at least some of them were celebrated in drama and song. This is altogether much more probable than the alternative: that the stories were consciously invented after the practice of historical writing had been introduced at the end of the third century. As for the authenticity of the stories ... they should not be dismissed out of hand. There existed more than one formal means of oral transmission, and there can be no objection in principle to the suggestion that the traditional stories might be based on fact.[18]

This is Professor Cornell's opinion and, although he would regard himself as a cautious scholar, certainly unwilling to accept these legends in uncritical fashion, he is at least prepared to consider the possibility that historical facts lay at the heart of the legendary founding of Rome. I would agree and take the argument one step further by proposing that we should not so readily dismiss such legendary material as a tool for historical reconstruction as many modern scholars tend to do these days. I realise it is not fashionable to take legends seriously, but they can complement and often enhance a history which is otherwise based predominantly on archaeological evidence (including contemporary texts where available). In the case of Rome, what those 'legendary' core facts do, at their most basic, is conform to the picture evolving out of the archaeological record where we see:

(1) a dramatic change in burial practice (cremation now in addition to inhumation) at the end of the Bronze Age, possibly due to an influx of new people into the Italian peninsula (though this in itself is a controversial issue);

(2) this 'Villanovan' culture then evolves into the Etruscan and Latial societies of the Early Iron Age; and

(3) Rome itself subsequently emerges as an urban centre towards the end of the Villanovan period in what is known as Latial Phase III (roughly dated to 650-620 BC).

This pattern is consistent with the basic tradition of (a) a migration of Achaeans (from the Greek mainland), Tursenoi (from Anatolian Arzawa) and Trojans (from Anatolian Wilusa) to Italy, practising cremation; followed by (b) the rise of both Etruscan and Latin kingdoms which evolved into (c) the city-states of Tarquinii, Caere (etc.) and Rome. However, as we have seen, the chronological imperative prevents this neat model from being straightforwardly accepted because the Late Bronze Age of (1) is separated from the Iron Age birth of Rome (3) by over four centuries. Hence the need on the part of the Roman chronographers to pad out the foundation epoch with what seems to be a long line of spurious kings of Alba and apparently exaggerated reign-lengths for the early Roman kings.

However, if we now apply the New Chronology dating to the Italian archaeological phases, a much more satisfying picture emerges. The Latial phases I to IVB would then have the following tentative historical (or rather legendary) links.

Latial Phase I	–	c. 900-860 BC	– Early trading and settlement of Bronze Age Greeks (traditionally led by Evander of Arcadia)
Latial Phase IIA	–	c. 860-820 BC	– Settlement of Trojan War refugees and Tursenoi of Arzawa (traditionally led by Aeneas and succeeded by Ascanius)
Latial Phase IIB	–	c. 820-650 BC	– Period of the Alban kings (traditionally 14 reigns)
Latial Phase III	–	c. 650-600 BC	– Founding of Rome and reigns of the first Latin and Sabine rulers (traditionally founded by Romulus)
Latial Phase IVA	–	c. 600-550 BC	– Early kings of Rome (Tullus to Tarquin I)
Latial Phase IVB	–	c. 550-510 BC	– Early kings of Rome (Servius to Tarquin II)

If we now add the artistic influences and cultural/demographic changes we can begin to see some interesting correlations with the traditional/legendary narratives.

I	– Bronze Age (Proto-Villanovan), pre-urban (c. 900-860 BC)
IIA	– Early Iron Age (Villanovan), pre-urban, cremation & inhumation burials (c. 860-820 BC)
IIB	– Early Iron Age (Villanovan), early proto-urban, cremation burials cease (c. 820-650 BC)
III	– Early Iron Age (Villanovan), proto-urban (c. 650-600 BC)
IVA	– Orientalising art, proto-urban (c. 600-550 BC)
IVB	– Archaic period, late orientalising art, urban (c. 550-510 BC)

This scheme would allow us to superimpose the traditions in what some would no doubt perceive as a superficially attractive manner, starting with Evander's pre-Trojan War migration to Italy and settlement on the hills of Rome – represented by the limited finds of Phase I (Proto-Villanovan) Bronze Age ceramics (including Mycenaean pottery); then, at the beginning of Phase IIA (Early

Villanovan), the arrival of Aeneas and his followers some forty years later – represented by the sudden appearance of cremation burials of warriors alongside the inhumations of the native population (the Latins under King Latinus); then the dynasty of Alban kings founded by Aeneas' son Ascanius – represented by Phase IIB (Middle Villanovan) when the cremation burials cease and the foreign warrior class seems to disappear from the archaeological record; then the foundation of Rome by Romulus – represented by Phase III (Middle Villanovan) with the ever-increasing urbanisation of the Early Iron Age villages (and the building of huts on the Palatine); then the dynasty of Roman kings – represented by Phases IVA (Late Villanovan) and IVB (beginning of the Archaic period) with the transformation of Rome into a true city with public buildings and civic planning (traditionally ascribed to Servius). The last two phases show strong orientalising influences which would find a ready explanation in the reigns of the Etruscan Tarquins that fall in the last century of the regal period. Etruscan culture exhibits many oriental features and, of course, legend places their origins in western Anatolia whilst archaeology produces clear evidence of contact with Corinth and its orientalising art.

In this scheme Romulus founds the city of Rome in around 650 BC at the beginning of Latial Phase III (a century after the traditional foundation date) when Cornell sees unambiguous signs of city-state urbanisation.

> Archaeological evidence clearly indicates that the site (of Rome) was permanently occupied centuries before 754 BC; on the other hand it was not until considerably later that any major change occurred in the organisation and structure of the community, of a kind that can be linked to the crucial processes of urbanisation and state-formation. These developments, which can legitimately be defined as the foundation of a

> city-state, cannot on present evidence be pushed
> back beyond the middle of the seventh century
> – that is, more than one hundred years after the
> so-called 'traditional' date.[19]

This presents us with an interesting situation. I previously argued that the preceding dynasty of Alba Longa was probably an invention of the later historians trying to fill out the gap between Aeneas and Romulus required by the traditional date for the Trojan War. We have now arrived at a date for Aeneas of *circa* 860 BC and a date for Romulus of *circa* 650 BC, leaving us with a gap of over two hundred years from the founding of Lavinium (*c.* 862 BC) to the founding of Rome. This could conceivably account for the Alba Longa dynasty of fifteen kings (averaging fourteen years of reign for each ruler). So we now have two possible models which need to be investigated:

(1) Accepting the traditional date of 753 BC for Romulus, we should test whether the legendary founder of Rome could have been the physical grandson of Aeneas (as in the oldest traditions). In this model the wattle-and-daub huts found on the Palatine hill and conventionally dating to *circa* 750 BC would represent the archaeological evidence for Romulus' foundation of Rome in the mid-eighth century as the long chronology of the regal period requires. However, with Aeneas founding Lavinium some 109 years earlier in 862 BC, there are obvious chronological difficulties which present themselves here. Ascanius was a child at the sack of Troy (say, aged six) and could not have been much more than fifteen at the death of Aeneas nine years later (in 855 BC). If Romulus was Aeneas' grandson, he would then have been born around ten years later in 845 BC, making him a ninety-two-year-old at the founding of Rome. This is just too great an age to accept and suggests that there must have been

at least two further generations between Ascanius and Romulus. The latter was not, therefore, the grandson of Aeneas but perhaps his great-great-grandson.

(2) Arguing for a foundation for Rome one hundred years later in 650 BC (as Cornell proposes), but accepting the tradition that the dynasty of Alba Longa intervened between the foundations of Lavinium and Rome (which Cornell rejects), we would then present Romulus as the eighth- or ninth-generation descendant of Aeneas through Ascanius, founder of the dynasty. This would require a similar down-dating of the Latial archaeological phases.

Having reviewed the evidence, I am personally drawn more to model (1) rather than (2) because it is in keeping with the earliest traditions. This book has been all about being prepared to give greater credence to the legendary histories of Western Civilisation than is currently acceptable – but within the framework of a revised chronology which actually makes those literary traditions perfectly tenable. Most of the perceived 'historical flaws' in the Classical legends are the result of an overstretched timeline which separates personalities and events from one another so that they are no longer chronologically feasible. Aeneas of Troy and the founding of Roman civilisation is a prime example of this phenomenon. The legend simply cannot be true because the chronological imperative prevents it. But, with the New Chronology as a powerful weapon against such scepticism, a new era could be dawning when our cultural heritage – that is, our legends – will be rehabilitated as the foundations of genuine history.

In that light I will go with my philosophical and emotional instincts and opt for Romulus (a genuine historical figure) as a close descendant of Aeneas and with a foundation date for Rome of 753 BC, just as the Romans themselves believed. That way I can look forward, one day, to standing beside the post-holes which once held the wooden pillars of Romulus' hut on the Palatine, where I can transport myself back to the days when the world's greatest Classical city was born. If you prefer to take the less romantic but more pragmatic approach of the 650 BC foundation date, then that is fine by me. Either way, both models are consistent with an Aeneas floruit in the second half of the ninth century BC – something quite impossible in the conventional scheme which places the Trojan War in the first half of the twelfth century.

Conclusion Thirty-Seven

The founding of Lavinium by Aeneas took place in *circa* 862 BC, some 109 years before the foundation of Rome in 753 BC. The Roman claims of Trojan ancestry are impossible within the conventional chronological scheme but well within the bounds of possibility once the New Chronology date of *circa* 864 BC for the fall of Troy is accepted.

Chapter Nineteen

LORDS OF AVARICE

ur long journey has finally come to an end before the temple of the eternal flame in the Roman Forum. The Vestal Virgins are long gone and the fire they tended within the sacred hearth of the Temple of Vesta has been extinguished for countless centuries. For two thousand years that flame – first lit in sacred Ilios – had burned. Aeneas had carried Hestia's flickering light from the ruins of Troy to Lavinium before its installation in the Temple of Vesta during Rome's regal period.

For the first thousand years (from their initial incursion at the end of the Early Bronze Age to the fall of Troy) the warlords who had lit the flame of Indo-European aspirations played a decisive part in the history of the ancient world as the 'sackers of cities' and plunderers of civilisation. For much of that time they were destroyers of culture and rarely builders. By the time of Agamemnon, the Achaean branch of the family had turned rape and pillage into an 'honourable profession' – at least in their own perceptions.

With the founding of Rome a new age had begun and the deeds of our avaricious Indo-European ancestors were assigned to legend. They had been real enough, but the mists of time had begun to shroud them in the camouflage of myth. However, archaeology and historical research are now beginning to reveal the fascinating past of these lords of avarice.

The complex history I have reconstructed in the six hundred or so pages you have read to reach this point may have, at times, seemed overwhelming and perhaps confusing. You have had to explore cultures and regions which are probably unfamiliar to you. Some of the four- and five-syllable names of the characters you have met along the way are hard to get your tongue around and I apologise for that (even though there is not much I could have done about it). If you have persevered to this point, then you are now fully equipped to follow the entire history of the Indo-European era in a single chapter.

So, with the hard work done, it is now time to bring all the evidence together and tell the story of the origins of Western Civilisation in a more broad-sweeping narrative. This story is reconstructed from the archaeological and textual evidence (including the legendary traditions of the Classical period) and is, in my opinion, consistent with that evidence. Of course, it may not be the only historical model capable of fitting the facts, but that is what history is all about. As I have said on numerous occasions before, 'history' is not the past – it is only our best guess as to what actually happened, based on the material bequeathed to us from that past. This is my historical interpretation of Bronze Age Greek, Cretan, Anatolian and Egyptian history. It is deliberately and unashamedly intended to be a colourful and personality-based history. I honestly admit to not being from the school of 'cultural change' or 'demographic trends'. Such anthropologically based perspectives of our past leave me cold. I make no apologies for believing that great men and women – good and bad – are the engines which drive civilisation forward (and sometimes backwards). History is about individuals and not 'trends'.

So, here goes. Please fasten your seat-belt and turn off all mobile phones for the duration of your journey.

In the Beginning …

The Indo-European speakers first appeared on the historical stage as princes of Kanesh in eastern Anatolia, mentioned in Old Assyrian period texts from the merchants' *karum* ('market quarter') below the citadel. The short text carved on a dagger belonging to Anitta, king of Kushara and Kanesh, heralds the linguistic arrival of the Indo-European aristocracy. These chariot-riding princes went on to establish the mighty kingdom of the Hittites under its legendary founder Labarna (perhaps one and the same as Hattushili I).

At around the same time, newcomers of similar ethnic and linguistic stock were entering Greece (from Anatolia or the Balkans), bringing with them their distinctive Grey Minyan ware. These people I have identified with the 'Divine Pelasgians' of Greek tradition who, in later times, were found to be settled on the Greek mainland, the Aegean islands (including Kalliste/Thera) and along the west coast of Anatolia (including Wilusa/Ilios). These newcomers were the destroyers of Troy II (mistakenly thought by Schliemann to be Priam's Ilios) and the distant ancestors of the Sea Peoples. They probably spoke an Indo-European language named Luwili in the Hittite texts and what scholars today call Luwian.

Some of their kin migrated from Anatolia into the Levant where they settled at the beginning of the Middle Bronze Age, later building large fortified strongholds with glacis ramparts and ruling over the indigenous Canaanite/Amorite population. Independent Indo-European kingdoms were set up along the coast in places like Ugarit and Byblos so as to exploit seagoing trade with their kin in Crete, Cyprus and coastal Anatolia as well as the Aegean (collectively known as Kaftara/Kaptor/Kaptara). Over the centuries, the Levantine branch of this aristocratic elite gradually assimilated into the Canaanite culture of the region and, in later generations, took West Semitic names (perhaps through intermarriage with the local Amorite dynasts). This minority element of mixed Indo-European warlords (allied to the Hurrians of the Zagros mountains) was technologically formidable with its horse-breeding skills and chariot warfare. They soon came to dominate the region.

The biblical author tells us that their chieftains were the mighty Rephaim and Anakim – Anatolian terms with Semitic plural endings which simply mean 'ancestors' and 'rulers'. Manetho later knew them as the Hyksos – 'rulers of the shepherd nomads' (*heka-shosu*), because they were a ruling aristocracy whose subjects were local Amalekite pastoralists of the Negeb. He correctly claimed that the Hyksos came from Phoenicia (that is, northern coastal Canaan) where they had first settled in the Fertile Crescent. These northerners, who would come to dominate the Egyptian delta during the Hyksos period, referred to themselves as *hekau-khasut* – 'rulers of foreign lands' or perhaps more correctly 'rulers of the mountain regions'. I believe that this term does not simply apply to 'hill countries' in general, as is often implied in the standard reference works, but to the northern mountains which stretch from Greece through to the western coast of Anatolia and beyond – in other words the original homeland of the Indo-European tribes and their Hurrian allies.

The Hyksos Domination

At the beginning of the MB IIB period, the first wave of foreigners – the Avvim (Hebrew *Awim*) of south-west Canaan – invaded a much-weakened Egypt, brought to its knees by a series of devastating natural disasters which the Bible associates with the departure of the Israelite slaves into Sinai. The drowning of the recently formed 13th Dynasty chariot force in the Yam Suph ('Sea of Reeds' – Lake Balah near Kantara) left the Egyptian delta open to invasion from the east. The Avvim, with their Shosu (Amalekite) infantry, surged across the border from their base at Sharuhen (Tell el-Ajjul near Gaza) and reached Memphis. They too had been put under pressure by the arrival in eastern Canaan of the former Israelite slaves on a mission to seize the 'Promised Land' for their tribal confederacy. These violent former slaves had spent the best part of forty years training a guerrilla army in order to ethnically cleanse the territory they intended to occupy. The Israelite army, under Moses, had already fought its way through Transjordan, slaughtering every living thing it found in its way. When the Israelites crossed the Jordan, led now by Joshua, and began to sack the fortified towns built by the Anakim, the latter were forced to move westwards, leaving the hill country to the Israelite newcomers. The principal Anak ('ruler') – Sheshi by name – having usurped power from the Avvim, fortified Sharuhen and made it the base (both by the sea and on the Via Maris) from which he could exploit the resources of recently conquered Egypt. His son Nehesi was put in charge of the delta, making his base at Avaris, the city which had been abandoned by the Israelites forty years earlier.

There, on behalf of his father, Nehesi built a great sacred compound dedicated to the storm-god of the northern mountains in his Canaanite personifications of Baal-Zaphon ('Lord of the North') and Baal-Hammon ('Lord of the Amanus Mountains' north of Ugarit). The Egyptians later identified this northern Baal with their indigenous god, Seth (Sutekh), whose temple was established next to the ruins of the Hyksos shrine. Seth – Lord of Avaris – had reigned in the eastern delta for four hundred years by the time of Haremheb when his vizier, Seti (later Pharaoh Seti I) came to Avaris to renew the foundation of the storm-god's sanctuary. It is widely believed by Egyptologists that the 19th Dynasty Ramesside kings were descended from Hyksos ancestors, which is why Ramesses II chose to establish his royal estate of Pi-Ramesse there.

Back in the Second Intermediate Period, the Lesser Hyksos ruled for over a century before a dynastic change took place. The original Canaanite Anakim of southern Palestine were themselves ousted by Aryan rulers from north-east Anatolia and their allies from the Aegean. These newcomers had met for a summit treaty on the earthly throne of Baal on the highest peak of the Amanus range (Mount Zaphon) overlooking the Canaanite coast. The scene is portrayed in the West House Miniature Fresco.

These were the rulers I have described as the Greater Hyksos whose founder was Salitis (the Sakil-Har/Shalek of the hieroglyphic texts and possibly one and the same as Caluti of the Umman Manda mentioned in an early Hittite tablet). These chariot warriors with their seafaring partners (principally from Thera) were more sophisticated than their Anakim forebears. They had vast trading links with Caphtor (Cyprus and southern Anatolia, Crete and the Aegean). In taking over the Egyptian delta, they saw an excellent opportunity to exploit the great wealth provided by the Nile valley and its contacts with African Kush. And the gold of the Middle Kingdom pharaohs awaited them, lying unprotected within their pyramid tombs. Organised gangs of 'miners' were despatched to remove the treasures of the 12th Dynasty from Dashur, Lisht, el-Lahun and Hawara. The unimaginable gold hoard was then smelted down and exported to eager royal customers scattered all around the eastern Mediterranean. Portraits of the plunderers were left on the walls of the Egyptian tombs to commemorate the deed.

The Lords of Avaris in Hyksos Egypt eventually made peace with the remnant 13th Dynasty pharaohs, now restricted to Upper Egypt (and labelled the 17th Dynasty by modern scholarship). This was accomplished in the usual way – through war followed by an imposed marriage alliance with an Aegean princess. Legend gives her the name Io (Greek Ya) and she became the eponymous ancestor of the Yawans (the Ionian Greeks). Io was brought to Egypt from Argos by Phoenician ship. This is the first of three notorious abductions from the legendary past. Indeed, there were five women in our story whose fate changed the course of human history. They were:

(1) Io/Ya the priestess, daughter of the Pelasgian Inachus, ruler (Anak) of the Argolid, abducted by 'Phoenician' seafarers and taken to Egypt where she married Telegonus and gave birth to Pharaoh Ahmose, founder of the 18th Dynasty.

(2) Europa, daughter of Agenor, the Hyksos ruler of Tyre, abducted by Greek Pelasgians ruling Crete and taken to that island where she married Asterius and gave birth to Minos the Elder.

(3) Helen, wife of Menelaus of Sparta, abducted by Paris and taken to Troy where her presence led to the greatest catastrophe in Greek and Anatolian history, contributing in a significant way to the collapse of Mycenaean power in the Aegean.

Two other women fell in love with heroes and died because of their rejection and abandonment. They were:

(4) Ariadne, daughter of Minos the Younger, who succeeded to the throne of Knossos following the death of her father and his successor, Deucalion. She married Theseus and left with him for Athens. She was then abandoned on Cyprus where she died in childbirth.

(5) Dido/Elissa, wife of the murdered Sicharbas of Phoenicia, who fled from Pygmalion of Tyre and founded Carthage. According to Virgil, she fell in love with Aeneas and committed suicide on a pyre when the Trojan hero left to fulfil his destiny in Italy. However, there is an alternative tradition which has her choosing to die in the flames rather than succumb to the amorous advances of a local ruler.

CHAPTER NINETEEN

The Hyksos Expulsion

In Avaris Io gave birth to Epaphus, successor of Yanassi who
was the son of Anak-idbu Khyan – the Inachus of Greek
legend. Thus Io/Ya was the mother of Auserre Apophis
(born as a result of the liaison between Io and a Phoenician
sea captain according to tradition), the sister of Yanassi and
the daughter of Khyan. That same legend has Epaphus
taken to Phoenicia which is difficult to explain historically.
There may be a confusion here with another Apophis.
Perhaps we may see the legendary Agenor – a Pelasgian
ruler who left Egypt to found Tyre – in a well-attested but
unpositioned king named Akenenre Apophis. It is not
difficult to imagine a Graecising of Akenenre into Agenor.
Perhaps the tale of Apophis' expulsion to Phoenicia is
derived from the tradition concerning Agenor's departure
from Egypt to Tyre. Another Hyksos king – Khamudy
– may be identified with 'Phoenician' Cadmos who sailed
to Greece (via Thera) bringing the knowledge of writing
with him (though there are chronological difficulties with
this equation).

In the meantime, back in the reign of Khyan or his
successor Yanassi, a cessation of hostilities had been
imposed between Avaris and Thebes with the betrothal of
the unmarried Io to Pharaoh Sekenenre Tela II of the 17th
Dynasty. In spite of this move to secure peace between the
two royal families, Sekenenre soon renewed hostilities with
the Hyksos of Avaris in a failed attempt to rid his country
of the foreign occupiers. This action had been forced upon
him by the taunts of his new overlord in the north – his
stepson, Auserre Apophis. Sekenenre was killed in battle
and honoured by the addition of an epithet to his nomen.
Thus Tela became Telaken – 'Tela the Brave'. Greek legend
knows him as Telegonus. Ironically, it was his Aegean
wife, the daughter of Inachus – here identified with Queen
Ahhotep ('Ya [the Pelasgian mood-deity] is Content') – who
continued the fight. She first supported her brother-in-law,

Kamose, who managed to retake Memphis and assault the walls of Avaris before suffering a reverse which may have cost him his life – possibly at the hands of the Kushite allies of Apophis. Then Ahhotep held the Egyptian kingdom together whilst her young son, Ahmose, grew to maturity and was finally successful in expelling the Greater Hyksos kings from Avaris. The Hyksos delta stronghold had been under prolonged siege (perhaps on and off for several campaign seasons) but was too strong to be taken by force. So, in Ahmose's eleventh year, a treaty was agreed which allowed the alien occupiers to depart from Egypt unmolested.

Some of the Hyksos (along with their Shosu allies) crossed northern Sinai to seek refuge in Sharuhen. These refugees by land became the Philistines of the book of Judges who, within a century or so, had established themselves in the Pentapolis of Philistia, ruled over by the Philistine *seranim* ('lords'). Thus, as the book of Genesis states, Egypt was the 'father' of the Caphtorim who became the Philistines. One band of their Hurrian and Solymite allies (the Solymi of Anatolia) settled in Jerusalem and are to be identified with the Jebusites of the Bible.

The main Greater Hyksos royal family left Avaris by sea (possibly in different fleets at different times), heading for coastal Phoenicia and the Aegean. Some returned to Thera/Kalliste whence they had originally set out decades earlier. It was perhaps from Avaris that Cadmus journeyed to Boeotia where he founded Cadmaean Thebes. The majority sailed on to the Peloponnese and made claim to their original homeland. Those arriving in Argos brought the mummified bodies of their ancestor-kings with them to avoid desecration at the hands of the Egyptians. Legend gives the name of Danaus to their leader and makes him the great-great-grandson of Inachus (through Io and her first son, Epaphus, and his son 'Baal', father of Danaus).

At this point it is important to emphasise that all these legendary personalities are almost certainly synonyms for either real historical figures whose names were lost when the legend took root, or aetiologies devised to explain ancestral origins. So, the name of Danaus' father – Baal – may be nothing more than a vague association with the Baal/Seth-worshipping Hyksos, just as Baal's mother – Libya – is clearly linked to the later land of Libya. Whether there was a real Hyksos queen called Libya, after whom the country was named, remains a matter of conjecture.

As a consequence it would perhaps be more prudent to think of the various relationships postulated in the Io legend in a rather less specific or literal sense. Thus, we might be safer in stating no more than that:

(1) an Indo-European princess connected with the Greater Hyksos (and perhaps mother of a Hyksos king named Apophis) married an Egyptian pharaoh named Sekenenre Telaken of the 17th Dynasty;

(2) the two royal lines (one Indo-European, the other native Egyptian) thus became linked by blood; and

(3) sons from both branches of the Indo-European root – personified in Princess Io (i.e. the Egyptian Queen Ahhotep) – then fought for control of Egypt until the Theban side of the family eventually succeeded in banishing their delta cousins resident in Avaris (the legend of Danaus and Aegyptus).

The Foundation of Mycenaean Greece

Those Hyksos refugees who reached the Argolid seized control from the indigenous ruling family (of King Gelanor) and ruled from Argos in their stead. This extended Hyksos family of Pelasgian nobility, displaying the ostentatious riches plundered from Egypt, were renamed Danaoi after their leader, Danaus.

For about a century, the burial site of the royal family in Argos had been located on the southern slopes of the craggy rock of Mycenae and it was there that the Hyksos royal mummies were communally interred in Grave Circle A found by Schliemann during that famous 1876 excavation season. The fabulous treasures adorning the bodies of the shaft-grave royalty were made from Egyptian gold plundered from the Middle Kingdom pyramids by those Hyksos 'miners' who had left their self-portraits (with characteristic Aegean Elvis quiffs) as the equivalent of 'Kilroy was here'. So the golden masks which covered the mummified faces of the male warriors found by Schliemann were not made in the likeness of Agamemnon and the returnees from Troy but are images of the Greater Hyksos Lords of Avaris. The legendary words uttered by Schliemann should really have been 'I have looked upon the face of wide-ruling Khyan'.

Danaus' two successors were perhaps buried in the neighbouring shaft-grave VI before Perseus, descendant of Danaus (through his mother Danae), founded a citadel palace at Mycenae from where the remainder of the dynasty (named after him) ruled. At this point the era of the Mycenaean tholos tomb was inaugurated, culminating in the 'Treasury of Atreus' – the actual burial place of Atreus, father of Agamemnon.

Less than a century after the death of Perseus, a new family (the Pelopids) took control of Mycenae and the Argolid following the death of the last Perseid king, Eurystheus. Atreus, son of Pelops (king of Elis and son of Tantalus of Anatolia), became ruler of Mycenae and constructed a massive defensive wall around the citadel. It was at this time that the shaft-graves of the Greater Hyksos and their queens were enclosed within the cyclopean wall and a sacred compound created over them. The new dynasty of Pelopid rulers constructed even more magnificent beehive tholos tombs for themselves as Golden Mycenae reached its zenith under Atreus and Agamemnon. Then came the Trojan War.

The bloody contest between the Achaiwoi of Mycenaean Greece and the Pelasgian/Luwian allies of Wilusa (Homer's

Ilios) in western Anatolia lasted, on and off, for ten years. In the end the Achaean victory was overshadowed by political collapse at home resulting from the distractions of foreign war. The organisations of state – themselves based on the needs and customs of the warrior elite – fell into decay and eventual ruin as a direct result of those warriors being absentee landlords preoccupied on distant shores with their habitual plunder and greed. Legend personifies the impending collapse with the murder of Agamemnon at the hands of his queen and her lover, the king's nephew. The great tholos intended for Agamemnon was then completed during the reign of the usurper queen and has become known by tradition as the 'Tomb of Clytemnestra'. When the archaeologists exposed the burial they found that the only skeleton was that of a woman.[1]

The Dorian Invasion

The returns (*nostoi*) of the victorious Achaeans could not sustain either the moral bankruptcy or the slave-based economy of the Mycenaean hegemony. Political infighting between the Greek kingdoms quickly led to assassinations and palace burnings. The Heracleidae – exiled in Anatolia since the ousting of the Perseid line by Atreus – seized their opportunity and, in concert with their Dorian allies, swept into the Peloponnese. The 'sons of Heracles' retook possession of their land, pushing the Achaeans into the western mountains and the safe haven of Athens. The Athenians held out against the invaders and initiated a migration of Achaean and local Pelasgian refugees across the Aegean Sea to coastal Anatolia where their kin had been living for some generations. There they founded new Ionian colonies at Smyrna (modern Izmir), Miletus, Halicarnassus (modern Bodrum) and Ephesus. Homer's parents were amongst the colonists settling in Smyrna. Fifty years later the great poet would be singing his stories of the Trojan heroes, just four generations after the great war which had brought Mycenaean power to an end. The full extent of the so-called Greek Dark Age lasted from the fall of Mycenae to the Dorians in around 820 BC and Homer's *floruit* in *circa* 750 BC.

The Sea Peoples' Invasion

In the meantime, other Achaean warriors, having participated in the Trojan War, had marched their troops into the lands of Pamphylia and Cilicia in southern Anatolia, founding cities as they went. Their most renowned leader was Mopsus of Colophon who had fought his way through Arzawa into the coastal plain of ancient Kizzuwatna where his descendants ('the House of Mopsus') ruled from their capital at Adana. Mopsus' men were the Danana of the Sea Peoples' confederacy whose devastating invasion of the Levant is recorded on the walls of Medinet Habu in Thebes. Ramesses III successfully repelled the famous attack of the Bronze Age Greeks and Anatolians in his eighth year (*c.* 855 BC) and Mopsus himself was killed at Ashkelon. However, some of the Akawasha (Achaiwoi), Peleset (Pelastoi), Shekelesh (Sagalassoi), Danana (Danaoi) and Tjekker (Teukeroi) settled in the coastal cities of Palestine amongst the descendants of their Pelasgian ancestors who had arrived in the region half a millennium earlier.

Colonisation of the West

This movement of Aegean and Anatolian peoples, scattered across the eastern Mediterranean, was the beginning of the colonisation movement which saw cities being founded on the north African coast, Sicily, Sardinia, Italy and Iberia. The Phoenicians established Carthage in *circa* 825 BC, but Aeneas, refugee from Troy, may have in reality preceded his legendary lover, the queen of that city, by a generation with his arrival on the shores of Hesperia (Italy) in *circa* 862 BC to found the city of Lavinium.

Aeneas' successors eventually built a settlement on the Palatine hill in *circa* 753 BC, looking down on the swampy ground which would later become the Roman Forum. The Romans held to the belief that their ancestors had come from Troy and the Julian clan of the first Caesars proclaimed descent from Iulus/Ascanius, son of Aeneas. This was no fantasy, no elaborate mythology designed to elevate the prestige of the influential Roman families. The emperors of Rome were indeed descended from the Indo-European sovereigns of windy Troy. They were both the last of the Divine Pelasgians from the ancient East and, at the same time, the first truly European monarchs of the modern West.

The BC era came to an end during the reign of the second emperor, TIBERIUS Caesar, the successor to AUGUSTUS Caesar in whose time Virgil composed the epic poem of Aeneas' journey to Italy. The ancient world had quietly passed away with the crucifixion, on a barren hill outside Jerusalem, of a little-known preacher and healer from Galilee. This event went unnoticed in Alexandria and Rome. Yet, within decades, the new Western World would change beyond recognition because of this man's simple teachings.

Part Five

Reference Section

ACKNOWLEDGEMENTS

This has been the longest of the three books in the *A Test of Time* series – not just in its physical length but also in the time it has taken to research, write and typeset.

The first reason for the time-lag between *Legend* (published in 1998) and *The Lords of Avaris* was the intervention of *The Lost Testament* – an historical overview of the Old Testament narratives set within the New Chronology model – which my editor, Mark Booth, requested because of all the interest engendered by the first two volumes in the series. This extra book took the best part of three years to write – quite some achievement when you consider that it took Moses forty odd years just to compose the Pentateuch (according to tradition).

The second reason is perhaps more mundane but has certainly turned out to be the more challenging of the two. In 2003 Ditas and I decided to up sticks from our comfortable existence in Kent and move to the Marina Alta in Spain. We now wake up to a breathtaking panorama overlooking a verdant valley of orange groves, beyond which lies the blue Mediterranean and (on a clear day) the cliffs of Ibiza upon the hazy horizon. That is where we are now, but it has been a nightmare getting there over the last three years. Yes, all the stories you hear about building in Spain are true and, in spite of the warnings and foreknowledge, we managed to get ourselves sucked into all the traps to such a degree that we only moved into our new retreat just this last summer (June 2006).

During those three years of nomadic existence – having found ourselves reluctantly playing the role of the new millennium's Shemau – I have been trying to write this book which covers two thousand years of history across the entire Mediterranean sea. Needless to say, the task has been nigh impossible. I have been denied access to my research library (locked away in storage), detached from the essential libraries of the Institute of Archaeology and

621

University College London, and unable to communicate with colleagues on a regular basis. As a result, it has felt at times as if this epic was never going to find its way onto the editor's desk. However, like Odysseus, battered and bruised, I made it home in the end.

Because of these difficulties I am sure that there will be mistakes and misunderstandings on my part throughout this very wide-ranging book. For those errors that have slipped through the editorial process I apologise (especially to the specialists in the various fields of Indo-European and Classical studies). However, such weaknesses should not detract from the obvious advantages which a new, lower chronology offers to ancient world scholarship, bringing the traditions of Greece and Rome much closer to historical reality than is the case with the currently accepted chronological model.

The Shemau in the Midst of the Aamu

It has to be said that I would have been unable to finish this book before the end of 2006 if it had not been for the support offered by family, friends and colleagues. They have redirected mail, photocopied papers to send out to Spain, endured long telephone calls to discuss this and that, and put us up in their homes when we have been back in the UK for breaks from the Spanish building trauma. We have also found some new friends here in Spain who have done all they can to make our nomadic sojourn on the coast of Phoenician Iberia as comfortable as possible.

The list is long but very necessary. Thank you so much to: John, Angela and Nora (my older siblings); Maurice, Beth and the boys; Eddie, Malou and the girls; John and Deirdre; Mike and Janet; Mick and Lynda; Barbara and Briony; Charlie, Profula and the kids; Margaret; Anthony; Peter, Friedrun and the boys; Tom, Lynn and Sarah; Norman and Karen; David and Rosita; Dave and Sandra; Heinz and Ingrid; Alan and Ulla; Ono and Marianne; Juan, Vicki,

Joan and Maria-Jose; Virginia; and Beverly. You all know who you are and how much we appreciate everything you have done.

Special recognition is due to several couples. Ditas' sister, Beth Kyle, and her husband, Maurice, have gone beyond the call of family duty by putting us up in their Leicester home whenever we came to visit. The same goes for our good friends Eddie and Malou Rogers whose door was always open to us when we turned up at Gatwick for a visit to southern England. John Smith and Deirdre Pelling also provided a comfortable bed and a place to relax in good company. Thank you for all your kindness and those gargantuan repasts at the Thai restaurant in West Wickham – especially the crispy-duck.

When we needed a retreat in the countryside to write and recuperate, Mick Fairfield and Lynda Howard offered us their delightful holiday cottage in the Lake District for several weeks at a time. It was just perfect.

I should also express my appreciation to colleagues who have aided and advised in regard to NC research: Peter van der Veen, Bernard Newgrosh, Bob Porter and David Lappin. My part-time researcher, Alda Watson, gave her time to source material on the internet and put us up in her Cretan home when we visited the island to take photographs. Much appreciated, Alda. And thanks to my long-time friend and colleague Mouna Mounayer for a place to rest in beautiful Lebanon – just a short drive from Byblos.

Special thanks must also go to graphic artist Mike Shepherd for his expertise in Photoshop. The beautifully-lit backgrounds to the statues and pottery reproduced in the plates of this book are the result of his tireless efforts on the magnificent Mac G5 computer.

Margaret Davies recently took over from Mike Rowland as the Legend Conferences Administrator. Mike was unfortunately too ill to continue in the post he had held for the last decade (in addition to his duties as ISIS Treasurer for more than twenty years). Thanks to you both for looking after this important organisation which enables myself and colleagues to present our ideas directly to a live audience. Margaret is continuing to look after Legend delegates and liaise with the conference centres where Legend events take place. If you would like to be kept informed as to what conferences and study tours are being planned, write to Margaret at: *megdavies@lineone.net*.

Mike Brown has also taken responsibility for putting the *Journal of the Ancient Chronology Forum* (where much NC research was published between 1987 and 2005) online at *www.newchronology.org* where you can access any *JACF* article or paper for a small charge.

Another great supporter is Cami McCraw of Texas who set up and moderates (with Richard Abbott) the New Chronology discussion group at Yahoo. This has been a very successful initiative and the group goes from strength to strength, making it one of the largest ancient history groups on the internet. To join this lively debating forum just log onto *http://tech.groups.yahoo.com/group/newchronology* – then follow the instructions to register and Cami will do the rest.

The Fount of Knowledge

Because this is the last volume in the *A Test of Time* series, it is perhaps the appropriate time to acknowledge the debt I owe to all those first-class academics who taught and encouraged me at University College London and the Institute of Archaeology, London, during the late 1980s and early 90s. To: Professors Harry Smith (Egyptian Language and Culture), Geoffrey Martin (Egyptian Archaeology), Amélie Kuhrt (Ancient Near Eastern History), Nicholas Coldstream (Mycenaean and Minoan Archaeology), Tim Cornell (Historical Methodology); Dr David Dixon (Egyptian Environment); Dr Riet van Bremen (Archaic and Classical Greece); Peter Parr (Levantine Archaeology); and to Egyptology postgraduates (now Drs) Mark Collier and Bill Manley. I am so very grateful to you all for passing on your knowledge and experience to this 'furry caterpillar in the Egyptological salad' as Anthony van der Elst put it whilst introducing my lecture at a recent conference held at Reading University. This seemed to amuse Professor Alan Lloyd greatly and did much to enhance my reputation as 'the dark side' of ancient world studies. Thank you, Anthony! Remind me to drop you in it next time we meet.

Professor Alan Lloyd too had a major part to play in encouraging my somewhat esoteric research interests. We met on an ISIS Nile cruise for which Alan was the guest Egyptologist. He delivered a handful of marvellous lectures which put Egyptian civilisation in a quite different light to that which you normally read about in popular books. Of course, Professor Lloyd (Swansea University and Chairman of the Academic Committee of the Egypt Exploration Society) is now a grandee in Egyptology circles but, even so, he has regularly supported Legend events by giving lectures and participating in conference study tours of Egypt. The man has a deep and unique understanding of the subject we all love and I am glad that I can call him a friend.

Other scholars and academics have also kindly offered their time to deliver presentations to ISIS and Legend delegates at lecture meetings and conferences, some travelling from abroad to do so. They are too numerous to mention individually by name, but thank you all for your support.

Specifically in terms of this book, a special word of gratitude must go to Professor Manfred Bietak, Director of the Institute for Egyptology, Vienna, and the Austrian Archaeological Institute in Cairo. A number of the photographs and drawings reproduced here come from the excavation archive of the Austrian archaeological mission at Tell ed-Daba and Ezbet Helmi which Professor Bietak has very kindly given me permission to use. Of course, this does not mean that Manfred Bietak necessarily agrees with all I have to say – though many of the ideas and views I have expressed in this book were first voiced by the excavator himself. However, such theories and working hypotheses were published or discussed in the more tempered tones of academia rather than the forthright style with which I have become identified. Nevertheless, Manfred is a friend and colleague whose archaeological discoveries have had a major influence on the ideas published in the *A Test of Time* series. Without him and his remarkable work over the past fifty years the story you have just read would have been a much more barren affair.

I need also to thank pottery artist Nikolas Gabriel for giving me permission to take photographs of his wonderful collection of replica pottery from all periods of Greek and Cretan history. This very talented craftsman has reproduced some of the most famous works of the ancient potters in superb detail and accuracy – many of which are used in this book where the originals were hard to photograph because of museum conditions or were not located on my travels. If you wish to visit Nik on your next trip to Crete, his shop 'Ceramica' is in the town of Ayia Nikolaos.

As always, a book is only as good as its editors, and I would, of course, wish to register my thanks to Mark Booth and Charlotte Haycock for all their help in putting this volume together. In addition, the scrutiny of Kate Truman, who has proofread all three books in this series, has been of great assistance.

Finally, as always, my thoughts turn to the long-suffering woman who has had to put up with all of this – my tireless and constant companion Ditas, who for the past twenty-one years has travelled all over the Middle East with me. She has had to endure long treks into the mountains of Kurdistan (on several occasions), numerous nights spent sleeping on the hard uncompromising floors of the Eastern Desert and Sinai, hiked across muddy fields in Italy and up precipitous mountain paths on Crete. And, after all that, she still manages to keep a smile on her face whilst typesetting these colossal, self-indulgent books for her eccentric husband. Oh for a quiet life! Thank you for everything, Ditas. This is one furry caterpillar who really appreciates it.

BIBLIOGRAPHY

A

Akurgal, E. – 1955: *Die phrygische Kunst* (Ankara).

Akurgal, E. – 1962: *The Art of the Hittites* (London).

Alt, A. – 1959: 'Die Herkunft der Hyksos in neuer Sicht' in *Kleine Schriften zur Geschichte des Volkes Israel* 3 (Munich).

Albright, W. F. – 1945: 'An Indirect Synchronism between Egypt and Mesopotamia *ca.* 1730 BC' in *BASOR* 99.

Albright, W. F. – 1954: 'Some Remarks on the Archaeological Chronology of Palestine before about 1500 BC' in R. W. Ehrich (ed.): *Chronologies in Old World Archaeology* (Chicago).

Albright, W. F. – 1957: 'Further Observations on the Chronology of Alalakh' in *BASOR* 146.

Astour, M.C. – 1981: 'Toponymic Parallels Between the Nuzi Area and Northern Syria' in Morrison, M. A. & Owen, D. I. (eds): *Nuzi and the Hurrians* (Winona Lake).

Aubet, M. E. – 1993: *The Phoenicians and the West: Politics, Colonies and Trade* (Cambridge, paperback edition 1996).

Austin, M. M. & **Vidal-Naquet, P.** – 1986: *Economic and Social History of Ancient Greece: An Introduction* (London).

B

Baillie, M. – 1989: 'Difficulties Associated with any Radical Revision of Egyptian Chronology: A Reply to B. Newgrosh' in *JACF* 3.

Barnett, R. D. – 1975: 'The Sea Peoples' in I. E. S. Edwards *et al.* (eds.): *CAH* II:2 (Cambridge).

Bartlett, J. – 1982: *Jericho* (Guildford).

Becker, H. & **Jansen, H. G.** – 1994: 'Magnetische Prospektion 1993 in der Unterstadt von Trois und Ilion' in *ST* 4.

von Beckerath, J. – 1964: *Untersuchungen zur politischen Geschichte der Zweiten Zwischenzeit in Ägypten* (Glöckstadt).

Beckman, G. – 1996: *Hittite Diplomatic Texts* (Atlanta).

Behr, H.-J. – 2003: *Troia: Ein Mythos in Geschichte und Rezeption* (Braunschweig).

Beloch, K. J. – 1913: *Griechische Geschichte* (Strassburg).

Bernal, M. – 1987: *Black Athena: The Afroasiatic Roots of Classical Civilization I: The Fabrication of Ancient Greece 1785-1985* (London).

Bernarbo Brea, L. – 1966: *Sicily Before the Greeks* (London).

Betancourt, P. P. – 1985: *The History of Minoan Pottery* (Princeton).

Betancourt, P. P. –1987: 'Dating the Aegean Late Bronze Age with Radiocarbon' in *Archaeometry* 29:2.

Bienkowski, P. – 1986: *Jericho in the Late Bronze Age* (Warminster).

Bienkowski, P. – 1989: 'The Division of Middle Bronze IIB-C in Palestine' in *Levant* XXI.

Bienkowski, P. – 1990: 'Jericho was destroyed in the Middle Bronze Age, not the Late Bronze Age' in *BAR* (Sept/Oct).

Bietak, M. – 1984: 'Problems of Middle Bronze Age Chronology: New Evidence from Egypt' in *AJA* 88.

Bietak, M. – 1986: *Avaris and Piramesse: Archaeological Exploration in the Eastern Nile Delta* (Oxford).

Bietak, M. – 1991a: *Tell el-Daba* V (Vienna).

Bietak, M. – 1991b: 'Der Friedhof in einem Palastgarten aus der Zeit des späten Mittleren Reiches und andere Forschungsergebnisse aus dem östlichen Nildelta (Tell el-Daba 1984-1987)' in M. Bietak (ed.): *ÄL* II (Vienna).

Bietak, M. – 1995: 'Connections Between Egypt and the Minoan World: New Results from Tell el-

627

Daba/Avaris' in W. V. Davies & L. Schofield (eds.): *EAL* (London).

Bietak, M. – 1996: *Avaris: The Capital of the Hyksos, Recent Excavations at Tell ed-Daba* (London).

Bietak, M. – 1997: 'Avaris, Capital of the Hyksos Kingdom: New Results of Excavations' in E. D. Oren (ed.): *The Hyksos: New Historical and Archaeological Perspectives* (Philadelphia).

Bietak, M. – 2000a: 'Rich Beyond the Dreams of Avaris: Tell el-Daba and the Aegean World – A Guide for the Perplexed: A Response to Eric H. Cline' in *ABSA* 95.

Bietak, M. & Marinatos, N. – 2000b: 'Avaris (Tell el-Daba) and the Minoan World' in *Krhth-Aigupto V, hgb. von A. Karetsou. (Essayband zu einer Austellung im Herakleion Museum)* (Athens).

Bietak, M. – 2001: 'Ausgrabungen in dem Palastbezirk von Avaris. Vorbericht Tell el-Daba/Ezbet Helmi 1993-2000' in M. Bietak (ed.): *ÄL* 11 (Vienna).

Bietak, M. – 2003: 'Science Versus Archaeology: Problems and Consequences of High Aegean Chronology' in M. Bietak & H. Hunger (eds.): *Proceedings of the SCIEM 2000 Euro Conference, Haindorf 2nd to 7th May 2001, in Contributions to the Chronology of the Eastern Mediterranean* IV (Vienna).

Bietak, M. & Marinatos, N. – 2003: 'The Minoan Paintings of Avaris' in B. Manley (ed.): *The Seventy Great Mysteries of Ancient Egypt* (London).

Bietak, M. & Forstner-Müller, I. – 2003: 'Ausgrabungen im Palastbezirk von Avaris. Vorbericht Tell el-Daba/Ezbet Helmi Frühjahr 2003' in M. Bietak (ed.): *ÄL* 13 (Vienna).

Bietak, M. – 2005a: 'The Tuthmoside Stronghold of Perunefer' in *EA* 26 (Spring).

Bietak, M. – 2005b: 'The Setting of the Minoan Wall Paintings at Avaris: Aegean Wall Painting – A Tribute

to Mark Cameron' in L. Morgan (ed.): *British School at Athens Studies* 13 (London).

Bietak, M. – 2005c: 'Bronze Age Paintings in the Levant: Chronological and Cultural Considerations' in M. Bietak & H. Hunger (eds.): *Proceedings of the SCIEM 2000 Euro Conference, Vienna 2nd to 7th May 2003, in Contributions to the Chronology of the Eastern Mediterranean* VII (Vienna).

Bietak, M. & Forstner-Müller, I. – 2005: 'Ausgrabung eines Palastbezirkes der Tuthmosidenzeit bei Ezbet Helmi/Tell el-Daba. Vorbericht für Herbst 2004 und Frühjahr 2005' in M. Bietak (ed.): *ÄL* 15 (Vienna).

Bietak, M. – 2006: 'Egypt and the Aegean: Cultural Convergence in a Thutmoside Palace at Avaris' in *Hatshepsut: Exhibition Catalogue of the Metropolitan Museum of Art* (New York).

Bimson, J. J. – 1990: 'The Philistines: Their Origins and Chronology Reassessed' in *JACF* 4.

Bittel, K. – 1970: *Hattusha: The Capital of the Hittites* (Oxford).

Blegen, C. W. et al. – 1958: *Troy* IV:1 (Princeton).

Blegen, C. W. – 1975: 'The Expansion of the Mycenaean Civilization' in I. E. S. Edwards *et al.* (eds): *CAH* II:2A (Cambridge).

Blegen, C. W. – 1995: *Troy and the Trojans* (London).

Boardman, J. – 1963: *On the Knossos Tablets: The Date of the Knossos Tablets* (Oxford).

Boardman, J. – 1980: *The Greeks Overseas* (London).

Boardman, J. – 1982: 'The Islands' in J. Boardman *et al.* (eds): *CAH* III:1 (Cambridge).

Boardman, J. – 1982: 'The Geometric Culture of Greece' in J. Boardman *et al.* (eds): *CAH* III:1 (Cambridge).

Brinkman, J. A. – 1981: 'Hurrians in Babylonia in the Late Second Millennium B.C.: An Unexploited

Minority Resource for Socio-Economic and Philological Analysis' in M. A. Morrison & D. I. Owen (eds.): *Nuzi and the Hurrians* (Winona Lake).

Brown, A. – 1983: *Arthur Evans and the Palace of Minos* (Oxford).

Bryce, T. – 1998: *The Kingdom of the Hittites* (Oxford).

Bryce, T. – 2006: *The Trojans and their Neighbours* (London).

von Burg, K. – 1987: *Heinrich Schliemann: For Gold or Glory?* (Windsor).

Burn, A. R. – 1930: *Minoans, Philistines, and Greeks: BC 1400-900* (London).

Burn, A. R. – 1965: *The Pelican History of Greece* (Harmondsworth).

Bury, J. B. & **Meiggs, R.** – 1900: *A History of Greece: To the Death of Alexander the Great* (London).

C

Cadogan, G. – 1976: *Palaces of Minoan Crete* (London).

Cary, M. & **Scullard, H. H.** – 1975: *A History of Rome: Down to the Reign of Constantine* (Basingstoke).

Catling, H. W. – 1975: 'Cyprus in the Late Bronze Age' in I. E. S. Edwards *et al.* (eds.): *CAH* II:2A (Cambridge).

Cline, E. H. – 1995: 'Egyptian and Near Eastern Imports at Late Bronze Age Mycenae' in W. V. Davies & L. Schofield (eds.): *EAL* (London).

Coldstream, J. N. – 1977: *Geometric Greece* (London).

Collon, D. – 1987: *First Impressions: Cylinder seals in the Ancient Near East* (London).

Collon, D. – 1994: 'Bull-Leaping in Syria' in M. Bietak (ed.): *ÄL* IV (Vienna).

Connor, W. R. – 1984: *Thucydides* (Princeton).

Cook, J. M. – 1973: *The Troad: An Archaeological and Topographical Study* (Oxford).

Cook, R. M. – 1972: *Greek Painted Pottery* (London).

Cornell, T. J. – 1995: *The Beginnings of Rome: Italy and Rome from the Bronze Age to the Punic Wars (c. 1000-264 BC)* (London).

Cotterell, A. – 1985: *Origins of European Civilization* (London).

Crossland, R. A. – 1971: 'Immigrants from the North' in I. E. S. Edwards *et al.* (eds.): *CAH* I:2B (Cambridge).

Culican, W. – 1970: 'Almuñecar, Assur and Phoenician Penetration of the Western Mediterranean' in *Levant 2*.

Cumming, B. – 1982: *Egyptian Historical Records of the Later Eighteenth Dynasty*, Fascicle I (Warminster).

Curtis, A. – 1985: *Ugarit, Ras Shamra* (Cambridge).

D

Davaras, C. – 1946: *Guide to Cretan Antiquities* (Athens).

Davison, J. M. – 1961: *Attic Geometric Workshops* (Newhaven).

Desborough, V. R. d'A. – 1972: *The Greek Dark Ages* (London).

Dever, W. G. – 1985: 'Relations Between Syria-Palestine and Egypt in the "Hyksos" Period' in J. N. Tubb (ed.): *Palestine in the Bronze and Iron Ages: Papers in Honour of Olga Tufnell* (London).

Dickinson, O. – 1994: *The Aegean Bronze Age* (Cambridge).

Dorpfeld, W. – 1902: *Troja und Ilion* (Athens).

Doumas, C. – 1978: 'The Stratigraphy of Akrotiri' in *Thera and the Aegean World* I.

Doumas, C. – 1992: *The Wall-Paintings of Thera* (Athens).

Drews, R. – 1988: *The Coming of the Greeks: Indo-European Conquests in the Aegean and the Near East* (New Jersey).

Drower, M. S. –1973: 'Syria *c.* 1550-1400 B.C.' in I. E. S. Edwards *et al.* (eds.): *CAH* II:1 (Cambridge).

Dunand, M. – 1968: *Byblos: Its History, Ruins and Legends* (Beirut).

E

Easton, D. F. – 1985: 'Has the Trojan War been found?' in *Antiquity* LIX.

Easton, D. F. *et al.* – 2003: 'Troy in Recent Perspective' in *AS* 52.

Edel, E. – 1966: *Die Ortsnamenliste aus dem Totentempel Amenophis*, iii (Bonn).

Edgerton, W. F. & **Wilson, J. A.** – 1936: *Historical Records of Ramses III – The Texts in Medinet Habu*, Volumes I & II (Chicago).

Epstein, C. M. – 1966: 'The Hurrians and the Development of Bichrome Ware' in *Palestinian Bichrome Ware* (Leiden).

Evans, A. J. – 1912: 'The Minoan and Mycenaean Element in Hellenic Life' in *JHS* 32.

Evans, A. J. – 1930: *The Palace of Minos* III (London).

Evelyn-White, H. G. (trans.) – 1982: *Hesiod: The Homeric Hymns and Homerica* (Cambridge, Mass.).

F

Farina, G. – 1938: *Il Papiro dei Re Restaurato* (Rome).

Fields, N. – 2004: *Troy c. 1700-1250 BC* (Oxford).

Finkelstein, I. & **Silberman, N. A.** – 2001: *The Bible Unearthed* (New York).

Finley, M. I. – 1956: *The World of Odysseus* (London).

Finley, M. I. – 1970: *Early Greece: The Bronze and Archaic Ages* (London).

Fitzhardinge, L. F. – 1980: *The Spartans* (London).

Fornara, C. W. (ed.) – 1977: *Archaic Times to the End of the Peloponnesian War* (Cambridge).

Forrer, E. – 1924: 'Vorhomerische Griechen in den Keilschrifttexten von Bogazköi' in *MDOG* 63.

French, E. – 2002: *Mycenae: Agamemnon's Capital* (Stroud).

Furumark, A. – 1980: 'The Thera Catastrophe – Consequences for European Civilization' in *Thera and the Aegean World* II.

G

Gamkrelidze, T. V. & **Ivanov, V. V.** – 1984: *Indoeuropeysky Yazyk i Indoeuropeytsy* (Tbilisi).

Garasanin, M. – 1982: 'The Early Iron Age in the Central Balkan Area, *c.* 1000-750 BC' in J. Boardman *et al.* (eds): *CAH* III:1 (Cambridge).

Gardiner, A. H. – 1909: *Admonitions of an Egyptian Sage* (Leipzig).

Gardiner, A. H. – 1959: *The Royal Canon of Turin* (Oxford).

Gardiner, A. H. – 1961: *Egypt of the Pharaohs* (London).

Garstang, J. & **Garstang, J. B. E.** – 1940: *The Story of Jericho* (London).

Garstang, J. & **Gurney, O.** – 1959: *The Geography of the Hittite Empire* (London).

Gimbutas, M. – 1997: *The Kurgan Culture and the Indo-Europeanisation of Europe: Selected Articles from 1952 to 1993*, (eds.) M. R. Dexter & K. Jones-Bley (Washington).

Gittlen, B. M. – 1981: 'The Cultural and Chronological Implications of the Cypro-Palestinian Trade During the Late Bronze Age' in *BASOR* 241.

Godart, L. & **Sacconi, A.** – 1999: 'La Géographie des États mycéniens', in *Académie des Inscriptions et Belles-Lettres. Comptes Rendus des Séances de l'Année*, April-June (published 2001), (Paris).

Godley, A. D. (trans.) – 1975: *Herodotus* Book I (Loeb Classical Library, Mass.).

Goedicke, H. – 1984: 'The Canaanite Illness' in *SAK* 11.

Goedicke, H. – 1986: 'The End of the Hyksos in Egypt' in L. H. Lesko (ed.): *Egyptological Studies in Honor of Richard A. Parker* (London).

Gordon Childe, V. – 1926: *The Aryans* (New York).

Grant, M. – 1969: *The Ancient Mediterranean* (New York).

Grant, M. – 1987: *The Rise of the Greeks* (London).

Grant, M. – 1989: *Myths of the Greeks and Romans* (London).

Graves, R. – 1960: *The Greek Myths*, Vols. 1 & 2 (London).

Green, A. R. – 1983: 'David's Relations with Hiram: Biblical and Josephan Evidence for Tyrian Chronology' in C. L. Myers & M. O'Connor: *The Word of the Lord Shall Go Forth – Essays in Honor of David Noel Freedman in Celebration of his Sixtieth Birthday* (Winona Lake).

Green, P. – 1973: *A Concise History of Ancient Greece to the Close of the Classical Era* (London).

Grene, D. (trans.) – 1987: *The History: Herodotus* (Chicago).

Grene, D. & **Lattimore, R.** (eds.) – 1954: *Sophocles I: Oedipus the King, Oedipus at Colonus, Antigone* (Washington).

Griffith, F. L. – 1898: *Hieratic Papyri from Kahun and Gurob*, 2 vols (London).

Gurney, O. R. – 1952: *The Hittites* (London).

Gurney, O. R. – 1973: 'Anatolia *c.* 1600-1380 BC' in I. E. S. Edwards *et al.* (eds): *CAH* II:1 (Cambridge).

Güterbock, H. G. – 1986: 'Troy in the Hittite Texts' in Mellink, M. J. (ed): *Troy and the Trojan War: A Symposium Held at Bryn Mawr College, October 1984.*

Güterbock, H. G. – 1990: 'Wer war Tawagalawa?' in *Orientalia* 59.

H

Haider, P. W. – 1988: *Griechenland-Nordafrika: Ihre Beziehungen zwischen 1600 und 600 v. Chr.* (Darmstadt).

Hainsworth, J. B. – 1982: 'The Greek Language and the Historical Dialects' in J. Boardman *et al.* (eds): *CAH* III:1 (Cambridge).

Hallager, E. – 1977: *The Mycenaean Palace of Knossos* (Stockholm).

Hallo, W. W. & **Simpson, W. K.** – 1971: 'Caravaneers and Conquerors of the Northland' in *The Ancient Near East* (London).

Hammond, N. G. L. – 1959: *A History of Greece to 322 BC* (Oxford).

Hammond, N. G. L. – 1982: 'Illyris, Epirus and Macedonia in the Early Iron Age' in J. Boardman *et al.* (eds): *CAH* III:1 (Cambridge).

Hammond, N. G. L. – 1982: 'The Peloponnese' in J. Boardman *et al.* (eds): *CAH* III:1 (Cambridge).

Hampe, R. & **Simon, E.** – 1981: *The Birth of Greek Art: From the Mycenaean to the Archaic Period* (New York).

Hankey, V. – 1995: 'Stirrup Jars at el-Amarna' in W. V. Davies & L. Schofield (eds.): *EAL* (London).

Hankey, V. & **Tufnell, O.** – 1973: 'The Tomb of Maket and Its Mycenaean Import' in *ABSA* 68.

Hankey, V. & **Warren, P.** – 1989: *Aegean Bronze Age Chronology* (Bristol).

Harden, D. – 1971: *The Phoenicians* (Harmondsworth).

Harding, A. F. & **Tait, W. J.** – 1989: 'The beginning of the end: progress and prospects in Old World chronology' in *Antiquity* 63.

Hawkins, J. D. – 1974: 'Assyrians and Hittites' in *Iraq* 36.

Hawkins, J. D. – 1982: 'The Neo-Hittite States in Syria and Anatolia' in J. Boardman *et al.* (eds): *CAH* III:1 (Cambridge).

Hawkins, J. D. & **Easton, D. F.** – 1996: 'A Hieroglyphic Seal from Troia' in *ST* 6.

Hayes, W. C. – 1955: *A Papyrus of the Late Middle Kingdom in the Brooklyn Museum* (Brooklyn).

Hayes, W. C. – 1973: 'Egypt: From the Death of Ammenemes III to Seqenenre II' in I. E. S. Edwards *et al.* (eds.): *CAH* II:1 (Cambridge).

Helck, H. W. – 1962: *Die Beziehungen Ägyptens zu Vorderasien im 3. und 2. Jahrtausend v. Chr.* (Wiesbaden).

Helck, H. W. – 1955: 'Die liegende und geflügelte weibliche Sphinx des Neuen Reiches' in *MIO* 3.

Helck, H. W. – 1979: *Die Beziehungen Ägyptens und Vorderasiens zur Ägäis bis ins 7. Jahrhundert v. Chr.* (Darmstadt).

Hermes, G. – 1935: 'Das gezähmte Pferd im neolithischen frühbronzezeitlichen Europa?' in *Anthropus* 30.

Hermes, G. – 1937: 'Das zug des

gezähmten Pferdes durch Europa' in *Anthropus* 32.

Higgins, R. – 1970: *The Greek Bronze Age* (London).

Hoffmeier, J. K. – 1989: 'Reconsidering Egypt's Part in the Termination of the Middle Bronze Age in Palestine' in *Levant* 21.

Hoffner, H. A. Jr., – 1982: 'The Milawata Letter Augmented and Reinterpreted' in *AO* 19.

Hölkeskamp, K.-J. – 2000: 'Von Palast zur Polis – die griechische Frühgeschichte als Epoche' in H.-J. Gehrke and H. Schneider (eds.): *Geschichte des Antike: Ein Studienbuch* (Stuttgart and Weimar).

Holloway, R. R. – 1994: *The Archaeology of Early Rome and Latium* (London).

Homer (trans. W. Shewring) – 1980: *The Odyssey* (Oxford).

Homer (trans. R. Fitzgerald) – 1984: *The Iliad* (Oxford).

Hood, S. – 1971: *The Minoans: Crete in the Bronze Age* (London).

Hooker, J. T. – 1976: *Mycenaean Greece* (London).

Houwink ten Cate, P. H. – 1983-4: 'Sidelights on the Ahhiyawa Question from Hittite Vassal and Royal Correspondence' in *Jaarbericht van het Vooraziatisch-Egyptisch Genootschap 'Ex Oriente Lux'* 28.

I

Iakovidis, S. – 1977: *The Present State of Research at the Citadel of Mycenae* (London,)

Isserlin, B. S. J. – 1982: 'The Earliest Alphabetic Writing' in J. Boardman *et al.* (eds): *CAH* III:1 (Cambridge).

J

Jablonka, P. – 1994: 'Ein Verteidigungsgraben in der Unterstadt von Troia VI: Grabungsbericht 1993' in *ST* 4.

James, P. *et al.* – 1991: *Centuries of Darkness* (London).

James, P. *et al.* – 1987: 'Bronze to

Iron Age Chronology in the Old World: Time for a Re-assessment?' in *JACF* 1.

Jánosi, P. – 1991: 'The Queens Ahhotep I & II and Egypt's Foreign Relations' in *JACF* 5.

Jeffery, L. H. – 1982: 'Greek Alphabet Writing' in J. Boardman *et al.* (eds): *CAH* III:1 (Cambridge).

Jidejian, N. – 1971: *Byblos Through the Ages* (Beirut).

Jones, H. L. (trans.) – 1932: *Strabo: Geography* (Cambridge, Mass.).

K

von Kamptz, H. – 1982: *Homerische Personennamen* (Göttingen).

Keenan, D. J. – 2003: 'Volcanic ash retrieved from the GRIP ice core is not from Thera' in *Geochemistry, Geophysics, Geosystems* (*Electronic Journal of the Earth Sciences*) 4, no. 11 (15th Nov.).

Keller, W. – 1970: *The Etruscans: A journey into history and archaeology in search of a great lost civilization* (London).

Kemp, B. J. – 1983: 'The Second Intermediate Period in Egypt' in B. G. Trigger *et. al.*: *Ancient Egypt: A Social History* (Cambridge).

Kempinski, A. – 1974: 'Tell el-'Ajjul – Beth-Aglayim or Sharuhen?' in *IEJ* 24.

Kempinski, A. – 1983: *Syrien und Palastina (Kanaan) in der letzten Phase der mittelbronze IIB-Zeit* (1650-1570 V.Chr.) (Wiesbaden).

Kempinski, A. – 1992: 'The Middle Bronze Age' in A. Ben-Tor (ed.): *The Archaeology of Ancient Israel* (New Haven).

Kenyon, K. M. – 1957: 'Israelite Pottery: Stratified Groups' in J. W. Crowfoot *et al.*: *The Objects from Samaria* (London).

Kenyon, K. M. – 1960: *Excavations at Jericho*, Vol. I (London,).

Kenyon, K. M. – 1965: *Excavations at Jericho*, Vol. II (London).

Kenyon, K. M. – 1970: *Archaeology of the Holy Land* (London).

Kenyon, K. M. – 1973: 'Palestine in the Time of the Eighteenth Dynasty' in I. E. S. Edwards *et al.* (eds.): *CAH* II:1(Cambridge).

Kenyon, K. M. – 1983: 'Palestine in the Middle Bronze Age' in I. E. S. Edwards *et al.* (eds.):*CAH* II:1 (Cambridge).

Kerényi, C. – 1959: *The Heroes of the Greeks* (London).

King, A. – 1982: *Archaeology of the Roman Empire* (London).

Kirk, G. S. – 1975: 'The Homeric Poems as History' in I. E. S. Edwards *et al.* (eds): *CAH* II:2B (Cambridge).

Kirkbride, D. – 1965: 'Appendix E: Scarabs' in K. M. Kenyon: *Excavations at Jericho*, Vol. II (London).

Kitchen, K. A. – 1967: 'Byblos, Egypt and Mari in the Early Second Millennium BC' in *Orientalia* 36.

Kitchen, K. A. – 1973: 'The Philistines' in D. J. Wiseman (ed.): *Peoples of Old Testament Times* (London).

Kitchen, K. A. – 1987: 'The Basics of Egyptian Chronology in Relation to the Bronze Age' in *High Middle or Low: Acts of an International Colloquium on Absolute Chronology Held at the University of Gothenburg 20th-22nd August 1987*, Part 1.

Korfmann, M. – 1996: 'TROIA – Ausgrabungen 1995' in *ST* 6.

Korfmann, M. – 1997: 'TROIA – Ausgrabungen 1996' in *ST* 7.

Korfmann, M. – 1998: 'Troia, an Ancient Anatolian Palatial and Trading Center: Archaeological Evidence for the Period of Troia VI/ VII' in *The Classical World* 91.

Kotter, W. R. – 1986: 'The Stratigraphic and Chronological Context' in *Spatial Aspects of the Urban Development of Palestine in the Middle Bronze Age* (Arizona).

Krauss, R. – 1985: *Sothis- und Monddaten, Studien zur astronomischen und technischen Chronologie Alt Ägyptens* (Hildesheim).

Kretschmer, P. – 1924: 'Alaksandus, König von Vilusa' in *Glotta* 13.

Kühnert-Eggebrecht, E. – 1969: 'Die Axt als Waffe und Werkzeug im alten Ägypten' in *MAS* 15.

Kuhrt, A. – 1995: *The Ancient Near East* c. *3000-330 BC* I (London).

Kupper, J.-R. – 1973: 'Northern Mesopotamia and Syria' in I. E. S. Edwards *et al.* (eds): *CAH* II:1 (Cambridge).

L

Labib, P. H. – 1937: *Die Herrschaft der Hyksos in Ägypten und ihr Sturz* (Glückstadt).

Lacy, A. D. – 1967: *Greek Pottery in the Bronze Age* (London).

Langdon, S. & **Fotheringham, J. K.** – 1928: *The Venus Tablets of Ammizaduga* (London).

Larsen, M. T. – 1976: *The Old Assyrian City-state and Its Colonies* (Copenhagen).

Lacy, A. D. – 1967: *Greek Pottery in the Bronze Age* (London).

Lappin, D. – 2002: 'The Decline and Fall of Sothic Dating: El-Lahun Lunar Texts and Egyptian Astronomical Texts' in *JACF* 9.

Latacz, J. – 1991: 'Hauptfunktionen des antiken Epos in Antike und Moderne' in *Der altsprachliche Unterrricht* 34/3.

Latacz, J. – 2001: *Troia – Wilios – Wilusa. Drei Namen für ein Territorium* (Basel).

Latacz, J. – 2004: *Troy and Homer: Towards a Solution of an Old Mystery* (Oxford, 2004).

Leclant, J. & **Yoyotte, J.** – 1954: 'Les Obelisques de Tanis' in *Kemi* 14.

Lehmann, G. A. – 1996: 'Umbrüche und Zäsuren im östlichen Mittelmeerraum und Vorderasien zur Zeit der "Seevölker"-Invasionen um und nach 1200 v. Chr. Neue Quellenzeugnisse und Befunde' in *HZ* 262.

Lehmann, J. (trans. J. M. Brownjohn) – 1977: *The Hittites:*

People of a Thousand Gods (London).

Leick, G. – 1999: *Who's Who in the Ancient Near East* (London).

Levi, P. – 1980: *Atlas of the Greek World* (Oxford).

Lewy, H. – 1980: 'Anatolia in the Old Assyrian Period' in I. E. S. Edwards *et al.* (eds): *CAH* I:2A (Cambridge).

Lewy, H. – 1980: 'Assyria *c.* 2600-1816 B.C.' in I. E. S. Edwards *et al.* (eds): *CAH* I:2A (Cambridge).

Lichtheim, M. – 1973: *Ancient Egyptian Literature* I (London).

Lichtheim, M. – 1976: *Ancient Egyptian Literature* II (London).

Littleton, C. S. (ed.) – 2002: *Mythology: The Illustrated Anthology of World Myth and Storytelling* (London).

Lorimer, H. L. – 1950: *Homer and the Monuments* (London).

Loud, G. – 1948: *Megiddo* II, Text (Chicago).

Luce, J. V. – 1969: *The End of Atlantis* (London).

Luce, J. V. – 1975: *Homer and the Heroic Age* (London).

Luckenbill, D. D. (ed.) – 1926: *Ancient Records of Assyria and Babylonia* I (Chicago).

M

Macalister, R. A. S. – 1913: *The Philistines: Their History and Civilization* (reprinted 1965, Chicago).

Macqueen, J. G. – 1975: *The Hittites and their Contemporaries in Asia Minor* (London).

Maguire, L. C. – 1995: 'Tell el-Daba: The Cypriot Connection' in W. V. Davies & L. Schofield: *EAL* (London).

Malek, J. – 1982: 'The Original Version of the Royal Canon of Turin' in *JEA* 68.

Mallory, J. P. – 1989: *In Search of the Indo-Europeans: Language, Archaeology and Myth* (London).

Mallowan, M. – 1972: 'Carchemish: Reflections on the Chronology of the Sculpture' in *AS* 22.

Manning, S. W. – 1999: *A Test of Time: The Volcano of Thera and the Chronology and History of the Aegean and East Mediterranean in the Mid Second Millennium BC* (Oxford).

Manning, S. W. – 1990: 'The Eruption of Thera: Date and Implications' in *Thera and the Aegean World* III:3.

Marinatos, N. – 1994: 'The "Export" Significance of Minoan Bull Hunting and Bull Leaping Scenes' in *ÄL* IV (Vienna).

Markoe, G. E. – 2000: *Phoenicians* (London).

Matyszak, P. – 2003: *Chronicle of the Roman Republic* (London).

McDonald, W. A. – 1967: *The Discovery of Homeric Greece* (London).

Mellaart, J. – 1980: 'Anatolia *c.* 2300-1750 B.C.' in I. E. S. Edwards *et al.* (eds): *CAH* I:2A (Cambridge).

Mellersh, H. E. L. – 1967: *Minoan Crete* (London).

Merrillees, R. S. – 2002: 'The Relative and Absolute Chronology of the Cypriote White Painted Pendent Line Style' in *BASOR* 326.

Michael, H. N. – 1980: 'Radiocarbon Dates from the Site of Akrotiri, Thera, 1967-1977' in *Thera and the Aegean World* II.

Mitchell, F. – 1956: 'Herodotus' Use of Genealogical Chronology' in *The Phoenix* 10.

Mitchell, T. C. – 1982: 'Cherethites' and 'Philistines, Philistia' in J. D. Douglas *et al.* (eds.): *New Bible Dictionary* (Leicester).

Mitchell, W. A. – 1989: 'Ancient Astronomical Observations and Near Eastern Chronology' in *JACF* 3.

Money, J. H. – 1973: 'The Destruction of Akrotiri' in *Antiquity* 47.

Montet, P. – 1928: *Byblos et l'Égypte* (Paris).

Montet, P. – 1957: *Géographie de l'Égypte ancienne*, 2 vols (Paris).

Montet, P. – 1928: 'Notes et Documents pour servir a l'Histoire des Relations entre l'Ancienne Égypte et la Syrie' in *Kemi* I.

Morgan, L. – 1995: 'Minoan Painting and Egypt: The Case of Tell el-Daba' in W. V. Davies & L. Schofield: *EAL* (London).
Morrison, M. A. & **Owen, D. I.** (eds.) – 1981: *Nuzi and the Hurrians* (Winona Lake).
Morrison, M. A. – 1983: 'The Jacob and Laban Narrative in Light of Near Eastern Sources' in *BA* 46:3.
Morwood, J. (trans.) – 2002: *Euripides: The Trojan Women and Other Plays* (Oxford).
Murnane, W. J. – 1980: *United With Eternity: A Concise Guide to the Monuments of Medinet Habu* (Chicago).
Murray, O. – 1980: *Early Greece* (London).

N

Na'aman, N. – 1980: 'The Ishtar Temple at Alalakh' in *JNES* 39.
Neumann, G. – 1999: 'Wie haben die Troer in 13. Jahrhundert gesprochen' in *WJA* 23.
Newgrosh, B. – 1988: 'Scientific Dating Methods and Absolute Chronology' in *JACF* 2.
Newgrosh, B. – 1989: 'Still at the Crossroads' in *JACF* 3.
Newgrosh, B. – 1999: 'The Chronology of Ancient Assyria Reassessed' in *JACF* 8.
Niemeier, W.-D. – 1982: 'Mycenaean Knossos and the Age of Linear B' in *SMEA* 23.
Niemeier, W.-D. – 1999: 'Mycenaeans and Hittites in War in Western Asia Minor' in *Aegaeum* 19.
Nilsson, M. P. – 1993: *Homer and Mycenae* (London).

O

Oldfather, C. H. (trans.) – 1933: *Diodorus Siculus, Books I-II* (Cambridge, Mass.).
Oliva, P. – 1981: *The Birth of Greek Civilization* (London).
Ogilvie, R. M. – 1960: 'Introduction' to *Livy: The Early History of Rome: Books I-V of The History of Rome from its Foundations* (London).

P

Page, D. – 1959: *History and the Homeric Iliad* (Berkeley).
Page, D. – 1959: 'The Historical Sack of Troy' in *Antiquity* 33.
Page, D. – 1978: 'On the Relation Between the Thera Eruption and the Desolation of Eastern Crete c. 1450 BC' in C. Doumas (ed.): *Thera and the Aegean World* I.
Palmer, L. R. – 1963: *On the Knossos Tablets: The Find-Places of the Knossos Tablets* (Oxford).
Pausanias (trans. P. Levi) – 1971: *Guide to Greece, Volume 1: Central Greece* (London).
Pausanias (trans. P. Levi) – 1971: *Guide to Greece, Volume 2: Southern Greece* (London).
Petrie, W. M. F. – 1890: 'The Egyptian Bases of Greek History' in *JHS* XI, (October).
Petrie, W. M. F. – 1892: in *The Academy* (25 June).
Petrie, W. M. F. – 1894: *Tell el-Amarna* (London).
Petrie, W. M. F. – 1939: *The Making of Egypt* (London).
Pictet, A. – 1859: *Essai de paléontologie linguistique* (Paris).
Pomerance, L. – 1978: 'Improbability of a Theran Collapse During the New Kingdom, 1503-1447 BC' in *Thera and the Aegean World* I.
Posener, G. – 1957: 'Les Asiatiques en Égypte sous les XIIe et XIIIe dynasties' in *Syria* 34.
Porter, B. – 2005: 'Thera and the End of the Middle Bronze Age' in *JACF* 10.
Pritchard, J. B. (ed) – 1969: *Ancient Near Eastern Texts Relating to the Old Testament* (3rd edition) (Princeton).

Q

Quagliati, Q. – 1900: 'Taranto: relazione degli scavi archeologici che si eseguirono nel 1899 in un abitato terramaricolo, allo Scoglio del Tonno, presso la citta' in *Notizie degli Scavi di Antichita.*

BIBLIOGRAPHY

R

Rackham, O. – 1978: 'The Flora and Vegetation of Thera and Crete before and after the Great Eruption' in C. Doumas (ed.): *Thera and the Aegean World* I.

Redford, D. B. – 1967: *History and Chronology of the Eighteenth Dynasty of Egypt* (Toronto).

Redford, D. B. – 1970: 'The Hyksos Invasion in History and Tradition' in *Orientalia* 39.

Redford, D. B. – 1979: 'A Gate Inscription from Karnak and Egyptian Involvement in Western Asia during the Early 18th Dynasty' in *JAOS* 99.

Redford, D. B. – 1992: *Egypt, Canaan, and Israel in Ancient Times* (New Jersey).

Reinach, S. – 1893: *Le Mirage Oriental* (Paris).

Renfrew, C. – 1987: *Archaeology and Language: The Puzzle of the Indo-European Origins* (London).

Rice, M. – 1998: *The Power of the Bull* (London).

Rohl, D. M. – 1995: *A Test of Time: The Bible – From Myth to History* (London).

Rohl, D. M. – 1998: *Legend: The Genesis of Civilisation* (London).

Rohl, D. M. – 2002: *The Lost Testament: From Eden to Exile: The Five-Thousand-Year History of the People of the Bible* (London).

Rose, H. J. – 1964: *A Handbook of Greek Mythology* (London).

Ryholt, K. S. B. – 1997: *The Political Situation in Egypt During the Second Intermediate Period* (Copenhagen).

S

Saghieh, M. – 1983: *Byblos in the Third Millennium: A Reconstruction of the Stratigraphy and a Study of the Cultural Connections* (Warminster).

Sandars, N. K. – 1978: *The Sea Peoples: Warriors of the Ancient Mediterranean* (London).

Save-Soderbergh, T. – 1951: 'The Hyksos Rule in Egypt' in *JEA* 37.

Schiering, W. – 1980: 'The Eruption of the Volcano on Thera and the Destructions on Crete' in *Thera and the Aegean World* II.

Schliemann, H. – 1976: *Ilios: The City and Country of the Trojans* (reprint, New York).

Schliemann, H. – 1976: *Tiryns: The Prehistoric Palace of the Kings of Tiryns* (reprint, New York).

Schliemann, H. – 1976: *Troja: Results of the latest researches and discoveries on the site of Homer's Troy* (reprint, New York).

Schuchhardt, C. – 1979: *Schliemann's Discoveries of the Ancient World* (New York).

de Selincourt, A. (trans.) – 1960: *Livy: The Early History of Rome: Books I–V* (London).

Shea, W. – 1979: 'The Conquest of Sharuhen and Megiddo Reconsidered' in *IEJ* 29.

Smith, S. – 1940: *Alalakh and Chronology* (London).

Snodgrass, A. M. – 1982: 'Central Greece and Thessaly' in J. Boardman *et al.* (eds): *CAH* III:1 (Cambridge).

Snodgrass, A. M. – 2000: *The Dark Age of Greece: An Archaeological Survey of the Eleventh to Eighth Centuries BC* (Edinburgh).

Starke, F. – 1997: 'Troia im Kontext des historisch-politischen und sprachlichen Umfeldes Kleinasiens im 2. Jahrtausend' in *ST* 7.

Stewart, J. R. – 1974: *Tell el-Ajjul: The Middle Bronze Age Remains* (Goeteborg).

Strabo, *Geographika*, Book V.

Strange, J. – 1980: *Caphtor/Keftiu: A New Investigation* (Leiden).

Strong, D. – 1968: *The Early Etruscans* (London).

Stubbings, F. H. – 1973: 'The Rise of Mycenaean Civilization' in I. E. S. Edwards *et al.* (eds): *CAH* II:1 (Cambridge).

Stubbings, F. H. – 1975: 'The Recession of Mycenaean Civilization, II: The Trojan War' in I. E. S. Edwards *et al.* (eds.): *CAH* II:2 (Cambridge).

T

Televantou, C. A. – 1990: 'New Light on the West House Wall-Paintings' in *Thera and the Aegean World* III:1.

Thackeray, H. St. J. & Marcus, R. (trans.) – 1934: *Josephus: Jewish Antiquities, Book V-VIII* (Cambridge, Mass.).

Thucydides: *History of the Peloponnesian War*, Book I.

Torr, C. – 1896 & 1988: *Memphis and Mycenae: An Examination of Egyptian Chronology and its Application to the Early History of Greece* (Cambridge); 2nd edition (eds. D. Rohl & M. Durkin, Whitstable).

Traill, D. – 1995: *Schliemann of Troy: Treasure and Deceit* (London).

Troy, L. – 1979: 'Ahhotep – A Source Evaluation' in *GM* 35.

Tubb, J. N. – 1995: 'An Aegean Presence in Egypto-Canaan' in W. V. Davies & L. Schofield: *EAL* (London).

Tubb, J. N. – 2004: 'Hyksos Origins: A Grave Issue', presented at the BM colloquium 'The Second Intermediate Period (13th to 17th Dynasties): Current Research and Future Prospects' (June).

Tufnell, O. – 1984: *Studies on Scarab Seals, Volume Two: Scarab Seals and their Contribution to History in the Early Second Millennium BC*, Parts 1 & 2 (Warminster).

V

Van Seters, J. – 1966: *The Hyksos: A New Investigation* (New Haven).

Vandersleyen, C. – 1971: *Les Guerres d'Amosis: Fondateur de la XVIIIe Dynastie* (Brussels).

Veenhof, K. R. – 1972: *Aspects of Old Assyrian Trade and its Terminology* (Leiden).

Velikovsky, I. – 1952: *Ages in Chaos* (London).

Vermeule, E. – 1964: *Greece in the Bronze Age* (Chicago).

W

Wace, A. J. B. – 1949: *Mycenae: An Archaeological History and Guide* (New Jersey).

Waddell, W. G. – 1971: *Manetho* (London).

Walberg, G. – 1991: 'A Gold Pendant from Tell el-Daba' in M. Bietak (ed.): *ÄL* II (Vienna).

Walberg, G. – 1991: 'The Finds at Tell el-Daba and the Middle Minoan Chronology' in M. Bietak (ed.): *ÄL* II (Vienna).

Ward, A. G. – 1970: *The Quest for Theseus* (London).

Warner, R. (trans.) – 1954: *Thucydides: History of the Peloponnesian War* (London).

Warren, P. M. – 1987: 'Absolute Dating of the Aegean Late Bronze Age' in *Archaeometry* 29:2.

Warren, P. M. – 1995: 'Minoan Crete and Pharaonic Egypt' in W. V. Davies & L. Schofield (eds.): *EAL* (London).

Warren, P. M. – 1984 'Absolute dating of the Bronze Age Eruption of Thera (Santorini)' in *Nature* 308.

Weinstein, J. M. – 1981: 'The Egyptian Empire in Palestine: A Reassessment' in *BASOR* 241.

Weinstein, J. M. – 1995: 'Reflections on the Chronology of Tell el-Daba' in W. V. Davies & L. Schofield (eds.): *EAL* (London).

Whiston, W. (trans.) – 1981: *Josephus* (London).

Wilhelm, G. – 1945: *The Hurrians* (Warminster).

Willcock, M. M. – 1976: *A Companion to the Iliad: Based on the Translation by Richmond Lattimore* (Chicago).

Willis, R. (ed.) – 1993: *World Mythology* (London).

Wilson, J. A. – 1969: 'Egyptian Historical Texts' and 'Egyptian Hymns and Prayers' in J. B. Pritchard (ed.): *ANET* (Princeton).

Winlock, H. E. – 1947: *The Rise and Fall of the Middle Kingdom in Thebes* (New York).

BIBLIOGRAPHY

Wood, M. – 1985: *In Search of the Trojan War* (London).

Woolley, L. – 1955: *Alalakh: An Account of the Excavations at Tell Atchana* (Oxford).

Wreszinski, W. – 1935: Atlas zur altägyptischen kulturgeschichte II (Leipzig).

Wunderlich, H. G. (trans. R. Winston) – 1983: *The Secret of Crete:* *A controversial account of archaeological detection* (Athens).

Z

Zielinski, G. A. & Germani, M. S. – 1998: 'New Ice-core Evidence Challenges the 1620s BC Age for the Santorini (Minoan) Eruption' in *JAS* 25.

ABBREVIATIONS

ABSA: Annual of the British School in Athens
AJA: American Journal of Archaeology
ÄL: Ägypten und Levante
ANET: Ancient Near Eastern Texts: Relating to the Old Testament
AO: Archiv für Orientforschung
AS: Anatolian Studies
BA: Biblical Archaeologist
BAR: Biblical Archaeology Review
BASOR: Bulletin of the American School of Oriental Studies
CAH: The Cambridge Ancient History
C & C: Chronology and Catastrophism (SIS)
EA: Egyptian Archaeology (EES)
EAL: Egypt, the Aegean and the Levant: Interconnections in the Second Millennium BC
EES: Egypt Exploration Society
GM: Göttinger Miszellen
HZ: Historische Zeitschrift
IEJ: Israel Exploration Journal
ISIS: Institute for the Study of Interdisciplinary Sciences
JACF: Journal of the Ancient Chronology Forum (ISIS)
JAOS: Journal of the American Oriental Society
JAS: Journal of Archaeological Sciences
JEA: Journal of Egyptian Archaeology (EES)
JHS: Journal of Hellenic Studies
JNES: Journal of Near Eastern Studies
JSSEA: Journal of the Society for the Study of Egyptian Antiquities
MAS: Münchner Ägyptologische Studien
MIO: Mitteilungen des Institut für Orientforschung
MDOG: Mitteilungen der Deutschen Orient-Gesellschaft
SAK: Studien zur Altägyptischen Kultur
SIS: Society for Interdisciplinary Studies
SMEA: Studi Micenei ed Egeo-Anatolici
ST: Studia Troica
WJA: Würzburger Jahrbücher für die Altertumswissenschaft

NOTES AND REFERENCES

Preface

1 N. Coldstream, 1977.
2 V. Hankey & P. Warren, 1989.
3 M. Bietak, 1996, p. 36.

Introduction

1 A. F. Harding & W. J. Tait, 1989, p. 147.
2 Herodotus, *Historia*, Book II:151-54.
3 W. M. F. Petrie, 1892, p. 621.
4 *Classical Review* VI (March 1892), pp. 127-31.
5 *The Academy* (14 May to 12 November 1892).
6 W. M. F. Petrie, 1892, p. 178.
7 C. Torr, 1892, p. 117.
8 W. M. F. Petrie, 1894, p. 17.
9 *Carnarvon Tablet*, trans. in J. B. Pritchard, 1969, p. 232.
10 H. E. L. Mellersh, 1967, p. 131.
11 J. Latacz, 2004, pp. 167-68.
12 In *A Test of Time, Volume One, The Bible – From Myth to History*, this date was given as *c*. 1192 BC. Further research undertaken since 1995 (especially involving astronomical dating) has required a lowering of this date by eleven years to *c*. 1181 BC.
13 A quote from Albert Szent-Gyoergi, Hungarian physiologist and Nobel Laureate in Medicine.

Chapter One

1 K. M. Kenyon, 1960, p. 479: 'The shaft had a uniform fill of powdery earth, *huwwar* chips and stones. There were MB sherds throughout the fill, indicating several stages of MB use. The blocking-stone of the doorway into the chamber was in place, packed round with smaller stones and sherds. At the level of the top of the door-blocking, were five vessels, two of them intact. Storage jar 1 was not only intact, but had the skin formed by the evaporating contents still in position. It therefore seems probable that this vessel belongs to the final use of the tomb, being put in the shaft because there was not room in the chamber; there do not in fact appear to have been any storage jars inside the chamber.'
2 *Ibid.*, p. 481: 'Within the tomb there was unfortunately a very heavy roof-fall, completely obliterating everything in the middle of the chamber. From what survives, however, it is clear that there was a final multiple simultaneous burial, for which earlier burials were swept on one side, resembling tombs G1 and H22. On the right-hand side bodies C1, B1, A1 and V lie side by side with legs to the centre; at the back V (*sic* according to the plan actually U – DR) and on the left-hand side M and A may also represent intact final burials. In addition to these, twenty-nine other bodies are represented by skulls. … The finds do not, however, suggest a long interval in time, for all seem to fall within the period of Group V.'
3 *Ibid.*, pp. 267-68.
4 D. Kirkbride, 1965 in K. M. Kenyon, Vol. II, p. 583: 'This scarab was found in Layer 1 of H 13, a tomb that was largely destroyed by roof-fall. Nevertheless, all the objects recovered lay within Group V, and the final burials, to one of which this scarab belonged, were of the multiple, simultaneous type; the result of some sudden disaster.'
5 K. M. Kenyon, 1960, p. 266: 'Many of the bodies had one or more scarabs, worn on the finger (though the bronze ring has usually decayed), round the wrist or round the neck; sometimes a scarab seems to have been suspended from a toggle pin.'
6 O. Tufnell, 1984, p. 81: 'Miss Kirkbride allocates the scarab

naming Sheshi, no. 3281 in the royal-name series (= no. 1773), to the top-most layer (1) (of Tomb H13), and to one of the final burials of the multiple simultaneous type which were considered the result of some sudden disaster. On all accounts the scarab would fit into the final stage of the tomb's use, and it probably marks the date of closure of the cemetery. ... the evidence at present suggests that the cemeteries at Jericho and Fara were closed at the same time and did not continue in use beyond the reign of ... Mayebre Sheshi.'

7   P. Bienkowski, 1990, pp. 45-46 & 69.

8   K. A. Kitchen, 1987, Part 1, p. 38: '... the 21-year reign of the founder of the 22nd Dynasty, Shoshenk I, can be set at *c.* 945-924 BC, thanks (i) to his synchronism with the detailed chronology of Judah and Israel, itself linked closely to a firm Assyrian chronology ... and (ii) to the series of known regnal years of his successors, which fill up the interval 924-716/712 BC almost completely.'

9   J. Bimson, 1992, pp. 19-22; D. Rohl, 1995, pp. 120-28.

10 I. Finkelstein & N. A. Silberman, 2001, p. 118.

11 *Ibid.*, p. 79.

12 P. Bienkowski, 1986, pp. 124-25: 'It appears extremely unlikely that there are any town walls at Jericho which could date to the Late Bronze Age. The actual area of occupation in this period seems to have been limited to the area around the Middle Building. ... Furthermore, only 8 out of 76 known LBA settlements in the whole of Canaan were fortified, and all but one of these were larger than one hectare. The vast majority of settlements were not fortified. It would seem, therefore, that a tiny unwalled Jericho fits the pattern in LB Canaan extremely well'; and p. 156: 'The evidence for Late Bronze

Age settlement at Jericho consists of three tombs originally used in the Middle Bronze Age and a small area of occupation on the tell, dated *c.* 1425-1275 BC. The settlement was unwalled and probably did not extend much further than the area of the "Middle Building". It seems to have been abandoned in early LB IIB. There is no archaeological evidence of fortifications or for a destruction.'

13 I. Finkelstein & N. A. Silberman, *op. cit.* [10], p. 77.

14 *Ibid.*, p. 73.

15 M. Bietak, 1996, p. 35.

16 M. Bietak, 1979, p. 295.

17 P. Bienkowski, *op. cit.* [12], p. 127.

18 A. H. Gardiner, 1909, pp. 3 & 18.

19 M. Lichtheim, 1973, p. 149.

20 J. van Seters, 1966, pp. 103-20.

21 *Ibid.*, p. 106.

22 Translation based on Lichtheim, *op. cit.* [19], pp. 149-63.

23 J. van Seters, *op. cit.* [20], p. 107.

24 H. E. Winlock, 1947, p. 101.

25 J. van Seters, *op. cit.* [20], pp. 108-09.

26 *Ibid.*, p. 115.

27 I. Velikovsky, 1976, pp. 25-39.

28 K. M. Kenyon, *op. cit.* [1], p. 267.

Chapter Two

1   K. S. B. Ryholt, 1997, pp. 40-50.

2   *Ibid,* p. 46.

3   *Ibid,* p. 43.

4   *Ibid,* pp. 252-54.

5   *Ibid,* p. 53.

6   *Ibid,* p. 51.

7   *Ibid,* p. 57.

8   M. Bietak, 1991a, p. 25.

9   This break occurs on the main Tell A and not in Area F where the occupation continues with Egyptian-style houses indicating an Egyptian presence there after the Asiatics of Tell A abandoned the site at the end of Stratum G.

10 Manetho Fr. 42 as quoted in Josephus: *Contra Apionem,* Book I:14.

11 M. Bietak, 1996, p. 36.

12 *Ibid,* p. 40.

13 M. Bietak, *op. cit.* [8], p. 25.

14 *Ibid.*, p. 39.

15 Manetho Fr. 42 as quoted in Josephus: *Contra Apionem,* Book I:14.

16 I am following Ryholt's new construction of the papyrus fragments here, though retaining Gardiner's original column numbering because I am not convinced that an extra column needs to be added to the beginning of the Turin Canon document as Ryholt proposes. I see no reason why the patch moved from Gardiner's column X cannot be accommodated at the top of his column I. As a result the column numbers remain as with Gardiner.

Chapter Three

1 A. H. Gardiner, 1959.

2 Published in G. Farina, 1938.

3 A. H. Gardiner, *op. cit* [1], p. 17.

4 Ryholt has proposed the insertion of an extra column between Columns I and II where he places the patch fragment bearing divine names. Because this does not affect the essential arguments I am putting forward here, and to avoid confusion over the numbering of the TC columns, I have retained Gardiner's original column numbers.

5 A. H. Gardiner, *op. cit* [1], p. 17: 'Down to IX:10 of the king-list the positions of the fragments as seen in F[arina] may be regarded as on the whole certain or at least plausible, but the arrangement of the remainder of Column IX and the whole of Column X must be regarded with the utmost scepticism. The scanty traces on the recto are wholly chaotic. In our Plates the positions given by Farina or Ibscher are retained, but only in order to avoid relegating to the Unplaced (Fragments) a number of pieces that undoubtedly belong to this papyrus.

... With the scanty material before us we see no solution to these problems.'

6 J. von Beckerath, 1964 and J. von Beckerath, 1984.

7 J. Malek, 1982, pp. 93-106.

8 K. S. B. Ryholt, 1997, pp. 24-25.

Chapter Four

1 W. G. Waddell, 1971, pp. 73-99.

2 M. Lichtheim, 1976, pp. 12-15.

3 W. C. Hayes, 1955.

4 F. L. Griffith, 1898.

5 B. J. Kemp in B. G. Trigger *et al,* 1983, p. 155.

6 G. Posener, 1957, pp. 145-63.

7 J. van Seters, 1966, p. 90.

8 W. C. Hayes, *op. cit* [3], p. 99.

9 J. van Seters, *op. cit* [7], p. 91.

10 *Ibid*

11 D. Lappin, 2002, pp. 71-84.

12 Actually 1320-1317 BC based on astronomers' more accurate calculations. The difference is due to the movement of Sirius itself on account of precession.

13 The dates used here are the low chronology of Krauss, 1985. For the higher chronology of Parker the reader should date the end of the 12th Dynasty to 1801 and the start of the 18th to 1550, giving an interval of 251 years in which to place the dynasties of the SIP. Krauss' dates are based on observations of the heliacal rising of Sirius at Elephantine whereas Parker locates the observations at Memphis or Itj-tawy.

14 K. A. Kitchen, 1987, pp. 43-44.

15 D. Lappin, *op. cit* [11], pp. 73-79.

16 This is the current NC date for Ramesses II. There is some discussion amongst NC researchers to see if this date can be raised by a few years (and possibly up to 25 years earlier). As work is 'still in progress' on this matter I have retained the current 943 BC date for Ramesses II's coronation here to avoid complicating the arguments.

17 Bernard Newgrosh, personal

18 W. A. Mitchell, 1989, pp. 7-26.
19 J. Leclant & J. Yoyotte, 1957, pp. 50-54.
20 P. Montet, 1957, p. 199.
21 J. van Seters, *op. cit.* [7], p. 101.
22 Disclosed by the excavator, Mohamed el-Maksoud, at a seminar held in the Egyptian Cultural Centre in London – May 1989.
23 M. Bietak, 1986, pp. 247-53.
24 W. G. Waddell, *op. cit.* [1], p. 90, note 3.
25 Needless to say, Mark Collier's and Bill Manley's live translation was not recorded, so I base this translation on J. B. Pritchard, 1969, p. 231.

Chapter Five

1 M. Bietak, 1996, p. 65.
2 D. Rohl, 1995, pp. 252-63.
3 Quoting Vivian Davies in *The Times* (London), 28 July 2003.
4 L. Troy, 1979, p. 83.
5 H. Goedicke, in L. H. Lesko (ed.), 1986, pp. 37-39.
6 On the other hand Vandersleyen, 1971, p. 34 and Redford, 1979, p. 274 opt for the fall of Avaris in Year 18 of Ahmose based on the same documentary evidence. Whichever date is correct, the simple fact is that the expulsion took place fairly late in the king's reign.
7 H. Goedicke, 1984, pp. 91-105.
8 H. Goedicke, *op. cit.* [5], pp. 37-47.
9 *Ibid.*

Chapter Six

1 P. Montet, 1928, pp. 90ff.
2 See. N. Jidejian, 1971, p. 28, note 15.
3 P. Montet in Wreszinski, 1935, pl. CXVII, p. 787.
4 W. F. Albright, 1945, p. 11.
5 S. Langdon & J. K. Fotheringham, 1928.
6 First published in W. Mitchell, 1989, pp. 7-26.
7 D. Lappin, 2002, pp. 73-79.
8 K. A. Kitchen, 1967, p. 41.

9 K. S. B. Ryholt, 1997, p. 73.
10 P. Montet, 1928, p. 155.
11 *Ibid.*, p. 157.
12 K. A. Kitchen, 1987, pp. 49-50.
13 M. Bietak, 1996, pp. 10-14.
14 J. B. Pritchard (ed.), 1969, pp. 149 ff.
15 R. Graves, 1960, p. 296.
16 N. Jidejian, 1971, p. 20.
17 M. Saghieh, 1983, p. 125.
18 P. Montet, *op. cit.* [3], pl. LXIX.
19 *Ibid.*, pl. LXX.
20 N. Jidejian, *op. cit.* [17], p. 22.
21 C. Schaeffer, 1949, pp. 49-120.
22 J. Tubb, 2004.
23 Quote from the abstract of *ibid.*
24 J. J. Bimson, 1990, pp. 58-76.
25 K. A. Kitchen, in J. Wiseman (ed.), 1973, p. 70.
26 K. M. Kenyon, 1970, p. 200.
27 M. Bietak, 1996, p. 63.

Chapter Seven

1 M. Rice, 1998.
2 M. Bietak, 2005a, p. 16.
3 W. M. F. Petrie, 1939, pp. 77-78.
4 Herodotus, *Historia*, Book I:1.
5 R. Graves, 1960, Vol. 1, p. 191.
6 *Ibid.*, p. 194.
7 N. G. L. Hammond, 1959, p. 87.
8 M. Bernal, 1987, p. 83.
9 R. Graves, *op. cit.* [5], p. 191.
10 F. H. Stubbings, 1973, p. 636.
11 P. Jánosi, 1991, p. 100.
12 M. Bietak, 1996, p. 65 and fig. 53.
13 P. Jánosi, *op. cit.* [11], pp. 102-03.
14 W. Helck, 1955, pp. 1-10; W. Helck, 1979, p. 58; and E. Kühnert-Eggebrecht, 1969, p. 92.

Chapter Eight

1 S. Manning, 1999.
2 See G. A. Zielinski & M. S. Germani, 1998, pp. 279-89; and D. J. Keenan, 2003.
3 D. Rohl, 1995, pp. 384-89.
4 Much of the material concerning the scientific dating debate for the Theran eruption was brought to my attention by Bernard Newgrosh who published with Mike Baillie a series

of commentaries and criticisms in *JACF* 2, 1988, pp. 60-68, *JACF* 3, 1989, pp. 37-41 and pp. 29-36 and *JACF* 4, 1990, pp. 15-28.

5   M. Bietak, 1996, p. 68.
6   *Ibid.*, pp. 74-75.
7   *Ibid.*, p. 79.
8   *Ibid.*, p. 78.
9   M. Bietak, 2005a, pp. 13-17.
10 Professor Jeffrey Soles, personal communication during the excavations at Mochlos, June 2004.
11 M. Bietak, *op. cit.* [5], p. 81.
12 Especially the presentation given at the Legend 'Lords of Avaris' Conference held in Manchester on 9 to 10 August 2003.
13 M. Bietak, *op. cit.* [5], p. 72.
14 M. Bietak, 2000a, p. 194.
15 P. M. Warren, 1984, p. 492.
16 S. W. Manning, 1990, p. 33.
17 L. C. Maguire, 1995, p. 55.
18 S. W. Manning, 1999, p. 129.
19 R. S. Merrillees, 2002, p. 1.
20 L. C. Maguire, *op. cit.* [16], p. 55.
21 M. Bietak, 2001, pp. 37-38. Translation by Peter van der Veen.
22 M. Bietak, *op. cit.* [9], p. 15.
23 H. Goedicke, 1984, pp. 94-95.
24 *Ibid.*, p. 99.

Chapter Nine

1   *Odyssey*, Book I:1.
2   J. H. Money, 1973, pp. 51ff.
3   D. Page, 1978, p. 697.
4   C. Doumas, 1980, p. 781.
5   An opinion strongly held by Professor Nicholas Coldstream at the Second Thera Congress; see *Thera and the Aegean World* II, 1980, p. 346.
6   A. Furumark, 1980, p. 669.
7   D. Page, *op. cit.* [3], p. 693.
8   O. Rackham in discussion at the Second Thera Congress; see *Thera and the Aegean World* II, 1980, p. 381.
9   N. J. Coldstream, 1980, p. 382.
10 C. Doumas, 1992, p. 25.
11 *Ibid.*, p. 47.
12 *Ibid.*, p. 27.
13 *Ibid.*, p. 48.
14 *Ibid.*

15 *Ibid.*
16 C. A. Televantou, 1990, p. 323.

Chapter Ten

1   Addressing the Asiatic Society in Calcutta on 2 February 1786.
2   V. Gordon Childe, 1926.
3   R. Drews, 1988, p. 124.
4   A. Pictet, 1859, pp. 753-54.
5   G. Hermes, 1935, pp. 803-23.
6   *Ibid.*, pp. 364-94; and G. Hermes, 1937, pp. 105-46.
7   M. Gimbutas, 1997.
8   C. Renfrew, 1987.
9   G. Wilhelm, 1989, p. 18.
10 J. P. Mallory, 1989, p. 38.
11 T. V. Gamkrelidze & V. V. Ivanov, 1984.
12 T. Bryce, 1998, p. 14.
13 R. Drews, *op. cit.* [3], p. 149.
14 W. F. Albright, 1957, pp. 30-31.
15 H. L. Ginsberg (trans.) in J. B. Pritchard, 1969, p. 143.
16 I am indebted to Peter van der Veen for bringing this discovery to my attention.
17 R. Drews, *op. cit.* [3], p. 83.
18 H. L. Lorimer, 1950, p. 307.
19 D. Rohl, 1995, pp. 285-86.

Chapter Eleven

1   V. Hankey & O. Tufnell, 1973, pp. 109-10.
2   Diodorus Siculus, Book IV:60 & Book V:80.
3   Herodotus, Book VII:71.
4   P. P. Betancourt, 1985, p. 115.
5   *Ibid.*, p. 159.
6   *Ibid.*, p. 171; O. Dickinson, 1994, p. 21.
7   L. R. Palmer, 1963.
8   *Ibid.*, p. 204.
9   *Ibid.*, p. 251.
10 O. Dickinson, *op. cit.* [6], p. 22.
11 E. Hallager, 1977.
12 W.-D. Niemeier, 1982, pp. 219-87.
13 M. Bernal, 1987, p. 79.
14 *Ibid.*, p. 77.
15 *Ibid.*, p. 83.
16 *Ibid.*

17 D. Collon, 1994, p. 84.
18 N. Marinatos, 1994, p. 92.
19 *Ibid.*, p. 91.
20 D. Collon, *op. cit.* [17], p. 81.
21 *Ibid.*, p. 81.
22 N. Marinatos, *op. cit.* [18], p. 92.
23 *Ibid.*, p. 90.
24 A. J. Evans, 1930, p. 205.
25 D. Collon, *op. cit.* [17], p. 84.
26 N. Marinatos, *op. cit.* [18], p. 89.
27 D. Collon, *op. cit.* [17], p. 83.
28 *Ibid.*, p. 84.
29 H. E. L. Mellersh, 1967, p. 125.

Chapter Twelve

1 J. Latacz, 2004, p. 49.
2 Schliemann, quoted in W. A. McDonald, 1967, p. 65.
3 A. Cotterell, 1985, p. 88.
4 A. J. B. Wace, 1949, p. 60.
5 Schliemann, quoted in W. A. McDonald, *op. cit.* [2], p. 65.
6 W. A. McDonald, *op. cit.* [2], p. 91.
7 A. G. Ward, 1970, p. 86.
8 A. Cotterell, *op. cit.* [3], p. 77.
9 F. H. Stubbings, 1973, p. 631.
10 *Ibid.*, p. 633.
11 *Ibid.*, p. 634.
12 R. Graves, 1960, Vol. I, p. 201.
13 F. H. Stubbings, *op. cit.* [9], p. 648.
14 R. Graves, *op. cit.* [12], p. 11.
15 *Ibid.*, p. 36.
16 *Ibid.*
17 *Ibid.*
18 *Ibid.*
19 Strabo, *Geographika*, Book V:2.
20 G. A. Lehmann, 1996, p. 4, n. 3; P. W. Haider, 1988, p. 10.
21 The inscription is from the funerary temple of the Pharaoh Amenhotep III, published in 1966 by Elmas Edel; see J. Latacz, *op. cit.* [1], pp. 130-31.
22 Strabo, *Geographika*, Book XII:8.
23 I. E. S. Edwards, 1971, p. 849.
24 R. Graves, *op. cit.* [12], p. 35.

Chapter Thirteen

1 F. H. Stubbings, 1975, p. 343.
2 T. Bryce, 1998, p. 394: 'In Homeric tradition, Troy and (W)ilios were two names for the same place. Wilios was an early form of the name Ilios before the initial w, representing the archaic Greek digamma, was dropped.'
3 J. Latacz, 2004, p. 289.
4 M. Wood, 1985, p. 228.
5 C. W. Blegen, 1995, pp. 143-44.
6 *Ibid.*, pp. 150-51.
7 Euripides: *The Trojan Women*, 1318.
8 M. Wood, *op. cit.* [4], p. 228.
9 N. Fields, 2004, p. 24.
10 *Iliad*, Book XIV.
11 T. Bryce, *op. cit.* [2], p. 399.
12 D. Easton, 1985, p. 189.
13 C. W. Blegen, *op. cit.* [5], pp. 163-64.
14 S. Iakovidis, 1977, pp. 134-35.
15 *Ibid.*, p. 105: 'Wace placed the construction of the Granary before the end of LH IIIA and its reconstruction during LH IIIB (1949:57). They continued to be used until well into the next period, LH IIIC, to the end of the 12th century, and were then destroyed by fire and abandoned (Wace, 1921-3: 40ff.), as was the palace. Therefore, concluded Wace, the citadel having been built as a whole at one and the same time and having served as the seat of the mighty kings of Mycenae for two and a half centuries, went up in flames around 1100 BC, probably as a result of the Dorian invasion.'
16 V. Desborough, 1972, p. 324.
17 I am following B. Newgrosh (forthcoming) and others who believe that the archaising elements in these texts do not imply a redating to the earlier period.
18 G. Beckman, 1996.
19 J. Latacz, *op. cit.* [3], p. 116.
20 See C. W. Blegen, 1975, p. 169 and Strabo, *Geographika*:412. There is mention of ships from 'Lower Thebes' which presumably means the lower city of Cadmaean Thebes. This in itself seems to support the idea that the upper royal city was no more at the time of the Trojan War.
21 J. Latacz, *op. cit.* [3], p. 126.
22 *Ibid.*, p. 244.
23 M. Wood, *op. cit.* [22], p. 181.

24 O. R. Gurney, 1952, p. 51.
25 On the other hand, New
    Chronologists have long suggested
    that this 60-year figure represents
    the combined reigns of all the
    Ramesside kings from Ramesses III
    to Ramesses XI, encompassed in the
    shortened chronology for the 20th
    Dynasty currently being constructed
    within the NC model.
26 H. Schliemann, 1976, p. 163.

Chapter Fourteen

1   W. M. F. Petrie, 1890, p. 271.
2   A. Snodgrass, 2000, p. 3.
3   *Ibid.*, p. 9.
4   M. Finley, 1981, p. 78.
5   V. Desborough, 1972, p. 322.
6   M. Nilsson, 1933, p. 69.
7   V. Desborough, *op. cit.* [5], p. 18.
8   *Ibid.*, p. 261.
9   A. Snodgrass, *op. cit.* [2], p. 21.
10 *Ibid.*, pp. xxiv-xxv.
11 *Ibid.*, p. xxxii.
12 P. James *et al.*, 1988, pp. 19 & 22.
13 D. Page, 1959, p. 31.
14 C. Blegen, 1995, p. 172.
15 C. Blegen *et al.*, 1958, p. 250.
16 J. N. Coldstream, 1977, pp. 326-27.
17 *Ibid.*, p. 20.
18 *Ibid.*, p. 346.
19 R. Hampe & E. Simon, 1981, p. 81.
20 J. N. Coldstream, *op. cit.* [16], p. 17.
21 A. Snodgrass, *op. cit.* [2], p. 31.
22 *Ibid.*, p. xxxi.
23 *Ibid.*, pp. 112-13.
24 *Ibid.*, p. 122.
25 *Ibid.*, p. 123.
26 *Ibid.*, p. xxv.
27 R. Cook, 1972, p. 262.
28 P. James et al., *op. cit.* [12], p. 29.
29 J. Davison, 1961, pp. 130-32.
30 A. Snodgrass, *op. cit.* [2], p. 6:
    'Eratosthenes, for example, placed
    the Homeric poems only a century
    after the Trojan War; Aristarchus
    made Homer contemporary with
    the Ionian migration, which meant
    a generation or so later than that,
    according to Greek chronological
    tradition, but would still leave
    Homer within the eleventh century

BC by our reckoning'.
31 A. Burn, 1930, p. 3.
32 J. N. Coldstream, *op. cit.* [16], p. 295.
33 *Ibid.*, p. 341.
34 R. Sealey, 1976, p. 28.
35 M. Grant, 1969, p. 152.
36 G. S. Kirk in Homer, 1980, p. xvi.
37 J. N. Coldstream, *op. cit.* [16], p. 342.
38 M. P. Nilsson, *op. cit.* [6], p. 53.
39 *Ibid.*, p. 26.
40 M. M. Austin & P. Vidal-Naquet,
    1986, pp. 37-38.
41 J. V. Luce, 1975, p. 45.
42 M. Wood, 1985, p. 143.
43 J. V. Luce, *op. cit.* [41], p. 130.
44 R. J. A. Talbert, 1985, p. 8.
45 M. I. Finley, *op. cit.* [4], p. 80.
46 R. Sealey, *op. cit.* [34], p. 30.
47 J. N. Coldstream, *op. cit.* [16], pp.
    349-50.

Chapter Fifteen

1   R. Graves, 1955, Vol. 2, p. 208.
2   V. R. d'A. Desborough, 1972, p. 21.
3   A. M. Snodgrass, 2000, p. 311.
4   Thucydides, Book I:12.
5   Diodorus Siculus, Book I:5.
6   A. R. Burn, 1930, p. 55.
7   A. R. Burn, 1965, p. 82.
8   A. M. Snodgrass, *op. cit.* [3], p. 13.
9   P. Oliva, 1981, p. 33.
10 N. G. L. Hammond, 1982, p. 705.
11 J. V. Luce, 1975, p. 135.
12 F. Mitchell, 1956, pp. 48-69.
13 V. R. d'A. Desborough, *op. cit.* [2], p.
    324.
14 A. M. Snodgrass, *op. cit.* [3], p. 11.
15 A. R. Burn, *op. cit.* [6], pp. 52-53:
    'Leonidas and Latychidas, kings
    in 480 BC, are fifteenth from
    Eurysthenes and Prokles, the first of
    the two (Spartan royal) lines; but the
    year of the conquest is given as 1104
    BC – allowing actually more than
    40 years per generation. The Trojan
    War, two generations earlier, is said
    to end in 1184.'
16 A. M. Snodgrass, *op. cit.* [3], p. 11.
17 J. Boardman, 1982, p. 789.
18 A. R. Burn, *op. cit.* [6], p. 28.
19 D. M. Rohl, 1995, p. 380.
20 According to the late Agiad dynasty

at Sparta, from Cleomenes III (235 BC) to Leonidas (488 BC) there are twelve kings over a period of 253 years, making an average reign-length of 21 years.

21 A. M. Snodgrass, *op. cit.* [3], p. 11.

22 N. G. L. Hammond, 1982, p. 642.

23 I am grateful to Richard Abbott for uncovering this genealogy in Pausanias and publishing his findings on the New Chronology Yahoo Groups site.

24 L. F. Fitzhardinge, 1980, p. 155.

25 Thucydides, Book I:12.

26 V. R. d'A. Desborough, *op. cit.* [2], p. 280.

27 J. B. Bury & R. Meiggs, 1900, p. 89.

28 P. Oliva, *op. cit.* [9], p. 63.

29 As summarised in R. Drews, 1988, pp. 206-07.

30 L. F. Fitzhardinge, *op. cit.* [25], pp. 24-25.

31 V. R. d'A. Desborough, *op. cit.* [2], p. 240.

32 M. I. Finley, 1981, p. 108.

33 *Ibid.*, p. 78.

Chapter Sixteen

1 J. A. Wilson (trans.), 1969, pp. 262-63.

2 Homer, *Iliad*, Book II:840.

3 Herodotus, *Historia*, Book II:56.

4 *Iliad*, Book X:429 & *Odyssey*, Book XIX:177.

5 See Albright: 'Syria, the Philistines and Phoenicia' in *CAH* II, Part 2, p. 513.

6 R. D. Barnett, 1975, p. 367.

7 *Ibid.*, p. 377.

8 M. Wood, 1985, p. 161.

9 Aeschylus: *Agamemnon*.

10 M. Grant, 1989, pp. 179-80.

11 R. D. Barnett, *op. cit.* [6], p. 364.

12 Herodotus, *op. cit.* [3], Book VII:91; *ibid.*, p. 365.

13 *Ibid.*, p. 364.

Chapter Seventeen

1 In the New Chronology it is argued that Assyria also practised this dual monarchy for a period following the assassination of Tukulti-Ninurta I when there was a line of warrior kings and a contemporary dynasty of priest-kings. See B. Newgrosh, 1999, pp. 78-106.

2 D. D. Luckenbill, 1926, p. 276.

3 D. M. Rohl, 1995, pp. 370-71.

4 M. Mallowan, 1972, p. 63.

5 J. D. Hawkins, 1974, p. 67.

6 R. A. Crossland, 1971, p. 856.

7 T. Bryce, 1998, p. 155-56; I am retaining the original identification of the Hittite king here with Arnuwanda III and not redating this text to Arnuwanda II, as is currently the fashion, for obvious reasons. It is ridiculous to have Phrygians arriving in Anatolia as early as the pre-Suppiluliuma I era, more than a century before the end of the Late Bronze Age. The Phrygian appearance in Anatolia is clearly a very late LB II and early Iron Age archaeological phenomenon.

8 R. A. Crossland, *op. cit.* [6], p. 857.

9 E. Akurgal, 1962, p. 124.

10 K. Bittel, 1970, pp. 137-38.

11 A. M. Snodgrass, 2000, p. 349: 'Professor R. S. Young, the director of the recent excavations at Gordion, had in his earlier work on Geometric Greece supported an unusually low chronology, and his conclusions as to relative dating now tend to favour Phrygian priority. In particular, by placing the rich and important burial in the Great Tumulus (MMT) at Gordion at *c.* 725 ... Midas who was the last king of the great period of Phrygia according to Greek tradition, and who was said to have committed suicide at the time of the disastrous Cimmerian invasion, which in turn tradition and archaeology agree in placing in the first quarter of the seventh century. But this King Midas is also known from the royal annals of Assyria, which mention one Mita, king of Musku (a country identifiable with Phrygia), under several different years; the earliest of these years is 717 BC, and so the

burial in the Great Tumulus must have taken place some time before then.'

12 V. R. d'A. Desborough, 1972, p. 121.

13 *Ibid.*, p. 120.

14 J. Boardman, 1982, pp. 774 & 83.

15 R. Hampe & E. Simon, 1981, p. 55.

16 M. E. Aubet, 1993, p. 169.

17 S. Reinach, 1893; K. J. Beloch, 1913.

18 M. E. Aubet, *op. cit.* [16], p. 167.

19 A. M. Snodgrass, *op. cit.* [11], p. 18.

20 W. Culican, 1970, pp. 28-36.

21 M. E. Aubet, *op. cit.* [16], p. 131.

22 Justinus, *Epitome*, XVIII:6.

23 For a discussion of Tyrian chronology, see A. R. Green, 1983, pp. 373-97.

24 This new link was brought to my attention by Peter van der Veen.

25 M. E. Aubet, *op. cit.* [16], p. 297.

26 G. E. Markoe, 2000, p. 129.

27 M. E. Aubet, *op. cit.* [16], p. 188.

28 R. D. Barnett, 1975, p. 368.

29 *Ibid.*, p. 369.

30 R. D. Barnett, *op. cit.* [28], pp. 360-61.

31 Herodotus, *Historia*, Book I:94.

32 W. Keller, 1975, p. 45.

33 *Ibid.*, p. 98.

34 *Ibid.*

35 R. D. Barnett, *op. cit.* [28], p. 368.

36 T. J. Cornell, 1995, p. 35.

37 I. Velikovsky, 1976; P. James *et al.*, 1991.

38 M. Austin & P. Vidal-Naquet, 1986, p. 58.

39 R. J. A. Talbert (ed.), 1985, p. 11.

40 M. M. Austin & P. Vidal-Naquet, *op. cit.* [38], p. 65.

41 Thucydides, Book I:12.

42 Strabo, *Geographika*, Book VI:1.

43 *Ibid.*, Book VI:3.

44 Thucydides, Book VI:2.

45 Q. Quagliati, 1900, pp. 411-64.

46 L. Bernarbo Brea, 1966, p. 130.

47 *Odyssey*, Book XIV:222.

48 *Ibid.*, Book IX:39-42.

49 N. K. Sandars, 1978, p. 143.

50 J. Boardman, 1980, pp. 35-36.

51 J. V. Luce, 1975, p. 54.

Chapter Eighteen

1 D. Strong, 1968, p. 39.

2 M. P. Nilsson, 1993, p. 42.

3 Livy: *The Early History of Rome*, Book I:3.

4 T. J. Cornell, 1995, p. 71.

5 *Ibid.*, p. 16.

6 M. E. Aubet, 1994, p. 189.

7 Dionysius, Book I:63.

8 R. M. Ogilvie, Introduction to *Livy*, 1960, p. 7.

9 *Ibid.*, p. 9.

10 Livy, Book V:43.

11 Cicero, *On the Orator*, Book II:52.

12 R. M. Ogilvie, *op. cit.* [8], p. 10.

13 C. S. Mackay, 1999, internet article.

14 *Ibid.* I have taken the liberty of correcting Mackay's mathematics by adjusting the figures by one year from the starting point of 117 BC for the accession of Tarquin I which he for some reason places in 616 BC.

15 T. J. Cornell, *op. cit.* [4], pp. 72-73.

16 T. J. Cornell, personal communication, 25 May 2004.

17 T. J. Cornell, *op. cit.* [4], pp. 10-11.

18 *Ibid.*, p. 12.

19 *Ibid.*, p. 80.

Chapter Nineteen

1 R. Hampe & E. Simon, 1981, p. 214.

GLOSSARY

12TH DYNASTY: NC – c. 1803-1632 BC; OC – c. 1937-1759 BC.

AEOLIAN: a dialect from north-central Greece which transferred to north-west Anatolia during the early Iron Age migrations of the Greeks.

AHMOSE: reigned NC – c. 1191-1168 BC; OC – c. 1539-1514 BC.

AHNENERBE: *Ahnenerbe Forschungs und Lehrgemeinschaft*, founded in 1935.

AKURGAL: (1911-2002).

ALBRIGHT: (1891-1971).

ALEXANDER THE GREAT: reigned 336-323 BC.

AMENEMHAT I: reigned NC – 1803-1774 BC; OC – 1937-1908 BC.

AMENHOTEP I: reigned NC – c. 1178-1158 BC.

APOPHIS: NC – c. 1199-1183 BC; OC – c. 1570-1535 BC.

ARDYS: (652-617 BC).

ARYAN: a term borrowed from Herodotus and from which the name Iran derives.

ASHLAR: blocks of stone cut with a saw.

ASHURBANIPAL: reigned 669-627 BC.

ASHURNASIRPAL II: reigned 883-858 BC.

AUGUSTUS: ruled 31-14 BC.

BITTEL: (1907-1991).

BRUGSCH: (1842-1930).

BURY: (1861-1927).

CASTOR AND POLLUX: celebrated twins renowned for their horsemanship and boxing skills, later deified by the Romans and given their own temple in the Forum Romanum.

CATO: (234-148 BC), Roman censor who was the first to write history in Latin prose.

CENSORINUS: c. AD 238; a Roman grammarian whose works also include *De Accentibus.*

CHAMPOLLION: (1790-1832).

CHILDE: (1892-1957).

DAHABIYA: a Nile sailing boat – the comfortable, stately mode of transport used by the first travellers to visit Egypt.

DIODORUS SICULUS: 1st century BC, who wrote *Bibliotheke* in Greek in forty books.

DIONYSIUS: born in the 1st century BC, and wrote in Greek a history of Rome from its beginnings to the First Punic War entitled *Roman Antiquities* which first appeared in 7 BC.

DROVETTI: (1776-1852).

DUNAND: (1898-1987).

ELIS: western Peloponnese.

EPIGONOI: the seven war-leaders who (according to tradition) fought against and destroyed Cadmaean Thebes in revenge for the deaths of their fathers, a generation earlier, who had attacked Thebes but were defeated and slain.

ERATOSTHENES: (276-194 BC).

EVANS: (1851-1941).

FELLOWS: (1799-1860).

FIBULAE: a large safety-pin clasp.

FIRST INTERMEDIATE PERIOD: NC – c. 2062-1830 BC; OC – c. 2150-1986.

FRANKFORT: (1897-1954).

FURUMARK: (1903-1982); devised the generally accepted (with up-to-date modifications) pottery chronology and classification of Aegean ceramics.

GALABEYAS: the typical long cotton gowns worn by Egyptian fellaheen.

GARDINER: (1879-1963).

GEOMETRIC GREECE: otherwise known as the Greek Archaic era, encompassing the Proto-Geometric, Early Geometric, Middle Geometric and Late Geometric periods, conventionally dated from c. 1050 to 700 BC.

GEORGE V: reigned 1910-1935.

GIMBUTAS: (1921-1994).

GYGES: (356-323 BC).

HATTUSHILI I: reigned NC – c. 1400-1367 BC; OC – c. 1650-1620 BC.

HA(T)WARE(T): usually written Hutwaret in the Egyptological literature but pronounced anciently with the vowel A rather than U in the word *hwt* = 'house' or 'temple'. The Ts were also unpronounced feminine endings – thus Haware would have been the most likely pronunciation.

HELCK: (1915-1993).

HIERATIC: a cursive form of hiero-glyphics used for writing on papyrus.

HIPPIAS: 5th century BC, a sophist and philosopher.

HOPLITE: a new type of infantry soldier devised by Spartan generals to fight in tight formation with long protruding lances.

HORACE: Quintus Horatius Flaccus (65-8 BC), Roman lyric poet and dramatic critic; a contemporary of Augustus.

IBSCHER: (1874-1943).

INDO-EUROPEAN: the term Indo-Europeans refers to peoples who once spoke a mother-tongue ancestral to the languages of Europe (Greek, Latin, German, Scandinavian and all those modern languages which derived from these sub-groups). The reason why this linguistic term contains the prefix Indo- is because the Late Bronze Age invaders of the Indus valley (enshrined in the Vedic tradition) also spoke an ancient dialect of Indo-European called Aryan. The language of the Vedic chariot lords evolved into Sanskrit which came to dominate the northern part of the Indian sub-continent. Thus the Indo-European language family extends from western Europe to central Asia and India.

Ir-Heba: 'Servant of the Hurrian goddess Heba(t)'.

JONES: (1746-1794).

JUSTINUS: third-century Roman historian.

KADESH-ON-THE-ORONTES: location of the battle between Ramesses II (NC – *c.* 943-877 BC) and the Hittite emperor, Muwatalli (NC – *c.* 966-937 BC).

KAMOSE: NC – *c.* 1194-1191 BC; OC – *c.* 1543-1539 BC.

KEMPINSKI: (1939-1994).

KENYON: (1906-1978).

KHAFRE: NC – *c.* 2444-2419 BC; OC – *c.* 2520-2494 BC.

KHUFU: NC – *c.* 2475-2452 BC; OC – *c.* 2551-2528 BC.

KORFMANN: (1942-2005).

KUSHITE: of the kingdom of Kush located on the upper reaches of the Nile in what is modern Sudan. The kingdom had its capital at different locations in different periods: first at Kerma, above the Third Cataract, then at Napata below the Fourth Cataract on the Dongola Bend, and finally at Meroe, south of the Atbara outflow into the Nile.

LACEDAEMON: or Laconia, south-central Peloponnese where the later kingdom of Sparta was located.

LEGRAIN: (1865-1917).

LIVY: Titus Livius, born at Padua in northern Italy in 59 BC, died AD 17 who composed the opus work *Ab Urbe Condita Libri* in 142 books.

LOWER EGYPT: the delta region north of Memphis.

MARIETTE: (1821-1881).

MARINATOS: (1901-1974).

MB IIB: in Egypt NC – *c.* 1445-1200 BC; in Syro-Palestine NC – *c.* 1460-1200 BC.

MEGARON: a large single-roomed building with pillared porch leading to a central hearth surrounded by four columns.

MENAHEM: reigned *c.* 740-731 BC.

MIDDLE KINGDOM: NC – *c.* 1830-1632 BC; OC – *c.* 1986-1759 BC.

MONTET: (1885-1966).

MONTUHOTEP II: NC – *c.* 1867-1816 BC; OC – *c.* 2007-1956 BC.

MURSHILI I: reigned NC – *c.* 1367-1338 BC; OC – *c.* 1620-1590 BC.

NEO-HITTITE: the 'afterglow' of the Hittite empire with kingdoms centred on cities such as Carchemish, Melid (Malatya), Kummukh (later Commagene), Samal (Zincirli) and Pattin.

NEW KINGDOM: NC – *c.* 1181-832 BC; OC – *c.* 1530-1069 BC.

OLD ASSYRIAN PERIOD: Erishum I to Shamshi-Adad, OC – *c.* 1939-1781 BC; NC – *c.* 1690-1533 BC, including the reigns of Sargon I to Erishum II (Kanesh II) and Shamshi-Adad (Kanesh IB).

OLD HITTITE PERIOD: OC – *c.* 1650-1500 BC; NC – *c.* 1400-1250 BC.

ONAGER: a wild donkey of the Zagros mountain region domesticated for use in trading caravans and for pulling carts, as seen on the Ur Standard drawing the royal wagon.

ORTHOGRAPHY: the way that words are written – i.e. spelling.

GLOSSARY

ORTHOSTATS: thin slabs of stone (plain or carved) set up on their edges to face a mudbrick wall at its lower courses, like a dado.

OSORKON II: 22nd Dynasty, reigned OC – 874-850 BC; NC – c. 784-760 BC.

OVID: Roman poet who lived between 43 BC-AD 17, patronised by the emperor Augustus but then exiled to the Black Sea coast in AD 8.

PALAEOGRAPHY: style of writing.

PARROT: (1901-1980).

PATINATION: the tan of a carving caused by the sun. The older the carving the darker the patination.

PENDLEBURY: (1904-1941).

PEPI II: reigned NC – c. 2168-2075 BC.

PETRIE: (1853-1942).

PHRAORTES: (675-653 BC).

PINUDJEM: reigned NC – c. 812-787 BC).

PITHOI: large storage jars.

POMPIUS TROGUS: a contemporary of Livy from Gallicia.

POSENER: (1906-1988).

PSAMTEK I: reigned 664-610 BC.

PYRRHUS: 'Red-head' also known as Neoptolemos 'renewer of war', the son of Achilles.

REZIN: reigned c. 755-730 BC.

RIG VEDA: 'Praise and sacred knowledge'.

ROWATY: ('Mouth of the Two Ways').

SARGON II: reigned 721-705 BC.

SCHLIEMANN: (1822-1890).

SCHOPENHAUER: (1788-1860).

SECOND INTERMEDIATE PERIOD or SIP: NC – c. 1632-1181 BC; OC – c. 1759-1530 BC.

SENUSERET III: reigned NC – 1698-1660 BC; OC – 1836-1817 BC.

SEPTUAGINT: the Greek translation of the Old Testament narratives made by Jewish scholars commissioned by the third century BC Ptolemaic pharaohs (also known as the LXX).

SHALMANESER III: reigned 858-824 BC.

SHOSHENK III: 22nd Dynasty, reigned OC – c. 825-773 BC.

SHULGI: reigned NC – c. 1882-1834 BC.

SHUPPILULIUMA I: reigned NC – c. 1030-993 BC.

SIAMUN: reigned OC – c. 1069 BC but NC – c. 778 BC.

SPENCE: (1930-1999).

STRABO: 63 BC-c. AD 24, writing in Greek and using now lost works such as those of Eratosthenes and Posidonius.

TAKELOT II: 22nd Dynasty, reigned OC – c. 850-825 BC; NC – 760-735 BC.

TELL ED-DABA: 'Mound of the Hyaena'.

THALASSOCRACY: sea-based sovereignty.

THEON: (c. AD 335-405), last Director of the Alexandrian Library; a mathematician and astronomer who wrote commentaries on his predecessors.

THIRD INTERMEDIATE PERIOD: NC – c. 820-664 BC; OC – 1069-664 BC.

THUTMOSE I: reigned NC – c. 1158-1146 BC.

TIBERIUS: ruled 14 BC-37 AD.

TIGLATH-PILESER III: reigned 744-726 BC.

TIMAEUS: (c. 355-260 BC).

TOGGLE-PIN: a bronze pin used to fasten a robe or cloak.

TUKULTI-NINURTA II: reigned 890-883 BC.

UPPER EGYPT: the Nile valley south of Memphis.

UR III: NC – c. 1900-1793 BC; OC – c. 2112-2004 BC.

VARRO: (116-27 BC), Rome's greatest antiquarian.

VELLEIUS PATERCULUS: (c. 19 BC-AD 31).

VIRGIL: Rome's greatest epic poet (70-19 BC).

WADDELL: (1884-1945).

WINCKLER: (1863-1913).

WOOLLEY: (1880-1960).

YOUNG: (1773-1829).

ZAMBEEL: a basket used to carry earth.

ZILE: the fortress which guarded Egypt's Sinai border with Canaan. The Egyptological literature commonly gives the name as Djaru, based on the hieroglyphic writing of the fortress' name. However, the Egyptian sign for Dj (as in Djoser) was probably pronounced Z (as in Zoser); the Egyptian sign for R could also be read as L; and the vowel marker at the end of the name need not render U but any vowel. So Djaru was probably pronounced something like Zile (as similarly transcribed in the Akkadian script of the Amarna Letters).

INDEX

R

Q